The New
JEWISH
CUISINE

Evelyn Rose has an international reputation as a writer, broadcaster and authority on food and wine. She is a specialist on Jewish food and food customs, and as Cookery Editor of the *Jewish Chronicle*, where she has a weekly column, she demonstrates and lectures widely on the subject. She writes a monthly column for the wine magazine, *Decanter*, and also for *Cheshire Life*, and contributes to other national magazines and newspapers. She has been cooking on television for many years and is a frequent contributor to both national and local radio. Active in consumer affairs, she is a member of the Consumers' Committee for Great Britain, and also of the Consumers' Committee of the Meat and Livestock Commission. She is a past National Chairman of the Institute of Home Economics and is a Fellow of the Institute. Evelyn Rose is married with three children, and lives in Manchester where she conducts Master Classes in Food and Wine.

Also by Evelyn Rose, and published by Robson Books

THE COMPLETE INTERNATIONAL JEWISH COOKBOOK
THE ENTERTAINING COOKBOOK
THE FIRST-TIME COOKBOOK (WITH JUDI ROSE)
THE ISRAEL GOOD FOOD GUIDE

The New
JEWISH CUISINE
Evelyn Rose

PAPERMAC

To my husband Myer and my daughter Judi,
who between them have advised, criticized,
encouraged, cajoled and supported me above and
beyond the call of family duty while I was
writing this book.

First published 1985 by Robson Books Ltd, London

First published in paperback 1988 by PAPERMAC
a division of Macmillan Publishers Limited
4 Little Essex Street London WC2R 3LF
and Basingstoke

Associated companies in Auckland, Delhi, Dublin,
Gaborone, Hamburg, Harare, Hong Kong, Johannesburg,
Kuala Lumpur, Lagos, Manzini, Melbourne, Mexico City,
Nairobi, New York, Singapore and Tokyo

British Library Cataloguing in Publication Data

Rose, Evelyn
The new Jewish cuisine.
1. Cookery, Jewish
I. Title
641.5'676 TX724
ISBN 0–333–46409–5

Typeset by Bookworm Typesetting, Manchester, England.

Printed in Hong Kong

All illustrations copyright © Stonecastle Graphics

CONTENTS

...owledgements

...ing a cookery book is essentially a solitary occupation but it demands a large ...pport team, and I have been very fortunate in the technical, literary and culinary ...ssistance that I have received from mine.

My husband, Myer Rose, worked with me at every stage of the preparation of the manuscript and without his tireless labour the book would not have seen the light of day. My daughter, Judi Rose, helped me with the initial selection of the recipes and the overall plan for the book and later gave me useful critical advice. My son, David Rose, gave me invaluable practical advice and encouragement. I owe a great debt to my colleague, Sula Leon, not only for her help in testing some of the recipes, but also for her generosity in allowing me to include those that were originally developed for our 'Master Classes in Food and Wine'.

Christine Windeler kept the domestic wheels turning; Mary Bagnall helped with the collation of material; Dawn Calmonson produced a superbly typed manuscript; Susan Rea was a most supportive literary editor; Jean Macqueen edited my copy with tremendous tact and efficiency.

The following people generously shared their family recipes and experiences with me; however, I take full responsibility for their present form which took shape only after many testing sessions in the kitchen and round the dinner table: Monty Alge, Roslyn Blain, Bayla Brandeis, Chana Cohen, Polly Conn, Risa Domb, Elizabeth Gibson, Maria Green, Shiphra Grosskopf, Hette Groswald, Frank and Ruth Hyams, Jill King, Agneta Levi, Phyllis Leigh, Edna Miller, Ernest and Fay Moritz, Christiana Rose, Hilde Rose, Magda Rubel, Sybil Shields, Frances Showman, Frank and Steffi Surkes, Sonia Szigeti, Janey Stevenson, Margaret Travis, Sylvia Wax.

I received helpful technical advice on the kosher food trade from meat executive Alan Factor, master butcher Jeffrey Holland, master baker Jack Maurer, and master fishmonger Sam Stoller.

Lawrence Shields gave me invaluable guidance on matters of food science and Dr Samuel Oleesky on those of medicine. Rabbi Felix F. Carlebach, M.A. advised me on Jewish religious law. To them all I give my heartfelt thanks.

The cover photograph was taken by Paul Turner.

The food was prepared by Judi Rose.

1985   EVELYN ROSE

Introduction

This is a book about a new international cuisine. It's a way of cooking that's been developed by ordinary people cooking for their families in their own kitchens in many different parts of the world, not by a celebrated chef in the kitchen of some great restaurant or hotel. Although its roots reach five thousand years back into the past, its wide-ranging repertoire of intriguing and mouth-watering dishes from almost every country on the globe faithfully reflects the way we Jews live here and now — and the way we hope to live in the future.

In most people's minds, Jewish food is a typical peasant cuisine, much of it heavy in fats, sugars and starches. But this new-style Jewish cuisine is leaner and lighter by far, with a strong emphasis on the more 'natural' foods that reflect our growing preoccupation with cooking for health as well as for pleasure. Yet although many everyday meals are now based on this approach to food, when it comes to high days and holydays the older, much-loved dishes 'like Momma used to make' still appear on the majority of Jewish family tables.

So into this book I have tried to distil the very best of this old-style, new-style Jewish cuisine. Although you will find many exciting and innovative dishes that are not usually thought of as typical Jewish food, I have also included some of the more famous traditional dishes such as chopped liver and fried fish, but with their ingredients and cooking methods tailored to fit in with today's more health-conscious meals. And I have reserved a special place for the glorious kuchens, kichlach and strudels of yesteryear.

Those old traditions that do still linger on are being kept alive and vigorous with the help of some very new machines. The kuchen dough is coaxed to rise in the microwave oven, the gefilte fish is chopped in seconds on the food processor, and enough chicken soup and matzah balls for a month of shabbats are stockpiled in the freezer. Today's cooks rely heavily on modern technology to eliminate the tedious and time-consuming drudgery of the past.

The recipes that you will find in these pages have been collected from cooks living all over the world. Among them you will find classic dishes from many famous cuisines, but they can all be prepared and eaten in the most Orthodox Jewish household. Yet because they hold up a mirror to the way ordinary people worldwide are cooking and eating today, they have a universal appeal which I hope will make them welcome in kitchens and around dinner tables wherever delicious home cooking is welcomed and enjoyed.

HOW TO USE THE RECIPES

● **Solid measures** are first given in spoons, pounds and ounces. **Liquid measures** are first given in spoons, pints or fluid ounces. Within the brackets that follow these measures, the first figure given is the metric equivalent and the second is the American equivalent measure in cups, e.g.

3 oz (75 g/⅓ cup) — solid measure;

¼ pint (150 ml/⅔ cup) — liquid measure.

● **American equivalent ingredients** are given in brackets, e.g.

glacé (candied) cherries;

double (heavy) cream.

1

- **Temperatures** are first expressed as a gas number and then in degrees, e.g. Gas No. 3, 325 degrees F, 170 degrees C.
- **Length measurements** are first given in inches and then in centimetres, e.g. 2 in (5 cm).
- **Spoon measures**: as I find the use of millilitres to express spoon capacity unnecessarily complicated, I have used household tablespoons and teaspoons throughout. All spoon measures are level. As the difference in volume is so small I have assumed British and American spoons to be interchangeable; however, some adjustment in the quantity of seasonings may be necessary to suit individual tastes.
- In calculating the **metric equivalents** of ounces or fluid ounces, I have worked out the *exact* equivalent in grams or millilitres, and then rounded it up or down to the nearest multiple of 25. For instance, 8 ounces exactly equals 226.80 g, which I give as 225 g; 10 fluid ounces equals 284.10 ml, which I give as 275 ml. In no case is there more than half an ounce or half a fluid ounce difference between the imperial and metric measures as stated, and this is not enough to make other than a trifling difference (in, for example, seasoning) to the recipe. However, it is not advisable to use a mixture of imperial and metric measures in the same recipe, as this may cause an imbalance in the proportions of solid to liquid ingredients.
- **Butter** is slightly salted, unless unsalted is specified.
- **Sugar** is granulated unless caster (superfine), icing (confectioners') or a variety of brown sugar is specified.
- **Eggs** are 'standard' (number 3) size (approximately 2 oz (50 g) in weight). The egg size is only critical when 4 or more eggs are used in a recipe — in that case, extra large (or small) eggs can upset the ratio of liquids to solids.
- **Flour** is plain (all-purpose), unless self-raising flour is specified; white, unless a brown flour is specified; regular, 'soft' white (as used for cakes and biscuits), unless a strong bread flour is specified.

    4 oz (125 g/1 cup) plain flour plus 1 level teaspoon baking
    powder = 4 oz (125 g/1 cup) self-raising flour.

- **Margarine** is a soft variety labelled 'high in polyunsaturates', unless a block of firm margarine is specified.
- **Tin and pan sizes** are given for guidance only, and those of approximately the same size can be used, provided they are the same depth or deeper than specified.
- **Oven temperatures** are given for guidance only, as different ovens vary in the distribution of heat and the time taken to complete the cooking of a particular food. This is most marked when a fan-assisted or forced-air oven is used, for which you should follow the manufacturers' instructions for cooking similar foods. In general this will mean setting the oven lower by 1 Gas No., 25 degrees F or 10 degrees C, and cooking for 5 or 10 minutes less for every hour of cooking time.

Food Storage Times

The recommended storage times given in the recipes are based on certain assumptions, listed below.
- **In the freezer**: all foods, whether cooked or raw, are stored in airtight containers, freezer storage bags or foil packages to prevent freezer 'burn'. The exceptions are soft or fragile foods that are 'open-frozen' until firm, and must then be packaged in the same way.

The recommended storage time is based on the maximum period after which deterioration of flavour or texture may take place. If foods are frozen for longer than recommended, they will not be dangerous to eat but they will be past their prime.

● **In the refrigerator**: all cooked and prepared foods are stored in airtight containers and covered with clingfilm (saran wrap) or foil to avoid dehydration and the transference of flavours and smells from one food to another. All raw fruits and vegetables are stored in plastic bags or containers, according to variety.

The recommended storage time is based on the maximum period during which the food is pleasant and *safe* to eat.

● Fuller details on food storage can be found in my *Entertaining Cookbook* (Robson Books).

ADAPTING GENERAL RECIPES FOR THE JEWISH KITCHEN

Many recipes are published in cookery books, newspapers and magazines which need adapting in some way before they can be used in the Jewish kitchen: they may contain non-kosher ingredients, or combine meat and dairy products in the same dish, or simply include a dairy food in a dish that is to be served as part of a meat meal.

It is then a question of finding suitable alternative ingredients which, while satisfying the requirements of the dietary laws, will not cause a radical alteration in the flavour and texture of the original dish. Here are my suggestions for overcoming the more common problems of this kind.

Butter

● To **fry meat and poultry**: for each 1 oz (25 g/2 tablespoons) butter, substitute 2 tablespoons oil or a chicken-flavoured vegetable fat.

● To **sauté vegetables** for a meat casserole or soup: substitute an equal amount of soft margarine.

● To **fry or roast potatoes**: for each 1 oz (25 g/2 tablespoons) butter, substitute 2 tablespoons oil and a nut of soft margarine.

● In a **pudding or cake** for a meat meal: substitute an equal amount of soft margarine; in addition use water to mix instead of milk. If only a small number of eggs is included in the recipe, substitute an extra egg for 2 fl oz (50 ml/¼ cup) of the milk.

● In **pastry** for a meat meal: for each 5 oz (150 g/⅔ cup) butter, substitute 4 oz (125 g/½ cup) soft margarine and 1 oz (25 g/2 tablespoons) soft white fat (shortening).

● In the **batter for crêpes** for a meat meal: substitute an equal amount of melted margarine.

● In a **chicken soup or sauce**: substitute an equal quantity of chicken-flavoured vegetable fat or soft margarine.

● To **fry pancakes** for a meat meal: substitute a flavourless vegetable oil.

● To **shallow-fry blintzes** for a meat meal: substitute an equal quantity of soft margarine and 2 teaspoons of flavourless oil (to prevent over-browning of the margarine).

Milk

- In a **batter** for crêpes, blintzes, ordinary pancakes or Yorkshire pudding to serve at a meat meal: for each 10 fl oz (275 ml/1¼ cups) of milk, substitute 8 fl oz (225 ml/1 cup) water plus 1 egg and 1 tablespoon flavourless oil. The blintzes and pancakes will be lighter and thinner, and fried stuffed blintzes will be crisper, than when made with milk. Yorkshire pudding will have a crisper crust, but a less spongy inside.
- In a **sauce or soup** that contains chicken or meat, or to serve at a meat meal: *either* substitute kosher non-dairy pouring cream, *or* substitute chicken stock but make the soup look 'creamy' by whisking in 1 egg yolk for each 5 fl oz (150 ml/⅔ cup) of liquid, and heat until steaming.

Cream

- To enrich a **chicken sauce, soup or casserole:** *either* substitute an equal quantity of kosher non-dairy pouring cream (*not* whipping cream); *or*, for each 2 or 3 tablespoons of cream, thicken the sauce with 1 egg yolk; *or*, for each 5 fl oz (150 ml/⅔ cup) double (heavy) or whipping cream, substitute the **nut cream** (but do *not* allow it to boil): liquidize for 1 minute at maximum speed ½ oz (15 g/1 tablespoon) soft margarine, 5 fl oz (150 ml/⅔ cup) water, 1 teaspoon sugar and 2 oz (50 g/½ cup) cashew nuts. Refrigerate for several hours to allow the cream to thicken.
- To substitute for whipped cream in a **cold dessert:** *either* for each 5 fl oz (150 ml/⅔ cup) double (heavy) or whipping cream, substitute 4 fl oz (125 ml/½ cup) of kosher non-dairy whipping cream; *or*, in a jellied (gelatine) dessert, for every 5 fl oz (150 ml/⅔ cup) of double (heavy) or whipping cream, substitute a meringue made by whisking 2 egg whites until stiff and then whisking in 2 teaspoons caster (superfine) sugar — this will produce a lighter, less unctuous texture than cream. I do not think any non-dairy cream is a worthwhile substitute for Crème Chantilly (sweetened whipped cream served to accompany another dish) and it is better to do without it altogether.

Chicken stock

- In a **milk soup or sauce**: substitute vegetable stock made with a cube or paste, or a chicken-flavoured 'parev' stock cube or powder.

Shellfish

- In a **fish cocktail or salad**: substitute an equal weight of fillets of a firm white fish such as halibut, bream or lemon sole, poached, then cut into small cubes or coarsely flaked.
- In a **creamed casserole or filling** for pastry cases or **fish pie**: substitute an equal quantity of fresh salmon, halibut or haddock, poached, then flaked or cut in 1 in (2½ cm) cubes.
- In a **deep-fried dish**: substitute an equal weight of raw fillets of lemon sole, plaice or baby halibut, cut into bite-size strips. Coat with batter or with flour, egg and breadcrumbs (as for Fried Fish in the Jewish Fashion, page 18) and fry as directed.

Smoked or salted meat

- In a **savoury flan**: substitute for bacon or ham a food with a salty tang such as black olives, smoked mackerel, smoked salmon or anchovies.
- In **mixed grills**: substitute an equal weight of smoked top rib for bacon.
- In a **salad** for a meat meal: substitute smoked turkey breast for ham.
- In a **meat or chicken casserole**: you can substitute an equal quantity of smoked top rib for bacon. Many people do not like a smokey flavour in a hot casserole, however, and there is no reason why it should not be omitted in dishes such as *coq au vin* and *boeuf Bourguignonne*.

Hindquarter meat cuts

If you live in a community where the 'porging' of hindquarter meat is not allowed, the following forequarter cuts can be substituted instead (kosher cuts are named first):

- **First-cut shoulder steak, blade steak, alki steak or bola (chuck)**: use in place of braising or stewing cuts, such as round steak.
- **Corner or prime bola (chuck)**: use for braising or pot-roasting in place of topside or silverside of beef.
- **Pickled brisket**: use in place of pickled silverside.
- **Boned and rolled wing rib**, well hung: use in place of sirloin or fillet for roasting.
- **Rib steaks**, well hung: use in place of rump, sirloin or point steak — 'entrecôte' steak is actually rib steak.
- **First-cut lamb chops and cutlets**: use in place of loin or leg chops.
- **Shoulder of lamb**: use in place of leg of lamb.
- **Boned shoulder of lamb**: use in place of boned fillet of lamb.
- **Boned shoulder or breast of lamb**: use in place of boned and cubed leg (for kebabs, for instance).
- **Boned-out veal shoulder chops**: use in place of leg of veal for escalopes, scallopini and schnitzel.
- **Boned shoulder or breast of veal**: use in place of boned-out leg of veal.
- **Minced bola (chuck)**: use in place of minced beefsteak.

CHECKING FOR KASHRUT

As methods of preparing pre-packed and ready-prepared foods are constantly changing, as are the ingredients and additives used in them, please consult a Rabbi if you are uncertain of the kashrut status of any item listed on any packet that does not carry a recognized certificate of kashrut. (For details of how to make kasher meat and poultry at home, see page 114.)

Old Traditions, New Machines

Using modern food-preparation machines to preserve old culinary traditions might seem a paradoxical notion. Yet the selective use of these machines turns them into your servants rather than your masters, and makes it possible to save many of the old labour-intensive dishes that might otherwise be as doomed as the dinosaurs.

There is nothing new about using machines, and most people are already familiar with the most useful ones such as the electric mixer and the indispensable freezer. But now there is a completely new generation of kitchen aids to be investigated and harnessed to the very special needs of the Jewish kitchen.

New skills — and a new time-scale — are needed, when you use the power and speed of electric machines to make dishes that were once prepared painstakingly by hand and cooked by methods perfected over a long period of time. And the very speed at which these new appliances operate is sometimes difficult to appreciate. For instance, it can take at least 10 minutes hard labour with a hand-held chopping knife to chop egg and onion to just the right texture, yet a food processor gives you the same result in just 10 seconds. Similarly, using a microwave oven, the time it takes to poach gefilte fish can be measured in minutes instead of hours.

In this chapter, therefore, I have selected some of the most popular traditional recipes such as borscht, gefilte fish and kuchens, and explained the techniques by which they can be prepared using some of the more revolutionary of these kitchen machines — the food processor, the deep-fryer, the forced-air oven, the re-designed pressure cooker, and — most mind-boggling of all — the microwave oven. In addition, I have given some guidelines to help you to adapt many of the other recipes in the book to this new high-speed style of cooking. Although these new machines sometimes seem a little daunting when you start to learn to use them, I hope this chapter will give you the confidence to master them so that you can harness their power to help you prepare *any* dish from your repertoire in a fraction of the time it once demanded.

THE FOOD PROCESSOR

Here are some special techniques for processing certain foods you may not find in your instruction book. The amounts suggested for processing at one time are based on the *liquid capacity* of the regular size domestic food processor — that is, 28 fl oz (800 ml/3½ cups), which may also be expressed in some brands as a total *bowl capacity* of 3 pints (1¾ litres/8 cups).

• Most machines now incorporate a **pulse action** which makes it much easier to control the degree of fineness to which foods can be processed. You will notice that the pulse action is frequently used in the techniques described here and in recipes throughout the book. If your machine does not have a built-in pulse switch, you can get the same result manually by operating the machine in short bursts instead of using a continual processing action.

• **A purée for soup** made with a food processor is *not* as fine as one produced on a blender; however, many people prefer a little texture in a soup. Strain the cooked vegetables into the bowl and add just enough of the cooking liquid (about ½ cup) to moisten them, then process until the mixture becomes a purée. Return to the pan and whisk to incorporate with the remainder of the cooking liquid.

• To **chop fish**, insert the metal blade, then put in the skinned and filleted fish cut into 1 in (2½ cm) chunks, only half-filling the bowl, and process for 5 seconds *only* or the texture will be ruined. Use this technique for Gefilte Fish (see page 12 for details). To **purée fish**, proceed as for chopped fish, but process for 10 seconds or until fish is reduced to a purée. Use this technique for smoked salmon or haddock mousse, or for making fish terrines or quenelles.

• It is difficult to achieve the evenness of texture of **minced raw meat** (ground meat) put through a butcher's mincer, but this is the best domestic technique to use. Trim the meat of fat and gristle and cut in 1 in (2 ½ cm) chunks. Insert the metal blade, put in about ½ lb (225 g) of meat (approximately 1 cupful) and *pulse* until it is finely chopped. Do *not* process continuously or the meat will become pasty and unsuitable for use.

• To 'mince' **cooked meat** proceed as above, checking the texture every second or two until it is as fine as you need. This is the method to use for meat fillings for blintzes, kreplach or shepherd's pie.

• To make fresh or dried **coating crumbs**, cut the bread in roughly even pieces and process with the metal blade, until as fine as required.

• There are three methods of grating **cheese**, depending on the kind of cheese you are using.

　1. This method is only successful with a hard-pressed cheese such as Cheddar. Cut the cheese in pieces to fit the feed tube, then put it in the freezer for 15 minutes, before placing it in the feed tube and grating with a fine or medium disc.

　2. This is for softer cheese such as Edam or Gouda, which is chopped rather than grated by the machine. Take the cheese from the refrigerator, cut it in 1 in (2½ cm) cubes, then process with the metal blade until as fine as you require.

　3. For Parmesan or other very hard cheese used as a topping, either use a special Parmesan grating disc, or leave the cheese at room temperature for 1 hour, then cut in 1 in (2½ cm) chunks and feed through the tube, with the machine running, on to the metal blade, and process until as fine as required.

• To grate **potatoes** for latkes, use a two-stage technique. First insert the grating disc, then insert the peeled potatoes (cut to fit) into the feed tube and grate into the bowl. Turn into another bowl. Now insert the metal blade, half-fill the processor bowl with the grated potatoes, then pulse until they are just a little coarser than a pulp.

• To chop **onions**, insert the metal blade, then add the peeled onions cut in 1 in (2½ cm) chunks and *pulse* until as fine as you require. Do *not* process continuously or the onions may be chopped too fine, and the excess moisture they exude will stop them from browning properly. Use the same technique for chopping other juicy vegetables.

• For **parsley** and other **herbs**, remove any stalks, wash and thoroughly spin-dry. Insert the metal blade and chop as finely as required. Chopped herbs are rather moist, so if they are not to be used within 24 hours, freeze them until required.

• The food processor makes short work of chopping or grinding **nuts**. If you have just blanched the nuts in boiling water, first dry them off for 10 or 15 minutes in a low oven (Gas No. 2, 300 degrees F, 150 degrees C) or in the microwave oven (turned to HIGH, laid on a paper towel, until dry to the touch). Use the metal blade and do not process more than ½ lb (225 g/2 cups) of nuts in a standard-sized machine. *Pulse* so that you can stop when they are chopped as finely as you require.

• **Hollandaise sauce**: the food processor offers you a foolproof method for a normally tricky sauce. Follow the instructions given for making Avocado Hollandaise on page 95, making sure that both the liquid and the fat are *very hot* when added to the egg yolks in the machine.

• The trick for slicing **apples** is first to cut the apple in half right through the stalk, then peel (if desired) and cut out the core. Cut a small slice from the side of the apple, then place it in the feed tube with this cut side downwards, against the slicing disc. In this way, the apple will sit evenly in the tube, and you will achieve perfect slices.

• Prepare **sorbets** following the detailed instructions for making the Apple and Cider Sorbet on page 223. The food processor can handle chunks of almost solid sorbet, and will process the mixture until it is as smooth as one made in a special *sorbetière*.

• **Chocolate** cannot be grated using the grating disc, as the chocolate starts to melt with the heat of friction. Instead, break it into 1 in (2½ cm) cubes, put in the bowl, and process with the metal blade until as fine as required.

• For **pasta (lokshen) dough**: see the recipe for Home-made Lokshen on page 10.

• For **short crust pastry**, I prefer to process both the dry and the liquid ingredients at the same time. This prevents the fat being rubbed in too finely, and so making shortbread rather than pastry. The use of a block margarine, rather than a soft one, will make the pastry easier to handle, but soft margarine can be used if you prefer it for dietary reasons. Insert the metal blade, and put the dry ingredients and the well-chilled fat (cut into 1 in (2½ cm) chunks) into the bowl. Mix the liquid ingredients well together, including eggs if used, then turn on the machine, and pour them down the feed tube, pulsing only until the mixture looks like a moist crumble, then tip it into a bowl and gather together into a ball. Flatten into a block, wrap in film or foil and chill for at least half an hour before rolling out. This makes a short but slightly flaky melt-in-the-mouth pastry that is easy to roll out.

• Using a food processor is the easiest way to make **choux pastry**. Follow the detailed instructions given in the recipe for Haddock Gougère (page 107), processing until the paste looks shiny and can be pulled up into floppy peaks.

• Different techniques are used to make **biscuit (cookie) dough**, depending on whether the dough is to be rolled, moulded or dropped from a teaspoon. For rolled doughs, follow the technique for pastry. For other doughs, follow the instructions given in individual recipes.

• You will find instructions for kneading **yeast doughs** in the recipes for kuchens, on page 16. Any of the bread doughs in this book can be made using a food processor, mixing and kneading in the same way as for kuchen.

• The technique below produces a rich 'creamed' **cake** with a larger volume and a more tender texture than when all the ingredients are processed together. I give it in detail as it is not the method usually advised in instruction books. It is important to have all the ingredients at room temperature — the butter or margarine should be almost as soft as mayonnaise.

1. Insert the metal blade.
2. Put the eggs and sugar in the bowl.
3. Process for 1 minute, scraping down the sides once with a rubber spatula — you should not be able to feel any grains of sugar in the egg by then.
4. With the motor running, add spoonfuls of the soft fat down the feed tube,

processing all the time. At this stage the mixture will look like mayonnaise.

5. Add any liquid and flavouring such as rind and essence and process until smooth.

6. Spoon the sifted dry ingredients on top of the creamed mixture.

7. *Pulse* until the mixture is blended, scraping down the sides of the bowl once; about 4 seconds.

8. Spoon into the prepared tin and bake in the usual way.

CHOPPED EGG AND ONION

SERVES 6 as a starter, 15 as a spread   *Will keep 1 day under refrigeration*

When preparing in a food processor any mixture which should be chopped rather than puréed, such as Chopped Liver or Chopped Herring, it is essential to pulse in the ingredients rather than to process them continually. This same mixture makes a delicious sandwich spread if the bulbs and 2 in (5 cm) of the green from a small bunch of spring onions (green onions) are used instead of ordinary onion, and the mixture is bound with soft butter or margarine. The Chopped Egg and Onion can be served with a spoonful of Chopped Liver for a special hors d'oeuvre, or spread on crackers or challah at a cocktail party.

*1 medium (5 oz (150 g)) onion, cut in 1 in
(2½ cm) chunks
8 hard-boiled eggs, shelled and halved*

*2 rounded tablespoons soft margarine,
rendered chicken fat or chicken-flavoured
vegetable fat
½ teaspoon salt; 10 grinds black pepper*

Put the onion into the bowl and pulse for 3 seconds until roughly chopped. Add all the remaining ingredients and pulse for a further 5 seconds, until finely chopped and blended together. Turn into a small gratin dish, smooth the top level and mark with a pattern using the blade of a knife. Cover with foil and chill for at least an hour before serving.

BORSCHT

SERVES 6–8

*Freeze 3 months
Cooked beet juice will keep 4 days under
refrigeration, the complete soup for 2 days*

By chopping the vegetables very finely in the food processor the flavour can be extracted from them very quickly, and the soup will have a very fresh taste. It is best to make the soup one day, then cool and reheat until steaming just before serving, on the next. Hot borscht is usually served with a garnish of sliced boiled potatoes, cold borscht with a swirl of soured cream.

2 lb (1 kg) old beets or 3 bunches of young beets
1 medium carrot, peeled
1 medium (5 oz (150 g)) onion, peeled
2½ pints (1½ litres/6 cups) water (for dairy borscht) or meat or chicken stock (for meat borscht)
15 grinds of black pepper

2 teaspoons salt (if water is used)
2 tablespoons sugar

TO THICKEN:
3 tablespoons lemon juice or 1 teaspoon citric acid crystals
3 whole eggs

Have ready a half-gallon (2¼ litre/10 cup) soup pan. Trim the beets, then peel or scrape. Cut all the vegetables into 1 in (2½ cm) chunks, then process in two batches until very finely chopped. Put in the pan with the water or stock, pepper, salt (if used) and sugar. Bring to the boil, cover and simmer for 20 minutes, until the vegetables are soft and the liquid is a rich dark red.

Pour the contents through a coarse strainer into a bowl and discard the vegetables, then return the strained beet juice to the pan and leave on a low heat. Put the lemon juice and the whole eggs into the food processor and process for 5 seconds, until well mixed. With the motor running, pour two ladles of the hot beet juice through the feed tube and process for a further 3 seconds, then add to the beet juice in the pan and heat gently, whisking constantly with a batter whisk until the soup is steaming and has thickened slightly. Do not let it boil, or it will curdle. Taste, and adjust the seasoning so that there is a gentle blend of sweet and sour. The soup reheats well.

HOME-MADE LOKSHEN EGG NOODLES

Makes about 12 oz (350 g) dry weight   *Keeps 4 days under refrigeration*

This may be counted a labour of love, but it's great fun to make, and there's none of the tedious kneading our grandmothers had to do when they made this dough every Friday, and left the noodles on teatowels to dry, festooned on the back of the kitchen chair!

8 oz (225 g/2 cups) plain (all-purpose) flour
2 eggs

Pinch of salt
1 tablespoon plus 2 teaspoons lukewarm water

With the metal blade, process the flour, eggs and salt until thoroughly blended, then slowly add the water through the feed tube until it forms a ball that leaves the sides of the bowl clear. If the dough is too sticky (it will depend on the absorbent quality of the flour), add a little more flour. Process for a further 40 seconds to knead dough, then turn it out on to a floured board. Knead briefly with the heel of the hand to ensure that the dough looks like chamois leather — that is, very smooth and springy. Cover with a large bowl and leave to 'relax' for 20 minutes.

To shape the lokshen Divide the dough in two for easier handling. Roll each piece until it is paper-thin and you can see the board through it. It will then be about 14 in (35 cm) square — if sufficiently kneaded, it will not stick to the board. Place a dry teatowel on the table and dust it lightly with flour. Place the squares of dough on top and sprinkle them with flour. Leave for a further 20 minutes, or until the surface no longer feels sticky to the touch. Roll each sheet into a loose, flattened 'Swiss roll', about 3 in (7½ cm) in diameter, and cut it into slices each ⅛–½ in (¼–½ cm) wide, using a sharp cook's knife, and then unroll. If you are going to cook the lokshen the same day, spread them out on the teatowel and leave for 5 minutes. If you wish to use them later, drape the towel over the back of a trolley handle or chair, and leave them until they are dry and brittle (about an hour). Cook the lokshen in boiling soup or salted water, until bite-tender.

VARIATIONS

Plaetschen (noodle squares)   Cut the rolled-out dough into strips ½ in (1½ cm) wide. Pile the strips on top of each other and then cut into ½ in (1½ cm) squares. When required, boil until tender and use as a garnish for a consommé or chicken soup.

Shpaetzlen (bow knots)   Cut the rolled-out dough into strips, 1 in (2½ cm) wide, and then into 1 in (2½ cm) squares. Pinch the squares with the fingers to make little bow shapes. When required, boil until tender and use as a garnish for a chicken or tomato soup.

Fingerhuetchen (thimble noodles)   Roll out the dough, but leave to dry for only 15 minutes, then fold in two. Using a floured thimble or tiny metal cutter, cut through both layers making little circles. Drop into deep fat heated to 375 degrees F, 190 degrees C (when a square of bread will brown in 30 seconds), and cook for a minute or until slightly browned. Drain on paper towels, then serve hot in chicken soup. They may be reheated in a moderate oven.

KREPLACH 'JEWISH RAVIOLI'

Makes 75 kreplach
SERVES 8 people, twice

Freeze cooked 3 months
Will keep 3 days, raw or cooked, under refrigeration

Affectionately known as 'Jewish ravioli', these three-cornered pastries are made in many households on Kol Nidre to garnish the soup served at the meal on the Eve of the Fast. Whether this is a form of penance on the part of the cook, I do not know, for they have always taken a deal of time and patience to prepare — at least in the past. Fortunately both are drastically reduced when the dough is kneaded in the food processor instead of by hand. The three-cornered shape is said to represent the Patriarchs Abraham, Isaac and Jacob, and on Shavuot they are made with a filling of cream cheese, to celebrate the giving of the dietary laws and the consequent distinction between meat and dairy foods. The meat filling for kreplach is made from shin beef which has first been cooked in water until tender, to make a stock for a meat soup.

1 recipe Home-made Lokshen

THE FILLING:
Half a medium (5 oz (150 g)) onion, peeled and cut in 1 in (2½ cm) chunks

1 lb (450 g) shin beef cooked and cut in 1 in (2½ cm) cubes
1 egg
½ level teaspoon salt; speck of white pepper

Pulse the onion and meat until finely 'minced' — after about 5 seconds — do *not* process until pasty. Add the egg and seasonings through the feed tube and process until evenly moistened and just beginning to cling together — another 3 seconds. Turn into a bowl.

Have ready a half-gallon (2¼ litres/10 cups) pan, half-full of boiling water with 2 teaspoons salt in it. Roll out the dough as thinly as for the lokshen, but do not leave it to dry. Instead, roll it into a flattened 'Swiss roll' and cut across into pieces 2 in (5 cm) wide, then unroll and pile these strips on top of each other and cut them into 2 in (5 cm) squares. Put a teaspoon of the meat filling in the centre of each square, then fold over into a triangle, pressing the edges securely to seal — dampen them with water only if necessary. As each krepel is formed, lay it on a sheet of greaseproof paper.

Add one-third of the kreplach to the boiling water, bring back to the boil, cover and cook for 15 minutes, tasting after 10 minutes to see if they are tender. Drain and reserve. Repeat with the remaining kreplach. Reheat in the soup for 5–10 minutes. Alternatively, the *uncooked* kreplach can be left out in the kitchen until the surface is quite dry — after about 2 hours (turning once or twice) — then stored in the refrigerator and cooked as required.

GEFILTE FISH MIX

2 lb (1 kg) fish makes 12–14 patties or balls	Freeze 3 months raw or cooked
6 lb (2¾ kg) fish makes 36–40 patties or balls	Fish, whether fried or stewed, will keep 3 days under refrigeration

Gefilte fish is one of the earliest forms of convenience food, and it is still the one traditional dish (besides Chicken Soup) that is eaten every week in the majority of Jewish households. It lends itself particularly well to preparation on the food processor, as the action of the metal blade almost perfectly duplicates the traditional method of chopping by hand with a 'hackmesser'. It is extremely quick and easy to prepare a large quantity that can be formed into patties and frozen raw; even 6 lb (2¾ kg) of fish can be mixed in less than half an hour. These patties can then be defrosted and fried, stewed or coated with a sauce as preferred. In addition it is useful to keep a small stock of ready-fried patties, which freeze particularly well and which will taste freshly cooked if crisped in a moderate oven just before they are served.

I find that 2 lb (1 kg) is the minimum of fish worth processing, and 6 lb (2¾ kg) the maximum that can easily be handled by one person at one time. Do not process the fish longer than stated in the recipe, or you will end up with puréed rather than chopped fish balls. To get the best results, allow the matzah meal to swell in the egg and onion purée, before adding to the fish. If you are short of time, the fish mix can be refrigerated overnight and then shaped and cooked or frozen the next day. I do not advise freezing the fish mix without shaping it, as it takes so long to defrost.

Equal quantities of haddock and cod make a tasty and relatively economical mixture. However, when small fillets of hake can be bought at a reasonable price, they can be used instead — they do give the dish a superior flavour and texture.

12

TO MAKE 36–40 PATTIES OR BALLS:
3 lb (1½ kg) haddock fillet, skinned
3 lb (1½ kg) cod fillet, skinned
3 medium (5 oz (150 g)) onions, peeled
6 eggs
6 teaspoons salt; ½ teaspoon white pepper
6 teaspoons sugar (or equivalent artificial sweetener)
3 tablespoons oil
6 oz (175 g/1½ cups) medium matzah meal

TO MAKE 12–14 PATTIES OR BALLS:
1 lb (450 g) haddock fillet, skinned
1 lb (450 g) cod fillet, skinned
1 medium (5 oz (150 g)) onion, peeled
2 eggs
2 teaspoons salt; pinch of white pepper
2 teaspoons sugar (or equivalent artificial sweetener)
1 tablespoon oil
2 oz (50 g/½ cup) medium matzah meal

Wash and salt the fish and leave to drain. Cut the onion in 1 in (2½ cm) chunks and put into the food processor, together with the eggs, seasonings and oil, then process until reduced to a smooth purée. (If you wish to make the larger quantity using a processor of standard (1½ pints, ¾ litre, 4 cups) liquid capacity, you will need to do this in two batches, using 3 eggs and 1½ onions each time — all the seasonings can go into one batch to avoid complicated arithmetic!) Pour this purée into a large bowl and stir in the matzah meal, then leave to swell.

Cut the fish into 1 in (2½ cm) chunks and put in the processor, half-filling the bowl each time. Process for 5 seconds, until the fish is finely chopped, then add to the egg and onion purée and blend in using a large fork. Repeat until all the fish has been processed, then mix thoroughly — if preparing a large quantity, this is most easily done with the widespread fingers of one hand. The mixture should be firm enough to shape into a soft patty or ball. If it feels too 'cloggy', rinse out the processor bowl with a tablespoon or two of water and stir that in. If it feels very soft, stir in a tablespoon or two of meal. Leave for half an hour, or overnight (under refrigeration) if preferred.

To shape into patties or balls Dip the hands into cold water and form the mixture into patties about 2½ in (7 cm) long, 1½ in (3 cm) wide and ¾ in (2 cm) thick, or into balls the size of a small apple. The fish can now be cooked or frozen raw.

To freeze raw Arrange the patties or balls side by side on a tray lined with greaseproof paper or foil. When the tray is full, cover with a layer of paper or foil and make another layer on top. Put the tray, uncovered, in the freezer for 2 hours or until the patties are firm to the touch. They can now be packed, 12 into a plastic bag, or they can be individually over-wrapped in clingfilm (saran-wrapped), to make it easy to remove a few at a time.

To defrost Lay the frozen patties side by side on a board. Leave either overnight in the refrigerator, or from 1 to 3 hours at room temperature, until they are soft all the way through.

To fry the patties This is most easily done in a deep-fryer, but you can use a deep frying pan (skillet). In either case, coat the patties evenly, either with fine dry breadcrumbs (easily prepared from dry stale challah on the food processor) or with medium matzah meal.

To use a deep-fryer Remove the basket, then heat the oil to 375 degrees F, 190 degrees C. Cook 5 or 6 patties at a time, allowing approximately 5 minutes or until a rich golden-brown.

To use a frying pan Heat oil 1 in (2½ cm) deep until it is hot enough to brown an inch (2½ cm) cube of bread in 30 seconds. Gently lower in enough balls to fill the pan without overcrowding it — usually 5 or 6 in a 9 in (22 cm) pan. Cook steadily over moderate heat, turning every 2 or 3 minutes, until the patties are an even brown, 7 or

8 minutes in all. In either case, drain the fish by standing it up round the sides of a dish lined with crumpled kitchen or tissue paper.

For traditional platter of Gefilte Fish, see page 314.

For Gefilte Fish in Pepper, Tomato and Mushroom Sauce, see page 312.

For Gefilte Fish Balls in a Lemon Sauce, see pages 26 and 216.

For Gefilte Fish poached in a fat-free Provençal sauce, see page 38.

POTATO LATKES

SERVES 4–6   *Freeze 4 months*

Potato latkes for Hanukkah used to mean raw knuckles from the 'rebeizen' — the hand grater which had to be used. Now the potatoes can be grated much more efficiently, if less excitingly, with the grating disc of the food processor. With most grating discs the potato pulp will be too coarse, however, so it is advisable to process it briefly as well, using the metal blade. The potatoes should be grated only 15 minutes before you cook them, otherwise they tend to go an unattractive brown.

4 large potatoes, peeled (weight about 1½ lb (675 g) — enough to fill a pint (575 ml/2½ cups) measure when grated)
Half a medium (5 oz (150 g)) onion, peeled and cut in 1 in (2½ cm) chunks
2 eggs

1 level teaspoon salt; speck of white pepper
4 tablespoons self-raising flour or 4 tablespoons plain (all-purpose) flour plus a pinch of baking powder
Any flavourless oil for frying

Cut the potatoes to fit the feed tube, then grate through the grating disc. Turn into a metal sieve, and press down firmly with a spoon to remove as much moisture as possible. Leave to drain.

Put the onion, eggs, seasonings and flour into the bowl and process with the metal blade until smooth, about 5 seconds. Add the drained potatoes, and *pulse* for 3 or 4 seconds, until the potatoes are much finer and are almost reduced to a coarse pulp. Put oil ½ in (1½ cm) deep into a 9 in (22 cm) heavy frying pan (skillet). Heat until a little of the raw mixture sizzles when it is put into the pan. Put tablespoons of the potato mixture into the pan, leaving room between for them to spread. Cook over moderate heat until the underside is a rich brown, then turn, and brown the other side. Drain on crumpled paper; then serve as soon as possible, or keep hot in a moderate oven, Gas No. 4, 350 degrees F, 180 degrees C, for 15 minutes.

To freeze   Cook the latkes, but only until they are a pale brown. Drain thoroughly, then open-freeze. When firm, put into plastic bags.

To reheat   *Either* put the frozen latkes into hot deep fat and fry for 2 or 3 minutes until a rich brown, *or* fry in shallow fat for 2 or 3 minutes on each side until a rich brown. Drain and serve.

To cook latkes for a party   The latkes are most quickly cooked in a deep-fryer, dropping large teaspoons of the mixture into fat heated to 375 degrees F, 190 degrees C. A batch will take about 4 minutes, and they can then be speared on sticks to serve.

To reheat a large number of latkes for a party   Defrost the latkes for 1 hour on a foil-covered baking sheet, then reheat at Gas No. 8, 450 degrees F, 230 degrees C, for 7 or 8 minutes, until crisp and brown.

CHOCOLATE LOAF WITH COFFEE FUDGE TOPPING

Cuts into about 15 slices

Freeze 3 months
Will keep 1 week in an airtight container

Both the cake and the topping are mixed on the food processor. This is the method to use for any rich cake that would normally be made by the creaming method — it produces a bigger cake, with a finer, moister texture than one made by the 'one-stage' method. This cake can be mixed in a regular-sized food processor.

3 eggs
7 oz (220 g/1 cup) dark brown sugar
6 oz (175 g/³⁄₄ cup) soft butter or margarine
3 tablespoons milk or water (for a meat meal)
1½ teaspoons vanilla essence (extract)
6 oz (175 g/³⁄₄ cup) special sponge (cake) flour or ordinary white self-raising flour, or
6 oz (175 g/³⁄₄ cup) plain (all-purpose) flour plus 1½ teaspoons baking powder
3 tablespoons cocoa

2 tablespoons drinking chocolate (instant chocolate)

THE TOPPING:
2 teaspoons instant coffee, dissolved in 2 teaspoons boiling water
2 oz (50 g/¼ cup) butter or margarine (for a meat meal)
6 oz (175 g/1½ cups) icing (confectioners') sugar
1 teaspoon vanilla essence (extract)

Preheat the oven to Gas No. 4, 350 degrees F, 180 degrees C. Grease a loaf tin measuring about 11 x 3 in (27 x 7 cm) across the base, and 3 in (7½ cm) in depth, and line the base and two short sides with a strip of silicone paper. (If you use a shorter loaf tin, making a deeper cake, bake the cake one Gas No., 25 degrees F, 10 degrees C lower.)

Put the unbeaten eggs and the sugar in the bowl of the processor, and process for 1 minute. With the motor running, add spoonfuls of the soft fat through the feed tube — the mixture will now resemble mayonnaise. Add the milk and the vanilla and process for a further 3 seconds. Take off the lid and add the flour sifted with the cocoa and drinking chocolate. Cover and pulse for 5 or 6 seconds, until the mixture is an even colour, scraping the sides down once with a spatula if necessary. Spoon into the prepared tin and level with the spatula.

Put into the oven, then reduce the heat to Gas No. 3, 325 degrees F, 160 degrees C, and cook for 20 minutes, then turn back up to Gas No. 4, 350 degrees F, 180 degrees C for a further 25 minutes until the cake is springy to gentle touch and a skewer inserted in the middle comes out clean. (The cooking time will vary according to the type of oven, but don't start testing until the cake has been in the oven for at least 40 minutes.) Turn the cake out on to a cooling rack.

While the cake is cooking, make the topping Without washing the bowl, put in all the ingredients and process for 15 seconds until smooth and fluffy. Pile on the cooled cake and rough up with a fork.

KUCHENS
DATE KUCHEN, CINNAMON RAISIN KUCHEN, POPPYSEED KUCHEN

Makes 2 large loaves

Freeze cooked kuchens for 3 months
Freeze unrisen dough 3 months
Freeze shaped but unbaked kuchens for 2 weeks
Will keep fresh 3 days under refrigeration

If you are shy of yeast cookery — particularly the kneading of the dough — this is a marvellous way to gain confidence, and to produce kuchens of professional standards from the start. This amount of mixture can be processed either on a large food processor (5 pints/2¾ litres/12 cups bowl size), or on a regular-sized one fitted with a special dough dome. Or half the mixture can be processed at a time, on a regular-sized (3 pints/1¾ litres/8 cups bowl size) machine, the two balls made into one, and then risen and shaped together as in the recipe. Rather less liquid is used in this dough than in one kneaded with a dough hook, as it is distributed so much more quickly and evenly by the food processor. If the dough does not form a ball immediately after all the liquid has been added, do not process it any further but add an extra 1 or 2 tablespoons flour and then continue to process until a ball is formed.

This recipe makes a very tender kuchen which is delicious when sliced and spread with butter, margarine or cream cheese. It is also good to eat if toasted when it begins to dry out after a few days. The dough can be risen and shaped on the same day, or left to rise overnight. Or the shaped kuchens can be frozen and then defrosted in the refrigerator overnight, or in 15-second 'bursts' on HIGH (100% power) in the microwave, with a 10-minute resting period in between, until the dough feels slightly warm again to the touch. It is then left to rise until spongy as described in the recipe.

2 eggs
5 fl oz (150 ml/²⁄₃ cup) milk and water (see method)
1 oz (25 g/2 cakes) fresh yeast or 2 sachets easy-blend dried yeast

1 lb (450 g/4 cups) plain (all-purpose) white flour or bread flour
1 level teaspoon salt
3 oz (75 g/¹⁄₃ cup) soft butter or margarine
3 oz (75 g/¹⁄₃ cup) caster (superfine) sugar

Break the eggs into a measuring jug, add approximately 3 fl oz (75 g/²⁄₃ cup) cold milk, whisk to blend, then make up to 9 fl oz (250 ml/1 cup plus 2 tablespoons) with *very* hot water (the liquid should now be pleasantly warm). Dissolve the fresh yeast, if used, in this liquid (don't add easy-blend yeast at this stage, however). Put the flour, salt, butter or margarine and sugar (and easy-blend yeast if used) into the bowl of the food processor, and process for 2 seconds to rub in the fat, then add the liquid through the feed tube and process until a soft ball of dough is formed round the knife. Add the extra flour if necessary, then process for a further 40 seconds, to knead the dough.

Lift out the knife, leaving the dough in the bowl, then flour your hand and lift out the dough. Knead for 30 seconds on a floured board, then put in a large lightly oiled bowl and turn over to coat with the oil. Cover the bowl with clingfilm (saran wrap).
To rise and shape the same day Leave the dough in the kitchen for 1 hour or until it has doubled in bulk, then put back on the food processor, and process for 30 seconds

(or knead by hand for 2 minutes). Put the dough back into the bowl, re-cover and leave to rise for a further 30 minutes — this second rising gives the dough a very fine texture, and it is now ready to shape into the kuchen.

To rise overnight   Leave in the least cold part of the refrigerator. Next day, allow the dough to come back to room temperature (after about 2 hours) or put on HIGH (100% power) in the microwave for 15 seconds, repeating at 10-minute intervals, or until slightly warm to the touch.

The dough is now ready to roll, fill and shape with either a date, a cinnamon and raisin or a poppyseed filling.

DATE FILLING:
½ lb (225 g/1⅓ cups) stoned dried dates, chopped
½ oz (15 g/1 tablespoon) butter or margarine
1½ level teaspoons cinnamon
3 tablespoons sultanas (white raisins)

Put all the ingredients into a small pan, cover and simmer, stirring occasionally, until the mixture forms a thick juicy paste. Allow to cool.

CINNAMON RAISIN FILLING:
1 oz (25 g/2 tablespoons) butter or margarine
2 oz (50 g/¼ cup) soft light brown sugar
1 teaspoon cinnamon
2 oz (50 g/⅓ cup) sultanas (white raisins)
2 oz (50 g/½ cup) flaked hazelnuts (filberts) (optional)

Mix all the ingredients together until spreadable.

POPPYSEED FILLING:
Make exactly as the filling for the Hamantaschen on page 366.

ICING TO DECORATE:
2 oz (50 g/½ cup) sifted icing (confectioners') sugar
2 teaspoons (approximately) lemon or orange juice
1 oz (25 g/¼ cup) chopped walnuts

To shape the kuchen   Grease two 2 lb (1 kg) loaf tins measuring about 9 x 5 x 3 in (22 x 12 x 7 cm). Roll out half the dough into a rectangle 1 in (2½ cm) wider than the base of the loaf tin and ½ in (1½ cm) thick. Spread with the chosen filling to within ½ in (1½ cm) of either side, then turn these sides over the filling to seal it in, and roll up tightly into a 'Swiss roll'. Lay in one of the tins, join side down. Repeat with the other half of the dough. Put the tins into a large plastic bag and leave until the kuchens look puffy and feel spongy to the touch — 30 or 40 minutes.

Meanwhile, preheat the oven to Gas No. 4, 350 degrees F, 180 degrees C. Bake the kuchens for 35 or 40 minutes until golden-brown and firm to gentle touch. Turn on to a cooling rack, and whilst still warm, spread with the icing made by adding enough fruit juice to the icing sugar to make a thick coating consistency. Decorate with the nuts.

THE DEEP-FRYER

FRIED FISH IN THE JEWISH FASHION, COOKED IN THE DEEP-FRYER

Freeze 3 months
Will keep fresh 3 days under refrigeration, 2 days in a cool cupboard

Jewish fried fish is still eminently edible 2 days after it has been fried, and this is entirely due to the use of *oil* rather than a solid fat as the cooking medium. Oil does not congeal when it cools, so although the fish is undoubtedly at its best the day it has been cooked, the coating will stay crisp for quite a long time.

The *frying* of the fish in an ordinary frying pan has always demanded a high degree of skill and experience, particularly to judge and maintain the correct temperature of the oil, which is essential if the fish is to be cooked *inside* at the same time as the coating *outside* turns the correct shade of brown. However, a thermostatically controlled deep-fryer ensures an absolutely constant temperature, so that provided the fish is properly coated to prevent any moisture from it escaping into the oil, even a beginner can produce crisp, perfectly cooked fish every time.

The procedure for *coating* fish is simple but specific: it is important to select three shallow containers slightly longer and wider than the fillet or steak of fish. These containers are arranged side by side with plain (all-purpose) flour in the first one, one beaten egg for each 6 pieces of fish in the second, and dried breadcrumbs (the colour of oatmeal) or medium matzah meal in the third. The fish is washed, lightly sprinkled with salt, then left to drain in a colander for half an hour. It then goes into the flour for a very thin coating, then into the egg, which is spread evenly over the entire surface with a pastry brush, and finally into the crumbs which are patted on in an even layer with the hands. Chopped fish balls are coated *only* with crumbs or matzah meal, as the matzah meal they contain prevents moisture in the fish from escaping.

The *frying oil* can be corn oil, sunflower oil or peanut oil — all give similar results. The frying basket is removed (as this reduces the capacity of the pan), and then the oil is preheated to the temperature recommended by the manufacturer — usually 375 degrees F, 190 degrees C. It is essential not to crowd the pan, as too much cold fish can drastically lower the temperature of the oil and so allow the fish to absorb some of it before the temperature can be restored. The pan is closed, and the timer set as follows:

5 minutes for chopped fish patties
7 minutes for fillets
8 minutes for steaks

While the fish is cooking, line a shallow casserole with crumpled paper towels or tissue paper. When the fish is cooked, lift it out with a fish slice or slotted spoon and lay it on its side, round the edges of the dish, so that any drops of free oil can drain away. After 5 or 6 minutes, the fish can be lifted carefully on to a serving dish. If the

18

fish is to be eaten within 2 days, I prefer to store it in a cool cupboard rather than a refrigerator, as it will keep crisper for longer if not exposed to a damp atmosphere.

THE FORCED-AIR OVEN
TURKEY ROASTED IN A FORCED-AIR OVEN

Freeze cooked 3 months
Cooked bird will keep 3 days under
refrigeration

When an oven is heated by hot air blown by a fan rather than by heating elements fixed to its walls, a very even temperature can be achieved throughout the entire oven cavity, so that the old idea that the hottest part of the oven is towards the top no longer applies. It also means that, provided they are placed on some kind of rack, meat and poultry can be roasted without being turned. A large turkey can therefore be placed at the very bottom of the oven and still be cooked at the same temperature as in a normal oven, but for only 15 minutes to the pound (450 g).

By using this method, a 12 lb (5½ kg) stuffed bird (giving 15 ample portions) will be cooked to perfection in 3 hours. It then has a 20–30 minute 'resting' period, to allow it to 'settle' and so become easy to carve. The 'rest' takes place in the oven itself (turned down to the lowest gas setting, 250 degrees F, 100 degrees C) or at the side of the oven with the bird lightly covered in foil.

I have tried every method of cooking a turkey, both with and without some kind of protection. I have found that a bird that is completely covered with buttermuslin (cheesecloth) (or a similar material) soaked in oil is the easiest to handle during the cooking period and turns a wonderful mahogany brown with succulent flesh.

1 fresh turkey of suitable size
Sea salt
A piece of buttermuslin (cheesecloth) large

enough to cover the entire bird, or light-coloured non-woven kitchen cloths of a similar size

To prepare the bird for the oven (this can be done the day before) If desired, stuff the neck and the cavity of the bird. Tie the legs together with string, then tie the wings close to the breast. Paint the bird all over with a thin layer of oil, then sprinkle liberally with sea salt. Cover completely with muslin (cheesecloth) or kitchen cloths, tucking the edges well in underneath. Put some oil into a small basin, then use a pastry brush to paint it in an even moist layer all over the cloth covering the bird. Either refrigerate overnight, or roast at once as follows: Preheat the oven for 10 minutes to its maximum temperature (usually Gas No. 4½, 375 degrees F, 190 degrees C). Lay the bird, breast up, on a rack standing in a roasting tin on the *bottom* shelf of the oven and immediately reduce the temperature to Gas No. 3, 325 degrees F, 160 degrees C.

Calculate the roasting time as follows For a bird up to 12 lb (5½ kg) (unstuffed weight) allow 20 minutes to the pound (450 g). For a bird 12 lb (5½ kg) and over (unstuffed weight) allow 15 minutes to the pound (450 g). I do not find it necessary to allow a longer cooking time if the bird is stuffed. Allow 20–30 minutes 'resting period' for any weight of the bird.

To baste the bird At least once an hour, baste the bird by moistening the cloth covering with the oil which will have collected in the bottom of the roasting tin. Try to ensure that this covering never completely dries out.

To test for done-ness Pierce the thigh with a skewer. If a creamy liquid oozes out, the bird is cooked; if it is faintly tinged with pink, leave it another 20 minutes and test again. Remove the cloth covering from the bird and leave to rest until it is carved.

You will find recipes for turkey stuffings and cooking times for use in a conventional oven in my *Entertaining Cookbook* (Robson Books).

THE PRESSURE COOKER
HANUKKAH PUDDING COOKED IN A PRESSURE COOKER

SERVES 8–10	Will keep in a cool larder for up to a year

A pressure cooker can cut the cooking time by two-thirds for this rich pudding, so that you will be using gas or electric heat for 2 hours, instead of the 6 needed to steam the pudding in the traditional way. The pudding is reheated on the day of service in 30 minutes under pressure instead of 2 hours in a steamer. (Or it can be reheated on HIGH (100% power) in the microwave for 3½ minutes.)

This is not a traditional Jewish recipe, but has been adopted by many Jewish households to serve at Hanukkah meals. It is rich and moist, and should be allowed to mature for at least 1 month before it is served, with either the Lemon Sauce or the Weinchadau on page 362. To achieve the best flavour, mix the pudding one day and cook it the next.

2 oz (50 g/½ cup) plain (all-purpose) flour
Pinch of salt
½ level teaspoon mixed sweet spice
¼ teaspoon each ground cinnamon and nutmeg
2 oz (50 g/1 cup) fresh breadcrumbs
4 oz (125 g/⅔ cup) each stoned raisins, sultanas (white raisins) and currants
4 oz (125 g/½ cup) vegetarian suet, white fat (shortening) or soft margarine

4 oz (125 g/½ cup) dark brown sugar
2 oz (50 g/¼ cup) carrots, peeled and finely grated
1 small (4 oz (125 g)) cooking apple, peeled, cored and grated
1 tablespoon marmalade
1 egg, beaten to blend
Grated rind and juice of half a lemon and half a small orange
2 tablespoons brandy or rum

Do not mix the pudding in a food processor, as it's impossible to avoid chopping the dried fruit much too finely. Use an electric mixer, or you can easily make the pudding by hand. Grease a 2 lb (1 kg) pudding basin of earthenware or heatproof glass. Have ready a piece of silicone paper and one of foil, large enough to cover the basin with 2 in (5 cm) all round to spare.

Sieve the flour, salt and spices into the mixing bowl, then add all the remaining ingredients in the order given. Mix thoroughly until all the ingredients are evenly blended. Spoon into the greased basin and cover first with the paper and then with the foil, tucking the excess under the rim of the basin to make the cover airtight. Leave at room temperature overnight.

Next day, put in the pressure cooker and steam for 15 minutes, then cook at pressure for 1¾ hours, according to the manufacturer's instructions for a similar type of rich pudding. Allow the pressure to reduce slowly. When the pudding is cold, remove the cover and replace it with fresh paper and foil. Store in a cool place until required. Reheat for 30 minutes, according to the manufacturer's instructions for a 2 lb (1 kg) rich fruit pudding.

THE MICROWAVE OVEN

In addition to those dishes for which I give detailed instructions, many other recipes in this book can be easily adapted for cooking in a microwave oven. These include many of the soups, casseroles and stews, as well as the poached and baked fish dishes, vegetables, fruit compôtes and cakes. I do not advise you to try and cook either two-crust pies or soufflés in the microwave, or any dish that depends on oven browning for its eye appeal — unless of course your particular oven has some kind of browning facility built-in.

• The first thing to do when you set out to **adapt a conventional recipe** for the microwave is to find a similar recipe in the instruction book that comes with your machine, and use it as a guide to power levels and cooking times — as a rule of thumb, you can estimate that the food will cook in a *quarter* of the time it takes in a conventional oven or on top of the stove.

• Unless you have no alternative method of cooking, don't use the microwave oven for a heavy load of food, such as 10 baked potatoes, a large turkey, or more than 1¾ pints (1 litre/4½ cups) of soup. Because of the volume of food there will be no saving of time.

• There are many different ways of expressing the **level of power** at which different foods should be cooked. For instance, the most common setting, using 100% power, may be called high, full or perhaps a number such as '9'. If you have a machine with only two settings, HIGH and DEFROST, then these are the equivalent of 100% power and 30% power respectively in the table below. For those with variable power, I list below the percentage of power indicated by the various terms used in my recipes. You can then match the percentage to the terms used to express it in your particular instruction book.

Microwave power settings

HIGH = 100% power (650 watts)	Used to bring liquids and sauces to the boil, cook soups, fruits, vegetables, fish, smaller tender roasts, poultry up to 3 lb (1½ kg) in weight, and most cakes, also to 'sauté' vegetables, minced (ground) meat and small pieces of meat
MEDIUM = 75–80% power (500 watts)	For roasting some joints, reheating cooked foods and leftovers, and for cooking food containing cream, milk and cheese

21

LOW	= 50–60% power (300–400 watts)	For defrosting small items such as rolls, defrosting and reheating casseroles, and cooking egg custards
DEFROST	= 30–40% power (200–250 watts)	Defrosting solid foods such as roasts and minced (ground) meat, pot-roasting, softening butter for spreading
WARM	= 10–20% power (75–100 watts)	For keeping foods warm for up to 30 minutes

• Make sure you have the kind of **dishes** that the instruction book advises are suitable for use in the microwave. There are special microwave-safe containers available now in every shape and size, but you may also find that you already have suitable ones in your cupboard, made of glass, china or pottery — china soufflé dishes, for example, make excellent cake 'tins'.

• Never use **metal containers** of any kind, or china which is decorated in any way with silver or gold. Because metal reflects microwaves, bouncing them off its surface, it prevents their absorption by the food. It may also cause 'arcing' — a rather frightening phenomenon — when sparks are produced which can damage the oven as well as blackening metal decorations.

• You may have to adjust the amount of **liquid** — for instance, in a casserole — as there is so much less evaporation in a microwave oven than in a conventional one. As a rough guide, allow 10 fl oz (275 ml/1¼ cups) of liquid to each pound (450 g) of meat. When preparing soups, use only enough of the total amount of liquid in the recipe to cover the ingredients as they cook. In this way you can save even more cooking time, as there will be less liquid to heat up — the remainder can be added when the soup has finished cooking.

• Always **arrange pieces of food** such as meatballs and baked potatoes evenly spaced out round the edge of the dish in an oval or a ring. In addition, arrange foods of uneven thickness, such as chicken legs and chops, with the thicker part towards the outside of the ring. This helps to ensure more even penetration by the microwaves, and therefore more even cooking.

• Always **cover food** when cooking or reheating, unless instructed otherwise. This keeps it from drying out, particularly during reheating, and also helps to speed up the cooking process by trapping the heat that is generated in the cooking dish. Exceptions to the rule are *foods with a high water content* such as puddings and cakes, which need to dry out as they bake, and *crisp foods* such as pastry, biscuits and rolls which might become soggy (see below). The covering can be a lid, clingfilm (saran wrap), a napkin or even a paper towel. Clingfilm should always be punctured before the dish is cooked, unless you have a machine with an auto-sensor and are advised otherwise.

• Always puncture **plastic bags** before putting them into the microwave oven, if the food in them needs cooking for longer than 5 minutes; this will prevent them bursting through a build-up of steam. Prick **whole vegetables** such as potatoes, tomatoes and aubergines (eggplant) and **fruit** such as apples for a similar reason — to prevent them from bursting as their liquid content heats up and expands.

• Always allow a longer **cooking time**, the greater the quantity of food — this takes a little getting used to, after using a conventional oven where this does not apply. As a rule of thumb, allow between a third and a half *extra* cooking time, when doubling the quantity of food; for example, allow 5 minutes for one potato, but 7 minutes for two. Conversely, allow a third *less* time, when you halve the quantity of food; for example, two trout take 6 minutes to cook, but one trout only 4 minutes. Fortunately most instruction books provide helpful tables relating cooking times to the weight of the different foods. In any case, once you are aware of the need, experience will very soon be your best guide.

- Always **undercook** food if you are in any doubt as to the exact cooking time it will require — you can always put the dish back into the oven for a further minute or two, if necessary, whereas food that is overcooked for even a short time may be dried out and completely ruined. This is particularly important when baking cakes; the recipes give guidance on testing for done-ness.
- Always allow food to **stand** for the time recommended in the recipe. This is because most foods continue to cook for 5 or even 10 minutes after they have been taken out of the oven, as the heat generated in the outside of the food (where the microwaves first penetrate) is slowly conducted to the centre. If you ignore this and remove the food from the oven only when it is completely cooked right through to the centre, you will probably find that the outside has overcooked and become very tough and dry. This applies in particular to 'dense' foods such as potatoes, roasts and poultry, as well as to cakes and large casseroles.
- Always **turn** or **reposition food** every 5 minutes, *unless* your microwave oven has either a turntable to rotate the food automatically, or a special built-in 'stirrer' of some kind, which equalizes the exposure of the different food surfaces to the microwaves.
- Add **herbs** and **spices** at the beginning of the cooking period, but do not add the **salt** until the end, as it has a toughening effect, particularly on fish and meat.
- Always **reheat** foods containing a lot of moisture such as rolls, bread or cakes on a paper napkin or towel, and cover them lightly with another napkin or piece of towel to absorb the moisture that is brought to the surface by the action of the microwaves.

And here are a few tricks of the trade:

- To **toast blanched almonds** or **cashews**, spread 4 oz (125 g/1 cup) out on a plate and cook on HIGH (100% power) for 4 minutes for flaked almonds, 5 or 6 minutes for whole or split almonds, stirring twice. To **toast sesame seeds**, place 2 oz (50 g/½ cup) on a plate, and cook on HIGH (100% power) for 2½ to 3 minutes, stirring twice.
- To **shell chestnuts**, make a slit through the skin with a sharp pointed knife. Place 12 on a plate and cook on HIGH (100% power), 1 to 1½ minutes according to size. The shells can then be removed as if by magic.
- To **soften butter**, remove 8 oz (225 g/1 cup) from the wrapper and place on a suitable dish. Microwave on LOW (50–60% power) for 30 to 60 seconds (depending on how cold it is).
- To **melt butter** place 4 oz (125 g/½ cup) in a bowl and heat on MEDIUM (75–80% power) for 1 or 2 minutes (depending on the softness of the butter at the start). Don't melt butter on HIGH, as it tends to spatter the oven walls.
- To **melt chocolate**, place 4 oz (125 g) in a bowl, and cook on HIGH (100% power) for 1½ minutes, then stir well. If the chocolate is melted with a liquid such as coffee, it will probably need another 30 seconds.
- To **melt kosher gelatine**, sprinkle it on water or fruit juice as recommended in the recipe, heat for 30 seconds on HIGH (100% power), then stir until the liquid goes clear and the gelatine is completely dissolved.
- To **toast croutons** without any fat, cut 4 large slices of brown or white bread into ½ in (1½ cm) squares. Spread out flat on a plate and cook on HIGH (100% power) for 4 minutes, stirring once. **Fresh breadcrumbs** can be converted into dry breadcrumbs in

the same way, but first lay a paper napkin or paper towel on the plate, and cook only until dry to the touch and lightly coloured — 2 to 2½ minutes.

● To help **bread** to rise, put the newly kneaded dough, covered with clingfilm (saran wrap), in the microwave. Cook on HIGH (100% power) for 15 seconds. If it does not feel slightly warm to the touch, repeat 10 minutes later. This method can also be used to defrost frozen doughs, or to bring refrigerated doughs back to room temperature. I do not like to rise a dough completely by this method, as the structure of the finished bread will not be as good as after a slower rise.

● To cook **breast of chicken** for salads or sandwiches, place on dish, brush with lemon juice and cook on HIGH (100% power), allowing 5 minutes to the pound (450 g), with 5 minutes resting time.

● To cook **'baked' cheesecake** (based on 1 lb (450 g/2 cups) cheese) on a crumb or sponge finger (ladyfinger) crust, cook on LOW (50–60% power) for 20 minutes, until just set.

● To **plump dried fruit** such as apricots or raisins, put in a dish, sprinkle with water, cover and cook on HIGH (100% power) for 45 seconds, then allow to stand for 2 minutes.

● To warm a **baby's bottle** (8 oz (225 ml/1 cup) capacity) to lukewarm, remove the cap and teat and heat at MEDIUM (75–80% power) for 45 seconds. Replace the teat, shake gently, then leave to stand for 1 minute.

Soups in the microwave oven

The advantage of making a soup in the microwave oven lies in the saving not so much of cooking time as of washing-up time — it can be cooked, allowed to mature for several hours and then reheated and served, all in the same casserole or tureen. Or, if you prefer, it can be cooked in a large basin and served from the kitchen.

If the soup vegetables need to be sautéed, heat the fat on HIGH (100% power) for 2 minutes, add the finely chopped vegetables, cover and cook on HIGH for a further 3 minutes before adding the other ingredients.

The use of *hot* stock will also help to cut the cooking time. If you are using home-made stock and there is no other source of heat available, it can be heated in the microwave on HIGH (100% power) for 3 or 4 minutes or until bubbling. Otherwise, use a stock cube and boiling water from a kettle.

To thicken a cream soup in the microwave, do not make the sauce with flour. Instead, mix half the quantity of cornflour (cornstarch) with the milk, add to the soup, cook on HIGH for 2 minutes, stir and cook for a further 2 minutes until thickened and bubbly, then leave to stand for a further 2 minutes.

COURGETTE AND LETTUCE SOUP

SERVES 6   *Freeze 3 months*
                                        Will keep 2 days under refrigeration

The method used to cook this soup in the microwave oven can be adapted for any puréed soup such as Chick Pea and Noodle Soup (page 69), and the one that follows, or Minted Cucumber and Pea Soup (page 44). I do not think it is satisfactory to microwave soups that need to be simmered for a long time to bring out their flavour.

Ingredients for Courgette and Lettuce Soup on page 44

Select an ovenproof casserole, large soufflé dish or small soup tureen of approximately 3 pints (1¾ litres/7½ cups) capacity. Into the dish put the thinly sliced courgettes (zucchini), the onion and ½ pint (275 ml/1¼ cups) of hot stock. Cover and cook on HIGH (100% power) for 8 minutes. Add the shredded lettuce, stir, cover and cook on HIGH for 3 minutes more. Liquidize or process until smooth, then pour back into the dish. Pour the remaining 1 pint (575 ml/2½ cups) stock into the machine with the salt and black pepper and process briefly to clean down the sides, then add to the purée with the herbs, stirring well.

To reheat from hot   Cover and cook on HIGH (100% power) for 3 minutes.
To reheat from cold   Cover and cook on HIGH for 8 minutes.

LENTIL AND PEPPER SOUP SPANISH STYLE

SERVES 4

Ingredients for Lentil and Pepper Soup, Spanish Style, on page 55 — use half-quantity

In a 3 pint (1¾ litre/7½ cup) casserole or large bowl put the vegetables and oil. Cover and cook on HIGH (100% power) for 7 minutes, stirring once. Mix in a jug ¾ pint (425 ml/1¾ cups) of the stock, the chopped tomatoes and the seasonings. Uncover the vegetables, add the rinsed and drained lentils, the liquid and seasonings, cover and cook on HIGH for a further 10 minutes, stirring once. Purée, using a sieve or food processor, then return to the casserole. Stir in the remaining 1 pint (575 ml/2½ cups) of stock and leave for several hours. Reheat on HIGH for 8 minutes. Stir in the parsley before serving.

GEFILTE FISH

| *SERVES 4–6 with 14 small patties or 7* | *Freeze 3 months* |
| *larger ones* | *Will keep 3 days under refrigeration* |

While I do not think the flavour is quite as deep as when the fish is stewed in the traditional manner, this is a marvellous way of cooking just enough fish for one meal, using your own ready-frozen Gefilte Fish Balls (as described on page 12). Both the stock and the fish can be prepared in the microwave in 30 minutes; however, you will need to leave the dish overnight if you wish the sauce to 'jell'. The fish is still delicious even if no fish skins and bones are available for the stock.

14 small patties or 7 large patties of raw
Gefilte Fish Mix (page 12)

THE STOCK:
1 lb (450 g) fish skins and bones, well washed

1 medium onion, thinly sliced
2 medium carrots, sliced ¼ in (½ cm) thick
2 level teaspoons each sugar and salt
Hot water to cover the bones

25

Put the skins and bones into a large bowl, barely cover with hot water then cook, covered, on HIGH (100% power) until boiling — about 4 minutes. Uncover, skim the top, then add the remaining ingredients for the stock. Cover and simmer on DEFROST (30% power) for 20 minutes. Strain out the skin and bones.

Arrange the fish patties in a round or oval dish, positioning them in a ring, then pour over the stock with the carrots and onions. Cover with clingfilm (saran wrap), pierce a hole in it, then cook on HIGH (100% power) for 5 minutes. Turn each ball round, then cook on LOW (50–60% power) for a further 5 minutes. Leave to stand, covered, until cold, then refrigerate until required.

VARIATION

Gefilte Fish Ring Instead of fish patties, approximately 1½ lb (675 g/3 cups) fish mix can be used to fill a microwave-safe ring mould. (There is no need to make any stock.) Lay a paper towel on top of the ring and cook it on HIGH (100% power) for 5 minutes, then turn down to LOW (50–60% power) for a further 8 minutes. Insert a knife and if it comes out almost clean, the ring is done; otherwise give it 2 minutes more, repeating the test until it is done. Leave covered until cold. This makes a delicious summer dish, with salad and 'chrane', and is particularly popular with those who like gefilte fish, but not the jellied stock.

GEFILTE FISH BALLS IN A LEMON SAUCE

SERVES 4–6

Do not freeze
Will keep 3 days under refrigeration

If you are preparing several varieties of gefilte fish for a Seder meal, the microwave oven offers a very speedy way of cooking this variation, and the results are quite superb, equal to the same dish cooked in the conventional way as described on page 216.

14 small or 7 larger patties of Gefilte Fish Mix (page 12)

THE POACHING LIQUID:
Half a thinly sliced onion
2 teaspoons sugar
1 teaspoon salt; speck of white pepper
½ pint (275 ml/1¼ cups) boiling water

THE SAUCE:
2 eggs
3 tablespoons sugar
8 fl oz (225 ml/1 cup) strained poaching liquid (see above)
2 teaspoons potato flour (or cornflour (cornstarch) during the rest of the year)
4 tablespoons fresh lemon juice

Arrange the patties in a circle or oval in a shallow gratin dish. Put the ingredients for the poaching liquid into a jug or bowl and cook on HIGH (100% power) until bubbling, about 2 minutes. Pour around the patties, cover with clingfilm (saran wrap), pierce a hole in it, then cook on HIGH for 5 minutes. Turn each ball over, re-cover, then turn the setting down to LOW (50–60% power) and cook a further 5 minutes. Leave to stand, covered, for 5 minutes.

Lift the patties from the dish, then strain 8 fl oz (225 ml/1 cup) of the poaching liquid into a jug. Return the fish to the dish. Put the potato flour (or cornflour (cornstarch)) into a bowl and gradually stir in the lemon juice, then whisk in all the remaining ingredients until smooth. (This can be done in the food processor.) Pour into the jug and microwave on LOW for 2 minutes, stir, and cook for a further minute or two until thickened to the consistency of a coating custard. Pour over and round the patties, cover and chill until required.

WHOLE POACHED SALMON

SERVES 6–7
                                                  Freeze 3 months
                                                  Will keep 2 days under refrigeration

Salmon 'poached' in the microwave has a most delicate texture, and is cooked in about a quarter of the normal oven-cooking time.

1 salmon, 3 lb (1¼ kg) weight
                                                  1 teaspoon dried tarragon
Fish seasoning salt

Have the fish cleaned, and the head removed (or leave it on if you prefer). Cover a large oval plate with clingfilm (saran wrap) and lay the salmon on top. Sprinkle the body cavity with fish seasoning salt and dried tarragon, then cover with clingfilm and pierce a hole in it. Cook on HIGH (100% power) for 11 minutes, then leave to stand for 5 minutes. Test by lifting a little of the skin and making sure that it is pale pink to the bone and can be easily flaked with a fork; if necessary cook it a minute or two longer. Uncover and leave to cool.

When required, skin and leave whole, or carve (see page 74), and arrange on a lettuce-covered platter garnished with stuffed eggs and sliced cucumber.

VARIATION
Salmon steaks First weigh the fish, to calculate the cooking time. Arrange the salmon steaks in a circle on a flat plate or quiche dish, with the thinner part of each steak to the centre, and sprinkle with lemon juice. Cover with clingfilm (saran wrap), pierce a hole in it, then cook on HIGH, allowing 5 minutes to the pound, or until the fish flakes easily with a fork. Allow to stand for 5 minutes, then season lightly with salt and black pepper. Serve warm or cold.

TROUT WITH ALMONDS

SERVES 2
                                                  Freeze 1 month
                                                  Will keep 2 days under refrigeration

The microwave cooks delicate fish like trout so that the flesh stays light and moist, and it does save preheating a conventional oven, particularly in the summer. A dieter can simply omit the fried almond garnish, pouring only the lemon juice over instead. If more convenient, the fish can be cooked earlier in the day, then the garnish can be poured over and the fish reheated for 2 minutes on MEDIUM (75–80% power).

2 trout, each 8–10 oz (225–275 g) in weight
1 tablespoon lemon juice
½ teaspoon dried tarragon
½ teaspoon fish seasoning salt

GARNISH:
1 oz (25 g/¼ cup) flaked almonds
1 oz (25 g/2 tablespoons) butter or
margarine

Have the fish cleaned and the heads removed. Wash the body cavities, sprinkle with
the dried herb and seasoning salt, then lay them in an oval serving dish, side by side.
Cover the fish with clingfilm (saran wrap) and pierce it, then cook on HIGH (100%
power) for 6 minutes. Let them stand, covered, for 5 minutes while you prepare the
garnish. In a small bowl cook the butter and almonds, uncovered, on HIGH for 3 or 4
minutes, stirring once or twice until golden-brown, then stir in the lemon juice.
Uncover the fish and carefully remove the top skin, then pour the buttered almonds
and lemon juice over it and reheat for 1 minute on HIGH. Serve at once.

BEEF IN BEER

SERVES 4–6

Freeze 3 months
Will keep 3 days under refrigeration

There is not a great deal of time to be saved when stewing or braising meat in the
microwave, certainly not more than 45 minutes to an hour. It does save using a
conventional oven on a hot day, however, and a casserole can be cooked in its
serving dish, with the very minimum of attention. To tenderize the tougher cuts of
meat, it is important to simmer the casserole on a 30–40% power setting. This is a
delicious dish in its own right.

2 tablespoons oil
1½ lb (675 g) first-cut braising steak, cut in
¾ in (2 cm) cubes
1 large onion, very thinly sliced
2 sticks celery, very thinly sliced
1 oz (25 g/4 tablespoons) flour
1 teaspoon salt; 15 grinds black pepper

1 level teaspoon tomato purée
1 teaspoon brown sugar
1 can (15 fl oz/425 ml/2 cups) brown ale
2 teaspoons soy sauce
1 clove garlic, peeled and crushed
2 bayleaves

Select a large casserole or microwave-safe bowl. Heat the oil in it for 2 minutes on
HIGH (100% power), then add the meat, stir well, cover and cook for 3 minutes,
stirring once. (This initial browning could be done on top of the stove.) Remove the
meat, add the vegetables, cover and cook for 5 minutes, until softened. Uncover,
return the meat to the dish, add all the remaining ingredients and bring to the boil —
about 7 minutes. Turn down to DEFROST (30–40% power) and cook, covered, until
the meat is just tender — about 1½ hours. Leave for 20 minutes to stand before
serving. May be reheated.

SAVOURY MEAT LOAF

SERVES 4

Freeze 4 months
Will keep 2 days under refrigeration

The texture of this meat loaf is excellent, whether it is served hot or cold. It can be mixed and cooked in less than half an hour, and is splendid to serve with salad, to take on a picnic, or for a hot mid-week meal with microwave-baked potatoes.

Half a medium (5 oz (150 g)) onion, peeled and cut in 1 in (2½ cm) chunks
1 large slice of brown bread or 1 oz (25 g/½ cup) fresh breadcrumbs
1 egg
1 teaspoon dry mustard
1 tablespoon tomato ketchup
2 teaspoons soy sauce
1 teaspoon chopped parsley

1 teaspoon salt; 10 grinds black pepper
Small sprig of parsley
1 tablespoon medium matzah meal or porage oats
1 lb (450 g) fresh minced (ground) beef

FOR COATING:
1 tablespoon tomato purée

In a blender or food processor, purée all the ingredients except the matzah meal (or porage oats) and the meat. Put in a bowl, stir in the meal (or oats), then add the meat and mix thoroughly. Put into a shallow container and form into a loaf shape, then spread the purée all over the top and sides. Cook on HIGH (100% power) for 12 minutes, then allow to stand for 5 minutes to complete the cooking. Serve hot or cold.

TAGLIATELLE RING WITH TOMATO AND HERB SAUCE

SERVES 4–5

Freeze meat filling and sauce 3 months, tagliatelle ring 1 month
Will keep 2 days under refrigeration

This makes a delicious mid-week meal, and is particularly useful if you have some savoury mince ready in the freezer. It looks particularly attractive when the noodle mixture is set in a plastic ring mould — these are cheap and widely available wherever microwave cooking equipment is sold.

6 oz (175 g/1½ cups) broad egg noodles or
fresh tagliatelle
1 egg
1 level teaspoon salt; 20 grinds black pepper
1 tablespoon chopped parsley

THE MINCE:
1 tablespoon oil
1 onion, finely chopped
1 lb (450 g/2 cups) minced (ground) beef
1 medium-sized green pepper, finely diced
2 rounded tablespoons tomato ketchup
2 teaspoons Worcestershire sauce

2 teaspoons salt; 10 grinds black pepper
1 tablespoon chopped parsley
5 tablespoons water

THE SAUCE:
1 can (14 oz (400 g)) chopped tomatoes
1 tablespoon tomato purée
1 tablespoon olive oil
1 level teaspoon each salt and sugar
10 grinds black pepper
1 level teaspoon mixed Italian herbs
1 clove of garlic, peeled and crushed
2 tablespoons chopped fresh parsley or basil

Heat the oil and cook the onion until golden, then add the meat and cook until it loses its redness, stirring all the time. Add all the remaining ingredients, stir well, cover and simmer for 15 minutes. (This is as quick to do on top of the stove as in the microwave.) Divide into two portions for freezing.

Cook the noodles according to packet directions. Put in a sieve and pour cold water through, then drain well. Put into a mixing bowl and add one portion of the defrosted meat and the beaten egg, salt and pepper. Turn into a lightly greased microwave-safe ring mould or casserole. Cover with clingfilm (saran wrap) and pierce a hole in it. Microwave on MEDIUM (75–80% power) for 8 minutes. Take out of oven and allow to stand for 3 minutes. Put all ingredients for tomato herb sauce in a jug and microwave on HIGH (100% power) for 6 minutes until thickened. Put the tomato herb sauce on a serving plate and arrange the ring on top. Sprinkle with the parsley.

LAMB CUTLETS IN A FRUITED BARBECUE SAUCE

SERVES 4   *Best eaten fresh*

The sauce gives the chops a lovely golden-brown colour. If you prefer them even darker, brown them under a hot grill for 2 or 3 minutes. Garnish them with orange segments dipped in chopped parsley.

6–8 first-cut lamb cutlets
Salt and black pepper
1 egg, beaten
Dry breadcrumbs

THE SAUCE:
4 fl oz (125 ml/½ cup) hot chicken stock
4 fl oz (125 ml/½ cup) orange juice

Grated rind of 1 orange
2 rounded tablespoons redcurrant jelly
1½ teaspoons lemon juice

GARNISH:
Segments from 1 orange
Chopped parsley

Trim off all the fat from the cutlets. Salt and pepper them, then dip them first in egg and then in fine, dry breadcrumbs. Arrange in a casserole or flan dish large enough to hold the cutlets in one layer. Put all the sauce ingredients into a basin and microwave on HIGH (100% power) for 4 minutes. Stir well, then pour over the cutlets. Microwave, uncovered, on MEDIUM (75–80% power) for 12 minutes, baste with the sauce, then microwave for a further 5 minutes on the same setting. Leave to rest for 5 minutes. Garnish with the orange segments and chopped parsley.

MICROWAVE-OVEN-FRIED CHICKEN

SERVES 4–6

Freeze 3 months, cooked or raw
Cooked chicken will keep 2 days under
refrigeration

If you have a stock of ready-prepared chicken joints in the freezer, they can be defrosted, then cooked, to make a delicious meal in half an hour. To get a rich colour on the chicken, I suggest using a kosher pack of chicken coating crumbs, adding more flavour to them with the seasoning given below.

4–6 chicken portions (2 lb (1 kg)
approximate total weight)
1 oz (25 g/2 tablespoons) margarine, melted
(may be omitted if the crumbs contain fat)
1 teaspoon microwave chicken browner

1 teaspoon each paprika and dried herbes de
Provence
15 grinds of black pepper
4 tablespoons ready-prepared chicken coating
crumbs

Weigh the chicken portions and allow 7 minutes to the pound (450 g) cooking time plus 5 minutes resting time. Have ready a shallow round casserole (such as a quiche dish) or a microwave roasting dish with a rack.

Melt the margarine in the microwave on HIGH (100% power) for about 30 seconds. Mix the coating crumbs with the remaining ingredients and put into a shallow dish. Brush each joint with some of the margarine and then roll it in the crumbs, patting them on well. Arrange in a circle with the thicker part of the joints to the outside, either on a rack or in a shallow dish lined with kitchen paper. Cook uncovered on HIGH for approximately 14 minutes (or as calculated). Leave to rest for 5 minutes. Serve hot or cold.

PINEAPPLE UPSIDE-DOWN CAKE, FRUIT SAUCE

SERVES 4–5

Freeze 1 month
Will keep 2 days under refrigeration

This is a very light sponge under a delectable butterscotch glaze. It is nicest served warm and may be reheated on MEDIUM (75–80% power) for 2 minutes.

31

THE GLAZE:

2 oz (50 g/¼ cup) butter (or margarine for a meat meal)

2 oz (50 g/¼ cup) dark brown sugar

2 level tablespoons golden syrup (corn syrup)

THE FRUIT:

1 small (8 oz/225 g) can pineapple (6 rings)

THE SPONGE CAKE:

4 oz (125 g/½ cup) soft margarine

4 oz (125 g/½ cup) caster (superfine) sugar

4 oz (125 g/1 cup) self-raising flour or 4 oz

(125 g/1 cup) plain (all-purpose) flour plus 1 teaspoon baking powder

2 eggs

½ teaspoon vanilla essence (extract)

THE SAUCE:

1 tablespoon cornflour (cornstarch)

2 tablespoons caster (superfine) sugar

1 tablespoon lemon juice

2 tablespoons orange juice

1 teaspoon each grated orange and lemon rind

Reserved syrup from the fruit (½ pint (275 ml/1¼ cups) liquid in all)

Use a soufflé dish or round microwave-safe plastic container (about 7 or 8 in (17 to 20 cm) across). Melt the butter (or margarine) in a small basin on HIGH (100% power) for 1 minute. Use a little to grease the chosen container. To the remainder, add the golden syrup and sugar, stir, then microwave on HIGH for 1 minute, stir and cook for a further 1 minute. Pour this butterscotch into the chosen dish.

Drain the pineapple, reserving the juice, and arrange on the glaze. Beat all the ingredients for the sponge cake together by hand or machine until smooth. Spoon on top of the pineapple and smooth level. Microwave on HIGH for 5 ½ minutes, or until a cocktail stick comes out clean from the centre. If still moist, give it another minute (there may still be areas of dampness on the surface which will disappear during the resting time). Allow to rest for 5 minutes, then turn out on to a serving dish.

To make the sauce   In the serving jug, mix the cornflour and sugar thoroughly, then stir in the liquids and rinds. Microwave on HIGH for 2 minutes, stir and cook for a further 2 minutes until bubbling and clear. Serve hot; may be reheated.

HAZELNUT STREUSEL KUCHEN

Freeze 3 months
Will keep fresh 2 days under refrigeration

This is an excellent cake to cook in the microwave as the cinnamon and brown sugar in the topping gives it a very pleasing colour. The texture of the kuchen is particularly light and fluffy when cooked in this way.

8 oz (225 g/2 cups) self-raising flour plus ½ teaspoon baking power or 8 oz (225 g/2 cups) plain (all-purpose) flour plus 2½ teaspoons baking powder

3 oz (75 g/⅓ cup) soft margarine

5 oz (150 g/⅔ cup) caster (superfine) sugar

1 egg

4 fl oz (125 ml/½ cup) milk

THE TOPPING:
1 oz (25 g/2 tablespoons) butter or soft margarine
3 oz (75 g/⅓ cup) dark brown sugar

1 oz (25 g/¼ cup) plain (all-purpose) flour
2 oz (50 g/½ cup) flaked or chopped hazelnuts (filberts)

Grease an 8 in (20 cm) round microwave cake dish of glass or plastic, and line the bottom with a round of silicone paper or a piece of clingfilm (saran wrap) pressed into shape.

Put all the cake ingredients into a bowl and beat by hand or machine until a smooth soft batter is formed (3 minutes by hand; 2 minutes by mixer, 15 seconds in a food processor). Spoon into the dish, smooth level, and cook on HIGH (100% power) for 4 minutes, until the top is just set. If not, give it another minute. Mix the topping ingredients together, sprinkle on top of the cake, and cook for a further 2 minutes. Leave on a cooling rack. Turn on to a plate, then turn right side up on to a serving dish.

LEKACH

Freeze 3 months
Will keep 1 month in an airtight container

For the reluctant baker, here is the painless way to make a home-made honey cake for Rosh Hashanah. Even though it is baked in the microwave, the dark sugar and honey give this cake a rich warm colour.

3 oz (75 g/⅓ cup) dark brown sugar
4 tablespoons any flavourless oil
2 eggs
½ lb (225 g/¾ cup) warm honey (see below)
6 oz (175 g/1½ cups) plain (all-purpose) flour

1 teaspoon bicarbonate of soda (baking soda)
½ teaspoon ground cinnamon and ginger
1 teaspoon mixed sweet spice
3 fl oz (75 g/⅓ cup) warm coffee

Select a dish measuring 9 in (22½ cm) round and 3 in (7½ cm) deep — a glass soufflé dish is ideal. Lightly grease it, then line the bottom with silicone paper or clingfilm (saran wrap). Measure the honey into a bowl then heat on HIGH (100% power) for 1 minute.

To mix by food processor   Put the sugar and oil into the bowl of the food processor and process for 20 seconds. Add the eggs and the honey and process for a further 5 seconds. Pulse in the coffee. Sift the flour with the bicarbonate of soda and the spices, then add to the bowl and pulse in for 5 seconds, until evenly mixed.

To mix by hand or electric mixer   Add the ingredients to the bowl in the order given, mixing until smooth after each addition.

Turn into the dish and cook on MEDIUM (75–80% power) for 9½ minutes — the top of the cake may still be slightly tacky on top and will set as it cools. When cold, turn out of the dish and wrap in foil. Leave 2 days, if possible, before cutting.

SPICY CASHEWS

Enough for 6

Will keep 6 weeks in an airtight container in the refrigerator

These are delicious to serve at a Festival, particularly the New Year.

½ lb (225 g/2 cups) cashew nuts
½ oz (15 g/1 tablespoon) butter or 1
tablespoon oil

SEASONINGS:
1 teaspoon each curry powder, ground cumin and fine salt

In a shallow dish, heat the butter on HIGH (100% power) for 1 minute. Add the nuts, stir well to coat with the fat, then cook on HIGH for 2 minutes, stir again, then cook a further 2 minutes or until golden-brown. Mix the seasonings together and sprinkle over the nuts, stirring well. Cook for a further 1 minute on HIGH. Drain on kitchen paper. When cold, store in an airtight tin.

Enjoy it in Good Health

'Do have a banana or an apple, darling,' my grandmother would coax as soon as she'd finished hugging me when I went to visit her every Shabbat afternoon. Of course she knew I wasn't hungry — I'd just enjoyed a good lunch at home. But to her, as to the other grandmothers of her generation, food was an expression of love and the more of it you could give, the better.

Cooking and serving food is still a labour of love for Jewish women, but it's undertaken in a spirit that would have been unthinkable even a short time ago. Now we are more concerned about the dishes we should *not* be cooking and the food — such as sugar and fat — that we should *not* be loading on to the family plates. And we worry: are we giving them enough dietary fibre? Are the blender and the food processor reducing everything to pap?

For although scientists differ about the strength of the link between certain foods and coronary heart disease (as well as some other medical conditions), everyone seems to agree that it can do nothing but good to *cut down* the proportions of fat and sugar in our daily food and at the same time to *increase* the amount of dietary fibre.

This is a message that has been quickly taken to heart by most women (and men), according to a recent survey which showed that because of this concern about diet, the pattern of weekly food preparation — even for Shabbat — has undergone a radical change in many Jewish homes. Some of the richer and sweeter traditional dishes such as fried fish and fruit pies are no longer prepared as a weekly routine, but appear on the table only for a special occasion or festival. Foods that are brown — such as wholemeal (wholewheat) flour, brown sugar, brown rice and wholemeal pasta — are seen to be better than their white counterparts, while fresh fruit and yoghurt have ousted puddings and strudels from their place at the end of the family meal.

We are beginning to practise a leaner kind of cuisine which is not concerned primarily with *dieting* but with a good healthy *diet*. Yet the basic framework of the Jewish style of diet, with its emphasis on a variety of simple home-cooked foods, is still nutritionally sound, even when judged by modern standards. So I look upon this new way of cooking as a modification of our old traditions rather than a radical change, and in this chapter I have set out to adjust the *balance* between the different ingredients in our family recipes, rather than trying to find ways to proscribe them altogether.

I started by experimenting with some of the dishes that we would still like to eat regularly, if only we could do so with a clear conscience from the dietary point of view. Now I've worked out a recipe for a low-fat chopped liver, as well as a challah that is made with wholemeal flour. And I've found a method of frying fish *in the oven* that uses a fraction of the oil that's needed when it's cooked in a pan. In addition I've taken a close look at many everyday dishes, such as soups, meats and desserts, to see if their positive contribution to our well-being can be improved in an easy way. From these experiments there have emerged some general guidelines which I hope you will find helpful in developing your own personal style of cuisine — one that can, to use a time-honoured phrase of well-wishing, be 'enjoyed in good health'.

TRADITIONAL FOODS TODAY

Measured even by a modern nutritional yardstick, there are many good things to be found in traditional Jewish food. There is calcium as well as vitamins A and D in 'smetana and kaes', and abundant vitamin B in rye bread. Borscht is very rich in iron, and there's plentiful cheap protein in pickled herrings — not to mention the vitamin A to be found in Tsimmes, and the fibre in the Shabbat Cholent.

The *bad* news is that many other favourite dishes — such as Chopped Liver and Chopped Fried Fish — contain unacceptable amounts of fat, and old-style cakes and pastries such as Lekach and Apfelstrudel are positively loaded down with sugar.

However, I have found that by using a few special techniques, you can cut down on the amount of fat normally used in these well-loved dishes, and still retain a great deal of their inimitable flavour. This kind of 'heimische' diet can also be improved by including more of those old-fashioned thick soups such as 'hobene gropen' and lentil, which happens to be particularly rich in fibre, and by baking with wholemeal (wholewheat) and other whole-grain flours. (I shall consider the more difficult problem of sugar reduction in a moment.)

Cutting down on fat

- **Chopped Liver** can be made with half the normal amount of fat, binding it instead with extra onions.
- **Chicken and meat soups** can easily be defatted if they are first frozen to solidify the fat.
- **The Shabbat fowl** does not take as kindly to freezing as the soup does, so it should only be refrigerated, and next day, carefully skimmed of its fat. The same technique can be used for removing the fat from any other casserole such as **braised steak, meatballs** and **carrot tsimmes with brisket**.
- Do not fry any **meat or poultry** before casseroling it; instead, put it raw into the simmering liquid. It may not be quite as tasty, but it will certainly contain less fat.
- Fried **steaks** and **fillets of fish** present a difficult problem, as there is no way of reducing the amount of oil needed to cook them in the traditional way. One solution is to oven-fry the steaks and fillets, a technique which uses a fraction of the normal amount of oil. **Chopped fish patties** can be cooked in a lemon sauce, or in a fat-free Provençal Sauce which can also be used for braising chicken joints, meatballs and steak.

You don't need fat to give flavour to food; you have a whole larder-full of ingredients to call upon. Here are just a few suggestions.
- **Herbs** of all kinds, both fresh and dried, can transform casseroles, soups, stews, scrambled eggs and dips.
- Use **cinnamon** and **nutmeg** in fruit compôtes made with brown sugar or artificial sweetener. Experiment with other spices too.
- **Tomatoes** — fresh, canned or puréed — and **tomato juice** are good for enriching barbecue sauces, soups and broths, and in the cooking liquid for braises and stews.
- Store-cupboard sauces such as **Worcestershire sauce, soy sauce** and **mushroom ketchup** are useful in all mince (ground meat) dishes, as well as for stir-frying.
- In place of fat, use **mustard powder** or **French mustard** to coat meat or fish before roasting or grilling.
- Don't forget to add **garlic** — enough to flavour, not to overwhelm — to salad dressings as well as to casseroles.

- Find new ways of using **lemon juice** — for example, to flavour stewed fruit, in fruit salads to draw out the natural juices from the cut fruit, and in all tomato dishes.
- **Mushrooms** are delicious served raw in salads; or sprinkle them with salt and cook them covered, in their own juice, for sauces, soups and omelette fillings.
- Give casseroles and dips a bite with **cayenne** or **paprika pepper** or with **tabasco sauce**.
- **Stock** made with chicken, beef and vegetable cubes or paste makes excellent cooking liquid for frozen vegetables; use it too as a basis for low-calorie home-made soups.
- Use **orange and lemon rind** to enliven meat and chicken casseroles, and in apple and other dried and fresh fruit compôtes.

Cutting down on sugar

What can you do when the texture of the cake largely depends on the sugar in it? Answer: Make the same recipe, but less often, and serve it in smaller portions. The plainer the cake, however, the less important is the sugar; so for kichlach, pies and family-style cakes, experiment and see how far you dare go — for a start try cutting the sugar content by a third. The sugar in a cheesecake can safely be reduced, as many traditional recipes were formulated in the days when 'kaes' was a much sourer cheese than the products we use today. Make more yeast cakes, which need far less sugar than conventional cakes do, and taste just as good.

And take a careful look at pages 204-36 of this book, where I have collected a whole range of mouth-watering desserts in which the emphasis is *not*, I promise you, on elaborate and heavily sweetened concoctions based on whipped cream, but which explores the delicious possibilities offered by the wide range of fruits of every kind, the lighter ice creams and simple, fresh-tasting sorbets (sherbets).

CHOPPED LIVER

SERVES 6–8 as a starter, 10–12 as a spread

Freeze 1 month
Will keep 5 days under refrigeration

In this version, the fat content is half the usual amount and extra onion is used as a binding agent — but you will not notice any difference in the taste. If you wish to make a smaller quantity, use half the ingredients, but two hard-boiled eggs.

1 lb (450 g) chicken livers
2 medium (5–6 oz (150–175 g)) onions, finely sliced
1 barely rounded tablespoon soft margarine or vegetarian 'chicken fat'

1 clove of garlic, crushed
1 teaspoon sea salt; 20 grinds black pepper
Good pinch of ground nutmeg
3 large eggs, boiled for 10 minutes, then shelled

Grill the livers to make kasher and cook them as on page 114. Melt the fat in a lidded frying pan, add the onions, sprinkle with the seasonings, then cover and cook over moderate heat for 10 minutes or until softened and golden-brown, stirring twice. Uncover; if the onions are not a rich brown, continue to cook them uncovered for a further 4 minutes.

Put the contents of the pan into the food processor and process until reduced to a purée, about 30 seconds. Add the grilled livers and the shelled and halved eggs, and process until they are either finely chopped (use a pulse action for better control) or puréed, as preferred; alternatively, put all the ingredients through a mincer. Turn into a bowl, re-season, then refrigerate for at least 6 hours.

OVEN-FRIED FISH

SERVES 4–6   *Freeze 3 months*
                                      Will keep under refrigeration for 3 days

This resembles ordinary fried fish in taste and texture, but uses only a fraction of the oil.

6–8 fillets or steaks of any white fish, such
as sole, plaice, haddock, halibut, cod
1 egg
3 tablespoons oil
8 oz (225 g/2 cups) dried breadcrumbs or

medium matzah meal
Rind of 1 lemon, finely grated
2 tablespoons chopped parsley
1 teaspoon paprika
1 teaspoon salt; ¼ teaspoon white pepper

Preheat the oven to Gas No. 7, 425 degrees F, 210 degrees C. Have ready two flat baking trays.

Wash and salt the fish and leave to drain. Whisk the egg with the oil and put in a shallow dish. Mix the breadcrumbs, lemon rind, parsley, paprika, salt and pepper. Put in another dish. Dry each piece of fish thoroughly with kitchen paper and dip in and out of the egg-and-oil mixture, draining well, then coat with the crumbs. Arrange the coated fillets or steaks side by side on the ungreased trays. Cook without turning for 20 minutes, or until the fish is a rich golden-brown. Serve warm or cold.

GEFILTE FISH POACHED IN A FAT-FREE PROVENÇAL SAUCE

SERVES 6–8   *Freeze 3 months*
                                      Will keep 3 days under refrigeration

This is most delicious when served cold.

8–10 patties of Gefilte Fish (made as on
page 12)

THE SAUCE:
1 can (5 oz (150 g)) tomato purée
2 cans of water
1 mild onion, thinly sliced

1 large green pepper, seeds removed, cut into
½ in (1 cm) cubes
1 tablespoon tomato ketchup
1 bayleaf
1 teaspoon salt; 10 grinds black pepper
½ teaspoon dried **herbes de Provence**
2 teaspoons brown sugar or equivalent in
artificial sweetener

Preheat the oven to Gas No. 4, 350 degrees F, 180 degrees C. Select an ovenproof dish large enough for the patties to sit side by side.

Put all the ingredients for the sauce together into a pan, and simmer, stirring, for 5 minutes or until of coating consistency. Arrange the patties in the dish, cover with the sauce, and then with foil. Bake for 45 minutes (basting once), and allow to cool. Store in the refrigerator, but serve at room temperature.

JOINT OF BEEF, BRAISED IN WINE

SERVES 6–8

Freeze 3 months
Cooked meat will keep under refrigeration for 3 days

A very lean joint — such as bola or chuck — can be made tender and succulent if it is braised in moist heat. Provided only a tiny amount of fat is used for browning the meat, this is probably the best way to enjoy meat on a low-fat diet. The bed of vegetables on which the meat is cooked can be puréed to make a beautiful sauce without any additional thickening. The meat is delicious whether served hot or cold.

If you do not wish to use wine (although this helps to tenderize the meat as well as to flavour it) you can use extra beef stock instead.

Braising joint weighing about 4 lb (2 kg), well dried and sprinkled on all sides with freshly ground black pepper
3 teaspoons paprika pepper
2 tablespoons oil
1 small onion, chopped
1 small carrot, chopped
Half a green pepper, seeds removed, chopped
2 sticks of celery, chopped

½ pint (275 ml/1¼ cups) dry red wine, such as Côtes du Rhône or Roussillon
½ pint (275 ml/1¼ cups) beef stock
2 teaspoons tomato purée or 2 squashy tomatoes
1 bayleaf
1 teaspoon mixed Italian herbs
2 teaspoons salt; 10 grinds black pepper
1 clove of garlic, peeled and crushed

Preheat the oven to Gas No. 3, 325 degrees F, 160 degrees C. Select a casserole (preferably flameproof) into which the meat will fit comfortably.

Pat the paprika pepper all over the meat. Heat the oil in the casserole, then brown the meat on all sides — this initial browning is important, as the joint will not brown very much in the moist atmosphere inside the casserole.

Lift the meat out on to a plate, then put the vegetables into the casserole and cook over moderate heat until they take on a little colour, about 5 minutes. Discard any remaining oil. Add the wine to the pan and bubble fiercely for 3 minutes to concentrate the flavour, stirring well to scrape up any residue. Finally add the stock, tomato purée (or tomatoes) and seasonings. Lay the meat on top, bring the liquid to the boil, then cover and transfer to the oven. Cook until the liquid is boiling, then turn the oven to Gas No. 2, 300 degrees F, 150 degrees C and continue to cook until the meat is tender, allowing 40 minutes to the pound (450 g) and 40 minutes over — a 4 lb (2 kg) joint will take 3 hours 20 minutes. You can tell when the meat is tender because it will feel very soft when gently prodded.

Lift the meat on to a serving dish and put it back into the oven. If you have more than 5 fl oz (150 ml/⅔ cup) of liquid left in the bottom of the dish, boil it hard to reduce it, then pour the vegetables and liquid into a liquidizer or food processor and process until smooth. Heat in a small pan until bubbling, adding a little more stock if the texture seems too thick. Serve the meat in slices accompanied by the sauce.

SAVELOYS AND NO CHIPS

SERVES 4–6

Good saveloys — or frankfurters — should be made almost entirely of meat; and as they must be poached, rather than fried, they're a good way of enjoying the spiciness of sausages without the fat. Unfortunately they're traditionally eaten with chips or latkes, which of course have to be fried in oil. However, they can be very delicious when served in the Spanish style, under a bed of spicy vegetables — they even taste good this way with a baked potato!

½ lb (225 g/1 cup) mixed (or stir-fry) frozen vegetables
8–12 oz (225–350 g) cocktail frankfurters or regular frankfurters (cut these in half after poaching them)
2 red peppers, seeds removed, cut in fine shreds

3 juicy 'beef' tomatoes, each cut into six and the pips removed
Pinch of salt; 10 grinds black pepper
Good pinch of cayenne pepper
6 eggs

GARNISH:
1 tablespoon chopped parsley

Preheat the oven to Gas No. 4, 350 degrees F, 180 degrees C. Have ready one large gratin dish or 4–6 individual small ones, very lightly greased, as well as foil to cover them.

Cook the vegetables according to the instructions on the packet, then drain them thoroughly. Simmer the frankfurters for 2 minutes in almost-boiling water (do not allow them to boil or they will burst), then arrange them on the bottom of the dish or dishes. Cover with the peppers, tomatoes and mixed vegetables and sprinkle lightly with the salt and black pepper.

Bake for 15 minutes to heat through; then take out of the oven. Break each egg in turn into a cup, and slide it on top of the vegetables, season again with the salt, black pepper and cayenne pepper, cover and bake for a further 10–15 minutes or until the whites of the eggs are set. Sprinkle with the parsley and serve at once.

CHICKEN ROASTED WITHOUT FAT

SERVES 4–6

Freeze 3 months
Will keep 2 days under refrigeration

The chicken is wrapped in foil and cooked in its own juices, then uncovered to brown at the last minute. The skin of a chicken counts for half the total calories it contains, so it is best to discard it. This is an excellent way to cook chicken for a salad, as the flesh is very soft and juicy.

1 roasting chicken, 3½–4 lb (1¾–2 kg) in weight	Salt and black pepper
Small bunch of parsley	1 tablespoon lemon juice
Small apple, cut in eighths	Freshly ground sea salt

Preheat the oven to Gas No. 8, 450 degrees F, 230 degrees C. Have ready a piece of foil large enough to enclose the chicken in a loose package.

Lay the chicken in the middle of the foil, sprinkle the body cavity with salt and pepper and then stuff with the apple and parsley. Sprinkle the bird all over with the lemon juice and sea salt. Fold the foil into an airtight parcel, but do not press it too closely to the bird — the air must be able to circulate round it.

Place the foil parcel on a rack in a roasting tin and cook for 1¼ hours, then uncover, pour off any juices that have collected in the parcel (keep these for gravy) and allow the bird to cook for a further 20 minutes or until a rich brown. Leave in a warm oven for 15 minutes before serving, or allow to go cold.

LOW-FAT, LOW-SUGAR CHEESECAKE

Freeze 3 months
Will keep 3 days under refrigeration

THE BASE:
½ lb (225 g) packet of trifle sponges or the same amount of sponge cake, cut in slices

THE FILLING:
2 eggs, separated
2 teaspoons caster (superfine) sugar
1 oz (25 g/2 tablespoons) soft butter or margarine
2 oz (50 g/¼ cup) light soft brown sugar

1 teaspoon vanilla essence (extract)
1 teaspoon each grated orange and lemon rind
2 tablespoons lemon juice
1 lb (450 g/2 cups) any fairly dry low-fat soft cheese, such as curd cheese, sieved or processed cottage cheese, or Quark
2 level tablespoons cornflour (cornstarch)
5 fl oz (150 ml/⅔ cup) low-fat natural yoghurt

Preheat the oven to Gas No. 4, 350 degrees F, 180 degrees C. Line the bottom of a 7 in (17½ cm) square, or 9 in (22½ cm) round, loose-bottomed or spring-form tin with silicone paper.

Arrange thin slices of the sponge on the bottom and round the sides of the tin. Whisk the egg whites until they hold stiff peaks, then whisk in the caster sugar. Put all the other filling ingredients (except the yoghurt) into a bowl and beat well to blend, then fold in the meringue and the yoghurt, using a rubber spatula. Spoon the cheese mixture on top of the sponge and smooth level.

Bake for 35 minutes, or until firm round the edge — the middle will firm up as the cake cools. Chill thoroughly before serving the cheesecake, either plain or with a topping of thinly sliced, very ripe strawberries.

LOW-FAT PÂTÉS

The best solution I've found to resisting fattening nibbles is to prepare a variety of low-fat savoury pâtés. These can either be spread on a low-calorie wholewheat (graham) cracker or thinned with a little natural yoghurt and used as a 'dip' for crudités. Refrigerate the pâtés for several hours to allow the flavour to develop.

- **Replace the butter** in a pâté with a low-fat soft cheese such as curd, Quark or cottage cheese, all of which have a fat content of 4% or less.
- Process lumpy soft cheeses (like **curd or cottage cheese**) for 10 seconds on a food processor to give them the texture of a double-cream cheese.
- The soured cream in a **smoked fish pâté** can be replaced by natural yoghurt.
- The fat in **liver pâté** can be replaced by an equal weight of hard-boiled eggs, counting each egg as 2 oz (50 g) in weight.

HERB AND SPICE CHEESE PÂTÉ

SERVES 4 as a starter, 6–8 as a spread or dip

Do not freeze
Will keep 1 week under refrigeration

8 oz (225 g/1 cup) low-fat soft cheese
½ teaspoon sea salt; 10 grinds black pepper
Pinch cayenne pepper
Half a crushed clove of garlic or a pinch of

garlic salt
2 teaspoons each chopped parsley and chives
Pinch of dried fines herbes *or* herbes de
Provence

Pulse all the ingredients until well mixed, or beat together by hand.

ANCHOVY AND CHEESE PÂTÉ

SERVES 4 as a starter, 6–8 as a spread or dip

Do not freeze
Will keep 1 week under refrigeration

8 oz (225 g/1 cup) low-fat soft cheese
2 teaspoons anchovy paste or purée or 3
canned anchovy fillets, finely chopped
2 teaspoons Dijon or English mustard

10 grinds black pepper
Pinch of celery salt
3 teaspoons paprika pepper
1 tablespoon snipped chives

Prepare exactly as for the previous cheese pâté.

SMOKED MACKEREL PÂTÉ

SERVES 4 as a starter, 6–8 as a spread or dip

Do not freeze
Will keep 1 week under refrigeration

Small bunch of parsley, stalks removed
½ lb (225 g) smoked mackerel, skinned and
cut in 1 in (2½ cm) chunks
10 grinds of black pepper

1 teaspoon white horseradish relish (not
'chrane')
4 oz (125 g/½ cup) low-fat soft cheese
1 clove of garlic or ⅛ teaspoon garlic salt

To mix in a food processor Process the parsley until chopped, about 5 seconds. Add all the remaining ingredients and process a further 10 seconds, scrape down the bowl and process for 10 seconds more. Spoon into a pottery bowl, cover with clingfilm (saran wrap) and chill for several hours to allow the flavours to develop.

To mix by hand Chop the parsley. Put the smoked mackerel into a bowl and flake with a fork until very fine. Add all the remaining ingredients and mix until smooth. Spoon into a pottery bowl, cover with clingfilm and refrigerate for several hours.

VARIATION

Tuna pâté Substitute 1 can (7½ oz (200 g)) light meat tuna (well drained) for the mackerel. Use all the remaining ingredients except the horseradish relish, but add ½ teaspoon sea salt, 1 tablespoon lemon juice and 1 small, finely chopped pickled cucumber pulsed in at the end.

LOW-FAT SOUPS

- Don't sauté **onion** in fat in the usual way to improve the flavour, but add minced dried onion to the liquid in its place.
- Don't **thicken** the soup with a roux-based sauce made with whole milk; use cornflour (cornstarch) and skim milk instead.
- **Purée meat and vegetable soups** such as Minestrone or Potage Garbure, to make them thicker and more satisfying without using flour.
- For a low-fat soup garnish, toast **croutons** of wholemeal (wholewheat) bread for 15 minutes in a moderate oven, instead of frying them in fat.
- **Garnish** puréed vegetable soup with a swirl of thick natural yoghurt instead of cream, then float cucumber or orange segments on top, and scatter with plenty of chopped fresh herbs.

CELERY SOUP

SERVES 4–6
Freeze 3 months
Will keep 2 days under refrigeration

This is a very low-calorie soup but a well-flavoured one. Some varieties of celery are very stringy and the soup may therefore need pushing through a sieve after it has been puréed. The soup thickens and improves in flavour if it is left to stand overnight, or for at least 4 hours.

1 fat head of celery including the trimmed base and the leaves
2 teaspoons dried chopped onion
2 pints (1¼ litres/5 cups) stock (all vegetable, or all chicken)

1 large bayleaf
½ teaspoon salt; 10 grinds black pepper
2 tablespoons chopped fresh lovage leaves or 1 tablespoon chives

Cut off ½ in (1 cm) from the 'root' of the celery and discard it. Wash the celery thoroughly, then slice as thinly as possible, using either a food processor or a large cook's knife. Put the stock in a soup pan and add the celery and all the remaining ingredients except the herbs. Bring to the boil and simmer until the celery is absolutely tender.

Remove the bayleaf. Liquidize or process the soup to a purée. Return to the pan, bring slowly to the boil and add the herbs. Serve piping hot.

COURGETTE AND LETTUCE SOUP

SERVES 6

Freeze 3 months
Will keep 2 days under refrigeration

When the courgettes (zucchini) in the garden start to swell like marrows and the lettuces are beginning to bolt, I transform them into this beautiful pale green soup, which is thickened only with vegetables. As it is 'parev' it can be served with either a meat or a milk meal.

When time presses, you can cook this soup even more quickly using the microwave oven — see page 24.

1 lb (450 g) fresh or frozen courgettes
(zucchini), unpeeled, and thinly sliced
1 tablespoon dried minced onion or 1
teaspoon onion salt
½ teaspoon salt (omit if onion salt has been
used)

15 grinds black pepper
1½ pints (850 ml/4 cups) vegetable stock
1 medium lettuce, finely shredded
2 teaspoons chopped parsley or snipped
chives
Extra stock if necessary

Put the courgettes, onion, stock, salt and pepper into a soup pan and simmer until the courgettes are soft — about 10 or 15 minutes. Add the lettuce, bubble uncovered for 3 minutes, then put in the blender or food processor and process until smooth. Return to the pan and leave to stand overnight or for at least 3 hours. Just before serving, reheat until bubbling, thinning down if necessary with a little more stock — it should be the consistency of single cream. Stir in the herbs, taste and re-season if necessary, then serve piping hot.

MINTED CUCUMBER AND PEA SOUP

SERVES 6

Freeze 3 months
Will keep 2 days under refrigeration

This is an excellent soup for late summer when cucumbers are cheap and fresh mint is still available. It has a very subtle flavour and a light texture.

1 large cucumber, thinly peeled, with 2 in (5 cm) cut into matchsticks for garnish
½ lb (225 g/1½ cups) frozen petits pois
Bunch of fresh mint about 3 in (7½ cm) in diameter
2 teaspoons dried minced onion
½ teaspoon salt; ¼ teaspoon white pepper
1 bayleaf

¼ teaspoon dried fines herbes
1½ pints (850 ml/4 cups) home-made vegetable stock or 2 vegetable stock cubes dissolved in 1½ pints (850 ml/4 cups) hot water
½ pint (275 ml/1¼ cups) skim milk
2 teaspoons cornflour (cornstarch)

Finely slice the cucumber, saving a 2 in (5 cm) piece for the garnish. Strip the mint leaves from the stalks. Put the cucumber, peas, mint leaves, onion, seasonings and stock into a soup pan, bring to the boil, cover and simmer until the cucumber feels tender when pierced with a sharp knife — about 10 minutes.

Remove the bayleaf, then purée the contents of the soup pan in a blender or food processor, and return to the pan. Put the cornflour in a small basin and slowly add the milk, mixing to a smooth cream. Add to the pan, then bring the soup to the boil, stirring constantly. Simmer for 2 or 3 minutes, then leave for several hours or overnight for the flavour to mature.

Just before serving, reheat to simmering point and serve garnished with the reserved cucumber cut into matchsticks, and with oven-toasted croutons (see page 23).

GOLDEN VEGETABLE SOUP

SERVES 6

Freeze 3 months
Will keep 2 days under refrigeration

As long as some carrots are used for colour and thickening, the other vegetables can be varied to what you have in hand — there should be about 3 cups of vegetables in all. Purée in the food processor if you like a soup with a slightly coarse texture, and in the blender if you prefer a very smooth one.

½ lb (225 g) carrots
White part of a fat leek (about 4 oz (125 g))
1 large green or red pepper
1 tablespoon dried minced onion
Water or vegetable stock
1 bayleaf

1 teaspoon salt; ¼ teaspoon white pepper; 20 grinds black pepper
1 teaspoon dried fines herbes
½ pint (225 ml/1¼ cups) skim milk
1 tablespoon chopped parsley

Peel the carrots, split the leek and rinse under the tap. Quarter the pepper, remove the seeds and white pith. Cut all the vegetables into approximately 1 in (2½ cm) pieces and chop on the food processor until the pieces are about ¼ in (½ cm) across (or cut them into dice by hand). Put in a soup pan with the dried minced onion and barely cover with hot water or stock. Add the bayleaf, salt, peppers and dried herbs, cover and simmer until the vegetables are tender, about 20 minutes. Put in the blender or food processor and blend or process until puréed.

Put the skim milk into the same pan, add the vegetable purée and bring slowly to simmering point. If the soup is too thick, add a little more milk. Taste, and adjust the seasonings. Stir in the parsley. Leave for several hours for the flavour to develop. Serve piping hot.

TOMATO SOUP WITH MEATBALLS

SERVES 8

Freeze 3 months
Will keep 3 days under refrigeration

This is a low-fat version of the soup on page 68. It is essential to chill the soup overnight so that any fat that comes out of the meatballs can be skimmed off the top.

THE MEATBALLS:
1 lb (450 g) raw minced (ground) beef
Half an onion
1 egg
½ teaspoon salt; 10 grinds black pepper
1 teaspoon soy sauce
1 slice wholemeal (wholewheat) bread

THE SOUP:
1 can or tube (5 oz (150 g)) tomato purée
½ pint (275 ml/1¼ cups) water
½ pint (275 ml/1¼ cups) tomato juice

1 tablespoon dried minced onion or 1 teaspoon onion salt
1 clove of garlic, peeled and crushed
4 strips of orange peel
1 bayleaf
1 teaspoon dark brown sugar
20 grinds black pepper
1 large sprig of parsley
1 teaspoon each dried basil and oregano, or 2 teaspoons herbes de Provence
2 pints (1¼ litres/5 cups) strong meat stock (made with cubes)

To make the meatballs Put the meat into a mixing bowl. Purée the onion, egg, seasonings and bread, using a blender or food processor, then add to the meat, stirring together with a large fork. Set aside for 30 minutes, then roll into balls as big as a marble.

To make the soup Put all the ingredients into a soup pan, cover, and simmer together for 30 or 40 minutes. Drop the meatballs into the simmering liquid, cover and cook gently for a further 30 minutes. Cool and refrigerate. Next day, skim off the surface fat and remove the parsley sprig. Taste and add salt if necessary, before serving piping hot.

LOW-FAT FISH

- To **grill (broil) white fish** without fat, brush them with lemon juice.
- Brush fillets of **fat fish** such as herring or mackerel with a mixture of mustard and Worcestershire sauce. (See the recipe for Devilled Herrings, page 106.)
- **Fry fish** in oil only occasionally; instead 'fry' it in the oven as described on page 38.
- **Poach fish** in a little water, flavoured with julienne strips of young vegetables such as carrot and leek, then enrich the cooking liquor with skim milk and chopped herbs.
- **Bake fish** such as salmon and small trout without any fat at all, either in a conventional oven or in the microwave. Serve with lemon sections or a low-fat mayonnaise, rather than with a thickened sauce.

SMALL TROUT COOKED WITHOUT FAT

Do not freeze

FOR EACH PERSON, ALLOW THE FOLLOWING:
1 trout, 8–10 oz (225–275 g) in weight, cleaned through the gills with the head left on

1 tablespoon lemon juice
Pinch each of fish seasoning salt, white pepper and dried fines herbes

To bake in the oven   Set the oven at Gas No. 4, 350 degrees F, 180 degrees C. Place each trout on a square of foil and sprinkle with the lemon juice and seasonings, fold into a loose but airtight parcel, then bake for 20 minutes. Unwrap, skin and serve with the juices.

To bake in the microwave   Lay the trout in a shallow casserole and sprinkle with the lemon juice. Cover and cook at full power according to the manufacturer's instructions. Allow to stand as directed, then skin, sprinkle with the seasonings and pour over the cooking liquid.

SMALL FISH FILLETS, GRILLED UNDER A CRUSTY CHEESE TOPPING

SERVES 4

Do not freeze
Leftovers keep 1 day under refrigeration

Any white fish fillets can be used for this dish, but it is especially suitable for small plaice (also known as 'dabs') which can often be bought very cheaply. Neither butter nor margarine is used, but the topping prevents the thin fillets from drying out and shrinking, and provides a low-fat 'built-in' sauce as well.

The recipe is equally successful if halved and cooked in a smaller dish. Serve with a baked potato, or with crusty brown bread and a large tomato and lettuce salad.

Fillets from two medium plaice (weight on the bone about 3 lb (1¼ kg) in all)
1 teaspoon oil for greasing grill (broiler) pan
1 teaspoon salt; ¼ teaspoon white pepper

2 tablespoons lemon juice
2 tablespoons (approximately) low-calorie (fat-reduced) salad cream
2 oz (50 g/½ cup) low-fat Cheddar cheese or Edam cheese, grated

Wash the fish, salt it and leave in a colander to drain. Fifteen minutes before the fish is required, grease the grill (broiler) pan with oil and put it under the grill to heat. After 3 minutes, lay the fillets in it side by side and sprinkle with the pepper, then brush with the lemon juice. Grill (broil) gently for about 7 minutes or until the fish is beginning to colour. Spread with an even layer of the dressing and scatter with the cheese. Continue to grill for another 3 to 5 minutes, or until the cheese has set into a crusty layer and is a rich brown.

HALIBUT CREOLE

SERVES 6   *Do not freeze*

Pieces of halibut (you can substitute haddock) are laid on a bed of mushroom and tomato sauce and then grilled (broiled) under a light coating of cheese. The sauce can be made earlier in the day and will heat up again as the fish is grilled (broiled).

6 pieces of halibut, ¾ in (2 cm) thick and weighing approximately 6 oz (175 g) each, washed and lightly salted, then left to drain

THE SAUCE:
1 oz (25 g/2 tablespoons) butter or margarine
3 spring onion bulbs (green onions), finely sliced
½ lb (225 g/2 cups) pinky mushrooms, thinly sliced
1 can (15 oz (425 g)) tomatoes, well drained
¼ pint (150ml/⅔ cup) dry white wine, such as Graves or Muscadet

1 red pepper, seeds removed, cut in ⅜ in (1 cm) dice
1 level teaspoon sea salt; 10 grinds of black pepper
½ teaspoon herbes de Provence
1 clove of garlic, peeled and crushed
2 tablespoons chopped parsley

THE TOPPING:
3 tablespoons lemon juice
1 teaspoon fish seasoning salt
3 tablespoons low-calorie (low-fat) salad cream
3 oz (75 g/¾ cup) low-fat Cheddar cheese or Edam cheese, grated

Have ready a gratin dish large enough to hold the fish in one layer. Melt the fat in a pan, add the onion, cover and cook until golden and soft, about 5 minutes. Add the mushrooms, stir well, cover and cook until they are softened too, about 5 minutes. Add the tomatoes, wine, red pepper, seasonings and garlic and cook uncovered until a thick sauce is formed. Stir in the parsley, then spoon over the bottom of the dish and lay the fish pieces on top, side by side. Refrigerate until 15 minutes before required.

To grill (broil) the fish Brush the fish evenly with the lemon juice and sprinkle with the fish seasoning salt. Grill for 7 minutes until the fish is beginning to colour, then spread evenly with the salad dressing and sprinkle with the cheese. Continue to grill for a further 3 to 5 minutes, until the cheese has set into a crusty layer and is a rich brown.

SPRING FISH CASSEROLE

SERVES 4   *Do not freeze*
                                                Leftovers will keep 1 day under refrigeration

Thick slices of filleted haddock are poached with a bouquet of spring vegetables, and the cooking liquor is enriched with a little herb-flavoured milk. The dish can be cooked very successfully in the microwave.

1 tablespoon butter or margarine
3 fat spring onions (green onions), finely
sliced (both bulb and green part)
1 in (2½ cm) of the white part of a fat leek,
thinly sliced
3 baby carrots, finely sliced
1 lb (450 g) haddock fillet, cut in 4 pieces,
washed, salted and left to drain
Speck of white pepper

½ teaspoon fish seasoning salt
1 small bayleaf
10 peppercorns
4 oz (125 g/1 cup) pinky mushrooms, thinly
sliced
4 fl oz (125 ml/½ cup) skim milk
2 teaspoons chopped parsley or snipped fresh
dill
½ lb (225 g/1½ cups) frozen petits pois

Melt the fat in a non-stick frying pan or heatproof casserole and add the onions, leek and carrots. Stir well, then cover and cook for 7 minutes until the vegetables have softened. Put in the pieces of fish, then turn them over so that they are coated on both sides with some of the softened vegetables. Sprinkle each piece of fish with the fish seasoning salt and the pepper, then add the mushrooms and enough hot water to cover the bottom of the pan. Tuck in the bayleaf and peppercorns, cover and simmer for 5 minutes, then turn the fish over again, re-cover and continue to cook for a further 5 minutes, or until the fish can be flaked easily with a fork and looks creamy. Add the milk and the peas, and cook for a further 5 minutes until the peas are tender, then taste and re-season if necessary. Sprinkle with the parsley or dill, then serve piping hot.

LOW-FAT MEATS AND POULTRY

• Eat more of the leaner meats such as young **lamb** and **veal**, and young **poultry** without any skin.
• **Trim** all meats of their visible fat before cooking them.
• Roast and grill (broil) all meats on a **rack**, so that as the fat melts from the joint it isn't re-absorbed.
• Protect roasts with a **coating of mustard** instead of fat or oil (see the recipe for Lamb Dijonnaise, page 117).
• Leave all meat sauces (such as Bolognese) and steaks cooked in wine or sauce to **chill** overnight, so that any free fat can be removed easily.
• **Don't brown** either meat or poultry before braising, if it is to be cooked in a richly coloured sauce.
• For **extra fibre**, use wholemeal (wholewheat) breadcrumbs to bind minced (ground) meat mixtures, instead of matzah meal which is made from white flour.

GRILLED ALL-BEEF BURGERS

SERVES 4–5   Freeze raw or cooked beefburgers 3 months

The finest quality of beef, coarsely minced (ground) to give a light mixture and mildly spiced, is grilled (broiled) without added fat. The beefburgers can be served plain or with the Pizzaiola Sauce on page 156. To allow any free fat in the mixture to drain away, grill the beefburgers either on a wire rack under a grill or on a ridged iron griddle set on top of the cooker. Serve with a green or tomato salad and baked new potatoes.

2 lb (1 kg) minced (ground) beef, put
through the mincer only once
1 tablespoon tomato ketchup
1 tablespoon soy sauce

½ teaspoon Worcestershire sauce (optional)
1 teaspoon salt; 10 grinds black pepper
1 level teaspoon yeast extract or vegetable
paste

Turn the meat into a bowl and mix in all the other ingredients, using a fork so that the mixture doesn't pack together. Form into 4 or 5 'steaks' each about ¾ in (2 cm) thick. Put under a hot grill (broiler) on a greased wire rack (or on a hot stove-top griddle) and cook to your taste — 5 minutes on either side for 'well done' and a rich brown.

MEXICAN MEATBALLS

SERVES 6–8

Freeze 3 months
Will keep 3 days under refrigeration

To cut down on fat, the meatballs are not sealed by frying in the usual way, but added to the simmering liquid. This is just as effective in preventing their juices from leaking into the sauce. For the finest flavour, make the casserole 24 hours in advance, then reheat until bubbly.

THE MEATBALLS:
1½ lb (675 g) minced (ground) beef
Half an onion
1 egg
1 thick slice of wholemeal (wholewheat) bread
1 teaspoon salt; 10 grinds black pepper
1 teaspoon soy sauce

THE SAUCE:
1 tablespoon oil
2 onions, thinly sliced
2 cloves of garlic, peeled and chopped

2 teaspoons dark brown sugar
1 large red and 1 large green pepper, seeds
removed, thinly sliced
2 cans (15 oz (425 g)) tomatoes in juice,
coarsely chopped
1 rounded tablespoon tomato purée
3 teaspoons mild chilli sauce
1 large bayleaf
1 teaspoon salt; 10 grinds black pepper
2 teaspoons paprika
1 can (14 oz (400 g)) red kidney beans,
drained

To make the meatballs   Use the method described in the recipe for Tomato Soup with Meatballs (page 46), but form into balls the size of an egg.
To make the sauce   Heat the oil for 3 minutes in a heavy lidded pan, then add the onion and garlic, cover and simmer until the onion is soft, about 10 minutes. Uncover and sprinkle with the brown sugar, then cook until the onion turns a golden-brown. Add the sliced peppers, chopped tomatoes, tomato purée, chilli sauce, bayleaf and seasonings. Bring to boiling point, then cover and simmer for 45 minutes, stirring once or twice. Add the meatballs and simmer, covered, for 30 minutes; then add the drained beans and simmer for a further 10 minutes.

ENTRECÔTE STEAK AND MUSHROOMS

SERVES 4

Entrecôte steaks are cut from the eye of the rib and they make very tender eating if the beef has been well hung. A non-stick or heavy stainless steel pan needs only a teaspoon of oil to grease it, and the mushrooms for the sauce are cooked in their own juice, without any fat at all.

4 entrecôte steaks, each weighing 6–8 oz
(175–225 g), cut ¾ in (2 cm) thick
Black pepper and beef seasoning herb
mixture
2 teaspoons oil
½ lb (225 g/2 cups) mature mushrooms,
thinly sliced
½ teaspoon sea salt

5 fl oz (150 ml/⅔ cup) dry red wine
4 tablespoons thin beef gravy or water plus
half a beef stock cube
1 teaspoon Worcestershire sauce
10 grinds black pepper
1 teaspoon Dijon mustard
2 teaspoons chopped parsley

Trim off most of the fat, then lightly sprinkle both sides of each steak with freshly ground pepper and the beef seasoning herbs and leave at room temperature for 1 hour.

About 15 minutes before you wish to serve the steaks, set the oven to low (Gas No. ¼, 225 degrees F, 110 degrees C) and put a serving dish to heat in it. Choose a heavy frying pan, either non-stick or stainless steel, which is large enough to hold the four steaks side by side, put it over a moderate heat, and brush it very thinly with oil.

After about 5 minutes, when you can feel a fierce heat on your hand held 2 in (5 cm) above it, put in the steaks, and press them down well so they are in close contact with the hot pan. Cook the steaks for 4 minutes, by which time they should be a rich brown, then turn and cook the other side in the same way. Nick one of the steaks with a sharp knife — it should be a pale pink in the centre. If it is still too rare for your taste, cook for a further minute on each side and then test again.

When the steaks are done to your liking, remove them to the warm serving dish and leave in the oven. Pour off any fat that might have accumulated in the pan, then add the sliced mushrooms and sprinkle them very lightly with sea salt to draw out their juices. Cover and cook gently for 5 minutes until the mushrooms are tender and are swimming in a rich juice. Add to the pan the wine, gravy (or water and stock cube), Worcestershire sauce, pepper and mustard. Stir well to incorporate all the delicious sediment sticking to the pan, then simmer until syrupy and well-flavoured — 3 or 4 minutes. Stir in the parsley and pour around the steaks. Serve at once.

LOW-FAT VEGETABLE IDEAS

• To sauté and brown **onions** in the minimum of fat, add only enough to make a film over the bottom of the pan, put in the onions, then cover and allow them to soften and colour in their own juice. Cook uncovered to evaporate the moisture and complete the browning.

• To cook **mushrooms** with no fat at all, put them in a pan (or in the microwave), sprinkle lightly with salt, cover and allow to cook in the juices that will be drawn out of them. Use this juice in a sauce, or boil it away to crispen the mushrooms.

- To cook **aubergines (eggplant)** in the minimum amount of fat, salt them and leave for 30 minutes, then rinse and pat dry — this reduces by half the amount of oil that is needed to fry them. But better still, grill (broil) them instead, in which case you need only brush them with oil on both sides.
- To make a **vegetable ragoût** of any kind, use dried minced onion instead of fresh onion sautéed in oil, but make up the flavour with plenty of dried and fresh herbs.

RATATOUILLE

SERVES 4–6

Freeze 3 months
Will keep 3 days under refrigeration

This is a most delicious version of the classic dish, yet it contains no fat at all. It makes an ideal accompaniment to grilled steak, beefburgers or roast chicken, or it can be served as a starter with coarse brown bread.

6 fresh 'beef' tomatoes, peeled and chopped, or 1 can (15 oz (425 g)) tomatoes, canned in juice
1 tablespoon tomato purée
5 fl oz (150 ml/2⁄3 cup) vegetable stock (made from a cube or 1 teaspoon vegetable paste)
1 fat clove of garlic, peeled and crushed
1 teaspoon salt; 10 grinds black pepper
1 tablet artificial sweetener
1 tablespoon dried minced onion

3 medium-sized red peppers, seeds removed, cut into slices 3⁄8 in (1 cm) wide
2 medium-sized green peppers, seeds removed, cut into slices 3⁄8 in (1 cm) wide
1½ lb (675 g) aubergines (eggplant), unpeeled, cut in 3⁄8 in (1 cm) thick slices
3⁄4 lb (350 g) courgettes (zucchini), unpeeled, cut in 3⁄8 in (1 cm) thick slices
1 teaspoon dried herbes de Provence
1 tablespoon chopped parsley or fresh basil
1 tablespoon lemon juice
2 oz (50 g/½ cup) black olives (optional)

Put the tomatoes, tomato purée, stock, garlic salt, pepper, artificial sweetener and onion into a fairly wide pan and bring to the boil. Add the peppers and aubergines, cover and simmer for 20 minutes. Add the courgettes and herbs, half-cover and simmer for a further 5–10 minutes until they are just tender. If the mixture is watery, uncover and bubble for 5 minutes or until it is thick but still juicy. Stir in the lemon juice and olives (if used). This dish may be reheated.

LOW-FAT SALAD DRESSINGS

- Make a **fat-free dressing** for sliced cucumber and tomato salads with slightly sweetened dilute wine vinegar (experiment with artificial sweeteners). Flavour the dressing heavily with black pepper and chopped dill or chives.
- For general use, make or buy a **low-fat dressing** (see recipe below, for example) and flavour with chopped herbs, diced pickled gherkins, capers or stuffed olives.
- Use **natural yoghurt** instead of soured cream for minted dressings for cucumbers.

TROPICAL SALAD PLATTER

SERVES 4

Do not freeze
Leftovers will keep 1 day under refrigeration
Salad dressing will keep 4 days

Serve this with a glass of tomato juice spiced with Worcestershire sauce, add a slice of wholemeal (wholewheat) toast and you have a satisfying and complete low-fat, low-sugar meal. Make the salad dressing first as it must be well chilled. Arrange the salads just before serving.

THE SALAD:
1 small Iceberg lettuce or 2 lettuce hearts
1 bunch watercress, washed and coarse stalks removed
1 lb (450 g/2 cups) cottage cheese or Quark
1 medium pineapple, cut into 4 sections lengthwise, core and skin removed
Half a cucumber, sliced
4 pickled or plain boiled beets, sliced
6 small firm tomatoes
1 fat red pepper, cut in very thin rings

¼ lb (225 g/¾ cup) each black and green seedless grapes
1 crisp apple

THE DRESSING (WITHOUT OIL):
1 egg yolk
1 tablespoon white wine vinegar
4 tablespoons skim milk
1 teaspoon sea salt
¼ teaspoon paprika
¼ teaspoon mustard powder
¼ teaspoon soy sauce
¼ pint (150 g/⅔ cup) low-fat yoghurt

To make the dressing Put the egg yolk into a pan and stir in all the remaining ingredients (except the yoghurt) in the order given. Put over medium heat and stir constantly (without allowing the mixture to boil) until it becomes the consistency of pouring custard and will coat the back of a wooden spoon. Take off the heat and keep stirring, then put in a bowl and chill for 5 minutes in the freezer, 15 minutes in the refrigerator. Stir in the yoghurt. Serve cold with the salad.

To arrange the salad Take four large plates and arrange a salad on each as follows. Cover the top half of the plate with shredded lettuce and the bottom half with watercress leaves. Arrange two scoops of cottage cheese in the middle. Cut the pineapple sections into small wedges, and arrange in an oval at the base of the cottage cheese. Arrange the sliced cucumber and beets in overlapping rows on opposite sides of the plate, with the tomatoes cut in quarters. Arrange the red pepper strips on the cottage cheese and tuck the black and green grapes in where they look most effective. Slice the apple and tuck that in too.

LOW-FAT, LOW-SUGAR DESSERTS
● For a really low-sugar dessert, eat **fresh or dried fruits** which are sweetened only by their natural fruit sugar.
● For a **low-sugar fruit salad**, stir two level tablespoons of light brown sugar into the juice of a lemon, then stir through the prepared fresh fruit. Leave at room temperature for 1 hour to allow the juices to flow, then refrigerate until required.

- Serve more **sorbets (sherbets)** containing fruit juices and purées, such as apple, damson and orange, instead of very sweet and creamy ice creams.
- Serve **fruit purées** such as strawberry, blackcurrant or apricot as sauces for other fruits or sorbets, instead of cream.
- Use **honey-sweetened yoghurt** instead of soured and sweet whipped cream. This is delicious stirred into a jelly (gelatine dessert) just before it sets, using 5 fl oz of yoghurt to every jelly. Stir in sliced fresh fruit such as strawberries, raspberries or redcurrants at the same time.

FRESH FRUIT SALAD

SERVES 6   *Leftovers will keep 1 day under refrigeration*

The permutation of fruits that can be prepared in this way are limitless; this is one combination which I have found looks extremely pretty, and provides a good contrast of taste and texture. The lemon juice and the tiny amount of sugar are used to draw out the natural juices from the fruit.

Juice of a whole lemon (3 tablespoons)
6 mint leaves, finely chopped
1 tablespoon dark soft brown sugar
1 large Red Delicious apple, unpeeled and very thinly sliced

½ lb (225 g/2 cups) fresh or frozen redcurrants
½ lb (225 g/1½ cups) well-flavoured grapes
2 large oranges, peeled and sectioned (see page 189)
2 medium-sized ripe bananas, peeled and sliced just before serving

Put the lemon juice into a bowl with the mint leaves, and stir in the sugar until it has dissolved. Add the sliced apple and stir well to coat with the lemon juice, then add the redcurrants, the pipped (or seedless) grapes and the sectioned oranges. Mix well, cover and leave at room temperature for 1 hour. Chill until required, then stir in the sliced bananas.

YOGHURT BERRY DELIGHT

SERVES 6–8   *Do not freeze*
                                        Will keep 2 days under refrigeration

When this low-fat, low-sugar dessert is spooned into long-stemmed glasses, it looks just as mouth-watering — and I think tastes even more delicious — as the most calorie-laden cream mousse. It is best to use fresh fruit in season, but frozen fruit can be used provided it has not been sweetened in any way — frozen strawberries will have a better texture if they are added to the jelly when still half-frozen.

1 kosher strawberry jelly (gelatine dessert mix) (preferably sugar-reduced)
2 tablespoons lemon juice
6 tablespoons orange juice

¼ lb (125 g/1 cup) each raspberries and sliced strawberries
2 cartons low-fat raspberry or strawberry yogurt

Dissolve the jelly in about half a pint of very hot water, stir in the fruit juices and then make up to either 15 fl oz (425 ml/2 cups) or 20 fl oz (575 ml/2½ cups) according to the packet instructions. Put the jelly in a shallow container and chill in the freezer until it is on the point of setting — about 30 minutes — it will then have the same consistency as unbeaten egg whites. Gently stir in the yoghurt and the fruit to create a marbled effect. Chill in the refrigerator for 30 minutes, then spoon into one large glass bowl or individual glasses. Leave to set completely, in another hour or two.

FIBRE WITH EVERYTHING

Once upon a time it was called 'roughage'; now it's been named *dietary fibre* and the medical profession is unanimous in urging us to eat it daily for the sake of our digestion.

If you consider what you had to eat yesterday, you'll probably find that however delicious the food was in itself, it lacked an element of *crunch* — or dietary fibre. The problem is that so many of the foods we eat today have much of the roughage refined out of them, compared with those that our parents and grandparents ate. We eat white bread instead of rye, breakfast cereals instead of porridge, cream soups with all the fibrous parts strained out instead of cabbage borscht and lentil soup, fruit juices instead of the whole fruit; and this new pattern of eating can have a disastrous effect on the digestive system. Our mothers were right, too, when they insisted on prunes for breakfast — dried fruits are a very good source of fibre.

Straight bran — which is an excellent form of dietary fibre — makes very monotonous eating; it's the stuff that horses feed on from their nosebags. But it is delicious toasted as a breakfast cereal; it will slip down very well as part of a bread, scone or biscuit; and Toasted Bran (or any other bran cereal) is quite delicious as part of the topping for a fruit crumble and the fibre content is even higher when it's made with wholemeal (wholewheat) flour.

SOPA DE LENTEJAS MADRILENA
LENTIL AND PEPPER SOUP, SPANISH STYLE

SERVES 6–8

Freeze 3 months
Will keep 3 days under refrigeration

This is a splendid high-fibre soup with spicy undertones which give it a flavour that is totally different from that of the rather bland Jewish-style lentil soup. The lentils do not need to be soaked overnight but are left in boiling water for 15 minutes before cooking. 'Green' lentils (which are in fact an olive-green) are used to make this soup in Spain, but red lentils can be used instead. The soup needs 12 hours to mature before it is served.

½ lb (225 g/1 cup) lentils, soaked for 15 minutes in double their volume of boiling water
1 tablespoon sunflower oil or olive oil
1 large (8 oz (225 g)) onion, finely chopped
1 large red or green pepper, seeds removed, cut in strips
1 can (14 oz (400 g)) tomatoes in juice

3 medium carrots (about 6 oz (175 g) total weight), thinly sliced
2 teaspoons dark brown sugar
1 teaspoon salt; 15 grinds of black pepper
1 large bayleaf
1 teaspoon fines herbes
3½ pints (2 litres/9 cups) hot water plus 3 vegetable or meat stock cubes

Heat the oil gently in a heavy soup pan, add the onion and pepper, then cover and simmer for 10 minutes, stirring once or twice, until the vegetables begin to take on a little colour. Meanwhile put the soaked lentils into a sieve (discard the soaking water), and rinse thoroughly with cold water. Add to the pan together with all the remaining ingredients. Bring to the boil, cover and simmer for 1½ hours. Cool a little, remove the bayleaf, and purée in a liquidizer or food processor. Leave to stand overnight, then reheat and serve.

THREE RECIPES WITH ADDED BRAN

CURRIED BRAN CRACKERS

Makes 24

Freeze 6 months
Will keep 2 weeks in an airtight container

These high-fibre, low-sugar biscuits are delicious spread with any of the low-fat pâtés whose recipes are given on page 42, and accompanied by slices of crisp unpeeled dessert apple.

6 oz (175 g/1½ cups) wheatmeal flour
1 teaspoon baking powder
2 oz (50 g/⅔ cup) porage oats
1 tablespoon Toasted Bran cereal
Pinch of sea salt

1 tablespoon soft light brown sugar
½ teaspoon mild curry powder
2 oz (50 g/¼ cup) each sunflower margarine
and white vegetable fat
2 tablespoons skim milk

Preheat the oven to Gas No. 6, 400 degrees F, 200 degrees C. Line two oven trays with silicone paper.

Mix all the dry ingredients, then rub in the fats by hand or machine until the mixture resembles coarse crumbs. Sprinkle with the milk, then gather into a dough, and knead lightly until smooth. Roll out ⅛ in (½ cm) thick on a board dusted with wheatmeal flour, then cut into 2 in (5 cm) plain rounds and prick all over with a fork. Arrange 2 in (5 cm) apart on the trays and bake for 15 minutes, or until brown at the edges. Allow to cool, then store in an airtight container.

BRAN SCONES

Makes 10–12

Eat the same day
Freeze 1 month

8 oz (225 g/2 cups) wholewheat flour
4 teaspoons baking powder
1 oz (25 g/¼ cup) Toasted Bran cereal
½ teaspoon salt

2 oz (50 g/¼ cup) margarine or butter
1 egg
5 tablespoons skim milk or natural yoghurt
Milk and demerara (brown) sugar for glaze

Preheat the oven to Gas No. 8, 450 degrees F, 230 degrees C. Have ready a greased baking tray.

Mix the flour, baking powder, bran and salt, then rub in the fat by hand or machine until it looks like oatmeal. Whisk together the egg and milk (or yoghurt), then add to the dough mixture all at once and mix to a soft dough. Knead lightly on a floured board until smooth and free from cracks, then roll out ½ in (1 cm) thick. Cut the scones using a fluted 2 in (5 cm) cutter and arrange on the oven tray. Brush with milk and scatter with demerara sugar. Bake for 10 or 12 minutes, until well risen and a rich brown on top. Serve spread with a low-fat soft cheese.

VARIATION
Cheese and Bran Scones   Use the same ingredients but add 2 oz (50 g/½ cup) low-fat Cheddar or Edam cheese, grated, and ½ teaspoon mustard powder. Brush the tops of the scones with milk and scatter with a little more cheese. Serve with one of the cheese pâtés on page 42.

BRAN HERB ROLLS

SERVES 6–8

Freeze filled rolls 1 month
Will keep 2 days in foil parcel under
refrigeration

Hot bran rolls filled with a savoury herb mixture make an excellent high-fibre accompaniment to soups and salads.

8 wholemeal (wholewheat) bran rolls
(obtainable at good stores and supermarkets)

THE FILLING:
4 oz (125 g/½ cup) soft margarine

or butter
2 level tablespoons chopped parsley
1½ teaspoons dried herbes de Provence
15 grinds black pepper
1 teaspoon paprika

Cut each roll into slices ⅜ in (1 cm) thick but with the cuts stopping at the base, as for herb bread. Cream the fat with all the remaining ingredients, then spread this mixture on one side of each slice of the rolls and dot any remaining mixture on top of them. Wrap the rolls in a foil parcel, and freeze until required.

Preheat the oven to Gas No. 7, 425 degrees F, 225 degrees C. Put in the parcel and bake for 12 minutes, then open it and allow the rolls to brown and crispen for a further 3 or 4 minutes. Serve warm, not hot.

Soups

Was Henry IV of France thinking of Jewish chicken soup when he declared that every peasant in his kingdom should have a fowl to put in the pot on Sunday? Probably not, because France had expelled its Jewish population in 1394, and was not to acquire Alsace (where the large Jewish community included many poultry farmers) until 1678, long after the end of his reign.

But soup was certainly the big dish in his day, for commoners if not for kings, and had been since Neolithic times. A recipe for this Neolithic broth is suggested by the French chef, Raymond Oliver, in his book *The French at Table*. This recipe, consisting mainly of vegetables and wild herbs, would have produced a soup not unlike those still made by country folk today, such as the *melokhia* prepared from a particular glutinous leaf by the peasant women in Egypt, the *schov* made from wild sorrel that my Lithuanian-born grandmother used to pick every summer, and the *soupe à la menthe* which is a speciality of the Tunisian Jewish kitchen.

In Henry IV's day, every household, rich or poor, had its soup cauldron, which was replenished daily with water, fresh vegetables and any meat, fat or bones that were available. But soup began to lose its importance, at least at the tables of the rich, as the art of the kitchen became more sophisticated and meat and fish could be 'promoted' to being a separate course in their own right. The English led the way early in the eighteenth century by serving soup as an appetizer which was then removed from the table before the main dish of meat or fish was carried in.

But for peasants and labourers it has remained the cheapest way to feed a large family on a small income. Such a vegetable *potage* (as it is still called in France) need be enriched with only a small piece of meat in order to provide a family with its main meal of the day.

The importance of soup in traditional Jewish cookery probably owes as much to this element of economy as to the delicious flavour for which we prize it today. Seventy years ago, at my grandparents' table, the custom still lingered of cooking and serving the meat with the soup, then eating the two together, rather like *pot au feu*. Most of these traditional western Jewish soups were based on pulses and cereals, high in energy value and rich in the vegetable proteins that could augment the small amount of meat most families could afford. After a period out of favour because of their high calorie content, these old-style soups are now being rehabilitated as part of a high-fibre diet. Young people have also discovered that, like the medieval cauldron soups, they can provide a constant supply of cheap 'fast food'.

In the general Jewish community, the soups in favour at present are lighter and less fattening than in the past. Before they are added to the soup pan, both poultry and meat are trimmed of their fat, and clear broths and the lighter kinds of vegetable soups are more frequently served. In Israel, the cold soups so popular during the summer in eastern Europe have become 'naturalized' as part of the national diet. When you have lunch in the street cafés of Jerusalem and Tel Aviv you will be offered 'Tarator' — a yoghurt and herb soup — and 'Marak Yayin Duvdivanim' made from morello (sour red) cherries and soured cream, rather than the barley Krupnik and Cabbage Borscht that were the favourites fifty years ago.

In the home, the tempo of soup cookery has changed. Now it is only Chicken Soup whose preparation is measured in hours. With the advent of the kosher soup cube and the food processor, most other soups can be put together in minutes (when they are not replaced entirely by a packet or a can). Provided they offer something more than packaged monosodium glutamate, I am all in favour of factory-made flavourings, for there is little room in most of our lives for the devotion to the kitchen that the stockpot demands.

In this chapter I offer you a soup collection which preserves some of the flavours of the past but also includes recipes using the foods and the technology of the present and the future. (Consult the index, too, for other delicious soup recipes.) I'm still prepared to simmer Chicken Soup for most of the day, but if time is short, I'm also content to cook it in the microwave, then strengthen its flavour with stock cubes.

What would my grandmother have said if she was offered one of these new-style recipes such as Mediterranean Fish Soup or Courgette and Lettuce Soup? Would she have shaken her head in disbelief? Or would she have been more likely, as I should like to think, to smack her lips in approval? For Jewish women have never scorned innovation. From every age and culture they have chosen dishes to adapt as food for their families. Let us hope that when our grandchildren look back on the soups of the twentieth-century Jewish table, they will say, as we do today of Cabbage Borscht and Krupnik: 'that's tradition!'

SOUP SENSE

• **Pans** with ovenproof lugs rather than handles are a wise investment, because they can also be used as tureens and casseroles (they should be heatproof up to Gas No. 8, 450 degrees F, 230 degrees C). My preferred materials are enamelled steel and stainless steel which are reasonably light in weight, easy to clean, make efficient use of fuel and have a stylish appearance.

• Always choose a pan of the right **capacity** for your purpose.

2 gallon (9 litres/40 cups), for preparation for the freezer
1 gallon (4½ litres/20 cups) holds up to 16 servings
5 pints (2½ litres/12½ cups) holds up to 10 servings
3 pints (1¾ litres/7½ cups) holds up to 6 servings

A pan of larger capacity than you estimate you require gives more flexibility than one of the exact size, and there is less danger of the soup boiling over.

• Good knives and a food processor together make **vegetable preparation** quick and efficient. Use knives for those slicing and chopping jobs where precise sizes are required or juicy vegetables are involved, that the food processor cannot do so well. A cook's knife with a 7 inch (17½ cm) stainless blade and a vegetable knife with a serrated edge are the minimum you will need.

• Use a blender for a smooth **purée**, a food processor for one with a little texture. A vegetable mill is useful for puréeing stringy vegetables like celery.

• A coarse round sieve will **strain** out vegetables and other solids from stocks and consommés.

• Look for those makes of **stock cubes and pastes** where monosodium glutamate does not head the list of ingredients. These are difficult to find when it comes to beef and chicken cubes but easier with vegetable cubes and pastes, certain makes of which (often to be found in health food shops) contain no monosodium glutamate at all.

• The most useful **herbs** to grow for soup are parsley, chives, tarragon, dill and basil.

• **Parsley** for long-term storage should be frozen whole. When it is required, crumble it into the pan while it is still frozen. Parsley for short-term (1 week) storage should be chopped, stored in a plastic container, then frozen. Whole parsley will keep fresh for a week in the refrigerator. Wash, dry and store in an airtight container.

• To freeze **chives** for winter use, tie them with string in bundles about 2 inches (5 cm) in diameter and 6 inches (15 cm) long. Cut them with a sharp knife whilst they are still frozen.

• Dried herbs have a more intense flavour, fresh herbs a more delicate one. So use the dried herbs in hearty soups like tomato and mixed vegetable, and fresh ones for garnishes and in the softer cream soups like cauliflower and courgette.

• To **freeze soup** choose containers that have a lid that is as wide as the base, so that the frozen blocks can be easily eased out into the pan. Leave an inch headroom between the surface of the soup and the lid to allow for expansion of the liquid in the freezer. Freeze some one-portion servings as insurance against unexpected guests or between-meal snacks. Where freezer space is limited store purées or concentrates, and dilute with stock, milk or sauce as required.

• **Thaw frozen soup**, for greatest ease, overnight in the refrigerator. Or thaw in the microwave. To reheat a thick frozen soup, cover the base of the pan with an appropriate liquid, add the block of soup, cover and put the pan on a very low heat. This stops the soup from 'catching' as it thaws.

CHICKEN SOUPS

Chicken Soup in the Jewish Fashion

Young babies are weaned on it, invalids are tempted with it, wedding guests celebrate with it, mourners are consoled with it . . .no wonder Chicken Soup — or 'Jewish penicillin' as it is affectionately known — is one of the most famous soups in the world.

Its genesis lies in the villages of the Russian Pale of Settlement, where for centuries poultry was the cheapest form of meat. From the weekly bird with its fat and giblets, a canny housewife could prepare an entire Shabbat meal, starting with Chopped Liver and 'grebenes' and going on to soup and matzah balls, stuffed helzel and the bird itself, made tasty with fried onions. The flavour of all these dishes depended on the fact that a mature *fowl* was used rather than a young *chicken*.

An older bird still makes the best soup, but as it is not so popular today because of its high fat content and coarse if flavoursome flesh, the old method of making the soup by simmering a fowl until it had given its all, and then using it as the main course, has been modified. And if the result is not *quite* as good as we *think* Mother used to make, it is still a memorable dish to come home to on a winter's night.

In this chapter, I emphasize the need to allow all soups to mature from one day to the next. Chicken Soup in particular isn't worthy of the name until it has had this resting period. It is then that the real metamorphosis from chicken *stock* to chicken *soup* takes place.

In earlier, less diet-conscious days, Chicken Soup reached its apotheosis when, crowned with golden beads of fat, this 'gilderne yoch' was brought forth in triumph at Jewish wedding feasts. Today it is still served at weddings, though without its golden crown; and it is still a traditional part of the Shabbat meal in most Jewish homes, though it is more likely to have come from the freezer than to have been freshly made from the weekly bird.

But despite all the new-found skills of the flavour chemist and the food factory technologist, it is still quite impossible to prepare an authentic brew of Chicken Soup in any way other than from homely ingredients simmered with a seasoning of love.

BATCH OF CHICKEN SOUP FOR THE FREEZER

Makes about 1 gallon (4½ litres/20 cups)   *Freeze 3 months*
before concentrating

It is really worthwhile to prepare and freeze a month's supply of Chicken Soup at one time, as all the tedious parts of the process — straining the vegetables, stripping the flesh from the carcase and the giblets, even washing up the pan — are only done once. Then you can divide the batch into convenient portions which, when required, need only be simmered for a short time with some fresh vegetables. Soup garnishes such as Knaidlach (soup dumplings, page 75) and Kreplach (Jewish-style ravioli, page 11) also freeze well, but freeze them separately as they may go soggy if left in the soup.

To make this quantity of soup you will need a pan of 1½ gallons (6 litres/30 cups) capacity, tall rather than broad so that the base diameter is equal to that of the gas ring or hot plate of the cooker. I use an enamelled steel pan with a white enamel interior which is particularly easy to clean. Small batches of Chicken Soup can be made successfully in a pressure cooker or slow cooker, but to my taste they do not have quite the same depth of flavour.

You can arrive at a perfect panful of Chicken Soup by different routes, as to some extent you can vary the ingredients according to what you have in stock. But for the finest flavour, it is advisable to use at least a portion of a fowl — also called a 'boiling hen' (stewing chicken). If you do not like it plain boiled, the cooked flesh can always be used in a pie or pilaff. But if you do not use any fowl at all, and rely solely on giblets, then you may need to add chicken stock cubes to deepen the flavour. It is important to be generous with soup vegetables, and always to include some ripe tomatoes or a little tomato purée to deepen the colour without giving the stock a *taste* of tomato.

3–4 sets of chicken giblets
The last wing joints previously cut from
chickens before they were roasted, then
frozen (if available)
Any carcases from roast birds in the freezer
1 whole or half a boiling fowl, together with
the feet
3 large onions, peeled but left whole

6 carrots, each cut lengthwise into 4
Leaves and top 2 in (5 cm) of the stalks from
a bunch of celery
2 oz (50 g) bunch of parsley, including the
stalks
4 very soft ripe tomatoes or 1 tablespoon
tomato purée
1 tablespoon salt; ½ teaspoon white pepper

Put the giblets, wings, feet, broken-up cooked carcases and fowl (if used) into the pan and cover with 8 or 9 pints (4½ litres/20 cups) of water — sufficient to come to within an inch or two of the top of the pan. Bring slowly to the boil, then remove the scum from the top with a wet metal spoon. Add the vegetables, herbs and seasonings, bring back to the boil, cover and simmer for at least 3 hours on top of the stove, 4 hours in the oven. (An oven set at Gas No. 2, 300 degrees F, 150 degrees C should keep the liquid at a slow bubble.)

At the end of the cooking time, lift out the giblets with a slotted spoon and put in a bowl. Lift out and discard any cooked carcases. Remove the cooked fowl and reserve for another purpose. Place a coarse sieve over a large bowl and pour the soup through to separate it from the vegetables (which can now be discarded, as all their goodness and flavour will be in the soup). Strip the meat from the giblets and wings, and refrigerate until it can be added to the defatted soup next day. If freezer space is at a premium, the soup can be boiled down to half its volume. In any event, chill it overnight so that the congealed fat can be removed next day.

Divide the defatted stock into convenient amounts allowing 2 pints (1¼ litres/5 cups) for 4–6 servings (1 pint (¾ litre/2½ cups) if condensed). Divide the giblet meat between the portions, label and freeze.

When ready to use the soup   Put the required amount of frozen soup into a pan and add the following:

1–2 good-quality chicken stock cubes (the   *cubes*
number will depend on the strength of the   *1 in (2½ cm) length of the white part of a*
soup)   *leek, finely shredded*
1 medium carrot, cut into ⅜ in (1 cm)   *Chopped parsley*

Bring the soup slowly to the boil with the vegetables and simmer for 30 minutes. Stir in the parsley and serve with the desired garnish, which can be farfel, lokshen, mandlen, knaidlach or kreplach.

CHICKEN SOUP TRADITIONAL METHOD

SERVES 4–6   *Freeze 3 months*

If you prefer to make sufficient for only one meal, then proceed as follows:

The feet, the last joint of the wings and the   *2 carrots, peeled and cut into 4*
giblets of a young fowl (4 lb/2 kg dressed   *Leaves and top 2 in (5 cm) of 2 stalks celery*
weight) or roasting chicken, plus a chicken   *1 sprig of parsley*
stock cube, or a whole or half fowl with the   *1 very ripe tomato*
feet, wings and giblets   *2 level teaspoons salt; pinch of white pepper*
3 pints (1½ litres/7½ cups) water   *Any soft eggs from the fowl*
1 whole onion, peeled

Put the water, salt and pepper into a large, heavy soup pan, add the feet, wings and giblets, and the bird or the stock cube. Cover and bring to the boil. Uncover and remove any froth with a large, wet metal spoon. Add all the remaining ingredients. Bring back to the boil, then reduce the heat so that the liquid is barely bubbling. Cover and continue to simmer for a further 3 hours, either on top of the stove or in a slow oven (Gas No. 2, 300 degrees F, 150 degrees C), or until the fowl (if used) feels very tender when the leg is prodded with a fork.

Strain the soup into one bowl and put the giblets and the carrots into another. The fowl, if used, should be put in a separate container for further use or for freezing. Refrigerate.

Next day remove any congealed fat, and return the soup to the pan. Add the cooked giblets and the carrot (cut into small dice), and reheat slowly before serving. The soup may be garnished with cooked lokshen (vermicelli or egg noodles, see page 10), mandlen or knaidlach (matzah balls, see page 6).

Second-day chicken stock can be made by simmering the stripped carcase of a casseroled or roast bird for 2 hours with vegetables, using the same mixture as for fresh chicken soup. This stock makes an excellent basis for Borscht and for tomato and vegetable soups, and can be strengthened if necessary with chicken or beef stock cubes.

AVGOLEMONO CHICKEN SOUP IN THE GREEK STYLE

SERVES 6–8   *Do not freeze, apart from leftovers*

This creamy-textured soup, which is thickened with eggs like Borscht, has a faint tang of lemon juice which is very refreshing for a summer dinner. It is important to use a well-flavoured chicken stock, so it is particularly successful when made with traditional chicken soup. Avoid chicken soup cubes if possible, as the high proportion of monosodium glutamate they contain tends to mask the delicate flavour of the soup.

3 pints (1¾ litres/7½ cups) Chicken Soup   *3 eggs*
(see recipes above)   *2 tablespoons fresh lemon juice*
Shredded meat from the giblets or the portion *2 tablespoons chopped parsley*
of fowl used in making the stock   *Salt and white pepper if necessary*
3 tablespoons long-grain rice

In a large soup pan, bring the chicken soup and the meat to simmering point. Add the washed rice, stir well, then simmer, covered, for 15 minutes or until a grain of the rice feels tender when chewed.

In a medium-sized bowl, whisk the eggs and lemon juice until thoroughly blended. Take the soup off the heat, and gradually add 2 ladlesful to the eggs, whisking all the time. Return the egg mixture to the pan, then reheat the soup slowly, stirring it constantly, until it is steaming and creamily thickened. Don't allow it to boil or it will curdle, in which case vigorous whisking may restore its creamy appearance. Taste and add salt and pepper if necessary, stir in the parsley and serve. The soup will reheat well but on no account allow it to come to the boil.

CHICKEN SOUP WITH HOBENE GROPEN

SERVES 8   *Freeze 3 months*

This is a 'creamy' soup with a very satisfying flavour that is especially rich in the B vitamins. It is made with a variety of oats known in Jewish households as 'hobene gropen' or 'hubergrits'; however, if you ask for it in the local health food shops, you will get better results by calling it 'pinhead oatmeal'. In appearance it looks rather like bits of broken barley because the grains are 'kibbled' or cracked, rather than milled like other cereals. Because it is a wholegrain cereal it does need to be simmered for several hours but the result is a wonderfully sustaining winter soup.

4 pints (2¼ litres/10 cups) Chicken Soup
6 level tablespoons hobene gropen (pinhead oatmeal)
4 oz (125 g/¾ cup) butter (Lima) beans soaked overnight in water to cover

1 teaspoon salt; good pinch of white pepper
1 large carrot cut in ⅜ in (1 cm) dice
1 tablespoon chopped parsley

Put the hobene gropen into a basin, cover with boiling water, then strain. Bring the soup to the boil, then add the strained hobene gropen, the strained butter beans and the salt and pepper, and simmer, covered, for 2 hours. Add the carrot, and simmer covered for a further hour. Taste and season if necessary; then stir in the parsley and serve piping hot.

Leftover soup will need to be thinned down with a ¼ pint (150 ml/⅔ cup) of water.

CHICKEN SOUP UNDER A PASTRY CRUST

SERVES 6–8   *Freeze without pastry 3 months*

A Moroccan chef cooking in a restaurant in Israel first prepared this exquisite soup for me. It is a perfect example of the synthesis of the Sephardi and Ashkenazi cuisines which is taking place there all the time. Each guest breaks through a golden crust of puff pastry to reveal the chicken soup bubbling underneath it. It is also excellent prepared with French Onion Soup. For a dinner party, the bowls can be filled with soup and topped with raw pastry well in advance, and then the soup is reheated and the pastry baked simultaneously just before the meal. A saucer can be used as a guide for the pastry rounds.

To prepare this dish it is essential to have heatproof soup cups each about 4 in (10 cm) wide.

2–3 pints (1¼–1¾ litres/5–7 cups) clear Chicken Soup
4 tablespoons giblet or chicken meat
2 tablespoons each fine julienne strips

of carrot and white leek
3 tablespoons medium-dry sherry
15–16 oz (450 g) puff pastry
1 egg, separated

Bring the soup to the boil, add the vegetables and simmer for 5 minutes or until barely tender. Stir in the sherry and the meat, and taste for seasoning; then divide between the soup cups, filling them three-quarters full, and allow to go cold.

Roll out the pastry ⅛ in (½ cm) thick and cut into circles about 2 in (5 cm) wider than the top of the soup cups. Whisk the white of egg until frothy, then use it to paint a 1 in (2½ cm) deep band all the way round the top of each cup. Take each circle of pastry in turn and place it, without stretching it, across the top of a cup, sealing it down the sides. Thin the egg yolk with a teaspoon of water and brush it all over the top of the pastry.

Turn the oven to Gas No. 7, 425 degrees F, 220 degrees C, and put a baking sheet in to heat up. When the oven has reached the required temperature, arrange the soup cups on the hot tray and bake for 15 minutes or until the pastry is a rich brown. Serve at once.

STRONG AND CLEAR SOUPS
BEEF, VEGETABLE AND NOODLE SOUP

SERVES 8   Freeze 3 months

Shin beef gives a rich, deep flavour to this light-textured yet satisfying soup.

1 lb (450 g) shin beef
5 pints (2½ litres/12½ cups) water
5 beef stock cubes
8 sticks of celery, thinly sliced
2 large carrots (8 oz/225 g) cut in ⅜ in (1 cm) cubes
1 rounded tablespoon tomato purée

1 medium (5 oz/150 g) onion, finely chopped
1 teaspoon Italian herb seasoning
15 grinds black pepper
½ lb (225 g) (2 medium) potatoes, peeled and cut in ⅜ in (1 cm) cubes
2 oz (50 g/1 cup) vermicelli or tagliatelle
1 tablespoon chopped parsley

Put the water and the shin beef into a soup pan and bring to the boil. Skim off the froth with a wet spoon, cover and simmer for 1 hour. Add the stock cubes, celery, carrots, tomato purée, onion, Italian herb seasoning and pepper and simmer for another 30 minutes. Add the cubed potato, re-cover and simmer for a further 30 minutes.

Lift out the meat with a slotted spoon, cut it in bite-sized pieces and then return it to the soup together with the noodles. Simmer uncovered for 5 minutes, then add the chopped parsley. Taste and add salt if necessary. Leave for several hours or (preferably) overnight for the flavour to intensify, then slowly reheat to simmering point.

SPECIAL CONSOMMÉ

SERVES 8   *Freeze 3 months*

The bones from the prime kosher beef roast — ribs of beef — can be recycled to provide the basis for a richly flavoured yet economical consommé. The flavour is even better if the bones are simmered together with two or three sets of chicken giblets and a mixture of mature — and therefore very tasty — vegetables. Once this stock has been strained to remove the vegetables and then chilled to make it easy to remove every speck of fat, it can be frozen for later use — without the vegetables it will stay in good condition for up to 6 months — or used at once to make the consommé.

THE STOCK:

Bones from a 5 lb (2¼ kg) roast rib of beef (approximate weight)
2 or 3 sets of chicken giblets
Water
2 teaspoons salt; 1 teaspoon slightly crushed peppercorns (use a mortar and pestle or the end of a rolling pin to crush them)

1 large onion, halved
6 coarse outside stalks of celery cut in 2 in (5 cm) lengths
2 large, mature carrots, cut lengthwise in quarters
Small bunch of parsley
1 bayleaf; 1 teaspoon dried fines herbes
3 or 4 very ripe tomatoes

Put the bones and the giblets in a large soup pan and cover generously with the cold water. Bring slowly to the boil with the lid half on (if the pan is sealed completely the liquid will boil over when a froth of scum forms on top of it). Remove the scum which has formed using a wet metal spoon, then add the vegetables, herbs and seasoning. Cover and simmer for up to 6 hours, but for a minimum of 3 hours. The finest flavour is developed if the stock is simmered *in the oven*. A liquid is at simmering point when *occasional* rather than continuous bubbles break on the surface.

Pour the cooked stock through a coarse sieve to trap the vegetables, which should then be discarded as by this time they will have given up all their flavour to the stock. (If the stock is to be frozen it should be brought back to the boil and then boiled down by half, to save freezer space.) Allow the stock to cool, then chill or partly freeze until the fat solidifies and can be easily removed with a spoon.

THE CONSOMMÉ:

The stock made up to 4 pints (2¼ litres/10 cups) (if necessary) with water
4 meat stock cubes
4 oz (125 g/1 cup) very fresh mushrooms, wiped with a damp cloth then very thinly sliced through the stalk
2 large carrots cut into ⅜ in (1 cm) thick cubes
2 unskinned courgettes (zucchini), about 5–6 in (12–15 cm) long, cut into ⅜ in (1 cm) thick slices
1 level tablespoon tomato purée
3 tablespoons medium-dry sherry
1 tablespoon chopped parsley

The day before the consommé is to be served, put all the ingredients (except the sherry and parsley) into a large soup pan and bring slowly to the boil, cover and simmer for 20–25 minutes until the carrots are tender — no longer, or the vegetables will lose their 'bite'. Refrigerate overnight.

Shortly before serving, bring slowly to the boil, taste and re-season with salt and black pepper if necessary, then stir in the parsley and the sherry. Serve piping hot.

Individual portions of leftover soup can be frozen to make satisfying low-calorie snacks.

TWO FOR THE DINNER PARTY
CHESTNUT AND ORANGE SOUP

SERVES 6–8   *Freeze 3 months*

The combination of chestnuts and orange give this delicate French soup a most unusual yet subtle flavour. It is very quickly made with canned chestnut purée, but it will take longer if fresh chestnuts (which need to be peeled) are used. The garnish of shredded orange peel and chopped parsley makes a dramatic contrast to the golden-brown soup.

1 oz (25 g/2 tablespoons) margarine
1 medium carrot
1 large onion
4 oz (125 g/1 cup) mushrooms with their stalks
2½ pints (1½ litres/6 cups) hot water
4 beef or vegetable stock cubes
½ teaspoon salt; 15 grinds black pepper
1 can (15 oz (425 g)) chestnut purée or 1¼ lb (550 g) fresh chestnuts, peeled (method below)

4 long strips of orange peel (orange part only, not the bitter white pith)
3 tablespoons medium-dry sherry
1 rounded tablespoon chopped parsley

GARNISH:
2 teaspoons each finely grated orange rind and chopped parsley

To skin the chestnuts Using a small knife with a serrated blade, cut through the skin right round the middle of each nut, then drop into a pan of boiling water. As soon as the cut widens to show the flesh (in about 3 minutes) take out the nuts one at a time and remove the outer and inner skin (this is easy providing the chestnuts are fresh). Or use the microwave method on page 23.

Chop the carrot, onion and mushrooms finely (this is done most easily in a food processor). Gently melt the fat in a large soup pan, add the vegetables and stir well, then sauté them uncovered over moderate heat for 10 minutes, when they should be a golden-brown. Add the purée (first mashed down with a large fork) or the peeled chestnuts, together with the water, stock cubes, strips of orange peel and seasonings. Bring slowly to the boil, cover and simmer for 30 minutes or until the vegetables (and the fresh chestnuts if used) are very tender. Remove the orange peel. Purée the soup in a blender or food processor, then refrigerate for several hours or overnight.

Shortly before serving, reheat slowly with the sherry and chopped parsley. Top each bowl of soup with a sprinkle of chopped parsley and grated orange rind.

SUMMER TOMATO SOUP WITH FRESH HERBS AND MINIATURE MEATBALLS

SERVES 8   *Freeze 3 months*

This is a wonderful soup to make at midsummer when tomatoes have grown sweet by ripening in the sun rather than merely reddening in colour (but without gaining any extra flavour) on the journey from the grower to the greengrocer. At this season fresh basil will be in its prime, ready to give its distinctive spicy flavour to the soup. This soup can be made with canned tomatoes and dried herbs but the flavour, though excellent, won't have the same summery freshness.

Because a certain amount of free fat from the meatballs will rise to the top of the soup it is essential to make it a day in advance so that the solidified fat can be removed before serving. It is best to prepare the meatball mixture first to allow it to firm up so that it can be easily formed into balls.

THE MEATBALLS:
Large sprig of parsley
Half an onion, cut in rough 1 in (2½ cm)
chunks
1 egg
1 large slice of brown bread
½ teaspoon salt; 10 grinds black pepper
1 lb (450 g) fresh minced (ground) beef

THE SOUP:
1 oz (25 g/2 tablespoons) margarine
1 large onion, thinly sliced
1 clove of garlic, peeled and sliced
3 teaspoons brown sugar

1½ lb (675 g) deep red, fully ripe tomatoes,
quartered, or 28 oz (800 g) can peeled plum
tomatoes canned in tomato juice
2 pints (1¼ litres/5 cups) hot water
4 beef stock cubes
1 tablespoon tomato purée
½ pint (275 ml/1¼ cups) tomato juice or
juice strained from canned tomatoes
1 bayleaf; large sprig of parsley
1 teaspoon salt; 15 grinds black pepper
1 teaspoon Italian herb seasoning
2 level tablespoons fresh basil or 2 teaspoons
dried basil

To make the meatballs Put the parsley in the food processor and process until chopped. Add the onion, egg, bread and seasonings, then process until a smooth purée is formed. Turn into a mixing bowl, then add the beef, mix thoroughly with a fork and set aside.

To make the soup Melt the fat in a large soup pan, add the sliced onion and garlic, sprinkle with the brown sugar, stir well, cover and cook for 10 minutes until the onion is softened and golden. Add the tomatoes, re-cover and simmer until the vegetables are quite soft, about 15 minutes. Push them through a sieve or a food mill, discarding the tomato skins and any onion debris that won't go through. Return this purée to the pan and add the water, stock cubes, tomato purée, tomato juice, bayleaf, parsley, salt, pepper, Italian herb seasoning and dried basil (if used). Simmer very gently for 30 minutes. Discard the parsley and the bayleaf.

Meanwhile with wetted palms, form the meat mixture into approximately 36 tiny balls, then drop them into the simmering soup, cover and cook gently for 30 minutes. Cool the soup and the meatballs, then refrigerate. Next day, skim off the

68

solidified fat, bring slowly to the boil and, just before serving, stir in the fresh basil.
Serve the soup with four or five meatballs per person.

SOUP FOR A WINTER'S NIGHT
TUSCAN BEAN SOUP

SERVES 6–8   *Freeze 3 months*

This is the Italian equivalent of the thick and satisfying lentil and barley soups of the
Jewish cuisine. The soup is thickened by puréeing half the beans, whilst the
remainder are left whole to give a more interesting texture. Any small dried white
beans can be used — although the Italian cannellini beans are the most authentic. I
have reduced the amount of oil that would be used in Tuscany.

*½ lb (225 g/1¼ cups) dried cannellini or
haricot (navy) beans
1½ tablespoons olive oil
½ medium (5 oz (150 g)) onion, finely
chopped
1 large carrot, cut in ⅜ in (1 cm) dice
2 sticks celery, cut in ⅜ in (1 cm) dice
2½ pints (1½ litres/6 cups) hot water*

*3 meat stock cubes or 3 teaspoons vegetable
stock paste
1 level tablespoon tomato purée
1 teaspoon salt; 15 grinds black pepper
1 tablespoon chopped parsley*

Soak the beans in cold water to cover overnight. Heat the oil in a large soup pan and
sauté the onion until golden, then add the carrot and celery dice and cook for a
further 5 minutes, stirring occasionally. Add the hot water and the stock cubes or
vegetable paste, the tomato purée, salt and pepper and bring to the boil. Drain the
beans, rinse under the tap, then add to the pot. Cover and simmer very slowly either
on top of the stove or in the oven until the beans are absolutely tender — about 1
hour.

Remove half the beans and a little of the soup and purée in a blender or a food
processor, then return to the pan with the chopped parsley. Leave for several hours,
then reheat slowly and serve piping hot.

CHICK PEA AND NOODLE SOUP

SERVES 6–8   *Freeze 3 months*

Chick peas, with their slightly sweet and earthy flavour, are perhaps most familiar as
a constituent of those famous Middle Eastern 'fast foods', hummus and felafel —
they are in fact native to that part of the world and are known to have flourished in
Ancient Egypt, nearly four thousand years ago. They are grown and eaten widely
and are variously known as 'garbanzos' (in Spanish-speaking countries and the
United States), 'Bengal gram' (in India), 'pois chiche' (in French-speaking countries)
and 'ceci' (in Italy). Unless you use a pressure cooker (when they become tender in

69

half an hour) they can take as long as 3 hours to cook, so it's easier to use the canned peas. This Italian soup has a true Mediterranean flavour. For a meat version, use beef stock and omit the cheese.

2 cans (14 oz (400 g)) chick peas (garbanzos), drained, or ¾ lb (350 g/1½ cups) dried chick peas, soaked overnight (see below)
4 cloves of garlic, peeled
5 tablespoons olive oil
1 teaspoon Italian seasoning herbs
1 teaspoon salt; 10 grinds black pepper
1½ teaspoons sugar

1 can (14 oz (400 g)) tomatoes in juice
1 pint (575 ml/2½ cups) and 2 pints (1¼ litres/5 cups) of vegetable stock
3 oz (75 g/1½ cups) egg noodles
5 tablespoons grated Parmesan cheese or finely grated Cheddar or Lancashire cheese

To cook dried chick peas   Soak the peas overnight in twice their volume of cold water. Next day, cook covered in plenty of boiling water until tender, when the point of a knife can break open a pea — after about 2 or 3 hours. Or cook in a pressure cooker for 30 minutes. Do not salt until after cooking.

To make the soup   Heat the oil in a heavy soup pan and fry the whole garlic cloves over a moderate heat until they are a rich brown, then discard them — the oil will now have a gentle garlic flavour. Add the tomatoes to the oil together with the herbs, cover and cook for 10 minutes. Add two-thirds of the chick peas and simmer uncovered for 5 minutes; then add the 1 pint (575 ml/2½ cups) of stock and the seasonings, cover and simmer for 15 minutes.

Purée the soup in a blender or food processor, then return it to the pan with the 2 pints (1¼ litres/5 cups) of stock and the whole chick peas. Bring to the boil, add the egg noodles, cover and simmer for 5 minutes or until the noodles are tender. Taste for seasoning, then stir in the grated cheese and serve at once.

Note   If you make the soup in advance, cook the noodles in it only just before serving or they will go soggy.

SMOOTH VEGETABLE SOUPS
DANISH CAULIFLOWER SOUP

SERVES 6–8   Freeze 3 months

It was in North Schleswig in Denmark, when I was on my way to visit a dairy producing kosher cheese, that I first tasted this unusual recipe. The milk and cream in the soup came from the cows on a most unusual dairy farm on the estate of Count Brockenhuus-Schack — his family, unusually for Denmark, has lived in the same castle since the fifteenth century. In a country where the average dairy herd consists of seventeen cows, the Count directs a 'cowtel' where, under one roof, no fewer than four hundred animals live in contented luxury — they are milked electronically, to the sound of music.

It is the superb milk from this dairy herd, scrutinized at every stage of production by a religious supervisor from the Jewish community of Copenhagen, that is used to make a range of strictly kosher Danish cheeses for the Orthodox Jews of North America. Cheese made under similar Rabbinical supervision, as well as some made with vegetable rather than animal rennet, is now produced all over the world. The best of this cheese is identical in flavour and texture to its non-kosher counterparts. So if there is no Danish blue cheese available, any other mild blue cheese can be used instead. This is a pale delicate soup with a note of agreeable sharpness provided by the cheese. For the finest flavour, choose a cauliflower with tight cream-coloured florets and a crisp bright green stalk.

1 large very fresh cauliflower
1 oz (25 g/2 tablespoons) butter
1 medium (5 oz (150 g)) onion, thinly sliced

SAUCE BASE:
1 oz (25 g/2 tablespoons) butter
1 oz (25 g/¼ cup) flour
1¼ pints (725 ml/3 cups) vegetable stock

1 pint (575 ml/2½ cups) cold milk
1 teaspoon salt; ¼ teaspoon each white pepper and ground nutmeg
1 teaspoon dried fines herbes
2 oz (50 g/½ cup) Danish blue cheese, crumbled

TO FINISH:
4 tablespoons single (light) cream
1 tablespoon finely cut chives

Divide the cauliflower into florets and cook them in boiling salted water for 8 minutes or until barely tender, then drain. Reserve 2 tablespoons of the florets for garnish. Melt the butter in a small pan and sweat the sliced onions covered for 5 minutes. Add the cauliflower, toss to coat in the buttery juices, then sauté *uncovered* for a further 5 minutes or until the cauliflower and the onion are golden and tender. Sieve, liquidize or process these vegetables using some of the measured stock.

Make the sauce base by putting the butter, flour and milk together with the remaining stock into a soup pan. Add the seasonings and bring to the boil, whisking all the time. Add the cauliflower purée, stir well and simmer for 5 minutes, then crumble in the cheese, stirring until it is dissolved in the soup. Leave for several hours for the flavours to develop, then reheat to simmering point and stir in the cream and most of the chives. Garnish each bowl with some of the reserved florets and a pinch of chives.

CREAM OF GREEN PEPPER SOUP

SERVES 6–7   *Freeze 3 months*

The first time I tasted this unusual soup I was convinced it was made with asparagus — it has a similar subtlety of flavour and it doesn't possess the acidity you would expect from green peppers. As it has a tendency to separate if overheated, it is important not to leave it on the boil. But provided it has not been left boiling too long, it should become smooth and creamy again with vigorous whisking.

2 large fleshy green peppers (12 oz (350 g)
total weight)
1 medium onion (5 oz (150 g)), finely
chopped
1 oz (25 g/2 tablespoons) butter
1 pint (575 ml/2½ cups) vegetable stock

SAUCE BASE:
1 pint (575 ml/2½ cups) cold milk
1½ oz (35 g/3 tablespoons) each butter and
flour
1 teaspoon salt; ¼ teaspoon white pepper
¼ teaspoon dried fines herbes
Good pinch of ground nutmeg

Halve the peppers and remove the seeds and white pith. Cut a quarter of one pepper into tiny cubes (for garnish), then cut the remainder into strips. Melt the butter in a soup pan, add the onion and pepper, cover and cook gently for 10 minutes until well softened. Purée in a blender or food processor with a quarter of the measured stock.

Make the sauce base in the soup pan by putting the milk, butter, flour and seasonings into it and whisking them together over moderate heat until thickened. Simmer for 5 minutes, then add the vegetable purée and the remainder of the stock and allow to stand for several hours. Just before serving, reheat with the raw pepper cubes, whisking well until it reaches simmering point.

TWO FRENCH COUNTRY POTAGES

Paris, 1946. In that bitterly cold December when butter was four pounds a kilo on the black market and sugar two pounds (when you could find it), there was no question of sitting down to *dîner* — it was *souper* or nothing at all. In the barely heated flat of the Family Filderman, where I was to have my first joyful encounter with the French way of eating, the Sèvres china soup tureen was reverently placed on the table, full to the brim with Potage Garbure. Madame Filderman inclined her head in my direction. '*Servez-vous*,' she said, as she offered me first dip into the bubbling soup.

That simple vegetable soup, enriched, it must be said, with a little black market butter, was served with the same pride in its preparation as the chef's tour de force of *saumon au Riesling* which I was to enjoy in Paris a more prosperous decade later. It was my first experience of *la cuisine familiale* and of the French housewife's genius in translating yesterday's leftovers into today's *plat du jour*. Ever since, I have had a special respect — and affection — for such homely soups made with whatever is to hand on the day. Potage Garbure is traditional in the Pyrenees and is the kind of thick potage that is almost a meal in itself, like Minestrone and the thick pea and pulse soups of Russia and Poland. Here are two versions, using respectively summer or winter vegetables. Though sustaining, they are lighter and therefore more in tune with today's eating habits than many of our traditional soups.

To make a meat version of either soup, use 3 tablespoons sunflower or olive oil instead of the butter and oil, use beef stock instead of the vegetable stock, and omit the cheese.

POTAGE GARBURE FOR SUMMER

SERVES 8   *Freeze 3 months*

1 oz (25 g/2 tablespoons) butter
1 tablespoon olive oil or sunflower oil
1 medium onion (5 oz (150 g)), finely
chopped
8 stalks celery, thinly sliced
1 large carrot, grated
1 medium-sized green pepper, pith and seeds
removed, cut in ¼ in (½ cm) cubes
1 rounded tablespoon tomato purée
3 pints (1¾ litres/7½ cups) vegetable stock

4 in (10 cm) section of Chinese leaves
(Chinese cabbage), very thinly sliced
1 tablespoon chopped parsley
1 tablespoon snipped chives
3 tablespoons fresh basil, finely sliced, or 2
teaspoons dried basil
1 tablespoon fine lokshen (vermicelli)
Salt and black pepper
Finely grated cheese

Melt the fats, add the onion and cover the pan; simmer for 5 minutes until the onion
is translucent, then cook uncovered for 2 minutes until golden. Add the carrot, celery
and green pepper and stir well to absorb the fat. Add the stock and tomato purée and
bring to the boil, then add the Chinese leaves. Cover and simmer for 20 minutes;
uncover, add herbs and lokshen and simmer for a further 15 minutes. Leave
overnight if possible, then reheat, taste and add salt and pepper if necessary, and
serve piping hot with the cheese.

POTAGE GARBURE FOR WINTER

SERVES 8   *Freeze 3 months*

1 oz (25 g/2 tablespoons) butter
1 tablespoon olive oil or sunflower oil
2 onions, thinly sliced
2 large carrots, diced
2 fat sticks celery, diced
½ lb (225 g) potatoes, peeled and diced into
½ in (1 cm) cubes
½ lb (225 g) cabbage, Savoy if possible,
shredded

2½ pints (1½ litres/6 cups) vegetable stock
1 teaspoon dried herbes de Provence
1 rounded tablespoon tomato purée
Salt and pepper
1 can (14 oz (400 g)) white Italian beans
1 tablespoon chopped parsley
1½ oz (35 g/¼ cup) very finely grated cheese

Melt the fats, add the onions and cover the pan; simmer for 5 minutes until they are
translucent, then cook uncovered for 2 minutes until golden. Add in turn the carrots,
celery and potatoes, cooking each one for 2 or 3 minutes before adding the next
vegetable. Then add the shredded cabbage and cook for a further 5 minutes, stirring
once or twice. Now add the stock, salt and pepper, bring to simmering point, cover
and simmer for 45 minutes.

   Fifteen minutes before serving, add the drained beans and the herbs, then recheck
the seasoning. Just before serving stir in the grated cheese.

WEST AFRICAN PEANUT SOUP

SERVES 6   *Freeze 3 months*

This is a favourite with our vegetarian friends. It has a subtlety of flavour that belies the speed and ease with which it can be prepared. Unlike all the other soups in this chapter it does not need time to mature but can be served immediately after preparation.

½ lb (225 g/1 cup) smooth peanut butter
1½ pints (850 ml/4 cups) vegetable stock
½ pint (275 ml/1¼ cups) milk

½ teaspoon salt; 10 grinds black pepper
Good pinch of nutmeg
2 teaspoons Madras curry powder

Put the peanut butter in a soup pan and gradually whisk in the stock, followed by the milk and the seasonings; then bring slowly to boiling point. Taste and re-season if necessary. The soup should have the consistency of thin cream. Serve with crispy French bread or bread sticks.

MEDITERRANEAN FISH SOUP WITH SAUCE ROUILLE

SERVES 6   *Freeze 2 months*

Nowhere that I know of in the Jewish cuisine is there a precedent for the type of fish soup that is served on the Mediterranean coast of France, so I set out without a model to reproduce the true Provençal flavour using only those kosher fish — that is, species that have both fins and scales — that I could find at my local fishmonger.

For the foundation of the soup I made a strong fish stock using the bones of several different kinds of fish, reinforcing the flavour with the typical Provençal ingredients of olive oil, tomatoes, wines and herbs. There are many versions of the 'Sauce Rouille', which together with toasted French bread and Parmesan cheese is the traditional accompaniment to the soup in Provence. The one I give below is hot and garlicky without being totally antisocial.

This soup reaches the peak of its flavour 48 hours after preparation.

1 medium onion, finely chopped
2 in (5 cm) white part of a leek, finely
chopped
3 fl oz (75 ml/⅓ cup) olive oil
2 large cloves garlic, peeled and crushed
1 can (14 oz (400 g)) tomatoes, drained
1 tablespoon tomato purée
3½ pints (2 litres/9 cups) water
6 large sprigs of parsley
1 bayleaf
1 teaspoon dried basil
¼ teaspoon dried fennel
2 strips of orange peel, about 2 in (5 cm) long
2 teaspoons proprietary fish seasoning salt
20 grinds black pepper
2 lb (1 kg) fish bones, heads and trimmings
(a mixture of white fish, herring, trout and
salmon)

1 medium potato, peeled (see Rouille recipe
below)
5 fl oz (150 ml/⅔ cup) medium-dry white
wine
2 oz (50 g/4 tablespoons) long-grain rice
1 lb (450 g) haddock or halibut fillet, cut in 1
in (2½ cm) chunks
3 tablespoons chopped parsley

SAUCE ROUILLE:
2 whole pimientos (canned in brine)
1 medium potato (cooked in soup above)
2 large cloves of garlic, peeled
½ teaspoon salt; ¼ teaspoon white pepper
¼ teaspoon cayenne pepper or ¼ teaspoon
Tabasco sauce
1 teaspoon dried basil
5 tablespoons olive oil

Heat the oil in a very large saucepan, then add the onion and leek and cook gently, uncovered, for 5 minutes until softened but not browned. Stir in the garlic and tomatoes, then turn up the heat slightly and cook for a further 5 minutes. Add the water, herbs and seasonings, fish bones, heads and trimmings and the potato.

Cook uncovered at a moderate boil for 20 minutes. (Remove the potato when tender.) Pour the mixture into a bowl, rinse out the pan and strain the soup and all its ingredients back into the pan through a sieve, pressing well down to get out all the juices. Boil until the liquid is reduced by half. Add the wine and rice.

Cook with the pan partly covered for a further 15 minutes, or until the rice is almost tender. Now add the fish and cook, covered, for 7 minutes or until the fish looks creamy. Add the parsley, cool, and refrigerate for 48 hours. Reheat before serving.

To make the sauce Put all the ingredients except the olive oil into a food processor, and process until smooth. Add the oil slowly, as for mayonnaise. Finally add 2 tablespoons of the hot soup and process until smooth and thick.

To serve Toast some slices of French bread on both sides and put the Sauce Rouille and some Parmesan cheese in two separate bowls. Ladle the soup and fish into soup bowls; then pass first the Rouille for each guest to spread on the toasted bread and float on the soup, and then the cheese to sprinkle on top.

Don't overlook the recipes for Kreplach (page 89) and Home-made Lokshen (page 10).

TRADITIONAL KNAIDLACH
SOUP DUMPLINGS TO SERVE IN CHICKEN SOUP

SERVES 6–8   *Freeze 1 month*
                                             Will keep 2 days under refrigeration

These soup dumplings are also known in different communities as 'halkes', 'matzah balls' and 'matzah kleis'.

The young husband savoured a mouthful of 'knaidl'. 'Very nice,' he assured his anxious bride, 'but not quite like Mother used to make.' So she tried again the following week, and again and yet again, but the response was always the same. By the fourth week her exasperation knew no bounds. 'That'll show him,' she wept, as she tipped the entire packet of matzah meal into the bowl and with great difficulty shaped balls out of the resulting 'concrete'. That night the young husband yet again savoured a mouthful of 'knaidl', this week so hard that his spoon could hardly penetrate it. A beatific smile spread over his face. 'At last you've got it right,' he beamed at her, 'these are *just* like mother used to make.' Undoubtedly one person's cannonballs are another person's perfect knaidlach!

The recipe below is, I hope a happy compromise, producing knaidlach that are firm yet tender. To make them firmer still, add another tablespoon of matzah meal; to make them softer, add a tablespoon less. But don't alter the amount of fat.

2 large eggs
2 very slightly rounded tablespoons rendered chicken fat, chicken-flavoured vegetable fat or soft margarine
4 tablespoons warm chicken soup or water
1 level teaspoon salt; ¼ teaspoon white pepper

¼ teaspoon ground ginger
1 oz (25 g/¼ cup) ground almonds
5 oz (150 g/1¼ cups) medium matzah meal

Whisk the eggs until fluffy, then stir in the soft fat, tepid soup or water, seasoning, ground almonds and matzah meal, and mix thoroughly. The mixture should look moist and thick, but should not be quite firm enough to form into balls. If too soft, add a little more meal; if too firm, add a teaspoon or two of water. Chill for at least an hour, but overnight will do no harm.

Half-fill a pan with water and bring to the boil, then add 2 teaspoons of salt. Take pieces of the chilled mixture the size of a large walnut, and roll between wetted palms into balls. Drop these balls into the boiling water, reduce the heat until the water is simmering, cover and simmer for 40 minutes without removing the lid. Strain from the water with a slotted spoon and drop into simmering soup.

For a small number or a special occasion, cook the knaidlach in chicken soup rather than in water. They will absorb some of the soup but with it also its delicious flavours.

KNAIDLACH MADE WITH OIL

SERVES 4–6   *Freeze 3 months*

It is traditional to use rendered chicken fat to make these exquisite soup dumplings. Many people now prefer to use oil instead, however. The result is a very light and tender knaidl, if perhaps a less full-flavoured one.

1 cup (8 fl oz (225 ml)) medium matzah meal   *2 tablespoons corn oil* or *sunflower oil*
1 cup (8 fl oz (225 ml)) boiling water   *1 teaspoon salt; speck of white pepper*
1 large egg, whisked until frothy

Put the matzah meal into a bowl and stir in the boiling water, followed by all other ingredients. Mix thoroughly, then refrigerate for 1 hour to allow the matzah meal to swell and the mixture to firm up. Have ready a large pan of boiling water containing 2 teaspoons salt. Roll the mixture into little balls about the size of walnuts. Drop into the boiling water and then simmer *uncovered* for about 20 minutes or until the knaidlach rise to the top of the pan. Drain, then put into simmering chicken soup.

To freeze knaidlach   Open-freeze the cooked and drained knaidlach until solid — about 2 hours — then put them into plastic bags.

To use   Defrost for 1 hour at room temperature then reheat in the simmering soup.

Starters

Of all the different kinds of food in this book, perhaps none reflects the cosmopolitan quality of the Jewish cuisine more than the 'forspeisse' with which we choose to start a meal.

Our predilection for these tasty starters probably dates from the Romans' occupation of Palestine, when their custom of eating a spicy or salty food to stimulate the appetite was adopted by the native population. Through the years and across the world, however, it has found its expression through many different foods. At one time the salt or smoked herring was the favourite hors d'oeuvre, but today it may be a more luxurious fish such as salmon, trout or mackerel, or smoked turkey or salami served with an exotic fruit. Sephardi cooks have introduced us to delicate stuffed vine leaves, and to courgettes (zucchini) stuffed in the Italian fashion. But still the old-time pâtés are enjoyed, albeit in a modern interpretation.

None of these dishes owes anything to the artifice of the chef. They attract the eye by the quality and freshness of their ingredients, and satisfy the palate with their well-matched and often intriguing flavours.

THE SMOKED SALMON STORY

Ever since the dawn of history, when man began to *prepare* food for eating, rather than consuming it raw, smoke has been valued for its preservative qualities which, when combined with salting and drying, allowed very perishable food, meat and fish in particular, to remain edible long beyond their normal season. Today, almost any food can have its life prolonged in the freezer or the refrigerator, so it's mainly for the flavour imparted by the smoke that smoked salmon and smoked sausages are so highly valued.

The smoking and pickling of meat and fish is an art for which Jews seem to have a special talent — and taste. Certainly it was one widely practised by the Jews of eastern Europe, on both a commercial and a domestic scale, and one they took with them when they emigrated to the United States and Britain at the end of the nineteenth century.

In the Twenties, the Russian-born grandfather of master salmon-smoker Michael Hyman prepared and sold smoked sausages from his small but renowned 'Titanic' delicatessen — so called to commemorate his rescue from the famous shipwreck — in Manchester, England. In the Forties, his son started to smoke Scotch salmon instead. Today Mr Hyman controls a salmon-smoking empire that gathers its raw materials from as far north as Alaska and markets the prepared fish as far south as the Gulf States. The selection of the most suitable fish is a vital factor in determining the taste and texture, and therefore the quality, of the finished product — even more important than the skills involved in the salting and smoking processes.

Recently a completely new dimension has been added to this process of selection: the farming of the salmon itself. Instead of having to stockpile fish in the freezer during its brief natural season, smokers can now buy fresh fish in almost every month of the year. In addition, instead of having to shop for the fish all over the world, those varieties whose size, colour and fat content are most suitable for smoking can be produced under virtually natural conditions.

There is now a bewildering choice of smoked salmon, varying widely in price. For example, you can buy Scotch salmon (considered by many connoisseurs to be the very best) wild or farmed, fresh or frozen, by the whole side or ready sliced. In addition you can buy packets of trimmings that are excellent for making pâtés, mousses and dips. As with most foods, the price usually reflects the quality.

Fresh smoked salmon has a shelf life of only 12 days, so it is essential to buy it from a shop with a large and constant turnover and then use it within 24 hours. Frozen salmon (provided it has not been thawed before purchase — it should then be treated as fresh) can be stored for up to 2 months in the domestic freezer.

Some serving suggestions for smoked salmon Freshly smoked top-quality salmon prepared from a fresh wild fish commands a price beyond the most expensive steak. But for a special celebration there is nothing, in my opinion, to equal a bottle of vintage champagne and a plateful of hand-carved smoked salmon, its only embellishments a squeeze of lemon juice, some freshly milled black pepper and thin slices of brown bread spread with unsalted butter. Allow 1½–2 oz (40–50 g) per person if served alone, 1 oz (25 g) if served as part of a mixed hors d'oeuvre.

SMOKED SALMON PÂTÉ

SERVES 8–10 *Freeze leftovers 2 months*

This is a smooth firm pâté that can also be served as part of a cold buffet or as a filling for tiny puffs of choux pastry. It is not necessary to use top-grade salmon as the fish is puréed and the flavour softened by the other ingredients.

12 oz (350 g) smoked salmon or Gravlax (see recipe on page 81)
3 oz (75 g/⅓ cup) unsalted butter
4 oz (125 g/½ cup) curd, Quark or cottage cheese

1 carton (5 oz (150 g/⅔ cup)) soured cream
15 grinds black pepper
Pinch cayenne pepper
1 lemon

First make 10 tiny rolls from rectangles of smoked salmon or Gravlax, and reserve. Put the rest of the salmon in a food processor and process until chopped. Add all the remaining ingredients and process until smooth. Either pack into a terrine or divide between 10 tiny soufflé dishes or cocottes. Chill overnight. Garnish with the salmon rolls and slices of lemon. Serve with hot toast or warm rolls.

AVOCADO AND SMOKED SALMON COCKTAIL

SERVES 6–8 *Do not freeze*

This is typical of the innumerable variations on the theme of soft cheese, vegetables and fish that are served at dairy meals in Israel, especially at the famous 'Kibbutz breakfast'. Served in wine glasses, it makes a dramatic start to a fish meal.

3 shallots or *half a medium (5 oz (150 g))*
onion, peeled
1 small green or *red pepper, pith and seeds*
removed
Medium-sized sprig of parsley
2 medium or *1 large avocado, peeled and*
stoned
½ lb (225 g/1 cup) low- or medium-fat soft
cheese
1 teaspoon salt; 15 grinds black pepper
2 tablespoons lemon juice

2 teaspoons snipped chives
Half a 5 oz (150 g/⅔ cup) carton soured
cream
4 oz (125 g) smoked salmon

GARNISH:
Shredded Chinese leaves (Chinese cabbage)
or crisp lettuce
Lemon slices or twists
Paprika

This can only be prepared using a food processor. Cut the onion and pepper into rough 1 in (2½ cm) cubes and pulse until finely chopped. Put in a bowl. Process the parsley until finely chopped, then add all the remaining ingredients (except for the smoked salmon and the garnish) and process until as smooth as whipped cream. Coarsely shred the salmon, then add it to the vegetables in the bowl together with the avocado mixture. Stir well to blend. Chill, covered, until required.

To serve Put shredded Chinese leaves or lettuce in the bottom of 6–8 tall wine flutes. Spoon the avocado mixture on top, or pipe with a half-inch (1¼cm) plain tube. Garnish each glass with a dash of paprika and a slice or twist of lemon. Serve cold.

SMOKED SALMON TERRINE

SERVES 6–8   *Freeze 1 month*

This moulded savoury mousse set with gelatine can be served on a long platter, or sliced and presented on individual plates.

3 fl oz (75 ml/½ cup) dry white wine
1 bayleaf
5 fl oz (150 ml/⅔ cup) fish stock, or water
plus 1 teaspoon proprietary fish seasoning
salt
2 teaspoons crushed black peppercorns
¼ teaspoon cayenne pepper
1 tablespoon fresh lime juice or *lemon*
juice
½ teaspoon tomato purée (for colour)
½ lb (225 g) smoked salmon

5 fl oz (150 ml/⅔ cup) double (heavy) cream
8 fl oz (225 ml/1 cup) thick set yoghurt or
soured cream
1 sachet (½ oz (15 g)) of unflavoured kosher
gelatine powder
3 fl oz (75 ml/⅓ cup) water
1 teaspoon oil

GARNISH:
Slices of lemon or lime, and sprigs of fresh
parsley

Boil the wine, bayleaf, stock, crushed black peppercorns, cayenne pepper and fruit juice in a saucepan for 3 or 4 minutes or until the liquid has reduced by half (approximately 4 fl oz (125 ml/½ cup)). Pour through a fine sieve, then stir in the tomato purée. If using smoked salmon pieces, remove any bones or skin. Purée the salmon with a mincer, food processor or mouli, then stir in the wine mixture. Whip the cream until stiff and fold in the yoghurt or soured cream. Fold this mixture into the salmon mixture and season to taste.

Sprinkle the gelatine powder on to 3 fl oz (75 ml/⅓ cup) of cold water in a saucepan. Gently heat without boiling until it looks clear. Allow to cool, then stir into the salmon mixture. Lightly oil a 1½ pint (850 ml/4 cups) or 2 pint (1¼ litres/5 cups) mould (a loaf tin 9 × 5 × 3 in (about 22 × 12 × 7 cm) is excellent) and pour the mixture into it. Allow to set for at least 4 hours in the refrigerator.

To unmould the terrine Loosen from the sides with a knife, then dip the mould briefly into hot water. Invert a serving plate over the mould, then holding the two together turn them the right way up. Shake gently to remove the mousse. Garnish with sliced lime or lemon sections and sprigs of fresh parsley. Serve with rye bread, melba toast or cheese bread.

SALMON CURED AT HOME
GRAVLAX

Yields about 3 lb (1½ kg) Gravlax from a 5 lb   *Freeze 3 months*
(2½ kg) (gross weight) fish

If you have the courage to buy a whole salmon — or even a half one — then you can be rewarded with one of the great delicacies of Scandinavian cuisine, Gravlax. The salmon is 'cured' by salting rather than smoking, then carved in thin slices like smoked salmon and served with a mustard and dill sauce. It is comparable in texture and colour to the smoked fish, but the flavour — as you would expect — is rather more delicate, and the cost is approximately one-third of the best grade of smoked salmon.

You don't need to cure a whole salmon; half a fish works equally well using half the amount of pickling mixture. Fresh dill imparts the finest flavour, but when it is out of season look for dried dill weed with a pronounced and pungent perfume — some brands look and smell like grass cuttings. Gravlax can be served in any presentation that calls for smoked salmon. It is also known as 'gravad lax' (in Sweden) and 'grav laks' (in Norway).

Gravlax needs no special equipment, only a refrigerator and some heavy weights. It is ready to eat after 4 days and can then be stored for another week under refrigeration.

3½–4 lb (1½–2 kg) filleted salmon or   *1 teaspoon ground white pepper*
salmon trout (weight of whole fish with head   *4 tablespoons brandy*
approximately 4–5½ lb (2–2½ kg))   *½ jar (approximately 1 tablespoon) dried dill*
4 oz (125 g/½ cup) sea salt   *weed or ¼ pint (⅔ cup) chopped fresh dill*
4 oz (125 g/½ cup) granulated sugar

Have the fish cleaned, scaled and filleted but not skinned. Do not wash it but wipe well with paper towels. Mix the salt, sugar, pepper and dill in a bowl.

Put a double layer of foil (large enough to parcel the fish) on a board, then lay the salmon fillets on it side by side, skin down.

Cover one of the fillets with the salt mixture in an even layer, then moisten with the brandy. Lay the second fillet carefully on top, but with the shoulder part to the tail of the bottom fillet. In this way the thick part of the upper fillet will be resting on the thin part of the lower fillet so that the complete salmon (or half-salmon) will be an even thickness all the way through. Wrap firmly in the foil to make a compact package.

Lay the package of salmon on a tray (small enough to fit in the refrigerator) to catch any drips of brine that may ooze out of the parcel. Place in the refrigerator and weight down with two bricks wrapped in plastic bags. After 24 hours, turn the fish over and then replace the weights. Do this again on the following two days, then leave undisturbed until the fourth day. Take out, unwrap and drain off any brine, then gently scrape off most of the pickle, leaving a thin sprinkling of dill on the fish.

To serve Using a knife with a thin flexible blade with a wavy edge, carve in thin slanting slices like smoked salmon, starting from the tail end. Serve with sections of lemon, or accompanied by this sauce:

DILL AND MUSTARD SAUCE:
4 rounded tablespoons mayonnaise
1 level tablespoon Dijon mustard
1 level tablespoon mild clear honey or caster (superfine) sugar

2 teaspoons light soy sauce
1 tablespoon fresh chopped or 1 teaspoon dried dill weed
3 rounded tablespoons soured cream (optional)

Put the mayonnaise into a bowl and stir in all the remaining ingredients. Leave covered for several hours for the flavour to mature.

To freeze Gravlax Use interleaving film to separate the slices. Divide in quarter- or half-pound amounts and wrap firmly in foil. Defrost in the refrigerator overnight or for 2 hours at room temperature.

FOUR MORE FISHY TALES
PICKLED HERRING SALAD IN SOUR CREAM SAUCE

SERVES 6–8   *Do not freeze*

Crisp and sweet dessert apples and spicy pickled herrings are combined in this delectable German-Jewish speciality. It is important to drain the herrings well, so that the sauce is not diluted, and to cut the herrings and apple into equal bite-sized pieces.

1 jar (16 oz (450 g)) pickled (rollmop) herrings
1 medium (5 oz (150 g)) mild onion, white or red salad variety if possible
4 crisp, tart dessert apples (about 1 lb (450 g) in weight), such as Granny Smith

THE SAUCE:
½ pint (275 ml/1¼ cups) soured cream

1 teaspoon white wine vinegar
½ teaspoon caster (superfine) sugar;
½ teaspoon Dijon or other mild mustard

GARNISH:
Shredded lettuce or radicchio

82

Drain the herrings thoroughly on paper towels, discarding the pickled onions and liquid from the jar. Slice the salad onion finely, then cut each slice into two or three sections. Core and peel the apples, cut each into eight and then cut each section across into ½ in (1 cm) slices. Cut the herring into slanting slices of a similar size. Put the herring, onion and apple into a large bowl. Stir the vinegar and seasonings into the soured cream then stir it gently through the apple and herring mixture. Refrigerate for several hours or overnight.

Spoon the salad on to a bed of shredded lettuce or radicchio arranged on individual plates, and garnish with a pinch of paprika pepper. Serve with buttered rye or wholemeal (wholewheat) bread.

AVOCADO MOUSSE WITH ANCHOVIES

SERVES 6–8   *Do not freeze*

I like to make this mousse when the black and knobbly-skinned 'Haas' avocados are in season as they have a particularly good flavour. Whichever variety you use, be sure the avocados are very ripe.

This is a rich mixture so it is advisable to serve only small portions.

3 large, or 4 medium, very ripe avocados
5 oz (150 ml/⅔ cup) carton whipping cream, whipped (8 rounded tablespoons whipped cream)
4 tablespoons mayonnaise
2 cans (2 oz (50 g)) anchovies, drained and cut in ¼ in (1 cm) pieces

THE VINAIGRETTE:
4 tablespoons wine vinegar
2 tablespoons lemon juice

¼ pint (150 ml/⅔ cup) mild olive oil
1 clove of garlic, peeled and crushed to a paste
1 teaspoon caster (superfine) sugar
1 teaspoon Dijon mustard
2 teaspoons chopped parsley
1 level tablespoon very finely chopped onion or shallots
½ teaspoon salt; 10 grinds black pepper

GARNISH:
Cucumber or pickled cucumber

Shake all the vinaigrette ingredients together in a screw-top jar until thickened (1 or 2 minutes). Early in the day, peel and stone the avocados, cut them into ⅛ in (½ cm) thick slices and put them with the vinaigrette in a covered plastic container. Turn in the vinaigrette, making sure they are well moistened to prevent discoloration. Leave at least an hour, preferably longer.

To make the mousse Put the avocados and the dressing into a blender or food processor and process until quite smooth. Stir in the cream and the mayonnaise. Taste. If necessary, add a squeeze of lemon juice. Stir in the anchovy pieces. Chill until required. (The mousse does not discolour.)

Just before serving, spoon into individual soufflé or other small dishes, and garnish with the fresh or pickled cucumber and a sprinkle of paprika. Serve with thinly sliced buttered brown or black bread.

VARIATION
Use 6 oz (175 g) slivered smoked trout instead of the anchovies.

SOUTH AFRICAN TUNA MOUSSE

SERVES 6–8   Do not freeze

This is one of many innovative recipes I have learned from South African Jewish friends. It is light in texture with an excellent flavour, and looks splendid turned out of a decorative mould or set in individual cocottes.

1 can (7½ oz (200 g)) tuna, drained
The washed can filled with
mayonnaise
2 teaspoons kosher gelatine
4 fl oz (125 ml/½ cup) tomato juice

Small bunch of spring onions (green onions),
bulbs only
2 teaspoons Worcestershire sauce
½ teaspoon salt; 10 grinds black pepper
2 tablespoons lemon juice

Mix the gelatine with the tomato juice in a small pan, then heat *very* gently until clear. Put all the ingredients into a food processor or blender and process until absolutely smooth. Put into a pottery bowl or divide between individual cocottes, or spoon into a mould. Turn out when set (allow 3 hours) and decorate with sliced stuffed olives.

PIMIENTO AND ANCHOVY ANTIPASTO

SERVES 6–8   Do not freeze

This is an antipasto true to the original concept of the dish as developed by the gourmands of Ancient Rome. It includes oil to insulate the stomach against alcohol, and herbs, spices and salty foods to stimulate the appetite without satiating it. It tastes superb, and it looks a picture in scarlet, black and brown.

3 cans (2 oz (50 g)) anchovies in olive oil
6–8 canned red pimientos (1–1½ 14 oz (400
g) cans)
18–24 Calamata olives
6–8 very ripe tomatoes

DRESSING:
2 tablespoons lemon juice
2 tablespoons olive oil plus oil from the
anchovies

2 tablespoons finely chopped spring
onion (green onion) bulbs or 2 shallots,
chopped
1 large clove of garlic, peeled and
crushed
15 grinds black pepper
1½ teaspoons finely chopped parsley and
snipped chives
1 tablespoon finely chopped fresh basil, if
available

The day before you plan to serve the antipasto, open the anchovies and drain off the oil. Put the anchovy oil into a screw-top jar and add all the remaining dressing ingredients. Shake until thick (1 or 2 minutes). Drain the peppers thoroughly, cut them into ½ in (1½ cm) strips and put them at one end of a shallow container. Put the anchovies at the other, pour the dressing over them both, cover and refrigerate.

Shortly before serving, arrange the platter of antipasto. Choose a large oval gratin or similar dish. Slice the tomatoes thinly and arrange around the edge. Spoon the peppers and dressing into the centre, covering the base of the dish. Criss-cross their surface with the anchovies and decorate with the olives. Lightly sprinkle the tomatoes with coarsely ground sea salt. Chill until required. Serve with coarse brown bread and butter.

MELON, SWEET AND SPICY

For the two recipes below, use Charentais-type melons such as Ogen or Galia, or cantaloupe melons, all of which have a musky perfume. If you are in doubt as to their ripeness, leave them at room temperature for 3 or 4 days until their smell becomes very pronounced and the green skin of the unripe Galia turns yellow. Refrigerate until required.

MELON AND SALAMI

Allow a 1½ in (3½ cm) thick wedge of melon for each person. Remove the seeds, then cut down through the flesh (but not through the skin) at 1 in (2½ cm) intervals. In each split put one thin slice of salami without rind. Chill, then leave at room temperature for 30 minutes before serving with fingers of challah or fresh rye bread.

MELON AND SMOKED TURKEY WITH MELBA TOASTS

SERVES 6–8

The musky flavour of the melon enhances the smokey flavour of the turkey.

6–8 slices (approximately) of smoked turkey, depending on size (allow 1½ oz (40 g)) per person
1 medium Galia, Ogen or Charentais melon
(muskmelon, cantaloupe)
½ lb (225 g) grapes, seedless if possible (otherwise cut in two and remove the pips)
A few cocktail gherkins for garnish

Halve, seed, then slice the melon into ½ in (1½ cm) thick crescents and remove the peel. Cut each slice of turkey into three, then arrange on individual plates, overlapping the slices of melon and turkey. Decorate with the grapes, speared on cocktail sticks, and two or three gherkins.

MELBA TOASTS:
6–8 slices thin or medium sliced bread

Toast each slice on both sides. Immediately remove the crusts and split the bread horizontally, making two slices from each one. Place on a baking tray, untoasted side up, and toast in a moderate oven (Gas No. 4, 350 degrees F, 180 degrees C) until golden-brown, about 20 minutes. The toasts will keep crisp in an airtight container for up to 5 days.

AVOCADO AND GRAPEFRUIT SALAD

SERVES 6   *Do not freeze*

Sweet-and-savoury salads made their first appearance in the 1940s when they were featured on the exotic menus of Hollywood film studio restaurants. Now they are popular all over the world, particularly in Israel, which produces avocados and grapefruit that rival those grown on the West Coast of America. If possible, use seedless grapefruit and a pear-shaped variety of avocado such as the 'Fuerte' which cuts neatly into crescents to match the segments of grapefruit.

3–4 pink or yellow grapefruit
3–4 medium-sized avocados

THE DRESSING:
4 tablespoons sunflower oil plus 1 tablespoon, huile de noix *(walnut oil), or 5 tablespoons sunflower oil*
1½ tablespoons each grapefruit juice and lemon juice
Pinch salt; 5 grinds of black pepper

2 teaspoons Grenadine (pomegranate flavour) syrup or 1 teaspoon caster (superfine) sugar
2 teaspoons chopped fresh mint or 1 teaspoon dried mint

GARNISH:
Curly endive or watercress leaves
18–24 black olives

Use a serrated-edged knife to peel both the pith and the peel from the grapefruit, then cut between the sections to release the segments of grapefruit. Squeeze the 'skeleton' of the fruit to extract the juice and reserve it for the dressing. Lay the grapefruit segments on a flat plate and cover with clingfilm (saran wrap).

Put all the dressing ingredients into a screw-top jar and shake for 1 minute until thickened. Cut each avocado in half, peel and stone it, then cut in thin segments. Arrange in a shallow dish and brush well with the dressing. Cover with clingfilm and chill.

To serve   On each plate lay a bed of curly endive or shredded Chinese leaves (Chinese cabbage). Arrange alternate slices of grapefruit and avocado in a 'sunburst' pattern and garnish with the black olives. Pass the remaining dressing for guests to serve themselves.

SPICED MUSHROOMS WITH CELERY AND GREEN PEPPER

SERVES 6–8   *Do not freeze*

Many people prefer this recipe to the more usual 'Champignons à la Grecque'. Serve it in individual soufflé dishes or cocottes, accompanied by French bread or challah to mop up the delicious juices. If preferred, omit the celery and green pepper and use 1½ lb (675 g) mushrooms.

1 lb (450 g/4 cups) mushrooms
1 heart of fresh celery, finely sliced
1 fat green pepper, quartered, seeds and ribs removed, cut into very thin strips, 1 in (2½ cm) long

THE DRESSING:
6 tablespoons salad oil (corn, sunflower, peanut)

3 tablespoons olive oil
3 tablespoons wine vinegar or cider vinegar
2 teaspoons lemon juice
1½ level teaspoons each of sea salt and sugar
20 grinds black pepper
2 teaspoons grated onion
2 cloves of garlic, peeled and crushed
2 tablespoons chopped parsley

Trim off the stalks of the mushrooms (use them in a stew or other savoury dish). Rinse the mushrooms quickly, then put in a pan, cover with cold water and add a squeeze of lemon juice. Cover, bring to the boil and simmer for 5 minutes, drain well, then add the prepared celery and green pepper.

Put all the dressing ingredients into a screw-top jar and shake vigorously until an emulsion is formed. Stir into the vegetables. Cover and refrigerate for several hours or overnight.

STUFFED!
BARCHETTE DI ZUCCHINE RIPIENE AL FORNO STUFFED COURGETTES

SERVES 6–8   *Leftovers may be frozen*

I have adapted this dish for the Jewish kitchen from a classic Italian recipe. It makes a superb hot starter before a cold fish meal.

10–12 crisp and shiny-skinned courgettes (zucchini), each 5–6 in (12–15 cm) long
2 cans (2 oz (50 g)) anchovies, drained (reserve the oil)
1 tablespoon each butter and oil from anchovies
3 shallots or half a medium (5 oz (150 g)) onion, finely chopped

THE SAUCE:
½ pint (275 ml/1¼ cups) milk
2 oz (50 g/½ cup) plain flour

1 oz (25 g/2 tablespoons) butter
¼ teaspoon ground nutmeg
½ teaspoon salt; good shake of white pepper
2 eggs, beaten
2 tablespoons Parmesan cheese, grated
2 oz (50 g/½ cup) mature Cheddar cheese, grated
4 rounded tablespoons fresh breadcrumbs, dried in the kitchen for 1 hour, and 1½ oz (35 g/3 tablespoons) butter, melted, both mixed well together

Wipe the courgettes, top and tail them and cut them in half crosswise. Scoop out the top of each with an apple-corer, leaving a boat-shaped shell about ⅜ in (1 cm) thick. Bring a large pan of water to the boil with 1 teaspoon salt and cook the courgette shells, covered, until they are barely tender, about 5 minutes. Drain well and arrange in a large buttered entrée dish that will hold them in one layer, or use individual shallow heatproof dishes.

Drain the anchovies and chop finely. Put their oil into a frying pan with the tablespoon of butter. Add the onion or shallots and the anchovies and cook until the onion is golden, then add the courgette flesh, finely chopped. Cook until the flesh falls and becomes creamy in texture and golden in colour. Remove the mixture from the pan with a slotted spoon, leaving any free oil behind.

Set the oven at Gas No. 6, 400 degrees F, 200 degrees C. Put the butter, flour and cold milk into a pan with the seasonings. Whisk over medium heat (use a balloon or batter whisk) until the sauce thickens smoothly, then change to a wooden spoon. Simmer, stirring constantly, for 5 minutes; then add the onion and anchovy mixture, the eggs and the cheese. Mix well and bring back to the boil, then take off the heat. Taste and add more cheese if preferred. Divide the filling between the courgettes, then sprinkle the whole dish with the buttered crumbs. (The dish may now be left for several hours, or overnight.) Bake for 20 minutes or until the topping is crisp and golden. Cool for 5 minutes before serving.

COLD STUFFED VINE LEAVES WITHOUT MEAT

SERVES 8   *Freeze 3 months*

To those Jewish cooks used to stuffing cabbage leaves, the delicacy and subtle flavour of the vine leaf will come as a revelation. Vacuum-packed vine leaves that keep under refrigeration for many months are now widely available and make a very acceptable substitute for the fresh leaves which are found only in certain Mediterranean countries. In this recipe, they are stuffed with a mixture of spiced rice and pine kernels (pine nuts), simmered slowly in olive oil and lemon juice, and then served chilled as an original and refreshing starter. Or they can be eaten as part of a Middle Eastern style 'mezze' with hummus and tahina, taramasalata and warm pitta bread.

1 vacuum pack (8 oz (225 g)) of vine leaves
1 medium onion, finely chopped
2 tablespoons sunflower oil
8 oz (225 g/1 cup) long-grain rice
3/4 pint (425 ml/2 cups) hot vegetable stock
(or sufficient to barely cover the rice)
1/2 teaspoon each allspice and ground cinnamon
1 teaspoon salt; 10 grinds black pepper

1 tablespoon tomato purée
2 oz (50 g/1/2 cup) pine kernels (pine nuts) or broken cashew nuts, toasted under the grill
4 tablespoons olive oil
1/4 pint (150 ml/2/3 cup) water
4 tablespoons lemon juice
1 teaspoon sugar
3 whole garlic cloves, peeled

Put the vine leaves in a bowl and cover them with boiling water. When they are cool enough to handle, separate them and lay them in a colander. Rinse thoroughly with cold water, then drain well and spread out on a board side by side, vein side up and with the stalk end towards you.

Set the oven at Gas No. 2, 300 degrees F, 150 degrees C.

Put the oil into a pan and sauté the onion until it is soft and golden. Add the rice and fry, stirring constantly, for 3 or 4 minutes. Add the hot stock, the spices and seasonings, cover and cook until the rice has absorbed the stock — it will be only partly cooked at this stage. Stir in the tomato purée and the pine kernels or cashew nuts.

To stuff the vine leaves Place a heaped teaspoon of filling towards the stalk end of each leaf; then turn in the sides and roll up into a tight little parcel rather like a fat cigar. Lay each stuffed leaf in turn in the palm of your hand and squeeze it lightly to seal it. Reserve any torn leaves.

Choose a lidded casserole about 8 in (20 cm) across, and line the bottom with torn or imperfect leaves. Arrange the stuffed vine leaves in layers, tucking one whole garlic clove into each layer. Mix together the oil, water, lemon juice and sugar and pour carefully over the stuffed leaves. Lay a small plate on top to keep them tightly rolled, then cover with the casserole lid or a piece of foil. Cover and cook for 2½ to 3 hours, or until the leaves are quite tender — by this time the cooking liquid will have been almost completely absorbed. Allow to cool, then refrigerate overnight. Serve each guest with 3 or 4 vine leaves, garnished with a section of fresh lemon.

THE OLD TRADITION — WITH A TASTE OF THE NEW
CALVES-FOOT JELLY

SERVES 6–8   *Do not freeze*

This is known variously as 'Fusnogge' (Yiddish), 'Ptchia' (Russian) and 'Sulze' (German). In her book Gastronomie Juive, Suzanne Roukhomovsky describes it as a dish very characteristic of the Jewish–Russian cuisine, but as there is a name for it in three different languages it would seem to have been popular with Jews living all over eastern Europe. This particular version was cooked for me by a friend whose family had fled from the town of Czernowitz in Bukovina (now Romania) to Vienna during the First World War, but it is almost identical to Madame Roukhomovsky's Russian recipe.

This dish arouses strong emotions — either you adore its jellied texture or you loathe it. It bears more than a passing resemblance to some of the terrines of the 'nouvelle cuisine'.

2 calf's feet (koshered), with cold water to cover them
1 large onion, peeled
1 fat clove of garlic, peeled
3 bayleaves
1 level teaspoon black peppercorns
2 level teaspoons salt

2 tablespoons lemon juice (or cider vinegar if preferred)
3 hard-boiled eggs

GARNISH:
Lemon quarters
Tomatoes and cress

It's easiest to use an oval heatproof casserole in which the cleaned feet can be laid without having to saw them up. Lay in the feet, cover with cold water and bring to the boil on top of the stove. Simmer for 10 minutes; then, using a wet spoon, skim off the froth. Add the onion, garlic, bayleaves, peppercorns and salt. Cover and simmer gently for a further hour, either on top of the stove or in the oven. Skim once more, partially cover, and continue to simmer for a further 2½ to 3 hours, or until the gristle and meat are coming away from the bone.

Lift out the bones and any meat attached to them and set aside. Strain the liquid into a bowl, then return to the washed pan together with the lemon juice and the meat, cut into ⅜ in (1 cm) cubes. Bring once more to the boil, then take off the heat altogether.

To set the jelly I use a narrow French pâté dish, 9 x 5 x 3 in (about 22 x 12 x 7 cm) in size. But a loaf tin of similar size is equally good, particularly if you wish to turn it out for slicing. Pour half the liquid into the dish, and leave in the refrigerator or freezer until it is beginning to set. Arrange a layer of hard-boiled eggs on top, and spoon over the remaining mixture, including the meat. Chill overnight in the refrigerator until firm. Slices can be cut from the dish, or the jelly can be turned out on to a platter and decorated with the cress, tomatoes and wedges of lemon.

CHICKEN LIVER AND WALNUT PÂTÉ

SERVES 6–8　　　　　　　　　　　　　*Freeze 2 months*

This is a richly flavoured, smooth-textured pâté with the walnuts adding a little welcome 'crunch'. It should be left for 24 hours for the flavour to develop. Unlike traditional Chopped Liver, it freezes well as it does not contain any hard-boiled eggs. Serve it as a spread on challah or toast fingers, or scooped from the dish in the French fashion.

1 lb (450 g) chicken livers	*2 tablespoons brandy*
6 oz (175 g/¾ cup) margarine	*4 tablespoons medium-dry sherry*
1 large clove of garlic, peeled and crushed	*2 eggs*
1 medium onion, chopped	*4 oz (125 g/1 cup) walnuts (finely chopped)*
2 bayleaves	

Grill (broil) the livers for 2 minutes on either side to make kasher. Melt the margarine and sauté the onion until soft and golden. Add the garlic, bayleaves and livers and toss to coat with the onion and fat. Leave until the mixture stops steaming, and then remove the bayleaves. Chop the walnuts by hand or food processor, and put aside. Put all the remaining ingredients into the processor or blender (with the blender, put the liquids in first; with the processor, the solids). Process until smooth; then add the nuts and process for another 2 or 3 seconds to blend. Turn into an ungreased terrine or small deep pâté dish.

Place the dish in a roasting tin half-filled with hot water. Cover the dish with foil. Bake at Gas No. 3, 325 degrees F, 160 degrees C, for 1 hour or until the pâté is beginning to shrink slightly from the sides and is firm to gentle touch. Chill overnight. Keeps under refrigeration for 5 or 6 days.

Fish

Fish is still an honoured dish at most Jewish tables and finding a good supply of prime fresh fish is of very great importance to the Jewish cook. This is why, despite the strong trend towards frozen fish amongst the general population, you will still find a traditional 'wet fish' specialist in any neighbourhood with a large Jewish community. When I visited such a shop in a London suburb, 50 different varieties of fish were listed on the board, and no fewer than 30 of them were on sale that particular day.

The trade of the traditional fishmonger has changed very little over the past fifty years, and in some ways it has come full circle. For although the travelling fishmonger who cried 'fresh fish' from his cart was replaced some years ago by the suburban shop, a new kind of *mobile* fish shop is once again delivering sea-fresh fish to some fortunate doors. But even though the varieties of fish are much the same, many of them now come from fish farms rather than from rivers and lakes. Bream and pike, known to our grandmothers as 'lesht' and hecht', are bred in Ireland, whilst fresh carp flown in from Israel are on sale in England 48 hours after they've been harvested. Fresh sardines are now brought in by land and sea, together with other varieties of Mediterranean fish which were not available even a few years ago. There is less smoked fish on sale, however, and very often it is merely whiting or cod masquerading as smoked haddock; only a few shops still sell the smoked sprats and buckling that were so dear to our parents.

But a good fishmonger will still dress the fish like his father did, and also offer additional services such as mincing fish and onion for 'chopped fish', cutting plaice and lemon sole into *goujons*, filleting a whole salmon for Graviax or for cooking *en croûte*. A few of the older fishmongers, who learned the skill from their foreign-born parents, will even 'pocket' a whole pike so that it can be stuffed with bream and poached to make the *authentic* Gefilte Fish.

The main fish revolution has taken place in the home, however. For the famous Jewish fried fish that we learned to cook in Ancient Egypt, or perhaps in medieval Spain, has finally fallen from favour. Most of us still cook it for Festivals, and some more conservative cooks prepare a platter of fried fish for every Shabbat. But many younger housewives have banished fish cooked in oil from their family meals, together with other fat-intensive preparations of the Jewish cuisine. Poaching, grilling and baking have superseded the traditional methods, and frying is reserved for a special treat. (It is ironic that this has occurred at the very time that the invention of the automatic fish-fryer has taken all the guesswork — and the smell — out of this messy and exhausting process.) Gefilte Fish is nevertheless still made in one form or another, and you will find a recipe for poaching it in the traditional fashion, as well as cooking it in a Provençal or Lemon Sauce, in other chapters of this book. (Consult the index, too, for other fish recipes.)

In this chapter, you will find recipes for baking and poaching farmed fish, as well as more elaborate recipes for cooking steaks and fillets of sea fish for family meals and for dinner parties. In addition there are some new ideas for cooking different kinds of fish in pastry, as well as for fish kebabs and soufflés and for a variety of interesting sauces to serve with hot and cold poached fish.

FISH FACTS

- As a general rule, **fish cutlets on the bone** and **whole fish** are more succulent than fillets. This is especially true of grilled, baked or fried fish, as poached fish is usually enriched again with a sauce.
- A large covered **frying pan** is very useful for poaching fish on top of the stove; if it is made of an attractive material such as ceramic, stainless steel or heatproof porcelain, it can also be used as a serving dish.
- A **gratin dish** is essential for oven cookery when fillets of fish are poached side by side. These dishes are usually 1½–2 in (3½–5 cm) deep, oval or rectangular in shape, and measure between 11 in (28 cm) (for 4 servings) to 14 in (35 cm) (for 6–8 servings) from end to end.
- **Cooking times** for fish depend on the thickness of the steak or the rolled fillet. As a rough guide, cook for the following minimum times before starting to test for done-ness (when the fish is coming away from the bone and can be easily flaked with a fork):

Baked fish Allow 13–15 minutes in a moderate oven (Gas No. 4, 350 degrees F, 180 degrees C) per inch (5–6 minutes per cm) thickness.

Steamed fish Allow 10 minutes for the first ½ in (1½ cm) and 6 minutes for each additional ½ in (1½ cm) of thickness.

SALMON, TROUT AND THEIR SAUCES

Wild salmon is one of the finest fish in the world, and some would say that salmon trout (or sea trout as it is also known) is the finest of them all. Salmon and salmon trout look very much alike and it takes an expert eye to distinguish between them. In fact salmon trout is not a salmon at all, but a variety of the European common trout which has gone to sea and grown larger, pinker and more delicious on the way.

By duplicating the conditions of its complicated life cycle, fish farmers have now made salmon (and salmon trout as well) available most of the year at an economic price. A wild salmon is conceived in fresh river water, swims out to sea and then comes back to the river again to breed. So at a fish farm the smolts (baby fish) are first bred in fresh water and then put into salt water, usually in a cage which is anchored in the sea. Here the fish are fattened on high-protein food and their flesh is firmed by the use of agitators which, in the calm water of the cage, duplicate the massaging action of the sea waves. Although the fisherman may rightly insist that nothing can compare with 'wild' brown trout caught in a mountain stream, even farmed rainbow trout, if properly fed and reared under the right conditions, will develop a pleasing succulence of flesh and subtlety of flavour. And there is never a hint of the 'muddiness' that sometimes affects fish born and bred in the wild.

Whether you go for the wild or the farmed fish in any particular week must depend on the judgement of your fishmonger. Fish is still one food speciality where the shopkeeper is not just a retailer selling a standardized product, but a craftsman who must have a trained eye for judging the quality of the fish in the market, as well as the consummate skill to dress it ready for the kitchen. On the other hand, if you have access to fish that has been caught locally and bypassed the market, lucky you!

POACHED SALMON

Freeze 3 months
Will keep 3 days under refrigeration

Place the washed and salted fish on a double piece of greaseproof paper or foil greased with a little oil, then fold into a parcel, securing it if necessary with loosely tied string. Put it in a pan and cover with cold water. Add 2 level teaspoons salt and a speck of pepper and bring slowly to the boil.

To serve hot Reduce the heat and allow to *simmer* (but never boil) for 6 minutes to the pound (450 g) and 6 minutes extra. Lift out, drain well, unwrap and serve.

To serve cold When the water comes to the boil, bubble for 3 *minutes only*, then remove from the heat and leave the fish in the covered pan until the liquid is cold, at least 3 hours. It can be kept in the liquid for up to 3 days under refrigeration. Skin, portion and foil-cover when required.

For instructions for poaching a whole salmon or salmon steaks in the microwave oven, see page 27.

To skin and bone a whole cooked salmon Follow this step-by-step procedure:

1. Using a long, thin-bladed sharp knife, cut through the skin along the length of the backbone, across the tail and around the head.

2. Using the blade of the knife, peel off the skin, and pull off the fins.

3. With the back of the knife, scrape away the shallow layer of brown-coloured flesh over the centre of the fish.

4. Turn the salmon over and repeat, and then cut down along the backbone.

5. Turn the knife flat, ease the fillet gently from the bone and lift off (with a large fish this will have to be done in two pieces).

6. At the head and tail, cut through the bone with scissors and peel the bones away. Replace upper fillet.

By tradition the fish is coated with aspic or aspic mayonnaise. However, it is much simpler — and very effective — to cover the fish completely with thin overlapping slices of cucumber, and present on a bed of curly lettuce leaves.

WHOLE SALMON OR SALMON TROUT BAKED IN FOIL

Freeze 3 months
Cooked fish will keep under refrigeration for
3 days

This is an excellent method of cooking several fish at once, or a single fish if there is no fish kettle available. You can use the method whether the fish is to be served hot or cold.

Lightly grease a sheet of foil (large enough to enclose the fish) using corn or sunflower oil if it is to be served cold, butter if it is to be served hot. Lay the fish on top and wrap securely so that no juices can escape, but do not mould the foil too close or the heat cannot circulate. Bake in a moderate oven (Gas No. 4, 350 degrees F,

180 degrees C) for 10 minutes to the pound (450 kg) and 15 minutes over. A 2 lb (1 kg) salmon trout with head will take 35 minutes, a 5 lb (2¼ kg) salmon 65 minutes.

If the fish is to be served hot, test by inserting a knife into the backbone — the fish should look pale pink and creamy and come away easily when lifted. If you are serving it cold, leave it to cool in the foil; to skin and bone a whole fish, see the recipe for Poached Salmon above.

SMALL TROUT BAKED IN FOIL

Freeze 1 month (but texture may deteriorate)

For chef and fisherman alike, the most popular way to cook a trout has been to fry it in shallow fat in a thin coating of flour or oatmeal. For most occasions, however, I prefer to bake it like a whole salmon in a sealed parcel of foil. Prepared in this way the fish can be cooked in the minimum of fat or indeed with no fat at all and, unlike trout that is fried, it requires no attention while it is cooking. In addition, the flesh is always moist and all the flavourful juices are conserved. The fat-free fish can be served to dieter and hearty eater, with the one choosing a garnish of lemon sections and the other a rich sauce.

FOR EACH PERSON:
1 trout (8–12 oz (225–350 g) weight), head removed and cleaned
1 tablespoon lemon juice

Fish seasoning salt and black pepper
Flavourless oil for brushing on foil
1 teaspoon dried onion flakes (optional)

Set the oven at Gas 4, 350 degrees F, 180 degrees C. Cut a piece of foil large enough to make a loose parcel around the fish. Grease it lightly with oil, lay the fish in the centre, season the inside lightly with the salt, pepper, lemon juice and onion flakes if used. Fold up into a loose but airtight parcel. Put in the oven and allow 20 minutes for an 8 oz (225 g) trout, 25 minutes for a 12 oz (350 g) one.
To serve Leave 5 minutes after taking from the oven; then unwrap, skin, arrange on a plate and serve with or without the juice as preferred. May be served hot or cold, with lemon sections, mayonnaise or a special sauce.

VARIATION
Trout baked with Wine and Cream Before enclosing each trout in foil, spoon over it 1 tablespoon of dry white wine and whipping cream and top it with a pinch of dried tarragon or a few leaves of the fresh herb. Cook in the same way, spooning the cream and wine mixture over the skinned fish. Serve hot.

SAUCES FOR SALMON, SALMON TROUT OR SMALL TROUT
HERB MAYONNAISE SAUCE

SERVES 6–8   *Do not freeze*

To serve with warm or cold fish.

2 tablespoons chopped fresh herbs (a mixture
of any of the following as available: parsley,
chives, tarragon, dill)
1 egg yolk
½ teaspoon salt

½ teaspoon dry mustard
Speck of white pepper
1 tablespoon white wine vinegar
3 oz (75 ml/⅓ cup) sunflower oil
5 fl oz (150 ml/⅔ cup) soured cream

In a blender or food processor put the yolk, seasonings and herbs and process until the herbs are chopped. Add the vinegar, then the oil a tablespoon at a time, processing all the time. Finally pulse in the soured cream until evenly blended. Taste and re-season if necessary. Allow to mature for several hours.

ANCHOVY SAUCE

SERVES 6–8   *Do not freeze*

To serve with warm fish.

1 can anchovy fillets, well drained
2 oz (50 g/4 tablespoons) unsalted butter
8 fl oz (225 ml/1 cup) dry white wine

2 tablespoons lemon juice
2 teaspoons chopped parsley
10 grinds black pepper

Rinse the anchovy fillets in cold water, then drain, dry and roughly chop. Melt the butter in a small pan, add the chopped anchovies and stir over a moderate heat until they form a smooth mixture, about 3 minutes. Add the wine and simmer for 5 minutes to concentrate the flavour. Finally stir in the lemon juice and herbs and season with the black pepper. Add any juices from the cooked fish, then reheat and serve.
Note The sauce can be made in advance and reheated with the fish juices just before serving.

AVOCADO HOLLANDAISE

SERVES 6–8   *Do not freeze*

This can be served with warm or cold fish. It requires a blender or food processor, but is very easy to prepare. The sauce can be made an hour in advance and left covered in the kitchen.

1 small very ripe avocado	9 oz (250 g/1 cup plus 2 tablespoons)
4 egg yolks	unsalted butter or soft margarine
1½ teaspoons caster (superfine) sugar	2 tablespoons lemon juice
¼ teaspoon salt	1 tablespoon plus 2 teaspoons white wine
	vinegar

Purée the avocado in a food processor or blender, then remove it. Process the yolks, sugar and salt for 2 seconds. Bring the butter or margarine to the boil in one small pan and the lemon juice and vinegar in another. Slowly add the boiling vinegar mixture to the yolk mixture, followed by the foaming butter or margarine, processing all the time, rather as you would when making mayonnaise. To this thick sauce add the avocado purée and process for 2 or 3 seconds until it is an even pale green in colour.

SALMON IN THE NEW STYLE
DARNE DE SAUMON, SAUCE AU CITRON VERT   SALMON STEAKS IN LIME SAUCE

SERVES 6–8   *Do not freeze*

This is a delightful cold salmon dish with an unusual bittersweet sauce that is most refreshing on a hot day. It is served in the style of the nouvelle cuisine, with the fish sitting on a pale green 'coulis', some of which is then gently trickled over the salmon.

6–8 salmon steaks, each ¾ in (2 cm) thick and 6 oz (175 g) in weight
2 teaspoons fish seasoning salt
8 fl oz (225 ml/1 cup) dry white wine such as Muscadet
4 fl oz (125 ml/½ cup) water or fish stock
2 shallots or 4 spring onion (green onion) bulbs, finely chopped
Butter for greasing cooking dish

THE SAUCE:
Juice and grated rind of 1 lime, or 2 tablespoons lime cordial (or 2 tablespoons

lemon juice, if preferred)
¼ pint (150 ml/⅔ cup) each of soured cream and double (heavy) cream
2 bunches very fresh watercress (leaves only)
3 teaspoons Moutarde de Meaux (or other whole-grain mustard)
½ teaspoon sea salt; 10 grinds black pepper

GARNISH:
1 lime (or lemon, if preferred)
Few sprigs of watercress (saved from one bunch)

The salmon can be cooked in a large frying pan on top of the stove or in a baking tin in the oven. Butter the chosen dish, and sprinkle the base with the chopped shallots and fish seasoning salt and arrange the salmon steaks on top. Add the wine and the water or fish stock, and bring up to the simmer on top of the stove. Poach covered for 10 minutes, turning once, or put in a quick moderate oven Gas No. 5, 375 degrees F, 190 degrees C for 15 minutes or until the fish flakes easily when tested with a fork. (The water should simmer, *never* boil.) With a slotted fish slice, transfer the fish to a plate, and remove the skin and centre bone whilst it is still warm. Cover loosely to prevent drying out.

To make the sauce Strain the poaching liquid into a small pan and bubble vigorously until there is about 3 fl oz (75 ml/6 tablespoons) left in the pan. Leave until it is quite cold. Cut the stalks off the watercress, saving a few sprigs for garnish. Put the remaining leaves into the food processor, then add the poaching liquid, lime juice and rind (or the chosen alternative), the creams, mustard, salt and black pepper and process until of *coating* consistency.

To mix by hand Whisk all the ingredients together until of coating consistency, having first finely chopped the watercress leaves.

To serve Spread three-quarters of the sauce on a large fish platter or divide between individual plates. Lay the salmon on top and drizzle the remaining sauce over it. Loosely cover and chill for 1 hour. Garnish with lime or lemon twists and watercress sprigs.

SAUMON EN CROUTE, HERB SAUCE

SERVES 6–8   *Do not freeze*

This is a magnificent presentation, the pastry crust shaped and marked so that it resembles a golden fish. Ask the fishmonger to fillet and skin the salmon. It can then be left overnight in the refrigerator. However, it is advisable to prepare the dish for the oven on the same day as it is to be cooked, otherwise water may ooze out of the fish and make the pastry soggy.

The dish should not be served straight from the oven, but just warm; so, for convenience, plan to have it ready 30 to 60 minutes before it is served — then keep it warm in a low oven, Gas No. 1, 275 degrees F, 140 degrees C. The sauce can be made in advance, then gently reheated.

1 salmon (or salmon trout) 3–3½ lb (1¼–1½ kg) in weight, filleted, skinned and lightly salted
1 can cut spears asparagus, drained
1 lb (450 g) approximately puff pastry

HERB BUTTER:
2 oz (50 g/¼ cup) soft butter
1 teaspoon fish seasoning salt
2 teaspoons chopped parsley
¼ teaspoon white pepper

GLAZE:
1 egg yolk

1 tablespoon cream (reserved from cream for sauce)

THE SAUCE:
2 shallots or 4 spring onion (green onion) bulbs, finely chopped
½ oz (15 g/1 tablespoon) butter
2 teaspoons cornflour (cornstarch)
¼ pint (150 ml/⅔ cup) each soured cream and whipping cream
3 teaspoons mixed fresh herbs (parsley and tarragon) or 3 teaspoons parsley and ½ teaspoon dried tarragon
½ teaspoon salt; pinch white pepper
1 egg yolk

Cream the butter with the herbs and seasonings. Lay the fillets skinned side up on a board and spread one of them with two-thirds of the herb butter. Arrange the drained asparagus on top of the butter, then cover with the second fillet. Leave to one side.

Roll out the pastry ¼ in (½ cm) thick and long enough and wide enough to enclose the salmon. Down the centre of the pastry spread the remaining herb butter in a strip the width of the fish, then lay the salmon on top. Damp the edges of the pastry, then fold it over to enclose the fish, cutting away any excess. Lay the fish on a damp baking sheet, seal side down. Mark fish scales all over it, using the rounded end of a potato peeler and cutting through the top layer of the pastry. Cut out a 2½–3 in (6–7½ cm) equilateral triangle from the pastry trimmings. Make markings with the tines of a fork to simulate a fish tail.

Stir egg yolk and cream together, then brush evenly all over the pastry, including the 'tail'.

To cook the fish Preheat the oven to Gas No. 8, 450 degrees F, 230 degrees C. Bake the fish and the pastry 'tail' for 15 minutes, then open the oven, quickly reglaze the fish and take out the 'tail', which should now be well browned. Turn the heat down to Gas No. 7, 425 degrees F, 210 degrees C, and continue to cook for a further 25 minutes until a rich brown. Remove from the oven and put the baking sheet on a cooling tray. Leave for 30 minutes. Serve the salmon on a long platter with its 'tail' in position — the fish may be left uncovered on the serving dish in a warming oven for up to 30 minutes.

The sauce can be made early and warmed up gently when required. Melt the butter in a small pan; then add the shallots (or spring onions) and cook 3 minutes until softened. Put the cornflour into a small basin and mix with 4 tablespoons of the cream, then add to the pan together with the remainder of the cream (leave 2 tablespoons of the cream in the carton), the herbs and the seasonings. Simmer for 3 minutes. Take half the cream left in the carton, add the egg yolk, mix well and stir into the sauce. Do not reboil.

FRESH SALMON KEBABS

SERVES 6–8   *Do not freeze*

This way of cooking salmon — or indeed a large halibut — is a revelation, as the flesh stays moist under a crispy and savoury coating. It also makes the fish go a very long way. Serve it with 1 cup of plain or herb mayonnaise.

1½ lb (675 g) centre slice of salmon or large halibut, 1 in (2 ½ cm) thick, filleted
1½ teaspoons fish seasoning salt; 15 grinds black pepper
4 oz (125 g/½ cup) melted butter
10 level tablespoons fresh breadcrumbs
2 teaspoons grated lemon rind
6 tablespoons sesame seeds
32 small mushrooms

8 wooden skewers about 9–10 in (25 cm) long

HERB MAYONNAISE (OPTIONAL):
8 fl oz (225 ml/1 cup) plain mayonnaise (see page 190)
4 tablespoons chopped fresh dill or 2 tablespoons each chopped fresh parsley and chives
½ teaspoon French mustard
5 fl oz (150 ml/⅔ cup) soured cream

Cut the salmon into 1 in (2½ cm) cubes and sprinkle with the fish seasoning salt and pepper. Melt the butter in a bowl. In another bowl mix the breadcrumbs, sesame seeds and lemon rind. Cut the stalks of the mushrooms level with the edges of the caps.

Put the cubes of fish into the butter, turn to coat them on all sides, then dip them into the breadcrumbs and lay on a board. Paint the mushrooms all over with the melted butter. Thread the salmon and mushrooms alternately on the skewers, leaving room in between so that the fish can cook evenly. Sprinkle with any remaining butter. Grill for 15 to 20 minutes, turning once or twice. In a fan-assisted oven, air-grill for 15 minutes according to directions.

To enjoy this dish at its best, serve the kebabs either hot off the grill, or at room temperature up to an hour later.

To make the herb mayonnaise Beat all the ingredients together.

FRESH SALMON SOUFFLÉ

SERVES 4 as a main dish, 6 as an entrée   *Do not freeze*

At the Hôtel de la Cloche in Beaune, chef-patron Robert Petit makes a superb soufflé de saumon with only egg whites, cream and salmon, but for preparing in the domestic kitchen I have found the following version (using a béchamel sauce enriched with egg yolks instead of whipped cream) more certain of success. The flavour is excellent, even when made with — dare I mention it — best canned salmon, and there is no need for an accompanying sauce. The outside of the cooked soufflé should be set and golden-brown, the inside slightly creamy.

2 oz (50 g/4 tablespoons) butter
2 shallots or 4 spring onions (green onions), finely chopped
1½ oz (40 g/⅓ cup) flour
¼ pint (150 ml/⅔ cup) each of salmon poaching or canning liquor and milk, or use all milk
1 level teaspoon salt; 10 grinds black pepper

2 teaspoons tomato purée
1 tablespoon finely chopped parsley
4 large eggs
7 oz (200 g) salmon (weight after cooking), skinned, boned and finely shredded
2 oz (50 g/½ cup) finely grated mature cheese plus a little extra cheese for coating the dish

Set the oven to Gas No. 6, 400 degrees F, 200 degrees C. Butter a soufflé dish of 3 pints (1¾ litres/7 cups) capacity (about 8 in (20 cm) wide x 3 in (7½ in) deep) and coat the buttered surface with a thin layer of the cheese.

Melt the butter in an 8 in (20 cm) pan with a heavy base, add the shallots or spring onions and cook gently until softened, about 3 minutes. Now add the flour and the cold liquid, and whisk over moderate heat using a batter or balloon whisk until a thick sauce is formed. Add the salt, pepper, tomato purée and parsley and continue to bubble for a further 2 minutes.

Have ready a large bowl. Separate the eggs, dropping the yolks into the sauce (whisking well after each addition) and the whites into the bowl. Add the salmon and all but 1 tablespoon of the cheese to the sauce. Add a pinch of salt to the egg whites and whisk them until they stand in stiff but still glossy peaks. *Stir* one-quarter of the egg white into the salmon sauce, then *fold* in the rest, using a rubber spatula. Gently coax the fluffy mass into the prepared dish, and smooth it level. Sprinkle with the remaining cheese.

Put the soufflé into the preheated oven, then immediately turn down the heat to Gas No 5, 375 degrees F, 190 degrees C, and bake for 35 minutes. It will then have risen well above the top of the dish and be a rich brown.

FRESH SALMON QUICHE IN A BROWN HERB PASTRY CASE

SERVES 8   *Freeze 3 months*

A mixture of wholemeal and white self-raising flour makes superb brown pastry for this unusual quiche.

THE PASTRY:

4 oz (125 g/1 cup) wholemeal (wholewheat) or granary flour
4 oz (125 g/1 cup) self-raising white or 81% extraction flour
½ teaspoon salt
2 teaspoons soft brown sugar
1 teaspoon each dry mustard, herbes de Provence *and* fines herbes
5 oz (150 g/¾ cup) butter or sunflower margarine
1 egg, beaten
1 teaspoon wine vinegar

THE FILLING:

½ lb (225 g/1 cup) cooked flaked fresh salmon (10 oz/275 g raw)
1 tablespoon cornflour (cornstarch)
8 fl oz (225 ml/1 cup) single (light) cream
2 large eggs
½ teaspoon salt; 10 grinds black pepper
2 tablespoons snipped fresh dill or *2 teaspoons dried dill weed*
4 oz (125 g/1 cup) grated Cheddar or Lancashire cheese
A little more finely grated cheese for topping

To make the case Choose a loose-bottomed quiche tin 9 or 10 in (about 25 cm) in diameter. By hand or machine, rub the fat into the mixed flours, salt, sugar, and seasonings until each particle is about the size of a small pea. Sprinkle evenly with the vinegar and egg and gather together into a dough. Flatten the dough into a round 1 in (2 ½ cm) thick, wrap in foil and chill for 1 hour.

Roll the chilled dough on a floured board into a circle 11–12 in (30 cm) in diameter, lift on to the rolling pin and then ease it into the tin, pressing it well into the sides. Trim off any excess, using a sharp knife. Prick the case all over with a fork, then line it with a piece of foil pressed into the shape, and covering the edges of the pastry. Freeze for at least 30 minutes, or more if convenient.

Preheat the oven to Gas No. 6, 400 degrees F, 200 degrees C and put a baking sheet in it to heat up at the same time. Lay the frozen case on the hot baking sheet and bake for 15 minutes or until the pastry is firm to gentle touch, then remove the foil, prick the base again and return to the oven for a further 8 to 10 minutes until crisp and dry. This case can now be frozen for later use or used at once.

To complete the quiche Preheat the oven to Gas No. 5, 375 degrees F, 190 degrees C. Put the cornflour into a bowl and slowly stir in the cream followed by the eggs, seasonings and dill, then whisk until smooth. Stir in the cheese and salmon. Pour carefully into the pastry case and sprinkle thickly with cheese. Bake for 25 to 30 minutes, or until puffed and golden and firm to gentle touch. Leave at least 15 minutes before serving. The quiche can be gently reheated in a moderate oven until warm to the touch.

(**Note   In a microwave** — remove the quiche from the tin and place on a piece of paper towelling. Reheat on LOW (50–60% power) until warm to the touch, about 4 minutes.)

VARIATION

Individual Salmon Quiches   These look splendid served with crisp mixed salad as a main course for a special luncheon or after-theatre supper. You will need eight individual loose-bottomed quiche tins 4 in (10 cm) in diameter and 1 in (2½ cm) deep.

Make the pastry and filling in the same way as for the large quiche, but bake the pastry 'blind' for only 12 minutes. Fill and bake in the same way for 25 minutes.

A FRESHWATER FISH
POACHED CARP IN THE POLISH FASHION

SERVES 6   *Do not freeze*

In pre-war Poland, a country in whose multitude of lakes and rivers this much-fancied fish thrives, it was the custom in Jewish homes to serve a dish of cold poached carp as part of the Eve of Shabbat meal on Friday night. The carp is not actually a native of Europe and only became established there in the Middle Ages, when it was bred by the monks in their monastery fishponds. Today it is farmed extensively in many parts of the world and especially in Israel, where the descendants of those Polish Jews produce it for export to Europe. The 'Spiegelcarp-fen' or 'mirror carp' is considered the finest species for the table, as it has only a few large scales and its flesh is particularly sweet.

Before you buy, make sure the fish is fresh by checking that the inside of the gills is pink in colour rather than red. For this dish the fish should weigh between 4 and 5 pounds (2–2½ kg) gross. The smaller, less mature fish have a poorer flavour and their tiny bones can make eating a problem, a fact I learned to my cost when the power failed in Israel one Friday night, just as I was preparing to tackle one of these baby carp!

1 carp (4–5 lb (2–2½ kg) weight)

THE POACHING LIQUID:
2 pints (1¼ litres/5 cups) (approximately) water
1 medium onion, thinly sliced

2 carrots, thinly sliced
12 black peppercorns
2 level teaspoons sugar
1 teaspoon salt

Ask the fishmonger to scale the fish and cut off the fins. (If you have to do it yourself, dip it quickly in and out of boiling water to help speed the process.) He should then cut off the head together with 1 in (2½ cm) of the body and cut off the tail in a piece 4 in (10 cm) long. The body of the fish should be cut into steaks each 1 in (2½ cm) thick.

Wash and salt the fish, then leave it in a colander to drain.

Put the ingredients for the poaching liquid into a frying pan (about 10 in wide and 3 in deep (about 25 cm x 7 cm)) that can hold the fish in a single layer. Bring the liquid to the boil, then add the fish which (apart from the thicker head section) it should barely cover. Add a little more water if necessary. Cover and simmer on a very low heat for 15 minutes. Test by piercing the fish with a skewer, which should go in without any resistance.

Turn off the heat and leave the fish in the covered pan for 30 minutes, then lift out the pieces and arrange in a shallow casserole. Pour over the poaching liquid and vegetables and leave to set, for several hours or, preferably, overnight.

VARIATION
Carp in the German Manner   The fish is poached whole and served with a sauce of melted butter.

FISH IN SAUCE

I suspect that many people are nervous about serving a hot fish main dish for a dinner party because of the difficulties it presents if a sauce has to be made at the last minute, just as the guests begin to arrive. I have found two different ways to solve this awkward problem.

Fillets (but they must be thick ones) can be lightly poached and sauced early in the day, then briskly reheated just before serving.

Thick cutlets or **small whole fish** such as trout can be cooked before anyone arrives, and can then be kept hot in a very low oven for up to 30 minutes without any loss of texture. The sauce can also be made at the same time and then reheated on top of the stove or in the microwave just before serving.

Full details of these techniques are given with each recipe.

LOUP DE MER, SAUCE BELLET
SEA BASS IN THE RIVIERA STYLE

SERVES 6–8   *Freeze leftovers 1 month*

This is a superb way to cook steaks of fish on the bone — hake is excellent, if sea bass is not available. The fish is first fried 'à la meunière' in a light coating of seasoned flour and then finished with a wine and cream sauce delicately flavoured with shallots and mushrooms.

Much of the distinctive flavour of the dish is due to the use of 'crème fraîche', the French cultured cream which is a close relation of Devonshire clotted cream. A mixture of sweet and soured cream gives a similar result.

6–8 steaks of fish, each ¾ in (2 cm) thick
and 6 oz (175 g) in weight
3 oz (75 g/¾ cup) flour seasoned with 1
teaspoon salt and ½ teaspoon white pepper
4 oz (125 g/½ cup) butter and 1 tablespoon
sunflower oil
3 oz (75 g) shallots or half a mild onion,
finely chopped
4 oz (125 g/1 cup) pinky mushrooms, finely
chopped

Half a clove of garlic, peeled and crushed
½ pint (275 ml/1¼ cups) medium-dry white
wine
5 fl oz (150 ml/⅔ cup) each whipping and
soured cream
2 teaspoons cornflour (cornstarch)
½ teaspoon salt; 10 grinds black pepper;
pinch of nutmeg
1 tablespoon chopped fresh fennel, dill or
parsley

Wash the steaks of fish, lightly salt them, then coat with the seasoned flour, patting off any excess. Heat the butter and oil in a 9 in (22 cm) frying pan. The moment the butter starts to foam, lower in the fish and allow to cook steadily for 4 minutes each side, until golden-brown. Remove to a serving dish about 1 in (2½ cm) deep and leave, covered with foil, in a low oven, Gas No. 1, 275 degrees F, 140 degrees C, while completing the cooking of the sauce. (The dish may be kept hot at this stage for up to 30 minutes.)

To the same pan add the shallots and mushrooms together with the garlic, and cook gently for 5 minutes until softened but unbrowned. Add the wine; stir well, then bubble for 5 minutes until greatly reduced. Put the cornflour in a small basin and gradually mix with the cream; then add to the pan together with the nutmeg, salt and black pepper. Bubble for 3 minutes or until the sauce is of coating consistency, then pour over the fish and sprinkle with the herbs.

HADDOCK FILLETS NORMANDY STYLE

SERVES 6–8   Freeze (leftovers only) 1 month

The cider sauce and the garnish of poached apples transforms the mundane haddock into a party dish.

2–3 lb (1–1½ kg) thick haddock fillet,
skinned, washed and lightly salted
¾ pint (425 ml/2 cups) well-flavoured dry
cider
1 teaspoon salt; speck white pepper
Sprig of parsley; 1 bayleaf; 1 teaspoon black
peppercorns

THE SAUCE:
Poaching liquor from the fish

1 oz (25 g/2 tablespoons) butter
1 oz (25 g/¼ cup) flour
¼ pint (150 ml/⅔ cup) whipping cream

TO FINISH:
3 oz (75 g/¾ cup) sharp cheese (mature
Cheddar, for example), grated
2 eating apples, peeled, cored and cut in
eighths
Squeeze of lemon juice
Sprigs of parsley

Cut the fish into 6 or 8 pieces and leave to drain in a colander for 10 minutes. Put the cider, seasonings and herbs into a wide frying pan, bring to the boil, then add the fish. Cover and simmer for 10 to 15 minutes or until the fish looks creamy and flakes easily with a fork.

Put the apple sections in one layer in another frying pan, then add a squeeze of lemon juice and enough water to cover the base of the pan. Cover and poach gently until tender, turning once, about 6 or 7 minutes. (Or poach in the microwave without water, for about 3 or 4 minutes.) Lift the cooked fish out of its pan with a slotted fish slice and drain thoroughly on paper towels, then arrange in a greased gratin or similar shallow heatproof dish. Cover with foil to keep warm.

Strain the poaching liquid into a small saucepan and boil vigorously for 3 or 4 minutes until only ½ pint (275 ml/1¼ cups) remains. Meanwhile work the butter and flour to a paste using a flexible knife or spatula. Add the butter/flour mixture to the pan a teaspoonful at a time, whisking constantly (with a balloon or batter whisk) over moderate heat. Bubble for 3 minutes, then stir in the cream and bubble again until the sauce is thick enough to coat the back of a wooden spoon. Pour over the fish. Scatter with the grated cheese and arrange the drained apple decoratively on top.

To serve at once   Grill gently until a rich golden-brown.

To serve later   Allow the dish to cool completely, and cover with foil. Half an hour before it is required, reheat until bubbly around the edges, 15 to 20 minutes in a moderate oven, 5 minutes in a microwave (covered in clingfilm (saran wrap)).

FILLETS OF WHITE FISH IN CHEESE SAUCE ON A BED OF SPINACH

SERVES 6–8   *Freeze leftovers 1 month*

Fillets of baby halibut, plaice or sole are delicious served in this way. The recipe is excellent if you do not wish to use either wine or cream, as the sauce is sharpened with lemon juice and enriched with egg yolk instead.

6–8 fillets of fish (cut from fish weighing
approximately 1½ lb (675 g) each), washed,
salted and dark skin removed
Butter for greasing dish
2 tablespoons lemon juice
1 oz (25 g/2 tablespoons) butter

1 teaspoon dry mustard; pinch of cayenne
pepper
1 teaspoon salt; pinch of white pepper
2 egg yolks
4 oz (125 g/1 cup) grated sharp cheese
(mature Cheddar, for example)

THE SAUCE:
15 fl oz (425 ml/2 cups) milk
Grated rind of half a lemon, small bayleaf, 6
black peppercorns and a sprig of parsley
1 oz (25 g/2 tablespoons) butter
1½ oz (40 g/6 tablespoons) flour

THE SPINACH BED:
8 oz (225 g) packet frozen chopped spinach
(defrosted)
Pinch of salt; 10 grinds black pepper
¼ teaspoon ground nutmeg
Nut of butter

Set the oven at Gas No. 6, 400 degrees F, 200 degrees C. Fold each fillet in half and lay them side by side in a 10–12 in (25–30 cm) long buttered gratin dish. Sprinkle with the lemon juice and dot with the butter. Cover with foil or buttered greaseproof (waxed) paper and bake for 20 minutes, basting once, until the fish looks creamy.

Remove from the oven and turn it down to Gas No. ½, 250 degrees F, 120 degrees C.

Meanwhile heat the milk with the flavourings until it steams, then leave it covered on a low heat to infuse for 10 minutes. Strain the milk into a bowl and rinse out the pan with cold water, then return the milk to it together with the butter, flour and the dry seasonings. Whisk together over moderate heat (using a batter or balloon whisk) until the mixture boils; then bubble, stirring with a wooden spoon, for 5 minutes. Leave on a very low heat. Put the spinach into a frying pan and boil away any free liquid over medium heat. Stir in the remaining ingredients and leave on a low heat.

Lift the cooked fish out of its liquor with a slotted fish slice and lay on paper towels to drain. Pour the strained fish liquor from the dish into the sauce. Wash the dish; then arrange the spinach bed on the bottom with the cooked fish fillets on top. Cover loosely again and keep warm in the oven. Add to the sauce 3 oz (75 g/¾ cup) of the cheese and the egg yolks. Reheat, stirring, until it begins to simmer again, then take it off immediately (to prevent toughening the cheese and yolks) and coat the fish with it in an even layer. Sprinkle with the remaining cheese.

To serve at once Grill gently until a golden-brown.

To serve later Allow the dish to cool completely, and cover with foil. Half an hour before it is required, reheat until bubbly round the edges, 15 to 20 minutes in a moderate oven, 5 minutes in a microwave (covered in clingfilm (saran wrap)).

FILLETS OF DOVER SOLE IN WINE SAUCE

SERVES 6–8   *Freeze (leftovers only) 1 month*

This is the quintessential recipe for the meal where nothing but the best will do — the necessary ingredients are a good dry white wine, prime Dover soles and highly concentrated fish stock. When I prepared this dish for a dinner of the International Wine and Food Society, several members voted it the finest fish dish they had ever tasted.

5½–6½ lb (2½–3 kg) whole Dover sole (2½ lb (1 kg) when filleted), giving 6 to 8 good-sized fillets or 12 to 16 smaller ones
Bones and head from the fish
2 tablespoons finely chopped shallots or spring onion (green onion) bulbs
5 fl oz (150 ml/⅔ cup) each dry white wine (Muscadet is excellent) and fish stock (see below)
A few black peppercorns
1 small bayleaf
Sprig of parsley
1 oz (25 g/2 tablespoons) butter for greasing the cooking dish

½ lb (225 g/2 cups) button mushrooms
Nut of butter

THE SAUCE:
½ pint (275 ml/1¼ cups) strained poaching liquid (see below)
1½ oz (40 g/3 tablespoons) butter worked to a paste with 1 oz (25g/¼ cup) flour
8 fl oz (225 ml/1 cup) double (heavy) cream
Salt and black pepper to taste
2 heaped tablespoons grated sharp cheese (mature Cheddar, for example)
Nut of butter

First make the fish stock Remove the dark skin from the fillets, then put it with the fish bones and heads into a pan, cover with 2 pints (1¼ litres/5 cups) of cold water and simmer, uncovered, until the liquid is reduced to a cupful. Strain and reserve.

To poach the fish   Set the oven at Gas No. 6, 400 degrees F, 200 degrees C. Butter a baking tin or dish just large enough to hold the rolled fish in one layer, and scatter the shallots on the bottom. Salt the fish lightly on both sides, then roll up (or fold in half if too thick) and lay on top. Pour in the wine and stock, scatter with the peppercorns and tuck in the bayleaf and parsley sprig. Cover with foil and cook for 20 minutes, or until the fish has lost its translucent appearance. Remove from the oven and turn the heat down to Gas No. ½, 250 degrees F, 120 degrees C.

While the fish is cooking, slice the mushrooms thinly into a pan containing the nut of butter. Sprinkle them lightly with salt (to bring out the juices), cover and simmer for 5 minutes, then uncover and cook until the liquid has evaporated. Put on the lid and keep warm.

Lift the cooked fish out of its liquor with a slotted fish slice and drain on paper towels. Arrange the cooked mushrooms in a 10–12 in (25–30 cm) long gratin dish and lay the cooked fillets side by side on top. Keep warm in the oven. Measure the fish cooking liquor into a small pan and bring to the boil, then add the creamed butter and flour mixture, a teaspoonful at a time, whisking constantly. Now whisk in the cream and bubble gently until the sauce will coat the back of the spoon. Add salt and pepper to taste, then pour the sauce evenly over the fish. Sprinkle with the cheese and dot with the butter.

To serve at once   Grill gently until a rich golden-brown.

To serve later   Allow the dish to cool completely, and cover with foil. Half an hour before it is required, reheat until bubbly round the edges, 15 to 20 minutes in a moderate oven, 5 minutes in a microwave (covered with clingfilm (saran wrap)).

VARIATIONS

Omit the mushroom bed. Instead, remove the pips from 6 oz (175 g/1 cup) muscatel grapes, then arrange in the centre of the dish, surround with the cooked fillets and coat with the sauce. Grill as described above.

If Dover Sole is not available, lemon sole or thick plaice can be used instead.

A FAMILY SPECIAL
DEVILLED HERRINGS

SERVES 4–6

Leftovers will keep 2 days under refrigeration

The creamy-fleshed herrings caught in early spring make a cheap and easy family meal when grilled (broiled) under this delicious mustard coating. Large 'beef' tomatoes can be grilled at the same time, with a purée of potatoes completing the main course.

4–6 fine herrings, filleted

THE TOPPING:
2 tablespoons sunflower oil
1 tablespoon cider vinegar or red wine vinegar

3 teaspoons Dijon or English mustard
2 teaspoons Worcestershire sauce
1 teaspoon soy sauce
½ teaspoon sea salt; 15 grinds black pepper

Wash the fish, salt lightly and leave in a colander to drain for 10 minutes, meanwhile mixing the topping ingredients together in small bowl.

Lightly grease a grill (broiler) pan, heat it up 2 in (5 cm) from the grill for 3 minutes, then lay the fish in it side by side and skin side down, and brush them thickly with the topping mixture. Grill (broil) for 10 minutes, until the fish is a rich brown. Serve at once.

SMOKED FISH
TARTE AU SAUMON FUMÉ
SMOKED SALMON TART

SERVES 6–8 as a main dish, 8–10 as part of a buffet   Freeze 1 month

This is based on the famous 'quiche au fromage blanc' of Alsace. I have 'modernized' it however by using a brown herb pastry and enlivening the cheese filling with smoked salmon and fresh herbs. The texture is best if the 'tarte' is baked in a 9–10 in (25 cm) metal quiche tin at least 1½ in (4 cm) deep. (Metal conducts the heat more efficiently than pottery does, so that the pastry is crisper when baked.)

1 baked brown pastry case (see page 100)
½ lb (225 g/1 cup) low- or medium-fat soft cheese such as Quark, fromage blanc or curd cheese
2 teaspoons cornflour (cornstarch)
3 egg yolks
1 whole egg

¼ pint (150 ml/⅔ cup) whipping cream
1 tablespoon finely cut fresh dill or chopped parsley
1 teaspoon lemon rind
Pinch of salt (omit if the smoked salmon is very salty)
15 grinds black pepper
3–4 oz (75–125 g) smoked salmon

Preheat the oven to Gas No. 6, 400 degrees F, 200 degrees C. Put the soft cheese into a bowl and stir in all the remaining ingredients except the smoked salmon, beating until smooth. Cut the salmon into thin strips and arrange on the bottom of the pastry case. Pour in the filling and bake for 20 minutes until puffy and golden-brown. Turn the oven down to Gas No. 4, 350 degrees F, 180 degrees C, and cook for a further 15 minutes. Serve warm or at room temperature.

SMOKED HADDOCK GOUGÈRE

SERVES 6–8   Do not freeze

Gougère is the famous savoury choux pastry of Burgundy where you may be offered it, in the shape of a large airy puff, as a kind of blotting paper to soak up your glass of mid-morning wine. Most Burgundians buy their gougères from the pâtisseries, but the dish is very easy to make at home, especially if you have a food processor. A strong bread flour will make a very light choux pastry because when it is baked it will hold the maximum amount of air. Here it forms a crisp case for a creamy smoked haddock filling.

THE PASTRY:

4 oz (125 g/½ cup) butter or margarine
½ pint (275 ml/1¼ cups) cold water
5 oz (150 g/1¼ cups) strong bread flour, sifted with 1 teaspoon salt, speck of white pepper
4 eggs
2 teaspoons Dijon mustard
4 oz (125 g /1 cup) cheese (Gruyère or Cheddar), coarsely grated

THE FILLING:

1½ lb (675 g) smoked haddock
6 spring onion (green onion) bulbs, finely chopped

2 oz (50 g/¼ cup) butter
2 oz (50 g/½ cup) flour
¾ pint (425 ml/2 cups) milk
1 teaspoon dry mustard
Pinch each of salt and white pepper
Good pinch ground mace or nutmeg
3 teaspoons chopped parsley
2 generous tablespoons double (heavy) cream (optional)
2 hard-boiled eggs, chopped

THE TOPPING:

4 tablespoons fairly coarse dry breadcrumbs
4 tablespoons any finely grated cheese

Cut the butter into 1 in (2½ cm) chunks and put into a strong pan with the cold water. Heat until the butter melts, then bring up to a fast boil. Immediately tip the flour in all at once, and beat vigorously with a wooden spoon for 1 minute or until the mixture forms a soft ball of the texture of mashed potato, that can be rolled round in the pan. Take off the heat and cool until you can hold your hand against the side of the pan.

To mix by food processor Put the paste into the bowl, and add the eggs one at a time, processing after each addition until the mixture is smooth again. Finally process for 30 seconds.

To mix by hand or electric mixer Whisk the eggs to blend, then add to the dough in four portions, whisking or beating after each addition until smooth and elastic.

Paste made by either method should be smooth and glossy and firm enough to be pulled into floppy peaks. Beat in the mustard and the cheese. Butter a 2 pint (1¼ litres/5 cups) gratin or other heatproof dish about 2 in (5 cm) in depth. Pipe or spoon the choux pastry in a thick border round the edge of the dish, then spoon the smoked haddock filling (see below) into the centre. Sprinkle evenly with the mixed crumbs and cheese. Bake in a preheated oven, Gas No. 7, 425 degrees F, 220 degrees C for 25 minutes, or until the gougère is well risen, brown and crisp to the touch.

To make the smoked haddock filling This can be prepared after the choux paste has been piped into the dish. Cover the haddock with water and bring slowly to the boil in a covered pan. Leave for 10 minutes in the hot water, then drain, remove the skin and any small bones and flake roughly.

Sauté the spring onions in the butter until softened, about 3 minutes, then stir in the flour, the milk and the seasonings and bring to the boil whisking constantly, then bubble for 3 minutes. Turn off the heat, and stir in the cream (if used), the parsley, the chopped eggs and flaked fish.

TUNA COULIBIAC WITH A MUSHROOM AND WINE SAUCE

SERVES 6–8   *Do not freeze*

The Coulibiac is a Russian fish pie which, like many other things 'à la Russe', became popular in England in Edwardian times when there were close ties between the British and Russian royal families. It has no Jewish connections.

The original recipe had a filling of fresh salmon and turbot mixed with hard-boiled eggs and buckwheat, which was encased in brioche pastry. This version is not as lavish as the original but it is extremely good to eat and looks most impressive for a supper party or as part of a fish buffet.

2 oz (50 g/¼ cup) butter
4 oz (125 g/⅓ cup) spring onion (green onion) bulbs, shallots or mild onion, peeled and finely chopped
3 oz (75 g/½ cup) long-grain rice
¼ pint (150 ml/⅔ cup) dry white wine (such as Muscadet)
½ pint (275 ml/1¼ cups) water
½ teaspoon fish seasoning salt
10 grinds black pepper
2 cans (7½ oz (200 g)) light-meat tuna
1 tablespoon each chopped fresh parsley and snipped chives
1 lb (450 g) (approximately) puff pastry
4 eggs, hard-boiled and sliced

Beaten egg for glaze

THE SAUCE:
1 oz (25 g/2 tablespoons) butter
2 shallots or 4 spring onion (green onion) bulbs, finely chopped
4 tablespoons medium-dry sherry
½ lb (225 g/2 cups) white button mushrooms, finely sliced
6 tablespoons dry white wine
5 oz (150ml/⅔ cup) single (light) cream
2 teaspoons cornflour (cornstarch)
Pinch each of salt, ground nutmeg and white pepper

To prepare the filling In a pan with a thick base sauté the onion in the butter until soft and golden. Stir in the rice and cook for 2 or 3 minutes; then add the wine, water and seasonings and bring to the boil. Cover and simmer for 15 minutes until the rice has absorbed the liquid and the grains are tender and separate. Cool. Drain the tuna, flake finely with a fork and mix with the herbs and a little salt and white pepper to taste.

To assemble the Coulibiac Divide the pastry in half and roll each portion into a rectangle 12 in long and 10 in wide (30 x 25 cm). Lay one rectangle on a damp baking sheet. Leaving a 1 in (2½ cm) margin on all sides, spread the rice on the pastry, cover it with half the tuna mixture, then the sliced eggs (lightly salted) and finally the remaining tuna. Re-roll the second portion of pastry so that it is 1 in (2½ cm) wider and longer than the bottom portion. Brush the edges of the bottom rectangle with beaten egg, then lay the second rectangle on top and seal the two firmly together with the side of the hand. Flake the two edges together with the back of a knife, then crimp or leave plain. Brush the top with beaten egg, then chill for at least 30 minutes.

To bake   Preheat the oven to Gas No. 8, 450 degrees F, 230 degrees C. Put in the Coulibiac, then turn the oven down to Gas No. 7, 425 degrees F, 220 degrees C, and bake for 35 minutes or until a rich brown.

The sauce   This can be made when convenient, then reheated. Melt the butter in a saucepan, add the onion and cook, stirring occasionally, until soft and golden. Stir in 3 tablespoons of the sherry and simmer until the volume is reduced by half. Add the sliced mushrooms and the wine and simmer gently for a further 10 minutes. Mix the cream with the cornflour, season with the salt, nutmeg and white pepper and add to the pan with the remaining tablespoon of sherry. Simmer for 3 or 4 minutes. Serve with the sliced Coulibiac.

TUNA AND GREEN PEPPER SOUFFLÉ

SERVES 4   *Do not freeze*

This is an excellent dish to prepare for unexpected guests or for a family meal on the day 'there isn't a thing to eat in the house'. The base of the soufflé can be made early in the day and then reheated to lukewarm, the egg white folded in and the mixture baked as directed below.

2 oz (50 g/4 tablespoons) butter
Half a large green pepper, seeds removed,
cut in small cubes or *2 canned pimientos,*
drained
2 shallots or *4 spring onions (green onions),*
finely chopped
2 oz (50 g/½ cup) mushrooms, roughly
chopped
1½ oz (40 g/⅓ cup) flour
¼ pint (150 ml/⅔ cup) milk

1 teaspoon each salt and Dijon mustard
10 grinds black pepper
1 tablespoon parsley, finely chopped
1 can (7 oz (200 g)) tuna, drained and
roughly flaked
2 oz (50 g/½ cup) sharp cheese (such as
mature Cheddar), finely grated, plus 2
tablespoons for coating the cooking dish
4 eggs plus 1 extra egg white

Set the oven at Gas No. 6, 400 degrees F, 200 degrees C. Butter a soufflé or other round ovenproof dish of 3 pint (1¾ litre/7½ cup) capacity (about 8 in (20 cm) in diameter and 3 in (7½ cm) deep) and coat with the two tablespoons of cheese.

In a large pan melt the butter, add the pepper, shallots and mushrooms and cook for 5 minutes until softened. Add the flour, milk, seasonings and parsley and whisk over moderate heat until a very thick sauce is formed. Boil for 3 minutes, then remove from the heat.

Have ready a large bowl for the egg whites. Separate the yolks and whites, stirring the yolks one at a time into the sauce and putting the whites in the bowl. Now stir the tuna and the 2 oz (50 g) cheese into the sauce. Whisk the whites with a pinch of salt until they hold stiff but still glossy peaks. *Stir* a quarter of this meringue into the sauce, then use a rubber spatula to *fold* in the rest. Spoon into the prepared dish and smooth level.

Put in the preheated oven, turn the temperature down to Gas No. 5, 375 degrees F, 190 degrees C, and bake for 35 minutes or until well-risen and a rich brown on top. Serve at once with crusty bread and crisp green salad.

110

Meat

The kosher butcher's shop has undergone a radical change of style in recent years, and a good butcher now cuts and presents his meat with a degree of artistry and sophistication quite unknown even a short time ago. Although only the forequarters of animals are available in most countries outside Israel — where the hindquarters can be 'porged' of forbidden fats and sinews, by agreement with the Rabbinical authorities — they are being cut in a much more imaginative way. With the exception of hindquarter cuts such as rump steak, fillet and sirloin, one can now buy almost as wide a variety as in the general butchers' shops, including entrecôte and 'minute' steaks of beef, pocketed shoulder, kebabs, rack and crown roast of lamb, and schnitzels and scallopini of veal. And this is true not only in the large cities with a big Jewish population but also — albeit in frozen packs — in even the smaller and more remote communities.

As a result, there is now a strong emphasis on the less traditional methods of cooking, such as roasting and grilling, which not only are quicker and more convenient to do than the 'old-fashioned' casserole or braise but also need the minimum of added fat or, in some cases, no fat at all. The fat, particularly on braising cuts like brisket, was once considered to be the tastiest part of the dish but now, because their customers demand it, butchers are having to trim it off before it can be sold, and meat such as veal and young lamb which comes from leaner animals is in much greater demand.

Because of the number of working wives who haven't the time to stand in their kitchen like their mothers did, the butcher has to do some of the preparation and cooking that used to be done in the home. So he stuffs joints, threads kebabs, roasts beef and chickens, and prepares smoked top rib, beefburgers and schnitzels ready for the pan.

This chapter offers you a range of recipes for cooking the newer kinds of kosher meat cuts, particularly those that can be roasted or grilled (broiled) or 'stir-fried' in the popular Chinese style; you will find still more if you consult the index to the book. Minced (ground) meat still accounts for some 30 per cent of all meat sales, so I have suggested some unusual ways of cooking it. But as the casserole is still, in my opinion, the most economical way of enjoying kosher meat, I have included a variety of dishes from different cuisines in which I have drastically reduced the amount of fat that is normally used, and suggested less familiar ways of flavouring them with unusual herbs and spices.

CHOOSING AND USING KOSHER CUTS OF MEAT

Many kosher butchers now sell meat in both fresh and frozen pre-packs which name the cut and the most suitable method of cooking it, so it's easier than it has ever been to pick what you need even if you don't have a thorough knowledge of the subject. This applies in particular to the more 'convenient' cuts which need only to be put in the oven or under the grill (broiler) to make the kind of quick and easy family meal which was unknown a few years ago. Yet there is a huge variety of other more 'old-fashioned' cuts such as shin or top rib which make less expensive yet extremely tasty eating, but which the butcher doesn't bother to pre-pack because housewives find they haven't the time to prepare them in the traditional manner. A good butcher can cut and trim even this kind of meat to make it easier to handle, however, and dishes can be made from it quite speedily, using modern time-saving equipment such as the slow cooker, the automatic oven, the pressure cooker and the microwave oven. That is why I have given below a detailed list of *all* the kosher cuts, as well as some guidance on the best ways in which to cook them.

Although the nomenclature used to describe the cuts of kosher meat may vary from town to town, as well as from one country to the next, I have tried to describe them in such a way that the part of the animal they come from can be easily identified. I have also given directions for making kasher meat and poultry.

All meats should be completely cooked before storage; partially cooking meat raises the internal temperature just enough to encourage the growth of bacteria, but not enough to kill them.

Beef

• **Fresh beef** is bright red when first cut, but darkens on standing.
• **Tender beef** is usually flecked with fat, rather like marble, and is surrounded by a creamy layer of fat, which may be removed before cooking. (Fatless meat cannot be tender, however, unless cooked by moist heat as in a casserole or braise.) The inside of the bones should be rosy, and the meat firm and moist to the touch, and very smooth.
• **Hanging** is essential to tenderize beef that is to be roasted or grilled, although it is not necessary for more naturally tender meat such as lamb and veal. The meat should be hung in the butcher's cold store for 10 to 14 days, at a temperature between 32 and 34 degrees F (0–1 degree C). It's a good idea to order large roasting joints well in advance so that the butcher will have time to hang the meat to your satisfaction.
• **Beef cuts:**
Shin beef: For soup and beef tea; makes a flavoursome, if rather fibrous stew; the traditional cut for Hungarian Goulash. Also used for Cholent.
Brisket: (a) Thin end. For Tsimmes — used sliced, trimmed of most of the fat. *(b) Point.* For covered roasting (in fat without liquid) or for pickling, or for overnight cooking in a Cholent or Dfina. Only economical in a joint weighing 3 lb (1½ kg) or over. Meaty but fatty (middle brisket has a thinner layer of fat).
Flank: Needs rolling. Cheap. Sweet when pot-roasted, but must be pressed and served cold, or it falls to bits; also for pickling (not as tasty as brisket).
Neck steak: For mincing (grinding) or stewing — has plenty of 'body'.
Chuck or back steak: Stew, mince (grind) or braise.
Shoulder steak: First-cut for braising, cut in ¾ in (2 cm) thick slices, or for stews, cut in 1 in (2½ cm) cubes. If hung for 10 days, it can be fried.
Blade steak: Braise in slices, or pot-roast in one piece. The thin gristle running through can be nicked out before serving.
Alki or round bola (part of shoulder steak), also known as *chuck:* Braise; good, whether served hot or cold. Thin slices can be cut into 'fairy' steaks which are beaten out to tenderize them and can then be fried.
Top rib: Similar to flank but with more flavour. For Borscht, Cabbage Soup, Cholent, Dfina. Smoked top rib looks like 'streaky' bacon and is said to have a similar taste.
Wing rib (standing rib): For roasting; can be boned out for spit roasting, or shortened rib on bone can be spitted — keeping bone in adds to flavour.
Lid of rib (top of back rib): Usually rolled, then roasted or spitted; excellent cold for

112

sandwiches. The joint weighs only 2½-3lb (1¼-1½kg), so is useful for a small family.

Rib or 'entrecôte' steaks: Boned out and cut ½–¾ in (1½–2 cm) thick for grilling (broiling) or frying. Must be hung for 7 to 10 days.

Bola (chuck): (a) Corner or *prime bola:* For braising, with plenty of vegetables. Hung bola can be dry-roasted very slowly, loosely foil-covered for half the time, allowing 40 minutes to the pound (½ kg), or it can be sliced and grilled (broiled). *(b) Slice:* For braising, in tomato or wine sauce. Bola, frozen and then cut paper-thin, can be used for minute steaks.

Liver: For chopping. Young beasts' liver need only be grilled (broiled); an older animal's liver should be grilled to make kasher, then simmered in salted water for half an hour. (See 'How to make kasher meat and poultry' below.)

Knuckle and shin beef: For soup.

Oxtail: For soup (not always available).

Minced (ground) beef should always be frozen or cooked as soon after mincing as possible, and never kept longer than 24 hours under refrigeration, as the large surface area makes it deteriorate more quickly than other meat.

Veal

- **Good veal** is between 6 and 8 weeks old, the flesh milky rather than pink in colour.
- An older animal which is too young to be classified as beef is called a 'sterk' — it's also known as 'baby beef'. Insipid in flavour, with tenderness its only virtue.
- **Veal cuts:**

Shank of veal: For use in thick soups such as barley and 'hobene gropen'; for Calves-foot Jelly or meat casseroles, such as Osso Bucco. It must be cut with an electric saw.

Shoulder: The thick part of the shoulder can be plain roasted; the blade end is best boned out, stuffed and braised. Flavour with bayleaf, carrots and onions, and cook in a covered casserole.

Breast: Have it boned and pocketed or boned and rolled, then stuff and braise it.

First-cut chops: Grill (broil) or fry; also use boned out for escalopes.

Shoulder chops: Boned out, made kasher, frozen and sliced for schnitzel or scallopini.

Calf liver: Grill (broil) to make kasher (see below for details), then smother with onions in the frying pan; or use for Chopped Liver or for pâté.

Lamb

- **Good lamb joints** have plenty of light pinkish meat, creamy fat, and very little bone.
- **Lamb cuts:**

Neck and scrag: For Scotch broth.

First-cut chops (cutlets): There are 24 in each animal. For grilling (broiling), frying, roasting (six to eight joined together make a 'rack' or a 'carré d'agneau'; six first-cut cutlets from each side joined together make a 'Crown of Lamb').

Middle neck: For casseroling.

Breast: Casserole with spring vegetables. Boned, stuffed and rolled, it makes a good roast for a small family.

Shoulder: Roast; can be boned and rolled, or boned, pocketed and stuffed. Also used cubed for kebabs.

HOW TO MAKE KASHER MEAT AND POULTRY

All pre-packed meat and poultry, and a very large percentage of the fresh supply which is available in the large centres of Jewish population, has already been made kasher under Rabbinical supervision and can therefore be cooked without any further ritual preparation.

If, however, the food does have to be made kasher at home or in an institution, the following procedures should be followed exactly.

Meat and poultry (including bones and giblets, but excluding liver and grilling (broiling) steaks, for which special instructions are given below). All poultry must be drawn before it is made kasher.

1. As soon as possible after the food has been delivered, put it into a deep plastic or enamel bucket and cover completely with cold water.
2. Leave it to soak for half an hour.
3. Take it out and place it on a wire or plastic draining grid, tilted so that the liquid can easily drain away. Leave it to drain for 5 minutes.
4. Thoroughly sprinkle every surface with koshering (coarse) salt. (This can be obtained from a kosher butcher or grocer.)
5. Leave for one hour.
6. Rinse the food three times in cold water, to remove all traces of salt and blood.

Meat and bones should then be well dried with a paper towel and either cooked at once, or stored until required in the refrigerator or freezer.

Poultry and giblets must additionally be scalded as follows:

7. Put the bird in a bowl and pour boiling water over it from a kettle.
8. When cool enough to handle, scrape the skin of the bird with a blunt knife, to remove any feathers or coarse bits of skin; remove the skin from the feet. Look inside the body cavity to make sure it is absolutely clean, and that no traces of the entrails remain. Trim off any loose skin from the giblets. Dry thoroughly, and either cook at once or store in the refrigerator or freezer.

Liver: As liver contains too much blood to be effectively made kasher by soaking and salting, the following method is used instead:

1. A thick piece of liver should be cut open, thinner slices should be cut across the surface to facilitate the removal of the blood.
2. Wash the liver thoroughly in cold water, then sprinkle it on both sides with cooking salt (koshering salt is too coarse for the purpose).
3. Place the liver on a wire grid set on a foil-lined grill (broiler) pan (both kept only for this purpose).
4. Grill (broil) gently until the liver changes colour and the surface looks dry, then turn and grill the second side in the same way. Discard the foil after use.

Alternatively, replace steps 3 and 4 by placing the salted liver in a wire basket or on a wire grid over a gas flame and cooking it in the same way, until it has changed colour on both sides. Afterwards, the wire basket or grid should be held over the flame to burn off any residue, then washed, wiped and stored. Chicken livers are made kasher in the same way.

Calf's liver can be served without further preparation, or it can be put in a frying pan and smothered with fried onions. Ox liver must be tenderized by simmering in salted water for half an hour. It can then be used for Chopped Liver.

Steaks: Steaks which are to be grilled (broiled) do not need to be soaked and salted. The grilling process draws out the blood from the meat, and this is considered to satisfy the requirements of kashrut. However, they will have been made kasher by

114

soaking and salting in the usual manner if they have been purchased from a shop selling only ready-koshered meat.

Note All utensils used to make food kasher should be kept exclusively for that purpose. After use, they should be washed and wiped with a special cloth, then stored separately from other kitchen equipment.

ROASTS
On Roasting:

- A **roasting tin** fitted with a metal rack keeps the joint above the fat as it is cooking, so that it doesn't have a chance to soak any of it up. The tin should be made of a heavy material such as *pressed* aluminium or stainless steel. (A standing rib roast does not need to be set on a rack as the curve of the rib bone will keep the joint suspended above the fat.) A tin measuring 13 × 10 × 2 in (33 × 25 × 5 cm) is a good average size and is large enough to accommodate a joint (or a chicken) weighing 3–5 lb (1½–2½ kg).
- A sliced onion strewn in the bottom of the tin halfway through the cooking period will give a rich colour and a good flavour to **gravy** made from the meat juices.
- A **meat thermometer** takes the guesswork out of roasting, especially if you are particular about the degree of done-ness you require.
- All roasts are easier to **carve** if they are left in a warm place to 'settle' after they have finished cooking. During this resting time, the juices which have been drawn to the surface of the meat by the heat of the oven will go back towards the centre of the joint so that they are not lost when it is carved.
- A good **carving knife** is a worthwhile investment. An electric carving knife is particularly useful for carving boned joints. Otherwise use a conventional carving knife, but buy an efficient knife sharpener.

ROAST RIB OF BEEF

SERVES 8   *Freeze 2 months*
                                     Will keep under refrigeration for 4 days

A wing rib is the prime roasting cut for the Jewish table, but it is also the most expensive. However, as it is difficult to roast a small joint and keep it succulent, I buy a large one with at least two ribs and serve it only on special occasions. To ensure that it is tender, the meat must be hung for 10 to 14 days after it is made kasher, so it is wise to order it well in advance. Have the rib bone 'chined' so that the meat will sit evenly in the roasting tin.

A meat thermometer is most helpful in ensuring the meat is done to your liking. I have carefully tested the timings I give below but, to get the correct results, the meat must be left at room temperature for 2 hours before cooking begins. The cooked joint will be a rich crusty brown and the meat will be tender and juicy whether it is served hot or cold.

115

6 lb (2¾ kg) wing rib of beef
2 tablespoons sunflower oil
Black pepper
2 teaspoons herb seasoning for beef (if available)
1 large onion, thinly sliced

6 tablespoons water or medium-dry red wine

THE GRAVY:
½ pint (275 ml/1¼ cups) beef stock mixed with 1 teaspoon cornflour (cornstarch)

If the meat has been frozen, allow it to thaw at room temperature overnight. Refrigerated meat must be left in the kitchen for 2 hours before cooking to bring it to room temperature.

Preheat the oven to Gas No. 7, 425 degrees F, 210 degrees C. Stand the beef in a roasting tin, paint it all over with oil, then sprinkle generously with freshly ground black pepper and the herb seasoning. Put in the hot oven to brown for 15 minutes, then add the sliced onion and the hot water or wine to the roasting tin and turn the temperature down to Gas No. 3, 325 degrees F, 160 degrees C. Continue to roast for a further 2½ hours (25 minutes per lb (450 g)) for medium beef, or for a further 3 hours (30 minutes per lb (450 g)) for well-done beef, basting every 20 minutes. *In either case,* lightly salt the meat, then leave it in a warm place, or in the turned-off oven to settle for 15–20 minutes. This makes it much easier to carve.

The gravy Pour off as much of the fat as possible from the tin and remove the onion. Pour in the stock and cornflour, stir very well to incorporate the crusty bits at the bottom of the tin, then simmer until thickened and well flavoured, about 5 minutes.

VARIATION

To cook a four-rib wing roast (weight approximately 11–12 lb (5–5½ kg): Brown for 15 minutes at Gas No. 7, 425 degrees F, 210 degrees C, then turn down the temperature as above and cook for 20 minutes to the pound (450 g) for medium beef, 25 minutes to the pound (450 g) for well-done beef. (*Total* cooking time for a 12 lb (5½ kg) rib: 4¼ hours for medium beef, 5¼ hours for well-done beef.)

ROAST LAMB WITH AN ORANGE GLAZE

SERVES 6–8

Freeze leftovers 2 months
Will keep 3 days under refrigeration

This is an excellent variation on plain roast lamb. The meat develops a wonderful colour and a very fresh and fruity flavour.

4 lb (1¾ kg) shoulder of lamb

1 tablespoon Worcestershire sauce

THE GLAZE:
2 oz (50 g/¼ cup) soft brown sugar
Juice of half a lemon
Juice of 1 orange

THE SAUCE:
½ pint (275 ml/1¼ cups) beef stock, made from a stock cube, if necessary
2 level teaspoons cornflour (cornstarch)
Salt and pepper

116

Preheat the oven to Gas No. 4, 350 degrees F, 180 degrees C. Place the joint in a baking tin just large enough to contain it. Mix the ingredients for the glaze and simmer for 2 minutes, then pour over the meat. Roast for 2 hours, basting every 30 minutes. Remove to a serving plate and keep hot.

Mix the cornflour with a little of the stock, then stir in the remainder. Pour into the roasting tin and deglaze, stirring well. Check the seasoning. Simmer for 3 minutes.

ROAST LAMB DIJONNAISE

SERVES 6

Freeze 3 months
Leftovers will keep 3 days under
refrigeration

This is a splendid dish to make with winter lamb, as its mature flavour marries so well with the savoury mustard coating with which the meat is covered. As this coating also prevents the meat from drying out there is no need to baste it, so it is an ideal dish to leave in a pre-set oven.

4 lb (1¾ kg) shoulder of lamb on the bone
1 large onion, thinly sliced

THE COATING:
4 level tablespoons Dijon mustard
1 tablespoon dark soy sauce
1 clove of garlic, peeled and crushed
½ teaspoon dried herbes de Provence

½ teaspoon dried herb seasoning for lamb (if available)
2 teaspoons grated fresh ginger or a good pinch of powdered ginger
2 teaspoons olive oil

THE GRAVY:
½ pint (275 ml/1¼ cups) lamb or beef stock

Two hours before you intend to start roasting the meat, put all the coating ingredients except the oil into a small bowl and stir to blend, then gradually beat in the oil. Paint this mixture all over the lamb with a pastry brush, making sure you cover the underside as well. Place the meat on a rack in a roasting tin, and leave at room temperature for 2 hours.

Preheat the oven to Gas No. 4, 350 degrees F, 180 degrees C. Put the onion under the rack to flavour the gravy, then roast the lamb for 2 hours (30 minutes to the pound (450 g)). If the lamb is to be cooked in a pre-set oven, add a further 15 minutes. To make the joint easier to carve, lift the cooked lamb on to a warm serving dish and leave to stand, loosely covered with foil, for 15 minutes.

Pour off any fat from the roasting tin, then pour in the stock, stir well, and allow to bubble until syrupy, about 5 minutes. Strain into a sauce boat and serve with the lamb.

SHOULDER OF LAMB STUFFED IN THE PERSIAN FASHION

SERVES 8

Freeze cooked meat 2 months
Leftovers will keep 3 days under
refrigeration

A boned shoulder of lamb is stuffed with a mixture of minced (ground) beef and spiced rice enriched with nuts and raisins. As it needs so little attention while it is cooking and is so easy to carve, this makes a superb dish for a dinner party.

Ask the butcher to bone the meat, if possible leaving a pocket for the stuffing. If this is not possible the boned meat can be stuffed and then rolled before roasting. The lamb is also delicious when cold.

3½–4 lb (1¾ kg) shoulder of lamb, boned
and pocketed or boned and left flat

3 oz (75 g/¾ cup) walnuts, coarsely chopped
1 egg, beaten

THE STUFFING:
1 tablespoon oil
1 medium onion, finely chopped
½ lb (225 g) raw minced (ground) beef
¼ lb (125 g/½ cup) risotto (Italian) or Patna rice
4 fl oz (125 ml/½ cup) hot water
1 teaspoon salt
½ teaspoon ground cumin
10 grinds black pepper
2 teaspoons chopped parsley
2 rounded tablespoons raisins

THE COATING:
1 teaspoon salt; 10 grinds black pepper
Dusting of flour
2 tablespoons oil
1 tablespoon demerara (brown) sugar

THE GRAVY:
2 teaspoons fat from the roasting tin
2 level teaspoons cornflour (cornstarch)
½ pint (275 ml/1¼ cups) cold water
1 crumbled beef stock cube
Salt and pepper to taste

To make the stuffing In a saucepan with a heavy base, cook the onion in the hot oil until soft and golden. Add the meat and cook, stirring with a fork, until it loses its redness. Add the rice and stir well, then cook for a further 5 minutes until the meat is brown. Stir in the hot water, salt, cumin, pepper and parsley, cover and cook very gently for 15 minutes, or until the rice is barely tender. Stir in the nuts and raisins and bind with the beaten egg.

To stuff a pocketed shoulder Sprinkle the meat lightly with salt, then pack the stuffing in loosely and sew up into a neat shape.

To stuff and roll a shoulder Lay the meat, skin side down, on a board, and cut out any lumps of fat. Spread the stuffing, evenly over the meat, pushing it into any little folds. Roll up neatly and sew into a compact shape, or skewer closed if this is possible.

To roast the meat Preheat oven to Gas No. 4, 350 degrees F, 180 degrees C. Put a rack in a roasting tin and lay the meat on top. Sprinkle with the salt and pepper, and dust lightly with flour, then pour over the oil. Roast the meat for 2 hours, then sprinkle with the sugar and increase the heat to Gas No. 6, 400 degrees F, 200 degrees C, then cook for a further 20–30 minutes until a rich brown. Leave in a warm place (or in the oven turned down to Gas No. ¼, 225 degrees F, 100 degrees C), for 15 minutes before carving.

To make the gravy   Pour off all but 2 teaspoons of fat from the roasting tin. Mix the cold water smoothly with the cornflour, then pour into the roasting tin and add the crumbled beef stock cube. Bring to the boil, stirring well, then season to taste with salt and pepper.

CARRÉ D'AGNEAU PROVENÇALE
RACK OF LAMB ROASTED WITH SAVOURY HERB COATING

SERVES 4 or 8

Will keep 2 days under refrigeration
Freeze leftovers 2 months

This is one of the most delicious and exciting ways of presenting roast lamb, as the meat is so succulent and the joint looks most impressive on the dinner table. A rack of lamb consists of seven or eight cutlets joined together — so one rack will serve four and you will need two for a dinner party of eight, with each guest receiving two chops.

As the meat will need careful preparation by the butcher, it's advisable to order it in good time. He will remove the backbone (to make it easier to carve) as well as the flap of meat and fat on top of the rack. If you wish to decorate the rack with cutlet frills, he should also remove the lower 1 in (2½ cm) of meat and fat from each individual chop and scrape the bone clean.

A rack of lamb is quick and easy to cook, but the timing must be precise. The initial browning of the meat can be done just before dinner, but to roast the meat so that each chop is faintly pink in the centre, you will need to allow exactly 35 minutes from the time it goes into a hot oven to the moment it is carved at the table. If you are cooking two racks at the same time, double all the ingredients but roast for exactly the same length of time. If you prefer, the rack can be carved in the kitchen but it does not look as elegant as when presented whole.

1 rack of lamb containing 7 or 8 cutlets, prepared as described above

THE COATING:
1 tablespoon Dijon or other French mustard
2 shallots or *large spring onion (green onion) bulbs, finely chopped*
3 tablespoons chopped parsley
½ teaspoon dried herbes de Provence

1 medium garlic clove, peeled and chopped
1 oz (25 g/4 rounded tablespoons) very fresh breadcrumbs
1 oz (25 g/2 tablespoons) margarine, melted
¼ teaspoon sea salt; 10 grinds black pepper

GARNISH:
4 fl oz (125 ml/½ cup) strong beef or lamb stock
1 bunch watercress, washed and well trimmed

Make the crumb coating by thoroughly mixing all the ingredients (except the mustard) in a bowl. Dry the meat well with paper towels.

Heat a heavy frying pan over moderate heat until you can feel the warmth on your hand held 2 in (5 cm) above it. Put in the rack, sprinkling it lightly with salt and black

pepper, and cook over high heat until the outside is seared and brown on all sides —
a pair of tongs will help you to turn it more easily. Lift the meat out and arrange it in
a roasting tin, flesh side up, then deglaze the pan with the stock, stirring well to
incorporate all the delicious sediment. Pour this sauce into a small pan ready to be
heated later. Spread the browned rack with the mustard and coat it with the crumb
mixture, patting it on firmly.

Preheat the oven to Gas No. 8, 450 degrees F, 230 degrees C. Put in the meat and
roast for 25 minutes, until the crumbs are a rich brown, then leave the rack to stand
in the turned-off oven for 10 minutes (or transfer it to a warming oven). If you have a
meat thermometer it should register 170 degrees F (78 degrees C) at the *end* of this
time. Serve the rack garnished with the watercress and accompanied by the reheated
sauce.

VEAU POÊLÉ À LA MATIGNON
ROAST VEAL WITH LEMON AND HERB STUFFING

SERVES 8

Freeze 2 months
Will keep 3 days under refrigeration

As veal is a very lean meat, it is much more tender and juicy if it is braised in moist
heat rather than roasted in dry heat like lamb or beef. The herb stuffing gives the
meat a delicious flavour. As the joint is boned, it is very easy to carve for a dinner
party.

1 boned-out shoulder of veal weighing about
4 lb (1¾ kg), pocketed
2 tablespoons oil
1 onion and 2 carrots, very finely chopped
4 tablespoons medium-dry sherry
1 teaspoon salt; 15 grinds black pepper
2 bayleaves

1 level tablespoon chopped parsley
½ level teaspoon dried mixed poultry
seasoning or *Italian herb mixture*
Grated rind of half a lemon
Half a large onion, finely chopped
2 oz (50 g/¼ cup) margarine
1 egg, beaten to blend

THE STUFFING:
6 oz (175 g/3 cups) fresh breadcrumbs
1 level teaspoon salt
¼ level teaspoon white pepper

THE SAUCE:
8 fl oz (225 ml/1 cup) meat stock
1 teaspoon cornflour (cornstarch) mixed with
2 tablespoons medium-dry sherry

First make the stuffing. Put the breadcrumbs in a bowl and mix with the herbs,
seasonings and lemon rind. Sauté the onion in the margarine until tender and
golden, about 5 minutes. Pour the onion and fat over the seasoned breadcrumbs and
stir well, then add the beaten egg to make a moist but not 'cloggy' mixture (you may
not need to use all the egg). Lay the veal on the table and stuff the pocket. If it is not
pocketed, lay the meat flat, spread with the stuffing then form into a neat shape. Sew
up or skewer closed. Dry well.

Preheat the oven to Gas No. 4, 350 degrees F, 180 degrees C. Heat the oil in a
heavy casserole and fry the meat over a moderate heat until it is a rich brown — don't
rush this process as it should take 10 to 15 minutes. Remove the meat from the
casserole, put in the vegetables and sauté until they are softened and golden. Add

120

the sherry and bubble until it has almost evaporated. Return the meat to the casserole, laying it on top of the vegetables. Sprinkle with the salt and pepper, then add the two bayleaves. Cover and cook in the oven for 2 hours. The veal is ready when it feels soft to the touch, by which time it will be a mahogany brown. If it's ready too soon, turn the oven down to Gas No. ¼, 225 degrees F, 100 degrees C, and keep it hot for up to 30 minutes.

When ready to serve, lift the meat from the casserole and keep it warm on a serving plate. Skim off as much fat as possible from the liquid in the dish, but do not discard the vegetables. Pour in the stock and the cornflour mixed with the sherry, stir well then simmer until thickened. Put this sauce into the blender or processor and process until smooth, then reheat and serve with the meat, which should be carved in fairly thick slices.

VEAL ESCALOPES
ESCALOPES DE VEAU, LE PALAIS
VEAL ESCALOPES ON A VEGETABLE RAGOÛT

SERVES 6–8

Do not freeze
Leftovers will keep 3 days under refrigeration

A true escalope is cut from the leg of veal but as this is not usually available as a kosher cut, it should be cut from the boned-out shoulder or from the eye of the chop instead. These thin slices of veal are simmered in white wine and then served on a juicy vegetable ragoût. The dish can be prepared early in the day and then gently reheated just before dinner.

6–8 escalopes, cut ⅜ in (1 cm) thick
2 oz (50 g/½ cup) flour seasoned with 1 teaspoon salt and 10 grinds black pepper
Sunflower oil for frying
¼ pint (150 ml/⅔ cup) each medium-dry white wine and chicken stock, or ½ pint (275 ml/1¼ cups) chicken stock alone

THE RAGOÛT:
3 tablespoons olive oil
2 medium (5 oz (150 g)) onions, thinly sliced
1 tablespoon brown sugar
1 lb (450 g) aubergines (eggplant), unpeeled, cut in 1½ in (3 cm) cubes

2 large green peppers, halved, seeded and cut in strips ½ in (1 cm) wide
2 medium courgettes (zucchini), unpeeled, cut in slices 1 in (2½ cm) thick
1 can (14 oz (400 g)) tomatoes, drained
1 large clove of garlic, peeled and crushed
2 teaspoons salt; 15 grinds black pepper
1 tablespoon each lemon juice and wine vinegar
4 oz (125 g/1 cup) black olives

GARNISH:
1 tablespoon chopped parsley

To prepare the vegetable ragoût Heat the oil in a heavy frying pan, add the onions, sprinkle with the sugar, then cover and cook until soft and golden, about 10 minutes. Add the aubergines, peppers, courgettes and tomatoes with the garlic, salt and black pepper, stirring well. Cover and simmer for 30 or 40 minutes, stirring occasionally, until the vegetables are tender but not mushy, and the ragoût is thick and juicy. If

121

there is too much liquid in the pan, boil it away. Stir in the vinegar and lemon juice together with the olives. The ragoût can now be left in the covered pan until required.

To cook the escalopes Cover each escalope with a piece of greaseproof (waxed) paper, beat it out with a cutlet bat or the end of a rolling pin until as thin as possible, then dip in the seasoned flour. Heat enough oil in a heavy frying pan to come to a depth of ¼ in (½ cm) and cook the escalopes in it until they are a golden-brown on both sides, removing each one to a plate as it is ready. Pour off any oil remaining in the pan, add the white wine (if used) and stock and stir well, then simmer until syrupy. Return the escalopes to the pan, cover and simmer very gently for 15 minutes until they feel tender when cut with a knife. Leave until required.

To serve the dish Reheat the ragoût until bubbly, either on top of the stove or in the microwave. Bring the meat to simmering point in the sauce, but do not allow it to boil as this would toughen it. Arrange the ragoût round the edge of a large dish, put the escalopes in the centre and spoon over the sauce. Sprinkle with the chopped parsley and serve.

VEAL AND MUSHROOMS CHINESE STYLE

SERVES 4

Freeze 2 months
May be reheated

Little pieces of veal are stir-fried in the Chinese fashion, then simmered briefly in a mushroom and Marsala (or sherry) sauce. Serve it with savoury noodles or Crispy Kataifi (see page 173).

1 lb (450 g) veal beaten out as for escalopes (see recipe above)
1 tablespoon cornflour (cornstarch); ½ teaspoon salt
4 tablespoons sunflower oil
½ lb (225 g/2 cups) mushrooms, thinly sliced

3 spring onions (green onions), trimmed then cut in 1 in (2½ cm) lengths
½ lb (225 g/1½ cups) frozen peas, defrosted
1 tablespoon dark soy sauce
2 tablespoons Marsala or medium-dry sherry
4 fl oz (125 ml/½ cup) veal or chicken stock
½ teaspoon salt

Cut the veal into pieces about 1 in (2½ cm) wide and 1½ in (3 cm) long, then toss in the seasoned cornflour. Gently heat 2 tablespoons of the oil in a wok or heavy frying pan, add the pieces of veal and cook until golden-brown on both sides. Remove.

Heat the remaining 2 tablespoons of oil in the pan until almost smoking, then add the mushrooms, onions and peas, and stir-fry for 5 minutes, tossing with two spoons so that they cook evenly. Add the veal, soy sauce, Marsala (or sherry) and stock, sprinkle with a little salt, turn down the heat and cook gently together for 3 or 4 minutes until the veal feels tender. Serve at once.

BEEF WITH PEPPERS AND BEANSPROUTS CHINESE STYLE

SERVES 4–5   *Leftovers keep 2 days under refrigeration*

Take a pound (450 g) of frying steak and stir-fry it in the Chinese fashion. The result is a delicious dish, and one that is original at least for the Jewish table. Allow half an hour to prepare the raw ingredients, but only 5 minutes to cook them. It is easier to cut the meat as thin as is necessary if it has been partly frozen (some butchers will cut the meat for you). Serve with fried rice or Crispy Kataifi (see page 173).

1 lb (450 g) frying steak
4 tablespoons oil plus extra oil if necessary
4 green peppers, seeds removed
1 carton of fresh beansprouts

THE MARINADE:
1 egg white
1 tablespoon red wine

1 tablespoon soy sauce
1 level tablespoon cornflour (cornstarch)

THE SAUCE:
1 tablespoon red wine
2 tablespoons soy sauce
2 level teaspoons sugar
½ teaspoon salt
Any remaining marinade

Slice the meat ¼ in (½ cm) thick, then cut into 'matchsticks' each 1–2 in (2½–5 cm) long. Shred the peppers in the same way. Put to one side.

Ten minutes before dinner, mix the marinade ingredients in a bowl, stir in the strips of beef and leave for 5 minutes. Five minutes before dinner, heat the oil in a wok or heavy frying pan, lift the meat from the marinade (reserving any not absorbed) and fry quickly over high heat, until the meat changes colour and becomes a pale brown. Lift out and put to one side. If most of the oil has been absorbed, add a further 2 tablespoons to the pan and sauté the green pepper strips over high heat for 2 minutes, until they are well coated with oil. Return the beef to the pan, and add the reserved marinade, the sauce ingredients and the beansprouts. Cook for a further 2 minutes, then serve. The dish can be reheated, preferably in a microwave oven.

STEAK FOR TWO, SAUCE FITOU

SERVES 2   *Do not freeze*

This is my simplification of the classic dish 'Tournedos Chasseur' using two well-matured steaks cut from the eye of the rib. It makes a very special dish for two. Serve with crisp green salad and Oven-crisp Potatoes (see page 176).

2 rib steaks, cut ¾–1 in (2–2½ cm)
thick
1 teaspoon herb seasoning for beef

THE SAUCE:
Nut of margarine
4 oz (125 g/1 cup) button mushrooms, finely
sliced

1 shallot, finely chopped, or the bulbs of 4
spring onions (green onions)
½ pint (275 ml/1¼ cups) of a 'meaty' red
wine
½ teaspoon dried tarragon or 2 teaspoons
fresh tarragon, chopped
2 level teaspoons finely chopped parsley
Sea salt and freshly ground black pepper

Dry the steaks thoroughly using paper towels and trim off most of the fat, leaving only a thin strip round the edge. Sprinkle the steaks with freshly milled ground pepper and the beef seasoning (if available).

Heat a heavy-based frying pan or cast-iron griddle until you can feel a good heat on your hand held 2 in (5 cm) above it. Spear some of the trimmed fat with a fork and grease the hot pan with it. Cook the steaks for 4 minutes on each side, when they should be a rich brown on the outside and pale pink on the inside (nick one and see). Don't cook them any further, as they must now be kept hot in a low oven while you prepare the sauce.

Pour off any juices that have collected in the bottom of the pan and reserve them. Put the nut of margarine into the pan, and cook the mushrooms and shallots (or spring onions) gently until softened — about 3 minutes. Add the wine, herbs and reserved pan juices and bubble until the liquid is reduced by half, by which time the mushroom mixture will be very soft. Add salt and pepper to taste and stir in the parsley. Pour any juices that have oozed out of the steaks into the sauce.

Arrange each steak on a hot plate and surround with the sauce. Serve at once with the salad and the sauté potatoes.

MINCED (GROUND) MEAT
BEEFBURGERS DE LUXE

SERVES 4–5

Freeze raw 2 months
Freeze cooked 1 month

Best-quality lean minced (ground) meat is mixed with a careful selection of seasonings, then grilled (broiled), fried on a griddle, or thermal-grilled in a forced-air oven. If you like an open texture have the meat minced once; if you like a smooth close texture, have it minced twice. Serve the grilled beefburgers with a Barbecue Sauce or a Pizzaiola Sauce (see page 155) or in warm buns, in the American fashion.

1 egg
Half an onion, cut in chunks
1 thick slice of brown bread
1 tablespoon tomato ketchup
2 teaspoons soy sauce

½ teaspoon Worcestershire sauce
1 teaspoon salt; 10 grinds black pepper
1 level teaspoon yeast extract or vegetable
paste
2 lb (1 kg) minced (ground) raw beef

Put all the ingredients, except the meat, into a food processor or blender and process until puréed. Turn into a large bowl and add the meat, mixing thoroughly together with a fork to avoid packing the meat too tightly. Form into 4 or 5 'steaks' each about ¾ in (2 cm) thick. Grill (broil) for 5 minutes on each side until a rich brown.

SINIYE BEEFBURGERS WITH TAHINA SAUCE

SERVES 4–5

Freeze raw meat mixture 3 months
Do not freeze with topping

This is a Middle Eastern dish which is very popular in Israel — I have had it at a five-star hotel, as well as for a simple family meal. Large beefburgers are grilled (broiled), then covered with a delicious Tahina (sesame seed) sauce. (Bottled Tahina can be bought from delicatessens and Middle Eastern grocers.)

THE MEAT MIXTURE:
1 egg
Half an onion, cut in chunks
Large sprig of parsley
1 clove of garlic, peeled
½ teaspoon cinnamon
1 level teaspoon yeast extract or vegetable paste

1 teaspoon salt; 10 grinds black pepper
2 lb (1 kg) minced (ground) raw beef

THE TOPPING:
4 level tablespoons pine kernels (pine nuts)
(optional)
8 fl oz (225 ml/1 cup) Tahina diluted with 3 tablespoons water

Make the meat mixture in the same way as the Beefburgers de luxe. Grease five individual gratin dishes, each 6 in (15 cm) in diameter, or one large gratin dish big enough to hold five patties side by side. Shape five patties each about ½ in (1 cm) thick, and lay in the bottom of the dish. Grill (broil) for 6 minutes or until a rich brown, then scatter with the pine kernels and top with the Tahina sauce. Continue to grill for another 5 minutes until the topping is bubbly and golden-brown. Serve at once with a green salad.

ORIENTAL MEAT STRUDEL

Makes 2 strudels each serving 3–4

Freeze raw 2 months
Will keep 1 day raw or 3 days cooked under refrigeration

This is an excellent dish for either a family supper, or to serve with cold cuts for a buffet meal. It can be prepared the day before, but should be baked just before serving. The meat mixture must be quite cold when it is used or the pastry will go soggy.

THE MEAT MIXTURE:
2 tablespoons oil
2 tablespoons pine kernels (pine nuts) or
broken cashews
2 medium onions, chopped
1 lb (450 g) lean minced (ground) meat
(lamb or beef)
2 teaspoons brown sugar
1 rounded tablespoon tomato purée
2 tablespoons water
2 teaspoons soy sauce
½–1 teaspoon salt; 10 grinds black pepper

1 tablespoon chopped parsley
1 teaspoon dried mint
1 clove of garlic
Pinch cayenne pepper
1 teaspoon ground cumin

THE CRUST:
2 packets (½ lb (225 g)) puff pastry

TO GLAZE:
1 egg yolk mixed with 1 teaspoon cold water
2 tablespoons sesame seeds

Heat the oil and brown the pine kernels or cashews. Drain on kitchen paper (paper towels) and reserve.

In the same fat, sauté the onion until a rich golden-brown, then add the meat, sprinkle with the sugar and cook over high heat, stirring with a large fork, until the meat browns. Add all the remaining ingredients. Cover and simmer for 15 minutes. Uncover and simmer for a few minutes without the lid until juicy but not wet. Allow to go cold, then divide into two portions.

To make each strudel Roll out ½ lb (225 g) of the pastry into a rectangle measuring about 12 × 9 in (30 × 22 cm). Spread the filling evenly all over, leaving a 1 in (2½ cm) border of pastry clear all the way round. Turn the border in over the filling on the short sides, then roll up into a flattened 'Swiss roll'. Transfer to a baking sheet. Paint all over with the egg glaze and scatter with the sesame seeds. Make six cuts, 2 in (5 cm) apart, through the top crust.

Preheat the oven to Gas No. 7, 425 degrees F, 220 degrees C. Bake for 15 minutes, then turn down to Gas No. 6, 400 degrees F, 200 degrees C, and continue to cook for a further 15 minutes until a rich golden-brown. Serve warm, in slices.

To freeze Glaze the strudel and scatter with the sesame seeds, then open-freeze for 2 hours. Wrap in foil and store in a plastic bag.

To defrost Place on a baking sheet and leave in the refrigerator overnight, or at room temperature for 2 hours.

SWEDISH MEATBALLS

SERVES 6–8

Freeze 3 months
Will keep up to 4 days under refrigeration

The meatballs are stewed in stock, which is then thickened to make a delicious sherry-flavoured sauce.

THE MEAT MIXTURE:

2 lb (1 kg) raw minced (ground) beef
2 slices of bread, each cut 1 in (2½ cm) thick
Half a large onion
2 large eggs
1 large sprig of parsley
1 level teaspoon salt; 15 grinds black pepper
1 teaspoon lemon juice
1 teaspoon Worcestershire sauce or
angostura bitters

TO COOK THE MEATBALLS:

1 tablespoon sunflower oil
15 fl oz (425 ml/2 cups) strong meat stock

THE SAUCE:

Stock in which the meatballs were
cooked
1 level tablespoon cornflour (cornstarch)
3 tablespoons medium-dry sherry

Put all the ingredients except the meat into a blender, or food processor and process until they become a smooth purée. Pour into a large bowl. Add the meat and mix with a fork until evenly blended. Leave for 30 minutes then shape between the palms into balls about 1½ in (3 cm) in diameter. Brown in the hot oil, then add the stock, cover and simmer for 30 minutes.

Lift the meatballs from the pan with a slotted spoon, and keep them warm. Skim off as much fat as possible from the cooking liquid. Mix the cornflour with the sherry and add to the liquid in the pan. Bring to the boil and simmer for 3 minutes. Return the meatballs to the sauce and reheat for 5 minutes over moderate heat. Serve with boiled rice or mashed potatoes.

SESAME SPICED RICE

SERVES 6–8

Freeze 3 months
Will keep 3 days under refrigeration

The addition of a little minced (ground) meat simmered in wine gives this rich casserole extra body and flavour. It is a perfect dish to serve at a buffet supper party with cold meat or poultry.

6 tablespoons sesame seeds
2 tablespoons oil
1 medium onion, finely chopped
½ lb (225 g) raw minced (ground) beef
12 oz (350 g/3 cups) Basmati or other
long-grain rice

½ pint (275ml/1¼ cups) full red wine, such
as Côtes du Rhône
1 tablespoon soy sauce
1 level teaspoon paprika
2 level teaspoons salt
1 pint (575 ml/2½ cups) beef stock

Set the oven at Gas No. 4, 350 degrees F, 180 degrees C. Put the sesame seeds on a baking tray and toast in the oven for 10 to 15 minutes or until golden-brown. Remove.

Meanwhile, gently heat the oil and sauté the onion until soft and golden. Add the meat and cook until it loses its redness and begins to brown, stirring with a fork. Now add the rice and cook until it loses its glassy appearance, stirring well. Pour in the wine and bubble fiercely until its volume is reduced by half. Add the seasonings and stock and bring to a full boil. Stir well and transfer to the oven. Cook, covered, for 30 minutes until the rice is tender and has absorbed all the liquid. Stir in the toasted sesame seeds.

The dish can be kept hot in a low oven for half an hour. To reheat, sprinkle the surface lightly with water, cover, then put in a moderate oven for 15 minutes or until warm.

EN CASSEROLE

The casserole or main dish in one pot has been a mainstay of Jewish cookery since the start of our recorded history. Even as early as the Book of Genesis, there are references to food cooked in this way, while in more recent times the Cholent and Tsimmes of the Ashkenazim and the Dfina and Tagine of the Sephardim have continued this culinary tradition.

Because most household cooking was restricted to the hearth until well into the Middle Ages, the earthenware cooking pots in general use were fashioned with a round bottom so that they could nestle in the ashes of the fire — Rebecca must have used a dish of this shape to cook the kid for Jacob to give to Isaac. It was only when ovens became more commonplace that pots were designed with a flat base that could sit evenly on the oven floor. Just such a casserole, which is almost identical to the glazed brown dish used by everybody's grandmother, is illustrated in the *Cuoco secreto de Papa Pio Quinto*, the sixteenth-century cookery book written by the chef to Pope Pius V. In the past fifty years, however, the materials used to make these ovenproof casseroles have changed more radically than in the whole of the previous sixty centuries. While glazed earthenware is in fashion once again in many kitchens, most stove-to-table casseroles are now made either of stainless steel or of enamel bonded to aluminium, iron or steel — a non-stick coating for the interiors is also widely used. Which kind of casserole you choose will probably depend on the price, the weight, and of course your personal taste. The most durable, such as enamel or iron, are usually the heaviest to lift and it's important to test the weight in your hand before you buy one, especially if you will have to lift it up into a wall oven. Some of the lightest and most attractive, as well as the most durable — though, alas, also the most expensive — are made of stainless steel, while the less costly but very practical dishes with non-stick interiors have a much shorter useful life. But whatever material the body is made of, the casserole will be much more useful if its base can withstand *direct* heat, so that it can be used to brown the food on top of the stove before it is transferred to the oven to finish cooking.

Unless it's for cooking hot-pots and stews, it's more practical to buy a dish which is wide rather than tall, so that the pieces of meat or poultry can be arranged in one layer and the minimum of cooking liquid can be used (too much can dilute the flavour).

A casserole of any kind should always *simmer* and never *boil*, as the food may be toughened or broken down by the action of violently bubbling liquid. For this reason, it's always a good idea to check the rate of cooking during the first hour the food is in the oven, and if necessary lower the temperature by one gas number, 25 degrees F or 10 degrees C. Chuck steak, blade steak, top rib and the first-cut shoulder steak of beef, and the middle neck and breast of lamb, are the best kosher cuts to use in a casserole as they are lean yet tasty, and their fibrous connective tissue is effectively softened by the moist heat inside the dish.

The flavour of any casserole is improved if it is left to stand for several hours and then reheated.

BEEF, SPANISH STYLE

SERVES 6–8

Freeze 2 months
Will keep 4 days under refrigeration

The bland flavour of red kidney beans is complemented by that of the tasty Queen olives in this delicious casserole. Double the quantities for a buffet dish to serve 12–16.

2 lb (1 kg) braising steak, cut 1 in (2½ cm) thick
2 oz (50 g/½ cup) flour mixed with 2 level teaspoons salt and 15 grinds black pepper
4 tablespoons oil
2 medium (5 oz (150 g)) onions, finely chopped
¼ pint (150 ml/⅔ cup) full-bodied red wine, such as Côtes du Rhône
8 outer stalks of celery, very finely sliced

1 can (14 oz (400 g)) tomatoes in juice
¼ pint (150 ml/⅔ cup) beef stock or thin beef gravy
2 teaspoons brown sugar
1 fat clove of garlic, peeled and crushed
1 can (14 oz (400 g)) red kidney beans
2 oz (50 g/½ cup) Queen olives, cut in pieces

Preheat the oven to Gas No. 3, 325 degrees F, 160 degrees C. Put the salt, pepper and flour into a plastic bag. Cut the meat in 1 in (2½ cm) cubes, and toss in the bag until evenly coated, then fry in the oil until a rich brown. Transfer to a casserole. Add the onion to the fat and cook until a rich gold, then stir in the wine, celery, tomatoes, stock, brown sugar and crushed garlic. Bring to the boil, then pour over the meat. Cover and cook for 2 hours. Add the beans and their juice with the pieces of olive, cover and cook for a further 30 minutes.

LAMB AND ORANGE CASSEROLE

SERVES 6

Freeze 2 months
Will keep 3 days under refrigeration

The meat from a boned shoulder of lamb — considered by connoisseurs to have the finest flavour — is cooked in a very refreshing orange and liqueur sauce. This is a sophisticated yet good-tempered dish for an informal supper, as it can be kept hot without spoiling for up to an hour. It also makes a splendid family meal using extra stock instead of the wine and liqueur. Serve with Rice steamed in the Persian Fashion (see page 126) or with new potatoes.

129

2 tablespoons sunflower oil
2 lb (1 kg) boned shoulder of lamb, cut in 1½
in (3 cm) chunks
1 medium onion, finely chopped
2 teaspoons dark brown sugar
8 fl oz (225 ml/1 cup) chicken stock plus ½
pint (275 ml/1¼ cups) medium-dry white
wine, or ¾ pint (425 ml/2 cups) chicken
stock
1 level teaspoon salt

1 large or 2 medium navel oranges
Zest of half an orange, cut in matchsticks
1 tablespoon cornflour (cornstarch),
smoothly mixed with 3 tablespoons cold
water
4 tablespoons Curaçao, Grand Marnier or
Cointreau liqueur

GARNISH:
1 tablespoon chopped parsley

Preheat the oven to Gas No. 3, 325 degrees F, 160 degrees C. Sauté the meat in the oil (in two batches) until it is a rich brown, then add the onion and the brown sugar and continue to cook until the onion is golden-brown. Remove the meat and onion to a plate and add the wine to the pan. Stir well to incorporate any bits on the bottom, then bubble for 3 minutes to reduce the wine. Add the meat, the hot stock and the salt, and bring slowly to the boil.

Meanwhile put the matchsticks of orange peel into a small pan, cover with cold water and simmer for 10 minutes to remove any bitter taste. Put in a sieve and rinse with cold water, then add to the meat. Remove all the pith from the orange, then cut between the sections to release the fruit. Add to the meat together with any juice that can be squeezed out of the orange 'skeleton'.

When the casserole is bubbling, cover it and transfer to the oven, then cook until the meat is very tender, about 1¾ hours. Add the cornflour dissolved in the water together with the liqueur, stir well, then simmer in the oven for a further 20 minutes. Just before serving, sprinkle with the chopped parsley.

LAMB IN THE PROVENÇAL FASHION

SERVES 6

Freeze 2 months
Will keep 3 days under refrigeration

This delicious casserole is made particularly savoury by the olive oil, garlic and herbs of Provence. If you do not wish to use wine, substitute an equal amount of chicken stock instead. The casserole can be cooked either on top of the stove or in the oven.

2 tablespoons olive oil
2 lb (1 kg) boned lamb, cut in 1½ in (3 cm)
cubes
1 medium (5 oz (150 g)) onion and 1 large
carrot, each cut in ⅜ in (1 cm) cubes
2 teaspoons brown sugar
½ pint (275 ml/1¼ cups) chicken stock
5 fl oz (150 ml/⅔ cup) medium-dry white
wine

1 tablespoon tomato purée
1 tablespoon chopped parsley
1 fat clove of garlic, crushed
1 teaspoon dried herbes de Provence
¼ teaspoon ground nutmeg
1 teaspoon salt; 15 grinds black pepper
4 oz (125 g/1 cup) button mushrooms, stalks
removed

If possible, use a stove-to-table casserole. Heat the oil until you can feel the heat on your hand held 2 in (5 cm) above it. Add half the well-dried meat and cook briskly until it is brown on all sides, then remove to a plate and fry the second portion of meat in the same way. Cook the onion and carrot in the same fat until they are softened and golden, sprinkling with the sugar to hasten the process.

Put the meat back on top of the vegetables and add the chicken stock, wine, tomato purée and seasonings. Bring to the boil then cover and simmer gently, stirring occasionally, for 1½ hours. (Alternatively, cook in the oven at Gas No. 2, 300 degrees F, 150 degrees C, for 2 hours.) Add the mushrooms during the last half-hour.

When the meat feels tender, uncover the dish and simmer for 5 minutes until the sauce is reduced to a coating consistency. If you prefer to thicken it even further, stir in 2 teaspoons cornflour (cornstarch) smoothly mixed with 2 tablespoons cold water and simmer for a further 3 minutes. Serve with new potatoes.

MEXICAN BEEF

SERVES 4

Freeze 2 months
Will keep 4 days under refrigeration

A tasty but economical dish with an interesting blend of spicy flavourings.

2 tablespoons olive oil
1 medium (5 oz (150 g)) onion, finely chopped
1 large green or red pepper, seeds and pith removed, then cut in small dice
1½ lb (700 g) braising steak cut in 1 in (2½ cm) chunks
1 can (5 oz (150 g)) tomato purée, diluted with 2 cans hot water
2 tablespoons tomato ketchup
2 bayleaves

1 clove of garlic, peeled and crushed
1 teaspoon chilli powder or ¼ teaspoon Tabasco sauce
2 teaspoons paprika
1 teaspoon curry powder
2 teaspoons Worcestershire sauce
1 teaspoon salt; 10 grinds black pepper
1 can (15 oz (425 g)) red kidney beans, drained
1 tablespoon chopped parsley

Set the oven at Gas No. 3, 325 degrees F, 170 degrees C. Use a stove-to-table casserole.

Cook the onion and the pepper in the hot oil until softened and golden, about 5 minutes. Add the meat and continue to cook until it turns a rich brown. Add all the remaining ingredients except the beans and the parsley. Bring to the boil, cover and simmer in the oven for 2 hours, although longer will do no harm. Add the drained beans and the parsley and simmer, covered, for a further 15 minutes. Serve with rice or mashed potato.

PERSIAN LAMB AND APRICOT POLO

SERVES 6–8

Freeze 3 months
Will keep 3 days under refrigeration

This dish, with its combination of dried fruits and lamb, is reminiscent of the Tunisian Tagine, a recipe for which is given on page 350. But it is really a Persian version of a pilau (or pilaf), with the rice cooked in the classic 'chilau' style which is given in detail on page 172. After they have been cooked separately, the meat mixture and the rice are steamed briefly together before they are served. If the meat and rice have been prepared in advance, they should be reheated separately, then treated as freshly cooked. The Polo can be kept hot for 30 minutes in a low oven (Gas No. ¼, 225 degrees F, 110 degrees C).

1 large onion, finely chopped
2 tablespoons oil
1½ lb (675 g) boneless lamb shoulder, cut in
1 in (2½ cm) cubes
4 oz (125 g/¾ cup) dried apricot halves
2 oz (50 g/½ cup) muscatel raisins
1 pint (575 ml/2½ cups) hot water
1 or 2 beef stock cubes

1 teaspoon cinnamon
1 teaspoon salt; 15 grinds black pepper
12 oz (350 g/1½ cups) Basmati rice
2 tablespoons salt

GARNISH:
2 oz (50 g/½ cup) pine kernels
1 tablespoon oil

To cook the meat   Preheat the oven to Gas No. 4, 350 degrees F, 160 degrees C. In a heatproof casserole, sauté the onion in the oil until golden, then add the meat, and continue to sauté, stirring occasionally, until the onion and the meat are a rich brown. Add the apricots, raisins, hot water, stock cubes and seasonings, and bring to the boil. Cover and cook in the oven for 1¼ hours or until the lamb is tender.

To cook the rice   Soak the rice in cold water for half an hour then drain well. Fill a large pan (the size used for cooking pasta) with water, add the salt and bring to the boil. Add the rice and cook uncovered, bubbling gently for 5 to 8 minutes, until almost tender. Test by biting into a grain — there should still be a little hard core in the centre. Turn into a sieve, rinse with warm water to remove any excess salt, then allow to drain well.

To complete the polo   Have ready a 3½ pint (2 litres/9 cups) oven casserole. Arrange one-third of the rice evenly in the casserole, cover with half the lamb mixture, then another third of the rice, then the remaining lamb and finally the rest of the rice. Cover the final layer of rice with a dry teatowel, tucking it well inside the casserole. (This makes the rice fluffy.) Cover with a lid and steam for 20 minutes on top of the stove (or for 25 minutes in the oven *without* the teatowel).

Meanwhile, gently heat the last 1 tablespoon oil and toss the pine kernels in it until golden-brown. When the polo is ready, take off the lid, remove the teatowel, scatter the top with the pine kernels and serve.

STIFADO (OR STIFATHO)

SERVES 6

Freeze 2 months
Will keep 4 for days under refrigeration

This traditional Greek casserole has a wonderful depth of flavour. It should be cooked very gently so that the meat which can be either lamb or beef, becomes meltingly tender in a rich dark brown sauce and the tiny onions stay whole. The olive oil is traditional and greatly adds to the taste of the dish.

2½ lb (1.1 kg) (2¼ lb (1 kg) when trimmed) braising steak or boned lamb, cut in 1½ in (3 cm) chunks
3 tablespoons olive oil
Very hot water
1 lb (450 g) small pickling onions or shallots, peeled
2 tablespoons tomato purée
5 fl oz (150 ml/⅔ cup) medium-dry fruity

red wine (such as Côtes du Rhône) or 5 fl oz (150 ml/⅔ cup) meat stock
2 cloves of garlic, peeled and crushed
2 bayleaves
1 stick cinnamon
½ teaspoon ground cumin seeds
1 tablespoon brown sugar
2 teaspoons salt; 15 grinds black pepper

Set the oven at Gas No. 3, 325 degrees F, 160 degrees C. Heat the oil in a frying pan or (preferably) stove-to-table casserole and quickly brown the meat on all sides — you will need to do this in two batches so as not to crowd the pan. Barely cover the meat with very hot water, cover the dish and transfer it to the oven. Cook for 1 hour.

Uncover the casserole and add all the remaining ingredients, stir gently, then cover and cook for a further 2 hours or until the meat is tender. (If the casserole is bubbling too fiercely at any time, turn the heat down.) When the meat is ready, add a little extra boiling water if the liquid has reduced too much — it should be a rich gravy. Remove the cinnamon stick and serve with rice or boiled potatoes.

Poultry

Although a bird of some kind is still cooked regularly for Shabbat in most Jewish homes, it is more often a roaster rather than the traditional fowl; however, this younger bird is usually casseroled rather than open-roasted in the conventional way. A fowl, or a portion of one, is still considered essential for making Chicken Soup.

Joints of chicken and the breast meat of both chicken and turkey are extremely popular for mid-week meals because they can be so quickly and easily prepared. Many poulterers also prepare chicken and turkey schnitzels, as well as boneless turkey 'roasts' which are so useful for the working wife. As a lean white meat, chicken is also enjoying popularity as a low-fat food. Chicken fat, on the other hand, has been largely superseded by vegetable oils and margarines, although if it is used in only small quantities, it still has an essential part to play in flavouring certain traditional foods such as knaidlach and Chopped Liver.

The dishes in this chapter, therefore, reflect this radical change in the kind of bird — and the way it is now cooked — in the majority of Jewish homes. There are recipes for cooking whole birds, both roast and *en casserole*, but there are more that use chicken portions, which are so useful when cooking for a large number of guests for parties and holydays. There is a variety of ideas for using the breast meat in kebabs, stir-fries and salads, and also suggestions for using chicken livers in quickly made main dishes.

ABOUT ALL KINDS OF POULTRY

- Most birds are now sold made **kasher** and ready to cook, but fresh birds are to be preferred to frozen as their texture and flavour are both definitely superior. (If necessary, see 'How to make kasher meat and poultry', page 114.)
- **Fowls** are specially bred for the Jewish market, unlike the non-kosher 'boilers' or 'steam roasters' which are often only mature laying hens. A fowl should weigh between 4½ and 5 lb (2¼–2½ kg) dressed weight. Pre-packed birds are sold without either feet or livers for reasons of kashrut.
- **Roasting chickens** to serve 4–6 should weigh between 4 and 5 lb (2–2½ kg) although birds weighing more than 6 lb (2¾ kg) are also available. For jointing into four use a smaller bird weighing between 3½ and 3¾ lb (1¾ kg).
- **Poussins** should weigh between 1¼ and 1½ lb (550–700 g) and will serve two if split down the back.
- **Chicken breasts** can be bought on or off the bone, while boned and skinned breast meat is sold by the pound, or cut for schnitzels, kebabs or salads.
- **Ducks** weigh between 4 and 6 lb (2–3 kg).
- **Turkeys** vary in weight between 8 and 20 lb (4–9 kg), though birds weighing as much as 30–40 lb (13–18 kg) are used by the butcher for schnitzels, rolls, roasts and goulash, as well as for smoking and sausage-making.
- **Game birds** are rarely available, though there is no reason why they cannot be used provided they have been slaughtered in the ritual manner.
- If you do have to buy frozen birds, here is a guide to **thawing times.** The bird is completely thawed when it feels cool (but not icy) to the touch and the legs feel pliable. The body cavity should be completely free from particles of ice.

Weight	At room temperature	In the refrigerator
2 lb (1 kg)	8 hours	28 hours
3 lb (1½ kg)	9 hours	32 hours
4 lb (2 kg)	10 hours	38 hours
5 lb (2¼ kg)	12 hours	44 hours
6 lb (2¾ kg)	14 hours	50 hours

- If you need to thaw a chicken urgently, and do not have a microwave, immerse it completely (still in its wrapper) in a bowl of cold water, changing the water several times until the bird is thawed (after 4 or 5 hours for a medium-sized bird).
- To thaw a turkey, allow between 24 and 48 hours in a cool larder, as size.
- Treat all thawed birds as fresh, and cook immediately or refrigerate until required.
- To **roast a chicken** to a mahogany brown and still keep it succulent, lay it on a rack in a roasting tin and paint it all over with a very thin layer of olive oil, then sprinkle it lightly with sea salt. Roast a 4 lb (2 kg) bird for 1½ hours at Gas No. 5, 375 degrees F, 190 degrees C, then baste it well and cook it for a further 15 to 20 minutes at Gas No. 6, 400 degrees F, 200 degrees C, until the skin is crisp and brown, and the juices run clear when the leg is pierced.
- A sliced onion laid beneath the bird will give a good colour to the juices from which the **gravy** can then be made.
- Always **rest** the bird in a warm place for 15 minutes before carving it. This allows the meat to 'settle' and makes it much easier to carve.
- **Poultry shears** are indispensable for portioning small cooked birds.

TWO ROAST CHICKENS AND A DUCK
POULET 'TRUFFÉ' AU PERSIL
PARSLEYED CHICKEN

SERVES 4–6   Freeze leftovers 2 months

This is my adaptation of a recipe by the high priest of 'cuisine minceur', Michel Guérard. A herb pâté is inserted between the flesh and skin of the bird, which keeps it juicy and flavoursome as it roasts without basting and in the minimum of fat to a wonderful mahogany brown. It is essential to use plenty of fresh herbs.

1 chicken (3½–4½ lb (1¾–2¼ kg) net weight)

1 level teaspoon sea salt; 15 grinds black pepper

THE STUFFING:
1 tablespoon soft margarine
4 rounded tablespoons chopped parsley (about 1 oz (25 g) of the fresh herb)
1 tablespoon snipped fresh chives
1½ tablespoons chopped fresh tarragon or 1½ teaspoons of the dried herb
2 shallots or half a small mild onion, finely chopped

FOR ROASTING:
2 teaspoons olive oil
1 onion, sliced

THE GRAVY:
8 fl oz (225 ml/1 cup) strong chicken stock or soup
1 tablespoon chopped parsley

135

Set the oven at Gas No. 5, 375 degrees F, 190 degrees C. Put the margarine into a small bowl and mix with all the other stuffing ingredients. Lay the bird on its back with its neck towards you. Starting at the neck, slip your fingers between the skin and the flesh and work them towards the tail to loosen the skin over the breast; then inserting your hand carefully, gently free the skin from each leg a little at a time, leaving the skin attached at the tip of the drumstick. Push the stuffing into place under the skin with the fingers of one hand, while moulding it evenly from the outside with the other hand. Paint the bird sparsely all over with the olive oil and sprinkle lightly with sea salt.

Place the bird in a roasting tin (preferably on a rack to allow air to circulate under the bird) and roast, breast side up, for 45 minutes. Turn it over, surround it with the sliced onion, and cook for another 45 minutes (30 minutes for a 3½ lb (1¾ kg bird). Turn breast side up again and turn the oven to Gas No. 6, 400 degrees F, 200 degrees C. Roast for another 15 or 20 minutes, or until the bird is a mahogany brown. Dish the bird and keep it hot in a warming oven (or turn the main oven down to Gas No. 2, 275 degrees F, 140 degrees C). Remove the onion from the roasting tin, and serve it separately if desired (it will have served its purpose of turning the juices from the bird a lovely brown).

The gravy Add the chicken stock and parsley to the juices in the tin, stir well and bubble until reduced by a third — in about 5 minutes. Serve to accompany the bird.

VARIATION

Poulet 'Truffé' à l'Hongrois (Chicken stuffed under the skin in the Hungarian manner) This is a more opulent recipe, prepared in exactly the same way as the Poulet 'Truffé' au Persil but using chicken liver pâté instead of the one made with herbs. Leave the bird to stand for 20 minutes before carving to allow the pâté to set; this makes it much easier to section the bird.

PÂTÉ:

8 oz (225 g) chicken livers
1½ oz (40 g/3 tablespoons) margarine, rendered chicken fat or chicken-flavoured vegetable fat

1 small (4 oz (125 g)) onion, coarsely chopped
1 fat clove of garlic, peeled and chopped
½ teaspoon salt; 10 grinds black pepper
Pinch each of ground nutmeg and dried tarragon

Grill (broil) the livers for 2 minutes on either side to make kasher and cook them (see page 114). Melt half the fat and slowly sauté the onion and garlic in it until they are a rich golden-brown. Put them in the food processor together with the cooked livers, the remaining fat and all the other ingredients, and process until absolutely smooth. Turn into a bowl and chill for 30 minutes, then use to stuff the bird as directed. Add 1 tablespoon of medium-dry sherry to the gravy.

PERFECT ROAST DUCK

SERVES 4

Do not freeze
Leftovers keep 2 days under refrigeration

Duck is not a favoured bird in the modern Jewish kitchen, perhaps because there are no traditional recipes for preparing it. However, inspired by a tasting of some new varieties of duck currently being bred for the table in Israel, I started on a quest to find the best way to roast this bird so that the flesh would be succulent and tender and the skin fat-free and a crisp mahogany brown. With a little help from the Chinese, who are the duck cooks par excellence, I discovered several very important secrets of success. Firstly, to dry the skin as thoroughly as possible — when they are preparing 'Peking duck' the Chinese spend 24 hours on this process, but I can never find anywhere in my kitchen to hang it for that long. Next, before it goes in the oven, to brush it with a sugar-and-salt glaze. Finally, at regular intervals, to pour off the fat that melts out of it, to prevent it from being re-absorbed into the skin.

1 duck, 5 lb (2¼ kg) in weight	**THE GLAZE:**
1 medium carrot, sliced	*1 tablespoon soft brown sugar and 1*
Good sprig of parsley	*teaspoon salt, dissolved in 3 tablespoons*
Salt and black pepper	*boiling water*
1 medium onion, sliced	

If the bird is frozen, defrost it overnight at room temperature or in the microwave, then refrigerate it until you are ready to prepare it.

To prepare the bird for the oven Dry the cavity of the bird with paper towels, then use fresh ones to dry the skin thoroughly, rubbing and blotting it as firmly as possible. Wrap the bird in more fresh paper towels and refrigerate it. An hour before you intend to cook it, take it out of the refrigerator and unwrap it. Sprinkle the body cavity with pepper and salt and insert the sliced carrot and the parsley. Set the bird, breast side up, on the rack of a roasting tin, paint it all over with the sugar-and-salt glaze, then leave it at room temperature until you are ready to cook it.

Set the oven at Gas No. 4, 350 degrees F, 180 degrees C. Allow 30 minutes roasting time to the pound (450 g). Put the bird in the preheated oven and leave for 30 minutes, by which time the fat under the skin will have started to melt. Take the duck out, close the oven door after it, then prick it all over with a sharp fork. Pour off any fat from the roasting tin, then put the tin back in the oven with the sliced onion beneath the bird. Pour off the fat in this way every 20 minutes. (The easiest way to do this is to lift the bird — still on the rack — on to an oven tray. It is then easy to tip the fat from the roasting tin into a bowl.)

Continue to cook for the calculated time, when the bird should be a rich brown with a very crisp skin — if you prefer it even darker, brush it with honey and turn the oven up to Gas No. 8, 450 degrees F, 230 degrees C for the last 20 minutes.

To section the roast bird This is best done in the kitchen. Use kitchen or poultry shears to cut along the breast bone, then cut through the backbone so that the bird is in two halves. To quarter, make a slanting cut between the ribs to separate the wing and the leg, so that each portion includes a share of the breast meat. The bird can now be kept hot for 20 minutes at Gas No. 1, 275 degrees F, 140 degrees C. Alternatively, cut off both legs, then carve off the breast meat in long thin slices. This is best done at the table.

SIMPLE DUCK SAUCE:
1 tablespoon duck fat
1 tablespoon flour
½ pint (275 ml/1¼ cups) duck stock

(made from the giblets) or ½ pint (275 ml/1¼ cups) chicken stock
1 tablespoon morello (sour red) cherry or apricot jam
Pinch of salt; 5 grinds of black pepper

Pour off all but 1 tablespoon of fat from the roasting tin, then stir in the flour and cook for 2 minutes until the flour begins to brown. Now add the stock, stirring well to incorporate any juices that have congealed on the bottom of the pan. Tip the sauce from the roasting pan into a saucepan, add the jam and bubble until reduced to a syrupy consistency, season and serve.

ORANGE LIQUEUR SAUCE:
1 oz (25 g/2 tablespoons) granulated sugar
1 tablespoon wine vinegar
¼ pint (150 ml/⅔ cup) each of duck (or chicken) stock and orange juice

2 tablespoons orange liqueur (such as Curaçao, Grand Marnier, Cointreau)

GARNISH:
1 orange, sliced, with its peel on
1 bunch of watercress

First make the caramel. (This stage can be omitted but it does give the sauce a wonderfully rich colour and flavour.) In a small heavy pan dissolve the sugar in the vinegar, and boil without stirring until the liquid turns a rich brown. Cover the arm holding the pan with a teatowel, then pour the orange juice all at once on to the caramel — the mixture will splutter violently! Stir over gentle heat until the caramel has dissolved, then add the stock (which has been swirled round the defatted roasting tin to gather up any of the juices). Simmer gently until syrupy, then add the liqueur and season to taste. Garnish the duck portions with the orange slices and sprigs of watercress and serve with the sauce.

CHINESE DUCK PANCAKES

SERVES 8   *Freeze unstuffed pancakes 3 months*

In China, even if a chicken or duck is roasted whole, it is always served cut up in little pieces to make it easy to manage with chopsticks. A favourite way of serving duck for a special occasion is to use it as a stuffing for an unusual kind of pancake which is made with a dough, rather than with the batter which is more usual in the West.

Although the Chinese serve these pancakes as part of the main course, they can also be served as a very original starter for a conventional western-style meal. The pancakes should be prepared while the duck is roasting and left ready under a teatowel not more than an hour before the meal.

THE PANCAKES:
1 lb (450 g/4 cups) plain flour
½ pint (225 ml/1¼ cups) boiling water
1 tablespoon sunflower oil
Oil for frying the pancakes

THE FILLING:
Crispy skin and little pieces of flesh carved from 1 duck, 4–5 lb

(1¾–2¼ kg) in weight, roasted as described on previous page
12 well-trimmed spring onions (green onions), cut into matchsticks, 2 in (5 cm) long
½ large cucumber, unpeeled, cut into pieces of the same size as the spring onions
¼ pint (150 ml/⅔ cup) (approximately) Barbecue sauce (also known as 'Hoi sin Sauce')

To make the pancakes Have ready a small crêpe pan, 6 in (15 cm) in diameter (non-stick if possible). Put all the ingredients into a food processor and process until

138

a dough is formed, then process (to knead it) for 1 minute.

(To mix by hand Put the flour into a bowl, mix the oil and water, then gradually add to the flour, mixing and kneading until a smooth dough is formed.) Divide the dough into three pieces and then cut each piece into eight. Roll each of these 24 pieces into a thin pancake, 6 in (15 cm) in diameter.

Heat the pan until you can feel strong heat on your hand held 2 in (5 cm) above it. Brush the pan lightly with oil, then turn the heat down to moderate, put in a pancake, then turn it over after 20 seconds when the underside will be a mottled brown. Cook the second side of the pancake in the same way, then insert it into a slightly damp folded teatowel to keep it soft until required. Repeat with the remaining pancakes.

To serve Remove the crisp skin and the flesh from the cooked duck, and cut into small pieces. Arrange them on separate plates with the matchsticks of spring onions and cucumber on two other plates. Fold the pancakes in half and arrange them on another plate. Each guest takes a pancake, opens it up, then spreads it with sauce, lays a little of the shredded vegetables on top followed by some duck and skin, then folds it in half before eating.

TWO WHOLE BIRDS EN CASSEROLE
POULET BONNE FEMME EN COCOTTE

SERVES 4–6   *Freeze 2 months*

It was the fond memory of his mother's kitchen and of the wonderful aroma that permeated it as she cooked a chicken en casserole that prompted a professional chef to adapt this peasant dish for the classic French cuisine. It's not surprising that this method of cooking the bird in a covered dish is very reminiscent of the Jewish housewife's traditional way with the Shabbat fowl, for it does not need the constant attention demanded by a plain roasted bird. The French country cook has always used a plump young chicken rather than a mature fowl to put in her pot, and now this practice has become more popular in the Jewish kitchen as an increasing number of younger birds are bred for the kosher market. It is a superb way of cooking chicken for a Friday night or a holiday meal; even a young bird remains succulent as it slowly turns to gold on a bed of tiny onions, new potatoes and fresh herbs.

1 roasting chicken (3½–4 lb (1¾–2 kg) net weight)
1 ripe eating apple
Olive oil
1 oz (25 g/2 tablespoons) margarine plus 2 teaspoons sunflower oil
2 dozen shallots or small pickling onions

1½–2½ lb (¾–1¼ kg) small new potatoes, well-scrubbed but unpeeled, or old boiling potatoes, peeled
Sea salt; black pepper
2 oz (50 g/4 tablespoons) margarine
2 teaspoons oil
4 sprigs of parsley
1 small bayleaf

Set the oven at Gas No. 3, 325 degrees F, 160 degrees C. Dry the chicken thoroughly, season the cavity with salt and pepper, then put in the apple, unpeeled and cut in

139

quarters. Tie the legs together so that the bird is a neat shape. Brush the skin lightly all over with olive oil — other oils can be used, but olive oil helps the bird to turn a very rich brown. Melt the margarine with the oil in a flameproof casserole just large enough to hold the bird, then lay the chicken in it breast side down. Cook for 2 or 3 minutes over moderate heat, then turn the bird over using two spoons so as not to pierce the skin. Continue turning and browning the bird until it is a rich golden-brown on all sides — don't be tempted to hurry the process, as it should take at least 15 minutes. Lift the browned bird out on to a plate and discard the browned fat left in the dish.

Meanwhile, prepare the onions and potatoes. Drop the peeled onions into a pan of boiling water and cook for 5 minutes, then drain. If old potatoes are used, peel them and cut in 1½ in (3 cm) cubes. Put the potatoes into a pan of *cold* water, bring slowly to the boil, then drain at once.

Put the 2 oz (50 g/4 tablespoons) margarine and the 2 teaspoons of oil into the casserole in which the bird was browned, add the potatoes and toss them in the fat for 2 or 3 minutes, until the surface is quite free of moisture and they are beginning to colour. Arrange round the sides of the dish and lay the browned bird in the centre with the drained onions on top. Season with coarse salt and pepper and add the herbs.

Cook on top of the stove until the fat at the bottom is sizzling, then put on the lid. Transfer to the oven and cook for 1 hour 30 minutes for a 3½ lb (1¾ kg) bird, or 1 hour 45 minutes for a 4 lb (2 kg) bird, basting once or twice during the cooking period — the leg will waggle easily in the socket when the bird is done. The bird can now be kept hot in the casserole in a low oven (Gas No. 1, 275 degrees F, 140 degrees C) for up to 30 minutes.

To serve Lift out the chicken and portion or carve as desired. Put on a hot dish surrounded with the potatoes and onions, and add the cooking juices from the casserole.

CASSEROLED FOWL, BURGUNDY STYLE

SERVES 6–8   *Freeze 3 months*

A fine plump fowl has perhaps more flavour than any other kind of bird. As its flesh tends to be dry, however, it is best braised slowly on a bed of lightly fried vegetables in a covered casserole. The bird can then be jointed, or the flesh taken off the bone, and masked with a sauce made from the puréed vegetables enriched with wine. It makes a simple but succulent dish. As a fowl is usually fat, it's best to cool the dish overnight, and then skim off the fat before finishing it next day.

1 fowl, 4½–5 lb (2¼–2½ kg) net weight
(any lumps of fat removed)
2 teaspoons each paprika and flour
1 level teaspoon salt; 15 grinds black pepper
1 tablespoon oil
1 large onion, thinly sliced
1 carrot, thinly sliced
2 soft tomatoes or 1 teaspoon tomato purée

1 medium green pepper, seeds removed, cut
into strips (optional)
3 stalks of celery, diced
1 bayleaf
1 clove of garlic, peeled and crushed
4 fl oz (125 ml/½ cup) chicken stock
8 fl oz (225 ml/1 cup) medium-dry red wine
2 teaspoons parsley or ½ teaspoon dried
fines herbes

Turn the oven to Gas No. 4, 350 degrees F, 180 degrees C. Mix together the flour, paprika, salt and pepper, and rub into the skin of the bird. In a heavy casserole just large enough to hold the bird, heat the oil and fry the bird until a pale gold all over. This will take about 15 minutes. Remove the bird from the casserole. In the same fat fry the onion until it is soft and golden, then add all the remaining vegetables, the bayleaf and the garlic and stir over gentle heat until they have absorbed most of the fat.

Put the bird back into the casserole. Pour the stock down the side of the dish, then cover and transfer to the oven. Once the liquid starts to bubble (after about 15 minutes) turn the oven down to Gas No. 1, 275 degrees F, 140 degrees C. Cook for 3 hours, turning once. Allow the bird to cool, then lift it out of the juices and wrap it in foil. Refrigerate. Purée the vegetables and juices from the casserole in a food processor or blender, then refrigerate overnight.

Next day, skin the bird, then joint or remove the flesh in large pieces. Lay in a shallow ovenproof casserole. Remove all the fat from the top of the vegetable purée. Put the purée into a small pan with the wine and heat until bubbly, stirring well. Taste and add the herbs. The sauce should be just thick enough to coat the bird; if not, thin it with a little chicken stock. Pour over the chicken pieces, cover and reheat in a slow moderate oven — Gas No. 3, 325 degrees F, 160 degrees C — for 30 minutes or until steaming hot. Don't allow it to boil or it will toughen the flesh of the fowl.

CHICKEN PORTIONS EN CASSEROLE

- It is useful to have a large, shallow, **flameproof casserole** or **sauté pan** in which the joints can first be browned and then cooked in the oven side by side. For large quantities, the portions can first be fried in the sauté pan, and then transferred to a very large roasting tin which can then be covered with foil.
- **Do not crowd the portions** in the sauté pan, or it will be difficult to brown them evenly on all sides, as they will give off too much steam.
- **Wine** gives a mellow flavour to a sauce, but chicken stock can be used instead if preferred.
- When **reheating** a casserole, bring it only to simmering point before serving it, as recooking may cause the flesh to become dry or to fall apart.

BIBLICAL CHICKEN

SERVES 6–8   Freeze 2 months

Honey, almonds and raisins are simmered in a lightly spiced orange sauce to make this exquisite dinner party dish. As the flavour of the sauce is so delicate I prefer to use only the breast portions of the chicken.

It is much easier to cut whole almonds into slivers if the blanched nuts are soaked in water for 15 minutes beforehand.

6–8 boneless and skinless chicken breast portions
2 tablespoons flour
1 teaspoon salt; 10 grinds black pepper
3 tablespoons oil plus a large nut of margarine
1/4 lb (125 g/1 cup) blanched slivered almonds
5 fl oz (150 ml/2/3 cup) orange juice
2 teaspoons grated lemon rind

1/2 pint (275 ml/11/4 cups) chicken stock plus 1/4 pint (150 ml/2/3 cup) medium-dry white wine or 3/4 pint (425 ml/2 cups) chicken stock
1 tablespoon liquid honey
2 small oranges, peeled, thinly sliced and the slices halved
3 oz (75 g/1/2 cup) raisins (muscatels if possible)
1 tablespoon lemon juice

Set the oven at Gas No. 4, 350 degrees F, 170 degrees C. Sprinkle the skinned and well-dried chicken portions with the flour seasoned with the salt and pepper, and leave.

Heat the fats gently, then sauté the slivered almonds until golden, remove and drain on kitchen paper. In the same fat, sauté the chicken portions on both sides until golden-brown. Remove the chicken from the pan. Discard as much of the fat as possible without pouring away the savoury brown bits in it, then add the orange juice, lemon rind, stock and wine (if used) and stir to incorporate any residue sticking to the pan. Stir in the honey and bring to the boil, then simmer for 3 minutes. Arrange the chicken portions side by side in a casserole and pour over the sauce. Cover and cook for 45 minutes.

Lift the chicken joints from the sauce on to a serving dish, arrange the orange slices on top, cover and keep warm in a low oven. Pour the sauce into a small pan with the lemon juice and raisins and bring to the boil. Simmer for 2 or 3 minutes until of coating consistency, re-season if necessary, then pour over the chicken, sprinkle with the nuts, and serve at once.

Note   For a dinner party, get the major part of the preparation over earlier in the day by frying the chicken joints, arranging them in their oven dish and making the sauce. When you are ready to cook the dish, heat up the sauce, pour it over the chicken, cover and cook as if newly fried.

CHICKEN WITH HERBS, COUNTRY STYLE

SERVES 4–6   *Freeze 3 months*

This is a simple dish with an uncomplicated flavour that can be cooked very comfortably on top of the stove or in an electric frying pan. There is no need for a sauce. The chicken joints are simmered in their own savoury juices together with mushrooms, potatoes and fresh herbs.

1 medium potato per person (1¼–1½ lb/ 550–675 g altogether when peeled)
4–6 chicken portions cut from a bird 4 lb (2 kg) in weight, or 4–6 breast portions on the bone
1 oz (25 g/¼ cup) flour seasoned with 1 teaspoon salt and 15 grinds black pepper

3 tablespoons oil
1 oz (25 g/2 tablespoons) margarine
4 oz (125 g/1 cup) mushrooms, quartered
2 tablespoons chopped fresh herbs (tarragon, basil, parsley, thyme) or 2 teaspoons mixed dried herbs

Peel the potatoes and cut into rough 1 in (2½ cm) cubes. Put in a pan of boiling salted water, bring back to the boil, cover and cook for 2 minutes, then drain well and dry off over a low heat. Coat the chicken joints thinly with the seasoned flour by shaking them together in a plastic bag. As each joint is coated, remove it from the bag and pat well to remove any excess flour.

Heat the oil in a wide frying pan or in an electric frying pan set at 360 degrees F, 180 degrees C. Add as many joints as will fit in without crowding the pan and cook until rich brown. As the joints cook, remove them from the pan. Add the margarine to the fat in the pan, put in the well-dried potatoes and turn in the fat until they go a pale gold, then lift out. Add the mushrooms and cook for 3 or 4 minutes until brown — they should absorb all the fat, but if not remove any remaining from the pan.

Put the chicken back in the pan, sprinkle with the fresh herbs, and surround with the potatoes. Arrange the mushrooms on top, then sprinkle lightly with salt and black pepper. Cover and cook gently for 10 minutes (300 degrees F, 150 degrees C in an electric frying pan), uncover, turn the chicken and gently stir the potatoes, then sprinkle again with salt and pepper. Cover and cook for a further 20 minutes or until the juices run clear and yellow from the dark meat and the legs feel tender. (If all white meat is used, it should be ready in a further 10 minutes only.) Uncover — the chicken will be sitting in a delicious sauce, and the potatoes will be crusty and tender.

Note The *frying* of the chicken can be done earlier in the day — if more than an hour in advance, refrigerate. Or the whole dish may be cooked in advance, and gently reheated when required.

CHICKEN RIVIERA STYLE

SERVES 6–8   *Freeze 2 months*

The chicken is cooked in a sauce flavoured with the first fresh vegetables of the Riviera spring. Of course, these are also available right through the summer months.

8 chicken joints (cut from two 3½ lb (1¾ kg) birds) or 6–8 breast portions (on the bone)
1 oz (25 g/¼ cup) flour seasoned with 1 teaspoon salt, 15 grinds black pepper, 1 teaspoon paprika pepper
4 tablespoons oil
1 large (8 oz (225 g)) onion, finely chopped
2 medium courgettes (zucchini), cut into ½ in (1¼ cm) cubes
1 red and 1 green pepper, seeds removed, cut in 1 in (2½ cm) wide strips
1 stick of celery, diced
5 fl oz (150 ml/⅔ cup) medium-dry white wine

2 large ripe tomatoes, skinned, seeds removed, and finely chopped or 4 canned tomatoes, drained and chopped
½ pint (275 ml/1¼ cups) chicken stock
1 large clove of garlic, peeled and crushed
1 sprig of fresh thyme or 1 teaspoon dried thyme
2 teaspoons herbes de Provence
1 level teaspoon salt; 10 grinds black pepper
20 whole stuffed olives
2 teaspoons cornflour (cornstarch), dissolved in 2 tablespoons cold water

GARNISH:
1 rounded tablespoon coarsely chopped parsley

Set the oven at Gas No. 6, 400 degrees F, 200 degrees C. Coat the chicken portions thinly with the seasoned flour by shaking them together in a plastic bag. Fry in the hot oil over medium heat until a rich brown. Remove from the pan, drain on paper towels and then put into a casserole.

Add the onion and all the vegetables (except the tomatoes) to the same fat and cook gently together until softened and golden, about 10 minutes. Add the wine to the pan and bubble fiercely for 2 minutes to concentrate the flavour. Now add the tomatoes, the stock and all the seasonings, and pour over the chicken joints — they should be half-covered by this sauce. Cover and cook in a quick oven (Gas No. 6, 400 degrees F, 200 degrees C) for 15 minutes or until bubbly, then reduce the temperature to Gas No. 3, 325 degrees F, 160 degrees C for a further 25 minutes or until a leg feels tender when pierced with a knife. (Allow 20 minutes if breasts only are used.)

Lift the chicken out on to a serving dish and keep warm. Add the dissolved cornflour to the sauce and bubble on top of the stove for 3 minutes, stirring in the olives so that they are heated through. Pour this sauce over the chicken and serve garnished with the chopped parsley.

Note If the chicken is to be frozen or left overnight and then reheated, do not add the cornflour mixture and the olives to the sauce until just before serving.

POULET À L'ESTRAGON
CHICKEN IN TARRAGON SAUCE

SERVES 6–8   *Freeze 2 months*

The delicate flavour of a young chicken cooked in a light wine sauce marries extremely well with that subtle herb, tarragon, to make a perfect dish for a summer's evening.

8 chicken portions (cut from two 3½ lb (1¾ kg) birds) or 6–8 breast portions (on the bone)
1 oz (25 g/¼ cup) flour seasoned with 1 teaspoon salt and 15 grinds black pepper
3 tablespoons oil
1 medium onion (5 oz (150 g)), finely chopped
½ pint (275 ml/1¼ cups) medium-dry white wine, such as white Bordeaux

½ pint (275 ml/1¼ cups) leftover chicken gravy, strong chicken stock or soup
1 fat clove of garlic, peeled and crushed
2 sprigs fresh tarragon or 1 teaspoon dried tarragon
1 bayleaf
Small bunch of parsley

GARNISH:
8 fresh tarragon leaves (if available)

Set the oven at Gas No. 6, 400 degrees F, 200 degrees C. Coat the chicken portions thinly with the seasoned flour by shaking them together in a plastic bag, then patting off any excess flour. Fry in the hot oil over medium heat until a rich brown. Remove from the pan, drain on paper towels and then put into a casserole.

Add the onion to the same fat and cook gently until softened and golden — about 5 minutes. Now add the wine to the pan and bubble fiercely for 2 minutes to reduce its acidity and also to concentrate the flavour. Add the stock, garlic, tarragon, bayleaf and parsley and pour over the chicken joints (which should be half-covered by the sauce). Cover and cook in a quick oven (Gas No. 6, 400 degrees F, 200 degrees C) for 15 minutes until bubbly, then reduce the temperature to Gas No. 3, 325 degrees F, 160 degrees C, for a further 25 minutes or until a leg feels tender when pierced with a knife (20 minutes if breasts only are used). Leave the lid off for a further 15 minutes to reduce the sauce. If it is still too thin, dish the chicken then boil down the sauce on top of stove until syrupy and pour over the bird.

Garnish with tarragon leaves.

For 12 servings Use three 3½ lb (1¾ kg) chickens, each cut into 4, or 12 breast portions. Double the other ingredients. Allow 25 minutes for the sauce to come to simmering point instead of 15 minutes, then complete the cooking as in the recipe.

COQ AU RIESLING CHICKEN IN RIESLING

SERVES 6–8   *Freeze 2 months*

This is a famous chicken speciality of Alsace, gently seasoned so as not to distract from the flavour of the incomparable wine. Alsatian Riesling is much drier than wine produced from the same grape grown in other parts of the world, so if it is not available use another medium-dry wine instead, rather than an ordinary Riesling which might well be too sweet.

8 chicken portions cut from two 3½ lb (1¾ kg) birds, or 6–8 breast portions (on the bone)
1 oz (25 g/¼ cup) flour seasoned with 1 teaspoon salt and 15 grinds black pepper
4 tablespoons oil
1 large (8 oz (225 g)) onion, finely chopped

½ lb (225 g/2 cups) button mushrooms
½ pint (275 ml/1¼ cups) Riesling d'Alsace or other medium-dry white wine
½ pint (275 ml/1¼ cups) strong chicken stock or soup
1 teaspoon dried herbes de Provence

Set the oven at Gas No. 6, 400 degrees F, 200 degrees C. Prepare and cook in the same way as 'Poulet à l'Estragon' except when the onion is softened and golden, add the whole mushrooms (stalks cut off level with the cap) and cook with the onions for a further 3 or 4 minutes until they have become softened, then add the wine and stock and continue as directed.

For 12 servings Use three 3½ lb (1¾ kg) chickens each cut into 4, or 12 breast portions, and the following ingredients:

3 medium (about 1 lb/450 g) onions
6 tablespoons oil
¾ lb (350 g/3 cups) button mushrooms

15 fl oz (400ml/2 cups) each wine and stock
1½ teaspoons herbes de Provence

Cook in exactly the same way as for the 12 servings of 'Poulet à l'Estragon'.

CRISP CHICKEN PORTIONS WITHOUT A SAUCE
CHICKEN OR TURKEY SCHNITZELS

SERVES 6   *Do not freeze*

Excellent schnitzels can be made by cooking chicken or turkey breast fillets in exactly the same way as the traditional veal. Israel, which has to import almost all its meat supplies from abroad, has pioneered the use of poultry as 'meat' in its own right, so if you order a schnitzel or escalope there it will almost certainly be turkey or chicken rather than veal. The schnitzels can be served either hot off the pan or at room temperature. They also make very elegant picnic fare.

146

6 chicken or turkey breast fillets, skinned
2 tablespoons lemon juice (about half a
lemon)
1 teaspoon salt; 15 grinds black pepper
Plain flour for coating
1 large egg, beaten

1 cup fine dry breadcrumbs or 1 cup medium
matzah meal
6 tablespoons sunflower oil

GARNISH:
Lemon slices
Chopped parsley

Lay each fillet between two pieces of greaseproof paper and pound with a cutlet bat or the end of a rolling pin until as thin as possible (this is important to ensure the schnitzel is cooked through in the brief time it is in the pan). Mix the lemon juice and seasonings in a shallow dish, turn the fillets in it to coat them, then leave in the dish for 30 minutes. Arrange the flour, beaten egg and crumbs (or meal) in separate shallow dishes, side by side. Toss each fillet lightly in the flour, patting off any excess with the hands, then brush with a thin layer of beaten egg and turn in the crumbs. Leave for at least 30 minutes for the coating to set, though longer (in the refrigerator) will do no harm.

In a large frying pan with a thick base, heat the oil until you can feel it comfortably warm on your hand held 2 in (5 cm) above the surface. Put in the fillets and cook steadily for 5 minutes on each side until crisp and brown. As they are cooked, put them side by side in a slow oven (Gas No. 1, 275 degrees F, 140 degrees C) to keep hot.

Garnish each schnitzel with a slice of lemon topped with a sprinkling of parsley. Serve them hot with new potatoes and a crisp green salad, or cold with a rice or tomato salad.

SESAME CHICKEN

SERVES 6   *Freeze 3 months (cooked or raw)*

These crunchy portions of chicken are coated with a mixture of sesame seeds, crumbs and herbs and are equally delicious hot or cold. They are cooked with only 4 tablespoons of oil yet they are as crisp as if they had been deep-fried. They make excellent 'freezer-fillers' because they can be frozen either cooked, or ready-coated and raw.

6 chicken portions or 6 boneless breasts,
skinned
4 tablespoons lemon juice

THE COATING:
1 egg
4 tablespoons sunflower oil
1 teaspoon salt; 20 grinds black pepper

6 heaped tablespoons coating crumbs or
medium matzah meal
6 heaped tablespoons sesame seeds
3 teaspoons dried mixed herbs or herbes de
Provence
1 teaspoon paprika
¼ teaspoon garlic salt or ½ teaspoon garlic
granules
Rind of 1 lemon, finely grated

To marinate the chicken 1 hour before cooking, put the lemon juice into a flat dish, turn the chicken pieces in it, then leave, turning once or twice during the hour.

To coat and cook the chicken   Set the oven at Gas No. 6, 400 degrees F, 200 degrees C. If matzah meal is used to coat the chicken or if the coating crumbs are very pale in colour, spread them out on a baking sheet, put in the oven as it heats up and toast until they are golden-brown (this gives a better colour to the cooked chicken).

Whisk the egg and oil together with the salt and pepper until well blended and then put in a shallow dish large enough to hold a portion of chicken. Mix the coating crumbs, sesame seeds, herbs and seasonings in a dish of a similar size. Have ready a lightly greased oven tray large enough to hold the portions, well spaced, side by side. Lay the chicken joints in the egg mixture one at a time, and use a pastry brush to coat them evenly with it, then roll them in the crumb mixture to coat them evenly, patting off any excess with the hands. Arrange on the baking sheet and cook for 40 minutes (30 minutes for the boneless breasts) until a rich brown. There is no need to turn the chicken as it will brown evenly on all sides. The chicken can be kept hot and crisp for up to 30 minutes in a warm oven, Gas No. ½, 200 degrees F, 110 degrees C.

USING CHICKEN BREASTS
GINGERED MUSHROOM AND CHICKEN KEBABS

SERVES 4 — *Do not freeze*

Fresh ginger, which is now widely available, adds a wonderful tang to the marinade for these juicy chicken kebabs. It will keep fresh for weeks if it is wrapped in foil and stored in the freezer. The ingredients can be speared either on four long metal skewers or on eight of the shorter wooden ones. Use either chicken breast fillets or four boned-out chicken breasts (which means the breast meat from two 3 lb (1 ¼ kg) birds). The grilled (broiled) kebabs will have a better colour if olive rather than sunflower oil is used for the marinade. For a low-fat diet, use only 1 tablespoon of oil but, as the kebabs are grilling, brush them frequently with extra lemon juice. Serve the kebabs on a bed of savoury rice, accompanied by a green or a tomato salad.

1 lb (450 g) skinned and boned chicken breast meat
3 tablespoons lemon juice
4 tablespoons olive oil
1 teaspoon salt; 15 grinds black pepper
Pinch of five-spice powder (if available)
1 tablespoon light soy sauce
2 teaspoons peeled and grated fresh ginger

½ lb (225 g/2 cups) firm mushrooms, each about 1½ in (4 cm) in diameter (stalks cut level with the cap)
1 each medium red and green pepper, seeds removed, cut in 1 in (2½ cm) squares

GARNISH:
1 tablespoon chopped parsley
4 lemon quarters

In a bowl, whisk together the lemon juice, oil, salt, pepper, five-spice powder, soy sauce and ginger. Cut the chicken into 1 in (2½ cm) chunks and add to the bowl, stirring well to coat it with the marinade. Leave at room temperature for 1 hour, stirring occasionally (longer in the refrigerator will do no harm).

148

When ready to grill (broil) the kebabs, lift the chicken pieces out of the marinade using a slotted spoon. Put the prepared vegetables into the remaining marinade, stirring well, so that the mushrooms in particular are well impregnated with it. Thread the vegetables and the chicken pieces alternately on the skewers, but to ensure that they brown evenly do not pack them too closely together. Cook for 10 to 12 minutes under a preheated grill (broiler), turning once or twice and brushing at the same time with the remaining marinade. (In a forced-air oven, grill for 15 minutes without turning but brush in the same way with the marinade.) Serve garnished with the parsley and lemon quarters.

STIR-FRIED CHICKEN BREASTS

SERVES 4   *Do not freeze*

Using the ancient Chinese technique of stir-frying, a superb dish for two (or more) can be cooked in less than 10 minutes. The secret is to have both the chicken and the vegetables cut into pieces of a similar size so that they cook in the same length of time, while the subtle flavourings of soy, fresh ginger, five-spice powder and chilli produce an almost 'instant' sauce. An equal amount of veal 'scallopine' can be substituted for the chicken.

A traditional wok is the ideal cooking utensil, but you can use a large frying pan with a thick even base (see 'Stir-frying', page 130) that can stand fierce heat instead.

½ lb (225 g/1⅓ cups) sliced chicken breast meat
½ teaspoon salt, 10 grinds black pepper and a pinch of paprika
1 tablespoon sesame oil
1 clove of garlic, peeled
1 in (2½ cm) length of fresh ginger root, peeled and cut in slivers
6–8 oz (175–225 g) of any fresh green or yellow vegetable such as broccoli,

cauliflower, courgettes (zucchini), mangetouts (snow peas) or carrots
Half each of a large red and a large green pepper, seeds removed
1 fat spring onion (green onion) trimmed
1 teaspoon sweet chilli sauce or a good pinch of cayenne
2 tablespoons light soy sauce
Good pinch of five-spice powder
2 teaspoons cornflour (cornstarch)
½ pint (275 ml/1¼ cups) cold chicken stock

To prepare the ingredients This can be done whenever convenient — it is the only time-consuming part of the recipe. Cut the sliced chicken into 2 × 1 in (5 × 2½ cm) pieces and sprinkle with the salt, pepper and paprika. Prepare the vegetables according to type as follows: Break the heads of broccoli in 1 in (2½ cm) pieces and slice their stalks ½ in (1 cm) thick. Break the cauliflower into tiny florets. Slice the unpeeled courgettes ½ in (1cm) thick. Leave the mangetouts whole or break in half. Cut the carrots, the peppers and the spring onion into julienne strips.
To cook the dish Heat the oil in a wok or heavy frying pan until it is almost smoking. Add the garlic and then the chicken and ginger, and stir-fry until the chicken loses its shiny appearance, after about 3 minutes. Add all the remaining ingredients (except for the stock and cornflour) and stir-fry until the vegetables are tender but still crisp, about 5 minutes. Mix the chicken stock gradually into the cornflour, then add to the pan. Cover and bubble for 1 minute. Serve at once with rice or noodles.

CHICKEN SANTA CRUZ, SAUCE SEVILLANA

SERVES 6–8 as a main dish, or 12–14 as part of a meat buffet

Freeze 2 months
The cooked chicken breasts will keep 3 days under refrigeration, the sauce 2 weeks

I have named this dish in memory of the Jewish inhabitants of Seville who were once confined in the 'Barrio de Santa Cruz' — the picturesque Jewish ghetto of that beautiful city. At the height of its fame in the fourteenth and fifteenth centuries, this community produced such illustrious Jews of the 'Golden Age' as the poet Aben Sharada, the mathematician Juda ben Balaam and the philosopher and statesman Isaac Abrabanel. By then the olives and oranges which figure largely in this dish had long been native to this part of Spain, and we know from their descendants, the Sephardim, that it was the custom amongst these Spanish Jews to cook with oil as in this recipe. But I cannot claim that this exquisite dish of fried breasts of chicken, stuffed with an olive and liver pâté and served with an orange sauce, can be linked with any degree of authenticity to that particular period.

The stuffed breasts are sliced and served at room temperature, accompanied by the cold fruit sauce. They look particularly fine set out on a large oval platter, as part of a buffet meal.

6–8 fairly thick boned chicken breasts
2 oz (50 g/½ cup) flour seasoned with 1 teaspoon salt and 10 grinds black pepper
1 egg, beaten
6–8 tablespoons dry coating crumbs or medium matzah meal
Oil for deep frying
½ lb (225 g) chicken livers
3 oz (75 g/⅓ cup) margarine or chicken-flavoured vegetable fat
Half a medium (5 oz (150 g)) onion, finely chopped
Half a clove of garlic, peeled

½ teaspoon salt; 10 grinds black pepper
1 bayleaf
2 tablespoons medium-dry sherry
2 oz (50 g/½ cup) stuffed olives

THE SAUCE:
Rind of half an orange and half a lemon
8 oz (225 g) jar redcurrant jelly
Juice of 1 orange and 1 lemon (5 fl oz (150 ml/⅔ cup) in all)
2 level teaspoons cornflour (cornstarch)
2 fl oz (50 ml/¼ cup) sweet Kiddush or port-type wine

To make the pâté This needs to be made first to allow time for it to firm up. Grill (broil) the livers to make kasher and cook them as on page 114, then cut each liver in half. Put half the fat into a frying pan and sauté the onion and garlic until they turn a rich golden-brown. Sprinkle with the pepper and salt, then add the livers and the bayleaf, and toss thoroughly together for 2 minutes. Remove the bayleaf, put the contents of the pan together with the sherry and the remaining fat into the food processor and process until it becomes a smooth pâté. Stir in the whole stuffed olives. Spoon into a basin and chill until firm, about 30 minutes.

To stuff and fry the chicken breasts Skin the breasts and trim off any fat. Using a small, sharp-pointed knife, make a horizontal slit half-way through each breast and insert a tablespoon of the chilled pâté, then press the opening closed. Have ready three containers, one containing the seasoned flour, one the beaten egg and one the coating crumbs. Coat each breast in turn, first with the flour, then the egg, and finally the crumbs, shaking off any excess. Chill the breasts for at least 30 minutes (more will do no harm) to set the coating.

Fry in two batches in the basket of a deep-fryer for approximately 8 minutes, or in a pan one-third full of oil heated to 375 degrees F, 190 degrees C (or when a small cube of bread will brown in 40 seconds) for 10 to 12 minutes, or until a rich brown. Lift out and drain on crumpled kitchen paper (paper towels). Leave at least 1 hour before serving. To serve, cut the stuffed breasts diagonally into ¼ in (½ cm) slices and garnish with strips of the blanched rinds.

To make the sauce This is served cold and will benefit by maturing in the refrigerator overnight. Use a potato peeler to remove the zest only (without any of the pith) from the fruit, then cut it into fine shreds and blanch in boiling water for 5 minutes. Turn into a sieve, rinse well under the cold tap and then drain and reserve. Put the redcurrant jelly into a small pan with the strained juices and bring to the boil, stirring until it has melted down. Mix the cornflour smoothly with the wine, then add to the boiling liquid and cook until clear, about 2 minutes, then cool and refrigerate.

CHICKEN SALAD, TAJ MAHAL

SERVES 6–8

Do not freeze
Keeps 2 days in the refrigerator

This splendid salad of curried chicken piled on a bed of savoury rice and garnished with slices of banana and red-skinned apple makes a magnificent presentation for a buffet lunch or after-theatre party. The particular kind of curry powder used is a matter of taste. I don't grind my own but use a very good proprietary brand.

1½ lb (675 g) cooked chicken breast meat or *the flesh from an entire roasted 4 lb (2 kg) bird*
½ pint (275 ml/1¼ cups) mayonnaise
1 tablespoon medium-strength curry powder
2 rounded tablespoons mango and ginger chutney
1 teaspoon grated peeled fresh ginger

THE RICE SALAD:
12 oz (350 g/2 cups) Basmati (long-grain Indian) rice

1¼ pints (725 ml/3 cups) chicken stock
1 large green pepper, seeds removed, finely diced
1 small can (8 oz/225 g) sweet pimientos, drained and finely diced
3 rounded tablespoons seedless raisins
6 tablespoons vinaigrette (see page 189)

GARNISH:
1 banana
1 red-skinned eating apple
Paprika pepper

To make the chicken salad The chicken can be roasted or poached as preferred. Remove all the skin and cut the flesh into bite-sized pieces. In a large bowl, mix together the mayonnaise, curry, chutney and fresh ginger. Stir in the chicken and leave covered until required. (This can be done at any time of the day, but allow enough time for the salad to stand for at least 30 minutes, to let the flavour develop.)

To make the rice salad   Bring the chicken stock to the boil and add the rice, cover and simmer for 15 minutes, then take off the heat and leave covered to steam for a further 5 minutes. Uncover — the rice will have absorbed all the liquid and can be fluffed up with a fork. Put into a bowl and add the green pepper, pimientos and raisins. Sprinkle with the vinaigrette, and mix gently with a fork or spoon. Refrigerate in a covered container for several hours.

To assemble the salad   Spoon the rice on to an oval platter, and pile the chicken salad on top. Just before serving, decorate round the edge with thin slices of unskinned apple and thicker slices of banana. Dust with paprika and serve.

POACHED CHICKEN BREASTS WITH MUSHROOM AND WINE SAUCE

SERVES 6–8   *Do not freeze*

To keep them tender and juicy the boneless breasts are cooked in individual foil parcels over a baking tin of steaming water. The steam creates a moist atmosphere in the oven so there is no danger of the chicken drying out. Served without the sauce, this is an excellent dish for a low-fat or slimming diet.

6–8 chicken breast fillets (about 4 oz (125 g) each), skinned

FOR EACH CHICKEN FILLET:
1 tablespoon medium-dry white wine
Sea salt and freshly ground black pepper
A square of foil large enough to enclose the fillet of chicken generously
A little oil

THE SAUCE:
8 oz (225 g/2 cups) white button mushrooms, thinly sliced

1 oz (25 g/2 tablespoons) margarine
4 shallots or the bulbs of 4 large spring onions (green onions), finely chopped
4 tablespoons medium-dry sherry
6 tablespoons white wine
5 fl oz (150 ml/²/₃ cup) chicken stock
2 teaspoons cornflour (cornstarch)
Good pinch of salt and nutmeg
Good pinch of white pepper
Juices from the chicken

Set the oven at Gas No. 4, 350 degrees F, 180 degrees C. Lay the squares of foil on the table and lightly brush with oil. Lay a chicken fillet on top of each and sprinkle with the sea salt and two or three grinds of black pepper. Gather up the sides of the foil to make a boat shape, then pour in the white wine. Seal the foil firmly into a crescent-shaped parcel, but do not press it too closely to the chicken as this would stop hot air circulating around it. Lay the parcels on a rack set over a roasting tin. Just before cooking, half-fill the tin with boiling water. Bake for 35 minutes. (The chicken fillets can be left in the foil in a low oven for up to another 30 minutes.)

Meanwhile, prepare the sauce. Over moderate heat, melt the margarine in a medium-sized pan, add the shallots and cook, stirring once or twice, for 5 minutes until they are softened and starting to turn colour. Add the sliced mushrooms and continue to cook until they too have softened, then add 3 tablespoons of the sherry and cook until there is only 1 tablespoon of liquid left in the pan. Add the white wine and simmer gently, uncovered, for a further 10 minutes, then stir in the stock mixed with the cornflour and seasonings. Simmer for 3 minutes, then add the rest of the sherry.

When the chicken is cooked, open the parcels, lift out the fillets and arrange on a serving dish, cover and keep warm in the oven now turned down low. Pour any juices from the foil into the sauce, bubble until of a coating consistency, then coat the chicken fillets with it and decorate with a little paprika and sprigs of parsley. Alternatively, the sauce can be served separately in a sauce boat.

CHICKEN LIVERS MAKE A MEAL
CHICKEN LIVERS WITH SAGE

SERVES 4   *Leftovers may be frozen for 2 months*

This is an Italian dish, prepared 'à la minute' and served with either savoury rice or new potatoes or a well-seasoned purée of potatoes or carrots.

1 lb (450 g) chicken livers
2 shallots or half a small onion, finely chopped
2 tablespoons rendered chicken fat or olive oil

12 garden-fresh or dried sage leaves
4 fl oz (125 ml/½ cup) Marsala or medium-dry sherry
Salt and freshly ground black pepper

Wash the livers thoroughly, cut in half if very large, then dry well. Grill (broil) for 2 minutes on either side to make kasher and cook them at the same time (see page 114 for details).

Heat the fat in a heavy frying pan and sauté the chopped onion or shallot over moderate heat until soft and golden. Add the Marsala or sherry and the sage leaves, stir well and boil briskly until only 3 or 4 tablespoons of syrupy liquid are left. Add the cooked livers, stir thoroughly to coat them with the sauce, season lightly with salt and black pepper and serve at once.

CHICKEN LIVER GOULASH WITH NUTTY RICE RING

SERVES 6   *Leftovers may be frozen for 2 months*

This rich and flavoursome chicken liver sauce can be served on a bed of noodles or boiled rice, but for a special occasion it looks splendid in a moulded ring of rice. This is an excellent dish for an after-theatre supper, served in individual cocottes and accompanied by hot herb rolls.

1 lb (450 g) chicken livers
3 tablespoons sunflower oil
1 oz (25 g/2 tablespoons) margarine
1 large onion, peeled and finely chopped
1 clove of garlic, peeled and finely chopped
1 large green pepper, seeds removed, cut in ½ in (1¼ cm) squares
½ lb (225 g/2 cups) mushrooms, thinly sliced, or ½ lb (225 g/2 cups) button mushrooms, stalks removed and left whole
5 fl oz (150 ml/⅔ cup) beef stock or chicken stock
1 teaspoon salt; 10 grinds black pepper
1 teaspoon dried Italian seasoning herbs

2 teaspoons tomato purée or tomato ketchup
3 fl oz (75 ml/⅓ cup) Marsala or medium-dry sherry
2 teaspoons cornflour (cornstarch)
2 teaspoons chopped parsley

THE NUTTY RICE RING:
2 oz (50 g/4 tablespoons) margarine
2–3 oz (50–75 g/⅔ cup) broken cashew nuts
1 small onion, finely chopped
12 oz (350 g/2 cups) long-grain rice
1¼ pints (725 ml/3 cups) boiling chicken stock
½ teaspoon salt; 10 grinds black pepper

Grill (broil) the livers for 2 minutes on either side to make kasher and cook them (see page 114). Cut them in two or three pieces according to size.

In a large frying pan or flameproof casserole gently heat the fats together, then add the onion and cook over moderate heat until it is soft and golden-brown. Add the garlic, pepper and mushrooms, stir well and cook for a further 5 minutes until softened. Add the cooked livers, the stock, seasonings, tomato purée or ketchup, and Marsala or sherry. Simmer, covered, for a further 10 minutes or until the peppers have softened but still retain a little crispness.

Mix the cornflour to a cream with 2 tablespoons of cold water and add to the pan, then bubble for 3 minutes to cook the starch. Stir in the chopped parsley. Turn off the heat and leave until required, then reheat until bubbling and use to fill the rice ring

To prepare the Nutty Rice Ring Heat the fat in a heavy stove-to-table casserole, and gently fry the nuts until golden. Remove with a slotted spoon. In the same fat, sauté the onion until soft and golden, add the rice and stir well, continuing to cook until the grains of rice look milky rather than translucent. Add the boiling stock carefully (it may spit), with the salt and pepper. Cover and put in a moderate oven, Gas No. 4, 350 degrees F, 180 degrees C, for 25 minutes or until the liquid has been completely absorbed.

Grease a 2½ pint (1½ litres/6 cups) ring tin very well, and scatter the base with the nuts. Put in the cooked rice, packing it down well. Foil-cover and return to the oven for 15 minutes. Turn out and fill with the chicken liver sauce.

To reheat the rice from cold Sprinkle the surface with 2 tablespoons water, fluff up with a fork, then cover and put in a slow moderate oven, Gas No. 3, 325 degrees F, 170 degrees C, for 20 minutes.

Vegetarian Dishes

THE NEW VEGETARIANS

Who are they, these new Jewish vegetarians, who are prepared to break with the eating traditions of three and a half thousand years? Most of them are not vegetarians in the strict sense of the word, for they do eat fish — and also meat — on very rare occasions. But they are part of a growing number of Jews who are making a conscious effort to eat less animal foods in favour of a higher proportion of the so-called 'natural wholefoods', a term that embraces a huge variety of cereals, pulses, fruits and vegetables which are relatively free of the chemical additives — stabilizers, emulsifiers, colourings, synthetic flavourings and preservatives — of the factory food technologist.

People have given me a variety of reasons for making such a radical change in their life style, apart from the ethical considerations that motivate the vegetarian movement as a whole. Many students find 'eating vegetarian' an acceptable way to stay within their budgets and skill keep kashrut; many young mothers believe that a modified vegetarian diet is good for their family's health; many older people find that the lighter, meatless meals make less demands on their digestion. So widespread is the interest among the Jewish community as a whole that the International Jewish Vegetarian Society has published a book entirely devoted to the subject of preparing traditional Jewish dishes, like Chopped Liver and Gefilte Fish, without any of the traditional ingredients — like liver and fish!

There are, however, no recipes of that kind in this chapter. Instead I have concentrated on dishes which are delicious in their own right because they are made from the freshest and most nourishing foods. Some of these dishes I have learned from friends who are vegetarians, and others I have adapted and adopted over the years from the cuisines of other food cultures. Others originate in Israel, where the number of people who have abandoned the meal patterns of their parents is now so great that they have more wholefood and vegetarian restaurants to cater for their tastes than can be found in the whole of London!

COURGETTE FRITTERS IN HAZELNUT SAUCE

SERVES 6–8   *Do not freeze*

It was while watching a woman frying a panful of 'churros' in the market in Mijas in Andalucia, that I suddenly realized that their crispness was due to the 'stretchiness' of the mixture, resembling a soft yeast dough, that she was using to shape them. At last I had solved the problem of how to make the perfect fritter batter!

In the recipe I worked out on my return home, bread flour is used to make the dough stretchy, and beer to give a similar effect to that of yeast. Vegetable fritters made with this batter will stay crisp after frying, even for up to an hour. The unusual nut-based mayonnaise comes from Turkey, where it is known as 'Khiyàr Terèturu'.

155

4 medium courgettes (zucchini)

THE BATTER:
4 oz (125 g/1 cup) bread flour
Pinch salt
2 tablespoons any oil
¼ pint (150ml/⅔ cup) beer
1 egg white

THE SAUCE:
3½ oz (100 g/1 cup) packet 'white'

hazelnuts (filberts) (that is, without skins)
2 cloves of garlic, peeled and crushed
2 oz (50 g/1 cup) fresh breadcrumbs
1 tablespoon water
4 fl oz (125 ml/½ cup) each olive and light oil (e.g. sunflower)
2 tablespoons wine vinegar
1 teaspoon salt
3–4 tablespoons water (as required)

Cut the courgettes in diagonal slices ⅜ in (1 cm) thick. Put all the ingredients for the batter, except for the egg white, into a blender or food processor and blend until smooth — about 1 minute (extra beating makes a better batter). When ready to cook the fritters, whisk the egg white until it holds stiff but glossy peaks, then fold into the batter.

Have ready a deep-fryer (or a pan one-third full of oil) heated to 360 degrees F, 180 degrees C, when a cube of bread will brown in 40 seconds. Using tongs to hold it, draw each courgette slice through the batter, shaking off any excess and put into the oil (don't crowd the pan). Cook until golden — about 4 minutes. Drain on kitchen paper. Transfer the fritters as they cook to a shallow dish placed in a slow oven, Gas No. 1, 275 degrees F, 140 degrees C (they will keep crisp for 1 hour).

To make the sauce Process the nuts on a blender or a food processor until they are ground fine, then with the machine still running, add the garlic, the breadcrumbs and the 1 tablespoon of water, followed by the oil, poured in a fine stream as for mayonnaise. Finally add the vinegar and the salt and process until light and creamy. Add extra water if necessary so that the sauce has the texture of whipped cream. Serve cold to accompany the hot fritters.

AUBERGINE FRITTERS WITH PIZZAIOLA SAUCE

SERVES 6–8

Do not freeze fritters
Freeze sauce 3 months

The cooked aubergine (eggplant) has a creamy texture which contrasts pleasingly with the crisp coating of batter.

1½ lb (675 g) aubergines (eggplant) (about 3 medium)
Fritter batter (see preceding recipe)

THE SAUCE:
1 can (15 oz (425 g)) tomatoes, canned in tomato juice

1 tablespoon tomato purée
1 tablespoon olive oil
1 level teaspoon each salt and sugar
10 grinds black pepper
1 level teaspoon mixed dried Italian herbs
2 fat cloves of garlic, peeled and crushed
2 level tablespoons finely sliced fresh basil **or** coarsely cut parsley

Peel and then slice the aubergines ⅜ in (1 cm) thick. Place a layer of the slices in a colander, sprinkle with salt, then cover with another layer. Repeat until all the slices are salted, then leave for 45 minutes before draining and patting dry.

Simmer all the sauce ingredients together in an uncovered pan until thick but still juicy, about 10 minutes on top of the stove, 5 minutes on full heat in a microwave.

Coat the aubergine slices with the batter and fry them as described for 'Courgette Fritters' (see preceding recipe). Serve warm, with the hot Pizzaiola Sauce.

CHAKCHOUKA   VEGETABLE RAGOÛT WITH EGGS

SERVES 4   *Do not freeze*

It can be eaten either hot or cold — as a starter with pitta or brown bread, as a low-calorie accompaniment to meat or fish instead of potatoes, or as a vegetarian lunch or supper dish. Chakchouka, a favourite dish in Israel, is a juicy vegetable ragoût topped with eggs, which are either stirred through the mixture (as in this Yemeni version) or left whole, as in the Moroccan and Tunisian Jewish cuisine. The combination of the sweet peppers and the hot cayenne pepper gives it a most pleasing flavour.

2 medium (5 oz (150 g)) onions, finely chopped
1 large clove of garlic, peeled and finely chopped
1½ tablespoons sunflower oil
2 large glossy green peppers
4 large tomatoes, skinned ('beef
variety is excellent) or 4 canned tomatoes, well drained
1 teaspoon salt; 10 grinds black pepper
¼ teaspoon cayenne pepper
2 tablespoons chopped parsley
4 eggs, whisked to blend yolks and whites

In an 8 in (20 cm) heavy-based saucepan or deep frying pan, heat the oil and cook the chopped onion with the garlic until soft and golden. Meanwhile halve the green peppers and remove the white pith and seeds, then cut into ½ in (1 cm) squares. Add to the softened onion, cover and cook for 5 minutes until the peppers have also softened and are beginning to colour. Add the quartered tomatoes, the salt, black pepper, cayenne pepper and parsley and simmer covered for a further 5 minutes. Uncover and continue to simmer until there is no free liquid and the mixture is soft and juicy. Add the eggs, then stir with a wooden spoon over a gentle heat until creamily set. Either serve at once, or allow to go cold.

To finish in the Moroccan or Tunisian style   Omit the whisked eggs. Break 4 eggs, and gently place each one on top of the simmering ragoût. Cover and poach until set, about 4 minutes. Serve hot.

HARICOT BEANS AND PASTA IN A HERB AND TOMATO SAUCE

SERVES 6   *Freeze leftovers 3 months*

I first tasted this quite wonderful dish in a vegetarian guest house in the romantically lovely setting of Keswick, the village which was one of Wordsworth's favourite haunts in the English Lakes. It was prepared for me by a man whom you might call an 'ultra-Orthodox' Jewish vegetarian, for he is also a Vegan and does not serve or cook with eggs. I certainly wasn't conscious of their absence in that day's lunch, which started with an apple, parsnip and potato soup with home-made brown rolls, went on to this bean and pasta main dish served with a green salad, and concluded with a chocolate chiffon flan set with extract of seaweed in a wholemeal (wholewheat) pastry crust. Mind you, after such a meal there was nothing for it but to take a quick walk up one of the local mountains!

There is no need to pre-soak the beans overnight for this recipe. After only 15 minutes soaking in boiling water, fresh (as opposed to stale) beans will have swelled to three times their size. The dish can be prepared well in advance and reheated. Otherwise allow 3 ½ hours cooking time from start to service.

10 oz (275 g/1½ cups) dried white haricot
(navy) beans, soaked for 15 minutes in
boiling water to cover
3 pints (1¾ litres/7½ cups) water
1 bayleaf
2 cloves of garlic, peeled
8 tablespoons olive oil
12 oz (350 g/3 cups) pasta (shells, bows or
wheels), cooked until tender

THE SAUCE:
12 oz (350 g) carrots
12 oz (350 g) celery

1 large onion
2 tablespoons olive oil
2 cloves of garlic, crushed
1 teaspoon sea salt; 20 grinds black pepper
1 teaspoon dried oregano
½ teaspoon dried basil
1 can (15 oz (425 g)) tomatoes, chopped
3 tablespoons tomato purée

GARNISH:
1 tablespoon chopped parsley
Bowl of finely grated cheese (optional)

Strain the beans and rinse them under the tap. Put them with the water into a large pan and bring to the boil, skimming off the froth with a wet metal spoon. Add the bayleaf and garlic and simmer gently for 15 minutes, then add the olive oil and simmer, covered, for a further 2¾ hours until the beans are tender. Discard the bayleaf and garlic floating on top. Drain the beans, reserving ½ pint (275 ml/1¼ cups) of the cooking liquid to use in case the finished casserole is too dry.

Meanwhile clean and chop the carrots and celery very finely — most easily done in a food processor. Chop the onion coarsely, and sauté gently in the olive oil in a deep pan until golden. Add the carrots and celery, the crushed garlic, and the salt and pepper. Sauté, covered, for 30 minutes; add the herbs, stir well, then add the chopped tomatoes and the tomato purée. Taste — you will probably need more salt as none was added to the cooking water for the beans (to avoid toughening their skins). Add the beans and the cooked pasta, and stir well. Add some of the reserved stock if necessary to make a thick, juicy mixture. Pile into a serving dish, scatter with the chopped parsley and serve with the cheese (if desired).

PISSALADIÈRE PROVENÇAL PIZZA

SERVES 6 as a main dish, 8 as a snack   *Freeze crust only 2 months*

This is the Provençal version of the Italian pizza. One of the more plebeian pleasures of a holiday on the Côte d'Azur is to munch a slice of Pissaladière hot from the oven of the local pâtisserie as you stroll through the Flower Market after a morning's sightseeing in Nice.

Do not let the yeast dough deter you from making this savoury pastry with its onion, olive and tomato topping flavoured with the aromatic herbs of Provence. The dough can be prepared whenever convenient, and then rolled out and stored in the freezer until you are ready to spread it with the topping. Allow an hour to defrost and then treat it as newly made. The 'easy-blend' yeast mentioned in the list of ingredients is treated like baking powder, and *must* be first mixed with the dry ingredients, unlike fresh yeast which can be mixed with the liquid.

If you do not wish to use the anchovies which are the traditional garnish to a Pissaladière, you can substitute sliced and sautéed mushrooms.

11 oz (300 g/2¾ cups) plain flour
1½ teaspoons each salt and sugar
1 sachet 'easy-blend' yeast (see page 265) or
scant 1 oz (25 g) fresh yeast
1 egg
2 tablespoons olive oil
5 fl oz (150 ml/⅔ cup) hand-hot water
2½ lb (1¼ kg) onions, peeled and very
thinly sliced (use food processor if available)
5 tablespoons olive oil
6 sprigs of parsley

Sprig of fresh thyme or ½ teaspoon dried
thyme
Small bayleaf
1 clove of garlic, peeled and crushed
1 can (7 oz (200 g)) tomatoes, drained
1½ teaspoons salt; 15 grinds black pepper
2 cans (2½ oz (65 g)) anchovy fillets,
drained, or 8 oz (225 g/2 cups) sliced
mushrooms
24 black olives (about 6 oz/175 g)
Little extra olive oil

To mix the dough: If fresh yeast is used Crumble the yeast into the bowl of the processor or mixer and add the sugar, water and a few tablespoons of the flour. Mix together, then add all the remaining ingredients and mix to a dough.
If 'easy-blend' yeast is used Put flour, salt, sugar and yeast into the bowl of the processor or mixer and process for 3 seconds or mix for 30 seconds. Add egg, oil and hand-hot water and mix to a dough.
To knead dough made with either yeast Process for 1 minute on the food processor or knead with dough hook for 5 minutes on mixer, adding 1 or 2 tablespoons extra flour if mixture is still too sticky. Turn out on to a floured board and knead lightly by hand for 30 seconds or until the underside of the dough is silky-smooth. Grease a large mixing bowl lightly with oil and put in the dough, then turn it over so that it is covered with a film of oil. Cover the bowl with clingfilm (saran wrap) and leave in a warm kitchen until the dough doubles in bulk — about 1 hour.
To prepare the topping Do this while the dough is rising. If mushrooms are used, sauté for 5 minutes in 1 tablespoon oil. Put the onions and oil in a frying pan with the

garlic and herbs. Cover, and cook gently for 25 minutes. Uncover, and stir in the tomatoes. Re-cover and cook slowly for a further 20 minutes until the onions are meltingly soft and have amalgamated with the tomatoes. Add the salt and pepper. Remove the bayleaf and the herbs. Turn into a bowl and leave to cool.

To assemble the Pissaladière Set the oven at Gas No. 6, 400 degrees F, 200 degrees C. Grease a shallow baking tin about 14 × 10 × ¾ in (35 × 25 × 2 cm) in size. Punch down the risen dough, then roll it out to fit the tin. Press it into the tin, making the edges rather thicker than the centre. Spread the onion mixture over the dough, arrange the anchovies or the sautéed mushrooms decoratively on top and sprinkle with a little olive oil to prevent the surface from drying out. Leave for 15 minutes, then bake for 20 minutes. Open the oven and quickly arrange the olives on top, then turn down to Gas No. 4, 350 degrees F, 180 degrees C, and bake for a further 15 minutes or until the edges are a rich golden-brown. Serve warm, cut into squares.

TYROPITTA CHEESE PIE, GREEK STYLE

SERVES 6–8   *Freeze raw 3 months*

You've been lying under a hot Greek sun all morning; now you lazily make your way to lunch, probably a buffet which the Greeks do so well, with all those delicious 'mezzes' - appetizers like taramasalata, hummus and the tiny vine-leaf dolmas. But perhaps the most delicious part of the meal will be the cheese pie with its spongy herb filling enclosed in layers of fragile fillo pastry, which the Greeks call 'Tyropitta'.

You may be surprised to learn that the wonderful filling is actually made with semolina (cream of wheat), enriched of course with eggs, herbs and feta cheese. If this Greek cheese is unobtainable, use a mixture of Cheddar and mild Lancashire instead. If you can't get fillo or strudel pastry, then flaky pastry can be substituted. The pie can be prepared and chilled the day before it is served, and then baked and served fresh the next day. Leftovers can be reheated.

3½ oz (100 g/½ cup) fine semolina (cream of wheat)
16 fl oz (450 ml/2 cups) milk
1 oz (25 g/2 tablespoons) butter
4 oz (125 g/1 cup) mature Cheddar cheese, grated
4 oz (125 g/1 cup) feta or Lancashire cheese, crumbled
1 oz (25 g/3 tablespoons) Parmesan cheese

4 eggs
¼ teaspoon ground nutmeg
8 tablespoons mixed chopped parsley and chives
1 teaspoon dried oregano
15 grinds black pepper; pinch salt (to taste)
12 sheets fillo or strudel pastry
About 3 oz (75 g/⅓ cup) butter, melted

Lightly grease with some of the melted butter a tin measuring 12 × 8 × 1½ in (30 × 20 × 4 cm); a roulade tin is excellent. Set oven when ready at Gas No. 5, 375 degrees F, 190 degrees C.

To make the filling In a heavy-based saucepan, mix the cold milk and the semolina with the butter. Stir constantly over moderate heat until thick and bubbly. Reduce heat and allow mixture to bubble for 2 minutes. Add the cheeses and stir until melted and smooth. Remove from the heat, and cool until steaming stops, stirring occasionally. Whisk the eggs to blend them, then stir in the nutmeg, herbs and

160

seasonings. Stir the egg mixture into the cooled cheese sauce.

To assemble the pie Take six sheets of the pastry and stack them on top of each other, first brushing each sheet thinly with some of the melted butter (leave the top sheet of pastry unbuttered). Lift these pastry sheets and place them in the baking tin, trimming off any excess — the pastry should cover the sides as well as the bottom of the tin. Pour in the cooled filling and spread it evenly over the pastry. Butter the remaining six sheets of pastry in the same way, then lay them on top of the filling, trimming them level with the rim of the tin. Brush the top layer with butter, then using a sharp knife cut through the top six sheets, marking them into squares. Sprinkle the top lightly with cold water to prevent the pastry curling.

Bake the Tyropitta for 40 minutes, then turn up the heat to Gas No. 8, 450 degrees F, 230 degrees C, for a further 8–10 minutes until crisp and golden-brown. Serve warm, cut in squares. May be kept warm in a low oven for up to 30 minutes.

MUSHROOM AND COURGETTE FLAN

SERVES 6   *Freeze 3 months*

Courgettes (zucchini) and mushrooms combine to give a very interesting flavour to this most delicious savoury tart, which is equally good served warm or cold. I have reduced the fat content of the filling by combining the eggs with a sauce, rather than the more usual cream. The pastry will be especially crisp (even though it isn't baked 'blind') if you use a dish made of brown ovenproof glass, as this absorbs the heat rather than reflecting it — as is the case with shiny metal or white pottery. The flan can be frozen but it is most pleasing when freshly baked, so I prefer to have a stock of the empty pastry cases in the freezer rather than the complete dish.

THE PASTRY:

8 oz (225 g/2 cups) wheatmeal (81% extraction) flour or 4 oz (125 g/1 cup) each wholemeal (wholewheat) and white flour
1 teaspoon baking powder
5 oz (150 g/½ cup plus 2 tablespoons) butter or sunflower margarine
1 teaspoon each dried herbes de Provence *and* fines herbes *or mixed herbs*
1 teaspoon dry mustard
1 teaspoon salt; 10 grinds black pepper
1 egg beaten to blend with 1 teaspoon vinegar and 1 tablespoon cold water

THE FILLING:

½ lb (225 g/2½ cups) each pinky mushrooms and fresh young courgettes (zucchini), thinly sliced
2 oz (50 g/¼ cup) butter or margarine
1 large onion, finely chopped
2 oz (50 g/½ cup) flour
½ teaspoon sea salt
Pinch of white pepper
¼ teaspoon ground nutmeg or mace
1 large bayleaf
¾ pint (425 ml/2 cups) plain or skim milk
1 tablespoon chopped parsley
2 large eggs, well beaten
2–3 tablespoons finely grated cheese for topping

The pastry Mix the flour(s) with the baking powder and seasonings. Use the fat straight from the refrigerator. Rub it in by hand or machine until no pieces larger than a small pea come to the surface when the bowl is shaken. *Don't* rub in further,

161

or the pastry will be difficult to roll out. Beat the egg with the vinegar and water to blend, then sprinkle on the flour mixture and gather into a ball. Roll out to fit a 10 in (25 cm) oven-to-table quiche dish. Prick the pastry all over, then chill for 1 hour or (preferably) freeze for several hours or longer as convenient.

The filling   (Allow to go quite cold before using.) In a lidded frying pan melt 1 oz (25 g/2 tablespoons) of the fat, add the chopped onion, then cook over moderate heat for 5 minutes until golden. Add the sliced mushrooms and courgettes, cover and cook for a further 5 minutes, until the courgettes are tender, then uncover and cook until the vegetables are colouring nicely and there is no free moisture in the pan. Put the remaining ounce (25 g/2 tablespoons) of fat, the flour, the milk and the seasonings into a saucepan. Whisk over moderate heat until a thick smooth sauce is formed, then bubble for 3 minutes. Remove the bayleaf, drop in the beaten eggs (reserve 1 tablespoon of egg for the glaze) and whisk until well blended, then reheat until simmering to cook the eggs. Add the cooked vegetables, stir well, then allow to cool.

Spoon the filling into the pastry crust, brush the surface with the reserved egg and sprinkle with the grated cheese. Bake in a quick oven, Gas No. 6, (400 degrees F, 200 degrees C) for 30 minutes or until golden-brown. Serve warm or at room temperature.

MUSHROOM CHAUSSON

SERVES 6–8   *Freeze 1 month unbaked*

In this exquisite dish, layers of puff pastry are sandwiched with sherry-flavoured creamed mushrooms. It can be made in a rectangle, rather like mille feuilles, but I think it looks more dramatic — and is easier to serve — when baked in a round as I describe below. To achieve a professional finish, use a glaze of egg yolk and cream.

Serve the chausson as a starter, or as a supper dish, with a green or tomato salad and wholemeal (wholewheat) bread.

1 lb (450 g) packet of puff pastry
1 egg yolk and 1 tablespoon reserved cream
Sesame seeds (about 2 tablespoons)

THE FILLING:
½ lb (225 g/2½ cups) open or closed
mushroom 'cups' sliced thinly through the
cap and stalks
1 oz (25 g/2 tablespoons) butter
2 teaspoons oil

2 tablespoons chopped shallots, spring onion
(green onion) bulbs or mild onion
3 tablespoons sherry
1 level tablespoon cornflour (cornstarch)
8 fl oz (225 ml/1 cup) single cream (light
cream or half-and-half) (save 1 tablespoon for
the glaze)
Pinch each salt and white pepper
¼ teaspoon ground mace or nutmeg
2 tablespoons chopped parsley

To make the filling   Melt the butter with the oil, then cook the shallots (or onion) gently for 2 or 3 minutes until softened but not browned. Add the mushrooms, stir well and continue to cook for a further 4 or 5 minutes until softened. Add the sherry and bubble for 3 minutes until it has almost evaporated — this concentrates the flavour. Put the cornflour in a small bowl and slowly stir in the cream. Add to the pan and cook for a further 3 minutes until thickened and smooth. Add the seasonings and the parsley. Allow to go quite cold.

162

To assemble the chausson   Set the oven at Gas No. 8, 450 degrees F, 230 degrees C. Have ready a baking sheet. Divide the pastry in half and roll into two circles, one (for the base) 10 in (25 cm) in diameter, the other (for the top) slightly larger. Lightly sprinkle the baking tray with water, then lay the pastry base on it, and spoon the filling on top, leaving a margin of about 1 in (2½ cm) wide all round. Brush this margin with water, then lay the second (larger) circle on top. Seal firmly together, then flake the two edges with a knife. (At this stage the chausson can be refrigerated and then baked later.)

Mix together the yolk and cream, then brush evenly over the chausson, avoiding the seal at the side (or it won't rise evenly). Scatter thickly with the sesame seeds. Bake for 15 minutes, then turn down to Gas No. 6, 400 degrees F, 200 degrees C for a further 15 minutes or until really crisp and richly browned. Cool for 10 minutes, then serve in slices like a pie. It may be kept warm at Gas No. 1, 275 degrees F, 140 degrees C, for up to 30 minutes.

MIXED VEGETABLE QUICHE IN A CRUMB CRUST

SERVES 6   *Freeze (cooked) 2 months*

For those who want a change from regular pastry, this nut-and-crumb mixture provides a delicious quickly made alternative. The filling has a very creamy texture — but it is made completely without cream!

THE PASTRY:
5 oz (150 g) fresh wholewheat breadcrumbs (made from 7 large slices)
4 oz (125 g/½ cup) soft butter or sunflower margarine
2 oz (50 g/½ cup) ground hazelnuts (filberts) or almonds

THE FILLING:
1 oz (25 g/2 tablespoons) butter or margarine
1 small pepper, seeds removed, cut into ⅜ in (1 cm) squares
1 small courgette (zucchini), thinly sliced (unpeeled)

4 oz (125 g/1 cup) pinky mushrooms, thinly sliced
1 packet (5 oz (150 g)) frozen spinach, defrosted and well drained
1 tablespoon snipped fresh dill or chopped parsley
1 lb (450 g) any low-fat soft cheese (such as Quark, sieved cottage cheese or curd cheese)
3 oz (75 g/¾ cup) mature Cheddar or Lancashire cheese, grated
2 eggs, well beaten
Good pinch of ground nutmeg
10 grinds black pepper; ½ teaspoon salt
Parmesan or other finely grated cheese

Set the oven at Gas No. 5, 375 degrees F, 190 degrees C. To make the case, process all the ingredients in a food processor or mixer, until they form a ball. Put this ball into a 9 or 10 in (about 25 cm) oven-to-table quiche dish, and spread with a fork to cover the bottom and the sides of the dish, just as though it were a regular pastry crust. Chill while you make the filling.

Sauté the pepper, courgette and mushrooms in the fat until softened, about 5 minutes, then add the spinach, and bubble until there is no free liquid left in the pan. Stir in the herbs and set aside. Put the cheeses into a large bowl and stir in the beaten eggs and the seasonings. Finally, add the cooked vegetables, mixing thoroughly. Spoon into the pastry case, and sprinkle thickly with the Parmesan cheese. Bake for 35 minutes or until the pie feels firm to gentle touch (don't worry if the centre is still a little soft). Remove from the oven and allow to cool on a rack for 20 minutes. Serve at room temperature with a salad and warm herb bread.

GNOCCHI VERDI AL BURRO E FORMAGGIO CHEESE AND SPINACH DUMPLINGS

SERVES 4–6 as a main dish, 6–8 as a starter

Freeze leftovers 1 month

These tiny cheese and spinach 'dumplings' are baked, without sauce, under a crisp coating of buttered crumbs. The dish can be prepared one day and baked the next. Serve it warm in the Italian manner, 10 minutes after baking rather than hot from the oven.

1 oz (25 g/2 tablespoons) butter
2 shallots or ¼ mild onion, finely chopped
1 packet (8 oz (225 g)) frozen chopped spinach, defrosted
8 oz (225 g/1 cup) ricotta or curd cheese
3 oz (75 g/¾ cup) plain flour
½ teaspoon ground coriander or nutmeg
1 teaspoon salt

2 egg yolks
1 oz (25 g/3 tablespoons) Parmesan or other sharp cheese, finely grated
3 oz (75 g/¾ cup) Cheddar cheese, grated
2 oz (50 g/4 tablespoons) butter, melted
2 oz (50 g/½ cup) Parmesan or other sharp cheese, finely grated
2 oz (50 g/½ cup) coarse dry breadcrumbs

Set the oven at Gas No. 5, 375 degrees F, 190 degrees C. Butter a large gratin dish.

Sauté the onion in the butter until it is a pale gold in colour, then add the spinach and cook, stirring, for 5 minutes or until it has absorbed the butter and there is no moisture from the spinach left in the pan. Transfer the mixture to a mixing bowl and stir in the ricotta (or curd cheese), the flour, coriander (or nutmeg) and salt, mixing thoroughly with a wooden spoon. Add the yolks and the grated cheeses and stir to blend. Transfer to a shallow container and put in the freezer for 10 minutes, to firm up.

Have ready a large pan containing 4 pints (2¼ litres/10 cups) of boiling water and 1 tablespoon of salt. Meanwhile make small pellets of the mixture, each 1½ in (4 cm) long and 1 in (2½ cm) wide, dipping your hands into flour only if the mixture is too sticky to mould. Drop 12 of the pellets into the boiling water and cook for 3 minutes *after* the water has come back to the boil. Lift out the gnocchi with a slotted spoon, lay in the buttered dish and add another 12 pellets to the pan. Repeat until all the gnocchi are cooked.

Mix the melted butter with the crumbs and stir in the cheese, then sprinkle the mixture in an even layer over the gnocchi. Bake for 15 minutes or until golden-brown and bubbly. May be kept hot for 20 minutes in a low oven (Gas No. 1, 275 degrees F, 140 degrees C).

MELANZANE ALLA PARMIGIANA
AUBERGINE, TOMATO AND CHEESE CASSEROLE

SERVES 6–8   *Freeze leftovers 3 months*

This famous Italian dish of aubergine (eggplant) layered with tomatoes and cheese is better served warm rather than hot, as it will then have set to an almost custard-like consistency — rather like lasagne al forno — and will be easy to slice. In the traditional recipe the aubergines are fried in oil, but to lighten the texture I prefer to grill (broil) them instead. The preliminary salting also helps to reduce the amount of oil that is required. If the cheese is too soft to grate easily, freeze it for half an hour beforehand.

3 lb (1½ kg) oval aubergines (eggplant), sliced diagonally ½ in (1 cm) thick
12 oz (350 g/3 cups) mozzarella or Edam cheese, coarsely grated
4 rounded tablespoons Parmesan or other finely grated cheese
3 oz (75 ml/⅓ cup) olive oil (for grilling the aubergines)

THE SAUCE:
2 tablespoons olive oil

2 medium onions, finely chopped
2 cloves of garlic, peeled and crushed
1 can (28 oz (800 g)) plum tomatoes, well drained
1 tablespoon tomato purée
2 teaspoons brown sugar
2 teaspoons dried oregano
1 teaspoon Italian seasoning
1 teaspoon salt; 15 grinds black pepper

Layer the aubergine slices in a colander, sprinkling each layer with 2 tablespoons coarse salt. Leave to sweat for 20 minutes. Meanwhile, set the oven at Gas No. 6, 400 degrees F, 200 degrees C, and make the sauce. Heat the olive oil and sauté the onions and garlic until soft and golden. Add all the remaining ingredients, cover and bubble gently, stirring occasionally, for 15–20 minutes until thick and juicy. If the mixture is too watery, boil it uncovered for a minute or two.

Wash the aubergine slices under running water to remove the salt, drain and dry either in a salad spinner or with a kitchen towel. Heat the grill (broiler) at the highest setting. Brush the slices on one side with olive oil and grill until golden-brown, about 3 minutes. Turn, brush with more oil and repeat with the second side. Continue until all the slices have been grilled.

To assemble the dish   Arrange a thin layer of tomato sauce on the bottom of a large gratin dish or individual dishes, then cover with a layer of aubergines, a layer of mozzarella (or Edam) cheese and a sprinkle of Parmesan. Repeat with remaining ingredients, ending with the cheese layer. Bake for 35–40 minutes until golden-brown and bubbly. May be served warm, reheated if this is convenient, or cold.

TOASTED SESAME AND BRAZIL NUT ROAST

SERVES 4   *Freeze leftovers 1 month*

This is a contemporary version of the traditional vegetarian standby, the nut roast, in which the sesame seeds are first toasted to bring out their otherwise elusive flavour. The 'roast' can be served plain with grilled (broiled) tomatoes, or accompanied by a Mushroom Sauce (see page 219).

2 oz (50 g/²⁄₃ cup) sesame seeds, toasted in a moderate oven or in a dry non-stick pan until golden-brown
6 oz (175 g/1¼ cups) Brazil nuts, grated coarsely
2 oz (50 g/1 cup) wholemeal (wholewheat) fresh breadcrumbs
3 tablespoons sunflower oil or margarine
1 large (7 oz (200 g)) onion, finely chopped

1 oz (25 g/4 tablespoons) wholemeal (wholewheat) flour
2 large fresh or 4 well-drained canned tomatoes, chopped
1 rounded teaspoon yeast extract dissolved in ¼ pint (150 ml/²⁄₃ cup) vegetable stock
20 grinds black pepper
1 tablespoon mixed chopped fresh herbs (parsley, chives, dill as available) or 1 teaspoon mixed dried herbs

Set the oven at Gas No. 5, 375 degrees F, 190 degrees C. Grease a loaf tin or small ovenproof casserole, about 2 in (5 cm) deep. Put the sesame seeds, nuts and breadcrumbs into a bowl. Fry the chopped onion gently in the fat until softened and golden, about 5 minutes. Stir in flour and mix well, then add the tomatoes and the hot vegetable stock, simmering for 3 minutes before adding the pepper and the herbs. Stir this sauce into the dry ingredients and mix well. Spoon into the dish, and bake until golden-brown, 30 or 40 minutes.

INDIVIDUAL MUSHROOM SOUFFLÉS

SERVES 4 as a main dish, 8 as a starter   *Do not freeze*

If you enjoy soufflés, then it is worthwhile investing in the larger individual soufflé dishes (of 12 oz (350 ml/1½ cup) capacity), which provide one person with a satisfying main course. However, if the soufflé is to be served as a starter or as part of a mixed vegetable platter, then the normal 6 oz (175 ml/¾ cup) capacity is quite adequate.

The sauce part of the soufflé can be made earlier in the day and left to stand, then gently re-warmed until tepid, and the egg whites folded in as described below. Even soufflés that are ready for the oven can stand without baking for 20 minutes, providing they are covered with a dry teatowel to protect them from any draughts. The perfect soufflé should be spongy to the touch but still slightly creamy inside when it is opened up.

8 oz (225 g/2½ cups) pinky mushrooms
Half a medium onion or 3 shallots, very
finely chopped
1 oz (25 g/2 tablespoons) butter
Squeeze of lemon juice
2 tablespoons medium-dry sherry

THE SAUCE:
1½ oz (40 g/3 tablespoons) butter
1½ oz (40 g/6 tablespoons) flour

8 oz (225 ml/1 cup) milk
1 level teaspoon salt; 10 grinds black pepper
Pinch of ground mace or nutmeg
2 tablespoons thick (heavy) cream (optional)
1 tablespoon chopped parsley or scissored
chives
2 oz (50 g/½ cup) well-flavoured grated
cheese
4 large eggs, separated, plus an extra white

Set the oven to Gas No. 7, 425 degrees F, 210 degrees C. Put in a baking tray to heat up. Butter *either* four soufflé dishes of 12 fl oz (350 ml/1½ cups) capacity *or* eight dishes of 6 fl oz (175 ml/¾ cup) capacity then coat them with finely grated Parmesan or other cheese. Melt the butter, add the mushroom, onions (or shallots), lemon juice and sherry, cover and cook for 5 minutes. Uncover and allow to bubble until all the moisture has evaporated (about 3 minutes). Put the flour, butter and cold milk into another pan, and whisk over gentle heat (using a balloon or batter whisk) until a thick sauce is formed. Add the seasonings, cream and herbs, bubble for 3 minutes, then take off the heat and stir in all but 1 tablespoon of the cheese, the 4 egg yolks and the mushroom mixture.

Whisk the whites with a pinch of salt until they hold stiff, glossy peaks. *Stir* a quarter of the whites thoroughly into the sauce, then gently *fold* in the rest. Turn into the individual soufflé dishes and sprinkle the surface of each soufflé with the remaining cheese. Put the soufflés on to the tray that has been heating up in the oven. Turn the heat down to Gas No. 6, 400 degrees F, 200 degrees C. Bake for 15 minutes for small soufflés, 18 to 20 minutes for the large ones, or until a rich brown. Serve at once.

TOMATOES STUFFED WITH PINE KERNELS AND RICE

SERVES 6–8   *Do not freeze*

This makes a refreshing summer supper dish, perhaps accompanied by baked new potatoes and a Carrot and Hazelnut Salad (see page 196). Because the nuts have first to be shaken out of the dried pine cones and then the kernels themselves extracted by machinery, pine kernels (pine nuts) are always expensive, but they do have a delicious slightly 'piney' flavour, especially when they have been fried or toasted. They keep best in an airtight jar in the refrigerator. Split almonds can be substituted, but the flavour is not the same. If Italian risotto rice is not available, use any long-grain rice.

12–16 fat 'beef' or Mediterranean-type squat ripe tomatoes

THE STUFFING:
2 tablespoons olive oil
1 medium (5 oz (150 g)) onion
2 rounded tablespoons pine kernels (pine nuts) or split almonds
7oz (200 g/1 cup) Italian risotto (preferably) or long-grain rice
2 medium cloves garlic, peeled and crushed

1 rounded tablespoon currants
1 teaspoon cinnamon
1 tablespoon chopped parsley
1 tablespoon dried basil or 3 tablespoons chopped fresh basil
1 teaspoon dried herbes de Provence
15 fl oz (425 ml/2 cups) hot water or vegetable stock
1 teaspoon salt; 10 grinds black pepper
A little olive oil

Set the oven at Gas No. 5, 375 degrees F, 190 degrees C. Cut a thin slice from each tomato to make a cap. Scoop out the pulp and seeds and reserve for other use. Sprinkle each tomato with salt, then turn upside down to drain for 30 minutes. (Put a piece of paper towelling underneath a cooling tray to catch the drips.)

Heat the oil in a heavy-lidded saucepan, add the onion and cook until soft and golden. Add the pine kernels (or almonds) and cook until pale golden — watch they don't burn! Now add the rice, crushed garlic, currants, cinnamon and herbs, and turn in the fried onion until the rice begins to colour. Add the water or stock, salt and pepper, bring to simmering then cover and cook until the water has just been absorbed, about 10 minutes. Taste and add extra seasoning if necessary.

Arrange the tomatoes side by side in a greased ovenproof dish. Fill with the rice mixture and top with the 'lid' of the tomato. Sprinkle with olive oil, and surround with 2 tablespoons of water. Bake for 30 minutes.

SCALLOPED MUSHROOMS

SERVES 2–3   *Do not freeze*

This is a simple but extremely tasty and quickly made dish. Serve for a light lunch with granary bread and tomatoes or as a starter before a fish meal.

1 medium onion, finely chopped
2 oz (50 g/4 tablespoons) butter
½ lb (225 g/2½ cups) very fresh, pinky mushrooms, sliced finely

Pinch of garlic salt
½ teaspoon salt; 10 grinds black pepper
2 slices brown bread
2 tablespoons grated cheese

Melt half the butter, then add the onion, cover and simmer for 10 minutes until very soft and golden. Add the mushrooms and toss in the oniony butter for a further 5 minutes. Season well with the salt, garlic salt and black pepper. Put in a small shallow greased ovenproof dish. Melt the rest of the butter in the pan and add the bread, broken up with the fingers into tiny pieces — or, if you have the patience, cut into ⅜ in (1 cm) squares. When golden, mix with the cheese and scatter over the mushrooms. Grill for 3 minutes until a rich crunchy brown.

HOME-MADE YOGHURT

Do not freeze

The best yoghurt I ever tasted was in a remote village in that part of southern Turkey which seems to have been caught in a 'time warp' since the fourth century B.C.E., when Alexander the Great passed through on his way to the Persian Wars. That particular yoghurt had the flavour of a good 'smetana' and the texture of well-set junket, but even though the Turks seem to have thrived on it for more than two thousand years, I didn't dare enquire too closely into the conditions surrounding its preparation!

Fifteen years on, and the yoghurt cult is now firmly established in the West. But as things seem to go when traditional food is subjected to the sophisticated techniques involved in modern mass production and marketing, some of the charm of the original has been lost, and what was once a sharp and refreshing milk product has too often deteriorated into over-sweetened goo. There are exceptions of course, and there is a choice — between one kind which is firmly 'set' in the individual carton, and the other which is first incubated in huge stainless steel churns and then mixed to a creamy consistency, often with crushed fruit or juice.

Recently I've been making my own yoghurt and I've found to my delight that it has a very similar texture and flavour to that I enjoyed in Turkey, but with the big bonus of western standards of milk hygiene. My first yoghurt-maker was a very simple affair — a large vacuum flask in which warm sterilized milk was mixed with a 'starter' of natural yoghurt, and kept at a constant temperature just long enough to allow it to set. This is, in essence, the same method by which my grandmother used to make 'smetana', but she had no need for a 'starter' as she used naturally soured milk (easy before the days of pasteurization) which was left to set in small bowls in the warmth of an old-fashioned kitchen range.

Now I have acquired a much more scientific — and convenient — machine which removes any margin for error. The yoghurt is made in individual pots, each kept at a constant temperature by an electrically heated base. To the standard recipe that comes with the machine I add a couple of tablespoons of dried skim-milk powder, and the result is a thick, clean-tasting yoghurt costing about a third of the price of the commercial product. To make this into a fruit yoghurt, I stir in a teaspoon of home-made jam — blackcurrant, cherry, raspberry and strawberry are particularly delicious.

You can use natural yoghurt in any uncooked sauce that calls for soured cream. The big advantage is in the lower fat content — between 0.5% and 1.5% for low-fat yoghurt, and about 3.5% for whole-milk yoghurt, compared with 18% in the soured cream.

YOGHURT CHEESE

Makes about 1 lb (450 g) soft cheese
Do not freeze.
Keeps 1 week under refrigeration

This delicious soft cheese, known as 'labneh' in the Middle East, is the perfect base for sweet and savoury dips — see, for instance 'Labneh with Fruit and Vegetables,

169

Israeli Style', page 232. It can be made from either commercial or home-made natural yoghurt.

1½ pints (850 ml/4 cups) natural yoghurt
1 level teaspoon salt

THE EQUIPMENT:
A metal strainer with a medium mesh

A double thickness of cheesecloth, butter muslin or non-woven disposable kitchen cloth, large enough to line the bowl of the strainer and extend about 9 in (22 cm) beyond the rim all the way round

Dampen the cloth, then use it to line the strainer. Place the strainer on a basin of slightly larger diameter. Mix the yoghurt with the salt, then pour it into the strainer. Cover it loosely with the excess cloth, then leave it in a cool place overnight, or until the whey has stopped dripping from it. Turn it into a basin and add more salt, if necessary. Use in place of any soft milk cheese such as Quark or *fromage blanc*.

Vegetables, Rice and Pasta

Vegetables aren't what they used to be. There are new varieties to tease the imagination, new ways of preparing them to conserve their colour and crunch, and a new and growing recognition — especially among young people — of the importance of their role in the quest for a higher level of vitality and good health.

It's not so long since every vegetable had its season, and after that it was only available in a frozen pack for the remainder of the year. Now, on every day, in every month, there is a profusion of these out-of-season vegetables to be seen in every suburban greengrocery and supermarket. Even in the bleakest months of winter, when once nothing more exciting was on sale than cabbage and root vegetables, there are aubergines (eggplant) from Israel, beans from Kenya, courgettes (zucchini) from Spain, even parsley from Cyprus, to free us from the tyranny of the freezer and set the imagination of even the most conservative cook alight with new ideas.

The Jewish kitchen has not been slow to respond to this challenge. *Everyone* is joining in the search for more innovative recipes which use different techniques to cook the vegetables, and for unfamiliar herbs, spices, nuts and seeds to garnish them.

In homes where cabbage was once only for stuffing, it's often stir-fried with a pinch of caraway seeds; green beans that used to be served plainly boiled may be stewed in a tomato ragoût or tossed with toasted sesame seeds. Even the new potato is no longer scraped bare of its skin, but is left in its jacket, crisped in a hot oven and then stuffed with a low-fat herb cheese.

I feel it in my own kitchen, this exciting wind of change. The only vegetable I boil with any regularity is the potato; the rest are steamed in a splash of water, either in a moisture-retaining stainless steel pan or in the microwave, or perhaps briefly stir-fried in a spoonful or two of oil — although fat as an ingredient has almost disappeared from my vegetable recipes. Even my freezer stock has changed. Now that it's no longer a mainstay of my cooking but only a 'safety net' for the busy day, it consists of little more than *petits pois* and the more interesting mixed vegetables, and my own garden beans and courgettes.

So in this chapter, I have considered vegetable cookery with new interest. I have concentrated on new techniques like stir-frying, new combinations of vegetables, new sauces that vegetables can actually be cooked in, new ways of presenting these foods for a special occasion. There are also suggestions for serving potatoes, rice and pasta — now rehabilitated as positive nourishment rather than just 'fillers' — for both family meals and dinner parties. Above all, I've concentrated on the texture and flavour of vegetables, to give them their rightful place among the most important of our daily foods.

THE GOOD COMPANIONS

Potatoes, pasta and rice are the traditional accompaniments to most main dishes of meat and fish, but today we expect them to contribute something more than calories

171

to a meal. That's why brown rice and wholegrain pasta are now prized for their fibre and protein, and why potatoes are so often cooked in their skins so that the vitamin C they contain can be eaten rather than thrown away. Potatoes were also cooked without peeling in the Jewish households of two generations ago, but that was to save time rather than food value. Now we do both by cooking them in their jackets in the microwave. The small *new* potatoes that have a smooth rather than a paper-thin skin are delicious when quickly baked in a conventional oven. Serve them with low-fat yoghurt flavoured with black pepper and chives, or with a pat of one of the low-fat cheese pâtés on page 42, or with a small ripe avocado puréed with an equal volume of a low-fat soft cheese such as Quark, and seasoned with a squeeze of lemon juice and a good pinch of cayenne pepper.

The nicest kind of pasta is freshly made rather than dried. It's now sold in many supermarkets and delicatessen, or you can make your own with a food processor as described on page 6. When you do buy the dried packeted pasta, make sure the label says it's made with durum semolina — the cheaper ones produced from softer flours can become gluey when they are cooked. Egg noodles make a particularly savoury accompaniment when they are cooked in meat or chicken stock and then tossed with a very little olive oil and plenty of black pepper and fresh chopped herbs.

Basmati rice is my favourite for all savoury dishes, except when making the creamier kind such as risottos for which the Italian round-grain rice is definitely the best. It's wise to buy brown rice in a packet rather than from a sack, as it is of a much more consistent quality than the bulk variety which can often take an interminable time to become tender. Ordinary boiled or steamed rice acquires a whole new image when it's cooked with a few cardamom pods and a tablespoon or two of sultanas (white raisins).

Or you can always try beans!

RICE STEAMED IN THE PERSIAN FASHION

SERVES 6–8   *Freeze 3 months*
                                           Will keep 2 days under refrigeration

This method of cooking, which is always used by Iranian Jews to this day, ensures absolutely separate grains of fluffy rice. The carefully selected packeted rice on sale today does not need to be soaked for as long as in the traditional recipe, but in every other way the method I give below is identical to the one that was practised in Persia for centuries. After the rice has been briefly boiled, it is steamed under a teatowel in a pan whose base is covered with a thin coating of butter or oil. As the rice cooks, the lower layer absorbs this fat and becomes a crunchy titbit to offer to the honoured guest.

In Iran 'chilau', as this steamed rice is called, is used as the foundation for other dishes such as the Lamb and Apricot Polo on page 131, or it is served with a variety of aromatic sauces or 'khoreshta'. But I find myself using it more and more (but omitting the oil) as one of the best and simplest ways of cooking rice for everyday use. The large quantity of salt is not a printer's error — it is put in the water to keep the grains of rice separate but it is not absorbed by them, and in any case the rice is well washed afterwards. The rice can be reheated for 20 minutes in a moderate oven or in the microwave — sprinkle a little water on top, then cover with a lid to create the steamy atmosphere.

12 oz (350 g/1½ cups) Basmati (long-grain) rice
2 tablespoons salt
2 tablespoons oil plus 2 tablespoons

extra or 1 oz (25 g/2 tablespoons) butter plus 1 oz (25g/2 tablespoons) extra (for a milk meal)
1 tablespoon water

Soak the rice in cold water for 30 minutes, then strain and rinse thoroughly under the tap until the water runs clear. Bring a large heavy pan or casserole of water to the boil with the salt. Add the rice and cook uncovered, bubbling steadily, for 7 minutes or until a grain feels almost tender but still has a little resistance at the centre, when chewed. Turn the rice into the strainer and rinse thoroughly under the hot tap, then drain well.

Put the first quantity of fat into the pan with the water and heat until it steams, then spoon in the rice and cover with the second amount of fat. Finally, cover the rice with a dry teatowel, tucking it in well under the lid. Allow the rice to steam over a very low heat for 20 minutes. Either serve it plain, scraping the bottom of the pan well to loosen the crispy layers, or stir in the following garnish.

Carrot Garnish The carrot adds a beguiling sweetness to the rice and also gives it a pleasing appearance, speckled with gold.

1 onion, finely chopped
1 tablespoon oil
¾ lb (350 g/4 cups) carrots, finely grated

2 teaspoons sugar
1 teaspoon salt
½ teaspoon allspice (pimento)

In a heavy pan, sauté the onion in the oil until golden, then add the grated carrots, cover and allow them to cook in their own juice until tender, about 15 minutes. Stir in the seasonings, then blend carefully into the rice.

CRISPY KATAIFI

SERVES 6–8

Kataifi, sometimes called 'shredded wheat pastry', is really a kind of Middle Eastern noodle which looks rather like unravelled knitting. It is made by pouring a flour-and-water batter through a sieve on to a heated metal surface. It is mainly used to make a variety of delicious pastries which are stuffed with nuts and soaked in syrup, but it is also excellent when crisply fried like Chinese noodles. It makes a beautiful garnish for a stir-fry of meat or chicken, and also makes a tasty salted nibble to serve with cocktails.

Kataifi pastry is now sold in frozen packs by many delicatessen and Middle Eastern grocers. It will keep almost indefinitely in the freezer, but should be used within 4 days once it has been defrosted and kept in the refrigerator.

8 oz (225 g) kataifi pastry
A pan one-third full of oil heated to 375 degrees F, 190 degrees C, or

a deep-fryer heated to the same temperature

Defrost the amount of pastry you require, then reseal the remainder and refreeze at once. Use your fingers to separate the strands of pastry, rather as you would unravel a skein of wool. Put a handful of pastry into the frying basket and cook in the oil until it turns golden-brown, then lift it out and drain on kitchen paper, repeating the process until all the pastry has been fried. Serve at room temperature or reheat in a moderate oven until warm to the touch.

POTATOES PURÉED IN THE FRENCH STYLE

SERVES 6–8   *Do not freeze*

This is a very versatile recipe which can be adapted for either a meat or a milk meal by varying the liquid, and equally well either for 'lean cuisine' by omitting the fat or, for a special dinner party, by including lots of butter and cream, which is how the French prepare it. When it is topped by a thick crust of grated cheese, it is a very good dish to serve as part of a vegetarian main course. However you choose to prepare it, it is important to use a good 'boiling' potato such as Maris Piper, and to mash the potatoes over the heat so that steam rather than cold air is beaten in to lighten them — a hand-held electric whisk (beater) gives the best results.

Like all purées, this one is best served hot off the pan, but if this is not practicable it can be reheated either in the oven or the microwave, not longer than an hour after preparation. Do not keep it hot in the oven for more than 15 minutes, however, or the fluffy texture will be ruined.

2½ lb (1¼ kg) Maris Piper or other good boiling potato (weight when peeled)
1 teaspoon salt
4 tablespoons skim milk, whole milk or half-cream (for a milk meal) or hot meat stock (for a meat meal)

1 oz (25 g/2 tablespoons) butter or margarine (for a meat meal)
½ teaspoon white pepper, ½ teaspoon ground nutmeg
1 whole egg

Peel the potatoes, cut them into quarters and put in a pan containing sufficient boiling water to cover them. Add the salt, bring back to the boil, cover and cook at a steady boil for 15 minutes, or until there is no resistance when a small sharp knife is plunged into the centre of a piece of potato. Drain the water off, then return the pan to the stove and shake over a gentle heat until all the surface moisture has evaporated from the potato. Pour the chosen liquid down the side of the pan and when it starts to steam, add the fat (if used), the pepper and nutmeg. Whisk the potatoes (still over low heat) using a balloon whisk or portable electric mixer, until they lighten in colour and look creamy in texture. Whisk in the egg. Pile into a dish — for a dinner party, the mixture may be attractively piped into a lightly greased gratin dish.
To serve immediately Put under a hot grill (broiler) and cook until tinged with brown.
To serve later Reheat in a quick oven (Gas No. 6, 400 degrees F, 200 degrees C) for 15 minutes or until golden-brown. Or reheat in a microwave until hot to the touch, then brown under the grill.

POTATO AND ALMOND CROQUETTES

SERVES 6–8

Freeze 3 months (cooked)
May be reheated

The basic mixture for these croquettes is similar to that for a purée, but much firmer, with a pasty rather than a fluffy texture. To cook to an even gold, the croquettes need to be fried in deep fat, but they can be kept hot or reheated without losing their crispness. They are therefore an excellent choice for a dinner party menu. Defrost frozen croquettes for 1 hour at room temperature before reheating.

2¼ lb (1 kg) potatoes (weight when peeled)
1 teaspoon salt
2 egg yolks
2 oz (50 g/¼ cup) butter or margarine (for a meat meal)
2 tablespoons hot milk or stock (for a meat meal) (if necessary)
¼ teaspoon each white pepper and ground nutmeg

FOR COATING:
2 oz (50 g/½ cup) flour

2 whole eggs, beaten
4 oz (125 g/1 cup) each finely chopped almonds and dry breadcrumbs, mixed together

FOR FRYING:
A deep-fryer or an ordinary pan one-third full of sunflower or corn oil, heated to 375 degrees F, 190 degrees C (at which temperature a cube of bread will brown in 40 seconds)
Kitchen paper for draining the fried croquettes

Peel and quarter the potatoes, put into sufficient salted boiling water to cover and cook until tender when pierced with a sharp, slim knife, then return to a low heat to dry off thoroughly. Using an electric whisk if possible, whisk in the egg yolks and the fat, adding the liquid only if the mixture is very stiff. Season with the pepper and nutmeg, and extra salt if necessary, then turn on to a floured board, and divide into 16–18 pieces. Leave until cold, about 1 hour.

To shape the croquettes Put the flour, beaten eggs and mixed almonds and breadcrumbs into three separate bowls. Flour the palms of your hands, then form the cooled potato mixture into balls. Coat thinly with flour, then with egg and finally with the almonds and breadcrumbs. Chill until required, then fry in the deep hot fat until a rich brown, about 5 minutes.

To keep hot and crisp Leave at Gas No. ¼, 225 degrees F, 110 degrees C, for 20 minutes.

To reheat if necessary Put in a hot oven, Gas No. 7, 425 degrees F, 220 degrees C, for 10 to 15 minutes, or toss in a greased frying pan until hot to the touch, about 5 minutes.

GRATIN OF POTATOES, SAVOYARD

SERVES 6–8

Do not freeze
Leftovers will keep 1 day under refrigeration
Best reheated in the microwave

This is a convenient dish to serve with roast or braised meat for a dinner party, as it requires very little attention. Thinly sliced potatoes are baked in stock until they become soft and savoury at the bottom of the dish and golden and crispy on the top. The authentic French recipe includes grated cheese but I have omitted it so that the gratin can be served with a meat meal. If you have an ovenproof dish that can also go on direct heat, the gratin can first be heated until bubbly on top of the stove and then baked in a hot oven (Gas No. 7, 425 degrees F, 220 degrees C) for only 30 or 40 minutes, but for a dinner party it is probably more convenient to cook it more slowly as the timing isn't then so critical.

2½ lb (1¼ kg) boiling potatoes, sliced ⅛ in (¼ cm) thick (most easily done on the food processor)
Half a clove of garlic, unpeeled
3 oz (75 g/⅓ cup) margarine
1½ teaspoons (approximately) salt; freshly ground black pepper

⅛ teaspoon ground nutmeg
1 pint (575 ml/2½ cups) beef stock (made with a cube)
A fireproof dish, about 11 in (27 cm) long but no more than 2 in (5 cm) deep, greased with a little of the fat

Set the oven to Gas No. 5, 375 degrees F, 190 degrees C. Put the potatoes into a bowl and cover with cold water. Spear the half-clove of garlic with a fork, and rub all over the inside of the dish. Drain the potatoes and then dry with a towel as thoroughly as possible. Arrange half of them in the bottom of the dish, then dot with half the fat and sprinkle with half the seasonings. Repeat with the remainder of the potatoes, the fat and seasonings. Pour the boiling stock carefully into the dish — it should come just level with the top layer of potatoes but should not cover them. Bake for 1–1¼ hours until the potatoes are tender and the top is crispy brown. If the top layer seems to be drying out during the cooking, add a little boiling water.

FAN POTATOES

SERVES 6–8

Do not freeze

This is a very attractive way of presenting roast potatoes at a dinner party. Each potato is cut like a fan, and opens up as it cooks. The potatoes can be cooked at whatever temperature is most suitable for any other foods that are in the oven at the same time — though the lower the temperature, the longer they will take to brown. I allow 2 potatoes for each man and 1 for each woman guest, but you can adjust the numbers as you wish.

9–12 medium-sized roasting potatoes   3 tablespoons oil
1 teaspoon salt
2 oz (50 g/¼ cup) margarine

Peel the potatoes and then cut a thin slice off the bottom of each, so that they will sit evenly in the roasting tin. Put the potatoes in a pan, cover with cold water, add the salt, bring to the boil and cook for 5 minutes. Drain, then dry them off in the pan over low heat. When they are cool enough to handle, take each potato in turn, and make deep parallel cuts about ⅜ in (1 cm) apart from the top almost to the bottom, leaving it intact at the base. Choose the temperature that you prefer and roast the potatoes according to the table below. Set the oven and put a roasting tin containing the fat to heat up at the same time. When the oven reaches the correct temperature, take out the tin, put in the potatoes and baste them with the hot fat, then sprinkle lightly with salt. Return the tin to the oven and roast the potatoes in the usual way, basting twice, for the time given below.

Temperature	Cook for
Gas No. 3, 325 degrees F, 160 degrees C	1¾ hours
Gas No. 4, 350 degrees F, 180 degrees C	1½ hours
Gas No. 5, 375 degrees F, 190 degrees C	1½ hours
Gas No. 6, 400 degrees F, 200 degrees C	1¼ hours
Gas No. 7, 425 degrees F, 220 degrees C	1¼ hours

OVEN CRISP POTATOES

SERVES 6–8   *Do not freeze*

Although a roast or braise of meat can be safely left to cook without attention, it's very difficult to achieve really crisp potatoes when you are not there to turn and baste them, for instance on the morning of a Festival. One solution is to fry them *partly* beforehand — it can be as far in advance as the day before — and then finish the cooking in a very hot oven in a brief half-hour after synagogue. This is also an excellent dish to serve for a dinner party, as you achieve the effect of a sauté of potatoes without having to hover over a frying pan at the last minute. This method produces the most delicious golden-brown potatoes which are given added flavour by the fried onions and chopped parsley.

3 lb (1½ kg) potatoes, boiled in their skins   *2 medium onions, finely sliced (for sliced*
and then either sliced or cut into ⅜ in (1 cm)   *potatoes) or chopped (for cubes)*
cubes (see method below)
1 teaspoon salt   **GARNISH:**
3 oz (75 g/⅓ cup) butter (or margarine) plus   *Little sea salt; 15 grinds black pepper*
3 tablespoons sunflower oil, or 6 tablespoons   *1 tablespoon chopped parsley*
sunflower oil

Scrub the potatoes, then cook them whole in their skins, covered with boiling salted water, until tender — 25 to 40 minutes. (Test with the point of a sharp knife.) Drain off the water, then return the pan to the heat, and dry them off. Leave until they are cool enough to handle, then skin, and cut into ⅜ in (1 cm) thick slices or cubes.

To sauté the onions and potatoes Put the chosen fat(s) into a frying pan and heat until the warmth can be felt on the hand held 2 on (5 cm) above it. Add the onion, and cook gently until soft and golden — about 10 minutes. Remove to an oven tray wide enough to hold the onions and the potatoes in one layer — a roulade tin measuring about 14 × 10 × 2 in (35 × 25 × 5 cm) is ideal. Put the potatoes in the frying pan, stirring frequently until they are a light golden colour — they should slowly absorb the fat rather than fry in it. Turn into the tin and mix well with the onions. Leave until 40 minutes before serving.

To crispen the potatoes Preheat the oven to Gas No. 7, 425 degrees F, 210 degrees C (a slightly lower temperature can be used to suit other dishes cooking in the oven, but the potatoes will then take longer to brown). Put the dish with the potatoes and onions into the oven and cook for 30 or 40 minutes, until crisp and golden, shaking occasionally. The potatoes can then be kept hot for up to 20 minutes in a moderate oven until required. Turn into a serving dish, season with a few shakes of sea salt and the black pepper and sprinkle with the parsley. Serve piping hot.

STIR-FRYING

Stir-frying, or 'chow' as the Chinese call it, is really a form of 'instant cuisine', newly popular in the West because the cooking time is so brief that there is an amazing saving in both fuel and time.

It is a particularly suitable technique for cooking vegetables — I now use it more often than any other method except the microwave. It keeps them crisp and juicy, conserves their vitamin and mineral content, and does it all using the smallest possible amount of oil. Because the vegetables are cut up so small, one can blend several different shapes and colours, producing a very beautiful and original dish.

• Choose vegetables that harmonize with each other in colour, texture and flavour. You can cut them into shreds, slices, dice or julienne strips as you prefer, but it is important that all the pieces are of a similar size.

• The traditional high-sided pan or **wok** used for the stir-fry is made of iron, which quickly becomes rusty without constant care. You can buy a westernized version made of aluminium, and this is a good choice if you cook by gas, when the heat can easily reach right up the high sides of the wok. With an electric hot plate or a ceramic hob, however, I prefer to use a heavy frying pan which has a larger base that can make good contact with this kind of heating surface — a conveniently sized pan measures 8½ in (20 cm) across the bottom and is 3 in (7½ cm) deep, with a lid which can be used to steam foods if necessary.

• Always use **oil** in a stir-fry; the Chinese generally use peanut oil, but any flavourless oil such as sunflower or corn oil is equally successful. Do *not* use solid fats of any kind as they start to decompose before they reach the very high temperature that is required.

• To stir as you fry, use a large **spoon and fork** made either of metal or, if the pan has a non-stick lining, of heat-resistant plastic. Or you can use chopsticks, like the Chinese!

• Start by heating a couple of tablespoons of oil almost to smoking point — this means that the oil does not soak into the vegetables as in a sauté, but only softens them by contact with its heat. Cook the vegetables briefly in this hot oil, putting the harder and more fibrous ones in the pan first. Finally, season them, usually with soy

178

sauce, and serve them immediately — their delicate texture does not stand up to a waiting period of any kind.

• A **single vegetable**, such as cabbage or mangetout (snow) peas, can be fried by itself for a family meal, or a **variety of different vegetables** can be combined to produce a more elaborate presentation, to accompany a Chinese-style meal, or to serve as a vegetarian main dish.

One thing is certain, it has taken me longer to explain the technique than for you to put it into practice.

STIR-FRIED CABBAGE

SERVES 4

This looks very pretty when prepared from a mixture of red and green cabbage.

*Half a medium-sized green hearted cabbage
or one-quarter each of a red and green
cabbage, finely shredded
2 tablespoons oil*

*1 whole clove of garlic, peeled
½ teaspoon salt; 10 grinds black pepper
Good pinch of caraway seeds (optional)*

Heat the oil in a wok or frying pan, together with the garlic. When it is almost smoking add the cabbage, stir to coat with the oil, then stir-fry briskly for 2 or 3 minutes or until it is beginning to colour. Cover for 5 minutes to steam through, then uncover, season with the salt and pepper and stir in the caraway seeds.

STIR-FRIED MANGETOUT PEAS

SERVES 4–6

This is a favourite Chinese vegetable.

*2 tablespoons oil
2 whole cloves of garlic, peeled*

*1 lb (450 g) mangetout (snow) peas
1 teaspoon each salt and sugar*

Put the oil in the pan with the garlic and cook until the garlic begins to colour. Add the mangetout peas, and sprinkle with the salt and sugar. Turn the heat to medium and cook the mangetouts until they begin to colour and a pod feels tender but still crisp when eaten. Serve at once.

VARIATION
Stir-fried beans Use 1 lb (450 g) thin whole beans instead of the mangetout peas. Cook as above, but cover for 3 minutes if the beans are still not quite tender after they have been fried. Stir in 1 tablespoon of chopped parsley just before serving.

SPECIAL STIR-FRY OF MIXED VEGETABLES

SERVES 4–6

The vegetables blend and contrast with each other to create a dish with strong visual and taste appeal. If the baby sweet corn cobs are not available, use half a can of whole-kernel corn (well-drained) instead.

2 tablespoons oil
1 large whole clove of garlic, peeled
3 spring onions (green onions) (including the green) trimmed, then cut in 1 in (2½ cm) lengths
1 small can baby corn cobs, drained
1 medium carrot, cut in julienne strips
¼ head of very fresh cauliflower, divided in tiny florets, or 4 oz (125 g) broccoli, cut in tiny sprigs, with the stalks finely sliced
4 oz (125 g/1 cup) mushrooms, thinly sliced

Half a green and half a red pepper, cut in julienne strips
6 oz (175 g) fresh beansprouts
1 can Chinese 'straw' mushrooms or bamboo shoots (optional, but they do add interest)
1 in (2½ cm) peeled ginger root, cut in fine slivers
2 tablespoons soy sauce; 10 grinds black pepper
Pinch of salt, to taste
Pinch of five-spice powder

Heat the oil and garlic until the garlic turns brown, add the spring onions, corn cobs, carrot, cauliflower (or broccoli) and fresh mushrooms and stir-fry briskly for 2 or 3 minutes. Then add the peppers, beansprouts, straw mushrooms (or bamboo shoots) and ginger and stir-fry for another 3 minutes. Turn down the heat slightly and add the soy sauce, the black pepper and the five-spice powder, taste and re-season if necessary — the vegetables should now be tender but still crisp. Serve at once.

GREEN BEANS AND PETITS POIS, CHINESE STYLE

SERVES 6–8   *May be reheated*

This is a more sophisticated stir-fry suitable for a special dinner. The unusual combination of vegetables and toasted sesame seeds looks superb and has a most original taste and texture. The sesame oil adds a very distinctive flavour, but it can be omitted. The dish reheats well, either on top of the stove or in the microwave.

1 oz (25 g/¼ cup) white sesame seeds
1 lb (450 g) each fresh or frozen green beans and petits pois (spring peas)
1 level tablespoon butter or margarine

1 tablespoon sunflower oil
1 teaspoon sugar
1 teaspoon salt; 15 grinds black pepper
1 teaspoon sesame oil

In an 8 in (20 cm) heavy saucepan or a deep frying pan with a lid, toast the sesame seeds over moderate heat, tossing them in the pan until golden. Reserve. In the same pan sauté the peas and beans in the very hot mixed fats over moderately high heat, stirring constantly for 1 or 2 minutes until they are very well coated with the fat and have lost their icy appearance. Sprinkle with the sugar, cover and steam in their own juices for 5 or 6 minutes or until a bean feels just tender when it is bitten. If there is any free liquid at the bottom of the pan, cook briskly until it has evaporated. Take off the heat, sprinkle with the salt and pepper, the sesame oil and the toasted seeds and stir again. Serve piping hot.

TWO SPECIAL BEAN DISHES
GREEN BEANS SAUTÉ WITH TOASTED ALMONDS

SERVES 6

This is an excellent vegetable dish for a special occasion, as most of the preparation can be done early in the day. The split almonds can be toasted in a moderate oven, or under the grill, or in the microwave (see page 21).

1 lb (450 g) bobo beans or French beans
1 oz (25 g/2 tablespoons) butter (or
margarine for a meat meal)

2 oz (50 g/½ cup) blanched almonds, split
and toasted
½ teaspoon sea salt; 10 grinds black pepper

Earlier in the day, top and tail the beans if necessary. Bring a large pan of water to the boil with 2 teaspoons salt. Add the beans slowly, bring back to the boil (half-covering the pan to hasten the process), then boil for 5 or 6 minutes or until just bite-tender. Turn into a colander and drench with cold water to stop the beans cooking and to set the colour. Drain well, then refrigerate. Just before the meal, melt the butter or margarine in a heavy pan until it turns a light hazel-nut brown. Add the almonds and the beans, and toss thoroughly over a low heat, seasoning with the sea salt and black pepper. When steaming hot, dish and serve at once (though they can be kept hot in a low oven for not longer than 30 minutes).

VARIATION
Green Beans with Garlic Butter Omit the almonds, and add a good pinch of garlic granules to the melted fat instead.

181

FRENCH BEANS WITH PEPPERS AND TOMATOES IN THE FLORENTINE FASHION

SERVES 6–8

Whole green beans are simmered in a juicy tomato sauce flavoured with garlic and herbs. They go well with grilled (broiled) and roast meat and chicken. This is another very useful recipe for a dinner party as it can be made early in the day and then successfully reheated, either in a microwave oven or on top of the stove.

1½ lb (675 g) whole slim green beans (fresh or frozen), strings (if any) removed
2 tablespoons olive oil
1 large (8 oz (225 g)) onion, thinly sliced
2 medium-sized green peppers, seeds removed, cut into long strips
1 can (14 oz (400 g)) whole tomatoes in juice
1½ teaspoons salt; 10 grinds black pepper

2 teaspoons brown sugar
1 clove garlic, peeled and crushed
1 teaspoon Italian seasoning

GARNISH:
1 tablespoon fresh sliced basil leaves or 1 tablespoon chopped parsley

Heat the oil and sauté the onion until golden, 10 to 15 minutes. Add the peppers, the tomatoes with their juice and the seasonings and cook uncovered until as thick as ketchup (about 10 minutes). Add the beans and mix to coat them with the sauce, then stir in 6 tablespoons water. Cover and simmer for 15 minutes or until the beans are tender. Taste and re-season if necessary, then turn into a gratin dish and sprinkle with the herbs.

THREE WAYS WITH COURGETTES
BRAISED COURGETTES WITH HERBS

SERVES 6–8

May be reheated
Do not freeze

The courgettes (zucchini) cook in their own juices, without any attention. The dish can be got ready even the day before, but it should be freshly cooked for the meal. Do not use very large courgettes for this dish, as they tend to give out too much liquid. It can be adapted for either a milk or a meat meal.

1½–2 lb (675 g–1 kg) courgettes (zucchini)
2 oz (50 g/¼ cup) butter or margarine (for a meat meal)

2 teaspoons salt; 15 grinds black pepper
1 teaspoon dried basil

Preheat the oven to Gas No. 4, 350 degrees F, 180 degrees C. Lightly grease a lidded casserole or an 8 in (20 cm) diameter soufflé dish, 3–4 in (7½–10 cm) deep.

Wash but do not peel the courgettes, then slice them ½ in (1½ cm) thick. Arrange the slices in layers in the dish, dotting each layer with tiny dabs of the fat and sprinkling with the salt, pepper and herbs. Bake covered for 1 hour, until the courgettes are tender and juicy. The oven may now be turned down to Gas No. ½, 250 degrees F, 120 degrees C, and the dish kept hot for up to 20 minutes.

CHEESEY COURGETTES

SERVES 6 as a vegetable, 4 as a vegetarian main course   *Eat fresh on the day of preparation*

This is a good accompaniment to grilled (broiled) fish such as plaice, haddock or herring.

2 oz (50 g/¼ cup) butter
2 teaspoons oil
1 medium onion, finely chopped
2 lb (1 kg) young courgettes (zucchini), unpeeled, cut into ½ in (1 cm) thick slices
Sea salt; black pepper
1 teaspoon dried Italian herb mixture
8 oz (225 g/2 cups) grated cheese such as Edam or Cheddar

Have ready a shallow ovenproof dish. In a large frying pan, melt the butter, then add the oil and onion, and cook gently for 3 or 4 minutes until the onion has softened and begun to colour. Add the courgettes and cook at a gentle sizzle, turning them over frequently so that they are evenly browned. During this time, the onion will turn a rich golden-brown. When the courgettes feel soft when pierced with a knife, season well with salt, freshly ground pepper and the dried herbs. Arrange in the dish and cover evenly with the cheese. Grill (broil) gently for 4 or 5 minutes, until the cheese melts into a golden topping. Serve warm.

KISHUIM REHOVOT SAVOURY COURGETTES

SERVES 6–8   *Freeze 3 months*
Keeps 4 days under refrigeration
May be reheated

This delicious if rather fiery Israeli vegetable ragoût can be served hot with roasts and grills, as a starter or to accompany cold meats and poultry. It is a good way to use the more mature, less tasty courgettes (zucchini) as most of the flavour comes from the sauce.

1 large (8 oz (225 g)) onion, finely chopped
1 fat clove of garlic, peeled and finely
chopped
2 tablespoons olive oil
2 red peppers, seeds removed, cut in ½ in (1
cm) cubes
2 lb (1 kg) courgettes (zucchini), unpeeled
but topped and tailed and cut in ½ in (1 cm)
slices

1½ teaspoons salt; 10 grinds black pepper
1 teaspoon brown sugar
Good pinch of cayenne pepper
2 rounded tablespoons tomato purée
¼ pt (150 ml/⅔ cup) water
1 tablespoon chopped parsley

Heat the oil in a deepish frying pan or stewpan and cook the chopped onion and the garlic for 5 minutes, until softened and golden, then add the peppers and cook for a further 5 minutes until they are beginning to colour. Add the courgette slices, the salt, black pepper, brown sugar and cayenne pepper and cook covered for a further 10 minutes. Add the purée diluted with the water and bubble uncovered for about 5 minutes until thick and juicy, like ratatouille. Stir in the parsley. Serve hot or cold.

PARTY PEAS
CUCUMBER AND MINTED PETITS POIS

SERVES 6–8   Will keep 1 day under refrigeration

This makes a very pretty presentation in two shades of green. The delicate flavour of both vegetables marries well with salmon, trout or spring lamb. The cucumber can be prepared and cooked in advance but, to preserve their lovely colour, the peas should be cooked only just before serving. Alternatively, the whole dish can be prepared in advance, and then reheated in the microwave as this does not affect the colour.

1 fat cucumber, peeled
2 oz (50 g/¼ cup) butter (or margarine, for a
meat meal)
1 lb (450 g/3 cups) petits pois (spring peas)

Large sprig of fresh mint or 2 teaspoons
dried mint
1 teaspoon sugar
1½ teaspoons salt
¼ teaspoon white pepper

Cut the cucumber into 1 in (2½ cm) thick slices, then cut each slice into ¼ in (½ cm) thick vertical slices first one way and then the other, so that the cucumber is cut into julienne strips each ¼ in (½ cm) thick and 1 in (2½ cm) long. Put these julienne strips into the inner section of a salad spinner or a colander, sprinkle lightly with salt and leave for at least 20 minutes (though overnight in the refrigerator will do no harm). Rinse off the salt, then spin or shake to remove the moisture.

Melt the butter or margarine in a lidded frying pan and, before it can turn colour, add the strips of cucumber, bring to the boil, then cover and simmer for 5 minutes until they become translucent. Add the peas, the seasonings and the mint, stir well, re-cover and cook gently until the peas are tender, about 5 minutes. Uncover the pan, lift the vegetables into a serving dish with a slotted spoon, and boil down the pan juices until about 2 tablespoons remain. Spoon over the vegetables and serve.

SWEET AND SOUR RED CABBAGE IN THE SWEDISH STYLE

SERVES 6–8

Freeze 3 months
Will keep 4 days under refrigeration

Swedish cooks use a conserve made from lingonberries to flavour this delicious cabbage dish, but as it is hard to find, I have used one containing cranberries — which are very similar — instead. It is important not to overcook the cabbage so that it still has a little 'bite' left in it. It is good to serve with almost any hearty meat main dish.

1 baking apple, peeled and sliced into eight
1 large (8 oz (225 g)) onion, finely chopped
1 oz (25 g/2 tablespoons) margarine
2 level tablespoons soft light brown sugar
2½ lb (1 kg) (approximately) red cabbage, quartered, cored and finely shredded

4 tablespoons red wine vinegar
8 fl oz (225 ml/1 cup) chicken stock
1 teaspoon salt
2 rounded tablespoons cranberry jelly or sauce
10 grinds of black pepper

Heat the fat in a large heavy pan, then add the apple and onion, cover and cook for 5 minutes, stirring occasionally. Add the sugar and the cabbage, cover and cook for a further 5 minutes, then add the vinegar and cook for another 5 minutes. Finally add the stock and salt, and cook, covered, stirring occasionally for 1 hour or until the cabbage is tender, but still has a little 'bite' left in it. Just before serving, stir in the cranberry jelly or sauce, sprinkle with the black pepper and taste to make sure the flavour has a good balance of sweet and sour.

To cook in the oven   Preheat the oven to Gas No. 5, 375 degrees F, 190 degrees C. Use a flameproof oven-to-table casserole; otherwise you will need to start the cooking in a pan. When the stock is added bring the mixture to the boil, then transfer to the oven for a further 1 hour, or until bite-tender.

TOMATOES PROVENÇALES

SERVES 6–8

Do not freeze
Leftovers can be reheated, preferably in the microwave

To enjoy these as you would in Provence, you need to use the large deep red 'beef' tomatoes which are similar to those grown in the south of France. Be prodigal with the herbs — they are what this dish is mainly about. The tomatoes, with their crispy topping, make perfect partners for robust baked fish such as mackerel, or for lamb chops or steaks. They can also be served as a starter, with 6 chopped anchovies added to the filling.

6−8 firm ripe red tomatoes about 2½−3 in (6−7½ cm) in diameter (beef tomatoes)
Salt and pepper

THE FILLING:
3 tablespoons olive oil plus 1 tablespoon extra
3 tablespoons finely chopped shallots or spring onions (green onions)

1 fat clove of garlic, peeled and crushed
4−5 tablespoons chopped fresh parsley
1 teaspoon herbes de Provence
1 teaspoon dried basil or 1 tablespoon fresh basil (if available)
Good pinch of salt; 15 grinds black pepper
3 oz (75 g/1½ cups) fresh white breadcrumbs

Cut the tomatoes in half and gently scoop out the juice and seeds with a teaspoon. Sprinkle the insides lightly with salt and pepper and turn the tomatoes upside down to drain on kitchen paper.

To prepare the filling Heat the 3 tablespoons oil in a frying pan and sauté the shallots until soft and golden. Add all the remaining ingredients and mix well. Fill each half-tomato with some of the filling, and sprinkle with a few drops of the remaining olive oil. They may now be left until 20 minutes before serving. Preheat the oven to Gas No. 6, 400 degrees F, 200 degrees C. Bake the tomatoes for 15 minutes until they are tender but still hold their shape and the breadcrumbs are lightly browned.

Salads

The only salad that I can remember my mother making, when I was a small girl, was a typically *English* mixture of lettuce, cucumber, tomato and hard-boiled eggs, accompanied by the ubiquitous bottled mayonnaise. This is not altogether to be wondered at because when *she* was a girl, together with the other children of immigrant Jewish parents who attended the 'Jews' School' in Manchester, she was taught to be a 'good plain English cook' — and salads didn't rate very highly in English household cookery at that time.

This is clearly emphasized in the list of contents of a Jewish cookery book for schools, published in 1895. For amongst the 350 'typically English' dishes such as rice pudding and Cornish pasties which had been specially selected to help anglicize the cooking of this first generation of English-born Jewish children, there is only one salad — and that is the very one I remember from my childhood meals!

Nor were there many traditional salad recipes to be learned at home. With the exception of a Russian or a potato salad bought at the local delicatessen, for the Jewish housewife born in the Pale of Settlement 'salad' was synonymous with a single dish — sliced radishes, spring onions (green onions) and cucumber in a 'smetana' dressing.

But the picture was soon to change. The American *Settlement Cookbook*, published in 1926, already lists a hundred different salads for the Jewish table. From 1933 onwards, refugees from many of the countries of Europe — and in particular those from Hungary, Germany and Austria, who had a richer food culture than the Russian and Polish Jews — brought with them to their new homes in Britain, Israel and the United States a host of new ideas which have since become part of a new salad 'tradition' in Jewish households worldwide. Today, whether it be a private dinner party or a public charity luncheon, no table is complete without some kind of salad, and the lesson that raw fruit and vegetables are good for your health has been taken to heart by every Jewish housewife worthy of the name. So, in this chapter, you will find a selection from the huge variety of dishes representing the salad scene on Jewish tables today.

THE WAY TO SUPERLATIVE SALADS

● For the crispest possible **salad greens**, thirty years ago, I would put my washed lettuce into a wire basket, take it into the garden and whirl it round my head until the leaves were completely dry. The invention of a purpose-designed salad spinner has put an end to all that. Now the greens are spun round in a perforated basket, like clothes in a spin-drier, and the water is effectively removed by centrifugal force. To crispen the greens, I then wrap them loosely in a teatowel and refrigerate them for several hours until they are required. This method *never* fails.

Salad Oils

● I use three **oils** in my salad dressings — sunflower, olive and walnut (*huile de noix*) — and I have only specified a particular oil where its flavour is essential to the recipe.

187

- **Sunflower oil** is light in texture, tasteless and relatively cheap. I use it as an all-purpose oil either by itself or mixed with the other two more highly flavoured and expensive oils.
- For many years I paid lip service to the virtues of **olive oil**, wondering meanwhile what all the fuss was about, until on a visit to the Italian town of Sorrento I was given a jar of oil produced from the first pressing of the olives that grow above the town. Experimenting on my return home with this fruity, golden-green oil, I discovered that when it was judiciously used, it really did add a new dimension both to the flavour and the texture of even the simplest vinaigrette. Connoisseurs may debate whether Tuscan or Provençal oil has the finer flavour, but providing it is cold-pressed virgin-oil — *huile vierge fine* as it is described on a French label, *olio extra vergine* on an Italian one — there is very little to choose between them. Spanish olive oil is generally rather strong in flavour, and Greek olive oil tends to be heavy and thick, at least for dressing salads. Virgin olive oil is now widely available and some of the very finest is sold by those wine merchants who also specialize in wines from the areas where the oil is produced. Provided it is protected from the light, olive oil will remain in good condition for many months.
- **Huile de noix** (not to be confused with 'nut oil' which is a flavourless oil made from peanuts) is pressed from the superbly flavoured walnuts that grow in the Dordogne, in France. Its nutty flavour marries very well with that of the avocado, and it is also excellent in certain fruit salads and in those green salads that have a garnish of chopped nuts. It is even more expensive than the best olive oil, however, and is usually sold only in speciality food and kitchen shops, but it will remain in good condition for as long as olive oil, provided it is refrigerated to prevent it from going rancid.

Salad Herbs

- **Fresh herbs** are a new concept in western Jewish cookery: the yellow sprig of dill floating in the jar of 'heimische' pickled cucumbers is one of the very few examples of their use that comes to mind, unless you include garlic — 'knobl', as it is known in Yiddish — which is an essential flavouring for pickled cucumber, pickled brisket and wurst. Today, however, a wide variety of herbs are grown and used in the kitchens of Israel. There, as in southern Italy and France, they can be cultivated under a sun so hot and powerful that it intensifies their flavour in a way that is just not possible during even the sunniest summer in a more temperate climate. That is why I try to buy dried herbs that have been grown near to the Mediterranean. But when it comes to fresh herbs, I grow as many varieties as the garden (and our northern English climate) can sustain.
- The most useful herbs for salads, and the easiest to cultivate in the average garden, are **mint, parsley** and **chives**. However, if you have a greenhouse or a propagating frame in which the herb seeds can get off to a good start, you can grow more delicate plants like **tarragon, dill** and **basil** as well. You can, of course, buy young herb plants ready to go into the garden.
- For the reluctant gardener, an increasing number of **cut herbs** are sold pre-packed ready for use. When you buy fresh herbs, treat them as though they were newly picked by washing, drying and refrigerating them in a covered container as soon as you get them home.
- Fresh herbs can be treated exactly like other salad greens, so that instead of adding the *chopped* herb to the salad dressing, *whole* leaves of plants such as **parsley,**

coriander and **basil** can be added to the salad bowl in little sprigs instead.

• If you have to substitute **dried herbs** for fresh in the salad dressing, allow them to steep in it for at least an hour to draw out their flavour, using 1 teaspoon of the dried herb in place of 1 tablespoon of the fresh.

More Salad Secrets

• In a salad dressing, I prefer the clean, unadulterated flavour of **sea salt** to that of ordinary 'cooking salt', which has to be mixed with an anti-caking agent to keep it running freely. But just because it contains no additives, the sea salt is actually more salty, and less of it should therefore be used than ordinary salt.

• Almost every salad dressing, except for the most delicate in flavour, is improved by the addition of **garlic** in one form or another. For the merest hint of flavour, steep a whole peeled clove in the dressing for several hours, then discard it before use. For a really robust flavour — and this is the method I prefer — crush the clove to a paste using either the tip of a flexible knife or a self-cleaning garlic press. For occasional use the dried granules of garlic, which have a much longer shelf life than the fresh bulbs, are both convenient and effective. Never keep fresh garlic in an airtight container or it will quickly go mouldy.

• To segment **oranges** or **grapefruit**, equip yourself with a small vegetable knife with a razor-sharp serrated blade (this kind of knife is also invaluable for slicing other juicy fruits such as tomatoes and strawberries). Peel the fruit completely, at the same time removing the bitter white pith that lies beneath the skin, then cut between the sections of the fruit so that the flesh can be removed in pith-free segments, leaving the inedible 'skeleton' of the fruit behind. Squeeze this 'skeleton' over a bowl and use any juice that comes out in the salad dressing.

SALAD DRESSINGS
BASIC VINAIGRETTE

Makes 8 fl oz (225 ml/1 cup)   *Keeps indefinitely under refrigeration*
Sufficient for 2 green salads each serving
6–8

If the dressing is to be stored for more than two days, do not add any fresh herbs, as they will become discoloured.

6 tablespoons sunflower oil
3 tablespoons olive oil
3 tablespoons wine vinegar, cider vinegar,
sherry vinegar or lemon juice

1 level teaspoon each of sea salt and caster
(superfine) sugar
15 grinds black pepper
2 teaspoons English mustard powder or 1
rounded teaspoon Dijon mustard

Place all the ingredients in a screw-top jar and shake until thickened (1 or 2 minutes).

VARIATIONS
Herb dressing Stir in 2 level tablespoons chopped mixed herbs — parsley, chives, tarragon or dill, or any combination of two or more of them.

Garlic dressing *Either* leave a peeled clove of garlic in the dressing for at least an hour, discarding it before dressing the salad, *or* crush a peeled clove of garlic to a paste and mix with the other ingredients.

SHARP HERB AND WALNUT OIL VINAIGRETTE

Enough for 6–8   *Use up within 2 days*

This is a superb sauce for artichokes or avocados, or to dress any cooked vegetable. If you cannot get walnut oil (huile de noix) use a fine virgin olive oil instead.

4 tablespoons white wine vinegar or cider vinegar
2 tablespoons lemon juice
4 fl oz (125 ml/½ cup) sunflower oil and 2 tablespoons walnut oil (huile de noix) or olive oil
1 fat clove of garlic, peeled and crushed

2 level teaspoons caster (superfine) sugar
1 teaspoon Dijon mustard
2 tablespoons very finely chopped shallots or spring onion (green onion) bulbs
2 tablespoons chopped fresh mixed herbs — parsley, chives, tarragon
1 level teaspoon salt; 20 grinds black pepper

Put all the ingredients into a large screw-top jar and shake together until thoroughly blended and thickened — about 1 minute. Leave at room temperature until required.

PROCESSOR OR BLENDER MAYONNAISE

Makes 12 fl oz (350 ml/1½ cups)   *Do not freeze*
                                           Will keep 1 month under refrigeration

The high-speed emulsifying action of a blender or food processor makes it easy to produce home-made mayonnaise that is thick and creamy, and completely removes the fear of failure so often experienced when making it by hand. The flavour can be varied by using different oils; the mixture of olive and sunflower oils in this recipe produces a pleasant fruity sauce, with a light texture. Use eggs and oil at room temperature.

1 egg
2 teaspoons mustard powder
1 teaspoon caster (superfine) sugar
1 teaspoon sea salt
10 grinds black pepper
Good pinch of cayenne pepper

1 tablespoon lemon juice
8 fl oz (225 ml/1 cup) sunflower or other light, tasteless oil
2 fl oz (50 ml/¼ cup) fruity virgin olive oil
1 teaspoon wine vinegar

190

Put the egg and the seasonings into the blender or food processor and process for 30 seconds, then add the lemon juice and process for a further 5 seconds. Put the oils into a jug and, with the motor running, pour in a thin but steady stream on to the egg mixture — the mixture should lighten in colour and become creamy and thick. Finally process in the wine vinegar. Taste and re-season if necessary, then store in an airtight container in the refrigerator until required.

GREEN SALADS
SHADES OF GREEN SALAD

SERVES 6–8

A variety of leaves in different shades of green are tossed with slivers of marinated avocado to make a salad with tremendous visual appeal. I like to serve it with grilled (broiled) salmon for a spring dinner party.

1 small head of curly endive
2 lettuce hearts
3 pieces of chicory
1 bunch watercress
4 in (10 cm) section Chinese leaves (Chinese cabbage)
1 small green pepper, seeds removed, thinly sliced
1 medium-sized avocado, ripe but not squashy, peeled and thinly sliced

THE DRESSING:
4 tablespoons sunflower oil
2 tablespoons olive oil
2 tablespoons lemon juice
1 teaspoon French mustard
1 clove of garlic, peeled and halved
1 tablespoon finely cut chives
1 teaspoon salt; 10 grinds black pepper

Wash and dry the salad leaves (you can substitute the equivalent quantity of other leaves, according to the season), wrap them in a teatowel, lay them in the salad bowl and leave to crispen in the refrigerator. Whisk all the dressing ingredients together in a small bowl until thickened, then spoon over the green pepper and avocado. Cover and leave for several hours.

To serve Arrange the leaves in a salad bowl, add the pepper, avocado and dressing (first removing the garlic), then toss together gently until the leaves are evenly coated.

GUINEVERE'S SALAD

SERVES 6–8   *Use within 48 hours of preparation*

Because of its overpowering flavour of liquorice I had avoided using raw fennel in a salad until Guinevere — a Cambridge don who brings her daunting intellectual powers to bear on haute cuisine and on Celtic poetry alike — suggested marinating it in lemon juice. The transformation was quite magical. This is an exciting and original salad to serve as a separate course, and because the dressing is in no way assertive, it can be happily partnered by a glass of wine.

2 bulbs of fennel
2 tablespoons lemon juice
2 oz (50 g/½ cup) blanched split almonds
1 medium Iceberg lettuce

½ lb (225 g/2 cups) black grapes, halved and pips removed
About 2 tablespoons mild olive oil

The night before, cut out and discard the core of the fennel, then shred the bulbs as finely as possible. Put into a container, toss with the lemon juice, cover and refrigerate overnight. Toast the almonds either under the grill or in a moderate oven until they turn a pale brown, sprinkle lightly with sea salt and leave aside.
To assemble the salad   Shred the lettuce, halve and pip the grapes. Put in a salad bowl with the fennel, lemon juice and salted almonds. Add enough olive oil to make the leaves glisten. Serve within an hour.

SALAD MIMOSA

SERVES 6–8   *Use on day of preparation*

This delightful salad gets its name from the garnish of finely chopped egg, which looks for all the world like a spray of mimosa blossom. It was introduced to me by a friend who is an inspired exponent of French family cooking. She served it to accompany a main dish of veal cutlets and sauté potatoes, with which it made a most refreshing contrast — the slightly astringent flavour of the chicory and watercress softened by the sweeter undertones of mushrooms and hard-boiled eggs.

1 medium Iceberg lettuce
4 medium heads chicory
1 bunch watercress
2 oz (50 g/½ cup) very fresh button
mushrooms, stalks removed
2 hard-boiled eggs

THE DRESSING:
4 tablespoons sunflower oil

2 tablespoons olive oil
1 tablespoon each wine vinegar and lemon juice
½ teaspoon each sea salt and sugar
10 grinds black pepper
2 teaspoons English mustard powder
1 tablespoon any mixture of fresh herbs, finely chopped, plus a good pinch of herbes de Provence

Shred the lettuce, slice the chicory across into ½ in (1½ cm) rings, wash the watercress and cut off the coarse stalks. Slice the raw mushrooms very thinly. Arrange the well-dried salad greens and the mushrooms decoratively in a bowl. Chill.

Put all the dressing ingredients (except the fresh herbs) into a screw-top jar and shake until thickened. Leave for several hours for the flavour to develop.

Just before serving, grate the hard-boiled eggs finely on top of the salad (most easily done in a small rotary grater). Add the fresh herbs to the dressing and toss with the salad at table.

A TASTE OF ISRAEL'S SALADS

Dip into the salad bowls of modern Israel and you can sample many of the strands of culinary history that are today being woven together in this most cosmopolitan of countries. From the cornucopia of fruits and vegetables that flourish in its fields and orchards, professional and domestic cooks from both the East and the West have created dishes with a variety of taste and texture that is perhaps greater than anywhere else in the world.

On a blazing summer's day it's a special delight to come into the cool of some simple café, perhaps by the Old Harbour at Jaffa or in the shaded *souk* by Acre's Crusader fortress, and dip warm pitta bread into a bowl of the smoky, sesame-flavoured aubergine (eggplant) purée, 'Baba Ghanoush'. Or sitting in the shaded rough stone dining-room of 'Mea Naftoah' overlooking the blue Judaean hills, one can enjoy a hot and spicy Moroccan Carrot Salad or a cool, minty Lebanese cracked wheat salad called 'Tabbouleh'. By the shores of Lake Kinneret, the dairy restaurant of Kibbutz Ginossar will serve you a carrot and raisin salad of impeccable American pedigree, whilst in the Philadelphia Restaurant in East Jerusalem, a rainbow platter of fifteen exotic fruit and vegetable mélanges salutes the fading memory of centuries of Ottoman Turkish rule.

The archetypal salad of twentieth-century Israel is less subtle and sophisticated: a bowl of every raw vegetable imaginable, accompanied by oil, vinegar, yoghurt and other seasonings suitable to prepare a do-it-yourself dressing. This salad was the mainstay of the menu in many of the early communal settlements because it was quick and easy to prepare and together with rough country bread it made a satisfying breakfast for the workers after their early morning labours in the fields. Today, in a more elegant reincarnation, it is served as part of the lavish so-called 'Kibbutz breakfast' in every Israeli hotel.

MINTED ORIENTAL SALAD

SERVES 6–8

This is a classic dish amongst Jews from Syria and Egypt. It differs from similar salads served in other countries round the Mediterranean in the size of the pieces of vegetable — in the Israeli version they are cut into tiny, even cubes instead of the larger chunks familiar in Greek and Turkish salads. In the streets of Tel Aviv and Jerusalem this salad is to be found on every felafel stall — you spoon some into the pouch of your pitta bread as a refreshing foil to that fiery Middle Eastern food.

In the home, the glistening red and green cubes in their minted dressing make a stunning buffet salad to serve with any cold dish of fish, chicken or meat. Be generous with the herbs — they are an integral part of the salad, not just a garnish.

The vegetables and the dressing can be prepared well in advance, even the day before, but they should not be combined until an hour before serving or the delightful crisp texture will be ruined.

1 long fat and straight cucumber, unpeeled
(unless the skin is coarse)
4 large firm but ripe tomatoes
1 red and 1 green pepper, halved, seeds and
white inner pith removed

THE DRESSING:
3 tablespoons sunflower oil
1 tablespoon fruity olive oil

1 tablespoon each wine vinegar and lemon
juice
1 fat clove of garlic, peeled and crushed
1 level teaspoon salt; 10 grinds black pepper
1 teaspoon caster (superfine) sugar
1 tablespoon finely snipped fresh mint or 1
teaspoon dried mint
2 tablespoons chopped parsley

Cut each of the vegetables into even ⅜ in (1 cm) cubes or squares, then put the tomatoes and peppers into separate bowls, cover and refrigerate. Put the cucumber cubes into a salad spinner or sieve, sprinkle with 1 teaspoon of coarse salt and leave for 30 minutes, then spin or drain, and refrigerate. In a screw-top jar, shake together until thickened all the dressing ingredients except the fresh herbs. Add the dried mint (if used), then leave for several hours to mature in flavour.

To assemble the salad Put the cucumber, pepper and tomato cubes into a large bowl, then stir in the chopped parsley and mint together with the dressing, and mix well, using two spoons. Arrange the salad in a fairly shallow dish — it looks particularly effective against black or white. Serve cool but not chilled.

TABBOULEH CRACKED WHEAT SALAD

SERVES 8   *Do not freeze*

Cracked wheat makes an unlikely but surprisingly delicious salad ingredient, with a fascinating flavour — quite unfamiliar in the West — that can only be described as 'earthy'. Parsley and lemon juice are added with a very lavish hand to give this salad its very special character. Serve it when you would otherwise serve one made with rice or potatoes. Tabbouleh seems to improve in flavour as time goes by, and will keep under refrigeration for up to 4 days. Cracked wheat is also known as 'bulgar' or 'bourghul' and is sold at vegetarian and health food shops.

½ lb (225 g/1 cup) cracked wheat
6 tablespoons olive oil
4 tablespoons lemon juice
1 small bunch of spring onions (green onion)
bulbs, finely chopped (about 4 tablespoons)
2 teaspoons salt; 20 grinds black pepper

2 tablespoons chopped fresh mint leaves
1 cup finely chopped parsley (about 2 oz (50 g)
of the whole herb)

GARNISH:
Black olives, tomato and cucumber slices

Well in advance, put the cracked wheat into a heatproof bowl, cover with boiling water and leave for 2 hours to swell. Drain, then dry as thoroughly as possible, first squeezing out the moisture with your hand and then laying the cracked wheat on paper towels and patting it well. Put it back into the bowl and stir in all the dressing ingredients, mixing thoroughly to blend the flavours. Taste and add more salt or lemon juice if necessary — it should be tart but not sour. Serve the chilled Tabbouleh piled in an oval gratin or decorative dish and garnish just before serving.

MOROCCAN CARROT SALAD

SERVES 6–8

Do not freeze
Keeps refrigerated for up to one week

This is a very unusual relish salad, fragrant with cumin and fiery with cayenne, that can be served with other salads as a starter, or to accompany cold meats.

1 lb (450 g/3 cups) slim young carrots,
peeled and sliced ¼ in (½ cm) thick
1 pint water to cover them
1 teaspoon salt

1 teaspoon salt
1 teaspoon ground cumin
½ teaspoon Tabasco sauce or ¼ teaspoon
cayenne pepper

THE SPICE PASTE:
2 fat cloves of garlic, peeled and crushed
2 rounded tablespoons chopped parsley

TO FINISH:
4 tablespoons sunflower oil
3 tablespoons lemon juice or wine vinegar

Cook the carrots in the salted water until barely tender when pierced with a knife, about 5 or 6 minutes. Put to one side in their cooking liquid. Pound the ingredients for the spice paste in a mortar, or crush them together with the end of a rolling pin. Heat the oil in a small frying pan, then slowly stir in first the spice paste, and then 8 fl oz (225 ml/1 cup) of the carrot cooking water. Bring to the boil, then add to the carrots and the remainder of the cooking water. Stir in the lemon juice or vinegar. Chill in a covered container. The salad is ready the same day.

CUCUMBER SALAD IN THE GERMAN STYLE

SERVES 6–8

The cucumber is marinated in a caraway-flavoured dressing, lightened with a very little sweet or soured cream (which can be omitted for a meat meal). This is excellent served well chilled with grilled or poached salmon or chopped fried fish.

1 large or 2 medium cucumbers

THE DRESSING:
4 tablespoons salad oil
1½ tablespoons wine vinegar
2 teaspoons lemon juice

1 teaspoon salt; 10 grinds black pepper
1 teaspoon each French mustard and caster
(superfine) sugar
1 tablespoon single (light) or soured cream
(optional)
1 tablespoon chives or chopped parsley
1 teaspoon caraway seeds

Slice the unpeeled cucumber wafer-thin on a mandoline or food processor, and put into a bowl. Put all the dressing ingredients into a screw-top jar and shake (lid on) for 1 or 2 minutes until they form an emulsion. Pour over the cucumbers. Leave at least 1 hour before serving.

CARROT, RAISIN AND TOASTED HAZELNUT SALAD

SERVES 6–8   *Do not freeze*

This is a very nutritious salad, rich in carotene, calcium, iron and vitamin C, and with plenty of 'crunch'. To cut the calories, the mayonnaise can be omitted from the refreshing sweet-and-sour dressing, and extra yoghurt used instead.

1½ lb (675 g/4½ cups) young carrots, peeled and coarsely grated
6 level tablespoons raisins (seeded muscatels if possible)
2 oz (50 g/½ cup) toasted hazelnuts (filberts) (see below)

THE DRESSING:
¼ pint (4 rounded tablespoons) each of mild mayonnaise and natural yoghurt or ½ pint (275 ml/1¼ cups) thick natural yoghurt
2 teaspoons each lemon juice and orange juice
2 teaspoons soft brown sugar

Put the dressing ingredients into a bowl and stir well to blend, then mix in the grated carrots and the raisins, cover and leave for several hours. Meanwhile, toast the hazelnuts as follows: place the nuts on a metal tray and leave for 15 to 20 minutes in a moderate oven (Gas No. 4, 350 degrees F, 170 degrees C) until the nuts are golden-brown and bursting out of the papery skins. Wrap in a teatowel, leave for 5 minutes, then rub vigorously to remove the skins. (If you can buy hazelnuts without skins, this last step can, of course, be omitted.) Chop the nuts coarsely and store in an airtight container (they will stay crisp for several weeks) until required.

To serve Pile the salad lightly into a bowl and scatter with the nuts.

TOMATO SALADS
TOMATO AND BASIL SALAD ON A BED OF FENNEL

SERVES 6–8   *Do not freeze*

The flavour and texture of this salad are at their peak an hour after it has been made.

2 fat bulbs of fennel
2 tablespoons lemon juice
1½ lb (675 g) tomatoes, ripe but firm
1 small bunch spring onions (green onions), trimmed

4 tablespoons vinaigrette dressing (see page 189) plus an extra 2 teaspoons caster sugar
A handful of basil leaves, finely sliced or 1 tablespoon chopped parsley and 1 teaspoon dried basil added to the dressing an hour before use

Remove the cores of the fennel bulbs, then shred them as finely as possible. Mix with the lemon juice and leave covered for several hours or overnight — this takes away

196

some of the aniseed flavour. Arrange in a gratin dish, and cover with thin overlapping slices of tomato. Scatter them with the finely sliced spring onions, using both bulbs and green. Finally, add the herbs to the dressing and pour over the top. Leave in a cool place but do not refrigerate.

MANGETOUT AND TOMATO SALAD

SERVES 6–8   *Do not freeze*

This is a colourful and refreshing salad, with the mint jelly adding sparkle to the dressing. Take care not to overcook the mangetouts; they should remain crisp.

1 lb (450 g) mangetout peas (snow peas),
strings removed but left whole
6 tomatoes
1 large green pepper

THE DRESSING:
6 tablespoons olive oil

3 tablespoon white wine vinegar
1 level teaspoon each sugar and salt
15 grinds black pepper
1 level tablespoon chopped onion
1 level tablespoon each chopped parsley and
snipped chives
2 teaspoons mint jelly (for recipe see page
283)

Boil the mangetouts rapidly in a large uncovered pan of boiling salted water until just bite-tender. Immediately turn into a colander and plunge it into a bowl of cold water for 2 minutes. This will set the colour of the mangetouts. Drain thoroughly. Shake all the dressing ingredients together until blended. Cut the tomatoes into 6 or 8, depending on size, and the pepper into very fine strips. Blend with the dressing and serve very cold.

TWO COOKED VEGETABLE SALADS
CORN AND RED BEAN SALAD

SERVES 4–6   *Do not freeze*
                               Refrigerate for up to 3 days

This hearty, high-fibre salad with its tomato-flavoured vinaigrette dressing makes a satisfying accompaniment to cold pickled brisket or hot frankfurter sausages for a Sunday evening supper in winter.

1 can (11 oz (300 g)) corn with peppers
1 can (15 oz (425 g)) red kidney beans

THE DRESSING:
2 tablespoons sunflower oil
1 tablespoon olive oil
1½ tablespoons red wine vinegar

1 tablespoon tomato ketchup
½ teaspoon salt; 10 grinds black pepper
2 tablespoons finely chopped mild onion or 2
teaspoons dried chopped onion flakes
Half a clove of garlic, peeled and crushed

GARNISH:
1 tablespoon chopped parsley

197

Put the corn and beans into a sieve and leave to drain thoroughly. Put all the dressing ingredients into a screw-top jar and shake together for 1 or 2 minutes until they form a thick emulsion. Put the vegetables into a bowl and moisten evenly with the dressing. Leave for several hours for the flavour to develop. Pile into a pottery bowl and garnish with the chopped parsley.

SUMMER RICE SALAD

SERVES 6–8 with another salad, 4 if served alone

Do not freeze
Refrigerate for up to 3 days

This looks most appetizing in shades of brown, beige and scarlet. It carries well, so it's ideal for a picnic or a barbecue. For a main dish salad for four stir in 8 oz (225 g/2 cups) cooked chicken breast or the remains of a roast bird, cut in ½ in (1¼ cm) cubes.

7–8 oz (225–250 g/1 cup) brown or white long-grain rice
1 teaspoon salt
2 cups water
3 tablespoons vinaigrette dressing (see page 189)
2 teaspoons wine vinegar or cider vinegar

½ lb (225 g/2 cups) pinky mushrooms
1 large red pepper, seeds removed, cut in ½ in (1¼ cm) squares
2 tablespoons currants or raisins
2 oz (50 g/½ cup) blanched split almonds, toasted until golden

Bring the water and salt to the boil, add the rice, stir well, then when boiling again cover and simmer until the liquid has been absorbed and the rice is tender but not mushy — 15 to 20 minutes for white rice, about 30 minutes for brown. Turn at once into a bowl and use a fork to mix with the dressing. Wash the mushrooms and cut off the stalks (if any). Leave whole if small, cut them in quarters if larger. Bring ½ pint (275 ml/1¼ cups) water to the boil, add 2 teaspoons wine or cider vinegar and then the mushrooms, cover and simmer 5 minutes. Drain the mushrooms well and add them to the rice together with the red pepper squares, the dried fruit and the toasted nuts. Taste, and add more salt and pepper if desired. Put into a covered container and refrigerate until required.

STIR-FRIED VEGETABLE SALAD, CHINESE STYLE

SERVES 6–8

Do not freeze
Store under refrigeration for up to 48 hours

The crispness of the lightly cooked vegetables and the subtle flavour of the dressing make this a very sophisticated salad to serve either as a starter or as part of a cold buffet. To enjoy at its best, serve it the day it is made when the vegetables are still fresh and crunchy.

1 lb (450 g) green beans
½ lb (225 g/2 cups) button mushrooms
2 red peppers, halved, seeds and pith
removed
2 oz (50 g/½ cup) blanched and split
almonds, toasted

THE SAUCE:
2 tablespoons light soy sauce

2 tablespoons medium-dry sherry
1 tablespoon soft brown sugar
2 tablespoons white wine vinegar

TO FINISH:
2 tablespoons sunflower oil
1 clove of garlic, peeled and finely chopped
Salt and black pepper if necessary

Slice the beans or break each into 2 or 3 pieces, according to length. Cook in a large pan of boiling water (with 1 teaspoon salt) for 4 minutes (only partially covering the pan to preserve the colour) until the beans are barely tender. Turn at once into a colander and drench with cold water to set the colour. Drain thoroughly. Wipe the mushrooms with a damp cloth, cut off ¼ in (1 cm) from the end of the stalk, and slice thinly. Cut the peppers into matchsticks. Mix together all the ingredients for the sauce.

Heat the oil and garlic in a large frying pan or wok and when the garlic begins to sizzle, add the nuts. When they are beginning to colour, add the mushrooms and peppers and stir-fry, tossing constantly with a spoon and fork for 4 minutes. Pour the sauce mixture into the pan and mix thoroughly with the vegetables and nuts; then pour the entire contents of the pan over the cooked beans. Taste and add salt and pepper only if necessary — soy sauce is salty itself. Chill well before serving.

TWO MUSHROOM SALADS
MUSHROOM SALAD IN A RED WINE DRESSING

SERVES 6–8 as a relish   *Refrigerate for up to 4 days*

To achieve the original flavour of this delicious French relish salad, tiny mushroom caps are first sautéed in a fruity olive oil and then cooked in red wine until they turn a rich garnet in colour. It goes well with pickled or spiced meat.

1 lb (450 g/5 cups) very fresh small
mushrooms
3 tablespoons olive oil
1 small clove of garlic, cut in slivers
6 fl oz (175 ml/¾ cup) dry fruity red wine,
such as Côtes du Rhône

1 level teaspoon salt; 15 grinds black pepper
2 level tablespoons chopped parsley
2 fat green or red peppers, halved, seeds
removed, cut in very thin strips
1 tablespoon lemon juice (depending on the
acidity of the wine)

If the mushrooms are bigger than buttons, cut each in quarters through the stalk. Heat the oil and toss the mushrooms in it until they have absorbed it and are beginning to colour. Add the garlic and wine. Allow to bubble briskly for 2 minutes, then turn down the heat and simmer, uncovered, for 5 minutes, until most of the wine has evaporated. Stir in the seasonings, parsley and peppers, adding the lemon juice if necessary. Serve cold.

MUSHROOMS AND PIMIENTOS IN CORIANDER DRESSING

SERVES 6–8   Refrigerate for up to 4 days

This interesting salad changes its character as the day goes by. When it is freshly made, the mushrooms are plump and white and mild in taste, but after an hour they become smaller and darker and begin to develop a 'pickled' flavour. As the mushrooms are not cooked in any way it is important that they should be very fresh with white unblemished caps and a firm texture.

1 lb (450 g/5 cups) button mushrooms
1 small can of sweet pimientos in brine

THE DRESSING:
6 tablespoons sunflower oil
2 tablespoons olive oil
2 tablespoons each lemon juice and wine
vinegar
1½ level teaspoons salt

1 teaspoon sugar
White part and 1 in (2½ cm) of the green
from a small bunch of spring onions (green
onions), finely sliced
1 fat clove of garlic, peeled and crushed
15 grinds black pepper
2 tablespoons chopped fresh coriander or
parsley
1½ teaspoons ground coriander seed

Trim off ¼ in (1 cm) of the stalk of the mushrooms. Leave whole, or cut into four if they are large. Drain the pimientos and cut in strips. Put all the dressing ingredients into a bowl and whisk for 2 minutes or until they form an emulsion. Add the mushrooms and pimientos and stir well to coat evenly. Leave at room temperature for 1 hour, stirring occasionally, then serve or refrigerate until required.

SALADS WITH FRUIT
ORANGE, CHICORY AND WATERCRESS SALAD

SERVES 6–8   Must be served the day it is prepared

This is refreshing to serve as a 'chaser' after a highly seasoned or rich main course.

12 oz (350 g) chicory (4 or 5 medium
heads)
2 large or 3 medium thin-skinned oranges,
seedless navels if possible
2 fine bunches of watercress

THE DRESSING:
3 tablespoons oil (huile de noix — walnut
oil — for preference, otherwise sunflower oil)
1 tablespoon lemon juice
1 teaspoon caster (superfine) sugar
½ teaspoon salt; speck of white pepper

Cut the ends off the chicory, then cut across in ½ in (1½ cm) slices. Peel the oranges as you would an apple, removing the pith as well, and section them (see page 189). Add any free orange juice to the dressing ingredients and whisk well to form a slightly thickened emulsion. Wash the watercress under the tap, then cut off the tough stalks and dry the leaves well. Arrange the chicory and the orange sections in a salad bowl — a glass one for the prettiest effect. Toss in the dressing. Decorate with the watercress leaves arranged round the edge of the bowl.

MINTED ORANGE AND TOASTED HAZELNUT SALAD

SERVES 6–8   *Use on day of preparation*

A refreshing salad to serve with grilled (broiled) lamb cutlets. It is possible on occasion to buy lettuce *hearts*, usually of the crisp 'Little Gem' variety, and these give this salad a pleasing texture.

2 flat lettuce or crisp lettuce hearts
1 bunch of watercress
4 medium navel oranges

THE DRESSING:
3 tablespoons sunflower oil and 1 tablespoon huile de noix *(walnut oil)*
2 tablespoons orange juice

1 tablespoon lemon juice
1 teaspoon bottled or fresh mint sauce *or* 2 teaspoons chopped fresh mint leaves
1 teaspoon sugar
½ teaspoon sea salt; 10 grinds black pepper
1½–2 oz (35–50 g/½ cup) hazelnuts (filberts), roasted and coarsely chopped (see page 196)

Put the shredded lettuce and the watercress leaves in a bowl and chill. Peel and then segment the oranges, saving any juice that comes out for the dressing. Chill separately. Shake all the dressing ingredients together in a screw-top jar until thickened. Just before serving, arrange the orange segments on the crisp greens, top with the nuts and toss with the dressing.

SALAD OF GRAPEFRUIT, CHINESE LEAVES AND WATERCRESS WITH HONEYED DRESSING

SERVES 6   *Use only on day of preparation*

A refreshing salad to accompany hot or cold roast chicken.

1 can grapefruit segments in juice
1 bunch of watercress, leaves only
Half a head of Chinese leaves (Chinese cabbage), finely shredded

THE DRESSING:
3 tablespoons sunflower oil
1 tablespoon grapefruit juice (from the can)
1 teaspoon lemon juice
1 teaspoon liquid honey
½ teaspoon salt; speck of white pepper

201

Arrange the watercress and shredded Chinese leaves in a salad bowl, top with the drained grapefruit segments and chill. Put the dressing ingredients into a screw-top jar and shake until thickened. Just before serving toss with the salad until it is evenly moistened.

ORANGE AND CUCUMBER SALAD WITH DILL DRESSING

SERVES 6–8   *Use up within 48 hours of preparation*

A gently flavoured summer salad in a light dressing of sweetened wine vinegar. Serve it with poached salmon or cold roast beef. It looks most effective with the slices of cucumber and orange arranged in concentric circles in a china flan dish or shallow gratin dish.

1 long straight and slim cucumber
4 large or 6 medium oranges

THE DRESSING:
2 level tablespoons caster (superfine) sugar

2 tablespoons boiling water
4 tablespoons white wine vinegar or cider vinegar
1 tablespoon finely cut fresh dill (or chives, if dill is unavailable)

Slice the unpeeled cucumber finely, using a mandoline or food processor. Peel the skin and pith from the oranges and cut the fruit into thin slices. Arrange the orange and cucumber slices in the chosen dish. To make the dressing, put the sugar in a basin and dissolve in the boiling water. Add the remaining ingredients and stir well, then pour over the salad. Chill for several hours.

OGEN SUMMER SALAD

SERVES 6–8 or 10 with other salads   *Use up within 48 hours of preparation*

A good salad for a barbecue. It can also be served in tall glasses as a summer starter. The melon balls are added only just before serving, or their juice would dilute the dressing.

1 medium Ogen or other cantaloupe-type melon
8 large stalks of celery from the heart
2 medium-sized crisp red-skinned eating apples
6 oz (175 g/1 cup) black grapes, halved and pipped
½ lb (225 g/1½ cups) strawberries, hulled

1 oz (25 g/¼ cup) walnuts, coarsely chopped

THE DRESSING:
¼ pint (150 ml/⅔ cup) mild mayonnaise
1 teaspoon each orange and lemon juice
1 teaspoon soft brown sugar
10 grinds of black pepper

Stir together all the dressing ingredients, then put to one side. Halve the melon, remove the seeds, then scoop out the flesh using a melon-ball cutter. Leave in a sieve to drain. Cut the celery in ⅜ in (1 cm) cubes. Core and then quarter the apples and cut into cubes of the same size. Put in a bowl with the grapes and mix with the dressing. Chill for several hours.

Half an hour before serving, stir in the melon, garnish with the strawberries (sliced only if large) and sprinkle with the nuts.

WINTER SALAD IN RED, GREEN AND GOLD

SERVES 8–10   *Refrigerate only leftovers up to 2 days*

This is a spectacular salad for a buffet table. It goes especially well with cold chicken and turkey.

1 head of curly endive
1 fresh pineapple, approximately 2 lb (1 kg)
in weight
1 small red pepper, seeds removed, cut in
julienne strips
2 large oranges, peel and pith removed and
cut in segments
2 oz (50 g/½ cup) walnuts, coarsely chopped

THE DRESSING:
3 tablespoons mayonnaise
5 tablespoons sunflower oil
1 tablespoon walnut oil (huile de noix)
3 tablespoons lemon juice
3 teaspoons soft light brown sugar
½ teaspoon salt; 10 grinds black pepper
¼ teaspoon paprika pepper

Make a vinaigrette by whisking together all the dressing ingredients, except the mayonnaise, until thickened. Wash the curly endive thoroughly under the tap. Separate into small sprigs, discarding the core, then drain and dry in a salad-spinner or a teatowel. Using a sharp knife with a serrated blade, peel the pineapple, cut it lengthwise into four, then cut out and discard the core and slice into fingers 2 × 1 × ⅜ in (5 × 2½ × 1 cm) thick. Section the oranges as described on page 189.

In a larger bowl combine the endive, pineapple, red pepper, oranges and walnuts. In a small bowl, blend the vinaigrette and the mayonnaise. Pour this dressing over the salad, then toss lightly until all the ingredients are well coated. Leave for an hour, then pile into a bowl and serve.

Desserts

A revolution has taken place in the Jewish dessert menu over the past twenty years. Long live the Revolution! For it has swept away from most family dinner tables the shalets and the kugels, the strudels and the blintzes which provided an earlier generation with their own personal 'central heating' but only served to pile unnecessary poundage on to their more cosseted descendants.

In most Jewish households today, the 'afters' are usually restricted to fresh and stewed fruits, and fresh and dried fruit salads, with something a little more lavish served on Friday night and Shabbat. Even at dinner parties and family celebrations the fashion has moved away from the pastries and gâteaux of yesteryear, and there is an increasing emphasis on exotic fruit presentations and on ices served in an eye-catching way. Only when it comes to a Festival such as Sukkot or Shavuot do most of us indulge in the rich delicious recipes that our mothers used to make.

That is why there are only four recipes for pastry desserts in this chapter, yet more than a dozen suggestions for presenting fresh and poached fruits, with the emphasis on their appeal to the eye as much as to the stomach. Even without a sorbetière, it is now very easy to make both dairy and non-dairy ice cream and sorbets (sherbets), as smooth as you can buy, by using either an egg mousse foundation for the ice cream or a food processor to whisk up the sorbet. And I have concentrated especially on giving these home-made ices a depth of flavour that you can rarely find in a commercial pack. But there are always the very special occasions for which the dessert must provide a memorable finale, and I have given recipes for some spectacular creations especially for this kind of meal.

For ideas for really low-calorie desserts, see pages 41 and 53. And there are many traditional (if high-calorie) desserts in the chapter on 'Festivals', pages 302–369.

SETTING THE SCENE FOR THE DESSERT

● **Bowls and plates of glass** show off fruit desserts particularly well. It's useful to have two or three bowls of different depths and diameters, and a bowl on a pedestal for soft fruits and sorbets (sherbets).
● **Wide plates with shallow rims** are good for whole fruits poached in syrup, or for slices of fruit which have been masked with a fruit sauce or 'coulis'.
● A **long or oval dish** of glass or wood is especially effective for larger fruits such as melon or pineapple halves.
● **Glasses** — wine glasses, triangular 'Manhattan' cocktail glasses, large brandy balloons — make stunning containers for ice creams, sorbets (sherbets) and Zabaglione.
● After a meat meal, any of the fruit dishes can be served plain; after a milk meal, they are more refreshing if accompanied by thick yoghurt or soured cream rather than by the richer dairy cream.
● **Non-dairy cream** makes an excellent substitute for dairy creams in ice creams, purées and mousses, but neither the texture nor the taste is very agreeable when it is served alone as a direct replacement for whipped dairy cream.
● **Kosher gelatine** is available in certain countries but not in others. Either persuade a traveller to bring some back for you, or substitute a kosher jelly (gelatine dessert

mix) instead. I have not been successful in using agar-agar on a domestic scale, although vegetable gelatines made from alginates are widely used in making commercial desserts.

• The judicious use of **liqueurs** flavoured with fruits, nuts, chocolate or coffee can transform an ordinary fruit salad or sorbet (sherbet) into a very special dessert. Too much will drown the taste of the food, however, so add it by the tablespoon, until the right balance of flavours has been achieved — taste it and see.

• The degree of **sweetness** in a dessert is a matter of individual taste. Where the sugar content is not important to the texture (as it may be in cakes and biscuits (cookies)), it can be reduced to some extent, particularly in the poaching liquid for fruit. I have also been successful in using the newer sugar substitutes based on aspartame, which has no aftertaste. If you wish to experiment, always add the sugar substitute *after* cooking.

FRESH FRUIT PRESENTATIONS
CARAMELIZED CLEMENTINES

SERVES 6–8

Do not freeze
Will keep 3 days under refrigeration

Tiny clementines are marinated overnight in a glistening caramel syrup, then served in a glass bowl decorated with their own bright green leaves. You can use any relation of the tangerine, but it should be seedless and without too much pith. Do not allow the water to boil before the sugar has dissolved or the sugar may crystallize into tiny lumps. Serve plain or with vanilla ice cream or orange and lemon sorbet (sherbet) (see page 159).

12–16 clementines (according to size)

CARAMEL SYRUP:
6 oz (175 g/¾ cup) granulated sugar
5 tablespoons water

1 tablespoon lemon juice
1 tablespoon orange liqueur (Cointreau,
Grand Marnier, Curaçao, Aurum)
(optional)
5 additional tablespoons hot water

Peel the clementines, remove as much pith as possible with the fingers, then arrange side by side in a wide container. Put the sugar and water into a small, thick-bottomed pan and stir until the sugar has dissolved, then bubble without stirring until the water evaporates and the sugar turns a rich caramel brown. Cover your hand with a cloth to protect it from spattering syrup, then add the 5 tablespoons of hot water and stir over moderate heat until the caramel has dissolved. Stir in the lemon juice and liqueur (if used). Taste and add a further tablespoon of liqueur if necessary. Pour immediately over the fruit. Leave for several hours, basting three or four times with the syrup, then chill.

MELON WITH CHERRY WINE SAUCE

SERVES 6–8

Do not freeze
Cut melon keeps 1 day, cherry sauce 4 days under refrigeration

A sunburst of melon crescents with a bowl of scarlet cherry sauce in the middle makes a dramatic — and refreshing — finale to a dinner party. Cream is not necessary, but a crisp biscuit provides a pleasant contrast to the juicy fruit.

The success of this simple dish depends on the quality and flavour of the fruit. I use a Charentais-type melon like the Ogen or the Galia, with sweet-sour morello (sour red) cherries, though choice black cherries sparked with lemon juice are also excellent. If the melon(s) are bought 3 or 4 days before they are required, fully ripe fruit can be refrigerated, and fruit that is under-ripe will have time to mature at room temperature.

1 very large ripe melon or 2 medium ones (Charentais or cantaloupe)

THE SAUCE:
3 teaspoons cornflour (cornstarch)
1 tablespoon soft light brown sugar
1 can (15 oz (425 g)) stoned morello (sour red) or black cherries in syrup, strained

2 strips of orange peel each about 1 in (2½ cm) wide (removed with a potato peeler)
1 stick of cinnamon or ½ teaspoon ground cinnamon
4 tablespoons of fruity red wine
2 tablespoons lemon juice for black cherries, 2 tablespoons more wine for morellos

Mix the sugar and cornflour in a small pan, then gradually add the syrup strained from the fruit, the orange peel, cinnamon, wine and lemon juice (if used). Bring to the boil, then simmer for 3 minutes until thickened and clear. Stir in the cherries. Chill overnight, then remove the cinnamon stick and peel, and spoon into a small glass or pottery bowl.

One hour before serving, cut the melon(s) in half, then in quarters and finally into crescents 1 in (2½ cm) thick. Carefully cut away the skin with a sharp pointed knife and arrange the crescents in a circle on a large flat plate, with the bowl of sauce in the middle. Chill for only 30 minutes. Serve 3 or 4 crescents with a spoonful of sauce to each guest.

WHOLE ORANGES IN LIQUEUR ON A BED OF PINEAPPLE

SERVES 6–8

Do not freeze
Will keep 3 days under refrigeration

This is a very refreshing and colourful dessert to serve after a hearty main course of chicken or meat.

6–8 large navel oranges
5 oz (150 g/²⁄₃ cup) sugar
¼ pint (150 ml/²⁄₃ cup) water
2 tablespoons smooth apricot jam
3 tablespoons lemon juice

2 tablespoons Cointreau or other orange-flavoured liqueur
6–8 slices peeled fresh or canned pineapple
A few black grapes

Peel the oranges with a small serrated knife, removing all the pith, then cut a tiny slice off the base of each orange, so that it will sit upright in the dish. Cut each orange crosswise into 4–6 slices, then put back into shape. Spear each orange with a cocktail stick to hold it in shape, and arrange in a shallow casserole. Dissolve the sugar in the water and add the apricot jam, then simmer for 5 minutes until it becomes a thick syrup. Remove from the heat and stir in the lemon juice and the liqueur. Pour this syrup over the oranges. Put the dish in the refrigerator and chill for several hours, basting the fruit with the syrup three or four times.

To serve Arrange a slice of fresh or canned pineapple on each serving plate. Stand an orange on it and pour over a little of the syrup glaze. Top with a tiny 'leaf' cut out of pineapple leaf, or with one or two pipped black grapes.

FRESH PINEAPPLE WITH APRICOT COULIS

SERVES 6–8

Freeze apricot coulis 1 year
The coulis will keep for 4 days under refrigeration

This beautiful yet simple recipe looks superb and has a wonderful contrast of flavours. It is important to use very choice apricots.

1 large choice pineapple

THE APRICOT COULIS:
1 can (15 oz (425 g)) choice apricots or
1 lb fresh apricots stewed with

4 oz (125 g/½ cup) sugar and ¼ pint (150 ml/²⁄₃ cup) water, stones removed
1 tablespoon lemon juice
2 tablespoons liqueur with a fruit or nut flavouring, such as Amaretto or apricot brandy (optional)

To make the coulis Drain the juice from the fruit, put into a pan and bubble until the flavour has intensified — about 3 or 4 minutes. Stir in the lemon juice and liqueur, if used. Put in a blender with the fruit and liquidize until thick and smooth — the mixture should find its own level when dropped from a spoon. Chill thoroughly.

To finish Peel the pineapple, cut in slices ½ in (1 cm) thick, remove the core and arrange on individual plates. Chill for 30 minutes before dinner. Just before serving, spoon a ribbon of the apricot coulis round the pineapple and serve either plain or with thick yoghurt and a crisp biscuit (cookie).

ZABAGLIONE WITH FRESH PEACHES

SERVES 6–8

Do not freeze
Poached peaches will keep 2 days under
refrigeration

This is a truly elegant dessert, but your guests must be prepared to wait for the 5 or 6 minutes it takes to prepare the Zabaglione. If the peaches are fully ripe, they need not be poached but only skinned after blanching for one minute in boiling water. Marsala all'Uova is used for sweet dishes as opposed to the Marsala Fine that is used for savoury ones.

6–8 large ripe peaches

2 tablespoons lemon juice

THE POACHING SYRUP:
8 fl oz (225 ml/1 cup) water
5 oz (150 g/²/₃ cup) granulated sugar

THE ZABAGLIONE:
6 egg yolks
6 tablespoons Marsala all'Uova
2 oz (50 g/¼ cup) caster (superfine) sugar

To poach the peaches   Put the sugar, water and lemon juice into a pan which is wide enough to hold the peaches in one layer side by side. Bring to the boil, then simmer for 3 minutes until slightly thickened. Add the whole peaches in one layer, cover and cook gently for 10 minutes, basting two or three times until just tender when pierced with a sharp knife. Drain the fruit well, slip off the skins, and arrange each peach in the bottom of a large goblet such as a brandy balloon, or in a shallow glass bowl.

To make the Zabaglione   Just before dinner put the yolks and the sugar into a large glass mixing bowl that will fit comfortably over a pan. Whisk the sugar and yolks together until they lighten and thicken, using either a hand-held electric whisk or a large balloon whisk, then whisk in the Marsala. Cover and set aside.

Put 3 in (7½ cm) of water into the pan and bring to the boil, then reduce the heat until the water is barely simmering, cover and leave on a very low heat until required. After the main course has been cleared, set the bowl over the pan of simmering water and whisk the egg mixture until it fluffs up and takes on the consistency of softly whipped cream — it should form soft mounds in the bowl when dropped from the whisk; this will take between 5 and 6 minutes. Spoon the Zabaglione over the peaches and serve at once.

208

CARAMEL FRUIT SALAD

SERVES 6–8   *Do not freeze*
                               Leftovers will keep 1 day under refrigeration

The flavour of a fruit salad depends to a great extent on the syrup in which it is marinated. This one has a rich caramel flavour, lightened by the juice that comes out of the fruit — this should have a basis of oranges but can be otherwise varied according to the fruit available. The mixture given is particularly delicious, and is very refreshing after a meat meal. Refrigerate leftover syrup and use another day, or stew apples in it.

THE FRUIT SALAD:
3 large or 4 medium oranges
1 small pineapple or half a large one
½ lb (225 g/1½ cups) grapes, pips removed
2 bananas, sliced

THE SYRUP:
Caramel made from ½ lb (225 g/1 cup)
granulated sugar and 4 tablespoons water
2 tablespoons lemon juice
Juice from the oranges
2 tablespoons any orange-flavoured liqueur
(Cointreau, Grand Marnier, Curaçao)
(optional)

To make the caramel   Have a bowl of cold water ready in the sink. Put the sugar and water into a pan with a heavy base and heat, stirring until the sugar has dissolved. Now continue to heat steadily, stirring only occasionally until the water has evaporated and the remaining liquefied sugar has turned a rich caramel brown. Immediately take the caramel pan to the sink, and plunge its base in the water to stop the caramel cooking any more. Cover the arm nearest the pan with a teatowel to protect from splashes, and then add the juice that has come out of the oranges while they were being prepared, together with the lemon juice. Stir over a low heat until the caramel has liquefied again, then add the liqueur (if used). Allow to go cold. This syrup can be used immediately or kept for up to a week under refrigeration.

To prepare the fruit   With a sharp serrated knife, peel both the rind and the pith off the oranges, revealing the flesh. Cut between the segments and remove the sections of orange, then put them in a bowl. Squeeze the 'skeleton' of the orange into a bowl and use to add to the caramel as described above. Peel the pineapple, remove the core and cut into ⅜ in (1 cm) chunks. Seed the grapes.

Put the oranges and pineapple into a bowl and pour over the cold caramel syrup. Lay the grapes on top but don't mix them in until just before serving (this keeps them crisp). Half an hour before serving add the peeled and sliced bananas, and stir well.

COMPÔTE OF SUMMER FRUITS POACHED IN WINE

SERVES 6–8

Do not freeze
Will keep 2 days under refrigeration

This compôte is delicious served plain, with soured cream or with natural yoghurt slightly sweetened with honey.

THE SYRUP:
5 oz (150 g/²⁄₃ cup) light brown sugar
½ pint (275 ml/1¼ cups) water
¼ pint (150 ml/²⁄₃ cup) any fruity dry or
medium-dry red wine, such as Cabernet
Sauvignon
1 stick of cinnamon or ½ teaspoon ground
cinnamon

THE FRUIT:
1 lb (450 g) ripe freestone plums, halved and
stoned — Zwetschken variety if possible
½ lb (225 g/1½ cups) each of blackberries,
raspberries, blackcurrants and pipped black
grapes
2 large oranges

Put the sugar, water, wine and cinnamon into a pan and bring to the boil. Simmer for 3 or 4 minutes until the mixture becomes a light syrup. Have ready a slotted spoon. Put the plums in the syrup and allow them to simmer for 3 minutes, then lift out with the slotted spoon and put in a serving bowl. Do the same with the raspberries, blackberries and currants in turn, but give them only 1 minute each. Now boil the syrup down until its volume is reduced by half. Allow to go cold and then pour over the fruit. Half an hour before serving, completely peel the oranges (taking off all the pith), then cut the fruit into thin slices. Add to the compôte with the grapes.

WINTER FRUITS AND NUTS IN SPICED WINE

SERVES 6–8

Do not freeze
Will keep under refrigeration for 2 days

This is very refreshing after roast or grilled (broiled) meat.

½ lb (225 g/1½ cups) green grapes, seedless
or pipped
½ lb (225 g/1½ cups) black grapes, pipped
3 navel oranges, peeled and segmented
1 can (14 oz (400 g)) lychees
3 bananas, peeled and sliced
2 oz (50 g/½ cup) pecans or walnuts, shelled
2 oz (50 g/½ cup) Brazil nuts, shelled

THE SYRUP:
5 fl oz (150 ml/²⁄₃ cup) fruity red wine, such
as Cabernet Sauvignon
5 fl oz (150 ml/²⁄₃ cup) lychee juice from the
can
3 tablespoons light brown sauce
1 tablespoon lemon juice
3 cloves
1 stick of cinnamon or a good pinch of
ground cinnamon

Prepare the fruit and put it into a bowl. Put the wine, juices, sugar and spices into a pan and simmer for 5 minutes to allow the flavour to concentrate. Cool, then pour over the fruit and refrigerate. Coarsely chop the nuts, toast them under the grill or in the microwave, and add just before serving.

COMPÔTE OF FRESH PINEAPPLE, LYCHEES AND KIWI FRUIT

SERVES 6–8

Do not freeze
Will keep under refrigeration for 2 days

The fruit is mixed with a citrus sauce and served in small pineapple halves, arranged on a long platter of wood or glass. For a buffet meal two large pineapples can be used instead.

3 or 4 small pineapples
1 can (14 oz (400 g)) lychees
4 kiwi fruit

THE SYRUP:
4 oz (125 g/½ cup) syrup from lychees

2 oz (50 g/¼ cup) sugar
Juice of 1 orange or 3 oz (75 ml/⅓ cup)
orange juice
Juice of half a lemon
3 teaspoons cornflour (cornstarch)
2 tablespoons Cointreau or Kirsch (optional)

Cut the pineapples lengthwise through the flesh and leaves. Scoop out the flesh with a grapefruit knife, remove the core, then cut into bite-sized pieces. Reserve the shells. Drain the lychees, reserving the syrup. Peel and thinly slice the kiwi fruit.

Dissolve the sugar in the lychee syrup over gentle heat, then add the orange juice. Mix the cornflour to a cream with the lemon juice and add to the hot fruit juice. Bring to the boil, stirring, and simmer for 2 minutes, then stir in the liqueur (if used). Put the pineapple and lychees into a bowl and pour on the hot sauce, stirring gently. Allow to go quite cold. To serve, fill the pineapple shells with the cold compôte and garnish with overlapping slices of kiwi fruit.

FRESH STRAWBERRY AND CHERRY CUP

SERVES 6–8

Do not freeze
Serve the day it is prepared

This is a most refreshing fruit salad with a delightful contrast of colour and texture. It looks very effective in a glass pedestal bowl.

1–1½ lb (450–700 g/3–5 cups) plump
strawberries, hulled and cut in half
1 lb (450 g/2 cups) fresh black cherries,
stoned

5 fl oz (150 ml/⅔ cup) water
Juice of 1 large lemon or juice of 2 fresh limes
2 tablespoons Cointreau or Kirsch (optional)

THE SYRUP:
4 oz (125 g/½ cup) sugar

Put the strawberries into a bowl with the cherries. Bring the sugar and water to the boil stirring constantly, then simmer for 2 minutes or until as thick as canned fruit syrup. Allow to go cold, then stir in the fruit juice and liqueur (if used) and pour over the fruit. Chill until ready to serve.

REDCURRANT AND RASPBERRY KISSEL

SERVES 6–8   *Freeze 3 months*

In this favourite Russian-Jewish dessert there is an interesting combination of summer fruits, some of which are puréed and some left whole, to provide a contrast of texture. A glass bowl filled with this delicate pink jelly makes a beautiful finale to a summer dinner party. Arrowroot is to be preferred to cornflour (cornstarch) as a thickening agent, as it has no taste of its own to mask the fresh fruit flavour, and it also sets to a very clear gel. If redcurrants are not available, blackcurrants (and Crème de Cassis rather than Framboise) may be used instead. Frozen fruits can be used in the winter. Serve with crisp biscuits (cookies) such as Praline Crisps (page 172).

THE FRUIT PURÉE:
1 lb (450 g/4 cups) redcurrants
½ lb (225 g/1½ cups) raspberries
15 fl oz (475 ml/2 cups) water
4–6 oz (125–175 g/½–¾ cup) sugar
(according to the tartness of the fruit)
2 oz (50 g/4 rounded tablespoons) arrowroot
or cornflour (cornstarch)
3 fl oz (75 ml/⅓ cup) fruity white wine such as Riesling

2 tablespoons fruit liqueurs such as Crème de
Framboise (optional)
A little caster (superfine) sugar

TO FOLD INTO THE PURÉE:
½ lb (225 g/1½ cups) raspberries
½ lb (225 g/1 cup) dessert cherries (stoned)

Put the currants and the first half-pound (225 g/1½ cups) of raspberries into a pan with water and bring to the boil. Bubble uncovered until the fruit is tender — about 5 minutes. Push the contents of the pan through the fine sieve of a food mill or through an ordinary fine metal sieve.

Return the purée to the pan with the sugar and bring to the boil. Mix the arrowroot or cornflour with the wine and add to the pan, stirring constantly, then cook until the mixture thickens and looks quite clear — after 1 minute with arrowroot, or 3 minutes if cornflour has been used. Cool until it stops steaming, then stir in the liqueur (if used). Pour into a bowl and leave until it begins to set, after 30 minutes, then stir in the whole fruit. Spoon into a bowl or individual glasses, then sprinkle with a little caster sugar to prevent a skin. Chill for several hours, preferably overnight.

PEARS IN RED WINE WITH CREME DE CASSIS

SERVES 6–8

Do not freeze
Will keep 2 days under refrigeration

The Crème de Cassis produced in Burgundy is considered to be particularly fine, as the blackcurrants from which it is made thrive in the same climatic conditions as the grapes used to make its incomparable wines. Crème de Cassis is only one of a number of similar liqueurs such as Framboise (raspberry), Myrtille (bilberry) and Guignolet (cherry), which are made by steeping fresh fruit in a flavourless alcohol and then sweetening the filtered liquid. All these fruit liqueurs make a delicious sauce for ice cream or sorbets (sherbets) or, as in this dish, they may be stirred into a compôte made from a complementary fruit.

6–8 firm pears, Conference variety for preference
½ pint (275 ml/1¼ cups) fruity red wine such as Côtes du Rhône
1 level tablespoon dark soft brown sugar
5 oz (150 g/⅔ cup) granulated sugar

2 pieces each of thinly pared orange and lemon rind, about ½ in (1 cm) in width
1 cinnamon stick
4 cloves
1 tablespoon lemon juice
2 teaspoons cornflour (cornstarch) or arrowroot
4 tablespoons Crème de Cassis

Peel the pears but leave them whole. Cut a tiny slice from the base of each, so they will stand evenly in the serving dish. Choose a pan large enough to hold the pears lying flat on the bottom. Put in the wine, sugar, peel, spices and lemon juice and heat gently until the sugar dissolves, stirring all the time. Add the pears, then top up with enough water to cover them. Bring to the boil, cover and simmer very gently, turning once or twice until the fruit feels just tender when pierced with a sharp narrow knife. This will take about 30 minutes for very hard pears, but start testing after 20. By this time the pears will be a beautiful pink colour. Take out and arrange in the chosen dish.

Bring the cooking liquid to the boil, then bubble until the volume is reduced by half and is of a syrupy consistency with a pleasing 'winey' flavour. Stir in the cornflour (or arrowroot), mixed smoothly with the Crème de Cassis, bubble until clear, then strain over the fruit. Chill well. The pears are delicious served plain or with soured cream or thick yoghurt.

HOT AND FRUITY
BAKED APPLES STUFFED WITH DRIED FRUITS SOAKED IN WINE

SERVES 4–6   *Will keep 2 days under refrigeration*

This is a delightful variation on a familiar theme which makes an excellent dessert after a Friday night meat meal.

4–6 medium baking apples, unpeeled
4–6 tablespoons each of raisins, chopped
walnuts and light brown sugar

4–6 tablespoons Kiddush or other port-type
sweet red wine
1 teaspoon ground cinnamon
1 tablespoon lemon juice

Preheat the oven to Gas No. 4, 350 degrees F, 180 degrees C. Select an oven-to-table dish large enough to hold the fruit side by side.

Put the raisins in a small pan, cover with the wine, then heat until steaming (or heat in microwave on full power for 1 minute). Leave for 5 minutes to soften in the wine, then stir in the sugar, cinnamon and chopped walnuts. Core the apples, then cut through the skin all the way round the centre of the fruit. Arrange them side by side in the baking dish, then stuff the core cavity with the raisin and walnut mixture, spreading any remaining on the bottom of the dish. Cover the base with a thin layer of water and sprinkle with the lemon juice. Bake uncovered for 1 hour, basting twice. Allow to cool for 15 minutes before serving.

CRUNCHY FRUIT CRUMBLE

SERVES 6   *Freeze 3 months*
                             Will keep 4 days under refrigeration

This is a dessert for the brown flour and fibre enthusiasts. Vary the filling by using sliced baking apples or rhubarb, or whole plums, damsons or gooseberries.

THE FRUIT MIXTURE:
1 lb (450 g) prepared fresh or frozen fruit
3 oz (75 g/⅓ cup) granulated sugar
4 tablespoons water
1 tablespoon lemon juice

THE TOPPING:
3 oz (75 g/¾ cup) wholemeal (wholewheat)
flour

1 oz (25 g/¼ cup) chopped
walnuts
1 oz (25 g/¼ cup) Toasted Bran cereal or
muesli
3 oz (75 g/⅓ cup) soft brown
sugar
3 oz (75 g/⅓ cup) butter or soft
margarine

Preheat the oven to Gas No. 5, 375 degrees F, 190 degrees C. Grease a gratin or other oven-to-table dish measuring 9 × 6 × 1½ in (about 22 × 15 × 3 cm).

214

Mix the fruit and sugar, then put into the dish and sprinkle with the lemon juice and water. Rub all the topping ingredients together by hand or machine until they form a crumble, then pat down on to the fruit. Bake for 35 minutes until golden-brown. Serve plain or with natural yoghurt.

SYRIAN STUFFED PRUNES IN WINE SAUCE

SERVES 6   *Freeze 3 months*
                                            Will keep 3 days under refrigeration

You need to have a strong pioneering spirit to find the tiny restaurant hidden at the back of Jerusalem's Jaffa Road where you can taste the definitive version of this unusual dessert. It is prepared by chef-patron Michael Cohen whose wonderful Syrian cooking — with its combination of French finesse and Middle Eastern flavours — has made his four-table restaurant a magnet for the political, intellectual and artistic élite of Israel.

Mr Cohen serves the prunes hot, with Turkish coffee flavoured with cardamom seed, but you can also serve them cold with whipped cream, or with yoghurt perfumed with citrus blossom water. The prunes need to be soaked overnight to make it easy to remove the stones, unless you use tenderized prunes, which only require 15 minutes soaking.

1 lb (450 g) jumbo prunes
Freshly made tea to cover them
¼ lb (125 g/1 cup) walnut halves — the same number as the prunes
¼ pint (150 ml/⅔ cup) each water and sweet red Kiddush or other port-type wine

2 level tablespoons caster (superfine) sugar
1 cinnamon stick or 1 teaspoon ground cinnamon
2 oz (50 g/½ cup) raisins

The day before, put the prunes in a bowl and pour the hot tea over them through a tea-strainer. Leave them to soften overnight. Next day, remove the stone from each prune and insert a walnut half in its place. Put the wine and water into a pan with the sugar and cinnamon, bring to the boil and simmer uncovered for 3 minutes, then add the prunes and raisins. Cover and simmer for 20 minutes or until the prunes are tender and have absorbed most of the syrup. Reheat if necessary before serving.

HOT PEACHES WITH ICED FLORADORA SAUCE

SERVES 6–8   *Freeze sauce 1 month*

In this simple dish the icy liqueur sauce makes a delicious contrast to the hot baked fruit. This sauce can also be served over baked bananas or a warm apple compôte. To prevent the sauce from separating after it has been made, prepare it not more than 2 hours in advance, then chill it. It can also be frozen beforehand, and then put in the refrigerator to soften 30 minutes before it is required.

THE SAUCE:
1 large egg, separated
2 level tablespoons caster (superfine) sugar
2 tablespoons Amaretto liqueur
4–5 oz (125–150 ml/½–⅔ cup) whipping cream

THE PEACHES:
1 large or 2 medium canned peach halves per serving
Syrup from the can
2 tablespoons lemon juice
2 tablespoons soft light brown sugar

To prepare the sauce Whisk the egg white until it holds stiff peaks, then whisk in the sugar 1 teaspoon at a time. Stir in the egg yolks until the colour is even. Put the cream into a small bowl with the liqueur and whisk until it holds soft peaks, then fold into the egg mixture. Pile into a serving bowl or sauceboat. Refrigerate or freeze until required.

To bake the peaches Preheat the oven to Gas No. 4, 350 degrees F, 180 degrees C. Arrange the fruit side by side in an oven-to-table casserole or gratin dish and surround with the syrup. Sprinkle with the lemon juice and the brown sugar, cover and bake for 30 minutes. Bring steaming to the table and serve with the chilled sauce.

SOUFFLÉ AU GRAND MARNIER

SERVES 6

This is 'le grand dessert' for the great occasion. To perfume the soufflé with the fugitive flavour of the liqueur, cubes of sponge cake are soaked in it and then concealed in the centre of the raw mixture. This first part of the preparation for the soufflé can be done early in the day, and the egg whites folded in shortly before baking. But even this final step can be done up to 45 minutes before the soufflé goes into the oven. This means that all the preparations can be completed before the guests arrive. If the soufflé is put in the oven at the beginning of the meal, it will be ready to serve for dessert, 35 minutes later.

THE SAUCE BASE:
2 oz (50 g/½ cup) plain (all-purpose) flour
4 oz (125 g/½ cup) caster (superfine) sugar
¼ pint (150 ml/⅔ cup) each milk and single (light) cream or evaporated milk
5 egg yolks
1 oz (25 g/2 tablespoons) soft butter
Rind of a large bright red orange, finely grated

THE FLAVOURING:
4 tablespoons Grand Marnier (or other orange-flavoured liqueur such as Cointreau, Curaçao or Sabra)

2 tablespoons cold water
2 oz (50 g) sponge fingers (ladyfingers), trifle sponges or stale sponge (yellow) cake

FOR THE MERINGUE:
6 egg whites
Pinch salt
2 teaspoons caster (superfine) sugar

TO COAT THE SOUFFLÉ DISH:
½ oz (15 g/1 tablespoon) butter
1 tablespoon caster (superfine) sugar

216

To prepare the sauce Mix the flour and sugar in a heavy pan. Gradually stir in the milk and cream (or the evaporated milk) together with the grated orange rind. Whisk constantly over moderate heat, then when it starts to boil, use a wooden spoon to stir until the flour is cooked, in 3 or 4 minutes. Separate the eggs, stirring the yolks into the sauce and putting the whites into a large mixing bowl. When all the yolks have been added, stir in the butter and 2 tablespoons of the liqueur. If the sauce is to be left during the day, save a little of the butter to dot on the top to stop a skin from forming (this is not necessary if the egg whites are to be added within an hour).

To complete the soufflé Cut the sponge fingers or cake into tiny cubes, and soak in the remaining liqueur mixed with the water. Butter a 2½ pint (1½ litres/6 cups) soufflé dish and coat with the caster sugar — this gives the soufflé something to cling to as it rises. If the sauce was prepared earlier in the day, warm it gently until it feels tepid when touched with the finger.

Preheat the oven to Gas No. 6, 400 degrees F, 200 degrees C. Add the extra egg white to the 5 whites already in the bowl, and whisk them with a pinch of salt until they hold stiff peaks. Whisk in the 2 teaspoons of caster sugar. Stir a large spoonful of the meringue into the sauce to lighten the consistency, then fold in the remaining meringue with a rubber spatula. Turn half the mixture into the prepared dish, arrange the soaked cubes of sponge on top and cover with the remaining mixture. Smooth the top level, then put in the oven. Bake for 35 minutes until well risen and brown. Sprinkle with icing (confectioners') sugar and serve at once.

VARIATIONS

Lemon or Lime Soufflé Substitute 4 tablespoons lemon or lime juice and 2 teaspoons finely grated lemon or lime rind for the Grand Marnier and the orange rind.

Almond and Praline Soufflé Substitute 4 tablespoons Amaretto liqueur and 2 tablespoons praline (crushed almond or peanut brittle) for the Grand Marnier. Omit the orange rind.

BANANA SOUFFLÉ OMELETTE

SERVES 4

This delicious soufflé cooks in only 5 minutes, but it must be served hot off the pan, although most of the preparation can be done before the meal. Because it uses ingredients that are likely to be in stock, it is a very useful — and delicious — dessert to make for unexpected guests.

THE FILLING:

2 large bananas, cut in ½ in (1 cm) chunks
½ oz (15 g/1 tablespoon) butter (margarine for a meat meal)
1 level tablespoon soft brown sugar
1 tablespoon lemon juice
1 tablespoon apricot jam
1 tablespoon Cointreau (optional)

THE OMELETTE MIXTURE:

4 large eggs, separated
1 level tablespoon caster (superfine) sugar
2 level teaspoons flour
Grated rind of half an orange
Nut of butter or margarine for frying

217

To prepare the filling Melt the butter or margarine in a small frying pan and add the bananas, tossing over moderate heat until a pale golden-brown. Add the brown sugar and continue to cook until an even brown, then add the lemon juice and apricot jam. Take off the heat and stir in the liqueur (if used). Keep in a warm place or reheat when required.

To prepare the omelette mixture Half an hour before dinner, get ready an 8 or 9 in (20–23 cm) frying pan. Beat the yolks and sugar with a whisk until thick and mousse-like, then beat in the rind and the flour. Whisk the whites until they hold stiff peaks, then fold into the yolk mixture. Cover with a large bowl until required.

To cook the soufflé omelette Have ready the warm filling. Heat the grill (broiler). Melt a nut of butter or margarine in the frying pan and spoon in the omelette mixture. Cook gently for 4 minutes until the bottom is golden-brown, then put under a hot grill (broiler) as near as possible to the source of the heat. Cook until just brown and set, about 30 seconds, make a nick in the omelette, then spoon on the warm filling. Fold in two, transfer to a hot serving dish and sprinkle with icing (confectioners') sugar. Serve at once.

FRUIT AND PASTRY DESSERTS
ISRAELI APRICOT FLAN

SERVES 9–10

Freeze baked or unbaked pastry case 3 months
Leftovers will keep 2 days under refrigeration

This is a stunning presentation for a special buffet display. The lightly poached fruit is arranged on a bed of pastry cream flavoured with liqueur, and is then covered with a clear fruit glaze decorated with toasted almonds.

The gift of some tree-ripened apricots from my cousin's plantation in Israel prompted me to devise this delectable flan when I flew home to England next day.

The unusual pastry cream has the taste and texture of the most extravagant crème pâtissière but is made with nothing more recherché than custard powder! The flan is best served slightly chilled, on the day it is prepared, though the pastry case can be made whenever convenient.

THE BISCUIT PASTRY:
8 oz (225 g/2 cups) plain (all-purpose) flour
Pinch of salt
5 oz (150 g/⅔ cups) butter or margarine
2 level tablespoons caster (superfine) sugar
1 egg
Half an egg-shell of cold water
1 teaspoon vinegar

THE FRUIT:
1½–2 lb (¾–1 kg) fresh apricots
6 oz (175 g/¾ cup) sugar
8 fl oz (225 ml/1 cup) water

THE PASTRY CREAM:
8 oz (225 ml/1 cup) milk
1 oz custard powder
1 tablespoon caster (superfine) sugar
2 tablespoons any fruit-flavoured liqueur or Amaretto (optional)
8 fl oz (225 ml/1 cup) double (heavy) cream whipped

THE GLAZE:
Syrup from the stewed fruit
2 tablespoons lemon juice
2 rounded tablespoons smooth apricot jam
1 oz (25 g/¼ cup) flaked or slivered blanched almonds, toasted

To make the pastry   Make by hand or food processor as described for the Tarte aux Cerises au Kirsch on page 220. Wrap in film, flatten and chill for 30 minutes. Have ready a deep 10 in (25 cm) flan tin, or a shallower 12 in (30 cm) one. Roll out the pastry ⅛ in (¼ cm) thick on a lightly floured board, lift it over the rolling pin and carefully ease it into the flan tin. To prevent the pastry from shrinking, take a little 'tuck' in it all the way round the bottom edge of the tin so that the case is slightly thicker near the bottom than it is at the top. Roll the rolling pin over the top of the tin to cut off any excess pastry. Prick the bottom and the sides of the case with a fork, then press a large piece of foil into its shape, completely covering the bottom and the sides of the pastry. Put in the freezer for 1 hour.

To bake the flan case   Preheat the oven to Gas No. 6, 400 degrees F, 200 degrees C. Bake for 15 minutes, then carefully remove the foil, prick the base again if it looks puffy, turn the oven down to Gas No. 5, 375 degrees F, 190 degrees C and cook for a further 15–18 minutes until an even golden-brown. If the sides start to brown before the base, lay a piece of foil lightly over the top. Put the cooked flan on a cooling rack, and when quite cold carefully ease out of the tin and put on a flat silver tray or serving dish. The flan is now ready to fill.

To make the pastry cream   Make a custard with the milk, custard powder and sugar, either on top of the stove or in the microwave. Put in the freezer to chill for 20 minutes. Fold the chilled cream until it holds soft peaks, then whisk in the liqueur. Take the chilled custard from the freezer and process or blend for 1 minute until it looks smooth and creamy. Fold it gradually into the whipped cream, then spoon the mixture into the flan case and smooth level. Chill until required — it can be left overnight at this stage.

To cook the fruit   Halve the apricots and discard the stones. Put the sugar and water into a wine shallow pan, bring to the boil, then bubble for 3 minutes. Add the fruit in one layer, and simmer covered for about 10 minutes, or until almost tender. Do *not* overcook or the apricots will go mushy and the appearance of the flan will be spoiled. Take the pan off the heat and keep it covered for 20 minutes — this will allow the apricots to soften without losing their shape. Lift them out and allow to drain and cool on a cooling rack, then arrange in concentric circles on the pastry cream.

To glaze the flan   Put the apricot syrup into a small pan with the lemon juice and the apricot jam. Boil rapidly until the mixture becomes a thick syrup that will coat the back of a wooden spoon. Sprinkle the apricots with the toasted almonds, then spoon the glaze over the top. Chill the flan until required.

STRAWBERRY, RASPBERRY OR LOGANBERRY FLAN

SERVES 9–10

Freeze baked or unbaked pastry case 3 months
Leftovers will keep 2 days under refrigeration

Tightly packed circles of soft fruit are arranged in concentric circles on the pastry cream, and then covered with a redcurrant glaze. Frozen raspberries or loganberries may be used out of season, but not frozen strawberries which become flabby and wet when they are defrosted. The flan will keep crisp from the morning until the evening of the day it is prepared.

1 pastry case prepared and baked as for the Israeli Apricot Flan
Cold pastry cream, as in previous recipe
1½ lb (700 g/5 cups) small choice strawberries or raspberries or loganberries

THE GLAZE:
½ lb (225 g) jar redcurrant jelly
2 level tablespoons granulated sugar
2 tablespoons lemon juice

Heat all the glaze ingredients together, stirring, then boil rapidly until sticky drops of jam-like consistency fall from the spoon — about 5 minutes. Cool slightly.

To assemble the flan Put the cooled flan case on a serving dish and spoon in the pastry cream, then smooth level. Arrange the fruit on top, tightly packed together, then spoon the tepid glaze over the fruit and allow to set. Chill until required.

TARTE AUX CERISES AU KIRSCH
CHERRY TART WITH KIRSCH

SERVES 6–8

Freeze unbaked pastry case only 3 months
Cooked tarte will keep 2 days under refrigeration

Dessert cherries are baked in an almond custard set in a biscuity case. The flavours of liqueur and vanilla sugar combined give the filling a very subtle, sophisticated taste.

THE PASTRY CASE:
4 oz (125 g/1 cup) plain (all-purpose) flour plus 4 oz (125 g/1 cup) self-raising flour or 8 oz (225 g/2 cups) plain flour plus 1 teaspoon baking powder
2 oz caster (superfine) sugar
5 oz (150 g/⅔ cup) butter or margarine
1 whole egg
Squeeze of lemon juice
1 oz (25 g/4 tablespoons) icing (confectioners') sugar

THE FILLING:
1 ½ lb (700 g) dessert cherries
3 whole eggs
6 tablespoons whipping cream
1 oz (25 g/2 tablespoons) vanilla sugar plus 1 oz (25 g/2 tablespoons) caster (superfine) sugar or 2 oz (50 g/¼ cup) caster sugar plus 1 teaspoon vanilla essence (extract)
5 tablespoons ground almonds
2 tablespoons Kirsch
1½ oz (40 g/3 tablespoons) melted butter or margarine

220

To make the pastry: To mix with food processor Cut the fat into 1 in (2½ cm) chunks and put into the bowl with the dry ingredients. Beat the egg and lemon juice together, then add to the bowl, pulsing until the fat has been rubbed in and the mixture has been evenly moistened and is beginning to cling together into little balls. Turn into the bowl and gather together into a ball.

To mix by hand or electric mixer Mix the flours and sugar. Rub in the fat until no pieces larger than a small pea come to the surface when the bowl is shaken. Beat the egg with the lemon juice, then sprinkle over the mixture, and gather into a ball.

Knead the pastry by hand for 30 seconds until smooth, then wrap in film, flatten and chill for 30 minutes. Have ready a loose-bottomed or decorative heatproof flan dish, 10 in (25 cm) in diameter. Roll the pastry to fit the flan dish — there may be some pastry left over. Prick the sides and bottom of the pastry case with a fork, then trim the edges neatly. Freeze until the filling is prepared. Preheat the oven to Gas No. 6, 400 degrees F, 200 degrees C.

To finish Stone the cherries and put them into a bowl. Whisk together by hand or processor the eggs, cream, sugar, ground almonds and Kirsch, then add the melted butter and stir or pulse until evenly mixed. Take the uncooked pastry case out of the freezer and sprinkle the base with the icing sugar. Arrange the cherries on top and gently pour on the custard. Bake for 30–35 minutes until the custard is set. Serve warm. May be reheated.

SPICY APPLES IN A BROWN PASTRY CRUST

SERVES 6–8

Freeze (cooked) 3 months
Cooked pie will keep 4 days under refrigeration

The brown flour pastry is crisp and very short for this 'wholefood' pie, and the apples are bathed in a sauce containing dried fruits and spice.

THE PASTRY:
4 oz (125 g/1 cup) each plain wholemeal (wholewheat pastry flour) and white self-raising flour or 8 oz (225 g/2 cups) plain wholemeal flour and 1 teaspoon baking powder
5 oz (150 g/⅔ cup) butter or firm margarine
2 level tablespoons icing (confectioners') sugar
1 egg yolk
2 teaspoons vinegar
3–4 tablespoons icy water

THE FILLING:
2 lb (1 kg) fine-flavoured baking apples (weight when peeled)

4 oz (125 g/½ cup) dark brown sugar
3 teaspoons cinnamon
2 teaspoons mixed spice
2 level teaspoons cornflour (cornstarch)
4 oz (125 g/¾ cup) mixed dried fruit
3 oz (75 g/¾ cup) chopped walnuts, toasted in a moderate oven for 8 minutes until crunchy and golden
Grated rind and juice of ½ lemon

THE GLAZE:
1 egg white
2 tablespoons golden granulated or demerara (brown) sugar

Make the pastry by machine or hand, following the instructions for the Tarte aux Cerises au Kirsch on the opposite page.

Have ready a decorative 9–10 in (about 22–25 cm) flan tin or pie dish at least 1 in (2½ cm) deep. Preheat the oven to Gas No. 7, 425 degrees F, 220 degrees C. Peel and core the apples, then cut in slices about ⅛ in (¼ cm) thick using a knife or food processor. In a large bowl, mix the sugar, spices and cornflour; then add the dried fruit, nuts, apple slices and lemon juice and rind, and mix together gently but thoroughly.

Divide the chilled pastry in half and roll out one portion to fit the bottom of the flan tin or pie dish. Arrange the apple mixture on top. Damp the edges of the pastry then roll out the remaining portion, lay on top of the pie and seal the edges well together. Make three small slashes in the centre of the pie to allow steam to escape. Whisk the egg white until frothy, then paint all over the top of the pie, and scatter with the sugar in an even layer. Bake for 10 minutes, then reduce the heat to Gas No. 5, 375 degrees F, 190 degrees C and bake for a further 40 minutes or until a sharp knife goes in easily through the pastry and the apple filling. Serve warm. May be reheated.

ICE CREAMS AND SORBETS (SHERBETS)

- It is important to **freeze** ice cream and sorbet (sherbet) mixture as quickly as possible so that the particles of ice that form in them will be as tiny as possible and the frozen mixture will be smooth on the tongue. To do this, set the freezer or the refrigerator to FAST FREEZE an hour beforehand.
- The **ice creams** in this section do not need to be beaten during the freezing process.
- To make the **sorbets** smooth, the mixture needs to be whisked twice, either with a food processor or with an electric or hand whisk. To whisk on a food processor, the mixture should be frozen almost solid and then cut into rough chunks and placed in the machine. If it is to be beaten with a whisk it must only be frozen to a mush or the whisk will not be able to penetrate it. With this second method, there is always the danger that the mixture will melt before it has been sufficiently whisked, so chill both the whisk and the bowl before use.
- A **stiffly beaten egg white** folded in at the last moment before re-freezing will help to lighten a sorbet and give it a 'creamy' texture.
- All frozen mixtures need to **ripen** from one day to the next, to allow the flavour to develop fully before they are served.
- The **texture** of both ice creams and sorbets should be 'creamy' rather than firm, so they need to be allowed to soften slightly in the refrigerator during the meal. Certain sorbets which freeze particularly hard may even need to be softened briefly at room temperature.
- Ices can be **scooped, piped** or **turned out of a mould**. This can all be done several hours before dinner and the ice cream or sorbet can then be left in the freezer until it is time to transfer it to the refrigerator shortly before serving, when the final garnish of fruit, nuts or cream can be added.
- A **bombe** is frozen in a special metal mould or a mixing bowl, then turned out and either surrounded with a ribbon of fruit sauce, or masked with it.
- Scoops of the ice can be piled up in a bowl and decorated with little sprigs of fresh currants or berries in season.
- An **ice cream slice** is frozen in a long loaf tin, then turned out on a narrow plate and decorated with small clusters of toasted nuts or with a complementary fruit.

- **Coffee demi-tasses** or little **porcelain pots** make charming containers for ice cream. They can be decorated with shavings of chocolate or with sugared fresh fruit.
- Sorbets can be frozen until they are the consistency of whipped cream then **piped in whirls** on a tray. The whirls are quickly re-frozen and then arranged just before serving in wine glasses or on individual glass plates and decorated with slices of exotic fruit.
- **Several scoops of different sorbets** look spectacular in long-stemmed glasses with wide, shallow bowls.
- A solid metal **ice cream scoop** is a useful investment. Otherwise use a spoon with a round bowl dipped in a jug of boiling water.

APPLE AND CIDER SORBET

SERVES 8   *Freeze 3 months*

This recipe contains less sugar than most sorbets do — it is mainly sweetened by the natural sugar in the apples — so provided you use a strong dry cider and well-flavoured fruit, you will be delighted with the tart refreshing taste. In Normandy they make this kind of sorbet with 'windfalls' and their own cider, and lace it with Calvados — the local apple brandy. I think that English apples have a better flavour and our cider is drier and stronger, and that we can therefore make apple sorbets that are superior to the French ones. The Calvados is nice, though, if you can get it, but it's best to buy it in Normandy, as it is a horrendous price outside France. Otherwise serve the ice decorated with a few sprigs of redcurrants. It's also excellent as an accompaniment to apple pie. To serve it as they do in Normandy, put a scoop of the sorbet in a small wine glass and pour a tablespoon of Calvados over it at the table.

2 lb (1 kg) eating apples, either Cox's or
Granny Smith's
3 tablespoons fresh or bottled lemon juice
Water to cover the apples
2 cinnamon sticks

½ litre (17½ fl oz/2¼ cups) strong dry cider
4 oz (125 g/½ cup) caster (superfine) sugar
4 tablespoons fresh lemon juice
Rind of 1 lemon, finely grated
2 egg whites

Set the freezer to FAST FREEZE. Core the apples but do not peel them. Slice each one into 12 segments, then put into a bowl and leave covered with the first quantity of lemon juice and water for 15 minutes (this keeps the apples white). Drain them and put in a stainless steel or enamel pan. Add the cinnamon sticks and half the cider. Bring to the boil, then simmer, partly covered, for 10 minutes or until the apples feel soft. Remove the cinnamon sticks. Purée the stewed apples and juice in a blender or food processor, then push through a sieve to remove the peel. Add the sugar, stir until it has dissolved in the hot purée, then stir in the remaining cider, the second quantity of lemon juice and the zest. Mix well, cool, then put in a fairly shallow dish and freeze until it is semi-frozen, after about 3 hours.

Turn into the food processor and process for 45 seconds until the mixture looks

223

creamy and lighter in colour. (Or use a large balloon whisk or electric whisk.) Freeze again until semi-frozen. Whisk the egg whites until they hold soft peaks that just tip over when the beaters are withdrawn. Process the sorbet again as before, then pulse in the egg whites until they disappear. Freeze again until required.

BLACKCURRANT SORBET

SERVES 6–8   *Freeze 3 months*

In Burgundy, they accentuate the fruity flavours of this sorbet with a spoonful of Crème de Cassis, the local blackcurrant liqueur which despite its name does not contain any cream.

1 lb (450 g/4 cups) fresh or frozen blackcurrants or ½ pint (275 ml/1¼ cups) unsweetened purée
2 tablespoons water

6 oz (175 g/¾ cup) granulated sugar
½ pint (275 ml/1¼ cups) water
2 tablespoons lemon juice
1 egg white

Set the freezer to FAST FREEZE. Set aside a few of the currants for garnish. Remove any stalks from the fruit, then put in a pan with 2 tablespoons of water, cover and simmer for 8 or 10 minutes until absolutely soft. Leave until the fruit stops steaming, then push it through a sieve or mouli to remove the skin and pips.

Heat the sugar and water together in a small pan, stirring until the sugar is dissolved, then boil without stirring for 4 minutes. Allow this syrup to cool to room temperature, then stir in the purée and the lemon juice. Put in a shallow plastic container and freeze until semi-frozen — about 3 hours.

Turn into the food processor and process for 45 seconds until the mixture looks creamy and lighter in colour (or use a large balloon or electric whisk). Return it immediately to the container and freeze for a further 1½ hours until semi-frozen again. Have ready the egg white, whisked until it holds soft peaks. Put the sorbet back in the food processor and process for 45 seconds as before, then pulse in the egg white until no trace of it can be seen. Re-freeze until firm, at least 3 hours. When you serve it, offer a bottle of Crème de Cassis for guests to pour over their sorbet at the table.

REDCURRANT SORBET

SERVES 6–8   *Freeze 3 months*

To complement the delicate flavour of the redcurrants, the syrup is made with a fruity white wine, although water can be used if preferred.

1 lb (450 g/4 cups) fresh or frozen redcurrants
½ pint (275 ml/1¼ cups) fruity white wine such as Riesling

4 oz (125 g/½ cup) granulated sugar
1 tablespoon lemon juice
1 egg white

Set the freezer to FAST FREEZE. Set aside a few currants for garnish, remove any stalks, then push the fruit through a sieve or mouli to remove the skins and pips (there is no need to cook the fruit). Make in exactly the same way as the Blackcurrant Sorbet, offering a bottle of Crème de Framboise (raspberry liqueur) instead of Crème de Cassis for guests to pour over their sorbet at the table.

DAMSON SORBET

SERVES 6–8   *Freeze 3 months*

This has a wonderful tart flavour, which goes well with a lacing of Damson Gin (see page 286).

1½ lb (700 g) fresh or frozen damsons
¼ pint (150 ml/⅔ cup) water plus 4 oz (125
g/½ cup) granulated sugar (to stew the
damsons)

½ pint (275 ml/1¼ cups) water plus 4 oz
(125 g/½ cup) granulated sugar (for the
syrup)
1 tablespoon lemon juice (optional)
1 egg white

Stew the damsons in the ¼ pint (150 ml/⅔ cup) water in a covered pan until the flesh of the fruit is absolutely tender and the stones have risen to the surface. Skim off as many stones as possible, then sieve the fruit or put it through a food mill, discarding the stones as they are freed from the pulp. Stir in the first 4 oz (125 g/½ cup) granulated sugar.

Make a syrup with the remaining sugar and water and complete the preparation of the sorbet in the same way as for the Blackcurrant Sorbet, offering a bottle of Damson Gin instead of Crème de Cassis for guests to pour over their sorbet at the table.

STRAWBERRY SORBET

SERVES 6   *Freeze 3 months*

1 lb (450 g/3 cups) fresh or unsugared frozen
strawberries or ½ pint (275 ml/1¼ cups)
unsweetened purée
6 oz (175 g/¾ cups) granulated sugar

½ pint (275 ml/1¼ cups) water
4 tablespoons lemon juice
1 egg white

Put the strawberries in a blender or food processor and process until they form a smooth purée. Make the syrup as for the Blackcurrant Sorbet, cool and stir in the purée and the lemon juice, then complete the preparation of the sorbet in the same way.

ORANGE AND LEMON SORBET

SERVES 6–8   Freeze 3 months

This is a particularly refreshing sorbet with a fine orange flavour sharpened with a hint of lemon. You can use 6 fl oz (175 ml/¾ cup) of frozen or bottled concentrated orange juice made up with water to ½ pint (275 ml/1¼ cups) instead of the liquid juice, but then use only 4 oz (125 g/½ cup) sugar for the syrup. The smooth creamy texture of this sorbet makes it taste almost like ice cream.

10 fl oz (275 ml/1¼ cups) orange juice
(fresh, carton or canned)
Grated rind of 1 orange
Rind of 1 large lemon, finely grated, and 5
tablespoons juice (about 1½ lemons)

6 oz (175 g/¾ cup) granulated sugar
½ pint (275 ml/1¼ cups) cold water
2 egg whites, whisked until they hold soft,
glossy peaks

Set the freezer at FAST FREEZE. Mix the orange and lemon juices with the grated rind and leave to stand. Put the sugar and water into a pan and bring to the boil, stirring constantly until the sugar is dissolved. Stop stirring and simmer steadily for 10 minutes, then cool the syrup until it stops steaming. Add the fruit juice mixture. Put into a container and freeze for 3 hours or until semi-frozen.

Put in the food processor and process for 45 seconds until it goes creamy and lighter in colour (or use an electric whisk). Immediately return it to the container and freeze for a further 1½ hours. Put back in the food processor and process for 45 seconds. Have ready the whisked egg whites, add them to the mixture and pulse for 3 seconds or until no trace of egg white can be seen. Freeze until firm, about 3 hours.

PEACH SORBET

SERVES 6–8   Freeze 3 months

To develop an intense taste in a sorbet made from a fruit with a delicate flavour, it's a good idea to marinate the fruit in the syrup for some time before the mixture is frozen. For a special occasion, scoops of this sorbet look especially enticing served in 'Manhattan' cocktail glasses, garnished with a few fresh peach slices and a tiny sprig of fresh mint.

4 medium-sized ripe peaches (about 1¼ lb)
(550 g)
½ pint (275 ml/1¼ cups) water

4 oz (125 g/½ cup) granulated sugar
2 tablespoons lemon juice
1 egg white

Set the freezer to FAST FREEZE. Put the whole peaches into a pan of boiling water, bring back to the boil and then simmer for 1 minute. Pour off the boiling water and cover the peaches with cold water. You will find that the skins will peel off easily with the help of a small knife. Cut the peaches in half and remove the stones or, if this is not possible, cut the flesh away from the stone in chunks.

Put the sugar and water into a pan and stir over moderate heat until the sugar is completely dissolved. Bring to the boil and boil for 4 minutes, and stir in the lemon juice. Add the skinned peaches to the syrup, bring back to the boil, cover, remove from the heat and leave to stand until cold.

Put the peaches and syrup into the food processor or blender and process until puréed. Put into a shallow dish and freeze until *almost* solid, about 2 hours. Cut in chunks and process in the food processor for 1 minute, until smooth and creamy in appearance (or use a large balloon or electric whisk). Re-freeze for a further 2 hours or until almost solid again. Whisk the egg white until it holds soft peaks. Put the sorbet back in the food processor and process for 45 seconds, then add the egg white and pulse until it just disappears. Re-freeze. The sorbet will be ready to serve in 3 or 4 hours.

BROWN BREAD ICE CREAM

SERVES 10–12   *Freeze 3 months*

The delicious flavour of this ice cream belies its unimaginative Victorian name. Crumbs from a brown loaf are grilled with brown sugar until they become crisp and caramelized. Do not use a dark brown sugar — it will burn before the breadcrumbs have become crisp. The ice cream can be served in scoops with fruit salad or caramel sauce, or frozen in little pots.

3 oz (75 g/1½ cups) breadcrumbs from a day-old brown loaf
3 oz (75 g/⅓ cup) light brown sugar
4 eggs, separated
Pinch of salt

2 oz (50 g/¼ cup) caster (superfine) sugar
1 teaspoon vanilla essence (extract)
½ pint (275 ml/1¼ cups) whipping cream or non-dairy cream

Mix the brown sugar and breadcrumbs thoroughly together, then spread out on a heatproof tray and put under a medium grill (broiler) until crisp and as brown as a burnished chestnut. Keep an eye on this process, stirring with a fork about once a minute to ensure the browning and crisping is even. When the colour is right, the mixture will feel crisp in the fingers. Allow to go quite cold, by which time it will be really crunchy in texture.

Whisk the egg whites with a pinch of salt until they hold stiff peaks, then whisk in the caster sugar 2 teaspoons at a time whisking until stiff after each addition, then stir in the yolks until the colour is even. Whisk the cream with the vanilla essence until it hangs on the beaters and is of a similar consistency to that of the egg mixture. Fold the crumbs into the cream, and then fold into the egg mixture. Turn into a plastic container and freeze for 6 hours, until firm.

COFFEE AND BURNT ALMOND ICE CREAM

SERVES 8–10   *Freeze 3 months*

Instant Espresso coffee is the best for flavour.

2 oz (50 g/½ cup) slivered almonds
Nut of butter or margarine
3 eggs, separated
Pinch of salt
3 oz (75 g/¾ cup) icing (confectioners')
sugar

8 fl oz (225 ml/1 cup) whipping or non-dairy
cream
1 tablespoon Tia Maria or Sabra, or any
coffee-flavoured liqueur (optional)
2 tablespoons instant coffee dissolved in 1
tablespoon boiling water

To prepare the almonds, melt the nut of fat in a small frying pan and toss the almonds in it until they turn a rich brown, then drain on kitchen paper. (Or brown them in the microwave.)

In a large bowl whisk the whites with a pinch of salt until they hold stiff, glossy peaks. Add the icing sugar, a tablespoon at a time, whisking after each addition until the meringue is stiff again, then stir in the yolks until the colour is even. Whisk the cream until it is stiff enough to hang on the beaters, whisk in the liqueur, then whisk in the *cool* coffee a tablespoon at a time (hot coffee may curdle the cream). Don't overbeat. Fold the cream into the meringue mixture followed by the burnt almonds. Turn into a plastic container and put in the freezer for 6 hours. Serve plain or with chocolate sauce.

VARIATION
Coffee and Burnt Almond Slice   Make the ice cream as above. Have ready a few extra burnt almonds and some glacé (candied) cherries. Spoon the ice cream into a deep ice tray or a long plastic container measuring about 11 × 4 × 1½ in (about 27 × 10 × 3 cm) (or use a long loaf tin) and put in the freezer until firm — about 3 hours. About an hour before serving (or earlier if more convenient), run a sharp knife round the sides of the container. Dip the base for 15 seconds in a bowl of hot water, then unmould on to a long serving dish. Decorate with the nuts and cherries. Return to the freezer. When you sit down to dinner transfer the slice to the refrigerator to soften slightly.

FRESH GINGER ICE CREAM IN GINGER BASKETS

SERVES 6–8   *Freeze 3 months*

This original dessert could provide the grand finale for a special dinner party. Both preserved and fresh ginger are used in it to make a smooth and creamy ice cream of superb flavour. The ginger baskets add a novel touch, but of course you can also serve the ice cream more simply in a stemmed glass, accompanied by a sponge finger (ladyfinger).

THE ICE CREAM:

4 oz (125 g/½ cup) stem ginger (drained from the syrup in the jar)
3 eggs, separated
Pinch of salt
2 tablespoons light brown sugar
½ pint (275 ml/1¼ cups) double (heavy) cream
1 teaspoon vanilla essence (extract)
2 tablespoons ginger syrup (from jar)
2 teaspoons grated fresh ginger root

THE BASKETS:

2 oz (50 g/¼ cup) butter
2 oz (50 g/¼ cup) golden syrup (corn syrup)
1½ oz (40 g/3 tablespoons) caster (superfine) sugar
2 oz (50 g/½ cup) less 2 teaspoons plain (all-purpose) flour
½ teaspoon ground ginger

GARNISH:

2–3 tablespoons of the ginger syrup
Slices of a decorative fruit such as star fruit, kiwi fruit or strawberry, and pieces of stem ginger

To make the ice cream Chop the stem ginger into little bits. Separate the eggs, putting the whites in one (large) bowl and the yolks in another (small) one. Whisk the whites with a pinch of salt until they hold stiff peaks, then whisk in the sugar a tablespoon at a time. Gently whisk in the egg yolks until the colour is even. Whisk the cream until it hangs on the beaters, then whisk in the vanilla, followed by the ginger syrup, whisking until stiff. Fold in the grated fresh ginger, then fold the cream into the egg white mixture. Turn the ice cream into a container and freeze until half-set, about 2 hours. Gently stir in the chopped stem ginger. Continue to freeze until firm, preferably leaving overnight for the flavour to mature.

To make the ginger baskets Weigh all the ingredients very carefully. Put the butter into a thick-bottomed pan and heat gently until it is just melted, then stir in the syrup and sugar and continue heating and stirring until the mixture is smooth and without graininess. Do not allow it to boil. Stir in the remaining ingredients. Cool for 10 minutes or until the consistency of putty.

Form into balls the size of a walnut — there should be 10 or 12. Arrange 4 in (10 cm) apart on lightly oiled baking trays. Bake at Gas No. 3, 325 degrees F, 160 degrees C for 10–12 minutes or until golden-brown. Leave to cool for 1 minute or until the biscuits (cookies) can be lifted off the tray with a spatula, then mould each one over the bottom of a small glass or an aluminium jelly mould, making little cups. When firm — after a minute or two — arrange carefully on a cooling tray. When quite cold, store in an airtight tin at room temperature — *not* in the freezer, which makes the baskets go soggy. They will keep for up to a month.

To assemble Arrange a basket on each plate. Just before serving, arrange 2 scoops of ice cream in each basket. Drizzle a little of the remaining ginger syrup on top and decorate with the fruit and stem ginger.

FROZEN ZABAGLIONE

SERVES 10   Freeze 3 months

This looks and tastes best when frozen in little pots or 'cocottes'. It is important to use the 'cream' Marsala rather than the dry 'fine' version which is used for savoury dishes.

6 egg yolks
2 oz (50 g/¼ cup) caster (superfine) sugar

6 tablespoons Marsala
¼ pint (150 ml/⅔ cup) double (heavy) or
non-dairy cream

If you have a metal bowl that will fit over a pan so much the better as it conducts the heat most effectively. Otherwise, use a glass mixing bowl. For speed, use a hand-held electric whisk if possible; otherwise use a rotary whisk or a batter whisk.

Put the yolks and sugar into the chosen mixing bowl and whisk until blended, then add the Marsala. Put over a pan of *simmering* water, and whisk until the mixture becomes as thick as softly whipped cream and has increased two or three times in volume — after 5 or 6 minutes. Remove from the heat.

Replace the water in the pan with cold water, then replace the bowl and continue to whisk until the mixture feels tepid to the touch. Whisk the chilled cream until it is of a similar consistency, then gradually fold in the Zabaglione with a rubber spatula. Spoon into the chosen containers and freeze 2–6 hours depending on size.

LEMON BOMBE, APRICOT COULIS

SERVES 8–10   Freeze 3 months

This ice cream has a very refreshing lemon flavour and a creamy texture. Just before it is served, some of the Apricot Coulis is spooned over the bombe and the remainder is passed in a sauceboat at the table. The delicate pastel colours make this a very effective dessert for a spring dinner party.

Rind of 1 lemon, finely grated
Juice of 2 lemons (5 tablespoons)
3 eggs, separated
Pinch of salt
3 oz (75 g/⅓ cup) and 1 oz (25 g/

2 tablespoons) caster (superfine) sugar
8 fl oz (225 ml/1 cup) double (heavy) or
non-dairy cream
1 recipe Apricot Coulis (see page 207), well
chilled

Grate the lemon rind very finely and juice the lemons, then leave the rind and juice together in a basin. Put the egg whites into a bowl with the pinch of salt, then whisk until they hold stiff peaks when the beaters are withdrawn. Add the 3 oz (75 g/⅓ cup) sugar a tablespoon at a time, beating until stiff after each addition. Gently whisk in the egg yolks until the colour is even. Put the cream and the further 1 oz (25 g/ 2 tablespoons) sugar into a second bowl and whisk until it starts to thicken, then add the lemon juice and rind and whisk until the mixture is thick enough to hang on the beaters when they are withdrawn from the bowl. Carefully fold in the yolk mixture. Turn the ice cream into a 2 pint (1¼ litres/5 cups) mixing bowl and leave to freeze for 24 hours.

Several hours before it is required, fill a plastic bowl with hot water. Loosen the ice cream from the edge of the mixing bowl using a sharp knife, then stand in the hot water and count 'one, two, three' slowly. Immediately turn out the bombe on to a serving dish. Put back into the freezer until required.

ORANGE BOMBE

SERVES 8–10   *Freeze 3 months*

Concentrated orange juice gives this bombe a wonderful flavour. It looks beautiful surrounded with a fresh pineapple and orange fruit salad or fresh strawberry compôte. For a different presentation, freeze the ice cream in demi-tasse cups or cocottes and decorate with a few sliced fresh strawberries.

5 tablespoons concentrated frozen or bottled orange juice
1 tablespoon lemon juice
Rind of 1 orange and half a lemon, finely grated

1 oz (25 g/2 tablespoons) plus 1 oz (25 g/ 2 tablespoons) caster (superfine) sugar
8 fl oz (225 ml/1 cup) double (heavy) or non-dairy cream

Make in exactly the same way as the Lemon Bombe.

DRAMATIC DESSERTS
HAZELNUT TORTE WITH APRICOT FILLING

SERVES 8–10   *Freeze filled torte 2 months*
                                     Will keep 3 days under refrigeration

The tart flavour of the dried apricot filling makes a pleasing contrast to the sweet nut meringue. It can be made equally well with dairy or non-dairy cream.

THE TORTE:
5 oz (150 g/1¼ cups) hazelnuts (filberts)
5 egg whites
10 oz (275 g/1¼ cups) caster (superfine) sugar
1 teaspoon lemon juice
1 tablespoon flaked hazelnuts

THE FILLING:
6 oz (175 g/1 cup) dried apricots

½ pint (275 ml/1¼ cups) water
1 strip lemon peel
2 tablespoons lemon juice
8 fl oz (225 ml/1 cup) whipping or non-dairy cream
1 tablespoon caster (superfine) sugar
2 tablespoons liqueur, apricot-, orange- or almond-flavoured (optional)

231

To make the torte Set the oven at Gas No. 3, 325 degrees F, 160 degrees C. Put the hazelnuts on a tray and toast in the oven for 20 minutes, or until the nuts have turned a golden-brown. Rub them vigorously in a teatowel to remove the skins, then grind them to a coarse powder in a liquidizer, nut mill or food processor (this can be done at any time and the nuts stored in an airtight container). Cut silicone paper to fit two baking sheets, trace a 9 in (22½ cm) circle on each piece of paper, then turn over and lay the circles on the baking sheets.

Whisk the whites until they hold stiff peaks, then whisk in half (5 oz/150 g/⅔ cup) of the sugar, a tablespoon at a time, whisking until stiff after each addition. Whisk in the lemon juice. Mix the ground nuts with the rest of the sugar, then *fold* into the meringue using a rubber spatula. Divide the mixture between the two circles, either piping or spooning it into a round about 1 in (2½ cm) high. Sprinkle one round with the flaked hazelnuts. Bake for 1–1¼ hours or until the tops of the meringue rounds are biscuit-coloured and crisp to the touch. Allow to cool, then lift off the paper and store either in an airtight tin (up to 1 month) or in the freezer (up to 3 months) until required.

To make the filling Put the apricots into a small pan with the lemon peel, lemon juice and water (no need to soak them first). Bring to the boil, cover, then simmer until the fruit feels tender when pierced with a knife, about 20 minutes. Discard the peel, then purée the apricots and their liquid in a blender or food processor, and allow to go cold. Put the cream, sugar and liqueur into a bowl and whisk until the mixture will hang on the whisk when it is lifted above the bowl. Fold in the apricot purée.

To assemble Place one meringue layer on a plate and cover evenly with the filling, then place the other meringue (the one that was decorated with the flaked hazelnuts) on top. Open-freeze, then wrap in foil and freeze until required. Defrost at room temperature for 30 minutes before serving.

LEMON SCHAUM TORTE

SERVES 8–10

Freeze 1 month
Leftovers will keep under refrigeration for
3 days

The meringue for this superb dessert is piped or spooned into a long rectangle which cuts into more attractive slices than does the traditional round Pavlova. The torte can be frozen for up to 1 month in advance and then left at room temperature for about 20 minutes. It should be served semi-frozen, so that the lemon filling has the texture of soft ice cream.

THE TORTE:
4 egg whites
¼ teaspoon cream of tartar
8 oz (225 g/1 cup) caster (superfine) sugar
mixed with 2 level teaspoons cornflour
(cornstarch)

THE FILLING:
4 egg yolks

4 oz (125 g/½ cup) caster (superfine) sugar
6 tablespoons lemon juice (2 or 3 large
lemons)
Grated rind of 2 lemons
½ pint (275 ml/1¼ cups) double (heavy)
cream or 8 fl oz (225 ml/1 cup) non-dairy
cream

To make the torte Preheat the oven to Gas No. 2, 300 degrees F, 150 degrees C. Line two baking trays with silicone paper, each piece of paper marked on the reverse side with a rectangle 11 in (28 cm) long and 5 in (12 cm) wide. Whisk the whites, sprinkled with the cream of tartar, until they hold stiff, glossy peaks. Mix the cornflour with the caster sugar, then add a tablespoonful at a time, whisking until stiff again after each addition. Use a large 'rose' nozzle to pipe the meringue in parallel lines across the width of the rectangles; alternatively, spoon the meringue on to the rectangles and use a fork to neaten and texture it. Place the meringues in the oven, reduce the temperature to Gas No. 1, 275 degrees F, 140 degrees C, and bake for 1 hour or until the slices are crisp to the touch and will lift off the paper easily. Remove to cooling trays and allow to go cold.

To make the filling Start this as soon as the meringue goes into the oven, as the custard must be quite cold before the cream is folded in. Put the yolks and sugar into a heavy-bottomed pan. Stir with a wooden spoon until creamy, then add the lemon juice and rind. Cook over gentle heat like a custard, stirring constantly until the mixture thickens like mayonnaise. Take off the heat and stir for a further minute, then turn into a basin and refrigerate or freeze until absolutely cold, about 30 minutes.

Whisk the cream until it stands in soft peaks, then beat in the cold lemon custard, a tablespoon at a time — it will now look like lemon-coloured whipped cream. On a tray, spread out a piece of foil large enough to enclose the finished torte. Place one rectangle of meringue on it, spread the filling evenly over it, then lay the second rectangle on top, piped side uppermost. Freeze uncovered until solid, then wrap in the foil. To serve, unwrap the frozen torte and carefully transfer it to a serving dish or tray. Leave at room temperature for 20 minutes, by which time the filling will have softened enough to slice.

STRAWBERRY SCHAUM TORTE

SERVES 8–10

Freeze 1 month
Leftovers will keep under refrigeration 3 days

Make the meringue layers in exactly the same way as for the Lemon Schaum Torte (page 232), but use this filling.

Juice and grated rind of 1 medium orange and half a lemon (4 fl oz (125 ml/½ cup) altogether)
2 tablespoons orange-flavoured liqueur, such as Grand Marnier, Curaçao or Cointreau (optional)
1 oz (25 g/2 tablespoons) caster (superfine) sugar

½ lb (225 g/1½ cups) strawberries, sliced and sprinkled with 1 tablespoon caster sugar
½ pint (275 ml/1¼ cups) double (heavy) cream or 8 fl oz (225 ml/1 cup) non-dairy cream

Put the juices, rind and liqueur (if used) into a mixing bowl and stir in the sugar and cream. Stir well, then whisk until the mixture stands in soft peaks. Fold in the sugared strawberries. Use to fill the layers of the torte.

LEMON AND CHERRY CHARLOTTE RUSSE

SERVES 8–10

Freeze 2 months (without glaze)
Complete sweet will keep under refrigeration
for 3 days

A delicate lemon mousse is set in a ring of sponge fingers (ladyfingers) and coated with a beautiful cherry glaze. This traditional English dessert, which is equally delicious whether made with dairy or non-dairy cream, makes an impressive feature on a buffet table.

THE MOUSSE:
1 tablespoon smooth apricot jam
1 packet langue de chat *biscuits* or *sponge fingers (ladyfingers)*
3 large eggs, separated
6 oz (175 g/¾ cup) caster (superfine) sugar
3 fl oz (75 ml/⅓ cup) lemon juice
2 teaspoons grated lemon rind
½ oz (15 g/1 level tablespoon) kosher gelatine or 1 lemon jelly (gelatine dessert mix)

3 fl oz (75 ml/⅓ cup) water
¾ pint (425 ml/2 cups) whipping cream or 12 fl oz (350 ml/1½ cups) non-dairy cream

THE GLAZE:
1 can (15 oz (425 g)) sweet black cherries, stoned
1 level tablespoon cornflour (cornstarch)
1 tablespoon lemon juice
1 tablespoon cherry brandy (optional)

To prepare the lemon mousse Have ready a 7 in (17½ cm) loose-bottomed round cake tin about 3 in (7½ cm) deep. Take each biscuit in turn and dab the centre of the sugared side with a little apricot jam, then stand it up vertically against the side of the tin. Repeat with the remaining biscuits until the inside of the tin is completely lined.

Whisk the egg yolks with an electric beater until well blended, then whisk in the sugar gradually until the mixture lightens in colour and becomes as thick as whipped cream. Gradually whisk in the lemon juice and rind — the mixture will thin down but it will still be of mousse-like texture. Put the water into a small bowl and sprinkle the gelatine on top, then heat over a pan of hot water or in the microwave until it looks clear. (If a jelly is used, heat it with the water until dissolved.) Whisk the dissolved gelatine or jelly into the lemon and egg mixture, then leave it in the refrigerator or freezer until as thick as unbeaten egg whites — about 10 minutes in the freezer, 20 minutes in the refrigerator. If it becomes too set, whisk it until smooth.

Whisk the egg whites until they hold stiff but still glossy peaks. Whisk the cream until it holds a soft peak. Fold two-thirds of the cream, followed by the beaten egg white, into the lemon mixture, using a rubber spatula to make sure it is gently but evenly mixed. Spoon into the biscuit-lined tin and chill until firm, about 3 hours.

To make the glaze Mix the juice from the cherries (made up with water to 8 fl oz (225 ml/1 cup) if necessary) with the cornflour and bubble for 3 minutes, then stir in the lemon juice and cherry brandy (if used). Allow to cool until it stops steaming, then stir in the cherries and spoon over the top of the chilled charlotte. Chill thoroughly — for another hour.

To serve When quite firm, run a knife round the sides of the tin, then place it on a

234

canister or tin of a smaller size and push up the base to free the sweet from the sides of the tin. Arrange (still on the base) on a serving dish. Re-whip the remaining cream until it holds firm peaks, then pipe or spoon on the dessert. Serve chilled.

PINEAPPLE AND KIRSCH CHEESECAKE

SERVES 6–8

Freeze 2 months
Will keep 2 days under refrigeration

This is a light, refreshing and elegant cheesecake using delicate sponge layers instead of pastry.

1 fatless sponge (yellow) cake, 9–10 in (22–25 cm) in diameter, home-made or bought

THE FILLING:
4–6 small slices fresh or canned pineapple
4 fl oz (125 ml/½ cup) water plus 3 oz (75 g/ ⅓ cup) sugar, or 5 fl oz (150 ml/⅔ cup) syrup from fruit
Juice of 1 orange (3 oz) (75 ml/⅓ cup)
Juice of half a lemon
1 level tablespoon cornflour (cornstarch)
2 tablespoons Kirsch (Cointreau may be used instead)

THE CHEESECAKE:
1 lemon jelly (gelatine dessert mix) dissolved in 3 tablespoons water or ½ oz (15 g/1 tablespoon) powdered kosher gelatine dissolved in 3 tablespoons lemon juice
1 lb (450 g) medium-fat soft cheese
2 oz (50 g/¼ cup) caster (superfine) sugar (an extra ounce (25 g/2 tablespoons) if lemon juice has been used)
Grated rind of half a lemon
1 teaspoon vanilla essence (extract)
5 fl oz (150 ml/⅔ cup) soured cream

To prepare the filling If fresh pineapple is used, slice it ¾ in (2 cm) thick, and remove the skin and core. Cut the pineapple into small pieces. Heat the water and sugar together (or heat the pineapple syrup, if used), then add the orange juice. Mix the cornflour to a cream with the lemon juice, and stir into the hot fruit syrup. Bring to the boil, simmer for 2 minutes, then take off the heat and stir in the liqueur. Pour over the fruit. Allow to go quite cold.

To make the cheesecake Dissolve the jelly in the water. (If gelatine is used, mix it with the lemon juice, then either stand it in a bowl over a simmering kettle, or heat in the microwave, until clear.) Put the soft cheese into a bowl, then stir in all the remaining ingredients. Put in the refrigerator to chill until almost set (about 30 minutes). Meanwhile, freeze the cake for about 30 minutes so that it is easy to cut into two even layers.

To assemble the cake Use the washed tin in which the cake was cooked or one that a bought cake will fit in — it must have a loose bottom. Put the bottom layer of the sponge into the tin. Spoon the half-set cheesecake on top and cover with the cooled pineapple. Finally lay the top half of the cake lightly on top. Refrigerate, preferably overnight. To serve, pull down the sides of the tin and place the cake (still on the base) on a serving dish. Sift a thick layer of icing (confectioners') sugar over it.

SUMMER PUDDING

SERVES 8

Freeze 4 months
Will keep 3 days under refrigeration

This classic English midsummer dessert is tasted at its best when it is prepared with bread made from a Jewish challah mixture! A pudding basin is lined with strips of this rich bread, and then filled brimful with sugared soft fruit. After the pudding has been left under a weight overnight, the juice permeates the bread, giving it a sponge-like texture. This is delicious served with thick natural yoghurt.

1 challah baked in a 2 lb (1 kg) loaf tin (also known as 'best bread'), at least 24 hours old
3 lb (1¼ kg) fresh or frozen soft fruit (a good mixture is 1 lb (450 g/3 cups) raspberries, 1 lb (450 g/4 cups) blackcurrants plus 1 lb (450 g/4 cups) redcurrants)

8 oz (225 g/1 cup) caster (superfine) sugar
4 tablespoons Kirsch or vodka (optional)
4 tablespoons any fruit juice or syrup (not necessary if fruit is frozen)

Select a pudding basin with a 2 pint (1¼ litres/5 cups) capacity (fill it with water to make sure). Cut a small disc of silicone paper to fit the base of the basin. Decrust the loaf, cut it in ⅜ in (1 cm) slices lengthwise, then cut these into wedges about 1 in (2½ cm) wide which can then be fitted tightly together round the sides of the basin, meeting at the bottom and covering it — it is important that there are no gaps in the bread lining to let the juices escape.

Pick over but do not wash the fruit, then put into a bowl and mix thoroughly with the sugar, liqueur and fruit juice (if used). (If the fruit looks rather dry, cook it lightly first; if, on the other hand, it is very juicy, as frozen fruit often is when defrosted, the fruit juice can be omitted.) Spoon the prepared fruit into the bread-lined basin, pressing it down gently with the back of a wooden spoon so that the juices begin to penetrate the bread. Cut slices of bread to make a 'lid' on top. To weight down the pudding, cover it with film or foil, put a small pan that just fits on top, and on top of that put either a 2 lb (1 kg) weight or a 1 kg bag of sugar. Refrigerate it for at least 24 hours, sitting on a plate to collect any juice that may overflow.

To serve Don't unmould the pudding until you are ready to serve it, as the case may collapse. Have ready a pie or flan dish about ½ in (1 cm) deep. Carefully run a knife round the inside of the bowl to make sure the lining will come away, then reverse on to the serving plate. Any juice that has overflowed can be spooned on top.

Biscuits and Cookies

It's not so long since the home-made butter biscuit (cookie) or the kichel made with oil was the small change of Jewish hospitality, always kept handy by the thoughtful hostess to offer to any casual callers with a cup of tea or a glass of schnapps. So closely is this kind of biscuit associated with Jewish cooking that the Danes, who are no mean biscuit-makers themselves, have named one of their most delicious varieties *jödekager* or Jewish cakes! Today, although the kichel is still popular for Kiddushim in the synagogue and also for family use in more traditional households — my local kosher baker makes 20 different varieties by hand each week — the baking of biscuits is no longer a weekly ritual in most Jewish homes, at least among younger housewives. 'They're time-consuming, fattening and full of "empty calories"', they insist, while the more dedicated dietary purists would say that whether they're bought or home-made, we shouldn't eat any biscuits at all.

But for most of us, life without a little sweetness in our diet would be boring indeed. So to salve my conscience as far as this chapter is concerned, the biscuits that are intended for everyday eating are made with as many wholefoods as practicable, including natural brown sugars, wholemeal (wholewheat) flours, peanut butter, nuts, sesame seeds, honey, oats and bran. And for good nutritional value, I'd back these home-made 'health' biscuits against any commercial product, however attractively packaged. I must be honest, however, and admit that others are intended for the special dinner party or the family celebration, and are frankly luxurious in their ingredients.

I have collected these recipes on my journeys in many different countries, and from friends who come from all over the world. For however outlandish their other foods may seem, when it comes to making biscuits, cooks of no matter which nationality all seem to speak the same language.

Most of these biscuits are very quickly made — dropped from a teaspoon, rolled into balls or crescents, cut into fingers, frozen and sliced, or pressed into a tin — anything to avoid rolling them out on a board! I've only suggested that kind of time-consuming operation if the result is a biscuit that's very special indeed. If you follow my guidelines for easier biscuit-making, however, even that kind of hard work will be minimized.

BISCUIT GUIDE LINES

• Although biscuits (cookies) can be made successfully either by hand or with an electric mixer, I generally use a **food processor** because a batch of even the most delicate biscuit dough can be prepared on it in little more than a minute. Specific mixing instructions are given with each recipe, but there is one important point to bear in mind: if you are preparing a dough that needs to be rolled, process the mixture only until it begins to form tiny balls, then tip these into a bowl and gather them up into a dough by hand. (If the mixture is processed until it forms one big ball, it becomes very soft and difficult to handle.)

• To ensure that biscuits bake evenly it is essential to use **baking trays** made of a heavy material, such as pressed aluminium, that won't warp in the heat. Buy the trays in a size as large as the oven can hold, so that the time needed to bake any one batch of biscuits is as short as possible.

- The use of **silicone lining paper** will ensure that even the most delicate biscuits will not stick to the tray. The paper also protects the tray from grease so that it is much easier to keep clean.
- A flexible **spatula** will make it easy to remove fragile biscuits from the baking trays without breaking them.
- Most biscuits will keep well for a month in an **airtight container** stored at room temperature, though after two or three weeks they may need to be 'refreshed' by giving them 5 minutes in a moderate oven and then allowing them to cool before use. If you are not sure how long you will have to store a batch, however, it's safer to keep it in the freezer — individual biscuits only take 15 minutes to defrost.
- Most cooked and uncooked biscuits will keep for up to 6 months in the **freezer**. Biscuits such as *tuiles* that go limp in a moist atmosphere are better stored at room temperature and used within the month, however. Instructions for storage are given with each recipe.

TO SERVE WITH COFFEE OR TEA
FRUIT AND NUT SHORTBREAD FINGERS

Makes about 36

Freeze 3 months
Will keep 4 weeks in an airtight container

These are very short, very buttery biscuits with the traditional shortcake texture, but they do not need to be rolled out in the time-honoured way — the butter is rubbed into the dry ingredients to the 'crumb' stage, and then the mixture is merely pressed into the tin — the heat of the oven does the rest.

8 oz (225 g/2 cups) plain (all-purpose) flour
Pinch of salt
3 oz (75 g/¼ cup) cornflour (cornstarch)
1 oz (25 g/¼ cup) semolina (cream of wheat),
ground rice or ground almonds
4 oz (125 g/½ cup) caster (superfine) sugar

8 oz (225 g/1 cup) waxy butter (cut in 1 in
(2½ cm) chunks)
2 oz (50 g/⅓ cup) glacé (candied) cherries,
finely chopped
2 oz (50 g/½ cup) walnuts, finely chopped

Preheat the oven to Gas No. 2, 300 degrees F, 150 degrees C. Have ready an ungreased baking tin measuring approximately 12 × 8 × 1 in (30 × 20 × 2½ cm).

Put all the dry ingredients into a bowl. Add the chunks of butter and rub into the flour mixture until a fine crumb is formed, using the finger tips, an electric whisk at low speed or the pulse action of a food processor. Stir in the cherries and nuts. Spoon the mixture into the tin and press down firmly until the crumbs pack together. Bake for 55 minutes or until very pale gold. Remove from the oven, mark into fingers 3 in (7½ cm) long and ¾ in (2 cm) wide and sprinkle with a thin layer of caster sugar. Place the tin on a cooling rack and remove the biscuits when they are cold.

TOLLHOUSE COOKIES

Makes about 40

Freeze 3 months
Will keep 2 weeks in an airtight container

These are slightly 'cakey' biscuits with a rich chocolate flavour — the nuggets of chocolate stay whole even after baking.

4 oz (125 g/½ cup) butter or soft margarine
3 oz (75 g/⅓ cup) soft light brown sugar
2 oz (50 g/¼ cup) caster (superfine) sugar
5 oz (150 g/1¼ cups) plain (all-purpose) flour
½ teaspoon each bicarbonate of soda (baking soda) and salt

1 egg
1 teaspoon vanilla essence (extract)
4 oz (125 g) plain (semi-sweet) chocolate chopped into rough ¼ in (½ cm) cubes or 4 oz (125 g) chocolate dots
2 oz (50 g/½ cup) walnuts, chopped

Set the oven at Gas No. 5, 375 degrees F, 190 degrees C. Lightly grease two baking sheets.

Put the butter (or margarine), the sugars, flour, bicarbonate of soda and salt into the bowl of a food processor or mixer and process or rub in until the mixture resembles fine breadcrumbs. Add the egg, vanilla essence, chocolate bits and walnuts, and pulse or mix to a dough.

Pinch off pieces of dough the size of a walnut and roll between the palms into small balls. Arrange them 3 in (7½ cm) apart on the baking sheets and bake for 12 minutes or until firm to the touch and golden-brown at the edges. Remove from the trays with a spatula and leave to cool on a wire rack.

ICED VANILLA RINGS

Makes about 36

Freeze 6 months (not iced)
Will keep 4 weeks in an airtight container

These are very thin, very crisp biscuits with a semi-transparent icing that makes them look most professional.

5½ oz (160 g/1¼ cups plus 2 tablespoons) plain (all-purpose) flour
Pinch of salt
4 oz (125 g/½ cup) butter or soft margarine, cut in 1 in (2½ cm) chunks
1½ oz (40 g/⅓ cup) icing (confectioners') sugar

½ teaspoon vanilla essence (extract)
1 egg yolk

THE ICING:
6 oz (175 g/1½ cups) icing (confectioners') sugar
1 tablespoon lemon juice
1 tablespoon hot water

Preheat the oven to Gas No. 6, 400 degrees F, 200 degrees C. Have ready two ungreased oven trays.
To mix the dough by hand or electric mixer Rub the fat into the flour, salt and icing

239

sugar until the mixture resembles fine crumbs, then mix to a dough with the vanilla essence and the egg yolk.

To mix by food processor Process all the dry ingredients for 5 seconds, then drop in the vanilla essence and egg yolk and process for 3 seconds, or until little balls of dough are beginning to form. Tip the mixture into a bowl and knead to a dough.

To make the biscuits Wrap the dough in foil and chill for 30 minutes, then roll out on a floured board ⅛ in (¼ cm) thick. Cut in 2 in (5 cm) circles, then remove the centre of each circle with a ½ in (1¼ cm) diameter cutter (or the biscuits may be left whole). Repeat until all the dough including the trimmings has been used. Arrange on the trays and bake for 10 to 12 minutes or until a pale gold, but still slightly soft to the touch.

To ice the biscuits While the biscuits are baking, put the icing sugar into a small pan, and stir in the lemon juice and then enough of the hot water to produce an icing thick enough to coat the back of a wooden spoon. Heat gently until the icing becomes runny; it can now be left white or tinted a pale pastel with a few drops of colouring. When the biscuits come out of the oven, dip them face down into the warm icing, then allow to set on a cooling tray.

WALNUT FREEZER BISCUITS

Makes 48

Freeze cooked or raw 6 months
Will keep fresh 1 month in an airtight
container

To make these very crisp, wafer-thin biscuits, the uncooked dough is shaped into a roll the same diameter as you would like the cooked biscuits to be and then briefly frozen until it is firm enough to slice. As the rolls of raw dough store so well in the freezer, they can be thawed, then cut and baked freshly as they are needed.

4 oz (125 g/½ cup) butter or soft margarine
6 oz (175 g/¾ cup) caster (superfine) sugar
2 eggs
2 oz (50 g/½ cup) walnuts, finely chopped

Rind of half a lemon, finely grated
1 teaspoon vanilla essence (extract) or ⅔ oz
(20 g) packet vanilla sugar
4 oz (125 g/1 cup) plain (all-purpose) flour

To mix by hand or electric mixer Cream the butter and sugar until fluffy, then beat in all the remaining ingredients until the mixture looks creamy.

To mix by food processor Process all the ingredients (except the walnuts) for 10 seconds, scrape down the sides of the bowl, then process for a further 5 seconds. Pulse in the walnuts for 3 seconds.

To shape the biscuits You will need a piece of silicone or greaseproof (waxed) paper about 12 in (30 cm) long and 6 in (15 cm) wide. Lay the biscuit mixture down the centre of the paper, fold over the sides to enclose it, then mould it gently with your hands into a roll 2 in (5 cm) in diameter. Freeze for 30 or 40 minutes, or until the roll of dough is firm enough to slice with a sharp knife. Cut into slices ⅓ in (1 cm) thick and arrange on greased trays — the biscuits do not spread in the oven. Bake for 10 to 12 minutes or until golden-brown. Leave on the baking tray for 10 minutes to cool and crisp, then store in an airtight container.

WALNUT TOFFEE BARS

Makes 15–20

Freeze 3 months
Will keep 2 weeks in an airtight container

A layer of shortbread is topped by a scrumptious nut caramel. Serve the biscuits with coffee, or accompanied by vanilla ice cream as a dessert after a light main course.

THE SHORTBREAD:
6 oz (175 g/1½ cups) plain (all-purpose) flour
2 oz (50 g/¼ cup) caster (superfine) sugar
4 oz (125 g/½ cup) butter (cut in 1 in (2½ cm) chunks)

THE TOPPING:
4 oz (125 g/½ cup) unsalted butter

4 oz (125 g/½ cup) soft medium brown sugar
2 level tablespoons golden syrup (corn syrup) or thin honey
1 tin (6 oz (175 g)) sweetened condensed milk
6 oz (175 g/1½ cups) walnuts, coarsely chopped
1 tablespoon lemon juice

Preheat the oven to Gas No. 5, 375 degrees F, 190 degrees C. Have ready a tin 12 × 8 × 1 in (30 × 20 × 2½ cm) in size.

To prepare the shortbread layer Put the flour and sugar into a bowl and rub in the butter until the mixture resembles fine crumbs (5 seconds on the food processor). Spoon the mixture into the tin, then pat into a firm layer. Bake for 20 minutes until firm, and golden-brown round the edges. Allow to cool while you prepare the caramel.

To make the nut caramel Put everything except the walnuts and lemon juice into a thick-bottomed pan and heat, stirring, until the butter has melted and the sugar has dissolved. Bring to the boil and cook for 7 minutes, stirring occasionally until the mixture becomes a golden-brown caramel colour. Take off the heat, add the nuts and lemon juice and beat thoroughly. Spread on the cooked shortbread, then return to the oven for a further 10 minutes. Put the tin on a cooling rack and leave for 10 minutes, then cut into squares.

HEALTHY BISCUITS
BRAN FLAP JACKS

Makes 50 fingers

Freeze 6 months
Will keep in an airtight container for 1 month

The bran adds to the crunchiness of these easily made biscuits.

4 oz (125 g/½ cup) butter or *soft margarine*
4 oz (125 g/½ cup) dark brown sugar
½ lb (225 g/⅔ cup) golden syrup (corn
syrup)
4 oz (125 g/1¼ cups) porage oats
4 oz (125 g/1 cup) Toasted Bran cereal
¼ teaspoon salt
½ teaspoon ground ginger

Preheat the oven to Gas No. 3, 325 degrees F, 160 degrees C. Grease a large shallow baking tin measuring approximately 14 × 9 × 1 in (35 × 22½ × 2½ cm).

Heat the fat, sugar and syrup until melted, either on the stove or in the microwave. Remove from the heat and add the remaining ingredients. Mix thoroughly. Turn the mixture into the tin and smooth level with a wet knife or spatula, and bake for 30 to 40 minutes until a rich brown. Leave to cool for 5 minutes. Cut into squares or fingers. Remove from the tin when cold.

CINNAMON CRISPS

Makes 24

Freeze 6 months
Will keep 1 month in an airtight container

These delicious biscuits can be made by even young members of the family — toddlers can make them under supervision, as it's just like moulding plasticine or 'play-dough'. The wheatmeal flour gives them an appetizingly nutty flavour.

5 oz (150 g/1¼ cups) wheatmeal flour plus 1
teaspoon baking powder, or 5 oz (150 g/1¼
cups) white self-raising flour
2 oz (50 g/⅓ cup) soft dark brown sugar
1 teaspoon ground cinnamon
½ teaspoon ground ginger

4 oz (125 g/½ cup) butter or *margarine, cut*
in 1 in (2½ cm) chunks

CINNAMON SUGAR:
2 tablespoons (superfine) sugar or
granulated sugar, plus 1 teaspoon
cinnamon, mixed together

Preheat the oven to Gas No. 4, 350 degrees F, 180 degrees C. Have ready two ungreased baking trays.

Mix the flour, sugar and spices with the baking powder (if used). Rub in the butter by hand or machine until the mixture looks like coarse damp breadcrumbs, then gather together and knead to a dough. Pinch off pieces the size of a small walnut and roll between the palms into little balls. Arrange the balls 2 in (5 cm) apart on the trays. Take a large fork and dip it into cold water, then press down on the balls first one way and then the other. In this way biscuits will be formed that are about ⅜ in (1 cm) thick. Bake for 15 minutes until set but not crisp. Remove from the oven and immediately scatter with the cinnamon sugar. Leave for 10 minutes to crispen up, then put on a cooling rack.

HEALTH NUT BISCUITS

Makes about 25

Freeze 3 months
Will keep 1 month in an airtight container

These biscuits resemble bars of muesli or Granola, with all the high fibre and vitamin B content that implies, not to mention the delicious flavour and crunchiness. The easiest method of weighing out the honey or syrup is first to weigh the sugar on the scales, then to pile the honey or syrup on top until the scales register another 3 oz (75 g) and finally to scoop up this mixture and tip it into the pan or bowl in which it is to be melted. If the cooked biscuit mixture becomes too firm before you can cut it, put the tray back in the oven for another 2 or 3 minutes, to soften it slightly.

5 oz (150 g/²⁄₃ cup) butter or margarine
3 oz (75 g/½ cup) medium brown sugar
3 oz (75 g/¼ cup) thin honey or golden
syrup (corn syrup)
2 oz (50 g/½ cup) sesame seeds

2 oz (50 g/³⁄₄ cup) desiccated (dried and
shredded) coconut
2 oz (50 g/½ cup) hazelnuts (filberts),
roughly chopped
6 oz (175 g/1³⁄₄ cups) porage oats

Preheat the oven to Gas No. 3, 325 degrees F, 160 degrees C. Grease a Swiss roll tin measuring approximately 12 × 8 × 1 in (30 × 20 × 2½ cm).

Melt the butter slowly, then add the sugar, honey (or syrup), sesame seeds, coconut and hazelnuts. This can be done on top of the stove or in the microwave. Stir well, then add the oats and mix thoroughly. Spoon the mixture into the tin, then press it level with a wet spatula or knife. Bake for 30 to 35 minutes or until a rich golden-brown. Cool 10 to 15 minutes, and slice the mixture into fingers with a knife. When quite cold, remove from the tin.

NUTTY OATMEAL CRUNCH

Makes 48

Freeze 6 months
Will keep 1 month in an airtight container

These crunchy bar biscuits are full of good things like oats, nuts and brown sugar, and both the taste and the texture are quite outstanding.

4 oz (125 g/½ cup) butter or soft margarine
½ lb (225 g/²⁄₃ cup) golden syrup (corn
syrup)
2 oz (50 g/¼ cup) each light brown and dark
brown sugar

5 oz (150 g/1½ cups) porage oats
1½ oz (40 g/¹⁄₃ cup) chopped walnuts
1½ oz (40 g/½ cup) desiccated (dried and
shredded) coconut

Preheat the oven to Gas No. 3, 325 degrees F, 160 degrees C. Have ready a shallow greased tin approximately 14 × 9 × 1 in (about 35 × 22 × 2½ cm).

Put the fat, syrup and sugar into a pan and warm together until smooth and free from graininess (this can be done in a basin in the microwave). Stir in the oats, chopped nuts and coconut and mix well. Spread the mixture evenly in the tin,

243

patting it down into an even layer. Bake for 30 or 40 minutes, or until a rich even brown. If the centre of the mixture is not quite brown enough when the outside is ready, turn off the oven and leave the tray in to finish browning. When firm enough to cut (after about 30 minutes) mark into fingers, each measuring approximately 2½ × 1 in (6 × 2½ cm).

PEANUT BUTTER CRUNCHIES

Makes about 30

Freeze 6 months
Will keep 1 month in an airtight container

A biscuit for the peanut lover which is light, crisp and very quickly made.

5 oz (150 g/1¼ cups) plain (all-purpose) flour
7 oz (200 g/1 cup) soft light brown sugar
½ teaspoon salt
½ teaspoon bicarbonate of soda (baking soda)

3 oz (75 g/⅓ cup) butter or soft margarine
5 oz (150 g/⅔ cup) smooth or crunchy peanut butter
1 egg
1 teaspoon vanilla essence (extract)

Preheat the oven to Gas No. 5, 375 degrees F, 190 degrees C. Have ready two ungreased baking sheets.

Put the flour and sugar into a bowl and mix in the salt and the bicarbonate of soda. Add all the remaining ingredients and mix by hand or machine until a medium-soft dough is formed, about 2 minutes by hand or machine, 15 seconds by food processor. Pinch off pieces of dough the size of a walnut, roll between the palms into balls 1 in (2½ cm) in diameter. Dip a large fork into cold water, then flatten the balls into biscuits by pressing down with the fork, once, and then again at an angle of 90 degrees — this makes a criss-cross pattern on top of the biscuits. Bake for 15 minutes or until the biscuits are just beginning to brown round the edges (they will still be soft). Leave on the trays for 10 minutes, then lift off and store in an airtight container.

TO SERVE WITH ICE CREAMS, SORBETS OR FRUIT SALADS
KOURABIEDES
SHORTBREAD SNOWBALLS, GREEK STYLE

Makes 36

Freeze 6 months
Will keep 1 month in an airtight container

I first tasted these delicious shortbread 'snowballs' at a Greek Orthodox wedding in the charming little town of Kyrenia in northern Cyprus — the Greeks and Greek Cypriots consider them to be their national biscuit and serve them on all important and religious family occasions. Their lightness of texture, unusual in such a rich biscuit, is achieved by first melting the butter and then mixing it with the other ingredients when it has only partly solidified. This technique, which is also used by Syrian Jews to make their speciality biscuits, 'gereybes', is probably of Turkish origin, as the whole of the eastern Mediterranean was for centuries part of the Ottoman Empire. If unsalted butter is not available you *can* use salted butter but be sure to discard the salty residue that will be left at the bottom of the pan or bowl of melted butter.

8 oz (225 g/1 cup) unsalted butter
1 egg yolk
3 oz (75 g/¾ cup) icing (confectioners')
sugar
½ teaspoon vanilla essence (extract)
½ teaspoon baking powder

10 oz (275 g/2½ cups) plain (all-purpose)
flour
2 oz (50 g/½ cup) chopped almonds (or
almond nibs), toasted, or 2 oz (50 g/½ cup)
walnuts, finely chopped
½ lb (225 g/2 cups) sifted icing
(confectioners') sugar

Heat the butter until liquid on top of the stove or in the microwave, then put in the freezer for 30 minutes or until it is the consistency of thick mayonnaise. Stir in the egg yolk followed by the sugar, vanilla essence and the baking powder, then add the flour a heaped tablespoon at a time, stirring well after each addition. Finally stir in the nuts, then chill for a further 15 minutes.

Preheat the oven to Gas No. 3, 325 degrees F, 160 degrees C. Have ready two ungreased oven trays. Pinch off pieces of the dough the size of a large walnut, and roll into balls between the palms of the hand.

To shape the biscuits

For round biscuits: put the balls 2 in (5 cm) apart on trays.

For *pear-shaped* biscuits: gently mould each ball into a pear shape and stick in a clove to represent the stalk of a pear. Put them 2 in (5 cm) apart on the trays.

For *curved* biscuits: form each ball into a pencil-shaped roll about 6 in (15 cm) long and ⅜ in (1 cm) thick, then curve it into the shape of an 'S'. Arrange the biscuits on the trays about 1 in (2½ cm) apart.

To finish   Bake the round and pear-shaped biscuits for 20 minutes and the S-shaped ones for 15 minutes, until barely coloured but easy to lift from the tray. Leave for 2 or 3 minutes, then dip into the icing sugar and turn to coat well on all sides. Put on a cooling tray and when quite cold dust thickly with the icing sugar once more. Allow to mature at room temperature for 48 hours in an airtight container.

NUSSKIPFERL   WALNUT CRESCENTS

Makes 36

Freeze 3 months
Will keep in an airtight container for 1
month

A little carefully measured hot water added to the dough gives these elegant biscuits a much lighter texture than the traditional Viennese Kipferl made with ground almonds.

8 oz (225 g/1 cup) butter or block margarine,
cut in 1 in (2½ cm) chunks
2 teaspoons hot water
2 oz (50 g/¼ cup) caster (superfine) sugar

1 oz (25 g) packet of vanilla sugar or 1
teaspoon vanilla essence (extract)
8 oz (225 g/2 cups) plain (all-purpose) flour
2 oz (50 g/½ cup) walnuts, finely chopped
Sifted icing (confectioners') sugar

Preheat the oven to Gas No. 3, 325 degrees F, 170 degrees C. Have ready two ungreased baking trays.

In the mixer or food processor, mix the butter with the water, sugars and essence (if used), but *only* until the sugar has been absorbed — do not *cream* them together or the texture of the biscuits will be wrong. Add the flour gradually and mix or process until a ball of dough is formed, then mix or pulse in the nuts. Wrap the dough in foil and leave in the refrigerator to firm up, for about an hour.

Pinch off small pieces of dough the size of a walnut and form into a pencil-shaped roll 3 in (7½ cm) long and about ¾ in (2 cm) thick, then curve each into a crescent. Arrange the biscuits on the trays 1½ in (3½ cm) apart — they do spread a little. Bake for 15 to 18 minutes until firm but still pale in colour. Cool on the trays for 5 minutes, then carefully lift off and dust with icing sugar. Coat again with the icing sugar when quite cold.

PRALINE CRISPS

Makes 27–30

Freeze 3 months
Will keep for up to a month in an airtight container

These delicious biscuits are perfect to serve with summer fruits. The praline is crushed most easily in a food processor. Otherwise, put it in a plastic bag and roll vigorously with a rolling pin.

4 oz (125 g/½ cup) butter or *soft margarine*
2 oz (50 g/¼ cup) caster (superfine) sugar
4 oz (125 g/1 cup) plain (all-purpose) flour
1 oz (25 g/4 tablespoons) cornflour
(cornstarch)

1 oz (25 g/¼ cup) ground almonds or
ground hazelnuts (filberts)
1 teaspoon cinnamon
2 oz (50 g) peanut brittle, crushed to a
powder

Preheat the oven to Gas No. 5, 375 degrees F, 190 degrees C. Grease two baking trays.

Rub the fat into the dry ingredients until the mixture resembles breadcrumbs, then gather into a ball. Pinch off walnut-sized pieces of dough and roll into balls between the palms of the hands. Flatten ⅛ in (¼ cm) thick with the tines of a large fork dipped in cold water. Scatter evenly with the praline. Bake for 15 to 20 minutes until golden, then remove to a cooling rack.

SESAME SHORTIES

Makes 30–36 according to size

Freeze 3 months
Will keep for up to a month in an airtight container

These crisp and thin melt-in-your-mouth biscuits crammed with toasted sesame seeds, are ideal to serve with ice cream or fruit salad as they are only slightly sweetened. To toast sesame seeds, toss them in an ungreased non-stick pan over moderate heat until they are golden-brown, or bake on an ungreased tray in a moderate oven (Gas No. 4, 350 degrees F, 180 degrees C) for 15 minutes.

6 oz (175 g/¾ cup) butter or soft margarine
2 oz (50 g/½ cup) icing (confectioners')
sugar
½ teaspoon vanilla essence (extract)

8 oz (225 g/2 cups) self-raising flour or 8 oz
(225 g/2 cups) plain (all-purpose) flour plus
2 teaspoons baking powder
2 oz (50 g/½ cup) sesame seeds, toasted until
golden

Preheat the oven to Gas No. 5, 375 degrees F, 190 degrees C. Have ready two ungreased baking sheets.

To mix by hand or electric mixer   Work the butter and icing sugar together with the vanilla essence, then add the flour and sesame seeds and work to a dough.

To mix by food processor   Process the fat, icing sugar and vanilla essence for 4 seconds, add the flour and process for 4 seconds or until it begins to form little lumps, then add the sesame seeds and pulse for 2 seconds. Tip on to a board and knead gently to form a dough.

To bake the biscuits   Roll out the dough about ⅛ in (¼ cm) thick on a floured board, then cut into smaller circles or half-moons with a serrated cutter. Place ½ in (1¼ cm) apart on the baking sheets. Bake for 9 or 10 minutes or until pale gold round the edges. Take from the oven and sprinkle with caster sugar.

SNICKERDOODLES

Makes 36

Freeze 6 months
Will keep fresh 1 month in an airtight
container

The fanciful name of these crisp and airy biscuits, or cookies, has no particular significance; according to the *American Heritage Cookbook* it's a tradition in New England, where they were invented, for cooks to give their dishes 'fun to say' names such as 'Tangle Breeches', 'Graham Jakes' and 'Kindawoodles'! In the oven, the little balls of dough spread to form round biscuits, as perfect in shape as if they had been laboriously rolled out.

4 oz (125 g/½ cup) butter or margarine
4 oz (125 g/½ cup) caster (superfine) sugar
1 egg
½ teaspoon vanilla essence (extract)
6 oz (175 g/1½ cups) self-raising flour plus
½ teaspoon baking powder or 6 oz (175
g/1½ cups) plain (all-purpose) flour plus 2
teaspoons baking powder

THE COATING:
2 tablespoons caster (superfine) sugar
mixed with 1 tablespoon ground
cinnamon

To mix by hand or electric mixer   Put all the ingredients into a bowl and beat until a soft dough is formed.

247

To mix by food processor Process all the ingredients together but *only* until small lumps of dough form, then tip them on to a large piece of foil and squeeze together to form a dough. In either case, wrap the dough in foil, flatten so that it will chill easily, then leave in the refrigerator 1 hour.

To bake the biscuits Preheat the oven to Gas No. 6, 400 degrees F, 200 degrees C. Grease two baking trays. Take teaspoons of the dough and roll between the palms to make little balls. Drop the balls, one at a time, into a small bowl containing the coating mixture, and turn until evenly coated. Place on the trays 2 in (5 cm) apart, and bake for 10 minutes until golden-brown on top and a pale gold underneath — lift one and see. Lift off with a spatula and leave on a rack to cool. The flavour is improved after 24 hours at room temperature.

PETITS FOURS
WALNUT TUILES

Makes about 24

Do not freeze
Will keep for 1 month in an airtight container

Making these is rather a labour of love as they need shaping when they are still pliable, so only a few can be baked at one time. However, you are rewarded with the perfect biscuit to serve with ice cream or sorbet for a special dinner.

3 oz (75 g/¼ cup) golden syrup (corn syrup)
2 oz (50 g/¼ cup) caster (superfine) sugar
2½ oz (65 g/5 tablespoons) butter or soft margarine

2 oz (50 g/½ cup) plain (all-purpose) flour
2 oz (50 g/½ cup) walnuts, finely chopped
½ teaspoon vanilla essence (extract)

Preheat the oven to Gas No. 3, 325 degrees F, 160 degrees C. Line two baking sheets with silicone paper.

Put the syrup, sugar and fat into a pan and bring slowly to the boil; alternatively, put them into a bowl and bring them to the boil in the microwave, stirring once. Remove from the heat and stir in the flour, walnuts and essence, mixing well. Drop level teaspoons of the mixture, 3 in (7 cm) apart, on to each tray. Put one tray in the oven and after 5 minutes put in the second.

After 10 minutes, when the biscuits on the first tray are golden-brown, remove it from the oven and allow them to firm up until they can be easily lifted off with a spatula — after about 2 minutes. Lay each biscuit in turn over a rolling pin and press firmly into a curved shape. After 2 or 3 minutes, when they are set, remove them from the rolling pin and put on a cooling tray, then shape the second batch of biscuits in the same way.

Repeat the baking and shaping with the remainder of the raw mixture.

CHOCOLATE AND TOASTED HAZELNUT TRUFFLES

Makes 32

Freeze 3 months
Will keep in the refrigerator for a week in an airtight container

These delicious bon-bons compare in both taste and texture with the finest hand-made truffles made by a professional chocolatier. I prefer the taste of milk chocolate and butter but after a meat meal, plain chocolate and margarine make acceptable substitutes.

6 oz (175 g) plain (semi-sweet) or milk
chocolate
1 oz (25 g/2 tablespoons) butter or
margarine
1 egg yolk
2 oz (50 g/½ cup) icing (confectioners')
sugar, sifted

2 oz (50 g/½ cup) ground almonds
2 oz (50 g/½ cup) hazelnuts (filberts),
skinned, toasted and finely chopped
1½–2 tablespoons any coffee or chocolate-
flavoured liqueur or rum or brandy
Drinking chocolate (instant chocolate) and
icing (confectioners') sugar

The chocolate is most easily melted in a microwave: break it up and put into a basin with the butter or margarine. Cook on full power for 2 minutes, then stir well. Otherwise, melt the chocolate and fat *very* gently in a small pan. Stir in the remainder of the ingredients and beat together until smooth. Taste and add more liqueur if you like. Chill or freeze until the mixture has the texture of plasticine (15 to 30 minutes).

Pinch off pieces of the mixture and shape between the palms into balls the size of large marbles. Roll half the balls in drinking chocolate and the other half in sifted icing sugar. Put in waxed paper petit four cases and arrange in layers in an airtight container. Refrigerate or freeze until required.

Defrost frozen truffles for 30 minutes before use. Serve chilled truffles straight from the refrigerator.

MORITZ MERINGUES

Makes 36–40

Do not freeze
Will keep 2 months in an airtight container

Saturday morning after synagogue was 'calling' time for the Jewish families of Offenbach, a pleasant town on the River Main where their community had flourished on and off since the thirteenth century.

Grandmother Mayer would receive her guests, sitting on a straight-backed ebony chair in the salon of the large house on the Frankfurterstrasse where the family had lived and prospered for nearly a hundred years. On these occasions, the conversation was as formal as the refreshments — a glass of Madeira and a dish of her incomparable chocolate and sugared almond meringues.

It was Grandmother Mayer's daughter who brought the family recipe to England just before the war. 'But how can an old German-Jewish recipe include drinking chocolate?' I asked her grandson. 'It used to be cocoa, but we brought it up to date,' he told me, 'how else do you think a medieval recipe could survive for so long?' And to survive is certainly what these beautiful little petits fours deserve.

3 egg whites
4 oz (125 g/½ cup) caster (superfine) sugar
4 oz (125 g/1 cup) drinking chocolate
(instant chocolate)
2 teaspoons instant coffee powder

4 oz (125 g/1 cup) flaked almonds or
blanched whole almonds, soaked in water for
15 minutes and shredded with a knife
4 oz (125 g/½ cup) caster (superfine) sugar
Few drops cold water

Set the oven to Gas No. 3, 325 degrees F, 160 degrees C. Cover two baking sheets with silicone paper.

Whisk the egg whites until they hold stiff glossy peaks, then whisk in the caster sugar a tablespoon at a time, whisking until stiff again after each addition. Finally fold in the drinking chocolate mixed with the instant coffee.

Put the almonds and the sugar in a frying pan with a heavy base, sprinkle with a few drops of cold water, then fry over moderate heat, stirring constantly, until the almonds turn a golden-brown and the sugar is beginning to caramelize. Fold into the chocolate meringue *at once*, or the mixture will set into a toffee. (If this should happen, gently heat it up until it melts again.)

Put out in large tablespoonfuls on the lined trays, leaving 2 in (5 cm) between meringues. Leave for 15 minutes for the surface to dry out, then bake for 30 to 35 minutes or until crisp to the touch and easily detachable from the paper. When cold, store at room temperature as freezer storage makes them go damp.

NUTTY BUTTER CRISPS

Makes 30

Do not freeze
Will keep for 1 month in an airtight
container

I make no apology for publishing this much improved recipe for an old favourite, for it is certain that whenever you serve them, the plateful will melt away like the proverbial summer snows! It is important to measure the ingredients extremely carefully or the biscuits will not keep their even shape. Silicone paper is far easier to use — and much less costly — than the rice paper on which I used to bake these delicious petits fours.

3 oz (75 g/⅓ cup) butter
3 oz (75 g/⅓ cup) caster (superfine) sugar

3 level teaspoons double (heavy) cream
4 oz (125 g/1 cup) flaked almonds

Preheat the oven to Gas No. 4, 350 degrees F, 190 degrees C. Lightly grease as many baking sheets as you can fit into the oven at one time, then line them with silicone paper.

Slowly bring the butter, sugar and cream to boiling point, stirring constantly. Add the nuts and cook at a fast boil stirring, for 1 minute, then immediately take off the heat. Leave to firm up for 10 minutes.

250

Use two teaspoons to shape the biscuits: scoop up a small amount of the mixture with one teaspoon, and push it off on to the tray in a neat pile with the other, leaving 3 in (7½ cm) between the biscuits to allow them room to spread. Bake for 12 minutes until golden-brown. Cool for 2 or 3 minutes, then use a spatula to lift them off the paper on to a cooling tray. Repeat, using the same silicone paper, until all the mixture has been baked.

SOLEILS DE NICE

Makes 14–16

Freeze 2 months
Will keep for 2 weeks in an airtight container

For the special dinner party, these moist macaroons, covered in a thick coating of toasted nuts, make elegant petits fours to serve with coffee.

4 oz (125 g/1 cup) ground almonds
4 oz (125 g/½ cup) caster (superfine) sugar
1 level tablespoon smooth apricot jam
1 egg white (unbeaten)
Few drops almond essence (extract)
½ teaspoon vanilla essence (extract)

FOR COATING:
1 oz (25 g/4 tablespoons) plain (all-purpose) flour
1 egg yolk mixed with 3 teaspoons cold water
6 oz (175 g/1¼ cups) (approximately) toasted chopped almonds or chopped hazelnuts (filberts)
2 tablespoons smooth apricot jam

Preheat the oven to Gas No. 5, 375 degrees F, 190 degrees C. Cover a baking sheet with silicone paper.

Mix the ground almonds with the sugar in a medium-sized bowl. Stir in the apricot jam, the essence, and enough of the unbeaten egg white to make a paste that can be moulded into balls. Roll this paste between the palms into 14–16 balls, each the size of a small plum.

Put the flour, the egg yolk mixed with the water, and the chopped nuts into three separate small bowls. Take each ball in turn, roll it in flour and dip it first into the yolk-and-water mixture and then into the nuts. Arrange the balls 2 in (5 cm) apart on the baking tray, and with the top of the finger make a 'dint' in the top of each biscuit. Bake for 10 to 12 minutes, or until the surface looks dry. Transfer to a cooling tray and fill the 'dint' on the top of each biscuit with ½ teaspoon of apricot jam.

Cakes

This chapter is one of the shortest in the book, not because there is any lack of delicious cake recipes, but because most of us no longer consider making cakes worth the time and effort, except for special occasions. For although a well-made cake is a delight to eat, its contribution to our well-being is almost nil. In fact, mainly because of the widespread interest in weight-reduction, both the making and the eating of cake have now largely gone out of fashion.

It was not always so. Sweetness has been equated with hospitality ever since the Jews came under Babylonian rule in the sixth century B.C.E. — for it was in that part of the world that sugar was first used as a sweetener and, because of its costliness, considered as a luxury food that one naturally offered to guests. So until recently, the more sweet cakes a hostess could set before her guests the more generous and welcoming she was considered to be. Today, although cakes are undoubtedly still widely eaten and enjoyed — despite the strictures of the nutritionists — most Jewish women restrict their baking to family cakes that can be quickly prepared or to special cakes for special occasions. Some of the most interesting cakes are baked only for the Festivals and recipes for them will be found in the appropriate chapters (consult the index for these). Each of the small number of cake recipes in the following pages is outstanding of its kind, and some have interesting culinary histories of their own.

SUCCESSFUL CAKEMAKING

If you do bake a cake, then you will want to do so in the quickest and most efficient manner. That is why I have given detailed instructions for mixing cakes with a food processor as, except for a very special recipe such as the Sachertorte, this is the quickest method I know. In addition, a great deal of time can be saved by using the most suitable equipment and ingredients.

- Because all cakes **freeze** so well, it's useful to make a large quantity at a time, some of it for immediate use and some to be saved for the future. Alternatively, leftover cake can be frozen for use on another occasion.
- The chapter begins with four recipes for **cake squares**, because these are particularly useful to serve a few at a time.
- The other cakes are all made in large tins, the most useful of which is the **spring-form** tin, which has a hinged side to make it easy to remove fragile or delicate cakes. A **long loaf tin** is also useful, as you expose only one cut surface of a loaf cake when you take a slice off it (unlike a round cake).
- A large **cooling tray** is essential to ensure that air can circulate round the warm cake so that it does not become soggy on the bottom.
- If you use a food processor, you will get a lighter cake with **soft margarine** rather than with butter, as these modern fats have air beaten into them during manufacture. **Butter**, however, gives a better flavour to a filling or frosting, where the air content is not so important.
- Always use **eggs** of a standard size — usually weighing about 2 oz (50 g) each. While the size is not so important in a small cake containing only two or three eggs, using too many over-sized eggs can upset the recipe balance of a large cake and may sometimes cause it to fall.

- There is a certain limited nutritional advantage in using **natural brown sugars** as not only do they taste delicious, but they contain molasses, which in turn contains certain essential mineral salts that are not found in refined white sugar.
- There is more nutritional mileage to be gained by using brown flours. These vary in their nomenclature and their food value, the latter depending on their extraction rate. Pure **white flour** has an extraction rate of 70% and contains mostly starch (and certain nutritional additives which are put in by law). **Wheatmeal flour** has an extraction rate of 81%, is creamy in colour and is almost as fine as white flour, but it does contain some wheatgerm and bran. **Wholemeal (wholewheat) flour** has a 100% extraction rate and contains *all* the nourishment and the bran contained in the grain of wheat. Some are apt to be coarse and heavy in texture, but special finely milled wholemeal flour (wholewheat pastry flour) is now becoming available for use in delicate cakes and pastries.

CAKE SQUARES
ALMOND AND PEACH SQUARES

Makes about 20 squares

Do not freeze
Will keep 3 days foil-covered in the refrigerator

A very spongy cake is baked with slices of fresh peach covered with a crunchy topping of almonds and brown sugar. Serve warm as a pudding or at room temperature as a cake.

6 oz (175 g/³⁄₄ cup) soft margarine or 3 oz (75 g/6 tablespoons) each soft butter and margarine
4 oz (125 g/½ cup) caster (superfine) sugar
Grated rind of half a lemon
2 eggs
8 oz (225 g/2 cups) self-raising flour or 8 oz (225 g/2 cups) plain (all-purpose) flour, plus 2 teaspoons baking powder

4 or 5 large peaches (1½ lb (675 g))
Juice of 1 large lemon (3 tablespoons)

THE TOPPING:
2 oz (50 g/¼ cup) demerara (brown) sugar
2 oz (50 g/½ cup) flaked almonds

Preheat the oven to Gas No. 4, 350 degrees F, 180 degrees C. Grease a tin measuring approximately 12 × 8 × 1½ in (30 × 20 × 4 cm).

Put the soft fat, sugar, rind, eggs and 2 heaped tablespoons only of the flour into a bowl and beat by hand, mixer or food processor until smooth. Add the remaining flour and *stir* it in (or pulse in for 3 or 4 seconds) until the mixture is smooth again. Spoon into the prepared tin and smooth level.

Cut the unpeeled peaches into slices about ½ in (1½ cm) thick and arrange in tightly packed rows over the cake mixture; the slices will shrink during baking so a generous amount of fruit is needed. Sprinkle evenly with the lemon juice. Mix the demerara sugar and nuts and sprinkle on top of the cake. Bake for 35 or 40 minutes until slightly shrunken from the sides of the tin and spongy to gentle pressure on top.

BANANA STREUSEL KUCHEN SQUARES

Makes about 12 servings

Do not freeze
Leftovers keep 3 days in the refrigerator if tightly wrapped in foil

It is to those German-born Jews who arrived in America in the middle of the nineteenth century, at the very time that modern baking powder was invented, that we owe the concept of a kuchen that is raised without yeast. A kuchen made with baking powder does not possess the same taste and texture as one made with yeast in the traditional way — but it is nevertheless a delicious cake in its own right, and it can be prepared in a fraction of the time. The crunchy streusel topping gives a streusel kuchen a special charm of its own; did it develop from a little lateral thinking on the part of some anonymous housewife with frugal ways? Why wash away all those little bits of dough that cling to the bowl after the kuchen mixture has been set to rise, she must have wondered, when by adding just a little bit of sugar, butter and spice, they can be crumbled into a delicious topping? She tasted the mixture and it was good, and kuchens have been topped with streusels ever since.

The baked bananas give this kuchen a very unusual flavour. Whether it is served at room temperature as a cake, or slightly warm as a dessert with ice cream or custard, it is at its best the day it is baked. Later it can be refreshed by reheating it until warm to the touch, in either the microwave or a regular oven.

THE CAKE MIXTURE:

8 oz (225 g/2 cups) self-raising flour plus 1 teaspoon baking powder or 8 oz (225 g/2 cups) plain (all-purpose) flour plus 3 teaspoons baking powder
3 oz (75 g/⅓ cup) soft margarine
Rind of 1 lemon, finely grated
4 oz (125 g/½ cup) caster (superfine) sugar
1 egg
4 fl oz (125 ml/½ cup) milk

THE TOPPING:

3 large bananas, peeled and sliced, about ⅜ in (1 cm) thick
2 tablespoons lemon juice
Scant 2 oz (50 g/½ cup) flour
2 level teaspoons ground cinnamon
2 oz (50 g/¼ cup) butter, cut in bits
4 oz (125 g/½ cup) light brown sugar

Preheat the oven to Gas No. 5, 375 degrees F, 190 degrees C. Grease a rectangular cake tin measuring approximately 11 × 8 × 2 in (28 × 20 × 5 cm) or a 9 in (22½ cm) square one of a similar depth.

Put all the cake ingredients into a bowl and mix by hand or machine until a thick smooth batter is formed (15 seconds by food processor, 2 or 3 minutes by hand or electric mixer). Spoon the batter into the chosen tin and smooth level.

Arrange the sliced bananas on top of the cake and sprinkle evenly with the lemon juice. Rub the flour, spice, butter and sugar gently together until they form a crumble. Sprinkle this evenly over the bananas. Bake for 40 to 45 minutes, or until golden-brown.

DUTCH GINGER SQUARES

Makes 24–30 small squares

Freeze 6 months
Will keep in an airtight container for 1 month

If you take a walk any Sunday morning in the old Jewish quarter of Amsterdam, quite near to Anne Frank's house you will come upon a kosher bakery selling cakes such as 'Bolas', 'Stuffed Monkey' and these delicious 'Ginger Squares' that are still made in the Dutch-Jewish tradition of 100 years ago.

During the seventeenth century, in the great days of the Jewish community, its members were closely involved in the economic life of Holland, many of them as merchants in the import and export trades. So it's not surprising that ginger, which was one of the most precious commodities to be imported from the Dutch colonies in the East Indies, figured largely in their wives' recipes. The original recipe for these exquisite pastries, popularized by a Jewish baker who emigrated from Holland to the East End of London before the First World War, called for a great jar of Chinese-style preserved ginger, but I have found that a good ginger preserve makes an equally delicious filling at less than half the cost.

I have developed this version especially for use with a food processor, but the pastry can be made equally well (if less quickly) with an electric mixer or by hand, rubbing the fat in as for shortcrust pastry.

8 oz (225 g/2 cups) self-raising flour or 8 oz plain (all-purpose) flour plus 2 teaspoons baking powder
2 oz (50 g/½ cup) ground almonds or hazelnuts (filberts)
6 oz (175 g/¾ cup) firm butter or margarine, cut in 1 in (2½ cm) chunks
4 oz (125 g/½ cup) light brown sugar
1 egg
2 tablespoons lemon juice

THE FILLING:
1 lb (450 g) jar best-quality ginger preserve

THE TOPPING:
Milk or beaten egg for brushing on pastry
2 tablespoons demerara or golden granulated (coarse) sugar
3 tablespoons flaked almonds

In the food processor put the flour and ground nuts, the butter and sugar. Pulse until the mixture resembles coarse crumbs. Beat the egg and lemon juice together, add to the machine and pulse until the crumbs are evenly moistened and just beginning to hold together. Tip the mixture out into a mixing bowl and gather it up with the hands into a ball. Divide in two and knead each ball lightly until smooth. Flatten the balls, wrap in film, then chill for 1 hour — this makes the pastry easier to roll out.

Preheat the oven to Gas No. 5, 375 degrees F, 190 degrees C. Get ready an ungreased shallow baking tin measuring approximately 12 × 8 in (30 × 20 cm), and about ¾ in (2 cm) deep. Roll out one portion of dough on a floured board until it is the size of the tin. Carefully transfer on to the tin, and trim level with the rim. Spoon the ginger preserve evenly all over the dough. Roll out the remainder of the dough and carefully lay on top. Again, trim level with the sides, then press with the tines of a fork to seal to the edge of the tin. Brush the top of the pastry with the milk or beaten egg, then scatter evenly with the flaked almonds, mixed with the sugar. Bake for 40 minutes or until golden-brown and firm to gentle touch. Leave for 15 minutes, then mark into 24 or 30 small squares. When quite cold, lift from the tin.

CHOCOLATE WALNUT SQUARES

Makes 16 squares

Freeze 3 months
Will keep fresh for 1 week in an airtight container

Dark brown sugar makes these spongy chocolate squares particularly moist and flavourful. The food processor method gives them an especially fine texture.

1 oz (25 g/2 tablespoons) and 4 oz (125 g/½ cup) soft margarine
4 level tablespoons cocoa
6 oz (175 g/¾ cup) soft dark brown sugar
2 eggs

1 teaspoon vanilla essence (extract)
2 oz (50 g/½ cup) plain (all-purpose) flour
2 oz (50 g/½ cup) walnuts, chopped medium-fine
Caster (superfine) sugar for sprinkling

Preheat the oven to Gas No. 4, 350 degrees F, 180 degrees C. Lightly grease an 8 in (20 cm) square tin, and line the bottom with silicone paper. Melt the 1 oz (25 g/2 tablespoons) margarine and stir in the cocoa, then set aside.

To mix by food processor Process the eggs and the sugar for 1 minute until thickened and lighter in colour, scraping down the sides after 30 seconds. Add the vanilla essence, and then the 4 oz (125 g/½ cup) margarine through the feed tube, 1 tablespoon at a time, processing constantly. The mixture will now resemble mayonnaise. Add the cocoa-and-margarine mixture, and process for 2 seconds. Spoon the flour on top, and pulse it in until evenly blended, about 5 seconds. Pulse in the walnuts for 2 seconds.

To mix by hand or electric mixer Beat all the ingredients together until evenly blended, about 2 minutes.

To bake the squares Turn into the prepared tin, smooth the surface level, then bake for 25 to 30 minutes or until the top springs back when gently pressed. Take out of the oven and sprinkle evenly with caster sugar. Cool in the tin for 10 minutes, then cut into 16 squares.

A 'HEALTH' CAKE
PASSION CAKE

Freeze 3 months
Will keep 1 week in an airtight container in the refrigerator

The carrots, bananas, nuts and natural brown sugar in this moist and tender cake transform the 'empty' calories found in most baking into positive nourishment.

2 oz (50 g/½ cup) walnuts or hazelnuts (filberts), chopped
2 large bananas, mashed
6 oz (175 g/¾ cup) light brown sugar
3 eggs
10 oz (275 g/2½ cups) plain (all-purpose) white or wheatmeal flour
Pinch of salt
1 teaspoon cinnamon
2 level teaspoons baking powder

1 level teaspoon bicarbonate of soda (baking soda)
6 fl oz (175 ml/¾ cup) sunflower oil
6 oz (175 g/1½ cups) finely grated carrots

THE TOPPING:
2 oz (50 g/¼ cup) soft butter or margarine
6 oz (175 g/¾ cup) any smooth soft cheese
4 oz (125 g/1 cup) icing (confectioners') sugar
2 teaspoons lemon juice

Set the oven at Gas No. 4, 350 degrees F, 180 degrees C. Grease and line a cake tin 3 in (7½ cm) deep and either 9 in (22½ cm) round or 8 in (20 cm) square.

To mix by hand or electric mixer Put the chopped walnuts (or hazelnuts) and the mashed bananas into a mixing bowl. Add the sugar and eggs, and the flour sifted together with the salt, cinnamon, baking powder and bicarbonate of soda. Add the oil, then mix well until absolutely smooth. Finally stir in the grated carrots.

To mix by food processor Process the walnuts until coarsely chopped. Remove. Put in the bananas cut in 1 in (2½ cm) chunks and process until puréed. Add the eggs and sugar and process for 1 minute. Add all the remaining ingredients (except the nuts) and pulse for 3 or 4 seconds only, until evenly mixed. Add the walnuts and pulse for 2 seconds.

To bake the cake Spoon the mixture into the chosen tin and smooth level. Bake for 55 to 65 minutes, or until golden-brown and firm to gentle touch — a metal skewer will come out clean from the centre. Put on a wire rack and leave until cold.

To make the topping Beat all the ingredients together until smooth. Use to ice the top and sides of the cake. For current use, keep in a covered container in the refrigerator. Leave at room temperature for 30 minutes before serving.

TWO NUT CAKES
UGAT SCHEKADEME
CHOCOLATE AND ALMOND TORTE

Freeze without icing 3 months
The iced cake will keep under refrigeration
for 1 week

I first tasted this wonderful cake at my cousin Chana's home in Israel, but it really originates in her home town of Kovno (Kaunas), once the most famous centre of Jewish culture in Lithuania. At the height of its influence, before the Second World War, no fewer than five Jewish newspapers were published daily for a community 38,000 strong, but today its only claim to fame is as the setting for some of the more apocryphal Yiddish tales.

As to this cake from Kovno, once baked by her mother at every family celebration, Chana covered it with a velvety chocolate cream, but I find it equally delicious when served quite plain. If fine matzah meal is used in place of breadcrumbs it becomes a marvellous cake for Passover. As there are so many egg whites to whisk, however, it is very tedious to make without an electric mixer.

7 oz (200 g/1¾ cups) ground almonds
2 rounded tablespoons fine dry breadcrumbs
7 oz (200 g) grated chocolate
7 eggs, separated
8 oz (225 g/1 cup) caster (superfine) sugar
Juice of half a lemon (2 tablespoons)

GANACHE CREAM:
3 oz (75 g) plain (semi-sweet) chocolate
1 tablespoon water
2 level tablespoons caster (superfine) sugar
8 fl oz (225 ml/1 cup) double (heavy) cream
1 tablespoon rum

Preheat the oven to Gas No. 4, 350 degrees F, 180 degrees C. Have ready an 11 in (28 cm) loose-bottomed spring-form tin or two 8 in (20 cm) loose-bottomed sandwich tins, greased and lined with silicone paper.

To make the cake   Mix the almonds, the crumbs and the grated chocolate. Whisk the egg whites until they hold stiff peaks, then add the sugar, a tablespoon at a time, whisking until stiff after each addition. Fold in the yolks, followed by the dry ingredients. Finally stir in the lemon juice. Spoon the mixture into the tin(s) and level off. Bake for 30 minutes until golden-brown and firm to gentle touch. Put the cake on a cooling tray and turn out of the tin when cold. Split and fill, or leave whole and dust with icing sugar.

To make the ganache cream   Put the chocolate, water and sugar into a small pan and heat gently until the chocolate melts, then add the cream. Bring to the boil stirring, then immediately take off the heat, and refrigerate overnight. Next day whisk until as thick as whipped cream, then whisk in the rum. Fill and coat the cake.

MAGDA'S NUT CAKE

Freeze 3 months.
Filling may be frozen 1 month. Will
keep for 1 week in an airtight container

This cake, which was served at home in Budapest by Magda's grandmother — and in her day by her grandmother's grandmother — is a Hungarian version of the 'Nusstorte' made by every Jewish cook whose family once lived in the Austro-Hungarian Empire. The ground hazelnuts (filberts) which are used in place of flour give the cake its typically moist texture. Whipped cream is the traditional accompaniment, but the cake is also very good served plain with a compôte of summer fruits. Ground hazelnuts are sold by many health food shops, but the nuts are very easy to grind on a food processor — as fine as wholemeal flour.

5 eggs, separated
5 oz (150 g/⅔ cup) caster (superfine) sugar
1 teaspoon baking powder
2 tablespoons rum
½ lb (225 g/2 cups) ground hazelnuts
Pinch of salt

WHIPPED CREAM WITH RUM:
5 fl oz (150 ml/⅔ cup) whipping cream, well chilled
12 teaspoon caster (superfine) sugar
1 tablespoon rum

Preheat the oven to Gas No. 4, 350 degrees F, 180 degrees C. Grease a 9 in (22½ cm) spring-form tin (2 in (5 cm) deep) and line the bottom with a circle of silicone paper.

Whisk together the egg yolks and the sugar until the mixture falls in a continuous ribbon when the beaters are lifted out of the bowl. Stir in the baking powder, then

258

rum and the ground hazelnuts. Whisk the whites with a pinch of salt until they hold glossy peaks that just tip slightly to one side when the beater is withdrawn. Fold this mass into the yolk mixture, using a ribber spatula. Pour the mixture into the prepared cake tin, and bake for 30 minutes, or until the cake has shrunk slightly from the sides of the tin and the top is golden-brown and firm to gentle touch. Serve plain or with whipped cream.

To make the rum-flavoured whipped cream Put all the ingredients into a small bowl and whisk until the mixture holds soft peaks. Pile into a small bowl and chill until required.

FOREIGN SPECIALITY CAKES
FRENCH ORANGE LOAF, WITH ORANGE LIQUEUR FROSTING

Freeze 3 months
Will keep fresh under
refrigeration for 1 week

This fine-textured cake looks most effective in the kind of long loaf tin popular in France. The cake can be made by the traditional if rather tedious creaming method, but the texture is just as fine if made in a food processor by the very quick method I give below.

THE CAKE MIXTURE:
2 eggs
5 oz (150 g/⅔ cup) caster (superfine) sugar
2 oz (50 g/4 tablespoons) each soft butter and margarine
Rind of half a large orange and 1 lemon, finely grated
2 tablespoons boiling water
6 oz (175 g/1½ cups) special sponge (cake) self-raising flour, or 5 oz (150 g/1¼ cups) self-raising flour plus 1 oz (25 g/4 tablespoons) cornflour (cornstarch), or 5 oz (150 g/1¼ cups) plain (all-purpose) flour, 1 oz (25 g/4 tablespoons) cornflour (cornstarch) plus 1 teaspoon baking powder

THE FROSTING:
2 oz (50 g/¼ cup) butter (unsalted for preference)
Rind of half an orange, finely grated
1 tablespoon cream or top milk
1 tablespoon orange liqueur, for example Cointreau, Grand Marnier or Curaçao
½ lb (225 g/2 cups) sifted icing (confectioners') sugar

FOR DECORATION:
Few crystallized orange slices
4 tablespoons chopped walnuts or toasted hazelnuts

Preheat the oven to Gas No. 3, 325 degrees F, 160 degrees C. Grease a loaf tin measuring 10 x 4 in across the top and 3 in deep (25 × 10 × 7½ cm) or 9 × 5 × 3 in (22½ × 12½ × 7½ cm), and line the bottom with a strip of silicone paper.

Process the eggs and sugar for 1 minute, until thickened and lighter in colour, scraping the sides down after 30 seconds. Add the soft fats 1 tablespoon at a time, processing after each addition until the mixture looks like mayonnaise. Pulse in the grated rinds and the boiling water. Spoon the flour (and cornflour and baking powder, if used) on top, then pulse it in until the mixture is even in colour, scraping

259

the sides down once. Turn into the prepared tin and bake for 40 to 45 minutes, or until the sides have shrunk slightly from the tin and the top is firm to gentle pressure. Turn upside down on a cooling tray and leave — it will fall out after about 30 minutes.

To make the orange liqueur frosting Heat all the ingredients except the icing sugar until the butter is melted and the mixture is steaming — this can be done in the microwave. Pour at once over the icing sugar and beat until smooth, either by hand or in the food processor. Leave to cool until it is thick enough to spread — after about 15 minutes. Put the cake on a tray with the base uppermost and spread both the top and the sides with the frosting. Decorate with the crystallized orange slices and the chopped nuts. Serve in thin slices.

IRISH FRUIT CAKE

Will keep in an airtight container for 3 months

This is an exceedingly well-flavoured semi-rich fruit cake with a very moist texture. It can be made either with an electric mixer or in a food processor with a large capacity (3–3½ litres/12–15 cups).

½ lb (225 g/1 cup) butter or soft margarine
½ lb (225 g/1 cup) soft light brown sugar
Rind of 1 orange and half a lemon, finely grated
4 eggs, whisked to blend
10 oz (275 g/2½ cups) plain (all-purpose) flour
2 oz (50 g/½ cup) ground almonds
½ level teaspoon baking powder
2 level teaspoons mixed sweet spice
4 tablespoons stout (e.g. Guinness)

DRIED FRUIT MIXTURE:
½ lb (225 g/1½ cups) raisins
½ lb (225 g/1½ cups) sultanas (white raisins)
4 oz (125 g/½ cup) glacé (candied) cherries, cut in quarters
4 oz (125 g/1 cup) walnuts, chopped

TO SOAK THE CAKE:
8 tablespoons stout (e.g. Guinness)

Have the butter or margarine at room temperature. Preheat the oven to Gas No. 3, 325 degrees F, 160 degrees C. Grease a 7–8 in (17–20 cm) diameter tin, 3 in (7 cm) deep, and line the bottom and sides with silicone paper or a bought paper case. Mix the flour, ground almonds, baking powder, spice and salt.

To mix with an electric mixer Cream the butter or margarine until it is like mayonnaise then gradually beat in the sugar until the mixture is fluffy. Add the orange and lemon rind, then beat in the eggs a little at a time adding a little of the sifted flour mixture after each addition to prevent curdling. Add the flour and fruit alternately. Finally stir in the 4 tablespoons of stout.

To mix by food processor (This method is possible on a large-capacity machine only.) Process the eggs and sugar for 1 minute until thickened and lighter in colour, scraping down the sides after 30 seconds. Add the fat, 1 tablespoon at a time, processing constantly — the mixture should now be the consistency of mayonnaise. Add the 4 tablespoons of stout and the grated rinds and process until evenly blended. Spoon the flour mixture into the processor, then pulse it until evenly blended, scraping the sides down once with a rubber spatula. Spoon in the dried fruit mixture, and pulse in until evenly blended.

To bake and complete the cake   Turn into the prepared tin, level off, then bake for 1 hour. Turn the heat down to Gas No. 2, 300 degrees F, 150 degrees C, and continue to bake for a further 1–1½ hours or until the top springs back when gently touched with the finger and a skewer comes out cleanly from the centre. (An 8 in (20 cm) cake needs 1 hour at Gas No. 3, 325 degrees F, 160 degrees C, and 30 minutes at Gas No. 2, 300 degrees F, 150 degrees C.)

Take the cake out and put on a cooling rack. When quite cold take out of the tin and turn over so the base is uppermost. Put a plate underneath the rack, then prick the cake all over with a skewer and gradually spoon over the remaining 8 tablespoons of the stout. Wrap in foil, then put in an airtight tin. Leave at least 10 days before eating.

SACHERTORTE   VIENNESE CHOCOLATE CAKE

SERVES at least 12

Freeze 3 months
Will keep 1 week in an airtight container

On my left, a 'Sachertorte' from the famous Hotel Sacher; on my right, a 'Sachertorte' from the equally prestigious Café Demel. Both of them are rich and rare chocolate cakes of almost identical taste and texture, but which one is the genuine article as first baked by Franz Sacher in 1832? I shall leave it to the Viennese to argue the toss — they've already enjoyed a famous lawsuit in pursuit of this truth. I shall take my cue from chef Sacher himself, who, when asked to describe how he had composed his culinary heirloom, replied, 'I just flung a few ingredients together and there you are!' So that's what I did and, with the taste of both cakes still fresh on my palate, I developed this version; if it doesn't come with an impeccable provenance dating back 150 years, it is still faithful, I believe, to Franz Sacher's original intentions when he set out to devise a silky-smooth chocolate cake for his master, Prince Metternich.

This is one cake I still make by the traditional creaming method; to use a food processor for a 'Sachertorte' would be sacrilege indeed.

6 oz (175 g/³/₄ cup) soft butter
3 oz (75 g/¹/₃ cup) caster (superfine) sugar
5 egg yolks
¼ teaspoon ratafia or almond essence (extract)
6 oz (175 g) plain (semi-sweet) chocolate, chopped up then melted
6 oz (175 g/1½ cups) ground hazelnuts (filberts)
2½ oz (65 g/½ cup plus 2 tablespoons) self-raising flour or 2½ oz (65 g/½ cup plus 2 tablespoons) plain (all-purpose) flour with ½ teaspoon baking powder
2 tablespoons cocoa

6 egg whites
3 oz (75 g/¹/₃ cup) caster (superfine) sugar

TO FINISH:
3 or 4 tablespoons apricot jam, sieved then warmed until semi-liquid

THE ICING:
3 oz (75 g/¹/₃ cup) butter
6 oz (175 g) plain (semi-sweet) chocolate
2 tablespoons brandy or rum

Set the oven at Gas No. 3, 325 degrees F, 160 degrees C. Grease a 9½ in (24 cm) spring-form tin and line the bottom with silicone or greaseproof (waxed) paper.

Cream the butter until it resembles mayonnaise, then add the first 3 oz (75 g/⅓ cup) portion of sugar, 1 tablespoon at a time, beating until soft and fluffy after each addition — the mixture should now resemble whipped cream. Add the yolks one at a time, beating after each addition, then beat in the essence, melted chocolate and the hazelnuts. Fold in the cocoa, flour (and baking powder, if used). Whisk the whites until they hold stiff peaks, then whisk in the second 3 oz (75 g/⅓ cup) portion of sugar, 1 tablespoon at a time, whisking until stiff after each addition. *Stir* one-quarter of this meringue into the cake mixture to lighten the texture, then *fold* in the remainder with a metal spatula to conserve its content of air. Spoon the mixture into the prepared tin, and level off with a small spatula or knife. Tap the tin gently on the counter to disperse any large air bubbles. Bake for 60 or 70 minutes, or until the top is firm to gentle pressure and a metal skewer inserted in the centre of the cake comes out clean (start testing after 60 minutes). Stand on a cooling rack until cold, then ease out of the tin.

If the top has shrunk slightly, turn the cake over and ice the bottom instead. Put a large plate under the cooling rack to catch any drips. Brush the top and the sides of the cake with the warm jam. Melt the butter and broken chocolate with the brandy or rum, either in a small pan on top of the stove, or in the microwave (2 minutes on HIGH) then stir well together until quite smooth. The mixture should be thick enough to coat the back of a wooden spoon; if it is too liquid, chill for about 10 minutes until it thickens slightly. Pour over the top and the sides of the cake, and allow to set.

SWISS CHOCOLATE AND BURNT ALMOND CAKE

Freeze 3 months
Will keep for 1 week in an airtight container

The milk chocolate and almond topping of this delicious cake closely resembles a well-known triangular Swiss chocolate bar!

6 oz (175 g/¾ cup) soft light brown sugar
3 eggs
6 oz (175 g/¾ cup) soft margarine
2 teaspoons instant coffee dissolved in 4 tablespoons hot water
2 teaspoons vanilla essence (extract)
8 oz (225 g/2 cups) self-raising flour or 8 oz (225 g/2 cups) plain (all-purpose) flour plus 2 level teaspoons baking powder
4 oz (125 g/1 cup) drinking chocolate (instant chocolate)
2 level tablespoons cocoa

THE ICING:
2½ oz (65 g/5 tablespoons) butter or soft margarine
3 tablespoons single (light) cream or evaporated milk
3 tablespoons cocoa
½ lb (225 g/2 cups) icing (confectioners') sugar, sifted
1 teaspoon vanilla essence (extract)
3 oz (75 g/¾ cup) almond nuts or finely chopped blanched almonds, toasted

262

Preheat the oven to Gas No. 4, 350 degrees F, 180 degrees C. Grease a 9 in (23 cm) loose-bottomed cake tin (5 cm) deep, or (preferably) a *moule à manqué* (sloping-sided tin) of the same size, and line the bottom with silicone or greaseproof paper.

To mix by food processor Process the eggs and sugar for 1 minute until thickened and lighter in colour, scraping down the sides after 30 seconds. Add the margarine through the feed tube 1 tablespoon at a time, processing constantly. The mixture should now resemble mayonnaise. Add the vanilla essence and the coffee mixture, and process until evenly blended. Sift the flour (and baking powder, if used) with the drinking chocolate and cocoa, then spoon over the batter and pulse it until evenly blended, scraping the sides down once.

To mix by hand or electric mixer Put all the ingredients in a bowl and beat until smooth and creamy, about 3 minutes.

To bake the cake Spoon the cake mixture into the prepared tin and smooth level. Bake for 40 to 45 minutes until springy to the touch. Turn on to a cooling rack and leave to go cold.

To ice the cake Melt the fat in the liquid, either in a small pan on top of the stove or in a bowl in the microwave. Put the cocoa, icing sugar and essence into a bowl and pour on the hot liquid, then beat until smooth, about 2 minutes. Stir in the toasted nuts. Place a plate beneath the cooling rack to catch any drips, then gently pour the icing on top of the cake so that it flows over the sides, coating it completely. Leave to set.

MANDELMARMORGUGELHUPF
ALMOND MARBLE CAKE

Freeze 6 months
Will keep for 1 week in an airtight container

This is a variation of the famous Viennese Cake, which is baked by tradition in a fluted ring tin. I have enriched the recipe with ground almonds so that the cake is not only delicate but also moist in texture. Serve this cake quite plain — it goes well with a glass of dessert wine (such as Madeira or Beaumes de Venise).

4 large eggs
8 oz (225 g/1 cup) caster (superfine) sugar
8 oz (225 g/1 cup) soft butter or margarine
Few drops almond essence (extract)
3 oz (75 g/¾ cup) ground almonds

5 oz (150 g/1¼ cups) self-raising flour or 5 oz (150 g/1¼ cups) plain (all-purpose) flour plus 1¼ teaspoons baking powder
1 level tablespoon cocoa
4 tablespoons drinking chocolate (instant chocolate)
1 teaspoon vanilla essence (extract)

Preheat the oven to Gas No. 4, 350 degrees F, 180 degrees C. Grease a 9–10 in (23½–25 cm) gugelhupf or ring tin, or an 8 in (20 cm) square tin, 2–3 in (5–7 cm) deep.

To mix by food processor Process the eggs and the sugar for 1 minute, until thickened and lighter in colour, scraping the sides down after 30 seconds. Add the soft butter or margarine, 1 tablespoon at a time, processing all the time, until the mixture resembles mayonnaise. Pulse in the almond essence. Put the ground almonds and flour on top and pulse until evenly blended with the first mixture,

263

scraping the sides down once. Spoon half the mixture, by the tablespoon, into the chosen tin, leaving gaps between the spoonfuls. Add the cocoa, the drinking chocolate and the vanilla essence to the remaining mixture and pulse until evenly blended.

To mix by hand or electric mixer Cream the butter or margarine until it resembles mayonnaise, then beat in the sugar and almond essence, creaming until like whipped cream. Add the eggs one at a time, beating vigorously after each addition, and adding 1 tablespoon of flour with each egg. Finally fold in the sifted flour and almonds. Spoon half the mixture into the chosen tin, leaving gaps in between the spoonfuls. Add the cocoa and drinking chocolate to the remaining mixture and stir well until blended.

To bake the cake Spoon the chocolate mixture into the gaps in the plain mixture, then level the top. Bake for approximately 45 minutes, or until the cake has shrunk from the sides of the tin and the centre springs back when gently pressed. Turn upside down on a cooling tray and leave until cold, then gently ease out of the tin. Serve sprinkled with icing sugar.

Bread and Yeast Kuchens

My local Jewish baker makes the finest challot you ever tasted, using a machine that mixes 70 pounds of dough in exactly 8 minutes. The queue forms at 7.30 on a Sunday morning for his poppyseed and rye bagels that are shaped automatically, 36 at a time, without any assistance from a human hand. The special 'kitke' — the ten-strand plait he bakes for Festivals and family celebrations — is gilded with an electric egg-wash spray, and is a joy to behold. Yet despite all the high technology, he's such a fine craftsman that he's been awarded a place in the *Guinness Book of Records* for plaiting a thousand challot *by hand* in 1 hour, 53 minutes and 17 seconds!

So why bother to bake your own bread and kuchens at home? Because baking with yeast is one of the most exciting and fulfilling of all cookery tasks. Yeast is a living thing, and it seems to inject some of that life into the cold, inanimate ball of dough, helping it to grow and rise before your very eyes.

Jews have always had a high regard for the 'staff of life', and 'shew bread' made with the finest flour and oil played an important part in Temple ceremonial. It was given the Hebrew name of 'lechem', meaning a choice or chief food, and the baking of bread for her family was considered one of the most important tasks of the mistress of the house. Most of us have long since relinquished that duty, and buy our bread from the baker instead. But every now and again, what a delight it is to fill the house with the entrancing smell of a tender, wholemeal challah or an almond-filled kuchen ring. And it really is very easy, with dough hooks and processors and freezers — and just a little time and patience.

ALL ABOUT YEAST

Many very experienced cooks associate yeast cookery with mystery and mumbo-jumbo and when they see the word in a recipe, they immediately turn the page. The trouble is that as yeast is a living organism, it will only flourish — and so make dough rise — if it is treated with understanding and care. Fortunately, yeast, both fresh and dried, is now of a much more consistent quality and needs far less attention than that in use even twenty years ago, and I hope this will be evident in the recipes in this chapter.

• **Fresh yeast** is now available almost everywhere, usually at the local health food shop. If it is tightly wrapped in foil it will keep in excellent condition, sweet-smelling, slightly moist and pale in colour, for up to a month in the refrigerator. It can only be **frozen** successfully for up to six weeks, although yeast doughs can be frozen for up to three months.

• There is now a new kind of 'easy-blend' **dried yeast** that is as simple to use as baking powder; it is even mixed with the dry ingredients in exactly the same way. This new-style dried yeast, which I prefer to the more familiar granular kind, is very finely powdered and hyperactive so that a tiny sachet weighing 6 or 7 grammes can replace 28 grammes (1 oz) of fresh yeast. Its shelf life is limited to six months, but it has a 'use by' date on the packet.

BREAD FLOUR

The 'whiteness' or 'brown-ness' of a flour depends on the proportions it contains of the three main constituents of the wheat grain — the starchy inner endosperm, the bran and the vitamin-rich germ. The flour itself can be produced either by roller-milling the wheat or by grinding it between stones — the method used from earliest times until roller-milling was invented in the nineteenth century. Stoneground flour is now enjoying an enormous revival with the great interest in foods produced by traditional methods.

- The more of its three main constituents a particular flour contains, the higher its **extraction rate** is said to be:
- **Wholewheat flour** (also known as **wholemeal** or **graham flour**) has a 100% extraction rate; it contains all the nourishment of the original grain.
- **Wheatmeal flour**, with an extraction rate of between 80 and 90%, hasn't got as much of the bran and wheatgerm as wheatmeal flour has, but it has enough to make a positive contribution to the diet.
- **Wheaten flour** is wheatmeal with extra pieces of whole wheat grain.
- **Granary flour** has malted wheat and rye grains added to wheatmeal flour.
- **White flour** with an extraction rate of approximately 70% is milled only from the starchy endosperm — it contains none of the bran or the wheatgerm. In Britain, however, some of the vitamins and minerals have to be put back into the flour by law.
- The best bread is made from a **strong flour**, which is usually labelled 'bread flour' on the packet. Bread made from wholewheat flour has a coarse, close texture; if it is made with wheatmeal flour, it is much spongier. Many people prefer a bread made from a mixture of brown and white flours. It is worth experimenting to find the mixture of flours you like the best.
- **Sweet (enriched) yeast doughs** can be made either with a white bread flour or with the plain white (all-purpose) flour normally used for cakes and biscuits.

MIXING WAYS

In the old days you had two alternative ways of mixing a yeast dough: you beat the softer doughs with a wooden spoon, and you kneaded the firmer doughs with your hand. Then came the electric mixer, with its beater and dough hook for performing the same functions mechanically, and now there's also the food processor. With the standard-size processor you can mix a bread dough based on 1 lb (450 g/4 cups) flour and a kuchen (enriched) dough based on ¾ lb (350 g/3 cups). With a large food processor, however, you can mix a bread dough based on 2 lb (1 kg/8 cups) flour and a kuchen dough based on 1½ lb (675 g/6 cups). The kneading is done by the metal knife, and only takes 1 to 1½ minutes to produce a smooth and silky dough. (See page 188 for full details.)

PLAITED BREADS

- The best way to learn how to plait bread is by example — watching someone demonstrate it to you. However, as this is not always possible, I have tried to put the method into words, with the help of a diagram for a four-strand plait that illustrates the general principle.

• The real secret of following a plaiting sequence is that you must always count the strands *as you see them on the board*: don't try to remember what their original positions were before you started to plait them. (This becomes very clear when you actually start to plait.) I have found it helpful to practise for the first time using strands of plasticine instead of dough.

• Before you start to plait, always prepare the strands of dough on the board as follows:

1. Start with dough that has had one rising. Divide it into as many pieces as you require strands, then shape each piece into a ball.

2. Roll each ball with your hands into a strand about 9 in (22 cm) long that tapers slightly at each end.

3. Fan out the strands evenly on the board, then pinch them firmly together at the top end — you may find it helpful to weight this end down with a heavy knife. (The exception is the seven-strand herringbone plait, which starts differently — see below.)

4. Count the strands from the left to right as you see them on the board. Remember that when you have moved a strand according to your chosen sequence you count all the strands as you *now* see them on the board. In other words, the 'number' of each strand changes from its starting 'number' as the plaiting proceeds.

5. Now follow the plaiting sequence of your choice.

• **Three strands**. Bring alternate outer strands between the remaining two and repeat until the ends of the strands are reached.

• **Four strands**. Prepare as usual, then plait as follows:

> strand 2 over strand 3
> strand 4 over strand 2
> strand 1 over strand 3

Repeat until the ends of the strands are reached.

• **Five strands**. Prepare as usual, then plait as follows:

> strand 2 over strand 3
> strand 5 over strand 2
> strand 1 over strand 3

Repeat until the ends of the strands are reached.

• **Six strands**. Prepare as usual, then plait as follows:

Preliminary move (not repeated):

> strand 6 over strand 1

then

> strand 2 over strand 6
> strand 1 over strand 3
> strand 5 over strand 1
> strand 6 over strand 4

Repeat the last *four* moves until the ends of the strands are reached.

• **Eight strands**. Prepare as usual, then plait as follows:

Preliminary move (not repeated):

> strand 8 under strand 7 and over strand 1

then

> strand 2 under strand 3 and over strand 8
> strand 1 over strand 4
> strand 7 under strand 6 and over strand 1
> strand 8 over strand 5

Repeat the last *four* moves until the ends of the strands are reached.

- **Seven strands** (herringbone plait). Arrange the strands side by side, then divide the bottom half with four strands on one side and three on the other (see diagram). Bring the outside strands alternately to the centre, starting from the side with four strands. Join the ends and turn the top half towards you, then divide this other half with four strands on one side and three on the other (see diagram). Bring the outside strands alternately to the centre, starting from the side with four strands.

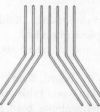

- After all the strands of dough have been plaited their full length, pinch all the free ends together, sealing them firmly. Turn the completed plait over on its side, then roll it gently to improve its shape.

BROWN CHALLAH OR TRADITIONAL TIN LOAF

Makes 2 plaited loaves each 12 in (30 cm) long or 2 medium tin loaves

Freeze 3 months
Will keep 4 days in bread bin or drawer

By tradition, a challah has always been made with white flour, partly in honour of Shabbat but also to make a distinction between it and the coarser brown bread eaten during the week. But now that brown flour is in greater favour than white, I see no reason why it should not be used for this special rich dough. However, if you prefer to make tin loaves from it rather than plaits, the directions for shaping them are given below. The dough can be left to rise in the refrigerator overnight, or it can be risen and baked on the same day.

THE DOUGH:
4 fl oz (125 ml/½ cup) boiling water made up to 12 fl oz (350 ml/1½ cups) with cold water
1 tablespoon dark brown sugar or honey
1 oz (25 g/2 cakes) fresh yeast or 2 sachets easy-blend dried yeast
6 oz (175 g/1½ cups) strong white (bread) flour plus 18 oz (500 g/4½ cups) wholemeal (wholewheat) flour, or 1½ lb (675 g/6 cups) wheatmeal or wholemeal flour

3 teaspoons salt
3 tablespoons any flavourless oil
2 eggs, beaten (saving 2 tablespoons for the glaze)

THE GLAZE:
2 tablespoons reserved egg
2 tablespoons poppy or sesame seeds

To make the dough Put the water, sugar or honey, and the crumbled fresh yeast (if used) into a large mixing bowl and add about a quarter (6 oz) (175 g/¾ cup) of the flour; mix to a smooth batter, cover with a teatowel and leave for 15 minutes until frothy. Uncover and add the salt, oil, eggs and remaining flour and mix to a spongy, scone-like dough. (If you use one of the new easy-blend dried yeasts, it *must* be

268

added to the dry ingredients, *not* the liquid, and the dough can then be mixed in one stage.) Knead the dough until it loses its stickiness and feels silky and smooth — 1½ minutes with the steel blade of a food processor, about 4 minutes with a dough hook, 10 minutes by hand. Turn the machine-kneaded dough on to a floured board and knead by hand for 30 seconds. Grease the mixing bowl with oil, put the dough back and immediately turn it over so that the top is covered with a film of oil (to stop it drying out). Cover the bowl with clingfilm (saran wrap) and leave to rise until it is double in bulk and will spring back when lightly prodded with a finger. Choose the time and method for rising the dough that suits you best, according to the following timetable:

Rising time for dough
In an airing cupboard 45–60 minutes   In a pleasantly warm kitchen 1½–2 hours
In a cold larder 8–12 hours   In the refrigerator 12–24 hours

Note   Dough that has risen in the refrigerator needs to be brought back to room temperature before shaping. This takes 1 hour in the kitchen or 2 minutes on DEFROST in the microwave.

To shape the bread   Divide the dough in two and knead each piece for 1 minute until it is smooth and elastic once more.

To make a four-strand plait   Divide one piece of dough equally into four. Flatten each quarter with the fist, then roll up into a little 'Swiss roll'. Flatten again, roll up as before, then shape into a ball — this greatly improves the texture of the loaf. Roll each ball into a 9 in (22 cm) strand that tapers slightly at each end. Join the four strands firmly together at one end, then fan them out on the board. Plait as shown on page 186. Arrange on a greased tray.

To make a tin loaf   Lightly grease a loaf tin measuring 9 × 5 × 3 in (about 22 × 12 × 7 cm). Divide the remaining dough into three and flatten each piece with the fist, then roll up into a little 'Swiss roll', flatten, roll up again, then finally roll into a ball. Arrange two of the balls side by side in the middle of the tin. Divide the third ball in two and shape into two smaller balls, then place one on either side of the centre balls.

To prove either the plait or the tin loaf   Slip the tray or the loaf tin into a large plastic bag and leave in the kitchen or airing cupboard for 45 minutes to 1 hour, or until puffy again. Remove from the bag, brush with the glaze and scatter with poppy or sesame seeds.

To bake the bread   Preheat the oven to Gas No. 6, 400 degrees F, 200 degrees C. Bake the *plait* for 25–30 minutes or until crusty and brown. Bake the *loaf* for 30–40 minutes, or until the bottom sounds hollow when tapped.

SESAME CHEESE BREAD

Makes 2 twists, or 2 loaves each serving 6–8   *Freeze 3 months*
Will keep 3 days under refrigeration

This is a beautiful bread with a 'vein' of herbs running through it. It is superb for a fish barbecue or to serve at an informal lunch or supper. Serve fresh, or reheat in the microwave for 2 minutes or (wrapped in foil) in a quick oven for 10 to 15 minutes. The bread can also be made in a large-capacity food processor. It can be shaped into either a twist or a simpler tin loaf.

269

THE DOUGH:

4 oz (125 g/1 cup) grated cheese
1½ lb (675 g/6 cups) wholemeal
(wholewheat) or wheatmeal flour
2 teaspoons brown sugar or honey
2 teaspoons salt
1 oz (25 g/2 cakes) fresh yeast or 2 sachets
easy-blend dried yeast
2 oz (50 g/¼ cup) soft butter or margarine,
or 3 tablespoons oil
5 fl oz (150 ml/⅔ cup) hot water
7 fl oz (200 ml/1 cup) milk
2 eggs

FOR SPREADING ON THE DOUGH:

2 oz (50 g/¼ cup) butter or margarine
4 tablespoons chopped parsley
1 teaspoon dried tarragon or 1 tablespoon
fresh tarragon, chopped

THE GLAZE:

1 tablespoon melted butter or margarine
A little sea salt
Sesame seeds

In the bowl of the mixer put the cheese, flour, sugar, salt and dried yeast (if used). Fix the dough hook and mix the ingredients to blend for 20 seconds. (With fresh yeast, mix the yeast until creamy with 3 tablespoons of the water cooled to lukewarm, then add with the liquids as described below.) Measure the milk into a jug, then make up to 12 fl oz (350 ml/1½ cups) with the hot water. Tip into the dry ingredients together with the soft fat or oil and the eggs, and knead at medium speed for 4 minutes (1½ minutes on food processor) or until the dough leaves the sides of the bowl clean.

Tip on to a floured board and knead with the hands into a smooth ball. Grease a large bowl lightly with oil, put in the dough, then turn it over so that the greased side is on top. Cover with clingfilm (saran wrap) and leave to rise in a warm kitchen until double in bulk (about 1½ hours). Turn the risen dough on to a floured board, punch down well with the fists to redistribute the air bubbles, then divide into two. Melt the 2 oz (50 g/¼ cup) butter or margarine and stir in the herbs.

To make a twist Have ready a greased oven tray. Roll half the dough into a rectangle about 20 in (50 cm) long and 9 in (22 cm) wide. Divide in two lengthwise, spread each piece with a quarter of the herb mixture, then roll each up tightly so that you now have two 'Swiss rolls', each 20 in (50 cm) long. Lay these side by side. Secure the two pieces at the top then twist together by lifting one side over the other. Seal at the other end, then twist into a ring, and place on the tray.

To make a loaf Have ready a greased loaf tin, measuring 9 × 5 × 3 in (about 22 × 12 × 7 cm). Roll out the other half of the dough into a rectangle about 10 in (25 cm) wide and ¾ in (2 cm) thick. Spread with the rest of the herb mixture, then roll up tightly into a 'Swiss roll', tuck in the ends to seal, then lay in the greased tin.

To prove the twist and the loaf Put into a large plastic bag and leave in the warm kitchen until they double in size and are puffy to the touch — 30 or 40 minutes. Brush with the melted fat and scatter with a little sea salt and the sesame seeds.

To bake Preheat the oven to Gas No. 6, 400 degrees F, 200 degrees C. Bake for 30–40 minutes, or until well risen and brown and the bottom sounds slightly hollow when it is tapped with the knuckle.

270

FRENCH CHEESE BRIOCHE

Makes 1 8 inch (20 cm) round brioche

Freeze 3 months
Will keep 3 days under refrigeration

The great delight of a true French breakfast — the brioche — is very complicated to make by the classic method and if there is a professional baker producing them in your neighbourhood, you won't need my recipe. But I have developed a method that is so easy and so certain of success that, although the loaf is not made in a traditional brioche mould, it brings the pleasure of making this kind of spongy bread well within the capability of the domestic baker.

The bread freezes and reheats well, and is delightful to serve at any time of the day. Serve it warm or reheated and cut in thick sections like a cake, or allow it to go cold and serve in thin lightly buttered slices.

3 tablespoons lukewarm milk
½ oz (15 g/1 cake) fresh yeast or
1 sachet easy-blend dried yeast
1 teaspoon sugar
1 oz (25 g/4 tablespoons) strong white (bread) flour
8 oz (225 g/2 cups) strong white (bread) flour
½ teaspoon salt

2 oz (50 g/¼ cup) soft butter or *margarine, cut in ½ in (1 cm) cubes*
2 eggs beaten to blend (save 1 tablespoon for glaze)
3 oz (75 g/¾ cup) Cheddar cheese, grated

THE GLAZE:
1 tablespoon reserved egg
1 oz (25 g/¼ cup) finely grated cheese
Good pinch of paprika

Put the milk into a basin and stir in the yeast. Add the sugar and flour, stir well, then leave until frothy, about 15 minutes. (If you use easy-blend dried yeast, omit this stage but stir 1 sachet of yeast with the dry ingredients and then mix to a dough with the milk, eggs and soft fat. If possible, use fresh yeast for this recipe, however; the sponge method described here produces a brioche with a finer texture.)
To mix by food processor Put the 8 oz (225 g/2 cups) flour, salt and butter (or margarine) into the bowl and process until the fat is rubbed in, about 5 seconds. Add the beaten eggs and the yeast mixture and process for 1 minute until the dough leaves the sides of the bowl clean. If it is still sticky, add a further 1 or 2 tablespoons of flour.
To mix with electric mixer Put the yeast batter, flour, salt, soft fat and eggs into a bowl and knead with the dough hook until the dough leaves the side of the bowl clean — about 4 minutes.
To finish the dough Turn on to a floured board and knead by hand for 30 seconds until the surface of the dough looks smooth and silky. Lightly grease a mixing bowl with oil, put in the dough and turn it over so that the top is covered with a thin film. Cover with clingfilm (saran wrap) and leave until the dough has doubled in size and will spring back when lightly pressed with a finger (for rising times see opposite). Turn out on the floured board again and knead in the 3 óz (75 g/¾ cup) of grated cheese (or you can do it in the food processor). Knead the dough into a ball.
To prove and bake Grease an 8 in (20 cm) diameter sandwich tin, put the ball of dough in it, and press down to fit. Put the tin into a large plastic bag and leave until the loaf is light and puffy again — about 30 minutes. Preheat the oven to Gas No. 6,

271

400 degrees F, 200 degrees C. When the loaf is ready, brush it with the reserved egg, scatter with the 1 oz (25 g/¼ cup) cheese and dust with paprika. Bake for 25 minutes until a rich brown.

BROWN CHEESE SCONE RING

Makes 1 ring of 12 scones   *Freeze cooked 3 months, raw 1 month*

This is a very tasty alternative to wholemeal (wholewheat) bread to serve with soups and salads. I like to use a mixture of wholemeal and white flours as this makes a lighter scone, but the choice is yours. The ring should be served slightly warm shortly after baking or reheated from frozen, either in the microwave (2 minutes on DEFROST) or wrapped in foil in a conventional oven, Gas No. 6, 400 degrees F, 200 degrees C, for 10 minutes. Or you can freeze the ring raw, then defrost it (overnight in the refrigerator, 1 hour at room temperature, 2 minutes on DEFROST in the microwave), and bake as directed.

12 oz (350 g/3 cups) wholemeal
(wholewheat), granary or 81% extraction
flour, or 6 oz (175 g/1½ cups) each
wholemeal flour and white (all-purpose)
flour
5 teaspoons baking powder
Large pinch each of salt and cayenne pepper
½ teaspoon herbes de Provence *(optional)*
1½ oz (40 g/3 tablespoons) margarine or
butter

4 oz (125 g/1 cup) Cheddar cheese, grated
1 egg
About 6 fl oz (175 ml/¾ cup) milk
1 teaspoon Dijon mustard

THE GLAZE:
1 oz (25 g/¼ cup) finely grated cheese
A little milk

Preheat the oven to Gas No. 7, 425 degrees F, 220 degrees C. Grease a 9 in (22½ cm) diameter loose-bottomed sandwich or cake tin.

Put the flour, baking powder, salt, cayenne pepper and dried herbs into a bowl. Add the fat and rub it in by hand or machine until no particles of fat larger than a flake of oatmeal are seen when the bowl is shaken. Mix in the 4 oz (125 g/1 cup) of grated cheese. Break the egg into a measuring jug and add sufficient milk to make up to 8 fl oz (225 ml/1 cup). Stir in the Dijon mustard and whisk to blend. Make a well in the centre of the flour mixture, pour in the liquid all at once, then use a knife to mix to a spongy dough.

Turn the dough out on to a board sprinkled with brown flour and knead until smooth, about 30 seconds. Roll the dough into a sausage and cut it into 12 equal pieces, then roll each piece into a ball. Place one ball in the centre of the tin and arrange the remaining balls around it so that they are barely touching. Brush with milk and sprinkle with the 1 oz (25 g/¼ cup) of cheese. Bake for 15–20 minutes, until golden on top.

FRESH HERB SCHNECKEN

Makes 24 rolls

Freeze baked rolls 3 months, unbaked rolls 2 weeks

These fluffy pinwheels with a pale green herb filling make an elegant accompaniment for soups or salads for a very special dinner party. For convenience, they can be prepared well in advance and frozen raw, then defrosted and allowed to prove before baking as if they were freshly made. The defrosting process can take place in the refrigerator overnight, or the rolls can be put on DEFROST in the microwave until they feel warm to the touch, usually after 3 or 4 minutes.

In this recipe, the fresh or dried yeast is mixed with all the other ingredients, just as though it were a cake mixture. Because it is allowed to rise slowly in the refrigerator before shaping, the dough is softer than an ordinary dough, and therefore makes fluffier rolls. They are served warm, either newly baked or reheated.

THE DOUGH:

1 lb 2 oz (500 g/4½ cups) any bread flour
1 oz (25 g/2 tablespoons) granulated sugar
1 oz (25 g/2 cakes) fresh yeast or 1 sachet easy-blend dried yeast
2 level teaspoons salt
3 oz (75 g/⅓ cup) soft butter or margarine, or 5 tablespoons oil
1 egg
8 fl oz (225 ml/1 cup) hand-hot water

HERB BUTTER:

4 oz (125 g/½ cup) butter or margarine (softened)
4 rounded tablespoons chopped parsley
2 tablespoons snipped chives
1 teaspoon dried herbes de Provence
½ teaspoon sea salt; 15 grinds black pepper

Put all the dough ingredients in the bowl of the mixer in the order given, and beat until the mixture leaves the sides of the bowl and the beaters are almost clean — it should be a soft scone-like dough. If too wet, add a further tablespoon or two of flour until the mixture can be gathered into a soft ball. Grease the inside of a mixing bowl, put in the dough, then turn it over so that it is coated on both sides with a little fat. Cover with clingfilm (saran wrap) and put in the refrigerator for 4 hours or overnight. Meanwhile, make the herb butter by beating all the ingredients together. Reserve 2 tablespoons for glazing the rolls. Grease 24 bun tins.

To shape the rolls Divide the chilled dough in half and work on one portion at a time. Roll into a rectangle 12 × 8 in (30 × 20 cm) and spread with half the remaining herb butter. Roll up, then cut in twelve 1 in (2½ cm) wide slices. Arrange in the bun tins, cut side up. Repeat with the remaining dough and herb butter. Slip the trays into a large plastic bag, leave for 45 minutes to 1 hour or until puffy. Bake at Gas No. 7, 425 degrees F, 220 degrees C for 15 minutes until a rich brown. Spread at once with the remaining herb butter.

273

THE VARIED DELIGHTS OF THE YEAST CAKE

Using one simple master recipe and an electric mixer, it's very easy to make a variety of the most glorious yeast cakes and rolls, light and fluffy in texture and surprisingly economical.

● If you're at home during the day, the dough can be left to **rise** in the kitchen; otherwise it can be put in the refrigerator to rise slowly overnight — the cold doesn't kill the yeast, it simply keeps it in suspended animation.

● From the master recipe you can make any *two* of the delicious possibilities that follow. The **Stollen** is rich with dried fruit and cherries and is served thinly sliced, either plain or with butter. **Butterscotch Schnecken** are stuffed with dried fruits and nuts and are covered in a butterscotch glaze. The **Almond Ring** has a luscious filling of almond paste and looks stunning with its topping of icing and toasted nuts. The **Apfelkuchen** has a spongy base thickly covered with apples and cinnamon sugar.

● All these cakes **freeze** well for up to 3 months. If they are to be kept in the freezer for more than a month, omit the icing (it tends to crumble in the cold) and put it on freshly after thawing.

● To **thaw** any of these cakes, leave in the packaging at room temperature for 2 or 3 hours. Or thaw on DEFROST for 2 minutes in the microwave. They will keep fresh for 2 days in the refrigerator.

● For instructions for mixing dough on a **food processor**, and for still more kuchen recipes, see pages 16–18.

MASTER RECIPE FOR SWEET YEAST DOUGH

Freeze unrisen dough 3 months
Freeze shaped but unbaked cakes for 2 weeks
Freeze cooked cakes 3 months
Will keep fresh 2 days under refrigeration

2 eggs
3 fl oz (75 ml/⅓ cup) cold milk
1 oz (25 g/2 cakes) fresh yeast or 1 sachet easy-blend dried yeast
3 oz (75 g/⅓ cup) soft butter or *margarine*

3 oz (75 g/⅓ cup) caster (superfine) sugar
Rind of 1 lemon, grated
1 lb (450 g/4 cups) plain white (all-purpose) flour
1 level teaspoon salt

Note   If you are using easy-blend dried yeast, mix it with the dry ingredients *before* adding them to the eggs and liquid in the bowl.

Break the eggs into a measuring cup, add the cold milk, whisk to blend, then make up to 10 fl oz (275 ml/1¼ cups) with hot water. Add the fresh yeast (if used) and stir until dissolved. In the mixer bowl put the flour, salt and sugar and mix thoroughly. Add the liquid, the soft butter and the lemon rind and beat for about 5 minutes until the dough is smooth and stretchy and leaves the bowl and the beater clean when pulled away. If too sticky, add a further 1 or 2 tablespoons of flour — the dough should be stiff enough to form into a soft ball.

To use at once Turn the dough on to a pastry board and knead for a few seconds — you will now have a satiny ball of dough. Grease a mixing bowl very lightly with oil, turn the ball of dough in it to coat it, then leave in the bowl and cover with clingfilm (saran wrap). It will take about 1½ hours in the kitchen to double in bulk. Then press the dough down, turn it over and knead it in the bowl for 1 or 2 minutes — this distributes the gas bubbles that have formed in the dough evenly throughout its mass.

To rise overnight Slip the dough into a greased polythene bag large enough to allow it to double in volume. Tie loosely and put on the bottom shelf of the refrigerator. Before using it next day, bring it out into the kitchen for 1 hour, so that it returns to room temperature. (If you have a microwave, you can hasten the process by putting it on DEFROST for 2 minutes.) Knead the dough for a further 1 or 2 minutes, as directed for the dough that has risen in the kitchen. In either case, leave the dough whilst you prepare the fillings for your chosen cakes.

STOLLEN

Half-quantity of risen sweet yeast dough
2 oz (50 g/½ cup) chopped walnuts or
toasted chopped almonds
4 oz (125 g/¾ cup) dried fruit mixture

Rind of 1 lemon, grated
2 oz (50 g/¼ cup) glacé (candied) cherries,
quartered
1½ oz (40 g/3 tablespoons) very soft butter

Turn the risen dough on to a floured board and knead in the nuts, fruit mixture and lemon rind (but not the cherries). Roll into a 10 in (25 cm) circle, spread with 1 oz (25 g/2 tablespoons) of the soft butter, then lay the cherries in a line down the centre. Fold the dough into three rather like an omelette, covering the cherries, and pressing gently to seal the top layer to the bottom one. Put on a greased tray, and brush with the remaining butter. Slip into a plastic bag and leave to prove until light and spongy to the touch, about 40 minutes. Bake in a quick oven, Gas No. 6, 400 degrees F, 200 degrees C, for 30 minutes or until brown. When cold, dredge thickly with icing (confectioners') sugar. Cut in slices and serve plain or buttered.

BUTTERSCOTCH SCHNECKEN

Makes 12

These are nicest either freshly baked, or reheated in the microwave or in a moderate oven (15 minutes in a foil parcel).

Half-quantity of risen sweet
yeast dough

THE GLAZE:
1 oz (25 g/2 tablespoons) each of butter,
brown sugar and golden syrup (corn syrup)

Put in a pan and simmer for 1 minute or until a rich golden-brown. Divide between 12 greased bun tins.

THE FILLING:
1 oz (25 g/2 tablespoons) soft butter
2 oz (50 g/¼ cup) caster (superfine) sugar

1 level teaspoon cinnamon
2 oz (50 g/⅓ cup) raisins
1 oz (25 g/¼ cup) chopped walnuts

Put the soft butter in a bowl and beat in the sugar and cinnamon, followed by the raisins and walnuts. Roll out the dough ⅜ in (1 cm) thick into a rectangle measuring 12 × 6 in (30 × 15 cm). Spread all over with the filling. Roll up lengthwise into a tight roll, then cut into twelve 1 in (2½ cm) slices. Arrange these, cut side up, in the bun tins. Slip the tray of tins into a plastic carrier bag and leave until puffy — 30 or 40 minutes. Bake in a quick oven, Gas No. 6, 400 degrees F, 200 degrees C, for 15–20 minutes, or until a rich brown. Allow 5 minutes for the glaze to set a little, then remove the Schnecken from the tins and leave them, with the glaze on top, on a cooling tray.

ALMOND RING

This is sliced and served either plain or with butter, as preferred.

Half-quantity of risen sweet yeast dough

THE FILLING:
3 oz (75 g/¾ cup) ground almonds or
hazelnuts (filberts)
Finely grated rind of half an orange
3 oz (75 g/⅓ cup) caster (superfine) sugar
1 egg yolk
½ teaspoon vanilla essence (extract)

THE GLAZE:
Few toasted flaked almonds
1 tablespoon orange juice
3 oz (75 g/¾ cup) icing (confectioners')
sugar

Mix the filling ingredients together to form a spreadable paste, adding a little cold water if necessary. Roll the dough into a rectangle measuring about 11 × 6 in (22 × 15 cm). Spread all over with the almond paste (leaving ½ in (1 cm) clear along each short side). Roll up lengthwise into a tight roll, then twist round to form a circle, sealing it well. Place on a greased tray. Using kitchen scissors, make cuts two-thirds of the way through the ring at intervals of 1½ in (4 cm). Slip the tray into a plastic bag and leave to rise until puffy, about 30 minutes.

Bake in a quick oven, Gas No. 6, 400 degrees F, 200 degrees C for 25 minutes or until golden-brown. Mix the sugar and juice to form an icing that will coat the back of the spoon. When the ring has cooled for 10 minutes, brush on the icing using a pastry brush and scatter with the almonds.

APFELKUCHEN

A very quickly made version of this recipe, made without yeast, is given on page 355.

Half-quantity of risen sweet yeast dough
4 large cooking apples, cored, peeled and
sliced ¼ in (½ cm) thick

4 oz (125 g/½ cup) caster (superfine) sugar
mixed with 1 level teaspoon cinnamon
Plum jam or ginger marmalade (ginger
preserve)

Roll the risen dough to a thickness of ⅜ in (1 cm) and use to line a Swiss roll tin measuring 14 × 10 in (35 × 25 cm), lightly greased. Allow the dough to rise again for 30 minutes, then spread with jam (or marmalade) and arrange the apple slices in overlapping rows on top. Sprinkle with the cinnamon sugar and leave for 10 minutes. Bake in a moderate oven, Gas No. 4, 350 degrees F, 180 degrees C, for 40 minutes. Serve warm or cold.

Preserves and Pickles

Preserving and pickling is a skill that seems to run in families, probably because — ideally — it needs to be learned by example rather than from a book. My husband had to apprentice himself to his father for a season before he was entrusted with the family recipe for pickled cucumbers. And when I wanted to put his mother's preserve recipes down on paper, there was nothing for it but to stand over her as she made her Lemon and Walnut Eingemachtes and write down exactly what she did, as she found it quite impossible to put the method into words (you will find the recipe on page 338). I had every sympathy with her, because each panful of jam I make seems to have a personality of its own and never behaves exactly as it says in the recipe.

From this you will gather that there is no tradition of jam-making in *my* mother's family, so I did have to learn it from a book. My own daughter, although a very keen cook, shows no interest in learning the art and I am sure the same is true for the majority of young women of her generation. But the old skills are disappearing for a reason more powerful than the changing fashions in food: the strong 'thumbs down' attitude that Jewish women now have to the use of too much sugar in their families' food.

It would be tragic, however, if this skill — which has been practised and perfected by countless generations of Jewish housewives — should be lost forever. So in this chapter you will find recipes for two uncooked jams whose sugar content I have managed to reduce, and which also contain significant amounts of vitamin C. I have included the other jams, jellies and fruit curds because not only are they outstandingly good to eat (if only on special occasions) but they are also suitable for making at Passover — *the* traditional time for making preserves in the Jewish home; more are to be found on page 338. The preparation of drinks based on fruit and alcohol is also a custom in many Jewish households, particularly in those families who once owned a 'shenk' — the Lithuanian version of an English country inn. I have included one recipe which dates back for more than a century, and another that is more modern in its origin.

THE PRACTICAL JOYS OF MAKING JAM

It is best to buy a specialist book if you wish to go into great depth on this subject. However, if you just want to make no more than the occasional panful of jam, you need only to follow a few simple guidelines to achieve success — and satisfaction.

• If you are offered a **preserving pan** (and have the room to store it) don't refuse it. But for making the moderate amounts of jam given in this chapter, any heavy-based half-gallon (2¼ litres/10 cups) capacity pan is perfectly adequate.

• Don't be tempted to buy **over-ripe fruit** just because it's cheap. Its jelling qualities will have deteriorated and you won't get a good set however long you boil the jam.

• **Preserving sugar** isn't essential, but it does reduce the amount of froth that has to be skimmed off the finished jam, a process which can be both tedious and wasteful.

• **Jam jars** with lids with built-in rubber rings are the most convenient to use. When the contents of the jar are cold this lid need only be screwed on tightly to provide a perfect seal. Select as many jars as you think you may need *before* you start to make the jam. Wash and rinse them, then leave them in a low oven (Gas No. ¼, 225 degrees F, 110 degrees C) to sterilize them, and also to heat them up ready for the hot jam. Don't put the jar *lids* in the oven, or the rubber rings may perish in the heat.

• To test whether the **setting-point** has been reached you have a choice of two homely though efficient methods: the saucer test and the flake test. While testing for the set by either method, be sure to remove the pan of jam from the heat to prevent it overcooking. If the jam fails the test, it can be returned to the heat to boil for 3 or 4 minutes more before testing again.

• **The saucer test:** Before starting to make the jam, put three saucers to chill in the freezer. When the correct time has elapsed, take out one of the saucers and put a teaspoon of jam on it, then return it to the freezer. After a further 3 minutes, take it out and push the jam gently with the finger. If the setting-point has been reached it will wrinkle slightly at the touch.

• **The flake test:** When the correct cooking time has elapsed, dip a wooden spoon into the jam, then lift it above the pan and twirl it round two or three times to cool it. Hold the spoon steady above the pan and let the cooled jam that is sticking to it drip back into the pan. If the jam has reached setting-point, drops of the jam will run together along the spoon to form a large *flake* that will break off sharply from the edge of the spoon. But if the jam runs off the spoon in *separate drops*, setting-point has not been reached and the jam needs further boiling. (Being of an impatient nature, I prefer the flake test to the saucer test, but both are equally reliable in practice.)

• **Whole fruit jams** should be cooled in the pan until a skin begins to form on the surface and only then ladled into the jar, so as to ensure that the fruit is distributed evenly throughout the jar. This applies equally to **jellies** that contain chopped herbs.

• To keep the jam in good condition from one season to the next, it should be **stored** in a dark, cool cupboard. If you don't have one, it is wiser to store the jam in the refrigerator.

TWO VERY SPECIAL PRESERVES
APRICOT AND AMARETTO CONSERVE

Makes 4 lb (2 kg/8 cups)

Will keep 12 months in a cool ventilated cupboard

This luxurious conserve, gently flavoured with an almond liqueur, is perfect to serve with warm croissants or bagels for a late Sunday breakfast or to spoon on fresh brown scones for Sunday tea. If Amaretto is not available, use either an apricot brandy or an orange-flavoured liqueur such as Cointreau. The dark sun-dried Turkish apricots have the finer flavour, the lighter oven-dried ones from California or Australia the prettier colour. You must make your own choice. If whole dried fruit is used, divide each apricot into two halves before soaking.

1 lb (450 g/3 cups) dried apricots
2 pints (1¼ litres/5 cups) cold water
2 lb (1 kg/4 cups) preserving sugar or granulated sugar

4 tablespoons fresh lemon juice
3 oz (75 g/¾ cup) almonds, blanched and split
2 fl oz (50 ml/¼ cup) Amaretto liqueur or Passover liqueur

The night before you plan to make the conserve, put the fruit in a preserving pan or other heavy pan of half-gallon (2¼ litres/10 cups) capacity and cover with the water. The next day, add more water if necessary, to ensure the fruit is barely covered, half-cover the pan, then bring to the boil and simmer until the apricots are absolutely tender — after 10 to 20 minutes. Meanwhile, wash and rinse sufficient jars, and put in a low oven, Gas No. ¼, 225 degrees F, 110 degrees C, to dry and warm.

Add the sugar to the tender fruit, stir until it has been dissolved, then add the lemon juice and almonds and boil hard until the jam will set (see opposite) — the liquid will then be a thick and viscous syrup. (Do not overboil or the sugar will begin to caramelize and spoil the delicate flavour of the conserve.) Stir in the liqueur. Put into the warm dry jars and cover at once with wax discs. Leave to cool, then cover each jar with cellophane or a lid with a rubber seal.

SPICED MORELLO CHERRY CONSERVE

Makes about 5 lb (2½ kg/10 cups)　　　　　　　*Will keep for 1 year in a cool, well-ventilated cupboard*

The tree in our garden bears between 30 and 40 pounds (15–20 kg) of deep red morello (sour) cherries every year. Most of these I freeze for winter compôtes and tartes, but I always reserve some of them to make this superb conserve. If you cannot get morellos, sweet black cherries can be used instead, but although the conserve will be delicious, it will not have the true sharp-sweet flavour. Over the years I have gradually reduced the sugar content of the conserve so that it is now tart and refreshing, in contrast to the cloying sweetness of so many factory-made jams.

It is worth investing in a really efficient cherry-stoner, preferably one with a plunger rather than a pincer action (the latter is tediously slow). It is not absolutely necessary to simmer the cracked cherry kernels with the fruit but they do undoubtedly improve the flavour.

4 lb (2 kg) morello (sour red) cherries (3 lb (1½ kg/6 cups) when stoned)
3 lb (1½ kg/7 cups) granulated or preserving sugar
Juice of 1 large lemon (3 tablespoons) or 1 teaspoon tartaric acid crystals or 1 teaspoon citric acid (sour salt) crystals

½ level teaspoon ground cinnamon
½ level teaspoon mixed spice
5 fl oz (150 ml/⅔ cup) juice (or juice and water)
1 bottle (8 fl oz (225 ml/1 cup)) liquid pectin

Wash the jars thoroughly, then put in a low oven, Gas No. ¼, 225 degrees F, 110 degrees C, to dry and warm whilst making the jam. Weigh the sugar and put that in the oven at the same time. Stone the cherries, reserving the juice. Make this up if necessary with water to 5 fl oz (150 ml/⅔ cup). Crush the stones, using a mortar and pestle, then tie in a piece of muslin or light-coloured disposable dishcloth.

Put the cherries and juice into the pan, bring to the boil, then simmer 5 minutes or until tender when rubbed between the thumb and forefinger. Add the sugar and the lemon juice or acid, stir until the sugar is dissolved, then add the bag of stones and the spices. Bring to a full rolling boil that cannot be stirred out. Boil hard for 3 minutes, then remove the bag of stones, stir in the pectin and continue to boil for a further 3 to 5 minutes or until the jam falls off the wooden spoon in flakes rather than in droplets. Leave in the pan until a skin begins to form on the surface — about 15 or 20 minutes. Take the hot jars from the oven. Put on a wooden board, then fill with the conserve. Cover each jar with a wax disc when hot and a lid when cold.

VARIATION
French Morello Cherry and Vanilla Conserve   Proceed exactly as for the Spiced Morello Cherry Conserve, but omit the spices. Add a vanilla pod to the pan together with the cherry stones. Remove the pod just before potting the conserve.

TWO UNCOOKED JAMS
Jams that can be made to set without boiling retain all the fresh flavour of the fruit, as well as their vitamin content, and there is no worry about finding the correct setting-point, as with a jam that has to be boiled. However, when these uncooked jams were developed about 40 years ago, they had a very high content of sugar which was thought necessary to help them to 'jell'. I have now reduced the proportion of sugar and find that I still achieve a well-set and fruity jam. Strawberry jam does not set easily even when cooked so the addition of some kind of jelling agent is essential, but as redcurrants are high in natural pectin, they do not need anything extra adding at all.

Uncooked jams are left to set at room temperature for 48 hours. They can then be stored in the refrigerator for up to 3 months, or they can be frozen and stored from one jam season to the next. Whether you pot jam for freezing in glass jars, plastic drinking cups or yoghurt pots, leave ¾ in (2 cm) of headroom to allow the jam to expand as it freezes. Otherwise it will break a glass jar or push the lid off a plastic one.

Frozen soft fruit can be used for making these jams as well as fresh fruit. Use the same weight of frozen redcurrants as specified in the recipe, but as the pectin content of frozen strawberries is diminished in the freezer, use an extra 10% weight of fruit but the same amount of sugar as in the recipe.

UNCOOKED STRAWBERRY JAM

Makes 6½ lb (3 kg/13 cups)

Freeze 1 year
Will keep 3 months under refrigeration

2½ lb (1¼ kg/8 cups) strawberries
3½ lb (1¾ kg/8 cups) caster (superfine) sugar

4 tablespoons lemon juice
1 bottle (8 oz (225 ml/1 cup) fruit pectin

Mash the strawberries with a fork (or process in the food processor for about 4 seconds), then turn into a large bowl and stir in the caster sugar. Leave for about 2 hours, stirring occasionally until all the sugar has dissolved. Add the lemon juice and the pectin and stir thoroughly, then divide between the chosen containers. Cover with the foil or lids and leave *at room temperature* for 2 days, then refrigerate or freeze as required. Stir the contents before using.

281

VERY LOW SUGAR REDCURRANT JELLY

Makes 1¾ lb (800 g/3 cups)

Freeze 1 year
Will keep 3 months under refrigeration

1 lb (450 g/4 cups) redcurrants
12 oz (350 g/1½ cups) caster (superfine) sugar

Put the redcurrants (defrosted if frozen) through the coarse sieve of a *mouli* or ordinary sieve, and then through the finer sieve — this removes all the skins and seeds. Add the sugar, and stir until quite dissolved — this cloudy mixture will clear after about 10 minutes. Put in containers and proceed as for the strawberry jam above.

PRESERVES TO SERVE WITH MEAT AND POULTRY

CRABAPPLE JELLY

Makes 1½ lb (675 g/3 cups)

Will keep for 1 year in a cool ventilated cupboard

If you were to plant a crabapple tree in the garden just for the sight of its crimson harvest, it would be enough. But there is an additional pleasure to be enjoyed when you use the fruit to make this delicate jelly and serve it the next winter with grilled or roast meats and poultry. Choose a variety such as John Downie, that bears bright red and yellow fruit, as this will make a beautiful rosy jelly which can be flavoured with herbs such as lemon balm, lemon verbena or mint.

If you intend to make jelly every year, then it's worth buying a proper jelly bag which ensures that a clear rather than cloudy juice is extracted from the fruit. Otherwise you will have to improvise a bag with a double thickness of buttermuslin (cheesecloth).

Pick the fruit when it is barely ripe as that is when it has the highest content of pectin — the natural jelling agent which helps to set the jelly. For the same reason do not peel or core the fruit as the peel and the core section are both rich in pectin.

THE CRABAPPLE JUICE:
2 lb (1 kg) crabapples
1 pint (575 ml/2½ cups) cold water, or just
enough to cover the fruit

THE JELLY:
1 pint (575 ml/2½ cups) crabapple juice
(prepared as described below)
Juice and grated rind of half a large lemon
1 lb (450 g/2 cups) preserving or *granulated*
sugar

Remove the stalks from the crabapples but leave the fruit whole. Wash them in cold water and drain in a colander, then place in a preserving pan, cover with the water and bring to the boil. Reduce the heat, then simmer very gently, stirring and crushing the fruit occasionally, until it is absolutely tender — this will take about an hour.

Dampen the jelly bag, then suspend it over a large bowl: an easy way to do this is to fix the loops over the legs of an upturned stool. Turn the fruit pulp into the bag and leave it to drip through overnight — do *not* press the juice through the bag, or the jelly will be cloudy.

Next day, measure the juice — there should be about 1 pint (575 ml/2½ cups). If it is only short of the amount by a tablespoon or two, make up the quantity with water; otherwise use proportionately less sugar. Set the oven to Gas No. ¼, 225 degrees F, 110 degrees C. Wash four small glass jars (each approximately 6 fl oz (175 ml/¾ cup) capacity), rinse them in hot water, then stand them upside down on an oven shelf to dry and heat through. Put the crabapple juice, lemon juice and lemon rind into the preserving pan and add the sugar, then cook, stirring, until the sugar has dissolved. Bring to the boil and cook without stirring until it will set (see page 279 for setting test) — about 8 or 10 minutes. Remove any scum from the surface with a wet metal spoon. Pour into the hot jars and cover each jar with a waxed disc. Cover with cellophane or lids when cold.

VARIATIONS
Lemon Balm Jelly   As soon as the sugar has dissolved flavour with 1 small bunch of lemon balm leaves. Remove before putting the jelly into the jars.
Rose-scented Geranium Jelly   Flavour as above, using 3 or 4 leaves. They can be left in the jelly.
Lemon Verbena Jelly   Flavour as above, using about 10 leaves — taste and see if more are necessary when the jelly is at setting-point. The leaves may be left in the jelly.

MINT JELLY

Makes about 1½ lb (675 g/3 cups)

This has an especially fine flavour when it is made with crabapple juice (see page 282) rather than ordinary apple juice. It has a sharp clean taste vastly superior to any commercial product. Serve it with roast lamb, grilled (broiled) lamb chops or to flavour a salad dressing (see, for instance, the recipe for Mangetout and Tomato Salad on page 197).

1 pint (575 ml/2½ cups) crabapple juice
Juice and grated rind of half a large lemon
2 tablespoons white wine vinegar

1 lb (450 g/2 cups) preserving or granulated sugar
2 tablespoons finely chopped fresh mint

Make in the same way as Crabapple Jelly, but add the wine vinegar with the lemon juice and rind. When the jelly has reached setting-point, stir in the chopped mint and leave the jelly in the pan until it is beginning to thicken — about 10 minutes. Stir well to distribute the mint evenly, and turn the jelly into the pots. Cover with wax discs and allow to go cold, then cover with cellophane or lids with rubber seals.

PICKLED DAMSONS

Makes 2 lb (1 kg)   *Will keep for a year in the refrigerator*

This spicy pickle, which can be made with either fresh or frozen fruit, makes a refreshing accompaniment to cold meats and poultry, or to serve with a 'ploughman's lunch' instead of chutney. The pickle is cooked in the oven to prevent the fruit from bursting their skins.

2 lb (1 kg) ripe damsons
1 lb (450 g/2 cups) soft light brown sugar
2 teaspoons lemon rind, finely grated

¼ teaspoon each ground cloves, allspice
(pimento) and ginger
½ teaspoon ground cinnamon
½ pint (275 ml/1¼ cups) white vinegar

Preheat the oven to Gas No. 4, 350 degrees F, 180 degrees C. Leave the damsons whole but prick each one all over with a fork. Put the sugar, lemon rind, spices and vinegar into a pan and heat until all the sugar has dissolved, stirring constantly. Arrange the damsons in one layer in a lidded heatproof casserole and pour the hot vinegar over them. Cover and cook in the oven for 35 minutes or until the damsons are tender but unbroken.

Meanwhile, wash and rinse two 1 lb (450 g) jars with lids. Put in the oven to heat through after the damsons have been cooking for 30 minutes. Spoon the damsons with the vinegar into the hot jars and cover tightly. When cold, refrigerate for 1 week before serving.

TWO FRUIT CURDS
TART LEMON CURD

Makes about 2½ lb (1¼ kg/5 cups)   *Keeps 8 weeks under refrigeration*

This is delicious as a spread on toast, scones or matzot. Combined with an equal volume of whipped cream it makes a superb filling for a sponge sandwich or small meringues.

Finely grated rind of 6 lemons
Juice of 6 or 7 lemons — 12 fl oz (350 ml/1½
cups)

6 oz (175 g/¾ cup) unsalted butter
1 lb (450 g/2 cups) granulated sugar
6 whole eggs

Put the juice and the grated rind into a bowl and leave for 2 hours, so that the oils in the rind can flavour the juice. Set the oven at Gas No. ½, 225 degrees F, 110 degrees C, and put in the sugar and 5 small jars to heat up. Pour the juice and rind through a fine strainer (discard the rind).

Melt the butter over gentle heat in a heavy-based pan, then add the warm sugar and the strained juice. Stir constantly until the sugar has completely dissolved.

Process the eggs on a food processor until thoroughly blended, about 10 seconds, then add a ladleful of the hot sugar mixture, processing all the time.
(To mix by hand Whisk the yolks and whites to blend, then add a ladleful of the hot sugar mixture, whisking constantly.) Tip the egg mixture into the pan and stir constantly over gentle heat until the mixture thickens to a pouring custard that will coat the back of a wooden spoon. *Do not allow the mixture to boil* or it will curdle.

Take off the heat and continue to stir for 2 or 3 minutes — it will thicken a little more with the heat from the pan. Pour the curd into the hot jars and cover with wax paper discs. When quite cold, cover with lids and refrigerate until required.

LIME CURD

Makes 1¼ lb (600 g) (3 small pots)   *Will keep under refrigeration for 2 months*

This is made in exactly the same way as the Lemon Curd, using fresh limes instead of lemons. To get the maximum juice from the limes, put them in the microwave on full power for 30 seconds, until they feel warm to the touch. You would need at least 12 limes to produce 12 fl oz (350 ml/1½ cups) juice, so I usually make only half the quantity of curd using:

6 limes   *8 oz (225 g/1 cup) granulated sugar*
3 oz (75 g/⅓ cup) unsalted butter   *3 whole eggs*

GRANDMA HYAMS' CHERRY BRANDY

Makes 1½ bottles cherry brandy   *Cherry brandy will keep at room temperature for several years*
Brandied cherries will keep in the refrigerator for up to six months

'Take 25 pounds of morello cherries and 5 bottles of brandy', said the original recipe that Mrs Hyams' parents brought with them from Russia in the early 1880s. And although she herself was born in England, she continued to follow the old tradition all her life, producing twelve glorious bottles of cherry brandy at a time to distribute amongst the family.

Alas, we no longer live in such expansive days, so we scaled down the recipe, bought a bottle of duty-free brandy on our way home from holiday, waited until the morellos were ripe, then started our preparations. It took from August until May to produce our one and a half bottles, but it was worth it. Not only did we have the cherry brandy but we also had a stock of wonderful brandied cherries as well.

The timetable

August	We mixed the cherries and sugar and left them to stand
September	Fermentation started
November	Fermentation ended
May	We bottled the cherry brandy

3 lb (1½ kg) morello (sour red) cherries
1¾ lb (750 g/3½ cups) soft light brown
sugar

11 fl oz (325 ml/1⅓ cups) brandy

Have ready a glass jar with a lid, big enough to hold all the cherries comfortably.

Wash and stem the cherries but do not stone them. Put into a colander, rinse thoroughly with cold water and drain well. Put a layer of the sugar in the bottom of the jar, and cover with a layer of cherries. Repeat until all the sugar and cherries are in the jar, ending with sugar. Put the lid on the jar but do not screw it on tightly.

Every 2 days, stir the contents of the jar gently but thoroughly, repeating until the sugar has completely dissolved, and then stir the mixture once a week until the cherries are completely covered with the liquid — from 3 to 6 weeks time, depending on the temperature of the room where the jar is stored. At this point, the mixture will start to bubble, a sign that fermentation has begun. Continue to stir, but now only once every 2 weeks. When the mixture stops bubbling, fermentation will have ceased, so the mixture can now be left for 3 or 4 weeks, until all the cherries have sunk to the bottom of the jar.

Pour the cherries and the syrup into a sieve over a large jug or bowl. Lift out the cherries and store in an airtight container in the refrigerator. Put a funnel in the neck of an empty 35 fl oz (1 litre) bottle, and fit a coffee-filter paper inside it. Slowly pour the syrup through the funnel to filter it. Measure the syrup, put it into a large bowl, and add 1 part of brandy to 3 parts of cherry syrup — you should have 33 fl oz (1 litre/4 cups) syrup and will therefore need 11 fl oz (325 ml/1⅓ cups) brandy. Bottle the cherry brandy and seal with tight-fitting corks. Leave for 4 months before drinking. Le 'hayim!

DAMSON GIN

Makes 35 fl oz (1 litre)   *Keeps for 1 year at room temperature*

Fresh or frozen damsons can be used to make this magnificent digestif. But beware — the taste may be fruity but the alcohol content is high! You will need either a sweet jar or a very large mayonnaise or coffee jar of 35 fl oz (1 litre) capacity in which to mature the gin.

1¼ lb (575 g) damsons
1 bottle (¾ litre) gin

10 oz (275 g/1¼ cups) granulated sugar

Remove the stalks, then wash and drain fresh damsons or defrost frozen ones. Prick the fruit all over with a sharp fork, then mix it in a bowl with the gin and the sugar. Transfer to the chosen jar, screw on the lid tightly and leave at room temperature for 4–6 weeks, stirring thoroughly once a week.

Stand a metal sieve over a very large jug or bowl and empty the damsons and the liquid into it. Put the damsons into a plastic container and refrigerate — they are delicious in a fruit salad. To filter the gin, place a funnel in the neck of a 35 fl oz (1 litre) bottle and line it with a coffee-filter paper. Slowly pour the gin through it into the bottle — the gin will be crystal clear. Cork and keep until required.

RUM OR BRANDY TOPF
FRESH FRUITS MACERATED IN ALCOHOL

Will keep for several months after preparation is complete, under refrigeration

As they come into season, summer fruits are added in sugared layers to a tall glass jar or a special pottery 'rumtopf', and covered with rum or brandy. After several months at room temperature the fruits will be swimming in a wonderful rum or brandy syrup and can then be used, either by themselves or mixed with other fruits, for a very special dessert. A 'rumtopf' started in mid-August will be ready by Hanukkah.

35 fl oz (1 litre/4½ cups) rum or *brandy*
½ lb (225 g/1 cup) sugar for every 1 lb (450 g) fruit used

CHOICE FRUITS IN SEASON (AS AVAILABLE):
1 lb (450 g) strawberries, washed, stems removed and large ones cut in half
1 lb (450 g) cherries, washed only if sandy, stems removed
1 lb (450 g) each apricots and peaches, blanched in boiling water for 2 minutes, then peeled, stoned and quartered

1 lb (450 g) each raspberries and blackberries, carefully sorted and imperfect berries removed
1 lb (450 g) each redcurrants and blackcurrants, washed and removed from their stems with a fork
1 lb (450 g) melon, seeds and peel removed and flesh cut into small dice
1 lb (450 g) plums, washed, halved and stems and stones removed
1 lb (450 g) grapes, washed and removed from the stems (use seedless grapes if available)
1 lb (450 g) pineapple, peeled and centre core removed and flesh cut into small sections or cubes

You will need a tall narrow jar, about 6 in (15 cm) in diameter and anything from 7 to 12 in (17–30 cm) high (an old-fashioned sweet jar is excellent). Prepare the first fruit in season (usually the strawberries) as follows (all other fruits are treated in the same way, after preparation according to variety): wash the fruit only if necessary, drain well, then put in a bowl and mix gently but thoroughly with ½ lb (225 g/1 cup) of the sugar. Leave for 1 hour, then put the mixture into the rumtopf. Pour on enough rum or brandy to cover the fruit by 1 in (2½ cm). To keep the fruit below the surface of the alcohol, cover it with a saucer; cover the pot itself with clingfilm (saran wrap) to stop the alcohol evaporating. Leave in a cool place, but do not refrigerate.

As each available fruit comes into season, add it to the rumtopf in a sugared layer, topping up with alcohol as necessary, so that the level is always 1 in (2½ cm) above the fruit. At the end of the summer, in about September, add the last layer of sugared fruit and alcohol, then leave undisturbed in a cool place until December. Refrigerate and use as required.

Party pieces

There are dinner party people and there are supper party people, and there are others, usually with more imagination than time, who can transform a workaday family meal into a feast for the unexpected guest. So when you're making your entertaining plans, it's worth asking yourself which kind of party person you are.

To give a successful dinner party, you need to be innovative yet well organized, able to compose an exciting but well-orchestrated menu in which each course is complementary and glides smoothly into the next. To plan a buffet supper party, you must have a good eye for colour and presentation as well as the stamina to stand up and prepare a wide variety of decorative dishes. Drinks parties are for those who enjoy planning their cast of guests and who find it no problem to put a variety of people at their ease while keeping up an endless flow of hot and cold finger food. If, however, your life is too full to mark off a corner and label it 'for entertaining only', then you will probably enjoy the challenge of the 'extended family' meal in which the mundane half-grapefruit is transformed with a sherry glaze, the mid-week stew is glorified with a flaky golden crust, and the 'end of the fruit bowl' fruit salad is given new interest with a dash of orange liqueur.

In my *Entertaining Cookbook* I have expanded at length on my own philosophy — and all the mechanics involved — in cooking for family and friends, and in *every* chapter of this book there are recipes (and quantities) for occasions that demand something more than everyday food. In this chapter, therefore, I have simply gathered together some of the more interesting party 'et ceteras' which I hope will add interest, and perhaps a little excitement, to a variety of entertaining occasions.

DIPS
BABA GHANOUSH AUBERGINE AND TAHINA DIP

SERVES 12–14 as a dip, 8 as a starter

Do not freeze
Keeps 1 week under refrigeration

Tahina is a purée made from crushed sesame seeds which has an elusive flavour that is hard to describe. For this famous dip it is mixed with aubergines (eggplant) which have been grilled over charcoal to give the dish its distinctive smoky flavour. However, if the aubergines are fat rather than long and thin they will cook more evenly in the oven.

Serve it either as a dip with crackers or crudités, or as a starter with scoops of warm pitta bread.

1½ lb (675 g) fine aubergines (eggplant)
Large sprig of parsley (enough to make 2 tablespoons when chopped)
2 cloves of garlic, peeled and halved
4 rounded tablespoons canned or bottled tahina
2 or 3 tablespoons lemon juice

½ teaspoon salt; 10 grinds black pepper
Pinch cayenne pepper
½ teaspoon ground cumin

GARNISH:
4 oz (125 g/1 cup) black Calamata olives

Preheat the oven to Gas No. 8, 450 degrees F, 230 degrees C. Prick the aubergines all over with a fork. Set on the oven shelf and cook for 25–30 minutes until they have begun to collapse and feel absolutely tender when pierced with a skewer. Leave until cool enough to handle, then cut in half and scrape the flesh out of the skins. Process (or blend) the aubergine flesh with the parsley, add the halved cloves of garlic and process until puréed — about 5 seconds. Now add the tahina and 2 tablespoons of the lemon juice alternately, processing all the time. Add the salt, the peppers and the cumin. Taste and add the final tablespoon of lemon juice if necessary — the mixture should have a little 'bite' but should not be sour. Cover and chill for several hours, then arrange in a pottery dish and serve garnished with the olives.

HONEYED ITALIAN DIP

SERVES 8   *Do not freeze*
                                      Will keep 6 weeks under refrigeration

While you're in the kitchen keeping an eye on the steaks, the rest of the company can take the edge off their appetites by dipping sticks of raw vegetable into this unusual dip. It's not very suitable for a cocktail party, however, as it does tend to drip as you dip!

5 fl oz (150 ml/²⁄₃ cup) lemon mayonnaise   **CRUDITÉS:**
1 level tablespoon thick (set) honey   *Raw carrot, green pepper and celery, cut*
½ teaspoon Worcestershire sauce   *into ½ in (1¼ cm) thick sticks*
2 teaspoons brandy   *Florets of raw cauliflower*
Few drops of lemon juice

Put the mayonnaise into a basin and stir in all the remaining ingredients (except the vegetables). Put into a small pot and refrigerate for several hours. Serve on a platter surrounded by the crudités.

SMOKED SALMON DIP

SERVES 8   *Freeze 1 month*
                                      Will keep 4 days under refrigeration

This is a pale pink, delicately flavoured mousse, with the consistency of softly whipped cream, which can be made from the cheaper 'titbits' of smoked salmon. It can only be prepared in a food processor or blender; if you use a blender, put the soured cream and the melted butter into the goblet before the other ingredients.

6 oz (175 g) smoked salmon pieces   *4 oz (125 g/½ cup) low- or medium-fat soft*
Large sprig of parsley or dill   *cheese*
1 teaspoon finely grated lemon rind   *2 oz (50 g/¼ cup) very soft or melted butter*
½ small clove of garlic, peeled   *5 fl oz (150 ml/²⁄₃ cup) soured cream or*
10 grinds of black pepper   *natural yoghurt*
                                             Crisps or tiny savoury biscuits (crackers) or
                                             toasts

Process or blend the salmon and the herbs until the fish is smooth and the herbs are chopped. Add all the remaining ingredients and process until smooth. Turn into a bowl and chill. Serve surrounded with the crisps or biscuits.

SPREADS

ANCHOVY AND PIMIENTO SPREAD

Sufficient for 40–50 crackers or slices of French bread

Do not freeze
Will keep 4 days under refrigeration

This can be either used as a spread, or packed into a pottery bowl and served as part of a cheese board.

1 can (2 oz (50 g)) anchovy fillets in olive oil, drained
1 large canned pimiento, drained on a paper towel

½ lb (225 g/1 cup) cream cheese, Quark or fromage blanc
10 grinds black pepper
1 tablespoon finely snipped chives

Cut the anchovies and pimiento in tiny cubes, then mix with the cheese and seasonings. Chill for several hours before use.

CHEESE AND SHERRY SPREAD

Sufficient for 40–50 crackers or slices of French bread

Do not freeze
Will keep 4 days under refrigeration

Edam, Cheddar or Lancashire cheese can be used as the foundation for this delicious spread which can also be served as part of a cheese board.

4 oz (125 g/1 cup) mature hard cheese, finely grated
4 oz (125 g/1½ cup) medium-fat soft cheese, Quark or fromage blanc
1 oz (25 g/2 tablespoons) soft butter or margarine
1 tablespoon medium-dry sherry

1 level teaspoon Dijon mustard
3 teaspoons finely snipped chives or a pinch of dried herbes de Provence
Pinch of salt; 10 grinds of black pepper

Put all the ingredients into a bowl and mix by hand or food processor until thoroughly blended. Taste and add more salt and pepper if necessary. Chill for 1 hour before use.

290

SARDINE SPREAD

Sufficient for 40–50 crackers or slices of
French bread

Do not freeze
Will keep 4 days under refrigeration

2 cans (4 oz (125 g)) sardines in olive oil
2 eggs, hard-boiled, then shelled
2 oz (50 g/¼ cup) soft butter or margarine

1 tablespoon lemon juice
1 teaspoon salt; 10 grinds black pepper
2 teaspoons chopped parsley

To mix by hand Mash the sardines thoroughly with a large fork, then add the mashed or sieved eggs followed by the remaining ingredients, and mix together until smooth.

To mix by food processor Put all the ingredients into a bowl and process until smooth.

VARIATION

Tuna Spread Substitute 1 can (7–8 oz (200–225 g)) light meat tuna for the sardines.

SAVOURY FILLO PASTRIES

Enchanting little pastries, stuffed with a variety of savoury fillings can be made with fillo (also spelled 'phyllo', 'filo' and 'fila'), a Middle Eastern pastry which is very similar to the *strudelteig* of Austria. Because the dough is made with only a very little vegetable oil, the paper-thin layers of fillo must be brushed with fat and then stacked on top of each other, or rolled up, to produce an effect very much like puff pastry. Because of its low fat content the raw fillo becomes very brittle on exposure to the air so it has to be handled with special care (see page 356 for details of how to store and use it). If it is unobtainable, however, thinly rolled puff pastry can be used instead.

The pastries can be filled and then frozen *raw* but not once they have been baked, as the pastry then becomes dry and crumbly. To prepare the pastries for the freezer, brush the tops with melted fat, open-freeze until solid (about 2 hours), then pack in layers in an airtight container. Defrost for 1 hour before baking. The pastries can be reheated in a moderate oven until warm to the touch, but *not* in the microwave as this makes the pastry lose its crispness.

SPANISH TUNA TRIANGLES

Makes 24 triangles

Freeze raw 3 months
Raw and cooked triangles will keep under
refrigeration for 3 days (brushed lightly with
fat if raw) and tightly covered with foil

---

8 sheets of fillo pastry (about ½ lb/225 g)
2–3 oz (50–75 g/¼–⅓ cup) unsalted butter or margarine, melted
1 tablespoon butter or oil
1 medium (5 oz (150 g)) onion, finely chopped
Half a medium-sized green or red pepper, seeds removed, cut in tiny cubes
1 can (7–8 oz (200–225 g)) light meat tuna in oil
½ teaspoon sea salt; 10 grinds of black pepper
Good pinch of ground nutmeg
2 tablespoons chopped parsley
2–3 tablespoons tomato ketchup

Cook the onion in the fat for 3 minutes, then add the pepper and continue to cook until the onion is soft and golden. Drain the tuna, put in a bowl and flake finely with a fork, then add the onion mixture and the seasonings. Bind with the tomato ketchup — the mixture should be moist enough to cling together. Set the oven at Gas No. 6, 400 degrees F, 200 degrees C. Have ready two oiled baking sheets.

To shape the triangles   Cut each sheet of fillo pastry into three long strips, each 5 in (12½ cm) wide. Brush very lightly but evenly with the melted fat, then fold in half lengthwise and brush with fat again. Put 1 heaped teaspoon of the filling at the bottom of a strip about 1 in (2½ cm) from the shorter edge and fold as illustrated.

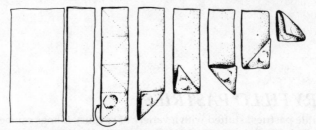

Put pastries on the trays and brush again with melted fat, then sprinkle with the sesame seeds. Bake for 20–25 minutes until crisp and golden. Serve at room temperature. May be briefly reheated.

VARIATIONS

Herbed Cheese Boreks   Make as for Spanish Tuna Triangles, but with a filling made by mixing together:

5 oz (150 g/³⁄₄ cup) herb-flavoured cream
cheese
4 oz (125 g/1 cup) crumbled Lancashire or
feta cheese

1 egg
½ level teaspoon salt; few grinds black
pepper

Vegetable Samosas   Make as for Spanish Tuna Triangles, but with this filling:

½ lb (225 g/1 cup) frozen mixed or stir fry
vegetables
1 tablespoon oil
1 medium onion, finely chopped
1 tablespoon ready-mixed mild curry

powder or ½ teaspoon each ground
coriander, cumin, fenugreek, turmeric, chilli
powder and white pepper
1 teaspoon fresh ginger, peeled and finely
chopped
Half a small potato (2 oz (50 g)), peeled and
cut in tiny cubes
½ teaspoon salt; 10 grinds black pepper

Cook the vegetables according to packet directions, then drain well. Sauté the onion in the oil until soft and golden, then stir in the curry powder (or the ground spices) and the ginger, and cook for 2 minutes. Add the potato cubes, cover and cook until the potatoes are tender, about 5 minutes. Uncover and cook until the potato cubes are golden-brown. Mix with the cooked vegetables, season and cool.

Using puff pastry   If fillo pastry is unavailable, you can make the Tuna Triangles, the Herbed Cheese Boreks and the Vegetable Samosas with puff pastry instead. Set the oven at Gas No. 7, 425 degrees F, 220 degrees C. Sprinkle two oven trays with cold water. Roll out 1 lb (450 g) puff pastry ⅛ in (¼ cm) thick and cut in circles with a 2½ in (6 cm) diameter plain cutter. Put 1 teaspoon filling in the centre of each circle, then fold over to form a semi-circle. Arrange on the trays, brush the tops with beaten egg, and scatter with sesame seeds. Bake for 15 minutes until puffed and golden-brown.

MEXICAN CIGARILLOS

Makes about 32 cigarillos

Freeze raw 3 months
Raw and cooked cigarillos will
keep under refrigeration for 3 days
if tightly wrapped in foil.

These tasty rolls have a hot and spicy filling which makes them wonderful finger food. They can also be served as part of a mixed hors d'oeuvres, accompanied by little pots of Baba Ghanoush (see page 288). If fillo pastry is unobtainable, use 1 lb (450 g) puff pastry rolled as thin as a knife blade and then cut in strips 5 in (12½ cm) wide and 6 in (15 cm) long. You will not need to brush this pastry with fat, but the tops of the cigarillos should be glazed with beaten egg before dipping into the sesame seeds.

293

8 sheets fillo pastry (about ½ lb/225 g)
3 oz (75 g/⅓ cup) margarine, melted
1 oz (25 g/¼ cup) sesame seeds

THE MEAT MIXTURE:
1 medium onion, finely chopped
2 tablespoons oil
2 teaspoons brown sugar
1 lb (450 g) lean minced (ground) meat
2 teaspoons paprika
Pinch of cayenne pepper

2 bayleaves
1 teaspoon mild curry powder
2 rounded tablespoons tomato ketchup
4 tablespoons raisins or currants
¼ pint (150 ml/⅔ cup) medium-dry red
wine
2 teaspoons soy sauce
2 teaspoons Worcestershire sauce
½–1 teaspoon salt; 10 grinds black pepper
1 tablespoon chopped fresh parsley
1 clove of garlic, peeled and crushed

Heat the oil, then add the onion and cook until soft and golden, about 5 minutes. Sprinkle with the sugar and add the meat. Cook, stirring with a fork until the meat loses its redness and begins to brown. Now add the wine and bubble until it is reduced by half. Add all the remaining ingredients. Cover and simmer for 15 or 20 minutes. Uncover and simmer for a few minutes without the lid — the mixture should be juicy but not wet. Allow to go cold.

To assemble the cigarillos Unwrap the fillo and divide each of approximately 8 sheets into long strips 4 in (10 cm) wide. Take each strip in turn and brush thinly with the melted fat. Arrange 1 tablespoon of the meat in a ½ in (1¼ cm) wide band 1 in (2½ cm) from the end of the strip nearest to you. Turn in the two long sides ½ in (1¼ cm) to enclose the filling, then roll up tightly into a cigar shape. Repeat with all the strips. Brush the tops thoroughly with the remaining fat. Put the sesame seeds in a small dish and press the cigarillos in them. Lay them on lightly greased baking sheets, about ½ in (1¼ cm) apart. Bake at Gas No. 6, 400 degrees F, 200 degrees C for 25 minutes or until a rich golden-brown. May be reheated.

MORE LITTLE PASTRIES
CHEESE AND OLIVE TARTLETS

Makes 24 tartlets

Freeze pastry for 3 months, baked tartlets with filling for 1 month

In the olive-packer's yard, inside the rows of barrels stretching as far as the eye could see, enough Manzanilla olives to fill the shelves of a thousand delis were fermenting to perfection under a baking Spanish sun, their dark green, bitter and woody flesh changing day by day to the familiar yellowy-green and tender delicacy that is so popular on the Jewish table. As for the little bit of red pepper that is stuffed in the middle, no longer is it cut by hand from strips of the cured pimiento flesh — it is produced by a machine which extrudes a continuous ribbon of minced pimiento paste. The stuffed olives still make delicious eating, however, especially in these savoury little tarts.

The same quantity of filling is sufficient for 8 larger (4 in/10 cm) quiches which, without the anchovies suggested in the recipe, will make a satisfying main course for a vegetarian meal.

THE PASTRY:

8 oz (225 g/2 cups) plain (all-purpose) flour
5 oz (150 g/²⁄₃ cup)butter or firm margarine
Pinch of salt
2 level teaspoons icing (confectioners') sugar
5 tablespoons iced water

THE FILLING:

1 oz (25 g/2 tablespoons) butter
2 shallots or half a small onion, finely chopped

1 tablespoon cornflour (cornstarch)
½ pint (275 ml/1¼ cups) milk
3 eggs
1 teaspoon Dijon mustard
Pinch of salt; 10 grinds black pepper
Pinch of cayenne pepper
6 oz (175 g/1½ cups) grated sharp cheese (Cheddar or Lancashire)
4 oz (125 g/1 cup) stuffed olives, sliced
6 anchovy fillets cut in ¼ in (½ cm) pieces (optional)

Make the pastry by the method on page 8. Chill it for 30 minutes, then roll out to fit 24 patty tins. At this stage, the cases can be chilled overnight, or they may be frozen. There's no need to defrost them before filling or baking. Preheat the oven to Gas No. 6, 400 degrees F, 200 degrees C.

To make the filling Melt the butter and gently sauté the shallots (or onion) until soft and golden. Put the cornflour into a bowl and gradually add the milk, stirring to blend evenly. Add the eggs, mustard, salt and peppers, then whisk to blend. Finally stir in the cheese, olives and anchovies (if used). Divide the mixture between the tartlets. Bake for 20 minutes until golden and puffed. Serve warm or cold. They may be reheated in a moderate oven until warm to the touch, or in the microwave.

DAIRY FINGER FOODS
SAVOURY PUFFS FILLED WITH MACKEREL MOUSSE

Makes 48–50   *Freeze the empty puffs for 3 months*

These are excellent finger food for a cocktail party or as a first course for an informal meal, served with drinks in the living room. The little puffs freeze to perfection, so it's worth making a large batch (as in this recipe) and using them as required — they can go straight from the freezer into a hot oven and after 4 minutes they will taste as though freshly baked. The mousse is also a good-tempered recipe, as it keeps for up to 5 days in the refrigerator. Fill the cold puffs with the mousse an hour or two before serving.

THE PASTRY:

½ pint (275 ml/1¼ cups) water
4 oz (125 g/½ cup) butter
5 oz (150 g/1¼ cups) strong (bread) flour
1 level teaspoon salt
Pinch each of ground nutmeg and white pepper
1 teaspoon Dijon mustard
4 eggs
Little Parmesan cheese for topping

THE MOUSSE:

2 large fillets smoked mackerel (12 oz (350 g) in all), skinned and cut in chunks
1 carton (5 oz) (150 g/²⁄₃ cup) natural set yoghurt
4 oz (125 g/1½ cup) curd or cottage cheese
2 oz (50 g/¼ cup) softened butter or margarine
2 teaspoons horseradish relish
10 grinds black pepper

Set the oven at Gas No. 7, 425 degrees F, 220 degrees C. Have ready two greased oven trays.

Put the water and fat (cut in chunks) into a pan and bring to the boil, when the butter should have melted. Take from the heat, add all the flour at once, together with the seasonings and mustard, and stir with a wooden spoon to make a smooth mixture. Return to the heat and cook for a further 2 minutes until the mixture forms a ball which can be rolled around the pan — the texture will be like thick mashed potato. Tip into the food processor and leave for 5 minutes or until it stops steaming.

Now add the eggs one at a time, processing after each addition until the egg is well incorporated. Process for 1 minute until the mixture is glossy and will just hold its shape. (If you are mixing by hand or electric mixer, drop in the eggs, one at a time, beating after each addition until glossy.)

Using a piping bag with a ½ in (1¼ cm) plain nozzle (or the tip of a spoon), pipe or spoon the mixture on to the trays in little mounds 1 in (2½ cm) in diameter and ¾ in (2 cm) high, leaving about 2 in (5 cm) between the puffs. Scatter the top of each puff with a little grated Parmesan cheese. Bake for 20–25 minutes or until crispy to the touch and a rich golden-brown. Take out, make a small slit with a knife in the side of each puff, turn off the oven, then return the puffs for a further 5 minutes to dry out. These can now be cooled and filled, or frozen until required.

To make the mackerel mousse Process all the ingredients together until smooth and fluffy. Chill for several hours, then use to fill the puffs through the slit in the side, using a piping bag (or cut the puffs in half and fill them with a spoon).

To serve Pile the filled puffs in a pyramid in an oval entrée dish.

VARIATION

Savoury Puffs with Tuna and Fresh Ginger Filling Make the savoury puffs as above. Fill them with a mixture of the following ingredients, mashed or processed together until fluffy.

1½ cans (7–8 oz (about 200 g)) light meat tuna, drained	5 tablespoons mayonnaise
4 oz cream cheese	3 teaspoons grated fresh ginger
	1 teaspoon salt; 15 grinds black pepper

VEGETABLE TORTILLA SQUARES

Makes about 40 little squares

I first tasted these delicious little morsels at the home of a Spanish Marquesa whose family claimed direct descent from Marrano Jews. The mixture is certainly very similar to the baked omelette or 'eggah' made by Sephardi Jews whose ancestors were expelled from Spain at the end of the fifteenth century. The dish probably has an even older, North African origin, however, having become 'naturalized' in Spain during the Moorish occupation. It is really a savoury egg and vegetable cake which can be eaten warm or cold, either as a supper dish or — as I had it in Spain — speared on cocktail sticks at a drinks party. It also makes wonderful picnic fare.

½ lb (225 g) packet frozen chopped spinach, defrosted
1 small onion, finely chopped
1 oz (50 g/2 tablespoons) butter
¼ lb (125 g/1 cup) mushrooms, thinly sliced or 1 can (10 oz (275 g)) cut asparagus spears, drained
3 eggs

1 packet (3½ oz (100 g)) herb- and garlic-flavoured cream cheese or 4 oz (125 g/½ cup) medium-fat soft cheese mixed with ½ teaspoon dried Italian seasoning and a pinch of garlic salt
½ teaspoon salt; 10 grinds black pepper
1 level teaspoon chopped parsley
6 oz (175 g/1½ cups) Cheddar cheese, grated

Set the oven at Gas No. 5, 375 degrees F, 190 degrees C. Butter a rectangular tin measuring 12 × 8 × 2 in (30 × 20 × 5 cm).

Put the defrosted spinach into a small frying pan and cook over moderate heat until most of the free liquid has evaporated. Remove. In the same pan cook the onion in the butter until soft and golden, then add the mushrooms (if used) and cook until the butter has been absorbed — after 2 or 3 minutes. Whisk the eggs in a small bowl. Put the soft cheese in a large bowl, add the eggs gradually, then stir in all the remaining ingredients, including the asparagus, if used. Pour into the prepared tin and bake for 30–40 minutes, or until golden-brown and firm to the touch. Cut in little squares and arrange on platters with cocktail sticks. Serve at room temperature.

TWO HOT MEAT FINGER FOODS
COCKTAIL MEATBALLS WITH AUBERGINE

Makes 36 little balls   *Freeze raw or cooked 3 months*

These delicious meatballs have a crispy outside and a soft and moist inside. Guests spear them with cocktail sticks and eat them plain or dipped into a barbecue or sweet-and-sour sauce.

1½ lb (675 g) aubergines (eggplant)
Sunflower oil
1 lb (450 g) fresh minced (ground) beef or lamb
1 medium onion, finely chopped

1 egg, beaten
2 heaped tablespoons (approximately) medium matzah meal or porage oats
Sunflower oil for frying the meatballs

Peel the aubergines, slice them ¼ in (½ cm) thick, put into a colander and sprinkle with salt. Leave for 30 minutes, then rinse and dry well.

Put oil to a depth ⅜ in (1 cm) in a heavy frying pan and cook the aubergine slices until soft and golden on both sides. Drain on kitchen paper (paper towels). If necessary, add a little more oil to the pan (there should be about 2 tablespoons), then fry the onion until soft and golden.

Put the meat into a large bowl. Chop the aubergines finely until a rough purée, then add to the meat together with the onion, the beaten egg and enough matzah meal or porage oats to make a soft tacky mixture that can be shaped into balls. Leave for 30 minutes for the mixture to firm up.

Cover a large plate with a thin layer of flour. With wetted hands, take a spoonful of meat mixture the size of a walnut and form into a ball between the palms, then drop on to the flour-covered plate. Repeat with the remainder of the mixture. Dry the hands, then toss each ball in the flour to coat it completely.

Fry the meatballs very gently in shallow fat until golden and crisp and cooked right through, about 10 minutes in all. Serve hot or cold. May be reheated in a microwave.

LAHMA BI AJEEN

SERVES 8–10　　　　　　　　　　*Freeze for 1 month either as raw dough or
cooked Lahma bi Ajeen*

These little meat-topped pizzas make wonderful cocktail finger food, or they can be served as a starter with Minted Oriental Salad (see page 193). They should be served warm and can be reheated for a few minutes in a moderate oven, or in the microwave.

THE DOUGH:
11 oz (300 g/2¾ cups) plain (all-purpose) flour
1½ teaspoons each salt and sugar
2 tablespoons olive oil
1 sachet dried easy-blend yeast or bare 1 oz (25 g/2 cakes) fresh yeast
1 egg
5 oz (150 ml/⅔ cup) hand-hot water

THE TOPPING:
2 medium onions, finely chopped

2 tablespoons oil
1 lb (450 g) lean minced (ground) fresh lamb or beef
1 tablespoon tomato purée
1 teaspoon brown sugar
1 teaspoon salt; 15 grinds black pepper
1 teaspoon allspice (pimento)
½ teaspoon ground cumin
Good pinch cayenne pepper
3 tablespoons parsley
1 tablespoon lemon juice

To prepare the dough with dried easy-blend yeast Put flour, salt, sugar and yeast into a bowl. Process 2 seconds (or mix for 30 seconds). Now slowly add egg, oil and hand-hot water and process 1 minute on food processor (or knead for 5 minutes on mixer), adding further 1 oz (25 g/4 tablespoons) of flour if mixture is sticky. Turn out on to the board and knead lightly by hand (about 30 seconds) until underside of dough is smooth.

With fresh yeast Put in bowl of processor or mixer with the sugar, hand-hot water and a few tablespoons of the flour. Process or mix until evenly blended, then add all the remaining ingredients. Process for 1 minute (or knead with dough hook for 5 minutes) until smooth and no longer sticky. Add 1 or 2 extra tablespoons of flour if dough is still sticky after kneading.

Grease a mixing bowl, put the dough in, turn over so the top is greased. Cover with clingfilm (saran wrap). Leave in a warm place until double in bulk, about 1 hour. Punch dough down.

To prepare the filling Do this while the dough is rising. Cook the onions in the oil until softened but not browned. Put in a bowl together with all the remaining ingredients, and knead by hand until well mixed.

To complete the dish Set the oven at Gas No. 8, 450 degrees F, 230 degrees C. Grease two baking sheets. Divide the risen dough into 20 pieces, each piece the size of a walnut. Roll or press each piece of dough into a very thin circle, 3 in (7½ cm) in diameter. Transfer the circles on to greased sheets. Top each circle with a thin layer of the meat mixture, covering the entire surface. Leave 15 minutes. Bake for 10 minutes until the dough is cooked but not crispy. Serve warm.

TWO NIBBLES
SESAME SEED CRISPS

Makes 36–40 (to serve 12)   *Freeze raw or cooked 3 months*

These flaky little biscuits (or crackers) make ideal 'nibbles' to serve with drinks.

4 oz (125 g/½ cup) butter or margarine
4 oz (125 g/½ cup) fairly dry cream cheese or curd cheese
5 oz (150 g/1¼ cups) plain (all-purpose) flour
1 teaspoon mustard powder

Good pinch each of sea salt and cayenne pepper

THE GLAZE:
1 egg yolk mixed with 1 teaspoon cold water and a pinch of salt
Small bowl of sesame seeds

Preheat the oven to Gas No. 7, 425 degrees F, 220 degrees C. Have ready two ungreased baking trays. By hand or machine, work together the butter and cheese until thoroughly mixed, then work in the flour sifted with the seasonings. Stop mixing immediately a dough is formed.

Turn on to a floured board, flatten into a rectangle 1 in (2½ cm) thick and wrap in film or foil. Chill for an hour, or leave for up to a week in the refrigerator, 3 months in the freezer.

Roll out ¼ in (½ cm) thick and cut in rounds about 1 in (2½ cm) in diameter. Brush the tops with the glaze, dip into the bowl of sesame seeds, then arrange on the trays. Bake for 15 minutes until a rich golden-brown. Serve within an hour of baking, or reheat in a moderate oven for 5 minutes.

SPICY CASHEWS

Enough for 30 (with other 'nibbles')   *Will keep for 6 weeks in an airtight container in the refrigerator*

These spiced nuts have a mild but very original flavour. You will find a version of this recipe that uses a microwave oven on page 23.

1 lb (450 g/3½ cups) cashew nuts
1 oz (25 g/2 tablespoons) butter or 2 tablespoons sunflower oil

2 teaspoons each curry powder, ground cumin and sea salt, mixed together

Set the oven at Gas No. 5, 375 degrees F, 190 degrees C. Put a baking tray in the oven with the butter or oil on it. When the butter has melted (or if using oil, when the oven has reached temperature), add the nuts and stir well to coat with the fat. Roast for 15 minutes, stir well and roast for a further 10 minutes or until golden-brown. Sprinkle with the seasonings, stir thoroughly to coat the nuts then roast for a further 5 minutes. Turn out on to a cooling tray and cover with a paper towel. Leave until cold, then store in an airtight container.

A SWEET ENDING
BONNES BOUCHES

Makes 30 tartlets

Freeze baked cases 3 months
Refrigerate complete bonnes bouches *for up to 24 hours*

Tiny cases of delicate almond pastry are filled with chopped glacé (candied) fruits folded into a fluffy pastry cream. They are delightful to serve with coffee at the end of a drinks party. Make the custard first, so that it has time to go quite cold before folding into the whipped cream.

THE PASTRY:
5½ oz (160 g/1 ⅓ cups) plain (all-purpose) flour
2 oz (50 g/½ cup) ground almonds
2 oz (50 g/½ cup) icing (confectioners') sugar
4 oz (125 g/½ cup) butter, cut in 1 in (2½ cm) chunks
1 egg yolk

THE FILLING:
8 fl oz (225 ml/1 cup) milk

1 oz (25 g/4 tablespoons) custard powder
1 tablespoon caster (superfine) sugar
8 oz (225 ml/1 cup) double (heavy) cream, whipped
2 teaspoons Amaretto liqueur or a few drops of almond essence (extract)
4 oz (125 g/½ cup) crystallized ginger, coarsely chopped
2 oz (50 g/¼ cup) glacé (candied) pineapple, coarsely chopped

Make the pastry either by hand by the method given on page 221, or, if using a food processor, by putting all the ingredients into a bowl and pulsing until the mixture begins to form tiny balls. Turn on to a floured board and gather together into a dough. Knead the dough until smooth, then wrap in foil or film (saran wrap) and chill for 1 hour.

Preheat the oven to Gas No. 4, 350 degrees F, 180 degrees C. Have ready some patty tins. Roll out the pastry ⅛ in (¼ cm) thick on a board sprinkled with icing sugar instead of flour. Cut in rounds to fit the patty tins, prick well and bake for 15–20 minutes, or until coloured a pale gold. Leave to cool before freezing or filling.

Make a custard with the milk, custard powder and caster sugar. Allow to go quite cold, then process or blend for 1 minute until smooth and creamy. Whip the cream with the liqueur or essence until it holds soft peaks, then fold in the custard, the crystallized ginger and the glacé pineapple. Divide between the pastry cases and chill until required.

To serve Put each tartlet into a paper case and arrange them on a silver or glass tray.

VANILLA FUDGE

Makes about 2 lb (1 kg)   *Will keep in an airtight container for as long as you leave it*

This is a very special treat for guests of all ages.

1½ lb (675 g/3 cups) granulated sugar   *3 fl oz (75 ml/⅓ cup) cold water*
3 oz (75 g/⅓ cup) butter   *2 teaspoons vanilla essence (extract)*
6 oz (175 g/¾ cup) can evaporated milk

Butter a 6–7 in (15–17½ cm) square tin. Have a large bowl of cold water ready in the sink, and a small bowl of cold water ready for testing.

Put all the ingredients (except the vanilla) into a pan with a heavy base and stir over moderate heat until the sugar has completely dissolved — when a little of the mixture rubbed between the thumb and forefinger no longer feels grainy. Once the sugar has dissolved and the mixture starts to boil, stir only when necessary to prevent it sticking to the bottom of the pan. Cook quite gently until a little of the mixture dropped into the small bowl of water can be squeezed together into a soft ball, or when a sugar thermometer shows 240 degrees F, 115 degrees C. (At this stage the mixture will be butterscotch in colour and will have started to come away from the sides of the pan.)

Take the pan to the bowl of water in the sink and submerge the base in it to stop it from cooking any further. Stir in the vanilla, leave to cool for 5 minutes, then start beating it with a wooden spoon until it begins to lose its gloss and thickens to the consistency of unwhipped double (heavy) cream. Pour immediately into the tin and level off with a knife heated under the hot tap. Allow to set for 15 or 20 minutes then mark into 1 in (2½ cm) squares. When quite cold, remove from the tin and store in an airtight container.

Festivals

The tapestry of Festivals that is woven through the Jewish year is probably the strongest link we have with the heritage from our past.

Festivals are mainly about families, and only partly about food. But it is the food that we eat as a family that gives them their special, unforgettable flavour. It is the images stamped on our minds from early childhood of the preparations that surround the Festivals and their special foods that we most vividly recall when far from home: of our mother testing the Passover sponge cake with an anxious eye, of our father mixing the charoset for the Seder with the ceremony of a master chef. We can conjure up the musky smell of melon and the perfume of the chrysanthemums that always fill the house at New Year and we can taste, as if we'd eaten them yesterday, that first yeasty bite of the Purim 'Hamantaschen', that first creamy mouthful of the Shavuot cheesecake.

In this chapter, you will find many traditional recipes you may remember from your own childhood, as well as others that may be less familiar but that can be eaten with the same spirit of love and celebration.

THE JEWISH YEAR

Pesach (Passover)	15th Nissan (March/April)
Shavuot (Pentecost, or Feast of Weeks)	6th Sivan (May/June)
Rosh Hashanah (New Year)	1st and 2nd Tishri (September/October)
Yom Kippur (Day of Atonement)	10th Tishri (September/October)
Sukkot (Tabernacles)	15th Tishri (September/October)
Hanukkah (Feast of Lights)	25th Kislev (December)
Purim (Feast of Lots)	14th Adar (February/March)

Many other traditional Festival foods and customs are described in my *Complete International Jewish Cookbook* (Robson Books)

PESACH

It's a truly magical moment when the house reveals its once-a-year Passover face, with the well-remembered plates and dishes brought out from their 51-week rest — including that little beehive jam pot, provenance unknown, in which the lemon curd has been served in our family for the past 50 years.

There's the prune eingemachtes to be admired and the medieval-style macaroons and sponge cakes to be savoured — for no matter how delicious they taste, they will only be prepared for this one week in the year. And what will the matzot taste like *this* year, we wonder, eyeing the stack of boxes as though, like wine, each season has its own elusive bouquet.

I love Passover because it is a truly family festival which demands a contribution of labour from every member — and that includes the menfolk preparing the charoset and tasting the salt water as well. But how I detest the growing commercialism of this festival of renewal, in which not so very long ago, each night — and day — was in truth different from every other night and day in the year. Who wants to eat the same year-round foods — but with a 'Kosher le Pesach' label? Who doesn't prefer a spoonful of homemade beetroot eingemachtes to the finest factory preserve? What cake mix can compare with the old family 'plava' recipe? What box of baker's fancies can equal our own home-rolled cinnamon balls? Yet sadly the list of Passover 'convenience' foods grows longer every year.

But now the white cloth has been laid on the table, the candles are ready and there's a glass for each guest with one for Elijah placed in the centre. Three separate matzot, representing the Jewish family world-wide, are concealed in the folds of the 'matzah dekke' and by the head of the family is set the special Seder plate arranged with the six symbolic foods. They carry the same message they have done for thousands of years: 'Remember we were slaves in Egypt, and yet we were brought forth to our Promised Land'. So we recall the bitter memories of slavery as we taste the salt water, and eat the horseradish and the charoset 'mortar', whilst our hopes for a safe and happy future are embodied in the cup of Elijah, set at its place of honour in the centre of the table.

Weighing Without Scales

Measure these foods with a tablespoon as follows:
1 oz (25 g) matzah meal (medium, fine or cake) = 1 heaped tablespoon
1 oz (25 g) potato flour = 1 rounded tablespoon
1 oz (25 g) ground almonds or hazelnuts (filberts) = 1 heaped tablespoon
1 oz (25 g) granulated or caster (superfine) sugar = 1 rounded tablespoon
1 oz (25 g) icing (confectioners') sugar = 2 rounded tablespoons
1 oz (25 g) desiccated (dried and shredded) coconut = 2 rounded tablespoons
1 oz (25 g) cocoa = 3 level tablespoons
1 oz (25 g) grated cheese = 1 heaped tablespoon
5 fl oz of any liquid = 8 tablespoons

To avoid having to duplicate cake tins and casseroles, use disposable foil sandwich, cake and quiche tins and lidded foil baking containers.

Setting the Seder Scene

At sundown on the 14th of Nissan, rather more than three thousand years ago, the Children of Israel made camp in Gilgal, on the Plains of Jericho. It was there, exactly 40 years after their Exodus from Egypt, that they celebrated the first 'Passover', following the instructions in Exodus, chapter 12: 'And they shall eat the flesh in that night, roast with fire, and unleavened bread, with bitter herbs they shall eat it'. Which is what we still do to this day.

On the ceremonial plate, which through the years has offered inspiration to many fine craftsmen in ceramic and metal, are set out the six symbolic foods, prepared according to tradition by the father of the family:

the shankbone of a lamb, usually represented today by a chicken's neck, is roasted until brown under the grill;

the 'roasted' egg, a symbolic 'burnt offering' for the Festival, is first hard-boiled and then browned under the grill;

the root of horseradish, which recalls the bitterness of slavery, is peeled and trimmed, then a 2 in (5 cm) length is set ready to cut into pieces during the service;

the dish of salt water, symbolizing the tears shed by the Israelites in Egypt, is taken from the larger quantity prepared for the Eggs in Salt Water (see over page);

the bitter herbs are represented in Ashkenazi households by small sprigs of parsley, and among the Sephardim by lettuce leaves;

the charoset is evocative in appearance (but certainly not in taste) of the mortar mixed by the Jewish slaves when they were forced to build the Egyptian treasure cities of Pithom and Ramses. It is made — at least by those Jews whose origins lie in eastern Europe — according to a recipe using apples, nuts and wine, which is inspired by two verses from the 'Song of Songs': 'Under the apple tree I awakened thee', and 'I went down into the garden of nuts'. The wine is used as a symbol of the miraculous parting of the Red Sea. However, it must be said that Sephardi communities make their charoset with different ingredients, which according to their geographical origin may include pine kernels (pine nuts), peanuts, chestnuts, dried apricots, coconut, raisins, dates, figs or bananas. Our family charoset is made by mincing or processing together 3 oz (75 g/⅓ cup) shelled walnuts and a small eating apple (peeled and cored), flavouring this pâté with 2 teaspoons each of sugar and ground cinnamon and moistening it with enough sweet red Kiddush wine to bring it to the consistency of mortar. This makes sufficient for two family Sedarim.

The **matzot** — three pieces of unleavened bread — are set out on the table, but concealed in the folds of a linen napkin or in a special 'matzah dekke'. They represent the three hereditary 'orders', dating from Temple times, into which Jews are still divided: the Kohanim (the priests), the Levites (their assistants) and the Israelites, who comprise the remainder of the population.

Many people are surprised to find that this unleavened bread is actually made from flour, whose use is otherwise not allowed during the Festival. However, this is very special flour whose production has been strictly supervised — in the case of the special 'Shemura' matzot eaten by very Orthodox Jews, from the moment that the sheaves of wheat are gathered in the field. This is to ensure that at no stage can either the grain or the flour become damp and ferment, causing the dough to rise and thus leavening the bread — which is, of course, strictly forbidden. For the same reason, once water has been mixed with the flour to make the dough, no longer than 18 minutes must elapse before the baked matzot are brought out of the oven. Because of the precise terms of the rules governing its manufacture, the matzah-baking process has barely changed throughout the centuries; in the remains of the matzah bakery attached to the fourteenth-century synagogue at Carpentras in Provence, one can see the remains of utensils that are almost identical to those still in use in some Chassidic communities today. I have watched the members of one such community preparing their own matzot as a special 'mitzvah', with hordes of little boys happily rolling the dough, each using a length of broom handle as a rolling pin. This community even won a special dispensation from the Clean Air Act to allow the matzot to be baked in a traditional wood-fired oven on the Eve of the Festival.

The serving of four ritual **glasses of wine,** as well as the custom of sitting on cushions and reclining to dine, is said to have originated in Graeco-Roman times. Certainly it has persisted to this day.

In our family, it is the custom to leave the table bare of cutlery and crockery until it is time for the meal. The cutlery for each guest is previously rolled in a linen napkin, and all the plates are stacked on a side table or trolley. As soon as the first part of the Seder service is completed, the wine glasses are removed to a place of safety and the table is quickly set. This method also gives the hostess time to organize the first course. The system works well for us, but you may have a completely different tradition in your family.

Full instructions for conducting the Seder service and meal are to be found in the Haggadah.

In all Passover recipes use ingredients specially packed for Passover.

Two suggestions for Seder menus

(Each one includes Eggs in Salt Water, wine and matzot)

Chicken Soup with Matzah Balls and Passover Lokshen
Chicken and Olive Casserole
Fan Potatoes
Green Beans sauté with Toasted Almonds
Braised Courgettes with Herbs
Almond Sponge Flan with Orange Glaze
Fresh Pineapple with Apricot Coulis

Cheese Soufflé Pancakes
Fresh Salmon with Green Herb Mayonnaise
New Potatoes
Shades of Green Salad
Mangetout and Tomato Salad
Cucumber Salad in the German Style
Chocolate Roulade with Strawberry Cloud Filling
Orange and Lemon Sorbet

You will find these recipes by consulting the index to this book.

EGGS IN SALT WATER

This delicious if unorthodox dish is *never* served except at this one time of the year. Whether you serve each guest with a whole egg and a bowl of the salt water, or slice the egg in the water to make a 'soup', the proportions remain the same. Allow one hard-boiled egg per person, with a third of an egg extra to allow for 'seconds', together with ½ teaspoon salt dissolved in 5 fl oz (150 ml/⅔ cup) cold water for each egg used. Put the salt and water in a very large bowl or tureen, and add the whole shelled eggs, or the sliced eggs, half an hour before the commencement of the Seder. Serve with a soup ladle.

AVOCADO EGG MAYONNAISE

SERVES 6–8

Do not freeze
Mayonnaise will keep under refrigeration for
2 days

This makes an excellent starter for Chol Hamoed.

6–8 eggs, hard-boiled
¼ pint (150 ml/⅔ cup) mayonnaise
1 large or 2 medium ripe avocados [making
approximately ¼ pint (150 ml/⅔ cup) of
purée]
2–3 teaspoons lemon juice
Half a clove of garlic, peeled
Pinch of cayenne pepper
½ teaspoon salt; ¼ teaspoon white pepper

GARNISH FOR EACH SERVING:
1 medium tomato
4 slices of pickled cucumber
3 black or green olives
3 slices red pepper, seeds removed
2 tablespoons Chinese leaves (Chinese
cabbage) or hearts of lettuce, shredded
Pinch of paprika pepper

Peel and stone the avocados, then cut in 1 in (2½ cm) chunks and put in the food processor with all the ingredients except the eggs and the garnish. Process until smooth, then cover and refrigerate until required — the mixture won't discolour. Shortly before dinner, divide the salad greens between 6–8 small plates. Cut the eggs in half and arrange on top, rounded side up, then coat with the avocado mayonnaise. Decorate with the garnish, arranging it around the edge. Sprinkle with paprika pepper.

PASSOVER CHEESE BLINTZES

Makes 12–14 blintzes
SERVES 6–8

Freeze empty crêpes 3 months, blintzes 1
month
Will keep filled but unbrowned 24 hours
under refrigeration

Crêpes made with potato flour are particularly light and delicate; the batter needs to stand for 30 minutes before it is fried. If the blintzes are put in the oven to brown at the start of the Seder service, they will be ready to serve as an entrée for the meal, either plain or with soured cream.

THE CRÊPES (PAREV):
3 eggs
8 fl oz (225 ml/1 cup) water
3 oz (75 g/¾ cup) potato flour, sifted with ½
teaspoon salt

THE FILLING:
1 lb (450 g/2 cups) cream cheese
Pinch each of sugar and salt

1 egg yolk
2 tablespoons cream or yoghurt (if mixture is
too stiff)

FOR FRYING THE BLINTZES:
A little oil

FOR BROWNING THEM:
2–3 oz (50–75 g/¼–⅓ cup) melted butter

To mix the crêpes Whisk the eggs to blend the yolks and whites, then whisk in half the water, followed by the salt and potato flour. Finally stir in the remaining water. Allow to stand 30 minutes. The mixture will be as thin as single cream.

To fry crêpes Use a 6 or 7 in (15–17½ cm) frying pan, preferably with a non-stick finish. Put the batter into a jug and stir thoroughly. Heat the frying pan for 3 minutes until you can feel heat on your hand held 2 in (5 cm) above it. Smear very lightly with oil. Pour a few tablespoons of batter into the pan. Swirl it round so that there is an even layer all over the bottom of the pan, then pour any liquid batter back into the jug — a thin layer will have set into a crêpe. When the sides of this crêpe begin to curl away from the edges of the pan, turn the pan upside down over a piece of greaseproof paper and the crêpe will fall out — you may need to loosen it a little from the side of the pan, but if it doesn't fall out easily it isn't cooked enough. Turn the crêpe over at once, so that the browned side is next to the paper.

Repeat with the remaining batter, keeping the pan over medium heat. As the blintzes stop steaming, they can be piled on top of each other. They can then be wrapped in foil and frozen or refrigerated until required, or they can be filled and then frozen. Defrost before reheating.

To fill and brown the blintzes Mix all the ingredients together. Place each crêpe, brown side up, on a board. Pipe or spoon a 1 in (2½ cm) band of the filling about 1 in (2½ cm) from the lower edge, then turn in the sides to enclose it and roll up. Arrange, join side down, on a greased oven tray, leaving 1½ in (4 cm) between the blintzes so that they can brown evenly. Refrigerate or freeze until required.

Preheat the oven to Gas No. 5, 375 degrees F, 190 degrees C. Brush each blintze thoroughly with the butter and bake for 25 to 30 minutes, until crisp and golden-brown.

VARIATION
Chicken Liver Blintzes Stuff the blintzes with Chopped Liver, using the recipe given on page 37. Brush them with 5–6 tablespoons oil (instead of the butter) before baking them. Serve plain or with any tomato sauce.

CHEESE SOUFFLÉ PANCAKES

Makes 12–14
SERVES 7–8

Freeze crêpes 3 months, filled pancakes 1 month

These make a superb entrée for the Seder or a main course for a light meal. They can be frozen well in advance and can then go straight from the freezer into a hot oven. If they are put in a preheated oven immediately the first part of the service is over, they will be puffed and ready after the Eggs in Salt Water have been eaten. When serving them at an ordinary meal it's better to give them time to become really golden and puffy and then keep them hot for 10 or 15 minutes if necessary, rather than serve them before the soufflé has set.

1 recipe potato flour crêpes (see preceding recipe)

3 eggs, separated
1 oz (25 g/2 tablespoons) butter

THE SOUFFLÉ MIXTURE:
1 slightly rounded tablespoon potato flour
6 fl oz (175 ml/¾ cup) milk
½ teaspoon salt; few shakes white pepper
5 oz (150 g/1¼ cups) grated Passover cheese, Cheddar or Edam

THE TOPPING:
2 oz (50 g/4 tablespoons) butter, melted
2 oz (50 g/½ cup) cheese, grated

In a small bowl, mix the potato flour to a smooth paste with a little of the milk. Heat the remainder of the milk until it is steaming, then pour it gradually on to the paste, with the salt and pepper, stirring all the time. Rinse out the milk pan, then pour in the milk mixture. Bring it slowly to the boil, stirring constantly, then bubble for 1 minute. Remove from the heat and add the cheese, stirring until smooth. Drop in the egg yolks, stirring, then return the pan to the heat, and cook gently until the mixture resembles a thick custard. Drop in the butter and stir well, then turn into a bowl and leave to cool a little; whisk the egg whites with a pinch of salt until they hold stiff, glossy peaks, then fold into the custard using a spatula or metal spoon.

Put a heaped tablespoon of the soufflé mixture on to the middle of each crêpe, fold one side over and then overlap with the other side. Arrange the crêpes, side by side on a greased baking sheet, brush with the melted butter and sprinkle with the 2 oz (50 g/½ cup) of cheese. Open-freeze for 2 hours, then cover with foil and leave.

To cook the soufflé pancakes Preheat the oven to Gas No. 6, 400 degrees F, 200 degrees C. Take the pancakes from the freezer and put at once in the oven, then bake for 20–25 minutes, or until puffed and golden — they will stay puffed in a low oven, Gas No. ¼, 225 degrees F, 110 degrees C for 15 minutes.

308

CREAM OF MUSHROOM SOUP

SERVES 6–8

Freeze 3 months
Will keep 2 days under refrigeration

You may prefer to omit the potato flour thickening, and purée the soup instead. If so, use ¾ lb (350 g/3 cups) mushrooms.

THE MUSHROOM MIXTURE:
1 oz (25 g/2 tablespoons) butter
4 spring onion (green onion) bulbs, finely chopped
½ lb (225 g/2 cups) very white mushrooms,
coarsely chopped
½ pint (275 ml/1¼ cups) water
1 mushroom soup cube

THE SAUCE:
1 oz (25 g/1 rounded tablespoon) potato flour
2 pints (1¼ litres/5 cups) milk
1 oz (25 g/2 tablespoons) butter
1½ teaspoons salt
1 small clove of garlic, peeled and crushed
¼ teaspoon white pepper
¼ teaspoon freshly milled nutmeg
2 tablespoons chopped parsley

Melt the butter in a soup pan, and cook the chopped spring onions, covered, for 5 minutes, then add the mushrooms, re-cover and simmer for a further 5 minutes. Stir in the water and mushroom soup cube and turn into a bowl.

Put the potato flour into a bowl and mix until creamy with some of the milk, then put it into the pan together with all the other ingredients except the parsley. Bring slowly to the boil, then simmer for 3 minutes before adding the mushroom mixture and the parsley. Leave for several hours or overnight. Reheat gently, and serve.

TOMATO AND LOKSHEN SOUP

SERVES 6–8

Freeze soup 3 months
Use lokshen when freshly made

This is an excellent 'second-day' soup, using leftover Chicken Soup. Or it can be made in a parev version, using vegetable stock instead. The lokshen is cut from a pancake made with cake meal.

THE SOUP:
2½ pints (1½ litres/6 cups) Chicken Soup or
2½ pints (1½ litres/6 cups) hot water plus
beef, chicken or vegetable stock cubes
1 can (15 oz (425 g)) peeled plum tomatoes,
puréed in blender or food processor
2 rounded tablespoons tomato purée
1½ tablespoons lemon juice

2 level tablespoons demerara (brown) sugar
15 grinds black pepper

THE PASSOVER LOKSHEN:
3 eggs
3 tablespoons water
Good pinch of salt
3 tablespoons matzah cake meal

To make the soup Put all the ingredients into a soup pan and simmer, covered, for 45 minutes, then leave to mature in flavour for several hours (or preferably) overnight.
To make the lokshen Whisk or process all the ingredients together until smooth,

then put in a jug. Lightly grease a round-sided frying pan with oil and heat until a drop of water sizzles when dropped on to its surface. Pour in some of the batter, then tip the pan so that any excess runs back into the jug, leaving a very thin layer behind. Cook this pancake gently until the bottom is a golden-brown, then turn and lightly cook the second side until just golden. Turn out on to greaseproof (waxed) paper and repeat with the remaining batter — you will have enough to make 4 pancakes. Allow to cool for 5 minutes, then roll up each pancake and cut in 'noodles' about ⅜ in (1 cm) wide.

Just before serving the soup, add the lokshen. Heat through for only 1 minute and then serve.

DAIRY MAIN DISHES
AUBERGINE, CHEESE AND TOMATO CASSEROLE

SERVES 4–6

Do not freeze
Leftovers will keep 3 days under refrigeration

This makes an excellent main dish with a salad and baked or new potatoes, or it can be served as an accompaniment to grilled (broiled) or fried fish. Allow the dish to cool for 10 minutes so that it can be cut evenly into squares. It can be prepared early in the day and baked freshly when required.

1½ lb (675 g) aubergines (eggplant), unpeeled, cut into slices ⅜ in (1 cm) thick
1 can (about 10 oz (275 g)) Passover tomato sauce
1 tablespoon tomato ketchup or tomato purée

½ teaspoon salt; 10 grinds black pepper
½ teaspoon sugar
1 tablespoon parsley, chopped
8–12 oz (225–350 g/2–3 cups) Gouda or Cheddar cheese, grated
Oil for grilling aubergines

Put the aubergine slices into a colander or salad spinner, sprinkling each layer with salt. Leave for 30 minutes, then rinse well, and pat or spin dry. Put the grill (broiler) on at high heat. Choose a shallow dish that will fit under the grill, and pour in enough oil to cover the base with a thin film. Dip each aubergine slice into the oil, then turn over so that each side is coated with oil. Grill (broil) the slices until golden-brown, then turn them and grill the other side. Drain on kitchen paper (paper towels).

Preheat the oven to Gas No. 6, 400 degrees F, 200 degrees C. Grease an ovenproof dish 8–9 in (20–22 cm) in diameter and 1½ in (3 cm) deep — a quiche dish is excellent. Mix together the tomato sauce, the ketchup (or purée), the seasonings and the parsley. Start with a layer of aubergines, and coat them with some of the sauce and a layer of the cheese; repeat, ending with a thick layer of cheese. Bake for 30 minutes, until a rich golden-brown.

VEGETABLE MATZAH LASAGNE

SERVES 8–10

Freeze uncooked 2 months
Uncooked lasagne will keep 24 hours under
refrigeration; leftovers will keep 2 days

This is a splendid main course for a vegetarian Seder, or it can be used as an entrée before a fish main course.

1 large (8 oz (225 g)) onion, finely chopped
2 cloves garlic, peeled and finely chopped
1 lb (450 g) aubergines (eggplant), peeled
and cut in ½ in (1 cm) cubes
¼ lb (125 g/1 cup) mushrooms, sliced
5 tablespoons oil
1 can (15 oz (425 g)) plum tomatoes
1 can (8 oz (225 g)) Passover tomato sauce
4 fl oz (125 ml/½ cup) dry red wine
(optional)

1 medium carrot, grated
3 tablespoons chopped parsley
1 teaspoon salt; 15 grinds pepper
9 sheets matzah, soaked in cold water for 1
minute, then drained and dried
1 lb (450 g/2) cups cottage or cream cheese
8 oz (225 g) Edam or Gouda cheese, cut in
thin slices
6 oz (175 g/1½ cups) Cheddar cheese, grated

In a large frying pan, cook the onion, garlic, aubergine and mushrooms in the oil over medium heat for 15 minutes, stirring frequently. Stir in the tomatoes, tomato sauce, wine, carrot, parsley, salt and pepper; bring to the boil, stirring to break up the tomatoes, then reduce the heat and simmer, covered, for 30 minutes. Uncover, and simmer to reduce the sauce until it is of coating consistency, then set aside.

Butter a 13 × 9 in (about 32 × 22 cm) baking dish. Spread a quarter of the sauce over the bottom. Arrange an even layer of 3 soaked matzot on top, trimmed to fit. Dot with one-third of the soft cheese. Arrange over this an even layer of one-third of the sliced cheese, and sprinkle with a quarter of the grated cheese. Repeat this procedure twice. Spread the remaining sauce evenly on top, and sprinkle with the remaining grated cheese. If made ahead, cover and refrigerate or freeze.

Preheat the oven to Gas No. 4, 350 degrees F, 180 degrees C. Bake the lasagne, uncovered, for 30–45 minutes, or until bubbly. If frozen, bake *unthawed* for 1–1½ hours. Let stand for 5 minutes, then cut into squares to serve.

PASSOVER CHEESE FRITTERS

SERVES 4

Do not freeze

These spongy little fritters make an excellent light lunch, or they can be served for dessert with a little eingemachtes or cinnamon sugar. Mix them just before you fry them, or the cake meal will make them stiffen up.

½ lb (225 g/1 cup) any low-fat soft cheese
2 eggs, whisked until fluffy
1 level teaspoon each sugar and salt
2 oz (50 g/½ cup) matzah cake meal

A little milk if necessary

FOR FRYING:
2 oz (50 g/¼ cup) butter and 1 tablespoon
oil, or 4 tablespoons oil

311

Put the cheese into a bowl, then gradually stir in the beaten eggs, the seasonings and the cake meal. The mixture should be like whipped cream. If it feels too solid, stir in a little milk. Heat the butter and the oil in a heavy frying pan and when the butter has melted, put in spoonfuls of the mixture, leaving room between them for the fritters to expand. Cook over moderate heat until the underside is a rich brown, then turn and cook the other side. Serve hot off the pan.

Passover Fish

- Passover is the time for **salmon,** and elsewhere in this book there are many dishes using this fish that are suitable.
- To make a **green herb mayonnaise** to serve with salmon, you can use the recipe on page 95. You will need to use a Passover oil, however, and omit the mustard.
- **Fried fish** should be coated first in cake meal, then in egg and finally in medium matzah meal, to achieve a really crisp coating.
- An **egg and lemon sauce** is usually served with halibut, but as this fish is often scarce, the same delicious sauce can be used with tiny balls of Gefilte Fish (see recipe on page 25).
- Gefilte Fish Balls can also be poached in a **pepper, tomato and mushroom sauce;** they are nicest served at room temperature rather than straight from the oven (see recipe below).

FILLETS OF WHITE FISH IN A PEPPER, TOMATO AND MUSHROOM SAUCE

SERVES 8–10

Do not freeze
Leftovers keep 2 days under refrigeration

This makes an excellent Seder dish which can be lightly cooked earlier in the day, then gently reheated during the Seder service. It's delicious made with fillets of plaice, bream or lemon sole.

2 fillets of fish per person, cut from fish
weighing approximately 1½ lb (675 g) each

THE SAUCE:
1 oz (25 g/2 tablespoons) butter or 2
tablespoons oil (for a meat meal)
1 medium onion, finely chopped
8 oz (225 g/2 cups) mushrooms, finely sliced
2 cans (10 oz (275 ml)) Passover mushroom
and tomato sauce
1 large red pepper, seeds removed, cut in
little cubes

2 level teaspoons each salt and sugar
1 tablespoon lemon juice
1 bayleaf
15 grinds black pepper

GARNISH:
1 tablespoon chopped parsley

312

Preheat the oven to Gas No. 6, 400 degrees F, 200 degrees C. Have ready a greased casserole large enough to hold the rolled fillets side by side.

Skin the fillets, wash and salt them lightly and leave them in a colander to drain, then roll up (or fold over, if very thick) and lay in the casserole side by side. Sauté the onion gently in the fat until golden, then add the mushrooms and cook for a further 3 or 4 minutes until softened and beginning to colour. Add all the remaining ingredients, then pour over the fish and cover loosely with foil. Bake for 20 minutes, basting once. Refrigerate until required.

Reheat covered in a moderate oven, Gas No. 3, 325 degrees F, 160 degrees C, for 30 minutes, or until bubbly. Garnish with the parsley.

VARIATION

Gefilte Fish in a Pepper, Tomato and Mushroom Sauce   Replace the fish fillets with Gefilte Fish Mix, prepared from 2 lb (1 kg) fish (recipe on page 12). Make the Pepper, Tomato and Mushroom Sauce as above. Preheat the oven to Gas No. 4, 350 degrees F, 180 degrees C. Form the fish into 12–14 balls and arrange them side by side in a large ovenproof dish. Pour over the warm sauce, cover loosely with foil and bake for 45 minutes, basting twice. Let go cold; the dish is best served at room temperature.

GEFILTE FISH BALLS IN A LEMON SAUCE

SERVES 8–10   *Will keep 3 days under refrigeration*

Little fish balls make a delicious — and economical — alternative to halibut steaks in this egg and lemon sauce. Allow the fish balls to soak in the sauce overnight. This dish can be cooked in the microwave as described on page 26.

Gefilte Fish Mix made with 2 lb (1 kg) fish, made into 22–24 oval-shaped little balls (see recipe on page 20)

THE POACHING LIQUID:
1 onion, thinly sliced
2 teaspoons sugar
2 teaspoons salt; speck of white pepper
1 pint (575 ml/2½ cups) water

THE SAUCE:
3 teaspoons potato flour
4 fl oz (125 ml/½ cup) lemon juice
3 eggs
4 tablespoons sugar
12 fl oz (350 ml/1½ cups) strained poaching liquid from fish

GARNISH:
1 lemon
Tiny sprigs of parsley

Preheat the oven to Gas No. 4, 350 degrees F, 180 degrees C. Bring all the ingredients for the poaching liquid to the boil on top of the stove, then pour into an ovenproof casserole. Add the balls, cover and bake for 40 minutes. Lift out the balls with a slotted spoon and arrange in a large entrée dish.

To make the sauce   Put the potato flour into a bowl and gradually stir in the lemon juice, then whisk with all the remaining sauce ingredients until smooth. (This can be done in 5 seconds in the food processor.) Heat the mixture gently in a small pan, stirring constantly until it thickens to a coating consistency.

313

To complete the dish Cover the fish balls with the lemon sauce and chill until required. Cut the lemon into thin slices, then make a slit to the centre of each slice and form the slices into twists. Arrange a cluster of lemon twists at one end of the dish and arrange two or three tiny sprigs of parsley around them.

TRADITIONAL PLATTER OF GEFILTE FISH

Makes 12–14 balls
SERVES 8–10

Freeze 3 months
Will keep 3 days under refrigeration

For many families, no Seder table is complete without its platter of poached Gefilte Fish. Gefilte Fish can be poached in the microwave as described on page 26, but the flavour is undoubtedly superior if it is simmered slowly on top of the stove in the traditional way. If you freeze the dish, you will need to restore the 'jell' to the stock when you are ready to use it: to do this, pour it into a pan, bring to the boil and cook for 1 minute, then cool and pour it over the fish. I do think the fish has a better texture if freshly poached, however, so I usually freeze the *uncooked* balls, then defrost them in the refrigerator overnight and poach them as though they were newly prepared. It is as well to order the head, skin and bones in advance.

Gefilte Fish Mix made with 2 lb (1 kg) fish
(recipe on page 12)

THE STOCK:
1 cleaned hake or haddock head

Skin and bones from the fish
1 medium onion, thinly sliced
2 medium carrots, sliced ¼ in (½ cm) thick
2 level teaspoons each sugar and salt
Water to cover the bones

The dish looks more attractive if the fish is shaped into balls rather than patties. To get the maximum flavour, first simmer the head, skin and bones of the fish with the salt and cold water to cover, for 30 minutes, then remove the skin and bones (leave in the head, as this helps the stock to gel). Add the onion, carrots, sugar and balls of fish. Bring to the boil, then turn the heat low, cover the pan and simmer for 1½ hours, uncover and simmer for a further 30 minutes to concentrate the stock. Lift out the balls and arrange them on a platter, topping each fish ball with a slice of carrot. Pour the stock through a strainer over the fish, then chill overnight before serving.

Passover Meat and Poultry Dishes

• Provided no beans, rice or pasta are used to accompany or garnish it, almost any meat and poultry dish can be adapted for Passover use. (Rice is eaten at Passover in Sephardi communities but it is *not* the custom amongst Ashkenazim.)

• In dishes where the meat or poultry is normally coated with flour, cake meal can be used instead.

• Sauces and gravies can be thickened by substituting an equal amount of potato flour for cornflour (cornstarch), and half the amount for flour. Use matzah meal instead of bread in minced (ground) meat mixtures, allowing 1 tablespoon medium meal to each pound (450 g) of raw meat.

314

CHICKEN IN A SWEET AND SOUR TOMATO SAUCE

SERVES 6–8 or 12

Freeze 3 months
Will keep 3 days under refrigeration

Since the destruction of the Second Temple in 70 C.E. there have, of course, been no sacrifices of the Paschal Lamb at Passover. Many Jews believe that it is forbidden to eat roast lamb at the Seder meal until the Temple is rebuilt, so it has become the custom to serve chicken as the main dish instead of red meat. This is a very tasty but uncomplicated dish which can be left in a low oven during the Seder service. I have given the quantities for 12 in square brackets.

6–8 chicken joints [12 joints]
3 tablespoons oil [4 tablespoons]
1 medium onion, finely chopped [2 small onions]
8 oz (225 g/2 cups) mushrooms, thinly sliced [12 oz (350 g/3 cups)]
2 teaspoons salt [3 teaspoons]
15 grinds black pepper [20 grinds]

2 tablespoons demerara (brown) sugar [3 tablespoons]
2 tablespoons lemon juice [3 tablespoons]
5 oz (150 g/⅔ cup) tomato purée [7½ oz (225 g/1 cup)]
½ pint (275 ml/1¼ cups) hot water [15 fl oz (425 ml/2 cups)]
1 chicken stock cube [1½ cubes]

Preheat the oven to Gas No. 4, 350 degrees F, 180 degrees C. Dry the chicken joints well, and fry in the fat in two or three batches until a golden-brown on all sides, then remove to an oven casserole or roasting tin large enough for them to lie side by side. In the same fat, sauté the onion until soft and golden, then add the sliced mushrooms and sauté until they have absorbed all the fat. Now add the remaining ingredients and bring to the boil. Simmer, uncovered, until as thick as ketchup, about 5 minutes.

Pour the sauce over the chicken joints, cover with a lid or foil, and cook for 45 minutes (1 hour for 12 joints), basting once. Reheat during the meal at Gas No. 3, 325 degrees F, 160 degrees C.

CHICKEN AND OLIVE CASSEROLE

SERVES 8–10

Freeze 3 months
Will keep 3 days under refrigeration

A glass of dry red Passover wine such as Cabernet Sauvignon will give a special flavour to this superb casserole. If you intend to cook it and then reheat it later, add the mushrooms and the olives as it is heating up ready to serve. It is most convenient to bring the dish to simmering before the commencement of the Seder service, and then to turn it down low, Gas No. 1, 275 degrees F, 140 degrees C, to keep it hot without spoiling, until the meal is served.

8–10 chicken portions
1 heaped tablespoon cake meal
1 teaspoon salt; 20 grinds black pepper
1 teaspoon cinnamon
4 tablespoons oil
2 medium onions, finely chopped
2 fat cloves of garlic, peeled and chopped
2 cans (15 oz (425 g)) tomatoes, well drained, then chopped

1 tablespoon demerara (brown) sugar
2 red peppers, seeds removed, cut in ½ in (1 cm) squares
15 fl oz (425 ml/2 cups) chicken stock
5 fl oz (150 ml/⅔ cup) red wine
1 lb (450 g/4 cups) button mushrooms, thinly sliced
6 oz (175 g/1½ cups) Queen olives, roughly chopped

Preheat the oven to Gas No. 4, 350 degrees F, 180 degrees C. Skin the chicken joints and mix the salt, black pepper and cinnamon with the cake meal; then coat the joints with the seasoned meal.

Heat the oil in a heavy frying pan and brown the chicken on all sides, then remove and drain on paper towels. In the same oil, gently sauté the onion and garlic until soft and golden, then add the tomatoes, sugar and red peppers and simmer uncovered for 15 minutes, or until the mixture is thick and juicy. Add the stock and wine and simmer for a further 3 minutes.

Arrange the chicken joints side by side in a large roasting pan and pour over the sauce — it should half-cover them, so add a little more stock if necessary. Cover with foil and cook for 45 minutes, basting once. Uncover, add the mushrooms and olives, and cook uncovered for a further 15 minutes. Serve garnished with chopped parsley.

PASSOVER APRICOT STUFFING

This is enough for a large chicken or a 4 lb (2 kg) shoulder of lamb, cooked as for Shoulder of Lamb in the Persian Fashion (see page 118).

4 oz (100 g/¾ cup) dried apricots, soaked overnight in sufficient water to cover
4 matzot
¼ pint (150 ml/⅔ cup) soaking water from apricots
1 medium onion, finely chopped

2 oz (50 g/¼ cup) margarine
Grated rind of half a lemon
½ level teaspoon salt; speck of white pepper
1 large egg

Crumble the matzot into a large basin, add the apricot soaking water and leave to soften. Meanwhile, cook the onion in the margarine until soft and golden. Add the seasonings and the beaten egg to the matzah mixture, then add to the onions in the pan and cook gently, stirring until the matzah starts to brown and loses some of its wetness. Stir in the apricots, roughly chopped.

VARIATION
Passover Pineapple Stuffing Make in exactly the same way but with these ingredients:

4 matzot
1 can (8 oz (225 g)) pineapple, drained and roughly chopped
2 tablespoons pineapple syrup from fruit
4 fl oz (125 ml/½ cup) water

1 medium onion, finely chopped
2 oz (50 g/¼ cup) margarine
Grated rind of half a lemon
½ level teaspoon salt; speck of white pepper
1 large egg

MUSHROOM AND MEAT LASAGNE

SERVES 6–8

Freeze 1 month
Leftovers keep 2 days under refrigeration

An excellent entrée or main course. Softened matzot make an excellent substitute for pasta.

6 matzot
2 tablespoons chopped cashew nuts
3 tablespoons oil
1 medium onion, finely chopped
½ lb (225 g/2 cups) mushrooms, sliced
1 lb (450 g) raw minced (ground) meat
(preferably beef)
2 tablespoons chopped parsley

1 clove of garlic, peeled and crushed
1 teaspoon salt; 15 grinds black pepper
2 tablespoons tomato ketchup
4 medium potatoes, boiled and mashed, or ½
packet reconstituted instant potatoes (about
½ pint (275 ml/1¼ cups))
2 eggs
2 tablespoons oil

Preheat the oven to Gas No. 4, 400 degrees F, 200 degrees C. Soak the matzot in cold water to cover for 1 minute, then lift out and pat dry with paper towels. Put 1 tablespoon of the oil into an oblong casserole 1½ in (3 cm) deep, and put into the oven to get hot whilst you prepare the filling.

Lightly fry the nuts in 2 tablespoons oil until golden-brown. Drain. In the same oil sauté the onion for 5 minutes, until soft and golden, then add the sliced mushrooms and fry for a further 2 minutes. Add the meat and cook briskly, stirring with a fork until it becomes a rich brown. Add the seasonings and the ketchup, bring to the boil and simmer for 5 minutes. Then add the mashed potato, and mix well.

Take the hot dish from the oven and line the bottom with two of the matzot, broken to fit. Spread half the meat mixture on top, and then another layer of matzot, followed by the rest of the meat. Top with the remaining two matzot. Beat the eggs with the 2 tablespoons of oil and pour over the top of the casserole. (The matzot will absorb this liquid.) Bake for 45 minutes, or until the top is a crisp golden-brown.

PASSOVER PINEAPPLE CHICKEN

SERVES 6

Freeze 1 month
Leftovers keep 2 days under refrigeration

A delicious mixture that can be topped with mashed potato and browned under the grill (broiler) or served with latkes or chips.

12 oz (350 g/1½ cups) cooked chicken or fowl (about half a cooked medium-sized bird)
2 tablespoons oil
2 tablespoons coarsely chopped almonds
1 medium onion, peeled, halved, then very thinly sliced
1 large green pepper, very thinly sliced

1 can (8 oz (225 g)) pineapple, cut up into small chunks
1 teaspoon potato flour
1 chicken stock cube
1 level tablespoon demerara (brown) sugar
2 teaspoons Passover vinegar
¼ pint (150 ml/⅔ cup) syrup from pineapple

Heat the oil and cook the nuts until golden. Lift out with a slotted spoon and drain on absorbent paper. In the same oil, cook the onion until softened but not brown (about 5 minutes), then add the pepper and cook a further 3 minutes. Add the chicken (cut into bite-sized chunks) and the pineapple, and allow to heat through gently.

In a small bowl put the potato flour, then add the sugar, vinegar and pineapple syrup. Crumble the chicken stock cube and add that too, then add to the chicken mixture in the pan and simmer 3 minutes. Stir in the nuts. May be reheated.

TWO SAVOURY SAUCES

Sauces can be thickened with either potato flour or egg yolks. Use an equal quantity of potato flour to replace cornflour (cornstarch), and *half* the quantity to replace flour. Do not make a roux, but mix the potato flour with some of the cold liquid, and then add it to the sauce and cook for 3 or 4 minutes more.

CHEESE SAUCE

Do not freeze
Will keep 2 days under refrigeration

This is excellent to serve either with vegetables such as cauliflower or courgettes (zucchini), or with grilled (broiled) fish. Reheat it either in the microwave or (very gently) on top of the stove, without allowing it to boil.

1 egg yolk
1 carton (5 oz (150 ml/⅔ cup)) natural yoghurt
2 oz (50 g/½ cup) Gouda or Cheddar cheese, grated

Good pinch each of salt, white pepper and freshly ground nutmeg

Put all the ingredients into a small pan, and heat gently, stirring all the time, until thickened to a coating consistency.

MUSHROOM SAUCE

SERVES 6–8

Do not freeze
Will keep 2 days under refrigeration

This is excellent for serving with oven-fried chicken.

2 oz (50 g/¼ cup) margarine
Half an onion, finely chopped
½ lb (225 g/2 cups) mushrooms, thinly
sliced
1 level tablespoon potato flour

5 fl oz (150 ml/⅔ cup) each white wine and
chicken stock or 10 fl oz (275 ml/1¼ cups)
chicken stock
½ teaspoon salt; 15 grinds black pepper
1 tablespoon chopped parsley

Melt the margarine, add the chopped onion, cover and simmer for 5 minutes. Uncover, and add the mushrooms. Stir well, cover and cook for 5 minutes. Uncover and bubble to boil away any liquid. Put the potato flour into a bowl and mix to a smooth cream with a little of the wine or chicken stock. Add the rest of the liquid to the mushrooms and bring to the boil. Pour the mixture on to the potato flour, then return it to the pan and bubble for 1 minute to cook the potato starch. Add the parsley, salt and pepper, then taste and re-season if necessary. May be reheated.

THREE COLD DESSERTS
BLUEBERRY CHEESECAKE

SERVES 10

Freeze 2 months without the topping
The completed cake will keep under
refrigeration for 2 days

This is a refreshing change from all the cakes with nuts and matzah meal. Blackcurrants, redcurrants or bilberries can be used instead of the blueberries, or the cake can be topped with slices of fresh or canned pineapple, brushed with a little apricot preserve. If you freeze the cake, put the topping on the day it is to be used.

Enough ⅜ in (1 cm) thick slices of sponge or
nut cake to cover the bottom and half-way up
the sides of a 9 in (22 cm) loose-bottomed
cake tin

THE CHEESECAKE:
2 eggs, separated
1 lb (450 g/2 cups) cream cheese
Juice and rind of half a lemon
2 oz (50 g/¼ cup) very soft butter
2–3 oz (50–75 g/¼–⅓ cup) caster
(superfine) sugar
2 packets (10 g) vanilla sugar
1 level tablespoon potato flour

Half a 5 oz (150 ml/⅔ cup) carton Passover
whipping cream, whipped, or 5 oz (150
ml/⅔ cup) soured cream

THE TOPPING:
¾ lb (350 g/3 cups) blueberries, frozen
without sugar
4 fl oz (125 ml/½ cup) water
2 oz (50 g/¼ cup) granulated sugar
2 teaspoons potato flour mixed to a smooth
cream with 2 tablespoons of lemon juice

319

To make the cheesecake Preheat the oven to Gas No. 5, 375 degrees F, 190 degrees C. Lightly butter a loose-bottomed cake tin, 9 in (22 cm) across and 3 in (7½ cm) deep, then arrange the cake slices on the bottom and half-way up the sides.

Separate the egg whites from the yolks and reserve. Put the cheese into a bowl and beat in the juice and rind of the lemon, the butter, egg yolks, sugars and potato flour. Stir in the cream. Finally whisk the whites until they hold stiff glossy peaks, then whisk in a further 1 level tablespoon caster sugar. Fold into the cheese mixture, then spoon on top of the cake, levelling the top.

Bake at Gas No. 5, 375 degrees F, 190 degrees C, for 25 minutes, or until the cake is set 1 in (2½ cm) round the edge. (The centre will set as it cools.) Leave in a draught-free place until cool, then chill several hours in the tin before covering with the topping.

To make the topping In a small pan, dissolve the sugar in the water, bring to the boil, then stir in the lemon juice and potato flour mixture and cook for 2 minutes until thickened and clear. Stir in the fruit, take off the heat, cover the pan and leave until cool but not set, then carefully spoon over the chilled cake and leave to set.

To unmould the cake Carefully run a knife between the outside of the cake and the tin, then stand the tin on a tall canister of a smaller diameter, and gently pull down the sides. Put the cake, still on the base, on to a serving dish and chill until required.

CHOCOLATE ROULADE WITH STRAWBERRY CLOUD FILLING

SERVES 8

Freeze 1 month
Leftovers will keep a day under refrigeration

A cake made entirely without flour commends itself at once for Passover use; however, this one is a masterpiece in its own right. Making a roulade may seem a daunting prospect, but I have carefully worked out this recipe so as to simplify it at every stage. The berries can be omitted and liqueur-flavoured whipped cream used as the filling instead. In either event, it's wise to make the roulade a day ahead so that it will be easy to slice.

The cake can only be made successfully in a roulade or Swiss roll tin not less than 1 in (2½ cm) deep.

THE ROULADE:
6 oz (175 g) plain (semi-sweet) chocolate
2 tablespoons hot water
5 eggs
6 oz (175 g/¾ cup) caster (superfine) sugar

THE FILLING:
½ lb (225 g/1½ cups) strawberries

2 level tablespoons caster (superfine) sugar
2 tablespoons orange juice
1 tablespoon lemon juice
1 teaspoon each grated orange and lemon rind
¼ pint (150 ml/⅔ cup) double (heavy) cream

Preheat the oven to Gas No. 4, 350 degrees F, 180 degrees C. Use silicone or greased greaseproof paper to line a roulade tin measuring 12 × 8 in (30 × 20 cm) across the base and 1–1½ in (2½–3 cm) deep, mitring the corners to make a neat fit.

320

Break the chocolate into a small basin, and melt it over a pan of simmering water or in the microwave (1½ minutes on full power, stirring once). Stir in the hot water. Separate the eggs, putting the yolks into a small bowl and the whites into a large one. Add the sugar to the egg yolks and beat with a batter whisk until the consistency of unwhipped double cream. Whisk the egg whites until they hold stiff, glossy peaks. Stir the melted chocolate into the egg yolk and sugar mixture, then stir in a large tablespoon of the meringue. Pour the chocolate mixture down the side of the bowl containing the beaten whites, then use a rubber spatula to fold the two together until the colour is even. Coax this fluffy mixture into the tin and spread it evenly — particularly in the corners. Bake for 20 minutes, or until a skewer comes out clean from the centre of the cake.

While it is baking, get ready a cooling tray, two sheets of greaseproof or silicone paper rather larger than the baking tin, a dry teatowel and a sifter of icing (confectioners') sugar. Remove the cake tin from the oven, put on to the cooling tray and cover lightly first with a sheet of paper and then the teatowel. Leave to go cold.

Meanwhile, prepare the filling. Slice the fruit thickly into a bowl and mix gently with the sugar, then pour on the fruit juices and rind. Leave while the cake is cooling, then drain off the juice. Put the cream into a bowl with the juice and whisk until thick and fluffy — it should hold a soft peak. When the cake is quite cold, turn it out on to a sheet of greaseproof paper thickly dusted with icing sugar. Peel away the baking paper with care. Spread the cake with the cream mixture and then cover it evenly with the sliced strawberries. Roll up the roulade with the help of the sugared paper. Carefully transfer to a serving dish, join side down. Chill several hours before serving.

TRIFLE FOR PASSOVER

SERVES 8–10

Do not freeze
Will keep 2 days under refrigeration

This is a delightful and relatively economical sweet for a fish supper. The jelly can be ommitted if preferred and more fruit used instead.

Enough stale sponge cake or Passover Victoria Sponge (page 332) to cover the bottom of a glass bowl about 7 in (17½ cm) in diameter
Jam
4 tablespoons kosher wine
Custard made with 1 pint (575 ml/2½ cups) milk (see below)
1 Passover jelly (gelatine dessert mix), any fruit flavour
Juice of a large lemon (3 tablespoons)
2 bananas
8 fl oz (225 ml/1 cup) whipping or double (heavy) cream

1 cupful fresh or canned mixed fruit, such as oranges and pineapple
4 tablespoons fruit syrup or juice

EGG CUSTARD:
3 whole eggs or 4 egg yolks
2 oz (50 g/¼ cup) sugar
1 level tablespoon potato flour
1 pint (575 ml/2½ cups) milk

GARNISH:
1 oz (25 g/¼ cup) slivered blanched almonds, toasted

Make the custard first. Whisk the eggs, sugar and potato flour until thoroughly blended. Heat the milk until it steams, then pour on to the egg mixture. Return to the pan and cook gently, stirring all the time, until the custard will coat the back of the spoon. *Do not* allow the custard to boil.

Slice the cake thinly, then sandwich the slices together with jam and arrange at the bottom of the glass dish. Spoon over the wine — the cake should be moist without being soggy. Pour over the warm custard, and leave several hours until cold and set.

Make up the jelly in the usual way, substituting lemon juice for an equivalent amount of water. (If canned fruit is being used, make up the jelly using the syrup in place of an equivalent amount of water.) Leave to chill in the freezer until almost setting, about 45 minutes. Fold in the sliced bananas, then pour the mixture over the custard and leave to set — another hour.

Whisk the cream until it hangs on the whisk, then whisk in the fruit syrup. Whisk until thick, then fold in the fruit, cut up into small pieces. Spoon over the jelly and decorate with the toasted almonds. Leave to chill for 2 or 3 hours.

THREE FRUIT FLANS
ALMOND SPONGE FLAN WITH ORANGE GLAZE

SERVES 8–10 with a fruit compôte or sorbet

Freeze 3 months without fruit
Will keep 2 days under refrigeration

You can make this delicious dessert, which is suitable for either a meat or a milk meal, equally well in a loose-bottomed tin or in an oven-to-table decorative dish. It can be made up to 24 hours in advance and is nicest served at room temperature.

Passover pastry (recipe on page 329)

Grated rind of half a lemon

THE FILLING:
4 oz (125 g/½ cup) soft margarine
3 oz (75 g/⅓ cup) caster (superfine) sugar
2 large eggs
4 oz (125 g/1 cup) ground almonds
1 sachet vanilla sugar
2 tablespoons potato flour

THE TOPPING AND GLAZE:
6 juicy oranges, pith and peel removed
1 tablespoon lemon juice
2 rounded tablespoons Passover apricot jam
1 tablespoon Passover apricot liqueur

Preheat the oven to Gas No. 5, 375 degrees F, 190 degrees C. Have ready a 9½–10 in (23–25 cm) diameter flan tin and a large piece of foil. Roll out the well-chilled pastry on a board sprinkled with cake meal, then carefully fit it into the chosen flan tin, and trim the edges with a knife. Prick all over with a fork, line with the foil moulded into the shape of the dish, then bake for 15 minutes. Remove the foil and continue to bake for a further 10 minutes until the pastry is golden. Lift on to a cooling rack.

Put all the sponge filling ingredients into a bowl and beat until smooth, about 2 minutes. Spoon into the flan case, turn the oven down to Gas No. 4, 350 degrees F, 180 degrees C, and bake until the top is golden-brown, about 25 minutes. Leave the tart to cool; lift out of the case if baked in a loose-bottomed tin.

Slice the oranges or section them, discarding the pith, then sprinkle them with lemon juice and leave for 30 minutes. Put the apricot jam, the liqueur and any juice that has come out of the oranges into a pan and bring to the boil, then simmer for 3 minutes, and cool until it stops steaming.

Arrange the flan on a serving dish and brush the almond topping with some of the glaze. Arrange the drained oranges in a design on top, then brush them with the remaining glaze. Leave in the refrigerator until the start of the meal, then leave in the kitchen until ready to serve.

PEAR AND ALMOND FLAN

SERVES 8–10 with fruit salad or ice cream   *Freeze pastry only 3 months*
                                                  Will keep 2 days under refrigeration

Poached pears are baked on top of an almond frangipane filling, making a dramatic Passover dessert with an interesting contrast of textures. The flan is suitable for either a milk or a meat meal.

Passover pastry (see recipe on page 329)
4 medium firm pears, Conference or William variety, peeled, halved and cores removed

THE POACHING LIQUID:
5 fl oz (150 ml/²⁄₃ cup) water
2 oz (50 g/¼ cup) demerara (brown) sugar
1½ tablespoons lemon juice

THE FRANGIPANE:
1½ oz (40 g/6 tablespoons) icing (confectioners') sugar
1½ oz (40 g/3 tablespoons) caster (superfine) sugar
1 packet (10 g) vanilla sugar
3 oz (75 g/¾ cup) ground almonds
2 oz (50 g/¼ cup) soft butter (or margarine for a meat meal)
1 egg

THE GLAZE:
3 tablespoons smooth apricot jam, warmed until runny

In a wide pan, dissolve the sugar in the water and the lemon juice, then add the pear halves in one layer and baste with the syrup. Cover and simmer until tender, about 15 minutes, basting and turning once or twice. Lift out the pears with a draining spoon and lay on paper towels. (The liquid can be used for poaching other fruit or for a fruit salad.)

Preheat the oven to Gas No. 5, 375 degrees F, 190 degrees C. Line a 10 in (25 cm) flan tin or a foil sandwich tin with the pastry and prick it well all over, then put in the freezer while you beat the ingredients for the frangipane together until they are smooth and creamy; then spread the mixture on the pastry base. Cut through the rounded side of each pear at ¼ in (½ cm) intervals (but leave the pear in one piece), then arrange on the frangipane. Press down on each pear in turn with the hand so that it spreads like a fan, then paint all over the fruit and frangipane with the melted apricot jam. Bake for 30 to 35 minutes until the pastry is golden-brown. Serve at room temperature.

PASSOVER TARTE ALSACIENNE

SERVES 10–12 with fruit salad

Do not freeze
Will keep 2 days under refrigeration

This is a tarte made in the tradition of the Jewish community in Alsace, which is mainly centred on Strasbourg. Sliced dessert apples are baked under a creamy custard topping, then glazed and decorated with toasted nuts. It makes a superb ending to a fish Seder meal.

Passover pastry (recipe on page 329), well chilled

½ pint (275 ml/1¼ cups) double (heavy) cream

THE FILLING:
2 lb (1 kg) Cox's or other dessert apples (weight when cored and peeled)
2 tablespoons granulated sugar
3 eggs
4 oz (125 g/½ cup) caster (superfine) sugar
⅔ oz packet (20 g/4 teaspoons) vanilla sugar

THE GLAZE:
2 tablespoons smooth apricot jam
2 tablespoons lemon juice
1 tablespoon sugar

TO DECORATE:
1 oz (25 g/¼ cup) toasted flaked almonds

Preheat the oven to Gas No. 6, 400 degrees F, 200 degrees C. Have ready a 12 in (30 cm) flan tin. Roll out the pastry, on a board sprinkled with cake meal, into a circle 14 in (35 cm) in diameter, then carefully ease into the flan tin, patching the pastry if necessary. Trim the pastry level with the sides of the tin, then prick lightly all over with a fork. Peel and core the apples, then slice them ¼ in (½ cm) thick. Lay the slices in concentric circles on the pastry, rounded side up. Sprinkle with the granulated sugar, then bake for 30 minutes until soft and lightly tinged with gold.

To make and bake the filling Whisk the eggs and sugars until smooth and creamy, then stir in the cream. Pierce the apples with a sharp knife to make sure they are tender, then carefully cover with the custard. Bake for a further 15 to 20 minutes, or until lightly set.

To glaze the tarte Allow to cool for 20 minutes, then put the jam, lemon juice and sugar into a pan, heat until smooth, stirring, then boil for 1 minute. Brush over the cooked flan with a pastry brush and sprinkle with the almonds. Chill before serving.

PASSOVER CRÊPES WITH APPLE AND WALNUT FILLING

Makes 15

Freeze 3 months
The filled crêpes will keep unbrowned for 1 day under refrigeration

These delicate crêpes with their juicy apple filling make a splendid milk or meat dessert, either for the Seder or for a mid-Festival meal. They can be filled and frozen in advance, then defrosted overnight in the refrigerator, or they can be filled early in the day. In either case the crêpes are browned in the oven just before serving.

1 recipe Passover crêpes (see page 327)
1 oz (25 g/2 tablespoons) butter or
margarine (for a meat meal)
1 lb (450 g) baking apples, cored, peeled and
finely sliced
½ teaspoon ground cinnamon

Grated rind and juice of half a lemon
2 oz (50 g/¼ cup) granulated sugar
1 rounded tablespoon apricot jam or
eingemachtes
1 oz (25 g/¼ cup) walnuts, chopped
2 oz (50 g/¼ cup) melted butter or 4
tablespoons oil

Melt the fat in heavy pan and add all the ingredients except the walnuts. Cover and cook gently until the apples are tender, after about 15 minutes, then add the walnuts and stir well to form a thick pulp. Allow the filling to cool, then spread each crêpe with a generous tablespoonful, roll up the crêpes and arrange 2 in (5 cm) apart on a greased oven tray.

Preheat the oven to Gas No. 5, 375 degrees F, 190 degrees C. Brush the surface of each crêpe with either butter or oil and bake for 30 minutes, or until golden-brown. May be kept hot for 15 minutes in a cool oven.

HOT LEMON SOUFFLÉ

SERVES 4–5

Do not freeze

A meringue is folded into warm lemon curd. The result is a 'sky high' soufflé with a superb flavour, suitable for either a meat or a milk meal. The lemon sauce can be made early in the day, then reheated until it feels warm to the touch, just before the meringue is folded in.

2 oz (50 g/¼ cup) butter or
margarine
4 oz (125 g/½ cup) sugar
6 tablespoons lemon juice (2 or 3 lemons)
Finely grated rind of 2 lemons

4 egg yolks
5 egg whites
Margarine (or butter) and caster (superfine)
sugar for lining soufflé dish

Grease a soufflé or other heatproof dish about 8 in (20 cm) in diameter and 3 in (7½ cm) deep, then coat it with caster sugar. Separate the eggs, putting the yolks into a small bowl and the whites in a large one. Add the extra egg white to this bowl. Beat the egg yolks to blend. In a pan (preferably not aluminium as this may cause discoloration) heat the butter or margarine with half the sugar, together with the lemon juice and the rind. When the mixture is liquid and without grittiness — a sign that the sugar has dissolved — pour half of it on to the yolks, stirring all the time, then return this mixture to the pan and cook very gently until as thick as double (heavy) cream; *don't* let it bubble, or it will curdle. (This could be done in a microwave.)

About 50 minutes before you intend to serve the soufflé, preheat the oven to Gas No. 6, 400 degrees F, 200 degrees C. Whisk the whites until they hold stiff peaks, then whisk in the rest of the sugar 1 tablespoon at a time, whisking until stiff after each addition. Now take a quarter of this meringue and *stir* into the egg yolk mixture — this will lighten it. Now pour it on top of the meringue and *fold* the two together, using a metal spoon or a rubber spatula. Coax this light mixture into the prepared dish and smooth it level. Put it in the oven, then immediately turn the heat down to Gas No. 5, 375 degrees F, 190 degrees C and cook for 35 minutes. Take from the oven, dust with icing (confectioners') sugar and serve at once.

A FAMILY SPECIAL
OLD-FASHIONED MATZAH PUDDING

SERVES 6	Freeze 3 months
	Leftovers will keep 3 days under refrigeration

A richly flavoured yet simple dessert that can be served either hot or cold.

4 matzot

6 oz (175 g/1 cup) Passover raisins (if available), soaked in boiling water for 5 minutes, then drained

1 cooking apple, peeled and coarsely grated

3 oz (75 g/⅓ cup) caster (superfine) sugar

2 oz (50 g/½ cup) chopped walnuts (optional)

1½ teaspoons cinnamon

1 rounded tablespoon apricot jam or marmalade

Juice and grated rind of half a lemon

3 eggs (whisked until thick)

3 level tablespoons matzah cake meal

3 oz (75 g/⅓ cup) margarine (melted)

1–2 tablespoons granulated sugar

Preheat the oven to Gas No. 4, 350 degrees F, 180 degrees C. Grease a tin or baking dish about 8 in (20 cm) square and 2½–3 in (6–7 cm) deep.

Pour *cold* water over the broken-up matzot in a mixing bowl and leave for 10 minutes, then drain well, and beat with a fork until smooth. Add all the other ingredients, except the margarine and granulated sugar, to the matzot in the order given, beating well. Stir in half the melted margarine, and turn into the chosen baking dish. Drizzle the remaining margarine over the top, and sprinkle with granulated sugar. Bake for approximately 1 hour or until a knife inserted in the centre comes out clean.

PANCAKES — LIGHT FOR BREAKFAST, RICHER FOR TEA
FEATHERLIGHT PANCAKES

SERVES 4   Do not freeze

It's a labour of love to get up half an hour early to mix these delicious pancakes ready for breakfast. If time is short, however, use an extra ounce (25 g/¼ cup) of meal, and mix the whole lot together including the eggs. After 5 minutes the mixture will be thick enough to fry, but don't expect it to be quite as light as the real thing! Serve the pancakes with cinnamon sugar (1 teaspoon ground cinnamon mixed with 4 oz (125 g/½ cup) caster (superfine) sugar), or with a spoonful of eingemachtes or strawberry jam.

2 oz (50 g/½ cup) fine matzah meal
½ teaspoon salt
3 eggs, separated

6 fl oz (175 ml/¾ cup) water
Butter and oil, or oil alone, for frying

Put the matzah meal and salt into a bowl. Whisk the yolks and the water together, then pour on to the meal and mix thoroughly. Leave to swell for 30 minutes. Whisk the egg whites until they hold stiff peaks, then fold into the meal mixture using a wooden spoon or a rubber spatula.

Put 2 oz (50 g/¼ cup) butter (or margarine) into a heavy frying pan and when melted add enough oil to come to a depth of ¼ in (½ cm) (or use all oil). Drop the mixture in the hot fat (it should bubble merrily when the mixture goes in). Cook over moderate heat until a golden-brown on all sides.

CHREMSLACH   FRUITED MATZAH FRITTERS

SERVES 4–6   Do not freeze

These make a delicious dessert after a light meal. They are pleasant served cold (but not chilled) for tea, or on a 'matzah picnic'. Serve them plain, sprinkled with caster (superfine) sugar or accompanied by a compôte of dried fruit.

4 matzot
2 oz (50 g/½ cup) chopped blanched almonds
1 tablespoon fine matzah meal
4 oz (125 g/½ cup) caster (superfine) sugar
2 tablespoons chopped raisins (if available)

1 rounded tablespoon apricot jam or marmalade
2 eggs, well beaten until frothy
Grated rind of 1 lemon
1 tablespoon lemon juice
Oil for frying ·

Break the matzot into pieces, put into a bowl and cover with hot water. Leave 1 minute, then squeeze out the moisture with the hands. Put into a mixing bowl and mix to a pulp with a large fork. Add all the remaining ingredients, mixing well.

327

Pour enough oil into a frying pan to come to a depth of ½ in (1 cm). When you can feel a good heat on your hand held 2 in (5 cm) above the pan, put the mixture in by tablespoons, flatten slightly, then cook at a gentle bubble until brown on both sides. Lift out with a slotted spoon and drain on crumpled kitchen paper (paper towels).

FIVE SPECIAL BISCUITS
ALMOND MACAROONS

Makes 12 or 13

Freeze 3 months
Keep moist for a week under refrigeration

The quantity of egg white is the important factor in producing macaroons that are crisp on the outside yet moist and chewy within. I have developed this method for the food processor, but the macaroons can be equally well made by hand, beating the mixture for 1 minute after each addition, using a wooden spoon.

4 oz (125 g/1 cup) ground almonds
1½–2 egg whites (1½–2 fl oz/40–50 ml),
broken up with a fork
5 oz (150 g/⅔ cup) caster (superfine) sugar

⅔ oz (20 g/4 teaspoons) packet vanilla sugar
Sifted icing (confectioners') sugar
12 or 13 halves of blanched almonds

Preheat the oven to Gas No. 6, 400 degrees F, 200 degrees C. Cover a baking tray with silicone paper.

Put the ground almonds into the food processor and process for 15 seconds or until very fine. (Omit this stage if mixing by hand — it is not strictly necessary, but it does make a biscuit with a finer texture.) Add about half an egg white, and process another 10 seconds. Then add half the caster sugar and the vanilla sugar, and process another 10 seconds. Add the second half egg white and the remaining sugar in the same way. Then add a further half egg white. The mixture will now be soft but just capable of being formed into balls with the hands; if it is too stiff add the remaining half egg white.

Take up pieces of the dough and roll between the hands into balls the size of a *large* walnut — you should get 12 or 13 balls. If you make more, they're too small, and should be re-rolled. Put the balls 2 in (5 cm) apart on the paper, and gently flatten with the fingers. Brush all over with cold water, then sprinkle with the icing sugar. Lay an almond half on each biscuit, or leave plain, as you prefer.

Bake for 16–17 minutes or until the tops are just lightly browned. (Over-baking will result in crisp instead of moist macaroons.) Remove from the tray using a spatula. When cold, store in an airtight tin.

PASSOVER CHOCOLATE BROWNIES

Makes about 24

Freeze 3 months
Will keep 1 week in an airtight container

These moist chocolate squares can be quickly mixed by hand. As they are 'parev', they're useful as an accompaniment to a fresh or dried fruit compôte after a meal.

3 eggs
4 fl oz (125 ml/½ cup) oil
7 oz (200 g/1 cup) caster (superfine) sugar
⅔ oz (20 g/4 teaspoons) packet vanilla sugar

Scant 2 oz (50 g/½ cup) matzah cake meal plus generous 1 oz (25 g/¼ cup) cocoa (3 oz (75 g/¾ cup) altogether)
2 oz (50 g/½ cup) walnuts, coarsely chopped
Caster (superfine) sugar

Preheat the oven to Gas No. 4, 350 degrees F, 180 degrees C. Grease a baking tin measuring about 11 × 7 × 1 in (27 × 17 × 2½ cm).

Whisk together the eggs and oil, then whisk in the caster sugar until the mixture has thickened slightly. Sift together the vanilla sugar, meal and cocoa, then stir into the egg mixture with the chopped nuts. Spoon into the tin and smooth level. Bake for 25 minutes until firm to gentle touch. Sprinkle with caster sugar, then cut into squares. Remove from the tin when cold.

ALMOND SLICES

Makes about 24 slices

Freeze 3 months
Will keep 1 week in an airtight container

An almond frangipane topping is baked on a very short and tender pastry base. It is not worth making a smaller amount of pastry; but you will have enough left over to make a dozen jam tarts, or a 6 in (15 cm) flan case, or a trayful of Coconut Fingers.

The pastry is so short that it is best to chill it overnight to make it easier to roll out.

THE PASSOVER PASTRY:
6 oz (175 g/1 cup) potato flour
2 oz (50 g/½ cup) cake meal
4 oz (125 g/½ cup) soft margarine or butter
3 oz (75 g/⅓ cup) caster (superfine) sugar
1 egg
3 tablespoons apricot jam

THE TOPPING:
4 oz (125 g/½ cup) soft butter or margarine
4 oz (125 g/½ cup) caster (superfine) sugar
2 eggs
4 oz (125 g/1 cup) ground almonds
2 tablespoons cake meal
⅔ oz (20 g/4 teaspoons) packet vanilla sugar
Sifted icing (confectioners') sugar

To make the pastry   Put all the ingredients into a bowl and work together with an electric mixer or wooden spoon until a dough is formed. Dust thickly with cake meal, wrap in foil, flatten into a block about 1 in (2½ cm) thick and chill in the refrigerator overnight.

To assemble the slices   Preheat the oven to Gas No. 4, 350 degrees F, 180 degrees C. Roll out enough of the chilled dough to fit the sides and base of a shallow tin measuring about 11 × 7 × 1 in (27 × 17 × 2½ cm) and spread with a thin layer of the jam. Put all the topping ingredients into a bowl and beat by hand or machine until smooth and creamy, then spread over the jam. Bake for 40–45 minutes, or until golden-brown. Cool for 5 minutes, then dust with a layer of icing sugar. Cool for a further 5 minutes, then cut into slices.

COCONUT FINGERS

Makes about 24 fingers

Freeze 3 months
Will keep 1 week in an airtight container

These have a macaroon-like topping on a pastry base. The pastry can be made fresh, or you can use that left over from the Almond Slices.

Passover pastry (see previous recipe)

THE TOPPING:
Lemon curd or tart jam
2 egg whites

4 oz (125 g/½ cup) caster (superfine) sugar
3 oz (75 g/1 cup) desiccated (dried and shredded) coconut
1 teaspoon grated lemon rind
1 oz (25 g/¼ cup) flaked almonds

Preheat the oven to Gas No. 5, 375 degrees F, 190 degrees C. Roll out enough of the dough to fit the sides and base of a shallow tin measuring about 12 × 7 × 1 in (30 × 17 × 2½ cm) — it will take about half the dough. Spread the surface of the dough with a thin layer of the lemon curd or jam. Whisk the egg whites until they hold stiff, glossy peaks, then whisk in the sugar, a tablespoon at a time, whisking until stiff after each addition. Fold in the coconut and the lemon rind, then spread evenly over the pastry and scatter with the flaked almonds.

   Bake for 15 minutes, then reduce the heat to Gas No. 3, 325 degrees F, 160 degrees C and bake for a further 10 minutes. Cut into 2½ × 1 in (6 × 2½ cm) strips when cold.

PASSOVER KICHLACH

Makes 40

Freeze 3 months
Will keep 1 week in an airtight container

These are very economical 'tin-fillers' that are very quickly made.

2 eggs, whisked well to blend
5 fl oz (150 ml/⅔ cup) oil
1 packet (20 g/4 teaspoons) vanilla sugar
Rind of half a lemon, grated
5 oz (150 g/⅔ cup) caster (superfine) sugar

4 oz (125 g/⅔ cup) potato flour
4 oz (125 g/1 cup) cake meal
1 teaspoon baking powder

TO GLAZE:
4 tablespoons each oil and granulated sugar

Preheat the oven to Gas No. 6, 400 degrees F, 200 degrees C. Grease two oven trays.

Using a fork, whisk the eggs until well blended, then stir in all the remaining ingredients — the mixture will be a thick batter. Drop by rounded teaspoonful on the baking sheets, leaving 1 in (2½ cm) between spoonfuls. Put the oil in one small bowl and the sugar in another. Dip the bottom of a glass first into the oil and then into the sugar, then lightly press it on to the top of each kichel, flattening it gently into a round. Renew the oil and sugar as required.

Bake for 8 to 10 minutes, or until golden-brown. Carefully lift off the trays on to a cooling rack. Store in an airtight container when quite cold.

TWO BISCUITS WITHOUT EGGS
HAZELNUT CRISPS

Makes 26

Freeze 3 months
Will keep 1 week in an airtight container

These crisp and airy biscuits (cookies) are very quickly made. Don't worry if you can't weigh the half-ounces (15 g) exactly — just make sure that the total weight of the potato flour and cake meal is correct.

4½ oz (5 oz less 1 level tablespoon) (140 g/⅔ cup less 1 tablespoon) butter or margarine
3 oz (75 g/⅓ cup) caster (superfine) sugar
4½ oz (140 g/¾ cup) potato flour
1½ oz (40 g/5 tablespoons) matzah cake meal

1½ level teaspoons Passover baking powder
2 oz (50 g/½ cup) ground hazelnuts (filberts)
1 packet (10 g (2 teaspoons)) vanilla sugar

Preheat the oven to Gas No. 4, 350 degrees F, 180 degrees C. Have ready two ungreased baking trays.

Cut the fat into 1 in (2½ cm) chunks and add to the dry ingredients in a bowl. Rub in the fat with the fingers until a dough is formed that can be gathered up. Pinch off pieces of the dough the size of a large marble and roll into balls between the palms, then arrange 2 in (5 cm) apart on the trays. Dip a large fork in cold water, then press it gently down on each ball, first one way and then the other, to form little biscuits.

Bake for 15 minutes until the tops are golden-brown and firm to gentle touch. Leave to firm up on the trays for 2 minutes, then lift on to a cooling tray with a spatula, and dredge lightly with caster (superfine) sugar. Store in an airtight tin when quite cold.

VARIATION
Lemon and Orange Crisps Use the same ingredients as for the Hazelnut Crisps, but omit the ground hazelnuts (filberts) and the vanilla sugar. Instead use 2 oz (50 g/½ cup) ground almonds, 2 teaspoons grated orange rind and 1 teaspoon grated lemon rind. Mix and bake in exactly the same way.
The following biscuits (cookies) are also suitable for Passover use:

Chocolate and Toasted Hazelnut Truffles (page 249). If an 8 oz (225 g) bar of Passover toasted hazelnut (toasted filbert) chocolate is used, the toasted hazelnuts can be omitted. Use a Passover liqueur, and coat the truffles with coconut instead of drinking chocolate.

Nutty Butter Crisps These can be made exactly as described on page 250.

Soleils de Nice (page 251). Omit the flour coating the biscuits and use 3 tablespoons of cake meal instead.

THREE CAKES TO MAKE IN MOMENTS
CHOCOLATE CAKE WITH MOCHA FROSTING

Freeze 3 months
Will keep 1 week under refrigeration

This is a moist and flavourful 'parev' cake that is really quick to make, even by hand. The recipe can easily be doubled and baked in two sandwich tins to make a gâteau, using 1½ times the amount of mocha frosting to fill and ice the cake.

THE CAKE:
1 oz (25 g/4 tablespoons) matzah cake meal
3 oz (75 g/½ cup) potato flour
1½ teaspoons Passover baking powder
6 oz (175 g/¾ cup) caster (superfine) sugar
2 tablespoons cocoa
⅔ oz (20 g/4 teaspoons) packet vanilla sugar
2 eggs

4 fl oz (125 ml/½ cup) Passover oil

THE FROSTING:
4 oz (125 g/1 cup) sifted icing (confectioners') sugar
1 tablespoon cocoa
2 oz (50 g/¼ cup) soft margarine
1 teaspoon instant coffee dissolved in 3 teaspoons boiling water
1 oz (25 g/¼ cup) chopped walnuts or toasted almonds (optional)

To make the cake Preheat the oven to Gas No. 4, 350 degrees F, 180 degrees C. Have ready an 8 in (20 cm) foil cake tin or an 8 in (20 cm) sandwich tin, 1½ in (4 cm) deep, greased and bottom-lined with silicone paper.

Put all the cake ingredients into a bowl and mix until absolutely smooth — about 2 minutes. Spoon into the tin, smooth level and bake for 35 minutes or until firm to gentle touch. Turn out on to a cooling tray.

To make the frosting Put all the frosting ingredients into a bowl and beat until smooth — about 1 minute. Spread on top of the cooled cake, rough up with a fork and, if liked, decorate with the walnuts or almonds.

332

PASSOVER VICTORIA SPONGE WITH GRILLED TOFFEE TOPPING

Will keep 1 week in an airtight container

A sponge cake with an intriguing nutty topping.

THE CAKE:
2 eggs
4 oz (125 g/½ cup) soft margarine
4 oz (125 g/½ cup) caster (superfine) sugar
1½ teaspoons Passover baking powder
Rind of half a lemon, grated
2 oz (50 g/½ cup) matzah cake meal

3 oz (75 g/½ cup) potato flour

THE TOPPING:
1½ oz (40 g/3 tablespoons) melted butter or margarine
4 level tablespoons desiccated (dried and shredded) coconut
4 level tablespoons caster (superfine) sugar
2 level tablespoons walnuts, finely chopped

Preheat the oven to Gas No. 4, 350 degrees F, 180 degrees C. Have ready an 8 in (20 cm) foil cake tin, or an 8 in (20 cm) metal sandwich tin, 1½ in (4 cm) deep, greased and bottom-lined with silicone paper.

Put all the cake ingredients into a bowl and mix until absolutely smooth and creamy, about 2 minutes. Spoon into the tin, smooth level and bake for 35 minutes or until firm to gentle touch. Turn out on to a cooling tray.

To make the toffee topping Melt the fat in a small pan, stir in the sugar and cook gently until smooth, then stir in the coconut and the chopped walnuts. When the cake has cooled for 10 minutes, spread it with the topping and grill (broil) gently for 4 minutes until golden-brown. The topping hardens as it cools.

PASSOVER FAIRY CAKES

Makes 18–20

Freeze 3 months
Will keep 1 week in an airtight container

As these do not contain nuts of any kind and have a very light texture they are particularly suitable for young children; adults will enjoy them as well!

5 oz (150 g/⅔ cup) soft margarine
6 oz (175 g/¾ cup) caster (superfine) sugar
3 eggs
4½ oz (140 g/1 cup plus 2 tablespoons) potato flour

1½ oz (40 g/5 tablespoons) cake meal
1½ teaspoons Passover baking powder
⅔ oz (20 g/4 teaspoons) packet vanilla sugar

Preheat the oven to Gas No. 6, 400 degrees F, 200 degrees C. Arrange 20 paper cases in bun tins or on flat baking trays.

Put all the ingredients into a bowl and beat by hand or machine until a smooth batter is formed (3 minutes by hand, 2 minutes by electric beater, 20 seconds by food processor). Bake for 15–20 minutes, or until golden-brown.

VARIATIONS

Lemon Cup Cakes   Omit the vanilla sugar, and stir in the grated rind of 1 lemon instead. Make a lemon icing with 6 oz (175 g/1½ cups) icing (confectioners') sugar mixed with 1 tablespoon lemon juice and up to 1 tablespoon water (the mixture should be thick enough to coat the back of a spoon). Spoon a little over each cake and allow to set.

Raisin Cup Cakes   Stir 4 tablespoons raisins (if available in a Passover pack) into the plain fairy cake mixture.

SUPERB SPONGE CAKES
FEATHERLIGHT PASSOVER SPONGE

Freeze 3 months
Will keep 4 days under refrigeration

This is a light, yet moist sponge (yellow) cake, perfect to serve plain for afternoon tea. It can also be split and filled with whipped cream or lemon curd, or soaked with syrup and served as a dessert.

5 eggs, separated
10 oz (275 g/1¼ cups) caster (superfine) sugar
1 tablespoon lemon juice

4½ oz (140 g/¾ cup) potato flour plus 1½ oz (40 g/5 tablespoons) matzah cake meal (6 oz (175 g/1 cup) altogether
2 tablespoons caster (superfine) sugar

Preheat the oven to Gas No. 4, 350 degrees F, 180 degrees C. Select a tin 9 in (22 cm) across and not less than 2 in (5 cm) deep. Grease it lightly with oil, then add a tablespoon of caster sugar and roll it round to coat the inside of the tin with a very thin layer.

Sift the meal and potato flour together. Put the egg yolks in one bowl and the whites in another. Put half the sugar into the bowl containing the egg yolks and whisk until thick and white, then whisk in the juice. (If an electric whisk is not available, stand the bowl over a pan of very hot water and whisk by hand.) Add a pinch of salt to the whites and whisk them until they hold stiff, glossy peaks when the whisk is withdrawn, then whisk in the remaining sugar, 1 tablespoon at a time, whisking until stiff after each addition. Fold this meringue into the yolk mixture. Now sprinkle on the meal and potato flour, a few tablespoons at a time, and cut and fold into the egg mixture — a rubber spatula is excellent. Turn the mixture into the prepared tin, and smooth level. Sprinkle the top lightly with caster sugar.

Bake for 1 hour 10 minutes until the cake has shrunk slightly from the sides of the tin, and the top is spongy when lightly pressed with a finger. Leave the cake in the tin standing on a cake rack until cold, then gently ease out of the tin.

PINEAPPLE LIQUEUR CAKE

SERVES 8–10

Freeze undecorated cake 3 months
Decorated cake will keep 3 days under
refrigeration

1 Passover Sponge (recipe above), freshly
baked

THE SYRUP:
4 oz (125 g/½ cup) granulated sugar
1 tablespoon smooth apricot jam
5 fl oz (150 ml/⅔ cup) water
2 tablespoons Passover liqueur, such as
apricot brandy (or orange juice)

1 tablespoon lemon juice

THE TOPPING:
5 fl oz (150 ml/⅔ cup) whipping or double
(heavy) cream, well chilled
2 slices fresh pineapple, cut up into little dice
2 teaspoons caster (superfine) sugar

Put the sugar, jam and water into a small pan and stir over gentle heat until the sugar is dissolved. Bring to the boil, then simmer gently for 5 minutes until a thick syrup is formed. Take off the heat and stir in the liqueur and lemon juice.

To soak the cake   When the cake comes out of the oven, prick it all over with the fork, then gently pour over the warm syrup. Cover and leave to go quite cold.

To make the topping   Sprinkle the fruit with the caster sugar, then leave at room temperature for 30 minutes. Put the cream into a bowl and pour in any juice that has oozed out of the pineapple, then whisk until it stands in soft peaks. Fold in the fruit and pile on top of the cake. Serve well chilled.

MOIST ALMOND SPONGE

Freeze 3 months
Will keep 1 week in an airtight container

This is a medium-sized cake, particularly suitable for the smaller family.

3 eggs, separated
6 oz (150 g/⅔ cup) caster (superfine) sugar
2 teaspoons lemon juice
3 oz (75 g/½ cup) potato flour

1 oz (25 g/¼ cup) matzah cake meal
3 oz (75 g/¾ cup) ground almonds
2 tablespoons caster (superfine) sugar

Preheat the oven to Gas No. 4, 350 degrees F, 180 degrees C. Oil a 7 in (17½ cm) loose-bottomed cake tin at least 2 in (5 cm) deep, and sprinkle with caster sugar.

Make the cake in the same way as the Featherlight Passover Sponge, page 334, but fold the ground almonds in with the meal and potato flour. Level the surface of the cake and sprinkle lightly with caster sugar, then bake for 45 minutes until the surface is firm to gentle touch. Leave the cake in the tin on a cooling tray until cold, then gently ease out.

PASSOVER CHIFFON SPONGE

Freeze 3 months
Will keep 1 week in an airtight container

This must be *the* perfect sponge cake to serve without any embellishment, except perhaps a dusting of icing sugar. It is light and airy with a delicate citrus flavour and a pleasing moistness provided by the oil. I have altered the ratio of the cake meal to the potato flour, so that it has an even finer texture than when I first developed it for an earlier book. An American 'angel food' cake tin is ideal to bake it in. If your cake tin is less than 3 in (7½ cm) deep, or if the eggs are very large, you may find the mixture will balloon over the top as it bakes. Don't worry about this, simply trim off any excess when the cake has cooled.

4 oz (125 g/⅔ cup) potato flour
1½ oz (40 g/5 tablespoons) cake meal
5 oz (150 g/⅔ cup) sugar
5 egg yolks
2 fl oz (50 ml/¼ cup) oil
2 fl oz (50 ml/¼ cup) orange juice

1 teaspoon each grated lemon rind and
orange rind
5 egg whites
Pinch of salt
2 oz (50 g/¼ cup) caster (superfine) sugar

Preheat the oven to Gas No. 3, 325 degrees F, 160 degrees C. Grease a 9 or 10 in (22 or 25 cm) ring tin, about 3 in (7½ cm) deep. Sieve the potato flour, cake meal and the 5 oz (150 g/⅔ cup) sugar into a large bowl, and mix well.

In a small bowl, mix together the egg yolks, oil, orange juice and the lemon and orange rind. Make a well in the middle of the dry ingredients, pour in the egg yolk mixture and stir with a wooden spoon until smoothly and evenly mixed. Whisk the egg whites with a pinch of salt until they hold stiff, glossy peaks, then whisk in the 2 oz (50 g/¼ cup) of caster sugar, a tablespoon at a time, whisking after each addition. Spoon this meringue on top of the first mixture, then fold the two together gently but thoroughly with a rubber spatula. Spoon into the prepared tin, smooth level, then bake for 1¼ hours, until firm to gentle touch. Put the cake, in the cake tin, on a cooling rack and leave until it feels cool to the touch, then loosen from the edges of the tin with the tip of a knife, and gently ease out. Store in an airtight container.

CHOCOLATE FEATHER SPONGE, LIQUEUR ICING

Freeze 3 months
Will keep 1 week under refrigeration

This cake is made only with potato flour and has an exceptionally tender texture and a rich chocolate flavour. It can be served plain with a dusting of icing sugar, or covered with the glossy liqueur icing.

4 oz (125 g/½ cup) unsalted butter	4 egg yolks
4 oz (125 g/½ cup) caster (superfine) sugar	1 teaspoon Passover baking powder
1 packet (10 g) vanilla sugar	2 oz (50 g/⅓ cup) potato flour
6 oz (175 g) plain (semi-sweet) Passover	4 egg whites
chocolate, broken in little bits	Pinch of salt

Preheat the oven to Gas No. 4, 350 degrees F, 180 degrees C. Grease the inside of an 8 in (20 cm) round loose-bottomed cake tin or an 8 in (20 cm) *moule à manqué* (French-style tin with sloping sides), and line the bottom with a circle of silicone paper.

In a small pan (or in a small basin if the microwave is used), melt the butter, then add the sugar, vanilla sugar and chocolate and melt gently together until smooth (2 minutes on full power in the microwave oven, stirring once). Stir in the egg yolks, the baking powder and the potato flour. Put the whites into a large bowl with the pinch of salt, and whisk until they hold stiff, glossy peaks, then use a rubber spatula to fold them gently but thoroughly into the chocolate mixture. When the colour is even, pour the cake mixture into the prepared tin and bake for 40–45 minutes, or until firm to gentle touch. Leave the cake, still in the tin, on a cooling rack for 5 minutes, then carefully ease out and leave until cold.

The liqueur icing Make the same icing as for the Sachertorte on page 261, but use only 4 oz (125 g) plain (semi-sweet) chocolate, 2 oz (50 g/¼ cup) butter and 1 tablespoon Passover liqueur. Pour this over the top or the bottom of the cake, whichever is the smoother.

Passover Preserves

● The making of **eingemachtes** — those thick and luscious fruit preserves made from beetroot, dried fruits or lemons — is one of the great traditions in the Passover preparations. I only hope it does not die out in this generation because of the ease of buying ready-made Passover jams. It was the custom in the past to offer a small dish of these preserves to eat with a spoon, together with a glass of 'Russian' tea. But nowadays it is more usual to serve it as a spread on matzot or crackers.

● The **apricot preserve** on page 279 can be made with the liqueur omitted, or replaced with Passover apricot brandy.

● The **lemon** and **lime curds** on pages 284-5 are delicious with matzot, but they can also be made into cake fillings by whisking 4 rounded tablespoons of the curd into twice the volume (a 5 fl oz (150 ml/⅔ cup) carton) of whipped cream.

● If you find all these recipes too sweet, and you have some unsweetened raspberries, strawberries or redcurrants in the freezer, then you can make either of the **uncooked jams** on page 281.

PRUNE EINGEMACHTES

Makes about 2 lb (1 kg)

Will keep for 1 year in a cool cupboard or the refrigerator

A true eingemachtes is not a jam in the usual sense, but whole or halved fruit suspended in a lightly set fruit jelly or syrup, which in this case is delicately flavoured with fresh lemon. If the prunes are tenderized and therefore need no soaking, add only ½ pint (275 ml/1¼ cups) of liquid to the pan.

½ lb (225 g/1¼ cups) jumbo prunes
1 pint (575 ml/2½ cups) water (to soak the prunes)
2 oz (50 g/½ cup) blanched and split almonds

2 large lemons plus an extra tablespoon of juice
1 lb (450 g/2 cups) granulated sugar

The night before you plan to make the preserve, cover the prunes with the water and leave to soak.

Next day, have ready four small jars washed, rinsed and put in a low oven, Gas No. ¼, 225 degrees F, 110 degrees C, to dry and heat. Also have ready four wax paper discs, and lids or cellophane circles to cover the jars. Remove the prune stones, and replace each with half an almond. Peel the lemons, remove all the pith, then slice, and cut each slice in half. Put the prunes and their soaking liquid into a 9 in (22 cm) heavy pan together with the sugar, lemon slices, juice and remaining almonds. Stir over gentle heat until the sugar dissolves, then cook uncovered at a fast boil until the syrup looks thick and viscous and a little will drop from the spoon in thick globules — it won't fall off in flakes like ordinary jam. (If it boils for too long and goes gluey, stir in a cupful of water, bring back to the boil and cook as before until **just** done.) Turn into the hot jars and cover with the wax paper discs. Cover with the lids when quite cold.

LEMON AND WALNUT EINGEMACHTES

Makes about 1 lb (450 g)

This is my mother-in-law's famous recipe; in her family it was always eaten with a spoon. Matzah crackers go with it exceptionally well; so does lemon tea.

4 oz (100 g/1 cup) walnut halves
12 oz (330 g/1½ cups) sugar

¼ pint (125 ml/⅔ cup) water
2 large lemons

Put the walnuts into a pan with enough cold water to cover, and bring to the boil. Stand for 1 minute, strain and set aside.

Remove the peel and pith from the lemons and reserve it; cut the lemon flesh into segments, reserving the membranes and pips. Tie up the lemon peel, pith, pips and membranes securely in a square of buttermuslin (cheesecloth).

Put the sugar and water into a large heavy-based pan and heat gently until the sugar has dissolved. Add the scalded walnuts, the lemon segments and the buttermuslin parcel. Boil gently, stirring from time to time, until setting point (see page 279) is reached; about 20 minutes. Remove the pan from the heat and take out the parcel. Allow to stand for 10 minutes, then put the preserve into small clean jars, previously warmed in the oven.

SHAVUOT

Milk, cheese and honey are the foods we enjoy at Shavuot, in celebration of the Giving of the Law to Moses on Mount Sinai. But this is also a festival of the spring harvest, rather quaintly known as 'The Time of the Giving of the First Ripe Fruits'. It is the custom to bring gifts of fruit and flowers to decorate the synagogue on the Eve of the Festival, and after the evening service, to enjoy cheesecakes, strudels and Israeli-style cheese dips before sitting down to read 'Tikkun leyl Shavuot' — passages from the Bible, the Talmud and Rabbinical writings — long into the night. Next day, a special 'dairy' breakfast of bagels, honey and cream cheese is served, to celebrate the giving of the dietary laws and the separation of meat from dairy foods.

CHEESE KNISHES

Makes 24

Freeze 3 months raw or cooked
Will keep 2 days under refrigeration

These tiny pastries are sometimes served as a soup accompaniment, at other times as a savoury mouthful to accompany a dairy meal. Knishes come in many flavours — including potato, chicken and meat — but at Shavuot they are naturally filled with a savoury soft cheese mixture. Many different doughs are used to make knishes, including a strudel dough and a kind of unsweetened biscuit (cookie) dough made with oil. But I prefer this flaky dough which can be made superbly well on the food processor.

THE PASTRY:
8 oz (225 g/2 cups) plain (all-purpose) flour
mixed with a pinch of salt
1 teaspoon icing (confectioners') sugar
5 oz (150 g/⅔ cup) firm butter or block
margarine, cut in 1 in (2½ cm) cubes
1 egg
1 teaspoon wine vinegar
1 tablespoon icy water
Further 1 oz (25 g/2 tablespoons) of firm
butter or margarine

THE FILLING:
Nut of butter

2 fat spring onions (green onions) including
some of the green, finely sliced
8 oz (225 g/1 cup) medium-fat curd cheese,
sieved cottage cheese or Quark
2 tablespoons chopped parsley
1 egg, beaten to blend (save 1 tablespoon for
glaze)
1 teaspoon salt; 15 grinds of black
pepper
Little soured cream or natural yoghurt

TO GLAZE:
1 tablespoon reserved egg
Sesame or poppy seeds

To make the pastry – to mix by food processor Put the dry ingredients and the 5 oz (150 g/⅔ cup) of fat cut in 1 in (2½ cm) cubes into the bowl. Whisk the egg, vinegar and water to blend, then sprinkle over the surface. Put on the lid, then pulse until the mixture is evenly moistened and looks like a crumble. Tip into a bowl and gather into a ball with lightly floured hands.

To mix by hand or electric mixer Sift the dry ingredients into a bowl and add the 5 oz (150 g/⅔ cup) of fat in cubes, then rub it in until no pieces larger than a small pea come to the surface when the bowl is shaken. Whisk the egg, vinegar and water to blend, sprinkle over the mixture in the bowl, then mix to a dough.

On a floured board, roll the dough mixed by either method into a rectangle about 12 × 6 in (30 × 15 cm) and spread the top two-thirds with little dabs of the extra 1 oz (25 g/2 tablespoons) of fat. Fold in three, as for flaky pastry, seal the ends and sides with the rolling pin, then gently flatten and roll out again. Fold in three once more, seal as before, then chill for at least 1 hour, or overnight. (The dough may also be frozen at this stage.)

To make the filling Heat the nut of butter and quickly sauté the onions until softened but not browned. Combine with all the other ingredients in a bowl and stir well to blend, adding the soured cream or yoghurt only if necessary — the mixture should be moist but thick enough to hold its shape.

To shape and fill the knishes Preheat the oven to Gas No. 7, 425 degrees F, 220 degrees C. Have ready two ungreased oven trays. Roll out the chilled pastry ¼ in (½ cm) thick and cut into 3 in (7½ cm) rounds with a plain cutter. Put a rounded teaspoon of the filling into the centre of each round, then fold into a half-moon and seal the edges. Arrange on the trays and brush with the beaten egg, then scatter with the sesame or poppy seeds. Bake for 15–20 minutes or until a rich brown. Cool for 15 minutes before serving, or reheat later.

FRUIT AND VEGETABLES IN LABNEH, ISRAELI STYLE

SERVES 8

Do not freeze
Any of the mixtures will keep under
refrigeration for 1 day

One of the more unusual delights of an Israeli breakfast, particularly in the big hotels, is to sample a variety of beautifully garnished dishes containing fruits and vegetables which have been mixed with a soft and creamy but slightly acid low-fat cheese made from yoghurt. I have given the recipe for making this cheese on page 169, but a reasonable facsimile can be made more quickly by blending any kind of soft cheese with yoghurt, 'smetana' or soured cream.

This is a joyous dish to serve for Shavuot, a worthy successor to the 'smetana and kaes' that my great-grandmother used to prepare for her little dairy in Manchester. First she would hang the curds and whey to drain in a pillowcase, then in true Lithuanian fashion, she would season the curds and put them in a muslin bag, to be pressed under a weight into a beautiful white cheese that tasted like solidified cream. Labneh has a pleasant texture of its own, however, and its content of fat is certainly more acceptable today than that of a rich cream cheese.

Arrange each flavour of the labneh in a pottery bowl or gratin dish, decorating the surface in a flower design made from strips of the different fruit or vegetable it contains. Serve at Shavuot breakfast either at the synagogue or at home, or as an accompaniment to a fish or dairy meal, or as part of a cheese board.

½ lb (225 g/1 cup) low-fat soft cheese,
cottage cheese processed until creamy, or
Quark

¼ pint (150 ml/⅔ cup) natural low-fat
yoghurt, smetana or soured
cream

Blend the cheese with enough of the yoghurt, smetana or soured cream to produce the consistency of softly whipped cream, then fold in any of the following fruits and vegetables, lightly seasoning the mixture to taste with salt and black pepper:

2 rings of fresh pineapple, finely diced, or
1 tablespoon finely diced green or red pepper,
with 1 medium pickled cucumber, or
2 in (5 cm) fresh cucumber, finely diced,

with 1 tablespoon chopped mint, or
2 tablespoons finely chopped spring onion
(green onion) including some green, with 1
tablespoon chopped parsley

CHERRY AND CREAM CHEESE STRUDEL WITH CHERRY BRANDY SAUCE

SERVES 8

Freeze leftovers 2 weeks
The strudel will keep 1 day, the sauce 4 days,
under refrigeration

This is an exquisite strudel, a true celebration of this happy Festival. The strudel is served warm or at room temperature, with either cherry brandy sauce or ice-cold soured cream. It can be reheated for 10 minutes in a moderate oven (*not* in the microwave, which makes it go soggy).

I have given full details of choosing and using fillo or strudel pastry on page 356. If you cannot buy this pastry, use puff pastry rolled paper-thin into a rectangle 14 in (35 cm) wide and about 14–16 in (35–40 cm) long.

6 sheets of fillo pastry, defrosted
2 or 3 oz (50–75 g/¼–⅓ cup) unsalted
butter, melted (melt the extra 1 oz (25 g/2
tablespoons) only if necessary)
1 can (15 oz (425 g)) pitted morello (sour
red) or black cherries
12 oz (350 g/1½ cups) curd or other low- or
medium-fat soft cheese
2 oz (50 g/¼ cup) caster (superfine) sugar
1 egg yolk
Grated rind of half a lemon
½ teaspoon vanilla essence (extract)
2 oz (50 g/1 cup) fresh breadcrumbs

1 oz (25 g/2 tablespoons) butter
1 oz (25 g/¼ cup) flaked almonds
Little melted butter
1 tablespoon granulated sugar, mixed with 1
tablespoon flaked almonds

THE SAUCE:
5 fl oz (150 ml/⅔ cup) cherry syrup (from
can)
2 teaspoons cornflour (cornstarch) mixed
with 1 tablespoon each lemon juice and
water
1 tablespoon cherry brandy

Preheat the oven to Gas No. 5, 375 degrees F, 190 degrees C. Have ready a lightly oiled baking sheet. Drain the cherries (reserving the syrup) and lay them on kitchen paper (paper towels) to absorb any moisture.

Mix together the cheese, sugar, egg yolk, lemon rind and vanilla. Melt the 1 oz (25 g/2 tablespoons) butter, add the crumbs and almonds and fry gently until golden-brown. Allow to cool.

Have ready six sheets of pastry, covered with a teatowel. Lay one sheet of pastry on a second teatowel and, with a pastry brush, paint the top surface very thinly with melted butter. Lay the next sheet on top, brush with butter, and repeat for each sheet in turn, stacking them one on top of the other until you have a pile of six. Leaving 2 in (5 cm) of pastry bare on the edge nearest to you, spread the *third* of pastry nearest to you with *half* the buttered nut and crumb mixture. On top of this mixture lay the cheese filling in a strip about 2 in (5 cm) wide. Lay the cherries on top of the cheese, and cover them in turn with the remaining crumbs.

Now lift up the teatowel and roll the bare pastry near you on to the filling, then turn in the sides and roll up the strudel. Place it, seam down, on the baking sheet. Paint it all over with a little more melted butter and scatter with the flaked almonds mixed with the granulated sugar. Bake for 20–25 minutes, or until golden-brown. (It doesn't take as long as Apfelstrudel does, as the cherries are already cooked.)

To make the cherry brandy sauce Put the cherry syrup into a small pan and bring to the boil. Stir in the cornflour mixed with the lemon juice and water, bring to the boil and bubble for 3 minutes or until the sauce looks clear. Stir in the cherry brandy. Serve warm or cold.

CREAM CHEESE STRUDEL IN FLAKY PASTRY

Makes 2 strudels about 14 in (35 cm) long
SERVES 12–14

Freeze 2 months
Will keep under refrigeration for 3 days

This is a very traditional strudel, perhaps a little more 'homely' in taste and texture than the one made with fillo pastry. Although the pastry is home-made, the strudel itself is very easy to prepare. It should be served warm, rather than hot, and can be reheated either in a moderate oven or in the microwave. Slice the strudel just before serving. Remember that the pastry needs to be chilled overnight before it is rolled out.

1 quantity of Soured Cream Flaky Pastry (page 359) formed into only two blocks and chilled overnight

THE FILLING:
1 lb (450 g/2 cups) medium- or full-fat cream cheese
1 oz (25 g/2 tablespoons) soft butter
1 egg

3–4 tablespoons caster (superfine) sugar, depending on the acidity of the cheese
Juice and grated rind of half a lemon
1 teaspoon vanilla essence (extract)
1 tablespoon cornflour (cornstarch)
4 tablespoons raisins

FOR DREDGING THE STRUDELS:
Sifted icing (confectioners') sugar

To prepare the filling Beat all the ingredients together until the mixture is smooth (this can be done at the same time that you make the pastry, and the filling left to mature overnight).

To complete the strudels Preheat the oven to Gas No. 6, 400 degrees F, 200 degrees C. Have ready two ungreased baking trays. Work on one block of chilled pastry and half the filling at a time. Roll the pastry into a *very* thin rectangle about 16 in (40 cm) wide and 9 in (22 cm) long — the pastry is very easy to roll. Leaving the 2 in (5 cm) of pastry nearest to you bare, arrange the filling in a band 2 in (5 cm) wide, leaving 1 in (2½ cm) of pastry bare of filling along each side. Fold in these sides, then fold the bare pastry nearest to you over the filling, then roll up like a flattened Swiss roll. You will now have a centre of filling surrounded by layers of very thin pastry. Lay the strudel on a tray, join down.

Make another strudel with the remaining pastry and filling in the same way. Prick them both all over with a fork. Bake for 10 minutes, then turn the heat down to Gas No. 4, 350 degrees F. 180 degrees C, and bake for a further 20–25 minutes, or until golden-brown. Leave for 5 minutes on a cooling tray, then sift an even layer of icing sugar over the top.

343

ALMOND AND LEMON CHEESECAKE

SERVES 8–10

Freeze 2 months
Will keep 3 days under refrigeration

This is my 'revised' version of the old-fashioned Russian-style cheesecake, baked in a pastry case with a good, solid filling made from home-made 'kaes'. I have lightened the filling with additional eggs, sharpened the rather bland taste of today's commercial 'kaes' with lemon juice, and added some ground almonds to enrich the flavour. The cake looks particularly splendid when it is made in a loose-bottomed flan tin about 1½ in (4 cm) deep, with sloping sides. Serve at room temperature or slightly warm, but it is not pleasant when chilled.

THE PASTRY:
6 oz (175 g/1½ cups) self-raising flour
4 oz (125 g/½ cup) butter or margarine
2 oz (50 g/½ cup) icing (confectioners') sugar
1 egg yolk and 1 tablespoon water (reserve the white)

THE FILLING:
¾ lb (350 g/1½ cups) low- or medium-fat soft cheese
2 oz (50 g/½ cup) ground almonds
1 oz (25 g/2 tablespoons) soft butter

2 oz (50 g/¼ cup) caster (superfine) sugar
2 tablespoons lemon juice
Grated rind of half a lemon
½ teaspoon vanilla essence (extract)
5 tablespoons sultanas (white raisins)
3 eggs

TO DECORATE THE CAKE:
1 tablespoon granulated sugar
1 oz (25 g/¼ cup) flaked almonds

To make the pastry, put all the ingredients into a bowl and work together until a dough is formed. Chill for 30 minutes. Preheat the oven to Gas No. 4, 350 degrees F, 180 degrees C. Have ready either a 9–10 in (22–25 cm) loose-bottomed flan tin about 1 in (2½ cm) deep, or an 8 in(20 cm) tin about 2 in (5 cm) deep, with sloping sides. Roll out the pastry on a lightly floured board to fit the tin, easing it in gently so as not to stretch it. Chill the pastry case while you prepare the filling.

Separate the egg whites from the yolks. Put the yolks and all the remaining ingredients (except for the sultanas) into a bowl and mix until thoroughly blended. Whisk the whites with a pinch of salt until they hold stiff glossy peaks, then carefully fold into the cheese mixture. Stir in the sultanas, then pour into the unbaked flan case.

Take the egg white left over from the pastry and whisk with a fork until frothy. Paint it over the cheese mixture, then sprinkle with the granulated sugar. Scatter the almonds. Bake the larger flan for 40 minutes; bake the smaller, deeper flan for 20 minutes, then turn the oven down to Gas No. 3, 325 degrees F, 160 degrees C and bake for a further 30 minutes. In either case, the cheesecake is ready when it is a pale gold colour and firm to gentle touch round the edges. (The filling continues to set as it cools.)

MALLAI ROMANIAN CHEESECAKE

SERVES 10

Freeze 1 month
Will keep under refrigeration 3 days

This very unusual Shavuot dish only survives, as far as I know, amongst Romanian-born Jews living in Israel. It is made with maize flour (corn meal) and can best be described as a sweetened form of 'mamaliga' — the Romanian equivalent of the Italian polenta — which is thought to have been brought to that part of Europe by the occupying Roman legions. Like all peasant dishes it is very easily made, with a satisfying texture and hearty flavour — the complete antithesis of the fluffy modern American-Jewish cheesecake.

Maize flour is generally sold in health food stores. The dish is served warm, either fresh from the oven or reheated, accompanied by a little more soured cream.

5 oz (150 g/1 cup less 2 tablespoons) fine maize flour (corn meal)
4 oz (125 g/½ cup) caster (superfine) sugar
Pinch of salt
3 packets (10 g/2 teaspoons each) vanilla sugar

1 lb (450 g/2 cups) medium-fat soft cheese or Quark
1½ 5 oz (150 g/⅔ cup) cartons soured cream (8 fl oz (225 ml/1 cup)) in all
2 large eggs
2 oz (50 g/¼ cup) butter or margarine

Preheat the oven to Gas No. 5, 375 degrees F, 190 degrees C. Have ready an ungreased rectangular oven casserole or baking tin approximately 10 × 8 × 2 in (25 × 20 × 5 cm).

Beat all the ingredients except the fat together until smooth, then spoon into the oven dish. Dot with tiny flakes of the butter or margarine. Bake for 45 minutes, or until golden-brown. Serve in squares.

LOGANBERRY AND SOUR CREAM TORTE

SERVES 10

Freeze 1 month but only leftovers — flavour and texture deteriorate
Will keep 2 days under refrigeration

'It can't work,' I thought when I first read this recipe. But then I had proof of this particular pudding when it was served at a dinner party, and for once 'quick and easy' really gives the best results. This pale pink cloud of fruit and cream makes a superb dessert for a Shavuot supper party.

THE BASE:
8 oz (225 g/16 biscuits) digestive biscuits
(graham crackers) or other semi-sweet
biscuits (cookies)
2 oz (50 g/4 tablespoons) butter, melted
1 teaspoon cinnamon

THE FILLING:
4 x 5 oz (150 ml/²⁄₃ cup) cartons soured
cream

6 oz (175 g/¾ cup) caster (superfine)
sugar
1 can (15 oz (425 g)) choice loganberries or
raspberries, well drained

THE TOPPING:
½ pint (275 ml/1¼ cups) whipping cream
1 oz (25 g/¼ cup) grated or flaked
chocolate

Preheat the oven to Gas No. 4, 350 degrees F, 180 degrees C. Grease a 9in (22½ cm) loose-bottomed tin at least 2 in (5 cm) deep. Crumb the biscuits either with a rolling pin or in the food processor. Mix in the cinnamon and moisten with the butter, then pat in a firm layer on the bottom of the tin.

To make the filling Process all the ingredients in a blender or food processor until smooth and evenly mixed. Pour into the tin and bake for 20 minutes — the centre will still be a little soft. Cool away from draughts.

To make the topping Whip the cream and fold in the flaked or grated chocolate. Pipe or spoon on top of the torte, then chill overnight. To unmould, stand the cake tin on a canister with a smaller diameter and gently pull down the sides, then transfer (still on the base) to a serving dish. Serve very cold.

ROSH HASHANAH

At the approach of a new year, people of every religion serve culinary tokens of hope for the future, and Jewish cooks are no exception. So the Tsimmes and the Tagine must be fruitier, the honey cake spicier, the apple cake sweeter than at any other time during the year. And for the second night of the Festival, there must be very special food, with a special prayer of thanks for the gift of life and the bounty which permits us to sit round the table with our families and to enjoy a Happy New Year.

NEW YEAR CHALLAH

Makes 2 medium loaves

*Freeze baked 3 months, or shaped and ready
for baking for 2 weeks
Will keep 3 days at room temperature in a
bread container*

Sweet on the tongue and light as air under a high-baked crust, the special challot baked in honour of the New Year are not plaited in the usual way but wound in a spiral, reaching symbolically towards heaven, the better to bear our hopes for a happy New Year. The baking of this bread used to be a traditional task in every Jewish kitchen on the eve of the New Year, but today it's usually left to the master bakers of the community! But if you have a mixer with a dough hook, the method is so easy — and the reward of taking the golden loaves from the oven is so great — that it's a 'mitzah' not to be missed.

In the 'old' days it would take 20 minutes to knead the dough by hand until it became like a springy silken ball. Today it takes just 5 minutes with a dough hook, and the bread will still have the same fine texture, almost like that of cake. The dough seems to make the very best bread if it can be left to rise slowly overnight as described in the recipe, but if time is short it can be allowed to rise in a warm kitchen, where it will take about 2 hours. Alternatively the bread can be shaped ready for the oven and then frozen until it is convenient to defrost it as described on page 24, before baking it as though it were newly prepared.

11 fl oz (300 ml/1⅓ cups) warm water
1½ lb (675 g/6 cups) white strong (bread) flour
1 oz (25 g/2 cakes) fresh yeast or 1 sachet easy-blend yeast
2 oz (50 g/¼ cup) sugar or 2 rounded tablespoons honey
1½ teaspoons salt

5 tablespoons oil
2 large eggs

TO GLAZE:
1 egg yolk mixed with 1 teaspoon water and good pinch of salt
Poppy seeds or sesame seeds

Attach the dough hook to the mixer, then put the water into the mixing bowl, followed by a third of the flour, the crumbled yeast and the sugar or honey. Mix until smooth, about 2 minutes, then cover with a teatowel and leave for 10 or 15 minutes, until it has frothed up. Add all the remaining ingredients for the dough.
(If you use easy-blend yeast Omit the preliminary mixing and rising. Mix the yeast thoroughly with the other dry ingredients, then add all the remaining ingredients to the bowl.) Now mix at low speed until a sticky ball begins to form, then turn to medium speed, and knead for 4 or 5 minutes until the dough is slapping against the edges of the bowl, leaving it clean as it goes round. If it looks sticky after this time, work in a further 1 or 2 tablespoons of flour.

Tip the dough on to a floured board and knead with the hands for a further minute until it is tight and springy with a silky feel. Grease a large bowl with oil, turn the dough in it to coat it (this stops the surface drying out), cover with clingfilm (saran wrap) and leave to rise in the refrigerator. If it rises before you have time to deal with it (it takes from 9 to 12 hours, but can be left for up to 24 hours), punch it down and leave it to rise again.

To shape the loaves Take the risen dough from the refrigerator and leave it to come to room temperature in the kitchen — about 1 hour. (Or put it on the DEFROST cycle of the microwave oven for 2 minutes, until warm to the touch.) Divide the dough in two and work on each half (to make 1 loaf) as follows: knead the dough by hand or machine for 2 minutes to break down any large bubbles of gas, then leave for 5 minutes to tighten up again under a cloth. Roll into a 'snake' about 18 in (45 cm) long, and 1½ in (3 cm) in diameter. Take the left-hand end of the 'snake' and start coiling it round on itself, making a spiral, so that when all the dough has been wound, the end you started with will be on top and the right-hand end can be tucked underneath. Repeat with the second piece of dough.

To prove and bake the loaves Arrange the loaves on one large or two smaller lightly greased trays, then slip the trays(s) into a large plastic bag and leave until the loaves have almost doubled in size, feel light and puffy to the touch and spring back immediately when lightly dented with the finger. This takes 30 or 40 minutes. Meanwhile, preheat the oven to Gas No. 7, 425 degrees F, 220 degrees C. Mix together the yolk, salt and water for the glaze, then paint the mixture all over the risen loaves and scatter with the seeds. Bake for 25 minutes, then turn the oven down to Gas No. 6, 400 degrees F, 200 degrees C for a further 10 to 15 minutes, or until the bread is a rich brown. Lift the loaves off the tray and tap the bottom. If the bread sounds hollow take them out. Otherwise turn them on their sides and leave them in the oven for another 5 minutes before removing to a cooling tray.

CHOPPED HERRING WITH CHERRY BRANDY

SERVES 8

Freeze 2 months
Will keep 3 days under refrigeration

The wooden chopping board and 'hackmesser' (hand chopper) my mother-in-law once used to make her chopped herring are now prized exhibits in a Jewish folk museum, and the very special texture of this wonderful dish can now be obtained equally well and with far less labour using a food processor — though truth to tell, most people buy it ready-made from the local delicatessen. But on special occasions — for breaking the fast or serving in the Sukkah — it's worth making this elegant version to serve on fingers of challah or black bread.

If you cannot get traditional salt herrings from the barrel, either use well-rinsed commercial pickled herring fillets (also known as rollmops) or soak fresh herring fillets in a salt-and-water brine (2 oz (50 g/¼ cup) salt to a pint (575 ml/2½ cups) water) for 2 hours, then treat as salt herring fillets.

6 salt herrings, soaked, filleted and skinned (see below)
1 medium (5 oz (150 g)) onion, peeled and cut in 1 in (2½ cm) chunks
2 medium (5 oz (150 g)) tart cooking apples (Bramley variety if available), cored, peeled and cut in 1 in (2½ cm) chunks
2 level tablespoons ground almonds

6 large eggs, hard-boiled, shelled and cut in half (reserve one yolk for garnish)
2 digestive (graham crackers) or Marie (semi-sweet) biscuits (cookies)
2 teaspoons 33% acetic acid
2 teaspoons caster (superfine) sugar
6 teaspoons cherry brandy
Pinch of white pepper

The day before you plan to make the dish, cut the head off each herring, slit the body and clean out well. Put the fish in a large glass casserole and leave under the cold water tap with the water running in a gentle trickle. Turn off the tap after an hour and leave the herrings, covered in cold water, in the refrigerator overnight.

Next day, lift them into a colander and drain well, then lay them on a board. Slit the skin down the centre back, peel it off from both sides. Flatten the back of each herring with the palm of the hand, then turn it over and lift out the centre bone. Cut each herring into rough 1 in (2½ cm) chunks.

On the processor pulse the onion until finely chopped, then remove it; chop the apple in the same way, then remove that also. Put the chunks of herring, the halves of hard-boiled eggs, the ground almonds and the biscuits into the machine with the acetic acid, sugar and cherry brandy. Pulse until finely chopped. Return the apple and onion to the machine, pulse briefly to blend, taste and re-season if necessary. Pile the chopped herring into a dish about 1 in (2½ cm) deep, cover with clingfilm (saran wrap) and chill.

Just before serving, sieve the remaining egg yolk over the top.

ADAFINA FROM GIBRALTAR

SERVES 8

Freeze 3 months
Will keep 3 days under refrigeration

The Adafina (or 'Dfina' as it is known outside Gibraltar) is the Sephardic version of the Ashkenazi Cholent — the Shabbat casserole which every Jewish community in the world has made, each to their own particular recipe, since the time of the Bible. It was particularly prized among North African Jews, who had a saying that 'un Sabbat sans dfina est comme un roi sans ville', and the village women in Morocco, Tunisia and Algeria would spend every Friday afternoon heating a special clay oven in which a *marmite* full of Dfina was left to cook from sundown until Saturday lunch.

In Gibraltar, however, it was the custom to send the Adafina to be cooked in the local baker's oven, and until recently every Saturday saw a procession of boys and family maids walking down Main Street, carrying steaming saucepans wrapped in blankets, for the ritual family lunch. Today, however, the Adafina is considered a special treat, at least by those Gibraltarians who, like the daughter of the family to whom this cherished recipe belongs, are now living in the West. She in fact only prepares it for special guests, or for festivals like Rosh Hashanah.

Adafina is a hearty, rib-sticking, extremely tasty dish, which turns a beautiful copper colour during its long stay in the oven. Connoisseurs particularly relish the 'hamine' eggs (a word derived, I wonder how long ago, from the Hebrew word 'ham' meaning 'hot') which are cooked in the heart of the Adafina still in their shells.

8 oz (225 g/1 cup) dried chick peas (garbanzo beans) soaked for 24 hours in 2 pints (1¼ litres/5 cups) cold water
3 tablespoons sunflower oil or corn oil
2 large (8 oz (225 g)) onions, thinly sliced
3 lb (1½ kg) piece of brisket or top rib
2 tablespoons ground paprika pepper
6 oz (175 g/¾ cup) long-grain rice, cooked in 15 fl oz (425 ml/2 cups) water seasoned with 1 teaspoon salt and ¼ teaspoon ground nutmeg

20 teaspoons salt; 20 grinds black pepper
1 teaspoon each cinnamon, allspice (pimento), chilli powder and brown sugar
6 oz (175 g/¾ cup) barley rinsed in cold water, then drained
1 whole head of garlic, unpeeled
8 raw eggs in their shells, well washed
8 medium potatoes, peeled
Boiling water

The day before they are required, put the chick peas to soak in the cold water — they will swell to three times their size. Start to prepare the Adafina 1½ hours before commencement of Shabbat (or if for a weekday Festival meal, whenever convenient the evening of the day before) — it needs at least 12 hours in the oven. You will need a 1 gallon (4½ litres/20 cups) capacity ovenproof pan or casserole.

Heat the oil gently in the pan, add the onions and fry slowly until a rich golden-brown. Rub the meat with the paprika pepper, then fry it briskly to seal on all sides. While it is browning, bring the water and seasonings for the rice to the boil in a small heavy pan. Add the rice, cover and simmer for 15 minutes until the water has been absorbed and the rice is barely tender. Wrap carefully in aluminium foil and prick all over with a fork so that the flavours from the Adafina can penetrate (or the rice can be wrapped in muslin (cheesecloth) in the traditional way). Mix together the salt, pepper, cinnamon, allspice, chilli powder and brown sugar.

Now start adding all the remaining ingredients to the pan, putting them around and on top of the meat and sprinkling each layer with some of the mixed seasonings. The eggs and the rice should be buried in the middle and the potatoes arranged on top. Add just enough boiling water to cover the potatoes, then cover the pan and bring to the boil on top of the stove. Simmer gently for 30 minutes, then transfer to a very slow oven (Gas No. ¼, 225 degrees F, 110 degrees C) and leave untouched until lunchtime the next day.

To serve Lift the meat on to a plate — it will be meltingly tender and practically falling apart like a French *daube* — and cut it into serving portions. Arrange the meat, potatoes and shelled eggs on a large platter on a bed of chick peas, barley and gravy. Serve the rice separately.

MOROCCAN LAMB AND PRUNE TAGINE

SERVES 6–8

Freeze 2 months
Will keep 3 days under refrigeration

This meat dish is served at Rosh Hashanah by Moroccan Jews for the same reason that Jews from Russia and Poland prepare their 'pflaumen tsimmes' — the dried fruits and honey it contains are symbols of hope for sweetness in the coming year. Jews of Moroccan descent never serve this on the Eve of the Festival but only on the second night, as according to their folk wisdom nothing black — like a prune — may be associated with the lightness and brightness of the first day of the New Year.

To make a traditional Tagine, a shoulder of lamb on the bone is cut up into small pieces and the stew is then simmered on top of the stove. I prefer to use boned meat, and to cook the Tagine in the oven where it needs far less attention. It's pleasanter to eat if the prunes are stoned, but if this cannot be done without them losing their shape, the dish will look better if the stones are left in. To get the correct dark colour and deep flavour, it is important to caramelize the onions by cooking them until they are a rich brown. The Tagine can be served from the casserole, or arranged in a large entrée dish.

1 very large (10 oz (225 g)) onion, finely
chopped
2 tablespoons sunflower or corn oil
2½–3 lb (1¼–1½ kg) boneless shoulder of
lamb, cut in 1 in (2½ cm) chunks
1–2 teaspoons salt; 15 grinds black pepper
1 teaspoon ground cinnamon

½ teaspoon ground coriander
¼ teaspoon ground ginger
1½ pints (850 ml/4 cups) hot water
½ lb (225 g/1¼ cups) dried prunes plus 1
teabag, or ¾ lb (350 g) packet
tenderized prunes
1 rounded tablespoon honey

GARNISH:
2 oz (50 g/½ cup) whole almonds, blanched
and toasted (optional)

Preheat the oven to Gas No. 3, 325 degrees F, 160 degrees C. If possible use a deep
oven casserole that can also be used to brown the meat on top of the stove.

Heat the oil in the casserole (or use a heavy frying pan) and sauté the onion until it
is soft and golden. Add the meat (in two batches if necessary so as not to crowd the
pan) and continue to cook until the meat is a golden-brown and the onions are an
even deeper colour. Sprinkle on the salt, pepper and spices, and cook, stirring, for a
further 2 minutes to release their aroma, then cover with the hot water. Bring to the
boil, then transfer to the oven. Cover and cook for 30 minutes then turn the heat
down to Gas No. 2, 300 degrees F, 150 degrees C, and cook for a further hour until
the meat is tender and the liquid has reduced to a rich sauce.

Meanwhile put the dried prunes in a bowl and cover with hot tea made with the
teabag. Leave for 30 minutes or until you can ease out the stone. (You can remove the
stones from tenderized prunes without having to soak them first.)

When the meat is tender, add the stoned prunes and the honey, then stir well, and
add another cup of boiling water if the liquid in the casserole has reduced too far.
Leave the dish in the oven for a further 20 minutes to cook the prunes. Serve
sprinkled with the nuts, if liked.

LEKACH FOR TODAY

Makes 1 loaf cake

Freeze 3 months
Will keep 1 month in an airtight container

Honey, spices and oil are the traditional ingredients for this cake, which has been
baked in celebration of the New Year ever since Ezra brought the Jews back from
Babylon in the fifth century B.C.E. That early 'lekach' was probably more like bread
than cake, as the only known raising agent at that time was yeast. The modern
version is lightened with bicarbonate of soda (baking soda) and eggs, which make it
moist and spongy, but it is still made with the same three ingredients Jewish
housewives have been using for more than two thousand years.

This is a particularly moist lekach, whose flavour is enhanced with ginger preserve
as well as the usual powdered spice. The cake rises at least 1 in (2½ cm) in the oven,
so to prevent the mixture bubbling over the sides, it is important to use the specified
size of tin. As it does not need maturing for more than a day, you can make it at any
time up to the Eve of the Festival, storing it well wrapped in foil. It can easily be

351

mixed by hand, but the ingredients can also be combined in an electric mixer or a large-capacity food processor.

To serve the lekach, cut it into slices ½ in (1 cm) thick and then into fingers.

9 oz (250 g/2¼ cups) self-raising flour or 9 oz (250 g/2¼ cups) plain (all-purpose) flour plus 2 teaspoons baking powder
2 teaspoons ground ginger
1 teaspoon cinnamon
½ lb (225 g/¾ cup) clear honey

4 fl oz (125 ml/½ cup) oil
3 oz (75 g/⅓ cup) soft dark brown sugar
1 egg
¼ lb (125 g/⅓ cup) ginger preserve
6 fl oz (175 ml/¾ cup) hot water mixed with ¼ level teaspoon bicarbonate of soda (baking soda)

Preheat the oven to Gas No. 2, 300 degrees F, 150 degrees C. Grease a 2 lb (1 kg) loaf tin measuring approximately 9 × 5 × 3 in (about 22 × 12 × 7 cm) and line the bottom and the two ends with one long strip of silicone paper.

Sift the flour and the spices into a bowl. Put the honey into another bowl, then add the oil, sugar, egg, preserve and half the flour mixture. Stir until smooth, then add the remaining flour mixture and the hot water mixed with the bicarbonate of soda, stirring until the batter is thoroughly blended — it will be very thin. Pour carefully into the tin. Bake for 1½–1¾ hours or until the top is springy to gentle touch and a skewer comes out clean from the centre. Place on a cooling tray and leave until cool.

LEKACH, ISRAELI STYLE

Makes 1 cake, to serve about 30

Freeze 3 months
Will keep 2–3 weeks wrapped in foil in an airtight container

If you travel to Israel over the New Year period you will be offered a slice of this celebration cake on your El Al plane, as this is the recipe used by their chefs. It is not a traditional lekach, but has the fine texture of a Madeira cake with a gentle flavour of honey and spice. To achieve that special texture it's best made by the creaming method — in any case, the quantity of mixture is too great for even the largest size of domestic food processor. Leave it to mature for at least a day or, better still, a week.

11 oz (300 g/2¾ cups) plain (all-purpose) flour
1 teaspoon baking powder
1 teaspoon each ground ginger and cinnamon
10 oz (275 g/1¼ cups) soft butter or margarine
7 oz (200 g/1 cup) caster (superfine) sugar

6 eggs
2 oz (50 g/½ cup) ground almonds
5 oz (150 g/½ cup) honey
3 oz (75 g/¼ cup) treacle (molasses) or golden syrup (corn syrup)
2 oz (50 g/½ cup) blanched, flaked or slivered almonds)

Preheat oven to Gas No. 3, 325 degrees F, 160 degrees C. Grease a tin measuring either 11 × 8 × 3 in (about 27 × 20 × 7 cm) or 12 × 10 × 2 in (30 × 25 × 5 cm), and line the bottom with silicone paper.

Sift together the flour, baking powder and spices and mix in the ground almonds.

In an electric mixer or by hand, cream the fat until it is the consistency of mayonnaise, then gradually beat in the sugar, creaming until the mixture is fluffy and light. Whisk the eggs to blend the yolks and whites, then gradually add to the creamed mixture, adding a little of the flour mixture after each addition to prevent the mixture curdling. Beat in the honey and treacle (or golden syrup), then gently fold in the remaining flour mixture. Pour in the tin, smooth level with a spatula, then scatter with the flaked or slivered almonds. Bake for 1¼–1½ hours in the deeper tin, 50–60 minutes in the shallower one, or until the surface springs back when lightly touched with the finger and the cake is a pleasant even brown. Put the tin on a cooling rack and leave for 10 minutes, then turn out the cake. Wrap in foil when cold. For the recipe for a lekach cooked in the microwave oven, see page 33.

CINNAMON APPLE SPONGE SQUARES

Makes 20

Freeze 3 months
Will keep 3 days under refrigeration

It was on the west coast of America that I first tasted these delectable fruit squares, which had been baked by a Jewish baker in an unfashionable sea-side resort, but I had to go to Israel to find the recipe. I suspect, however, that it is really of Russian origin, as oil was widely used there in the nineteenth century to make 'parev' cakes before the invention of vegetable oil margarine. Tart apple slices, spiced with cinnamon, are sandwiched between layers of moist yet fine-textured sponge cake.

The squares can be served warm with ice cream or cinnamon-flavoured yoghurt as a dessert, or covered with a brown sugar and walnut topping and passed round for afternoon tea.

THE CAKE:
4 eggs
10 oz (275 g/1¼ cups) caster (superfine) sugar
8 fl oz (225 ml/1 cup) any vegetable oil
8 oz (225 g/2 cups) self-raising flour
1 teaspoon vanilla essence (extract)

THE FILLING:
2¼ lb (1 kg) baking apples (2 lb (0.9 kg) weight when cored and peeled)
4 tablespoons granulated sugar mixed with 1 teaspoon cinnamon

TOPPING IF SERVED AS A DESSERT:
2 tablespoons granulated sugar

TOPPING IF SERVED AS A CAKE:
Scant 2 oz (50 g/¼ cup) melted butter or margarine
Scant 2 oz (50 g/½ cup) walnuts, coarsely chopped
1 teaspoon cinnamon
3 oz (75 g/⅓ cup) soft light brown sugar

Preheat the oven to Gas No. 4, 350 degrees F, 180 degrees C. Grease a tin measuring approximately 9 × 13 in (22 × 32 cm) across the top and 1½ in (3 cm) deep.
First prepare the filling Core and peel the apples, slice them on a food processor or grate them very coarsely, then mix thoroughly with the cinnamon sugar.

353

To make the sponge This can be done either with an electric whisk or in a large-capacity food processor.

To mix by electric whisk Whisk the eggs and sugar until thick and lemon-coloured, then mix in the oil followed by the flour and vanilla essence.

To mix by large food processor Process the eggs and sugar for 1 minute, until no grains of sugar can be felt in the mixture. Pulse in the oil to blend, then pulse in the flour and vanilla essence until the mixture is smooth and even.

Pour half the sponge mixture into the prepared tin, smoothing it well into the corners with a rubber spatula. Lay the apple filling on top in an even layer, then cover it with the remainder of the sponge mixture. If the squares are to be served as a *dessert*, sprinkle the top of the batter with the granulated sugar. Bake for 55 minutes or until well risen and firm to gentle touch in the centre. If it is to be served as a *cake* bake in the same way (omitting the sprinkled sugar topping), leave the baked cake to cool for 10 minutes, brush with the melted butter or margarine, then sprinkle with the walnuts mixed with the cinnamon and brown sugar. Grill (broil) gently for 2 minutes, then allow to go cold. Cut in squares or fingers as required.

SUKKOT

As they wandered in the wilderness for 40 years, our ancestors were forced to live in makeshift huts — the 'sukkot' — from which this Festival gets its name. Yet for us, it is a very special joy to enter the flower-scented Sukkah, and to recite together the blessing over the bread and the wine. Then it's time to enjoy a platter of stuffed vegetables and strudels, filled to bursting with the good fruits of the earth.

STUFFED AUBERGINES IN THE TURKISH STYLE

SERVES 6–8

Freeze 3 months
Will keep 3 days under refrigeration

The tradition of stuffed vegetables for Sukkot is a common bond between the Ashkenazi and the Sephardi communities. In Turkey, where a Jewish community of mainly Sephardic origin has lived for more than 400 years, the chosen vegetable is the aubergine which can vary in colour from snow white (hence its American name of 'eggplant') through palest pink to the more familiar dark purple variety grown in the West. When I visited a Jewish home in Istanbul, I saw great copper pans of these stuffed vegetables, which are simmered for hours to develop a succulent texture and rich, mellow flavour.

The stuffed aubergines are served at room temperature as an appetizer, so this is a good dish to come home to, after the Sukkot service. The slower the dish is cooked the better, and a day in the refrigerator will intensify the flavour. Serve on individual plates with a little of the sauce spooned over and around each aubergine half, and thick fingers of challah to mop up the delicious juices.

3 or 4 oval aubergines (eggplant), weighing
8–10 oz (225–275 g) each

THE FILLING:
2 medium onions, very thinly sliced
4 tablespoons oil
Scooped-out aubergine flesh, finely chopped
2 cloves of garlic, peeled and crushed
1 can (15 oz (425 g)) tomatoes in juice
½ teaspoon salt; 15 grinds of black pepper
2 teaspoons brown sugar

½ teaspoon ground allspice (pimento) or
cinnamon
4 tablespoons currants
2 tablespoons chopped parsley

THE COOKING LIQUID:
4 tablespoons olive oil made up to ¼ pint
(150 ml/⅔ cup) with water
1 teaspoon salt
1 teaspoon brown sugar
2 tablespoons lemon juice
2 bayleaves
1 clove of garlic, peeled and halved

Cut the prickly stalk end from each aubergine, then cut it in half lengthwise. Use a
spoon to scoop out the flesh, leaving a shell ½ in (1 cm) thick all the way round, then
chop the flesh fairly finely with a knife or food processor. Heat the oil in a heavy
frying pan, and cook the onions over moderate heat until soft and golden. Add the
aubergine flesh to the pan and cook, covered (except to stir occasionally), until it is
meltingly tender — about 10 minutes. Uncover and add all the remaining filling
ingredients, then cook briskly without the lid, stirring until the mixture is thick but
juicy.

Preheat the oven to Gas No. 3, 325 degrees F, 160 degrees C. Select a roasting tin
large enough to hold the aubergine halves side by side. Lay them in this tin and
divide the filling between them. Mix all the ingredients for the cooking liquid, then
pour it round them. Cover the tin with foil and cook for 1½ hours, turning the oven
lower if the liquid is bubbling too quickly around the aubergines. Baste them with the
liquid and cook uncovered for a further 30 minutes. Leave, covered, in a cool place
overnight.

APFELKUCHEN SQUARES

Makes 24 squares

Freeze 3 months
Will keep 3 days under refrigeration

A very thick layer of apple slices is sandwiched between a sponge base and a crunchy
walnut topping. The kuchen is so simple and uncomplicated to make that it can
easily be prepared on a large scale in a synagogue kitchen to serve for Kiddush in the
Sukkah. If the squares are served at home, they can be briefly reheated either in a
microwave or in a quick oven.

You will find another version of Apfelkuchen, made with a yeast dough, on
page 277.

8 oz (225 g/2 cups) self-raising flour
6 oz (175 g/¾ cup) soft margarine or butter
4 oz (125 g/½ cup) caster (superfine) sugar
Grated rind of half a lemon
3 eggs
2 lb (1 kg) baking apples (weight when peeled
and cored), thinly sliced
3 rounded tablespoons granulated sugar

2 tablespoons lemon juice
2 rounded tablespoons apricot jam

TOPPING:
2 oz (50 g/¼ cup) demerara (brown) or
golden granulated sugar
2 oz (50 g/½ cup) walnuts, finely chopped

Preheat the oven to Gas No. 4, 350 degrees F, 180 degrees C. Grease a tin measuring approximately 12 × 8 × 1½ in (30 × 20 × 4 cm).

Put the flour, fat, caster sugar, lemon rind and eggs into a bowl and beat by hand, mixer or food processor until smooth. Take two-thirds of the mixture and spread it thinly over the base of the tin. Arrange the sliced apples in an even layer on top, sprinkle with granulated sugar and lemon juice and dot with the jam. Drop the remaining cake mixture in teaspoonfuls all over the apple filling and put in the oven.

After 10 minutes, open the oven, quickly smooth the blobs of cake mixture over the top of the apples with a large fork, then sprinkle evenly with the mixed nuts and sugar. Close the oven and bake for a further 30 minutes, or until the cake is golden-brown and the apples feel tender when pierced with a sharp knife.

Cut into 2 in (5 cm) squares to serve.

ALL ABOUT FILLO AND STRUDEL PASTRY

These are both paper-thin pastries which are used to make Middle Eastern delicacies such as the Baklava Slices on page 359 and Austrian specialities such as the Cherry and Cheese Strudel on page 341. As they are made in a very similar way and with almost identical ingredients, they are completely interchangeable, and may be sold either as 'fillo' or 'strudel', so for the present purpose I shall consider them as one. The pastry is still made by hand by some very skilled pastry chefs, as well as by a dwindling band of Jewish cooks from Austria and Hungary who can still remember how their mothers used to make it. If you didn't learn its mysteries at your mother's knee, however, it's a far more satisfactory option to buy one of the commercial packs which are sold at speciality food shops and delicatessens, as well as at some of the more 'up-market' supermarkets.

This is a fascinating pastry to use, and requires no special skill, but as it behaves in a rather different way from more familiar pastries such as shortcrust, here are a few guidelines on choosing and using it.

● **How it's sold:** Usually in 1 lb (450 g) packs, containing approximately 16 sheets which vary in size between the different brands, but are usually either 14 or 16 in (35 or 40 cm) square.

● **How to store it:** The pastry is usually frozen before it leaves the factory, but as the distribution network isn't always as sophisticated as with more well-established foods, it may be defrosted by the time you get it home. If it is not to be used within the next few days, refreeze it at once — it will keep for up to a year. For more immediate use, it can be stored in the refrigerator for a maximum of 6 days. After that it may develop mildew and will have to be thrown away.

● **How to defrost it:** As the sheets of pastry cannot be separated while they are frozen, they will need to be completely defrosted before you can use them, so leave the packet in the refrigerator overnight, or at room temperature for 2 hours. In an emergency the pastry can be defrosted for 3 minutes in a microwave oven, and then left at room temperature until it feels pliable — between 45 minutes and 1 hour. If only part of a packet is used, the remainder should be tightly resealed with freezer tape and either refrozen at once, or refrigerated and then used within 6 days.

• **When it's in good condition:** Each sheet will feel slightly moist and can be screwed up in the hand like tissue paper without cracking or breaking. But if it feels dry and brittle the moment you take it from the pack, or if some of the layers are 'glued' together, then it's probably been subjected to fluctuations in temperature before you bought it and it will be most unsatisfactory to use, so take it back to the shop and get it replaced. Don't worry about the white powder that can be seen between the sheets, however — this is only a dusting of cornflour to stop them sticking together.

• **Protecting the pastry from the air:** As it contains only a tiny amount of vegetable oil or fat, the pastry starts to dry out the moment it is exposed to the air. So as soon as you take any of the sheets from the packet, put them under a teatowel and keep them there until you're ready to brush them with a protective layer of fat.

• **The role of fat:** This produces the wonderful flakiness for which this pastry is famed, as well as stopping the sheets of pastry from drying out. You can use unsalted butter or margarine or (for some savoury dishes) oil. Any salt present in the fat that is brushed on will make the pastry brown unevenly, so if you cannot get any unsalted fat and have to use a salted butter or margarine, be sure to discard any of the salty residue that sinks to the bottom after it has been melted.

• **The amounts of fat:** You will need far less than you think — just enough to coat each sheet of pastry with a very thin layer. Use a 1 in (2½ cm) pastry brush to do this, wielding it as though applying a coat of paint, and removing any puddles of fat from the surface of the sheet. If the fat is applied sparingly in this way you can achieve a result similar to puff pastry, but using only half the quantity of fat. However, it is essential to brush every surface of the pastry that is exposed to air, particularly if it is not to be cooked at once but stored in the freezer or the refrigerator.

• **Storing raw and cooked pastries:** Raw pastries (well coated with fat) keep well under refrigeration — see individual recipes for the exact length of time. Cooked pastries, unless they are soaked with syrup like the Baklava Slices, tend to crumble at very low temperatures, so they are better refrigerated and used up within the recommended storage time.

• Then **is it worth all the trouble?** Yes indeed, because as long as you take suitable precautions and treat it with care, you will find this classic pastry will provide an 'open sesame' to some of the most exquisite dishes in the culinary repertoire.

AUSTRIAN APFELSTRUDEL

SERVES 8–9

Do not freeze as it tends to crumble
Will keep 3–4 days under refrigeration, but reheat before serving

Purists may quibble, but I have managed to reduce the amounts of both fat and breadcrumbs — and also increased the amount of fruit — in this delectable version of the classic dessert. Whatever the width of your brand of pastry, overlap two pieces to make one sheet about 24 in (60 cm) wide. The strudel is nicest served in 2 in (5 cm) wide slices, thickly sprinkled with icing (confectioners') sugar. It may be reheated in the oven, but it tends to go soggy in the microwave.

8 sheets of fillo pastry, defrosted
4 oz (125 g/½ cup) unsalted butter or
margarine, melted

THE FILLING:
5 oz (150 g/⅔ cup) granulated sugar
1 teaspoon ground cinnamon

Rind of 1 lemon, finely grated
1½ lb (675 g) baking apples, cored, peeled
and coarsely grated or thinly sliced
3 oz (175 g/½ cup) raisins, sultanas (white
raisins) or chopped dates
2 oz (50 g/½ cup) walnuts or hazelnuts
(filberts), coarsely chopped
2 oz (50 g/1 cup) fresh breadcrumbs

Preheat the oven to Gas No. 5, 375 degrees F, 190 degrees C. Grease a large oven baking tray with oil. Mix together the sugar, cinnamon and lemon rind in a large bowl, then mix in the apples and dried fruit, coating them with the cinnamon sugar (this is best done just before the filling is required, otherwise juice may ooze out of the fruit and make the pastry soggy).

Lay a teatowel on the table, open the packet of pastry, remove eight sheets and lay them on top of the teatowel, then cover with another towel. Take two of the sheets, place them on a board and overlap them by about 4 in (10 cm), to make one sheet 24 in (60 cm) wide. Brush this sheet very sparingly with the melted fat, then lay the next two sheets, overlapping, on top and brush them with fat in the same way. Continue in the same way with the remaining four sheets, brushing the last two also with fat.

Sprinkle the half of the pastry nearest to you with half the crumbs and nuts, leaving a strip 3 in (7½ cm) wide clear at either side. Arrange the apple filling in a band about 3 in (7½ cm) wide in the centre of the crumb mixture, then sprinkle it with the remainder of the nuts and crumbs. Fold the edge of the pastry nearest to you over the apples, then fold in the uncovered 3 in (7½ cm) strip on either side. Brush these strips with fat, then roll the pastry up into a strudel with a slightly flattened rather than a rounded contour, and with the join underneath. Carefully transfer the strudel to the baking sheet, and brush it all over with a thin layer of fat (too much will stop it browning evenly). Make diagonal slashes, about 2 in (5 cm) apart, through the top layers of pastry.

Lay a piece of greaseproof (waxed) or silicone paper on top, then bake for 40 minutes, when the pastry should be golden and a small knife pushed through one of the slits will go right through the filling — if it is not ready give it another 5 minutes.

ISRAELI NÜSSE STRUDEL

Makes 4 strudels, cutting into about 36
slices

Freeze 3 months
Will keep 3 days in an airtight container, 1
week in the refrigerator

The fat is *cut* rather than rubbed into the flour to make this unusual pastry, which can be rolled out paper-thin to make a crisp and flaky case for the delicious nut filling. Although the soft dough needs to be chilled well overnight, it then becomes extremely easy to handle. The filling can be made at the same time as the pastry, then left to mature until next day. Fresh pecans were used to make the filling when I first tasted this strudel in Israel, but I have made it very successfully at home using walnuts instead.

THE PASTRY:

12 oz (350 g/3 cups) self-raising flour or 12 oz (350 g/3 cups) plain (all-purpose) flour plus 3 teaspoons baking powder
7 oz (200 g/¾ cup plus 1 tablespoon) firm margarine or butter, cut in 1 in (2½ cm) chunks
5 fl oz (150 ml/⅔ cup) soured cream

THE FILLING:

8 oz (225 g/2 cups) walnuts or pecans, coarsely chopped
3 oz (75 g/½ cup) raisins

4 oz (125 g/½ cup) granulated sugar
1 scant tablespoon thin honey
2 teaspoons grated lemon rind

FOR SPREADING ON THE DOUGH:

Apricot or another tart jam

TO GILD THE STRUDEL:

1 egg yolk mixed with 1 teaspoon cold water

To make the pastry Mix the flour with the chunks of fat and rub in or pulse until the particles of fat are the size of a hazelnut (filbert) kernel. Tip into a bowl and mix to a dough with the soured cream — the bits of fat should be visible as in rough puff pastry. Divide into four, form each piece of dough into a little block about ½ in (1 cm) thick, then wrap in foil and refrigerate overnight.

To make the filling Mix all the ingredients together to form a slightly tacky mixture, cover, and leave.

To prepare the strudels Preheat the oven to Gas No. 6, 400 degrees F, 200 degrees C, and have ready two ungreased oven trays. Roll out each portion of pastry in turn, on a lightly floured board to make a rectangle about 11 in (27 cm) wide and 6 in (15 cm) long. Spread the dough with a thin layer of jam, leaving ½ in (1 cm) clear all the way round, then sprinkle it with a quarter of the filling. Turn in the ends and roll up, then lay, join side down, on the tray. Repeat with the remaining three pieces of dough and the rest of the nut filling.

Prick the strudels all over with a fork, brush them with the yolk-and-water mixture, then bake for 10 minutes. Turn the heat down to Gas No. 4, 350 degrees F, 180 degrees C, and bake for a further 25 minutes or until the strudels are a rich brown. Carefully transfer to a cooling tray and allow to go cold. Cut the strudels into slices just before serving them, either plain or with a dusting of icing (confectioners') sugar.

BAKLAVA SLICES

Makes 18 slices

Freeze 3 months
Will keep 1 week under refrigeration

Those Jewish families whose history is rooted in the Middle East — Syria in particular — still make great trays of Baklava filled with a luxurious mixture of ground nuts and spices in celebration of Sukkot, just as Ashkenazi cooks stuff their strudels with other good things such as apples and dried fruits. This is an interesting variation of the traditional recipe — the filling is encased in pastry which is then rolled like a strudel, instead of being sandwiched between the layers in the more familiar way. The slices are very easy to prepare with commercial fillo or strudel pastry, and when they are soaked in a fragrant citrus blossom syrup, they make a memorable end to a Sukkot meal. Citrus blossom water (also known as 'orange flower water') is sold by chemists and some delicatessens, but lemon juice can be used instead.

8 sheets of fillo pastry (about ½ lb (225 g)), 12–14 in (30–35 cm) wide, defrosted
4 oz (125 g/½ cup) (approximately) unsalted butter or margarine (for a meat meal)

1½ oz (35 g/3 tablespoons) caster (superfine) sugar
½ teaspoon ground cinnamon
2 teaspoons citrus blossom water

THE FILLING:
4 oz (125 g/1 cup) walnuts
4 oz (125 g/1 cup) blanched almonds
1 egg white

THE SYRUP:
½ lb (225 g/1 cup) granulated sugar
6 fl oz (175 ml/¾ cup) water
1 tablespoon lemon juice
1 teaspoon citrus blossom water

Grease a roulade or Swiss roll tin about 12 × 8 ×1 in (30 × 20 × 2½ cm). Preheat the oven to Gas No. 3, 325 degrees F, 160 degrees C.

To make the filling Process or grind the nuts separately as they are of different degrees of hardness. They should *not* be ground as fine as commercial ground nuts, but should be more like coarse sand. Whisk the egg white until it holds stiff peaks, then whisk in the sugar a teaspoonful at a time. Add it to the nuts, add the cinnamon and citrus blossom water, and mix to a coarse paste.

To make the Baklava rolls Open the packet of pastry and take out eight sheets. Immediately re-seal the packet and refreeze at once (or refrigerate, then use within 5 days). Cover the pastry immediately with a teatowel to prevent it from drying out. Melt the butter or margarine, then butter the top of each piece of fillo in turn, laying them on top of each other until you have a stack of eight sheets. Spread three-quarters of the top of this pastry, stack with the filling, leave the quarter of pastry furthest away from you quite bare, then roll up into a tight 'Swiss roll', finishing with the join underneath. Cut the roll into 18 slices each rather more than ½ in (1 cm) thick, then lay the slices side by side without touching in the tin, brushing the tops and sides lightly with butter. Bake for 30 minutes, then turn up the heat to Gas No. 7, 425 degrees F, 220 degrees C and bake for a further 10 minutes until the slices are golden-brown.

To prepare the syrup Do this as soon as the Baklava Slices go into the oven as it must be allowed to cool to room temperature. Put the sugar and water into a medium-sized pan and heat, stirring, until the sugar has dissolved. Add the lemon juice and bubble gently for about 12 minutes until the syrup will thickly coat the back of a wooden spoon, then stir in the citrus blossom water and leave — as it cools it will thicken to the consistency of thin honey. When the Baklava Slices come out of the oven, leave them in the tin for 5 minutes to cool, then pour the syrup over them and allow it to soak in for 2 hours, basting once or twice. Serve at room temperature with the bottom of each roll to the top.

HANUKKAH

We gather round the great Hanukkiah in the synagogue and sing the famous hymn of praise, 'Maoz Tzur', but the real celebrations for this happy family Festival only start when we get home and get out the frying pan — after all, how can you fry latkes for a whole congregation? The famous victory of Judah Hamaccabee must not be celebrated with any common fare — nothing less will do than Potato Latkes for the Ashkenazim and cheesy Sambusak for the Sephardim, followed by rich puddings capped with wine sauces, and Sufganiyot — doughnuts — bursting with jam.

CHEESE AND POTATO LATKES

Makes 14 latkes   *Freeze 4 months*

These are quite delicious, with an intriguing flavour. For a recipe for traditional potato latkes, see page 14.

2 large potatoes
1 large egg
½ level teaspoon each baking powder and
salt

Pinch of white pepper
2 tablespoons plain (all-purpose) flour
6 oz (175 g/1½ cups) very finely grated
cheese

Grate the potatoes very finely, by hand or in a food processor, then turn into a sieve and leave to drain for 15 minutes. Whisk the eggs with the seasonings, then stir in the rest of the ingredients. In a large frying pan put oil to the depth of ½ in (1½ cm). When you can feel a comfortable heat on your hand held 2 in (5 cm) above it, put tablespoons of the mixture into the oil, flattening each latke with the back of a spoon so it will cook evenly. Fry at a steady bubble until a rich brown, then turn and fry the second side. Do not attempt to turn the latkes too soon or they may stick to the pan.
To freeze Cook the latkes as above, but only until they are a pale brown on each side. Drain thoroughly, then open-freeze. When firm, put in plastic bags.
To reheat Either put the frozen latkes in hot deep fat and fry for 2 or 3 minutes until a rich brown, *or* fry in shallow fat as above for 2 or 3 minutes on each side until a rich brown. Drain and serve.
To reheat latkes for a party Defrost the latkes for 1 hour on a foil-covered baking sheet, then reheat at Gas No. 8, 450 degrees F, 230 degrees C for 7 or 8 minutes until crisp and hot.

RÖSTI FOR HANUKKAH

SERVES 4–5   *Freeze 3 months*

The Swiss may call their famous dish 'rösti', but anyone can see it is really a monster potato latke! It requires far less pan-watching and uses much less oil than individual latkes and provided that it is cooked steadily until crispy brown on both sides, I think it is equally delicious. It can be reheated and crispened after freezing by thawing at room temperature for 1 hour, and then reheating in an ungreased non-stick pan for 5 minutes on each side. However, it is at its best eaten hot off the pan, as a light supper dish or to accompany cold roast chicken or meat.

2½ lb (1 kg) potatoes (weight before peeling)
(a waxy chipping variety if possible)
Sunflower oil or corn oil to come to a depth
of ¼ in (½ cm) in the frying pan

1 oz (25 g/2 tablespoons) butter (or
margarine for a meat meal)
Salt, black pepper and nutmeg
1 extra tablespoon oil

Have ready a heavy 8 in (20 cm) frying pan. Peel the potatoes but leave them whole. Put in a pan of cold, unsalted water, cover and bring slowly to the boil, then boil for 6 minutes or until they can be pierced with a knife but are still firm. Drain and allow them to go quite cold. Use a coarse grater with ½ in (1½ cm) holes or the coarse grater of a food processor to grate them into a bowl.

Put the oil and the solid fat into the pan and heat until the butter (or margarine) has melted and the foam has subsided. Immediately put in the grated potatoes and pat them into an even layer, pushing the edges together to form a cake that just fills the pan. Cook over a moderate heat until the bottom of the potatoes is a rich brown — not less than 7 minutes.

Sprinkle the top of the Rösti with a little salt, black pepper and grated nutmeg, then sprinkle it with 1 tablespoon of oil. Lay a plate of slightly larger diameter on top of the pan, then turn the pan over so that the Rösti is on the plate, cooked side up. Carefully slide it back into the pan so that the uncooked side is to the bottom. Continue to cook slowly but steadily for a further 5 to 7 minutes until the second side is equally brown. Slide on to a hot plate and serve, cut in wedges like a cake.

TWO SAUCES FOR HANUKKAH STEAMED PUDDING
A recipe for Hanukkah Pudding can be found on page 20.

WEINCHADAU

SERVES 6–8   Do not freeze

This is a famous German-Jewish sauce which is similar to a Zabaglione. The addition of a pinch of arrowroot or cornflour (cornstarch) helps the sauce to keep its mousse-like texture. It is best made just before serving, however — it only takes 3 or 4 minutes with a strong hand or a portable electric whisk.

3 egg yolks
3 oz (75 g/⅓ cup) caster (superfine) sugar
½ teaspoon arrowroot, potato flour or
cornflour (cornstarch)

5 fl oz (150 ml/⅔ cup) sherry or medium-
sweet white wine, such as hock
1 tablespoon brandy or liqueur

Put the egg yolks and sugar into a basin or the top of a double saucepan and whisk by hand or electric whisk until pale and mousse-like. Whisk in the arrowroot (or potato flour or cornflour) and wine. Stand the basin (or pan) over a pan of simmering water and whisk constantly until the mixture becomes thick and foamy. Remove from the heat, add the liqueur or brandy and whisk for another 2 minutes. Serve at once.

FRESH LEMON SAUCE

SERVES 6–8   *Do not freeze*

A beautiful golden sauce with a fresh fruit flavour.

1½ tablespoons cornflour (cornstarch)
4 tablespoons cold water
8 fl oz (225 ml/1 cup) boiling water
Rind of 1 lemon, finely grated

Juice of 2 lemons (5 tablespoons)
3–4 oz (75–125 g/⅓–½ cup) caster
(superfine) sugar
1 egg yolk
Nut of butter or margarine

Put the sugar, boiling water and lemon rind into a pan over moderate heat. Gradually add the cold water to the cornflour, then add this liquid together with the lemon juice, to the pan. Bring to the boil and simmer for 3 minutes until clear. Put the egg yolk in a small basin, and stir in about a quarter of the hot sauce. Return to the pan and cook, stirring, until steaming. Remove from the heat, then mix in the butter (or margarine), stirring well.

SUFGANIYOT ISRAELI-STYLE DOUGHNUTS

Makes 24   *Freeze raw 1 month, cooked 3 months*
                              Will keep fresh 2 days under refrigeration

These jam-filled doughnuts are eaten in Israel at Hanukkah instead of the more familiar latkes. They are a fascinating example of today's developing synthesis of Sephardi and Ashkenazi food customs — a happy result of the increasing rate of intermarriage between the two cultures. For sweet fritters soaked in syrup have long been part of the Sephardi tradition, whilst fritters filled with jam — or doughnuts — were often eaten at Hanukkah in many pre-war Jewish communities in Europe; the oil in which both are fried provides the common symbol of the Festival. This particular version is of Hungarian origin, and like all .the sweet things from that particular cuisine, it is rich with butter and eggs.

As the Sufganiyot freeze extremely well, it's worth making a large batch. Otherwise, simply halve all the ingredients but still use 1 oz (25 g/2 cakes) fresh yeast. Eat some of the Sufganiyot on the day they are made — although they stay quite fresh for up to 2 days in the refrigerator. Alternatively, as they freeze extremely well, take them from the freezer as they are required, and reheat either in the microwave or uncovered in a moderate oven.

1 oz (25 g/2 cakes) fresh yeast or 2 sachets
easy-blend yeast
10 fl oz (275 ml/1¼ cups) warm milk
1 teaspoon sugar
4 egg yolks
1 oz (25 g/2 tablespoons) caster (superfine)
sugar
1 lb (450 g/4 cups) plain white (all-purpose)
flour

Pinch of salt
4 oz (125 g/½ cup) very soft butter
Oil for deep-frying
Tart jam such as apricot or blackcurrant
Caster (superfine) sugar for coating the
doughnuts

Put the fresh yeast (if used), 2 fl oz (50 ml/¼ cup) of the warm milk and the 1 teaspoon sugar into a bowl, stir well, then leave to rise for 10 minutes. Put into the mixer bowl with all the remaining ingredients.

(If you use easy-blend yeast Omit the preliminary rising. Mix the yeast thoroughly with the other dry ingredients, then add all the remaining ingredients to the bowl.) Now beat everything together for 5 minutes, until the very soft dough looks smooth, shiny and elastic and will leave the sides of the bowl and the beater clean — this can be done with a wooden spoon or your hand, but it's hard work! Leave in the bowl, covered with clingfilm (saran wrap), and allow to rise until double in bulk, about 1½ hours.

Turn out on to a floured board and if the dough is at all sticky, work in a little more flour so that it is soft but easily rolled out. Roll out this dough to ⅜ in (1 cm) thick and cut into rounds about 2 in (5 cm) across. Leave the rounds on the board, covered with a teatowel, and let them rise until puffy, about 20 minutes.

Have ready a pan one-third full of oil, or a deep-fryer, heated to 360 degrees F, 170 degrees C (when a cube of bread browns in 40 seconds) — it should not be quite as hot as for fried fish. Fry the doughnuts in batches, leaving room for them to swell. They should be covered until the first side has browned — about 4 minutes — then uncover, turn them over and allow the second side to brown, then lift out and drain well on kitchen paper. Make a little slit in each doughnut and insert a teaspoon of the jam, then roll in the caster sugar.

PURIM

To celebrate the foiling of the plot to exterminate the Jews of the Persian Empire in the fifth century B.C.E. joy is supposed to be unconfined, and this is the only time in the year when Jews are encouraged to drink — so much that they can't tell the difference between Mordechai, the hero, and Haman, the villain of the story.

In former days, the women of the 'shtetl' would get together in one another's homes to bake 'Hamantaschen' — three-cornered pastries that are such a delicious feature of this Festival. Today, many synagogues hold communal 'bake-ins' instead. Then, on the Eve of the Festival, a blessing is recited over special sweetened raisin bread and the whole congregation can enjoy the Hamantaschen, which strangely are only eaten on this one occasion during the year.

KALISCHBROD   PURIM BREAD

*Makes 1 large loaf, or 1 smaller loaf plus 6
large Hamantaschen*

*Freeze 3 months
Will keep fresh 2 days under refrigeration*

This special challah which is used to make 'hamotzi' (a blessing) over, at the Purim meal, is half-way between a bread and a kuchen — it is probably a descendant of the 'artologanus' or 'cake bread' made by the bakers of ancient Rome. The dough is mixed with raisins which have been steeped in water to plump them up; very observant Jews do not mix the dough with this water or it would be classified as 'mezones' — a yeast dough mixed with raisin water which the Rabbis classify as cake, and it could not then be used to make a blessing for *bread* at the meal (yet another example of the maze of complexities facing a Jewish cook!).

When Jewish village life was at its height in the nineteenth century, the women would vie with each other in making elaborately plaited Purim bread which they would take to the baker's oven — one of my friends remembers his mother making a twelve-strand plait, with a five-strand plait on the top! No domestic oven today can accommodate bread of that size, which was probably made with 3 lb (1¼ kg/12 cups) of flour — nor do most of us have a large enough family to eat it. So from one batch of dough I have made a Purim bread and a batch of Hamantaschen as well. Although this is a traditional recipe, it has been modernized so that it can be made easily with the assistance of a dough hook and a refrigerator — the chilling seems to give it a better texture as well as making it easier to handle.

THE DOUGH (PAREV):

*1½ lb (675 g/6 cups) plain white (all-
purpose) flour*
1½ teaspoons salt
*1½ oz (40 g/3 cakes) fresh yeast or 2 sachets
easy-blend yeast*
3 oz (75 g/⅓ cup) caster (superfine) sugar
2 eggs
*9 fl oz (250 ml/1 cup plus 2 tablespoons)
warm water*
*3 oz (75 g/⅓ cup) lukewarm melted
margarine*

FOR THE BREAD ONLY:

2 oz (50 g/⅓ cup) raisins

THE GLAZE:

1 egg yolk
1 teaspoon water
2 tablespoons poppy seeds or sesame seeds

Fix the dough hook on the mixer and put the flour and salt into the bowl. Make a well in the centre and crumble in the fresh yeast (if used), then cover it with a tablespoon of the surrounding flour. Put the sugar on top and the unbeaten eggs at the side. Turn on the mixer, then add the water alternately with the margarine, kneading with the dough hook until the dough leaves the sides of the bowl clean and looks smooth and shiny — about 4 minutes.

(If you use an easy-blend yeast Mix the yeast with the flour and salt in the bowl, then add all the remaining ingredients, turn on the mixer and knead to a dough as described.)

Turn the dough out on to a floured board and knead by hand for 30 seconds. Place the dough in a large, lightly oiled bowl and then turn it over to coat it with a thin film of oil (this will stop it drying out). Cover the bowl with clingfilm (saran wrap) and refrigerate for at least 3 hours (or overnight) during which time the dough will double in size. While the dough is rising, cover the raisins with boiling water and leave them to plump up. Turn the risen dough on to a floured board and knead for 1 minute, then cut it in half. Use half to make the Purim bread and set half aside for Hamantaschen.

To make the Purim bread Take half the dough and knead in the well-drained raisins, then divide equally into four. Flatten each piece with the fist, then roll it up into a little Swiss roll. Flatten and roll up again, then form into a ball. Take each ball and roll into a 9 in (22 cm) strand that tapers slightly at each end. Make a four-stranded plait as shown on page 186. Seal the end nearest to you, then roll the plait over on its side to improve its shape.

Arrange the plait on a greased oven tray, slip into a large plastic bag and leave in the kitchen for 1 hour or until spongy to the touch. Meanwhile, preheat the oven to Gas No. 5, 375 degrees F, 190 degrees C. Brush the loaf with the yolk-and-water glaze, scatter with poppy or sesame seeds and bake for 25 to 30 minutes, or until a rich brown.

To make Hamantaschen The filling can be made when the dough is rising in the refrigerator, as it must be cold when it is used.

FILLING FOR HAMANTASCHEN

4 oz (125 g/1 cup) whole or ready-ground poppy seeds
4 fl oz (125 ml/1 cup) water
1 oz (25 g/2 tablespoons) margarine
2 oz (50 g/¼ cup) sugar
1 rounded tablespoon golden syrup (corn syrup) or honey
2 oz (50 g/⅓ cup) raisins
1 teaspoon vanilla essence (extract)

Grind the whole poppy seeds in a nut or coffee mill until they are of the consistency of ground almonds. Put into a pan with all the remaining ingredients, and simmer for 5 minutes, stirring all the time, until a thick paste is formed. Leave to go cold.

Divide the second half of the dough into six equal pieces and knead each piece into a ball. Roll each ball into a circle ¼ in (½ cm) thick, then spread with the filling and bring the edges of the circle together to form a triangle (see diagram). Seal the edges well, then arrange well apart on a greased tray. Place the tray in a plastic bag and leave until puffy, about ½ hour.

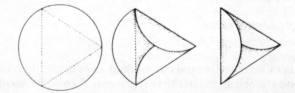

Remove from the bag, then bake at Gas No. 5, 375 degrees F, 190 degrees C, for 25 minutes. Brush the hot Hamantaschen with a thin coating of golden syrup or honey. Serve in slices, either plain or buttered.

FRUITY HAMANTASCHEN

Makes 18 small Hamantaschen

Freeze 3 months
Will keep 2 days under refrigeration

These spongy little Hamantaschen are filled with dried fruits instead of poppy seeds. This is an uncomplicated dough which can easily be mixed with a strong right hand or with an electric mixer — it is a little too soft to mix in a food processor, as it tends to make the motor labour.

THE DOUGH:

1 oz (25 g/2 cakes) fresh yeast or 1 sachet
easy-blend yeast
2 tablespoons boiling water mixed with 4
tablespoons cold milk (4 fl oz (125 ml/½ cup)
in all)
¾ lb (350 g/3 cups) plain (all-purpose) flour
2 eggs, beaten to blend
3 oz (75 g/⅓ cup) butter, melted, then cooled
to lukewarm
3 oz (75 g/½ cup) caster (superfine) sugar
Rind of half a lemon, finely grated
½ teaspoon salt

THE FILLING:

2 oz (50 g/¼ cup) butter, melted
3 oz (75 g/⅓ cup) caster (superfine) sugar, 1
teaspoon ground cinnamon and 3 oz (75 g/½
cup) mixed dried fruit, mixed together

THE GLAZE:

Honey, golden syrup (corn syrup), or 4
tablespoons milk plus 1 tablespoon sugar,
warmed together

Into the mixing bowl put the fresh yeast (if used), milk and water, a quarter of the flour and 2 teaspoons of the sugar. Beat until a smooth batter is formed after a minute, then cover with a teatowel and leave for 10 minutes or until it has frothed up. Beat in the eggs, the melted butter, the rest of the sugar and flour, the grated lemon rind and the salt. Beat for 4 minutes, by which time you will have an elastic batter which leaves the beaters or a wooden spoon quite clean without any stickiness when pulled away. If it is still a little sticky (perhaps the eggs were very large) beat in 1 or 2 tablespoons of extra flour.

(If you use easy-blend yeast Mix the yeast with the flour, sugar and salt in the bowl, then add all the remaining ingredients, turn on the mixer and beat to a dough as described.) Cover the mixing bowl with clingfilm (saran wrap) and leave in the kitchen to rise for 1½ hours or until the dough has doubled in bulk and will spring back when lightly touched with the finger.

Turn on to a lightly floured board and knead for a minute or two, to redistribute any large bubbles of gas that might spoil the texture. Divide the dough into eighteen equal pieces, and knead each piece in turn into a little ball, then roll it out into a small circle ¼ in (½ cm) thick. Spread the circle of dough with some melted butter, then arrange a spoonful of the sugared dried fruit on top. Draw up the circle into a three-cornered shape like a tricorne hat (see diagram opposite). Arrange the Hamantaschen on lightly greased oven trays, leaving room for them to expand. Slip each tray into a large plastic bag and leave for another30 minutes or until puffy again.

Meanwhile, preheat the oven to Gas No. 4, 350 degrees F, 180 degrees C. Bake the

Hamantaschen for 20 minutes, or until a rich brown. As they come out of the oven, brush them with a thin layer of honey or golden syrup or with the milk-and-sugar syrup. Eat the same day, or refrigerate or freeze until required.

QUICK HAMANTASCHEN WITH A BRANDIED FRUIT FILLING

Makes about 30

Freeze 3 months
Will keep fresh for 4 days in an airtight container

These little pastries are made in the traditional Romanian-Jewish style with a crisp *muerberteig* (a continental-style shortcrust pastry) instead of a yeast dough. The filling should be matured for at least 2 days, but it will keep for at least 6 months under refrigeration. These pastries keep fresh longer than yeast Hamantaschen do, and can be refreshed by warming either in a moderate oven or in the microwave.

THE FILLING:
¾ lb (425 g/2 cups) mixed dried fruit
1 apple (5 oz (150 g)), peeled and grated
2 oz (50 g/¼ cup) walnuts, coarsely chopped
1 oz (25 g/2 tablespoons) soft brown sugar
1 tablespoon each ginger marmalade (ginger preserve) and warm golden syrup
½ teaspoon each cinnamon and mixed spice
Pinch of ground nutmeg
Grated rind and juice of half lemon
1 tablespoon each brandy and kosher or port-type wine
1½ oz (40 g/3 tablespoons) melted butter or margarine

THE PASTRY:
¼ lb (125 g/1 cup) each self-raising and plain (all-purpose) flour
3 oz (75 g/⅓ cup) butter or margarine
2 oz (50 g/¼ cup) white fat
1 level tablespoon icing (confectioners') sugar
2 tablespoons water
1 egg yolk

THE GLAZE:
1 egg white
Granulated sugar

To make the filling Combine all the ingredients in the order given. Leave in a covered bowl for 2 days to mature.

To make the pastry Cut the fats into 1 in (2½ cm) cubes. By hand or by machine, rub them into the flour until the mixture looks like breadcrumbs, add the sugar, then mix to a dough with the yolk blended with the water. Knead lightly until smooth, then chill for 30 minutes.

To bake the Hamantaschen Preheat the oven to Gas No. 6, 400 degrees F, 200 degrees C. Have ready two ungreased oven trays. Roll the pastry out ¼ in (½ cm) thick on a board lightly dusted with icing sugar and cut into 3 in (7½ cm) circles, gathering up the trimmings and rerolling and cutting until all the pastry has been used. Put a spoonful of filling on each circle and draw up to form a triangle, pinching the edges firmly together in the shape of a tricorne hat (see diagram on page 248). Arrange on the trays.

Whisk the egg white until frothy, then paint all over the Hamantaschen and sprinkle with granulated sugar. Bake for 20 minutes, or until golden-brown. Allow to cool.

HUNGARIAN MOHN STRUDEL
POPPYSEED STRUDEL

*Makes 6 strudels each about 12 in (30 cm)
long*

*Freeze 3 months
Will keep fresh for 4 days under refrigeration*

This is a traditional Hungarian recipe using a delicious beaten yeast pastry thinly rolled to make a very luscious strudel stuffed with poppy seeds. When it is very fresh it can be eaten plain; later it can be thinly sliced and buttered.

*15 fl oz (425 ml/2 cups) lukewarm milk
2 oz (50 g/4 cakes) fresh yeast or 2 sachets
easy-blend yeast
1 egg yolk
6 oz (175 g/¾ cup) soft butter
4 oz (125 g/½ cup) caster (superfine) sugar
1½ lb (675 g/6 cups) plain (all-purpose)
flour
2 teaspoons salt*

THE FILLING:
*½ lb (225 g/2 cups) ground or whole poppy
seeds*

*8 fl oz (225 ml/1 cup) milk
4 oz (125 g/½ cup) caster (superfine) sugar
(or to taste)
Rind of 1 lemon, finely grated
6 oz (175 g/1 cup) raisins or sultanas (white
raisins)*

TO SPREAD ON THE DOUGH:
*1½ oz (40 g/3 tablespoons) melted butter
Tart jam such as damson or 'povidl'
(continental plum preserve)*

GARNISH:
Sieved icing (confectioners') sugar

To make the dough This is best made with an electric mixer or wooden spoon, as it is rather too soft to use a dough hook. Put the warm milk and the fresh yeast (if used) in the mixing bowl and stir until the yeast has dissolved. Add all the remaining ingredients.
(If you use easy-blend yeast Mix the yeast with the flour, caster sugar and salt in the bowl, then add all the remaining ingredients.) Now beat until the dough is smooth and stretchy and can be pulled away from the beaters leaving them almost clean. This will take about 5 minutes. Tip the dough out of the bowl, grease the bowl with oil, then put the dough back in and turn it to cover it lightly with oil. Cover with clingfilm (saran wrap) and leave in a warm kitchen until it has doubled in volume, about 1½ hours.
To make the filling If the poppy seeds are whole, grind them in a nut or coffee mill until they are like ground almonds, then put them in a pan with all the remaining ingredients. Bring to the boil, stirring, then bubble for 5 minutes until the filling is thick but juicy. Allow it to go cold.
To assemble the strudel Tip the risen dough on to a floured board and knead with the hands for 2 minutes, then divide into six equal pieces (weighing approximately 8 oz (225 g) each). Knead each piece into a ball. Roll each piece into a rectangle, ⅛ in (¼ cm) thick and measuring 11 × 6 in (27 × 15 cm). Spread first with a thin layer of melted butter and then with some jam, then spread *thickly* all over with the filling. Turn in the short ends and roll up into a strudel. Put the strudels on greased sheets, join side down, leaving room for each strudel to almost double in size. Put each tray in a large plastic bag and leave for 30 minutes or until the strudels are puffy and will spring back when gently pressed with the finger.

369

Meanwhile, preheat the oven to Gas No. 6, 400 degrees F, 200 degrees C. Put the strudels in the oven, turn the heat down to Gas No. 5, 375 degrees F, 190 degrees C and bake for 25 minutes or until rich brown. Turn the strudels over for 5 minutes if necessary to brown the bottom. Cool on a wire rack. Just before serving, sprinkle thickly with the icing sugar.

Rescue Operations

If the overheated gelatine speckles the mousse with pellets of glue and the ginger cake erupts like Vesuvius and flows out of its undersized tin, it's best to cut your losses and start again, for these two particular kitchen disasters will not respond to any kind of first-aid treatment, or even to the most dedicated intensive care.

It *is* often possible to retrieve the apparently irretrievable, however, if you only know what has gone wrong and why. So in this chapter, I have listed some of the crises that can arise in even the best-regulated kitchens, with suggestions for resolving them more or less happily or, if the damage is beyond repair, for preventing it from happening again.

SOUP

- If it is **too thick,** it may only be due to pulses or vegetables having solidified on standing. Heat the soup gently to see if this does the trick, but if it doesn't thin it down with an appropriate liquid such as stock or milk, until it's the consistency of pouring (light) cream.
- If it's **too thin,** either whisk a tablespoon or two of instant potato into the bubbling soup, or stir in 2 teaspoons of cornflour (cornstarch) mixed to a cream with a little cold water, adding more if it still isn't thick enough after simmering for 3 minutes.
- If it **burns** — a not-infrequent occurrence with thick soups made with split peas or lentils — do *not* stir the pot, as this will distribute the burned bits right through the entire panful. Instead, pour the soup into another pan, leaving the burned-on crust behind. If you *have* inadvertently stirred the burned bits through the soup, put it all through a coarse sieve to trap them.

  Next time, cook the soup on a lower heat or in a thicker pan.
- If it's **too salty,** cut a peeled potato in half and simmer in the soup for 10 minutes. Or, if appropriate, add a tablespoon of rice or 2 oz (50 g/½ cup) of fine pasta.

  Next time, add the salt half a teaspoon at a time, being particularly cautious if you have used a highly concentrated stock.
- If a meat soup **lacks flavour,** add one or two extra stock cubes, or stir in some leftover gravy or 2 teaspoons of tomato purée.

  Next time, cook it in the oven instead of on top of the stove and then leave it to mature overnight — the colour and the flavour will be vastly improved.
- If a soup **curdles,** try whisking it vigorously with an electric hand whisk or a rotary whisk. If this does no good, give it a whirl for a minute on a blender or food processor.

  Next time, if it's a soup thickened with eggs such as Borscht, add a little of the hot soup to the beaten eggs (never vice versa), then return it to the pan and reheat only until it is steaming; *never* let it boil. If the temperature of the eggs is raised too quickly, or if that of the soup goes beyond 180 degrees F, 80 degrees C (steaming point), the egg protein will be toughened, and cannot then thicken the soup. If, however, it's a cream soup containing an acid vegetable such as green pepper, be careful not to let it boil for too long, as this concentrates the acidity and may curdle any milk it contains.

FISH

• If it's **soggy and limp** after it's been fried, drain it, reheat the oil to a higher temperature (375 degrees F, 190 degrees C, when a cube of day-old bread browns in 30 seconds), and then re-fry the fish until it becomes stiff and crisp.

Next time, make sure the oil is at the correct temperature and don't crowd the pan — too much fish in too little oil lowers the temperature, so that the fish absorbs the oil instead of frying in it.

• If it's crisp when it comes out of the pan and becomes **soggy** on standing, it's not been drained correctly, and will need to be fried again briefly.

Next time, lay it to drain on crumpled (not flat) paper towels or tissue paper, so that it does not re-absorb the oil as it drains off.

• If the **oil froths** as soon as you put in the fish, take it out and recoat it — the froth is caused by moisture from inadequately coated fish seeping into the hot oil.

Next time, coat fish fillets and steaks first in flour, then in beaten egg and finally in dry crumbs or medium matzah meal; coat chopped fish balls only in matzah meal.

• If poached or baked fish is **dry** and too **firm** in texture, there's little you can do, as it's been toughened by cooking at too high a temperature for too long.

Next time, when poaching steaks or fillets, don't let the water boil, only let it simmer. When cooking a whole fish or cut of salmon, let it boil for only 2 minutes, then complete the cooking by leaving the fish in the cooling liquid. Whole fish can also be baked in foil in a moderate oven, but for not longer than an hour, unless they are more than 5 pounds (2½ kg) in weight. Again, the fish should be left to finish cooking wrapped in the foil until it is cool. (See page 93 for details.)

MEAT AND POULTRY

• If **steaks or roasts are tough** to eat, persevere with them this time.

Next time, make sure the butcher has hung the meat for at least 10 days, and don't overcook it — the more heat you apply to tender meat after the inside has reached the right temperature, the tougher it becomes. If you are unsure about testing for the 'done-ness' of roasts, invest in a meat thermometer and cut out the guesswork.

• If a **stew, braise or meatball casserole is greasy** when it is cooked, blot the fat from the surface with paper towels.

Next time, make it well ahead of time, put the entire dish (when cool) in the freezer until the fat has solidified enough to be scraped off, then gently reheat when required.

• If **lamb chops are very greasy** when cooked, pat off the excess fat with paper towels.

Next time, trim off all the visible fat apart from a thin edging, then grill (broil) on a rack so that any remaining fat can drain away. The same applies to roasts of both meat and poultry.

• If a **roast isn't properly cooked** in the specified time, you can finish it off in the microwave. Otherwise the guests will have to wait.

Next time, make sure that the meat is left at room temperature for 2 hours before it goes in the oven — cold meat can play havoc with recommended cooking times.

• If **meatballs are tough,** you'll just have to bite on the bullet.

Next time, lighten the mixture with a thick slice of crumbled bread to each pound (450 g) of meat, and mix the meatball mixture with a fork, rather than packing it solidly together with a spoon.

- If the **chicken is pale and flabby** when cooking time is up, remove it from the oven, paint it with olive oil and sprinkle with a tablespoon of lemon juice, then turn up the oven as far as it will go and roast the bird for a further 10 minutes. If a **duck isn't brown**, do the same but paint it with honey mixed with a little soy sauce.

Next time, dry the raw bird well, paint on the glaze before it goes into the oven, then cook the bird at a moderate temperature for the whole of the time.

VEGETABLES

- If **potatoes start to disintegrate** in the water before they're tender, drain off the liquid and let them steam in their own moisture under a teatowel until cooked.

Next time, choose a reliable boiling potato like Maris Piper, and don't let the cooking water boil too vigorously.

- If **potatoes are soggy** when mashed, put them in a greased casserole, then dry and crispen them under a hot grill.

Next time, beat *hot* rather than *cold* liquid into them, trickling it down the side of the pan until it bubbles, then whip the potatoes over a low heat so that they are lightened by the steam.

- If **roast potatoes are soggy** rather than crisp, drain them from the fat and set aside. Turn up the oven temperature to Gas No. 7, 425 degrees F, 220 degrees C, reheat the fat in the baking tray on top of the stove, then put the potatoes back in it, turn them in the hot fat (it should be bubbling around them), and then return to the oven until crisp and brown.

Next time, get the fat really hot while you're preheating the oven, so that the potatoes won't absorb it when they are put in.

- If by mischance you **overcook** a vegetable so that it is unpleasantly soft, purée it with a little fat, salt and pepper.

Next time, cook it for a shorter time than you think it will need — it's easy to cook for an extra minute, but you can't turn back the clock.

CAKES

- If a cake mixture **curdles** when you add the eggs stir in a little flour until it comes together again.

Next time, make sure all the ingredients, including the eggs, are at room temperature before you start.

- If a cake has a **shiny humped crust** and a **tough texture,** serve it warm as a pudding with stewed fruit and custard, or use it for a trifle.

Next time, fold rather than beat in the flour, as beating toughens the gluten in the flour, causing the dry, bread-like texture. This is particularly important when making cakes with a food processor. If all the ingredients are processed together, it should only take 15 seconds. Or do it my way, as described on page 8.

- If a cake **burns on top,** grate off the blackened part.

Next time, have your oven thermostat checked first. It's better to bear the expense rather than the constant exasperation and sense of failure.

- If the cake *cracks,* this may be because the oven was too hot, so that the top set before the cake was fully risen, and then cracked open when the uncooked mixture underneath tried to rise. Cover the top with a butter icing or even sifted icing (confectioners') sugar, and nobody will notice (except yourself).

Next time, cook the cake in a slightly cooler oven (set it one Gas No., 25 degrees F, 10 degrees C lower) but for a longer time. This is particularly important with cakes cooked in loaf tins which have a high proportion of 'inside' compared to crust.

● If a **cheesecake cracks,** cover it with soured cream or a fruit glaze.

Next time, use a drier cheese, and cook the cake for a shorter time; it has baked for long enough when a 1 in (2½ cm) band of filling next to the edge of the tin is firmly set — the remainder will set as it cools.

● If a cake rises but then **falls,** simply turn it over and treat the flat bottom as the top, providing, of course, that it is cooked in the middle.

Next time, don't use quite such large eggs — there can be a ½ oz (15 g) difference in weight between a large and a *very* large egg, and that is quite enough to upset the ratio of liquids to solids in a large cake. Or you may need to measure your raising agent more carefully — too much will produce more gas than the framework of the cake can sustain.

● If a ginger cake **overflows** in the tin — there is nothing to be done. Go and buy one.

Next time, measure the bicarbonate of soda (baking soda) with special care, and don't use self-raising flour or baking powder unless it is specified. Make sure that the tin is the size recommended by the recipe; this kind of cake has a very high rise.

PASTRY

● If pastry **keeps on breaking** as you roll it, simply pat and patch it into the dish.

Next time, don't go on rubbing in the fat until the mixture looks like bread-crumbs — stop when each particle is as small as a tiny pea; the mixture will then be able to absorb all the recommended amount of liquid, and will be pliable and easy to roll.

● If the pastry is **too sticky** to roll out, don't add any extra flour (which will toughen it). Instead, flour your *hands,* then pat and patch it into place.

Next time, cut down the amount of caster (superfine) sugar in the recipe, or substitute icing (confectioners') sugar instead. If will help if you chill the dough well before attempting to roll it out.

● If the pastry is **hard** when it is baked, you must grin and bear it.

Next time, increase the proportion of fat to flour — I like to use just over half the weight of fat to flour. Be sparing with the flour on the pastry board and rolling pin. Check the oven temperature; if it is too low the fat may run out of the dough, making it tough and hard.

● If pastry made on a food processor becomes **sticky** and **unmanageable,** turn it into a bowl and gently knead in a tablespoon or two of extra flour. This is only first aid so don't expect perfect results.

Next time, after adding the egg or water to the dry ingredients, process only until the mixture begins to form tiny balls — once it becomes one big ball it will be too soft to handle. Tip these tiny balls into a bowl and knead gently together by hand before attempting to roll it out.

● If a quiche or flan case **shrinks** in the oven, forget it this time.

Next time, gently ease the round of pastry into the tin without stretching it, then make a little pleat where the base and the sides meet, all the way round. Line the case with a piece of foil which has been tightly pressed into its shape, and *freeze* it for at least an hour before you bake it.

● If the puff pastry lid of a deep meat or fruit pie **slips into the filling** as it cooks, don't show it to the guests — it will still taste good.

Next time, make sure that the filling is quite cold before you put on the lid — otherwise it will start melting the fat out of the pastry, causing it to slither down. Try not to stretch the pastry as you lay it on top of the pie, and support it from below with a pie funnel.

YEAST DOUGHS

● If the dough stays **cold and flabby** and doesn't seem to rise, turn the oven on at its lowest setting, and put a bowl of hot water in it. When it is at temperature, turn it off and put in the dough, covered in clingfilm (saran wrap). Or put the dough on the DEFROST cycle of the microwave oven for 2 minutes. If after this the dough still hasn't 'moved' after half an hour, throw it away — if you used *fresh* yeast you have probably killed it with water that was too hot (it should feel gently warm like a baby's bath); if you used *dried* yeast, it may well have been stale.

Next time, make sure that fresh yeast is a creamy fawn in colour and slightly moist in texture — if it's brown and dry, throw it away. Check that you haven't exceeded the 'use by' date on the container of dried yeast. And check the temperature of liquids with care.

● If the dough is still **sticky** after the recommended kneading or beating time, add a little more flour — it won't harm the dough.

Next time, make sure you use a real bread flour, if that is recommended.

● If the food processor **seizes up** when you're mixing a dough, turn it off and leave it to cool down for a few minutes, then throw in a little more flour — a sticky dough makes the motor labour and finally come to a halt. When making a dough on a food processor, it's advisable to reduce the liquid by a tablespoon or two; you can always add it back if necessary.

● If a refrigerator dough doubles in volume and **threatens to overflow** the bowl before you're ready to shape it, punch it down, turn it over and leave it to rise again.

● If bread or kuchen is too **close in texture,** make the best of it — it will still taste good if you toast it.

Next time, make sure it is really puffy and light before it goes in the oven.

MERINGUES AND PAVLOVAS

● If egg whites **won't beat up,** wash the beaters thoroughly in hot water, transfer the whites to another clean bowl and try again. If this doesn't work, discard them and start again with fresh whites.

Next time, make sure your bowl and beaters are scrupulously clean — even a drop of grease will prevent egg whites beating up. So if you need to beat both egg whites and cream, whisk the whites *first* and then (without washing the beaters) you can whip up the cream.

● If you leave egg whites **whisking without sugar** and the meringue breaks down into a liquid, there's nothing for it but to throw them away.

Next time, turn off the beaters before you answer the phone. If the egg whites are already whisked stiff and you're called away, turn the bowl, with the beaten whites in it, upside down on the counter — they will still be firm when you return up to 15 minutes later.

● If you **add the sugar too quickly** and firm meringue turns into marshmallow, turn the mixer up to full power, walk away and leave for 5 minutes. If if hasn't become stiff by then, it never will.

- If a Pavlova **cracks** in the oven, forget it this time and fill and serve it as though it were perfect.

Next time, measure the cream of tartar with special care, and don't bake the meringue in a hotter oven than specified.

- If the meringue **'weeps'**, it's only undissolved sugar that's causing the tears.

Next time, add the sugar a tablespoon at a time, beating until stiff after each addition.

- If the meringue **sticks to the tin**, cook it a little longer in a low oven — when it's cooked enough, it should be easy to lift off. If this doesn't work, rescue as much as you can and keep it in a tin to crumble into fruit fools and mousses.

Next time, use silicone paper to line the baking tray and follow method and cooking times exactly. Pavlovas and meringues will then lift off like a dream.

- If you **overbeat the cream** for the filling and it starts to curdle, buy some more and start again.

Next time, use the cream straight from the refrigerator, particularly on a warm day. Whisk small quantities by hand, you'll have more control. Whisk large quantities by machine, but *only* until the cream hangs on the whisk, then finish by hand.

SAUCES

- If a sauce goes **lumpy**, beat it vigorously with a batter whisk. If that doesn't work and there's too much to throw away, put it on a food processor or blender and process until it is smooth. Or you can sieve it to remove the lumps — a horrible job — and you may then need to thicken it with a little cornflour (cornstarch) dissolved in cold water or milk, as the lumps you threw away will have included some of the flour intended to thicken the sauce.

Next time, do it my way by putting the fat, flour and cold liquid into the pan together, and whisking over moderate heat until thickened and smooth.

- If the sauce is **too thick** or **too thin**, treat it as described in the section of this chapter on reducing soups (page 371).

Next time, measure the thickening more accurately.

- If **mayonnaise won't thicken** or it **curdles**, tip it out of the bowl and put in another egg yolk, then gradually whisk or process the curdled or thin mixture into it — it will become very thick.

Next time, be sure to add dry mustard to the yolks before you add any oil — this helps the emulsion to 'take'. As a further precaution, add the first third of the oil a drop at a time (even when using a blender or food processor) until you can see or hear that it has begun to thicken — the tone of the motor will change. Only then is it safe to add the remainder of the oil in a constant thin stream, processing all the time. And never take eggs for mayonnaise straight from the refrigerator — let them come to room temperature before you use them.

- If a **vinaigrette dressing** is **too acid**, add a pinch of sugar and a little more oil and shake well.

Next time, use half each of vinegar and lemon juice, and if it's for dressing a green salad, use at least three times their combined volume of oil.

- If **herbs have gone grey** in a vinaigrette that's been stored for a few days, simply add more fresh herbs — the older ones will still taste all right, it's only their colour which has been bleached by the acid in the dressing.

- If an **egg custard curdles**, try whisking it smooth by hand or machine; next, try blending it on the processor or blender. If this doesn't work, throw it away.

376

Next time, make sure the mixture doesn't come to the boil — it will thicken at 180 degrees F, 80 degrees C (steaming point), which is well below boiling point. Heat it *slowly*, so that there are no 'hot spots' in the sauce that may cause it to curdle even though the whole panful has not come yet to the boil. If in doubt, cook it over hot water — it will need a much longer cooking time, however. Another precaution: adding a teaspoon of cornflour (cornstarch) to the beaten eggs also helps to prevent curdling. To make a really smooth custard with whole eggs, whisk them with the sugar for 1 minute in the food processor or blender, pour on the steaming milk and process until blended, then turn the mixture into the pan and heat slowly until it thickens; you'll know when that moment is about to arrive as all the froth on top of the liquid will suddenly disappear as if by magic.

MELTING MOMENTS

● If **gelatine goes lumpy** as you try to dissolve it, throw it away — you've overheated it and it will remain as tough as old boots whatever you do.

Next time, sprinkle the gelatine on to the liquid (*not* vice versa), then heat until the cloudiness disappears, standing it in a pan of simmering water, or in the microwave oven (about 30 seconds on full power).

● If **chocolate goes hard** when heated, instead of liquefying, drop in a tablespoon of white fat or butter and keep stirring, and it will become liquid again.

Next time, don't let the chocolate come directly into contact with the hot bottom of the pan, but add it after the water or melted fat.

LARGE-SCALE DISASTERS

● If you find you've overdone the amount of **chilli powder** in a party-sized casserole, don't be tempted to add more meat — you'll never get it right. Instead, drain off half the sauce, and replace it with freshly made sauce with no chilli in it.

● If a large quantity of **meat won't brown** in the pan, remove half and fry it in two small batches. Better still, get out another frying pan and use the two in tandem.

Next time, don't be tempted to crowd the pan, as the steam generated by a large quantity of tightly packed meat will inhibit browning.

● If you're left with a load of **ripe avocados** after a party, peel and stone them, then purée them with 1 tablespoon lemon juice to each 2 avocados. Freeze the purée in convenient amounts ready to make into guacamole, avocado mayonnaise or even soup — puréed avocados freeze for 3 months, but whole avocados go black at once.

● If an **avocado dip goes brown** on the surface, wait until just before you serve it, then mix the brown part in — it won't taste or show, as the discoloration is only due to oxidation.

Next time, mix the dip with something acidic like lemon juice or mayonnaise, and brush a little lemon juice on the surface before covering it tightly with foil.

And finally:

If you weep over **chopped onions,** *don't* rub your eyes with an oniony hand.

Next time, freeze the peeled onion for 20 minutes before chopping it and you will banish your tears.

INDEX

379

chicken breast cooked in
microwave oven, 24
chicken in Riesling, 146
chicken in sweet and sour
tomato sauce (Passover), 315
chicken Riviera style, 144
chicken roasted without fat, 40
chicken salad, Taj Mahal, 151
chicken Santa Cruz, sauce
Sevillana, 150
chicken schnitzels, 146
chicken soup (traditional
method), 62
in Greek style, 63
in Jewish fashion, 60
to prepare for freezer, 61
to remove fat, 36
under pastry crust, 64
with hobene gropen, 64
chicken stock, substitutes for, 4
chicken with herbs, country
style, 143
coq au Riesling, 146
gingered mushroom and
chicken kebabs, 148
microwave-oven-fried chicken,
31
pineapple chicken (Passover),
317
poached chicken breasts with
wine and mushroom sauce,
152
poulet à l'estragon, 145
poulet bonne femme en
cocotte, 139
poulet 'truffé' à l'hongrois, 136
poulet 'truffé' au persil, 135
roast chicken, 135
sesame chicken, 147
stir-fried chicken breasts, 149
stuffings for chicken
(Passover):
apricot stuffing, 316
pineapple stuffing, 316
summer rice salad with
chicken, 198
chicken livers:
chicken liver and walnut pâté,
90
chicken liver blintzes
(Passover), 307
chicken liver goulash with
nutty rice ring, 154
chicken livers with sage, 153
chopped liver (low-fat), 36, 37
chicory:
orange, chicory and watercress
salad, 200
shades of green salad, 191
chiffon sponge cake (Passover),
336

chilli powder, to correct excess,
377
Chinese duck pancakes, 138
Chinese leaves:
salad of grapefruit, Chinese
leaves and watercress with
honeyed dressing, 201
shades of green salad, 191
chives, to freeze, 60
chocolate:
almond marble cake, 263
chocolate and toasted hazelnut
truffles, 249
for Passover, 331
chocolate brownies (Passover),
329
chocolate cake with mocha
frosting (Passover), 332
chocolate feather sponge,
liqueur icing (Passover), 337
chocolate loaf with coffee
fudge topping, 15
chocolate roulade with
strawberry cloud filling
(Passover), 320
chocolate walnut squares, 256
ganache cream, 258
mandelmarmorgugelhupf
(almond marble cake), 263
Moritz meringues, 249
Sachertorte (Viennese
chocolate cake), 261
Swiss chocolate and burnt
almond cake, 262
to grate, using food processor,
8
to melt, 377
using microwave oven, 23
tollhouse cookies, 239
ugat schekademe (chocolate
and almond torte), 257
chopped egg and onion, 9
chopped herring with cherry
brandy, 348
chopped liver (low-fat), 36, 37
choux pastry, 295
for gougère, 107
chremslach (Passover), 327
cigarillos, Mexican, 293
cinnamon apple sponge squares,
353
cinnamon crisps, 242
cinnamon raisin kuchen, 16
clementines, caramelized, 205
cocktail meatballs with
aubergine, 297
coconut fingers (Passover), 330
cod, oven-fried, 38
coffee:
coffee and burnt almond ice
cream, 228

coffee and burnt almond slice,
228
coffee fudge topping for
chocolate loaf, 15
compôte of fresh pineapple,
lychees and kiwi fruit, 211
compôte of summer fruits
poached in wine, 210
consommé, special, 66
cookies, see under biscuits and
cookies
coq au Riesling, 146
coriander dressing for mushroom
and pimiento salad, 200
corn and red bean salad, 197
coulibiac, tuna, with mushroom
and wine sauce, 109
courgettes:
barchette di zucchine ripiene al
forno, 87
braised courgettes with herbs,
182
cheesey courgettes, 183
courgette and lettuce soup, 44
cooked in microwave oven,
24
courgette fritters in hazelnut
sauce, 155
kishuim rehovot, 183
mushroom and courgette flan,
161
ratatouille, 52
stuffed courgettes, 87
crabapple jelly, 282
cracked wheat, in tabbouleh, 194
cream, substitutes for, 4, 204
cream cheese strudel in flaky
pastry, 343
cream of green pepper soup, 71
cream of mushroom soup
(Passover), 308
crêpes, see under blintzes, crêpes
and pancakes
crispy kataifi, 173
croquettes, see under fritters and
croquettes
croutons, to toast, in microwave
oven, 23
crudites, with honeyed Italian
dip, 289
crunchy fruit crumble, 214
cucumber:
cucumber and minted petits
pois, 184
cucumber salad in German
style, 195
minted cucumber and pea
soup, 44
minted Oriental salad, 193
orange and cucumber salad
with dill dressing, 202

385